Popular New Orleans

New Orleans is unique – which is precisely why there are many Crescent Cities all over the world: for almost 150 years, writers, artists, cultural brokers, and entrepreneurs have drawn on and simultaneously contributed to New Orleans's fame and popularity by recreating the city in popular media from literature, photographs, and plays to movies, television shows, and theme parks. Addressing students and fans of the city and of popular culture, *Popular New Orleans* examines three pivotal moments in the history of New Orleans in popular media: the creation of the popular image of the Crescent City during the late nineteenth century in the local-color writings published in *Scribner's Monthly/Century Magazine*; the translation of this image into three-dimensional immersive spaces during the twentieth century in Disney's theme parks and resorts in California, Florida, and Japan; and the radical transformation of this image following Hurricane Katrina in public performances such as Mardi Gras parades and operas. Covering visions of the Crescent City from George W. Cable's *Old Creole Days* stories (1873–1876) to Disneyland's "New Orleans Square" (1966) to Rosalyn Story's opera *Wading Home* (2015), *Popular New Orleans* traces how popular images of New Orleans have changed from exceptional to exemplary.

Florian Freitag is Professor of American Studies at the University of Duisburg-Essen in Germany.

Routledge Studies in Cultural History

90 Negotiating Memory from the Romans to the Twenty-First Century
   Damnatio Memoriae
   Edited by Øivind Fuglerud, Kjersti Larsen, and Marina Prusac-Lindhagen

91 Cultures and Practices of Coexistence from the Thirteenth Through the Seventeenth Centuries
   Multi-Ethnic Cities in the Mediterranean World, Volume 1
   Edited by Marco Folin and Antonio Musarra

92 Controversial Heritage and Divided Memories from the Nineteenth Through the Twentieth Centuries
   Multi-Ethnic Cities in the Mediterranean World, Volume 2
   Edited by Marco Folin and Heleni Porfyriou

93 History as Performance
   Political Movements in Galicia Around 1900
   Dietlind Hüchtker

94 The Cultural Life of Risk and Innovation
   Imagining New Markets from the Seventeenth Century to the Present
   Edited by Chia Yin Hsu, Thomas M. Luckett, and Erika Vause

95 Popular New Orleans
   The Crescent City in Periodicals, Theme Parks, and Opera, 1875–2015
   Florian Freitag

For more information about this series, please visit: www.routledge.com/Routledge-Studies-in-Cultural-History/book-series/SE0367

Popular New Orleans
The Crescent City in Periodicals,
Theme Parks, and Opera, 1875–2015

Florian Freitag

NEW YORK AND LONDON

First published 2021
by Routledge
52 Vanderbilt Avenue, New York, NY 10017

and by Routledge
2 Park Square, Milton Park, Abingdon, Oxon, OX14 4RN

Routledge is an imprint of the Taylor & Francis Group, an informa business

© 2021 Taylor & Francis

The right of Florian Freitag to be identified as author of this work has been asserted in accordance with sections 77 and 78 of the Copyright, Designs and Patents Act 1988.

All rights reserved. No part of this book may be reprinted or reproduced or utilised in any form or by any electronic, mechanical, or other means, now known or hereafter invented, including photocopying and recording, or in any information storage or retrieval system, without permission in writing from the publishers.

Trademark notice: Product or corporate names may be trademarks or registered trademarks, and are used only for identification and explanation without intent to infringe.

Library of Congress Cataloging-in-Publication Data
Names: Freitag, Florian, author.
Title: Popular New Orleans : the Crescent City in periodicals, theme parks, and opera, 1875–2015 / Florian Freitag.
Other titles: Routledge studies in cultural history ; 95.
Description: New York, NY : Routledge, 2021. | Series: Routledge studies in cultural history ; 95 | Includes bibliographical references and index.
Identifiers: LCCN 2020026041 (print) | LCCN 2020026042 (ebook) | ISBN 9780367437718 (hardback) | ISBN 9781003005650 (ebook) | ISBN 9781000196917 (adobe pdf) | ISBN 9781000196931 (mobi) | ISBN 9781000196955 (epub)
Subjects: LCSH: New Orleans (La.)—In popular culture.
Classification: LCC F379.N54 F74 2021 (print) | LCC F379.N54 (ebook) | DDC 976.3/35—dc23
LC record available at https://lccn.loc.gov/2020026041
LC ebook record available at https://lccn.loc.gov/2020026042

ISBN: 978-0-367-43771-8 (hbk)
ISBN: 978-1-003-00565-0 (ebk)

Typeset in Sabon
by Apex CoVantage, LLC

 Printed in the United Kingdom
by Henry Ling Limited

Contents

List of Figures   vi
Acknowledgments   vii

    Introduction   1
1 Scribner's Illustrated New Orleans   26
2 Disney's Immersive New Orleans   132
3 *Wading Home*'s Post-Katrina New Orleans   232
    Conclusion   333

Index   341

Figures

1.1 Lafcadio Hearn's tour of "The Scenes of Cable's Romances." 26
2.1 New Orleans Square (Disneyland). 132
3.1 Dallas Arts District. 232

Acknowledgments

In *Why New Orleans Matters*, Tom Piazza writes: "Long before I visited New Orleans I would visit it in my imagination." One of the first times I made that imaginary journey was while reading Kate Chopin's short stories about the city, sometime in 2010, when I was preparing for my Ph.D. oral examination at the University of Konstanz. A few years later, I went to Disneyland in California in order to conduct field research for a project on theme parks, and while wandering through the streets of New Orleans Square, I again imagined myself visiting the Crescent City. In 2015, finally, I traveled to Dallas in order to attend the premiere of an opera about New Orleans, which once more imaginatively transported me to the city. By that time, I already knew that my next book would be about New Orleans, but what I did not know was that I had already, and unintentionally, retraced the different steps in the history of New Orleans in popular culture that I would eventually examine in this book. Also, I still had to actually visit the place I had been thinking and dreaming about for so long. Research for *Popular New Orleans* would eventually take me to New Orleans, but also to many other places that I had never thought I would see: New York City, Orlando, even Tokyo. In all of these places, I have met people who, in one way or another, share my fascination with the Crescent City and who, more importantly, have become wonderful colleagues and friends: Rosalyn Story, Mary Alice Rich, Barbara Hill Moore, Mark Noonan, and Bryan Rice. Thanks are also due to the German Research Foundation, the Volkswagen Foundation, and Johannes Gutenberg University Mainz, which supported my travels with their generous grants. Traveling was important, and fun as well, but most of the reading and writing that has gone into this book was done at home, in the small town of Lingenfeld in southern Germany. There, too, some extraordinary friends and colleagues have provided advice, support, and friendship: Filippo Carlà-Uhink, of course, but also the Bauer family and particularly the group of senior citizens who gather at the local Görtz bakery and café. Jutta Ernst has guided me through the process of writing this book with patience, indulgence, and resilience; and Ines Fricke-Groenewold, Marisa Mählck, and Cornelius Beckers were invaluable proofreaders. Finally, my parents have always kept me going by telling me how much they look forward to reading *Popular New Orleans*, although they do not speak a word of English.

Yet another place that has proven indispensable for *Popular New Orleans* is Hamburg. Hamburg has nothing to do with New Orleans (as far as I know), but it is the place where Alex lives, and how could I have ever written this book without him?

Introduction

On "Popular"

Popular culture is popular nowadays – with audiences (some popular culture artifacts more so than others), with creators (especially those artifacts that are also popular with audiences), as well as with students (and, hence, with university and departmental managers).[1] Yet, popular culture is particularly popular today with scholars. Indeed, the past few years have seen the publication of an impressive number of monographs and edited collections that propose to examine, according to their titles, the portrayal of some topic or other "in [American] popular culture." The range of subjects thus analyzed is nothing short of astonishing: from aunts and stepmothers to fathers (see Sotirin and Ellington; Lindenauer; and Tropp and Kelly), from zombies and vampires to werewolves (see McMahon-Coleman and Weaver; Bacon; and Bishop), from single women in the 1960s and 1970s to twenty-first–century men (see Lehman; and Watson and Shaw), from Catholicism to Asian religions (see A.B. Smith; and Iwamura), from international politics, war, and corporations (see Sachleben and Yenerall; Stahl; and Clare) to alcohol, James Bond, and Las Vegas (see Black; Weiner, Whitfield, and Becker; and Gragg). There has been, to my knowledge, no study yet of the representation of popular culture in popular culture, although Katrin Horn's recent examination of the role of camp in popular culture comes fairly close to this.

As much as these and similar studies may tell us about the individual popular culture artifacts they have ventured to explore, they offer precious little information about popular culture itself; that is, on how precisely they define this obviously popular, yet apparently vexed, phrase. Studies on popular culture tend, in short, "to focus on examples . . . rather than on the concept" (Storey, *Popular* 3). The reason for this may well be that, as Fred H. Schroeder already pointed out in 1980, "[d]efinitions of popular culture abound, and to those who have arrived at a satisfactory working definition, the subject is wearisome" (50). Another, related, issue may be that like most other people, scholars have an implicit sense, an intuitive understanding of what popular culture is, an understanding that they reasonably assume to share with their readers – after all, popular culture is, John Clarke writes, "a field in which we are all 'experts'" (20). In fact, there seems to exist a sort of tacitly operating canon of art forms or media that can be legitimately analyzed and labeled as "popular culture" in academic research and publishing – a canon that, if accepted and adhered to, appears to almost automatically relieve the researcher from the burden of having to engage in cumbersome definitory attempts and theoretical debates.[2] Thus, most of the monographs and edited collections mentioned previously discuss movies, TV shows, and print (newspapers, magazines, fiction), with digital material (video games, websites), pop music, and performances (theater, minstrelsy, musicals) being only slightly less "popular," while e.g., poetry, painting, or opera are never even mentioned – except to point out that they are not considered popular culture (see, for instance, Cullen, "Introduction" 3). Larry Gragg's *Bright Light City* (2013) is fairly representative in this respect: in order to discover patterns of images of the city of Las Vegas in American popular culture, Gragg examined "150 films, over 200 television programs, over 200 novels, nearly 1,500 newspaper articles, and over 200 magazine articles" (xi).

If this introduction does engage in (hopefully not-so-cumbersome) definitory attempts and theoretical debates, it is not only because *Popular New Orleans* at least partially violates the unwritten canon of popular art forms or media – examining, as it does, periodicals and theme parks, but also opera. It is also because I believe that especially in the field of popular culture, such conceptual discussions can prove both insightful and productive, opening new perspectives with occasionally surprising implications – for instance, the realization that in some respects, theme parks can be considered less popular than opera. Evidently, much depends on the way one understands and uses the term popular. According to John Storey, the meaning of "popular" has expanded from its origins as a legal term in late fifteenth-century England, where it referred to "a legal action that could be undertaken by anyone," to describing anything "that is widespread or generally accepted" by the early seventeenth century, to designating, from the early nineteenth century onwards, "forms of entertainment that are said to appeal to the tastes of ordinary people" (*Popular* 4). Over the course of its history in the English language, then, "popular" has come to connote "originating from the people" and "commonly liked by the people," as well as "created for the people" (see also Jenkins, McPherson, and Shattuc 27; Miller 2). All of these connotations can be seen reflected in the various concepts or theories that have been suggested and discussed at some point in the field of popular culture studies.

Thus, for some critics, popular culture has simply been culture that is "liked by many people" – i.e., they have treated the question of how to define popular culture as a purely quantitative one. In a 1988 article, for instance, Harold E. Hinds, Jr., has declared popularity the *"sine qua non"* of popular culture: popular culture should be defined, according to Hinds, as "those aspects of culture . . . which are widely spread and believed in and/or consumed by significant numbers of people," with "adoption/ consumption in more than one regional culture and by more than one narrow socio-economic group" constituting the "minimum" requirements for considering an artifact popular (*"Sine Qua Non"* 363; and 364). Although in a later article Hinds, Jr., has identified more precise standards for applying the criterion of popularity to popular culture research (see "Key Concept"), other scholars have either criticized this definition for its vagueness (see e.g., Storey, *Popular* 5) or have altogether rejected the quantification of popularity (see e.g., Browne and Browne 2).

The idea of popular culture as culture "originating from the people," in turn, first emerged in late-eighteenth-century Europe in the context of growing anthropological interest in peasant or folk cultures (see Jenkins, McPherson, and Shattuc 28). Conceptualized as the "authentic" expression of the life experiences of a stable, traditional social community (see Szeman and O'Brien 7) and inextricably linked with nineteenth-century romanticism and nationalism (see Storey, *Popular* 5), "folk culture" has subsequently been regarded as a subcategory of popular culture (see e.g., Schudson 86) or, conversely, as the pre-industrial equivalent of modern, mass-produced popular culture: in a 1992 article, for example, Lawrence Levine ("Folklore" 1369) has defined popular culture as the "folklore of industrial society" (see also Cullen, *Art* 21). More recently, notions of popular culture as culture "originating from the people" have informed Henry Jenkins's concept of "fan cultures" (as developed in his 1992 *Textual Poachers*), but also John Fiske's revisionist model of popular culture as consumer resistance (as developed in his 1989 *Understanding Popular Culture* and *Reading the Popular*): drawing on de Certeau's guerilla tactics of everyday life (1984), Fiske defines popular culture as "made by various formations of subordinated or disempowered people out of the resources, both discursive and material, that are provided by the social system that disempowers them" (*Reading* 1–2).[3] Thus conceived, popular culture "is not folk culture," as Fiske points out, but like the latter, it is "the culture of the people" (*Understanding* 176).

Of course, the very resources that Fiske's guerilla consumers use to produce what he terms popular culture are precisely what an entire host of earlier intellectuals and scholars, from Matthew Arnold and Frank R. Leavis to the Frankfurt School, Leo Lowenthal, and Dwight Macdonald, had conceived of as popular culture – namely, the mass-produced cultural commodities "created for the people" by the so-called culture industries (see Storey, *Inventing* 16–29). Depending on their location on the political spectrum, these critics viewed "mass culture" either as a threat to established cultural standards or as a depoliticizing narcotic: while in 1869, "mass culture" made Arnold fear for "our sentiment for beauty and sweetness," as well as "our sentiment against hideousness and rawness" (62), MacDonald, in 1953, railed against the "Lords of *kitsch*," who "exploit the cultural needs of the masses in order to make a profit and/or maintain their class rule" (60). The association of popular culture with industrially produced and mass-distributed items is still prevalent in much contemporary popular culture research (see previous); especially mass culture theorists' conceptualization of audiences as passive, non-discriminating, and easily ideologically manipulated, however, has been widely rejected as too simplistic (see Storey, *Popular* 6).

Rather than exclusively focusing on popular culture and implicitly reflecting the various connotations of the term popular, another strand of thought has taken a wider perspective, one from which the field of culture is viewed as polarized or subdivided into different, mutually sustaining categories – most frequently, "high" or "elite," and "low" or "popular," culture: "'High' needs to distinguish itself from 'low' in order to be what it is, and . . . 'low' or 'pop' also needs 'high' to have its own presumably separate identity" (Meisel 59). Some scholars have sought to attribute fixed inventories of specific creators, audiences, and particularly aesthetics to each category (see e.g., Harmon 65–7). In its most radical form, however, this school of thought has seen these categories as basically empty containers, to be filled "in a wide variety of often conflicting ways" depending on the specific historical and cultural context (Storey, *Introductory* 1), yet always so as to "sustain the distinction" and "continually mark the difference between them" (S. Hall 232). Ultimately inspired by the work of French sociologist Pierre Bourdieu (1979), then, this scholarship has identified popular culture as a relational, culturally specific, historically contingent, and discursively and institutionally constructed category that helps create and maintain social distinctions.

For instance, in the 1980s, scholars like Paul DiMaggio and Lawrence Levine have examined how certain forms of culture have moved "up the cultural escalator" (S. Hall 232) in nineteenth-century America as a result of their "sacralization" through such nonprofit cultural institutions as fine arts museums and symphony orchestras (Levine, *Highbrow* 134; see also DiMaggio). In the early 2000s, Jim Collins, Paul Lopes, and John Storey have performed similar work for twentieth- and twenty-first–century America (see Collins; Storey, "'Expecting'"; and "Social Life"; and Lopes). In addition to Shakespeare's plays, one of the most frequently used examples for the contingency of cultural categorization and hierarchization in American culture – and, hence, for the non-essentiality of the category of popular culture – has been (Italian) opera. Performed, consumed, and conceived of as both popular entertainment *and* high art throughout much of the nineteenth century in the United States (see Levine, *Highbrow* 86), opera was subsequently "*made* unpopular" (Storey, "'Expecting'" 37; emphasis original) by elite social groups which introduced normative forms of production and reception (see Levine,

Highbrow 101–102). In the late twentieth and twenty-first centuries, measures undertaken by opera houses (for instance, the use of surtitles) as well as by stakeholders in the cultural market (the use of opera in film, for example) have sought to make opera once again accessible to broader demographic segments (see e.g., Storey, "Social Life" 5; Black-Sotir).[4]

Hence, accessibility, its restriction and increasing, has been key to the un- and subsequent repopularization of opera in nineteenth-, twentieth-, and twenty-first–century America – as well as, I would suggest, to the (un/re)popularization of culture in general. Between what is referred to as "high" or "elite," and "low" or "popular," culture, there are, as Raymond Williams already noted, "evident and important differences of degree of access" (174; see also Levine, *Highbrow* 234). I would therefore agree with Paul J. Ramsey, who has recently defined popular culture quite simply as "media, art, and entertainment that is accessible to the masses" (ix). What exactly does "accessibility" entail, however, and how can we determine whether a given artifact is generally "accessible" and may therefore be considered popular culture? Using as a starting point the list of signs or attributes that Arjun Appadurai has compiled for his definition of luxury goods as a "special 'register' of consumption" (38),[5] one may distinguish four different aspects or levels of accessibility: (1) material or physical accessibility, including issues of price and media distribution, but also, and especially in the case of place-based artifacts, transportation; (2) intellectual or cognitive accessibility, which entails the readability, relatability, and/or recognizability of content and which may be assured through the use of formulas, among others;[6] (3) access to or availability of various modes of reception, i.e., the freedom to receive or consume cultural artifacts in whatever way one wishes;[7] and (4) access to production, i.e., the general availability of the means, processes, and structures to produce cultural artifacts.[8]

To be sure, accessibility is always relative. Art forms inevitably come, as Appadurai had already pointed out, down a specific "path" (28) and with a well-established cultural categorization that is powerfully lingering precisely because it had been originally established as "objective" and "natural" (see Levine, *Highbrow* 229; or indeed, the "tacitly operating canon of popular culture" evoked earlier). Yet (un)popularization measures accompanying specific cultural artifacts may, if not totally erase the ingrained memory of media hierarchy, at least invite diversions from the path – and thus momentarily reconfigure the cultural field by increasing or, indeed, decreasing the accessibility of a specific work.[9] This is why *Popular New Orleans* ultimately argues for a radically case-based definition of popular culture, one that takes into account both the previous path as well as diversions from it in the case at hand. In this sense, the opera examined in Chapter 3 – presented, as it was, in English, for free, and in a socially "neutral" venue, as well as dealing, as it did, with a highly relatable topic – may indeed be considered popular;

whereas, for instance, some of the themed entertainment spaces examined in Chapter 2 – restricted, as they are, to visitors who can afford the extraordinarily steep membership fees – may appear not so accessible or popular after all.[10]

On "New Orleans"

New Orleans, too, is popular with scholars nowadays (as well as with journalists, intellectuals, political commentators, and, of course, a lot of other people). In the preface to his seminal *New Orleans: The Making of an Urban Landscape*, written in 1973, geographer Peirce F. Lewis comments on "the dearth of scholarly writing about New Orleans" (xiii; see also 3). It was only in the context of a reprint of the original preface, however, that this phrase could still be legitimately used in the second edition of Lewis's volume, which was published 30 years later, in 2003 (see xi) – and thus even before in 2005 Hurricane Katrina and the subsequent flooding of much of New Orleans turned the eyes of scholars and of the rest of the world on the city. The almost-death of New Orleans due to the Katrina disaster would, as Thomas Ruys Smith has rightly observed, indeed not only mark a caesura in the history of the Crescent City and catalyze an "outpouring of cultural production both by and about New Orleans and New Orleanians," but also spur a "profound revitalization of interest" in scholarly circles that would eventually lead to a new "high-water mark for scholarship" about the city (3).[11] Nevertheless, already during the years before Katrina, New Orleans – both the city itself and its representation in the arts – had found itself at the center of much scholarly debate.

Until at least the turn of the millennium, this debate had positioned New Orleans primarily within a national framework, whereby the city somewhat inevitably appeared as exceptional, different, exotic, insular, unique – in short, as un-American. New Orleans's difference was seen as cutting across a large number of dimensions, but was mainly located in the early political, social, and cultural history of the city and that history's present-day repercussions: for example, New Orleans's origins as a colony of France, and later Spain, its tripartite system of racial classification, its layout and architecture, the use of French as the predominant language among its inhabitants and their practice of Catholicism, their customs and celebrations, etc. (see Thompson 152–3). Lewis himself had argued in the first edition of his groundbreaking study that "[f]rom the outset, New Orleans was a foreign city, and it has never completely lost its foreign flavor" (3). A "good share of the city" still looked to him, in the mid-1970s, "like nothing else in North America" (5). Yet the city's "physical situation," too, was judged "geographically exceptional" and "quantifiably unique" (Campanella 12; 178; see also Colten 2). Even when placed in the more limited, subnational frame of the South, New

Orleans was still considered "anomalous," a counterpoint to the rural, Anglo-Protestant, and morally rigid culture of the Southern states, an exception to the exception (of the South) to the exception (of the United States; see e.g., McCullough 65).

To be sure, scholars were merely echoing what other commentators had been saying about the city for a long time, since the early nineteenth century, at least: in 1833, for instance, Scottish officer and traveler James E. Alexander cautioned his readers to not "judge of America from New Orleans, for it is altogether *sui generis*" (31); in 1858, the *New York Times* editorialized that "New Orleans is, unquestionably, the most un-American city in our whole Confederacy" (qtd. in Stanonis, *Creating* 9); in 1893, *Harper's* declared that New Orleanians were "not like the rest of us" (Ralph 365); in 1968, Walker Percy saw the Crescent City as "both intimately related to the South and yet in a real sense cut adrift not only from the South but from the rest of Louisiana" ("Amour" 11); and in 1999, Randall Kenan described it as "the center against which America defines itself," "our most foreign city" (504). New Orleans, then, had "always stood apart in [U.S.] national discussions" (Kelman 215), had always sat uncomfortably within "the frames of U.S. nationalism, as well as their affiliated divisions into regional characteristics" in public debates (Gruesz, "Delta" 53).

Rather than resorting to the negative rhetoric of "un-Americanness," scholars – as well as others – had also described the city's uniqueness in positive terms – for example, as French: New Orleans was, Helen Taylor notes, "known from its earliest period as 'Paris-in-the-Wilderness,' [and] in the mid-nineteenth century it was called 'the American Paris'" (93). Thadious M. Davis, by contrast, has argued that "New Orleans viewed as a Caribbean city seems closer to both past and present actualities than the conception of New Orleans as 'America's European Masterpiece'" (200). Still others sought to capture the city's distinctive character by switching its continental affiliation to Africa, with e.g., Gwendolyn M. Hall and Danille Taylor calling New Orleans "the most African city within the United States" and "the most African of American cities," respectively (G. Hall 59; Taylor qtd. in Gotham 3). Yet, as Ottmar Ette and Gesine Müller have pointed out, regardless of whether it was labeled French, Caribbean, or African, the city was still viewed as "exotic and different" ("Introduction" 9).

To some extent, contemporary – that is, post-2000 and post-Katrina – criticism still relies on this discourse of uniqueness and un-Americanness: Dianne Guenin-Lelle, for instance, begins the preface to her *The Story of French New Orleans: History of a Creole City* (2016) with the following sentence: "New Orleans is a city like no other in North America" (xiii); on the same page, she quotes from two more recent publications – namely, Errol Barron's *New Orleans Observed* (2011) and Richard Megraw's *Confronting Modernity* (2008) – in which the city is referred to as "the least

American place in America" and "America's most foreign city," respectively. Even the city's designed landscapes, its public squares and private gardens, have lately received that most New Orleanian of epithets: "unique" (Douglas 3). As Mark L. Thompson somewhat wistfully asserted in 2010, the "aged ideology of nationalism" is "alive and well, as is the romantic, exotic, exceptional image of New Orleans" (167).[12]

And yet, in the years leading up to Katrina, two new lines of scholarly inquiry emerged. On the one hand, in the wake of the transnational turn in American Studies and particularly in Southern studies,[13] critics have been much less likely to discuss New Orleans within a nationalist framework and as exceptional or aberrant, but have rather placed the city, its history and its culture within broader, transnational contexts. Moving outward from the city in larger and larger concentric circles, important frames of reference have included the (circum)Caribbean and the Western hemisphere, the (circum- or French) Atlantic, and, finally, the globe. One of the most immediate effects of this paradigmatic readjustment of perspectives has been a "de-exceptionalization" of New Orleans and its main characteristics. In the introduction to *Look Away! The U.S. South in New World Studies* (2004), for instance, Jon Smith and Deborah Cohn have pointed out that "Virginia and Louisiana might well be said to have less in common than . . . Cuba and Louisiana, Havana and New Orleans" (3). While several voices, including those of Martha Ward, Kirsten Silva Gruesz, and Ned Sublette, have also warned against "sweeping . . . claims to connectivities and diasporic connections" (Regis 4; see also Ward; Gruesz, "Delta"; and "Gulf"; and Sublette 114), scholars such as the authors of *Blues for New Orleans* (Abrahams et al.), John Lowe, Berndt Ostendorf, and Nathalie Dessens have made strong cases for considering New Orleans not "the southernmost city in North America but rather the northernmost city of the Caribbean" (Ostendorf, "Mysteries" 278; see Abrahams et al.; Lowe, "Introduction"; and *Calypso*; Ostendorf, *New Orleans*; and Dessens).

Likewise, New Orleans has been examined in even broader, hemispheric and circum- or French Atlantic contexts: some of the contributors to William Boelhower's *New Orleans in the Atlantic World* (2010), Cécile Vidal's *Louisiana: Crossroads of the Atlantic World* (2014), Ottmar Ette and Gesine Müller's *New Orleans and the Global South* (2017), and Juliane Braun's *Creole Drama: Theatre and Society in Antebellum New Orleans* (2019), for instance, have successfully continued and extended the pioneering scholarship of Arnold R. Hirsch and Joseph Logsdon's *Creole New Orleans* (1992; see especially 189) and Joseph Roach's *Cities of the Dead: Circum-Atlantic Performance* (1996). From these and similar transnationally oriented critical endeavors, New Orleans has emerged, not just as a "paradigmatic metropolis of the Global South" (Ette and Müller, "Introduction" 9), but even as a paradigmatic global city (see White 186; 190–1).

Rather than to "de-exceptionalize" New Orleans by resituating the city within transnational contexts, another – albeit much smaller group – of scholars has sought to explore the sources and origins of the Crescent City's image of uniqueness by examining what had, over the course of the second half of the twentieth century, slowly but steadily replaced port commerce and petrochemical production as the city's most important economic sectors: the tourism industry. Of course, the fact that New Orleans has not exactly remained unaware of or stood aloof vis-à-vis its image of uniqueness and difference, but has rather embraced and reproduced this image, proudly "perform[ing] as a simulacrum of itself" (Roach 180), had not been lost on earlier scholars. Neither had earlier criticism ignored that standing behind these "self-conscious exotica" (Percy, "Why" 6) were also quite unexotic financial interests. In an interesting case of scholarly synchronicity, however, the mid-2000s saw the publication of no fewer than three studies that all focus on how New Orleans tourism boosters, in the interest of enhancing the city's appeal to visitors, not just exploited and further perpetuated but actively shaped and engineered public perceptions of the Crescent City: Jonathan M. Souther's *New Orleans on Parade* (2006), Anthony J. Stanonis's *Creating the Big Easy* (2006), and Kevin Fox Gotham's *Authentic New Orleans* (2007). Lynnell L. Thomas's *Desire & Disaster in New Orleans* was also researched and drafted around 2005, but not printed until 2014; Martine Geronimi's *Québec et la Nouvelle-Orléans*, written in French and already published in 2003, discusses tourism in New Orleans, but also in Quebec City.

Irrespective of whether they ultimately locate the beginnings of what Gotham has termed modern New Orleanian "touristic culture" (20) in the 1920s (Stanonis), the 1940s (Souther), or the 1960s (Gotham), these scholars all stress how from rather conventional strategies of place promotion and marketing during the late nineteenth century (e.g., hosting fairs and expositions), New Orleans eventually switched to projecting a highly selective and carefully crafted vision of itself to a touristic audience – a vision that, in turn, also impacted the city itself. Gotham, for instance, discusses "the rise of urban branding as a major promotional strategy used by powerful tourism organizations to transform urban culture into an abstract sign to entertain visitors and build attractions" (20). Similarly, Stanonis insists that the popular image of New Orleans as unique was the result of "the hard work of shrewd New Orleanians" rather than a "gift from the past": "In short, the Big Easy was made" (*Creating* 244). Souther, finally, views New Orleans as a city "on parade" that actively created an "aura of urban distinctiveness" which it then projected "to the rest of the nation" (*New Orleans* 4).

At the same time, Souther, Stanonis, and Gotham – as well as other scholars – have also intimated that the boosterism of local tourism actors was by no means the only or even the earliest source of New Orleans's "aura of urban distinctiveness" (Souther, *New Orleans* 4). Stanonis, for example, asserts that "such legends had existed prior to 1920" (the year he identifies as marking the beginnings of a touristic culture in the Crescent City) and that it was "[George Washington] Cable, along with another popular author, Lafcadio Hearn, [who] crafted the first romantic, exotic images of New Orleans" (*Creating* 2; 18). Similarly, Souther maintains that "the popular image of New Orleans predated the 1940s" (his choice of years for when mass tourism in the city took off) and that, for instance, the French Quarter had long been "captured in popular literature, notably in George Washington Cable's short stories" (*New Orleans* 2; 8). Gotham, too, ultimately locates the origins of the "stereotypical image" of the city not in "the rise of urban branding as a major promotional strategy" during the 1960s, but in the fictional writings of earlier New Orleans writers such as Cable and Hearn (65; 20; see also 74).[14]

Not all critics have agreed. Notably, Rien Fertel, in *Imagining the Creole City* (2014), has identified nineteenth-century Creole historian Charles Gayarré as "the primary architect of the New Orleans mythos" (4). Starting with *Romance of the History of Louisiana* (1848) and "continuing well into the 1890s," Fertel notes, "Gayarré published English-language popular histories" that "oozed exceptionality" and that due to their local and national success forever "changed the way Creoles and Americans, citizens of Louisiana and the world, thought about New Orleans" (4; 13; 14). Daniel Usner also lists Gayarré among the nineteenth-century historians of Louisiana whose works would "continue to influence twentieth-century literary and popular impressions and to benefit the local tourist and recreation industries" (17).[15]

And yet late-nineteenth–century popular fiction, and specifically the names of Cable and Hearn (as well as that of Grace Elizabeth King), come up again and again in scholarly debates about the origins of New Orleans's image of uniqueness. W. Kenneth Holditch notes that popular visions of the French Quarter "owe more to Cable's writing than to any other source" (50); S. Frederick Starr credits Hearn with having "invented" New Orleans; and Ostendorf claims that Cable and Hearn "did much to popularize this urban culture" (*New Orleans* 23). What is striking, however, is not only that these writers all lived in (and, in the case of Cable and King, even came from) New Orleans, wrote in the vein of what would eventually come to be known as "local color," and published these writings mainly in the northeastern United States. They were also, in one way or another, all connected to (as well as to each other via) the very same New York-based popular literary magazine: *Scribner's Monthly/The Century Illustrated Monthly Magazine*. This last observation constitutes the starting point for my discussion of popular culture depictions of New Orleans in *Popular New Orleans*.

On "Popular New Orleans"

Popular New Orleans traces the development of the image of New Orleans in popular culture artifacts from the late nineteenth to the twenty-first century. Given the popularity of both "popular culture" and "New Orleans," particularly among scholars, it may seem rather surprising that – to my knowledge, at least – there has not yet been published a study based on the intersection or combination of these two topics, i.e., a systematic critical examination of New Orleans *in* popular culture. But then, this very popularity, as well as the popularity of the Crescent City with creators of popular culture artifacts, may have been precisely the problem. Of course, countless scholarly articles, edited collections, and monographs have discussed the portrayal of the city in individual popular culture artifacts or in art forms and media commonly considered popular. A bibliography of David Simon's and Eric Overmeyer's HBO series *Treme* (2010–2013) alone – not to speak of depictions of New Orleans on the big and the small screen in general – would fill many pages. And for a truly comprehensive study of the image of the city in popular culture, one would certainly have to take into account even more than, for instance, the already overwhelming "150 films, over 200 television programs, over 200 novels, nearly 1,500 newspaper articles, and over 200 magazine articles" that Gragg has examined for his investigation of Las Vegas in popular culture (xi), as previously mentioned.

Therefore, but also and especially in light of the strictly case-based model of popular culture introduced earlier, my approach will be selective rather than comprehensive, as well as case-specific rather than generic. More precisely, *Popular New Orleans* will take an in-depth look at what I consider three pivotal moments in the history of New Orleans in popular culture – three moments that, as eclectic and disparate as they may appear at first sight, and particularly in their specific combination in this study, have all marked turning points in the public imagination of the city and have thus, each in its own way, made a decisive impact on the popular image of New Orleans, even as the latter continued to evolve. First and foremost, then, the three case studies that compose *Popular New Orleans* seek to indicate the broad ways in which the image of the city, as portrayed in popular culture artifacts, has developed over time. Moreover, the three case studies will also illustrate the fascinating richness, density, and variety of the popular culture response to the Crescent City: from nineteenth-century illustrated magazine features to twentieth-century themed entertainment spaces to twenty-first–century opera performances, the cultural artifacts discussed in *Popular New Orleans* were all realized in different art forms or media, and hence required and used vastly diverse and medially specific methods or processes of producing, conveying, and making broadly accessible their respective ideas of "New Orleans."

Consequently, rather than imposing a streamlined and unified, "one-fits-all" approach on the individual case studies, *Popular New Orleans* proposes to thoroughly engage with the theoretical and methodological apparatuses that have, over time, crystallized around the various art forms or media discussed in each case study, and to address at least some of the most pressing problems and questions that have lately been identified in each particular field of study – e.g., the issue of what I will refer to as the "rhizomatic turn" in research on periodical print (Chapter 1), the problem of the "textualism" of much research on theme parks and immersive spaces (Chapter 2), and questions about the "efficacy" of performances in investigations of public performances and rituals (Chapter 3). Ultimately, then, *Popular New Orleans* seeks to contribute at least as much to the fields of periodical studies, theme park studies, and performance studies as to those of popular culture and New Orleans studies, with each of the following chapters prominently featuring a subsection that offers an introductory review of relevant discussions and developments, publications, and representatives, as well as steps in the academic institutionalization in and of each field. Partly in order to compensate for the resulting theoretical and methodological variety of *Popular New Orleans* and partly in order to further elaborate, refine, and concretize my case-based model of popular culture as the "culture of accessibility," the remainder of this introduction will especially focus on how the various aspects or levels of accessibility outlined in this paragraph figure in the individual popular culture artifacts examined in each case study.

As has already been intimated, Chapter 1, entitled "Scribner's Illustrated New Orleans," will take us back to the origins of the popular image of New Orleans in the late nineteenth century. Using a periodical studies approach to discuss the veritable stream of Crescent City-related illustrated features published in *Scribner's Monthly, an Illustrated Magazine for the People* (later renamed *The Century Illustrated Monthly Magazine*) from the early 1870s to the early 1890s, this chapter will particularly examine how the local-color fictions of George Washington Cable and Grace Elizabeth King – notably, Cable's *Old Creole Days* and *The Grandissimes*, as well as King's *Balcony Stories* – interacted with the other literary, journalistic, and pictorial texts about New Orleans printed in the magazine. Despite the large number of periodical actors involved in the creation of "Scribner's Illustrated New Orleans" and despite the striking variety of their relationships to, investments in, and views on the city, these texts nevertheless project, as I will argue, a remarkably unified image of New Orleans as French and, at the same time, of New Orleans's Frenchness as past. "Scribner's Illustrated New Orleans" thus employed both fictional and non-fictional writing, as well as illustrations to depict the city's past as French and the city's French as past.

Scholars have long made a case for the centrality of late-nineteenth-century periodical print in the development of an American mass culture and have even identified magazines as "the first national mass medium" (Ohmann, *Selling Culture* vii; see also Ohmann, "Where"), compiling entire lists of social, political, economic, and cultural factors that contributed to making magazines more materially and physically accessible from roughly the 1880s onwards (see e.g., Hinnant and Hudson 113; 128). Hence, it is on the generation of magazines that *followed* upon that of *Scribner's/Century*, the so-called ten-centers, that this discussion about the role of periodicals in U.S. popular culture has mostly concentrated (see Zboray and Zboray 32). This should not, however, blind us to the fact that older magazines, and particularly *Scribner's/Century*, frequently played a pioneering role in the popularization of periodical print, thus paving the way for their successors and contributing, somewhat ironically, to their own demise: notably, Mark Noonan has emphasized the manifold ways in which *Scribner's/Century*'s long-time business manager Roswell Smith experimented with marketing and business techniques to propel the magazine's circulation to ever new heights, up to 222,000 in 1887 (7; 187).[16] Moreover, the specific literary genre that dominated "Scribner's Illustrated New Orleans" – namely, local color – has not only been considered exceedingly accessible to readers (through its formulaic descriptions of the surface particularities of individual U.S. regions and their inhabitants), but also to aspiring writers: regional fiction, Richard Brodhead has noted, "served as the principal place of literary access in America in the postbellum decades" (116; see also e.g., Bold 10), and "Scribner's Illustrated New Orleans" provides, as I will show, an especially striking illustration of this.

During the mid-twentieth century, Violet Bryan maintains, New Orleans "was a choice subject for popular fiction, histories, and films" (119; see also Taylor 101). Yet the man "most credited with vulgarizing the romance of the city" (Dawdy 76) chose to depict New Orleans in a different, entirely new popular art form that was just emerging at the time: the theme park. Entitled "Disney's Immersive New Orleans," Chapter 2 will take an integrated and historical approach to themed and immersive spaces to analyze the production, depiction, and reception of the city in Disney's theme parks and resorts in California, Florida, and Japan. As it stresses the gradual "Frenchifying" of Disney's New Orleans-themed spaces, the story of "Disney's Immersive New Orleans" will be, in a way, the story of the gradual translation of "Scribner's Illustrated New Orleans" into three dimensions: from Disneyland's "New Orleans Street" and "New Orleans Square" to the New Orleans-themed area of Tokyo Disneyland and Walt Disney World's "Port Orleans – French Quarter," Disney's immersive spaces, too, have depicted the city's past as French and the city's French as past.

Disney is one of the very few companies – McDonald's is another one (see Ritzer) – whose name has served as the basis for a term that designates, among other things, the process of making content more intellectually or cognitively accessible. Coined by Richard Schickel in 1968 (220), "Disneyfication" has frequently been used to criticize Disney parks, as well as theme parks in general, for formularizing, oversimplifying, and even grossly misrepresenting their themes in the interest of mass appeal and, hence, profitability (see, to give but one example, Wallace). As commercial place-based entertainment facilities, theme parks have also taken special care to be as physically accessible as possible, often establishing themselves close to large population centers (see Kagelmann, "Themenparks" [1993] 407). Even the strong cultural pressure to visit (Disney) theme parks as a sort of modern pilgrimage sites (see Moore), however, can only partly compensate for their rather limited material accessibility (mostly due to their increasingly high entrance fees).[17] In addition, during the past decade, larger theme park complexes such as Walt Disney World have introduced more or less mandatory reception protocols via online reservation systems that, while ostensibly assisting customers in making their theme park experience more personal and pleasurable, have also made it virtually impossible to visit the facilities without extensively engaging with them and their offerings prior to the visit.[18] With the "full" enjoyment of the (Disney) theme park thus restricted to initiates only, the medium may have started to become much less accessible than heretofore, if only in terms of accessibility of reception.

These recent developments notwithstanding, theme parks – as well as illustrated magazines, for that matter – are probably still considered much more accessible and popular than, for instance, opera. The aura of exclusiveness that continues to surround this art form is precisely the reason why the creators and producers of the opera premiere discussed in Chapter 3, entitled "*Wading Home*'s Post-Katrina New Orleans," made every conceivable effort to render the event as accessible as possible, particularly in comparison with other such performances (see earlier). The result was a hugely popular opera premiere (in terms of visitor numbers) with a remarkably diverse audience, but also one that, in the wake of Hurricane Katrina, thoroughly reconfigured the popular image of New Orleans. Indeed, using a performance studies approach to examine the 2015 premiere performance of Mary Alice Rich's (music and libretto) and Rosalyn Story's (libretto) *Wading Home: An Opera of New Orleans* in Dallas, Texas, "*Wading Home*'s Post-Katrina New Orleans" will discuss the event against the horizon of post-Katrina cultural production to show how it depicted the Crescent City both before and after the 2005 Katrina disaster as exemplary rather than exceptional, as American rather than French. Already, the opera itself (like the novel on which it is based) stresses the representative Americanness of the city by arguing that displacement and dispossession have been ubiquitous experiences for African Americans both before and after Katrina, as well as both in the Southern cityscape and in the rural South. The *performance* of this opera in Dallas further solidified *Wading Home*'s take on the exemplarity of both Katrina and New Orleans by subtly pointing to the links and parallels between the place where it is set (New Orleans) and the place where it was staged (Dallas). Moreover, as I will show, just like "Disney's Immersive New Orleans" translated the particular popular vision of the city as French – a vision inaugurated by, among others, "Scribner's Illustrated New Orleans" – into three-dimensional, real-life places, "*Wading Home*'s Post-Katrina New Orleans" used the power and efficacy of activist performance to transfer its own, almost diametrically opposed vision of the Crescent City as American into a lived reality. Popular New Orleans today is not just a place that one can visit "in [one's] imagination" (Piazza 5), then. Much like the "real" city of New Orleans, it has become a place – several places, in fact – that one can actually travel to, experience, and enjoy, in places as far away from the actual city as Texas, Florida, California, and Japan – and even, as I will argue in the Conclusion, in New Orleans itself.

Ultimately, then, *Popular New Orleans* is about the multi-leveled globality of popular New Orleans. This globality first of all applies to the changing images of the city in popular culture artifacts themselves: relying on the historical origins of the city during the eighteenth-century wave of European global expansion, for instance, older popular visions of the Crescent City regularly stressed the latter's exceptionality via its French past. More recently, in the wake of Hurricane Katrina, popular culture artifacts have engaged with the city's (and the disaster's) exemplarity on a national scale – but also on a global scale. The globality of popular New Orleans also and especially applies, however, to the widespread dissemination of public imaginations of the city. Complementing recent scholarship that views the Crescent City as a paradigmatic global urban space (see previous), the case studies in this book demonstrate that popular New Orleans could and can be found all over the world, from the New York offices of a late-nineteenth–century literary magazine to a mid-twentieth–century theme park in Japan to a twenty-first–century opera stage in Dallas. Even before local tourism boosters and business elites put their city "on parade" and projected their version of it "to the rest of the nation" and to the rest of the world (see previous), the rest of the nation and the world had come up with their own New Orleans. It is this New Orleans – popular New Orleans – that most people have visited and, quite probably, will ever visit. And, as *Popular New Orleans* will hopefully show, it is a New Orleans that is by no means any less worth the journey and the scholarly examination than the real one.

Notes

1. According to Imre Szeman and Susie O'Brien, "one institutional explanation for why courses in popular culture are quietly popping up alongside (and sometimes in place of) more traditional courses in subjects such as, say, medieval history," is that they attract large numbers of students from different

disciplines: "they are popular in the same commercial sense that [the American TV series] *NCIS* is popular, which is to say they are profitable" (17).
2. Holt N. Parker even maintains that "scholars of popular culture and cultural studies have taken a certain perhaps perverse pride in not defining their subject" (147).
3. Fiske's work thus also stands in the tradition of British cultural studies, which mainly developed out of the Centre for Contemporary Cultural Studies, founded in 1964 at the University of Birmingham. Drawing on Antonio Gramsci's concept of hegemony, Birmingham school theorists saw popular culture as "an arena of negotiation and struggle between . . . the imposition of dominant interests and resistance of subordinate interests" (Storey, *Popular* 11–3; see also Jenkins, McPherson, and Shattuc 35–7). In fact, in *Understanding Popular Culture*, Fiske writes that popular culture "always bears traces of the constant struggle between domination and subordination, between power and various forms of resistance to it or evasions to it" (19).
4. In Holt N. Parker's terms, then, opera has been "(un)authorized." Parker defines popular culture as "authorized culture":

> That is, popular culture consists of the paintings of those not recognized as artists by the artworld, the poems of those not recognized by whoever is responsible for recognizing poets, the medicine of those not recognized as physicians, the religion of those not recognized as priests, to which we might add the scholarship of those not recognized as scholars by the proper institutions.
>
> (165)

My own approach differs from Parker's mainly in that it goes beyond purely discursive issues to also take into account practical or material questions such as the price of a cultural artifact.
5. In his introduction to *The Social Life of Things: Commodities in Cultural Perspective* (1986), Appadurai identifies the following attributes as signs of luxury goods:

> (1) restriction, either by price or by law, to elites; (2) complexity of acquisition, which may or may not be a function of real "scarcity"; (3) semiotic virtuosity, that is, the capacity to signal fairly complex social messages (as do pepper in cuisine, silk in dress, jewels in adornment, and relics in worship); (4) specialized knowledge as a prerequisite for their "appropriate" consumption, that is, regulation by fashion; and (5) a high degree of linkage of their consumption to body, person, and personality.
> (38)

My own list of aspects or levels of accessibility differs from Appadurai's mainly in that it also takes into account access to the production of cultural goods.
6. Starting with John G. Cawelti's seminal "The Concept of Formula in the Study of Popular Culture" (1969), the use of formulas, conventions, stock plots, etc., has been viewed as one of the hallmarks of popular culture aesthetics. My point here is, however, that a cultural artifact does not have to be formulaic in order to be accessible, but can also be *made* accessible through, e.g., accompanying translations (cf. English surtitles in opera) or explanatory guides.
7. Levine argues that one of the central elements of the "sacralization" of certain forms of culture in nineteenth-century America was the "disciplining and training" of audiences: "'Silence in the face of art,' was becoming the

norm and was helping to create audiences without the independence to pit their taste, publicly at least, against those of critics, performers, and artists" (*Highbrow* 184; 195).
8. Jim Cullen has repeatedly pointed out that in contrast to other "sites of everyday life," including the labor market, residential patterns, and politics, popular culture "affords a unique degree of economic, social, and even political access for those otherwise marginalized in U.S. society" (*Art* 16), thus becoming a sort of cultural "gateway" ("Introduction" 6–7; see also Heffernan 355). In the late nineteenth century, for instance, photography was considered a "threat" by "those who were sacralizing art" because it:

> could give a wide spectrum of people the very means of *creating* art. It was the perfect instrument for a society with a burgeoning middle class, which could now satisfy itself with processes and images that had previously been confined to elite circles.
> (Levine, *Highbrow* 161; emphasis original)

In the twenty-first century, the invention of comparatively cheap (mobile phone) cameras and the development of easy-to-use photo, sound, and video editing software, as well as the launch of Web 2.0 with its "participatory culture" (Jenkins, *Convergence* 257) of YouTube, Myspace, and Instagram, has greatly increased access to the production of (visual) art.
9. In *Popular Culture and High Culture* (1974), Herbert J. Gans suggests – and subsequently rejects – a policy of "cultural mobility," according to which "American society should pursue policies that would maximize educational and other opportunities for all so as to permit everyone to choose from higher taste cultures" (128). Thus, Gans locates the issue of accessibility more on the consumers' side. By contrast, my model focuses more on what producers (can) do to make a specific cultural artifact accessible to a broad audience.
10. "Club 33," the themed restaurant and bar in question, constitutes but one small element of Disneyland's New Orleans Square, which is why I nevertheless consider the epithet popular justified in connection with Disney theme parks in general.
11. Critical debates about Hurricane Katrina and the artistic responses to the disaster will be discussed in more detail in "*Wading Home*'s Post-Katrina New Orleans" (Chapter 3).
12. On the dangers of this continued reliance on the exceptionalist narrative, see Lightweis-Goff.
13. Among the numerous programmatic delineations of transnational American studies, see especially Ickstadt; Radway's and Fisher Fishkin's presidential addresses to the American Studies Association in 1998 and 2004, respectively; Hornung; Elliott; and Fluck. See also such edited collections and monographs as Rowe's *Post-Nationalist American Studies* (2000) and *The New American Studies* (2002); Ostendorf's *Transnational America* (2002); Siemerling's *The New North American Studies* (2005); *Transnational American Studies*, edited by Fluck, Brandt, and Thaler (2007); *Re-Framing the Transnational Turn in American Studies*, edited by Fluck, Pease, and Rowe (2011); and Hebel's *Transnational American Studies* (2012); as well as the journals *Comparative American Studies* (published since 2003) and the *Journal of Transnational American Studies* (published since 2009). For the first signs of the transnational turn in Southern studies, see particularly the 2006 special issue of *American Literature* (McKee and Trefzer). As I have argued elsewhere (see Freitag, "New Approaches"), the transnational turn in (new) Southern studies is also reflected in the titles of a number of essay collections

(e.g., Jon Smith and Deborah Cohn's *Look Away: The U.S. South in New World Studies*, 2004) and monographs (e.g., James L. Peacock's *Grounded Globalism: How the U.S. South Embraces the World*, 2007), some of which appeared in the newly established series "New Directions in Southern Studies" and "The New Southern Studies" by the University of North Carolina Press and the University of Georgia Press, respectively.
14. L.L. Thomas, somewhat less specifically, speaks of the "image of the city that had been cultivated by writers and tourism boosters [and that] left a lasting imprint on the national popular imagination" (1).
15. In fact, in his final "Drop Shot" column for the New Orleans *Picayune*, published on 25 February 1872, George Washington Cable himself alludes to Gayarré as the only man who up to that point had "uncovered the mines of romance" of "Louisiana's brief two centuries of history" (qtd. in Cleman, *Cable* 19; see also Fertel 79). Cable would, of course, soon extensively work these mines for his contributions to "Scribner's Illustrated New Orleans" (see Chapter 1).
16. It was for a reason *Scribner's* called itself "an Illustrated Magazine *for the People*" (emphasis added), a title that was first suggested by the magazine's founding editor-in-chief, Josiah G. Holland, in a letter to publisher Charles Scribner from 26 July 1896. In the same letter, Holland proposed to make the magazine "popular in materials" and "the delight of the people" (qtd. in Noonan, *Reading* 4). This attitude persisted even after the name change to *Century*: in a letter from 31 January 1894, then associate editor Robert Underwood Johnson told L. Edwin Dudley that the magazine was "a little shy of [printing] old letters [of famous men] as they are apt to be deceptive as to popular interest" (Century Company Records, Series I, Box 51).
17. As early as 1999, the authors of the *Let's Go: USA* travel guide quipped that "Disney's price inflation rates make college tuitions look stable" (Hahn 366).
18. Aldo Legnaro and H. Jürgen Kagelmann have conceptualized this required engagement as "Erlebnisarbeit" ("experience work") and "Spaß-Arbeit" ("fun work"), respectively; see Legnaro 293; and Kagelmann, "Themenparks" (2004) 174–5.

Bibliography

Abrahams, Roger D., Nick Spitzer, Robert Farris Thompson, and John F. Szwed. *Blues for New Orleans: Mardi Gras and America's Creole Soul*. Philadelphia: U of Pennsylvania P, 2006. Print.

Alexander, James E. *Transatlantic Sketches*. Vol. 2. London: Bentley, 1833. Print.

Appadurai, Arjun. "Introduction: Commodities and the Politics of Value." *The Social Life of Things: Commodities in Cultural Perspective*. Ed. Arjun Appadurai. Cambridge: Cambridge UP, 1986. 3–63. Print.

Arnold, Matthew. *Culture and Anarchy*. London: Cambridge UP, 1932. Print.

Bacon, Simon. *Becoming Vampire: Difference and the Vampire in Popular Culture*. Oxford: Lang, 2016. Print.

Bishop, Kyle William. *American Zombie Gothic: The Rise and Fall (and Rise) of the Walking Dead in Popular Culture*. Jefferson: McFarland, 2010. Print.

Black, Rachel, ed. *Alcohol in Popular Culture: An Encyclopedia*. Santa Barbara: Englewood, 2010. Print.

Black-Sotir, Carolyn. "Opera in America: Music of, by, and for the People." Diss. University of Maryland, 2012. https://drum.lib.umd.edu/bitstream/handle/1903/13414/Black-Sotir%2c%20Carolyn.pdf?sequence=2&isAllowed=y. Web.

Boelhower, William, ed. *New Orleans in the Atlantic World*. London: Routledge, 2010. Print.

Bold, Christine. "Introduction." *The Oxford History of Popular Print Culture*. Vol. 6: US Popular Print Culture 1860–1920. Ed. Christine Bold. Oxford: Oxford UP, 2012. 1–19. Print.

Bourdieu, Pierre. *La distinction: Critique sociale du jugement*. Paris: Minuit, 1979. Print.

Braun, Juliane. *Creole Drama: Theatre and Society in Antebellum New Orleans*. Charlottesville: U of Virginia P, 2019. Print.

Brodhead, Richard. *Cultures of Letters: Scenes of Reading and Writing in Nineteenth-Century America*. Chicago: U of Chicago P, 1993. Print.

Browne, Ray B., and Pat Browne. "Introduction." *The Guide to United States Popular Culture*. Ed. Ray B. Browne and Pat Browne. Bowling Green: Bowling Green State U Popular P, 2001. 1–4. Print.

Bryan, Violet Harrington. *The Myth of New Orleans in Literature: Dialogues of Race and Gender*. Knoxville: U of Tennessee P, 1993. Print.

Campanella, Richard. *Time and Place in New Orleans: Past Geographies in the Present Day*. Gretna, LA: Pelican, 2002. Print.

Cawelti, John G. "The Concept of Formula in the Study of Popular Culture." *The Journal of Popular Culture* 3.3 (1969): 381–90. Print.

Century Company. *Century Company Records*. New York Public Library MssCol504.

Clare, Ralph. *Fictions Inc.: The Corporation in Postmodern Fiction, Film, and Popular Culture*. New Brunswick, NJ: Rutgers UP, 2014. Print.

Clarke, John. "Approaches to Interpreting Popular Culture." *Major Problems in American Popular Culture*. Ed. Kathleen Franz and Susan Smulyan. Belmont: Wadsworth, 2012 [1990]. 16–25. Print.

Cleman, John. *George Washington Cable Revisited*. New York: Twayne, 1996. Print.

Collins, Jim. "High-Pop: An Introduction." *High-Pop: Making Culture into Popular Entertainment*. Ed. Jim Collins. Oxford: Blackwell, 2002. 1–31. Print.

Colten, Craig E. *An Unnatural Metropolis: Wrestling New Orleans from Nature*. Baton Rouge: Louisiana State UP, 2005. Print.

Cullen, Jim. *The Art of Democracy: A Concise History of Popular Culture in the United States*. New York: Monthly Review, 1996. Print.

———. "Introduction: The World Wide Web of Popular Culture." *Popular Culture in American History*. Ed. Jim Cullen. Malden: Blackwell, 2001. 1–9. Print.

Davis, Thadious M. *Southscapes: Geographies of Race, Region, and Literature*. Chapel Hill: U of North Carolina P, 2011. Print.

Dawdy, Shannon Lee. *Patina: A Profane Archaeology*. Chicago: The U of Chicago P, 2016. Print.

Dessens, Nathalie. *Creole City: A Chronicle of Early American New Orleans*. Gainesville: UP of Florida, 2015. Print.

DiMaggio, Paul. "Cultural Entrepreneurship in Nineteenth-Century Boston: The Creation of an Organizational Base for High Culture in America." *Media, Culture and Society* 4 (1982): 33–50. Print.

Douglas, Lake. *Public Spaces, Private Gardens: A History of Designed Landscapes in New Orleans*. Baton Rouge: Louisiana State UP, 2011. Print.

Elliott, Emory. "Diversity in the United States and Abroad: What Does It Mean When American Studies Is Transnational?" *American Quarterly* 59.1 (2007): 1–22. Print.

Ette, Ottmar, and Gesine Müller. "Introduction." *New Orleans and the Global South: Caribbean, Creolization, Carnival.* Ed. Ottmar Ette and Gesine Müller. Hildesheim: Georg Olms, 2017. 9–11. Print.

———, eds. *New Orleans and the Global South: Caribbean, Creolization, Carnival.* Hildesheim: Georg Olms, 2017. Print.

Fertel, Rien. *Imagining the Creole City: The Rise of Literary Culture in Nineteenth-Century New Orleans.* Baton Rouge: Louisiana State UP, 2014. Print.

Fishkin, Shelley Fisher. "Crossroads of Cultures: The Transnational Turn in American Studies – Presidential Address to the American Studies Association, November 12, 2004." *American Quarterly* 57.1 (2005): 17–57. Print.

Fiske, John. *Reading the Popular.* Boston: Unwin Hyman, 1989. Print.

———. *Understanding Popular Culture.* Boston: Unwin Hyman, 1989. Print.

Fluck, Winfried. "Inside and Outside: What Kind of Knowledge Do We Need? A Response to the Presidential Address." *American Quarterly* 59.1 (2007): 23–32. Print.

Fluck, Winfried, Stefan Brandt, and Ingrid Thaler, eds. *Transnational American Studies.* Tübingen: Narr, 2007. Print.

Fluck, Winfried, Donald E. Pease, and John Carlos Rowe, eds. *Re-Framing the Transnational Turn in American Studies.* Hanover, NH: Dartmouth College P, 2011. Print.

Freitag, Florian. "New Approaches to the South." *Amerikastudien/American Studies* 60.2/3 (2015). http://dgfa.de/wp-content/uploads/Hardwig_UND_Noonan_UND_Zacharasiewicz_und_Irmscher_Review.pdf. Web.

Gans, Herbert J. *Popular Culture and High Culture: An Analysis and Evaluation of Taste.* New York: Basic Books, 1974. Print.

Geronimi, Martine. *Québec et la Nouvelle-Orléans: Paysages imaginaires français en Amérique du Nord.* Paris: Belin, 2003. Print.

Gotham, Kevin Fox. *Authentic New Orleans: Tourism, Culture, and Race in the Big Easy.* New York: New York UP, 2007. Print.

Gragg, Larry Dale. *Bright Light City: Las Vegas in Popular Culture.* Lawrence: UP of Kansas, 2013. Print.

Gruesz, Kirsten Silva. "Delta *Desterrados*: Antebellum New Orleans and New World Print Culture." *Look Away! The U.S. South in New World Studies.* Ed. Jon Smith and Deborah Cohn. Durham, NC: Duke UP, 2004. 52–79. Print.

———. "The Gulf of Mexico and the 'Latinness' of New Orleans." *American Literary History* 18.3 (2006): 468–595. Print.

Guenin-Lelle, Dianne. *The Story of French New Orleans: History of a Creole City.* Jackson: UP of Mississippi, 2016. Print.

Hahn, Irene J., ed. *Let's Go: USA.* New York: St. Martin's, 1999. Print.

Hall, Gwendolyn Midlo. "The Formation of Afro-Creole Culture." *Creole New Orleans: Race and Americanization.* Ed. Arnold Hirsch and Joseph Logsdon. Baton Rouge: Louisiana State UP, 1992. 58–87. Print.

Hall, Stuart. "Notes on Deconstructing 'the Popular.'" *Popular Culture: Critical Concepts in Media and Cultural Studies.* Vol. 1: History and Theory. Ed. Chris Rojek. London: Routledge, 2012 [1981]. 224–36. Print.

Harmon, Gary L. "On the Nature and Functions of Popular Culture." *Popular Culture Theory and Methodology: A Basic Introduction.* Ed. Harold E. Hinds, Jr., Marilyn F. Motz, and Angela M.S. Nelson. Madison: U of Wisconsin P, 2006 [1983]. 62–74. Print.

Hebel, Udo J., ed. *Transnational American Studies*. Heidelberg: Winter, 2012. Print.

Heffernan, Nick. "Popular Culture." *A New Introduction to American Studies*. Ed. Howard Temperley and Christopher Bigsby. London: Pearson Longman, 2006. 352–75. Print.

Hinds, Jr., Harold E. "Popularity: How to Make a Key Concept Count in Building a Theory of Popular Culture." *Popular Culture Theory and Methodology: A Basic Introduction*. Ed. Harold E. Hinds, Jr., Marilyn F. Motz, and Angela M.S. Nelson. Madison: U of Wisconsin P, 2006 [1994]. 371–81. Print.

———. "Popularity: The *Sine Qua Non* of Popular Culture." *Popular Culture Theory and Methodology: A Basic Introduction*. Ed. Harold E. Hinds, Jr., Marilyn F. Motz, and Angela M.S. Nelson. Madison: U of Wisconsin P, 2006 [1988]. 359–70. Print.

Hinnant, Amanda, and Berkley Hudson. "The Magazine Revolution." *The Oxford History of Popular Print Culture*. Vol. 6: US Popular Print Culture 1860–1920. Ed. Christine Bold. Oxford: Oxford UP, 2012. 113–31. Print.

Hirsch, Arnold R., and Joseph Logsdon, eds. *Creole New Orleans: Race and Americanization*. Baton Rouge: Louisiana State UP, 1992. Print.

Holditch, W. Kenneth. "*The Grandissimes* and the French Quarter." *Southern Quarterly* 18.4 (1980): 34–50. Print.

Horn, Katrin. *Women, Camp, and Popular Culture: Serious Excess*. Cham: Palgrave Macmillan, 2017. Print.

Hornung, Alfred. "Transnational American Studies: Response to the Presidential Address." *American Quarterly* 57.1 (2005): 67–73. Print.

Ickstadt, Heinz. "American Studies in an Age of Globalization." *American Quarterly* 54.4 (2002): 543–62. Print.

Iwamura, Jane Naomi. *Virtual Orientalism: Asian Religions and American Popular Culture*. Oxford: Oxford UP, 2011. Print.

Jenkins, Henry. *Convergence Culture: Where Old and New Media Collide*. New York: New York UP, 2006. Print.

———. *Textual Poachers: Television Fans and Participatory Culture*. New York: Routledge, 1992. Print.

Jenkins, Henry, Tara McPherson, and Jane Shattuc. "Defining Popular Culture." *Hop on Pop: The Politics and Pleasures of Popular Culture*. Ed. Henry Jenkins, Tara McPherson, and Jane Shattuc. Durham: Duke UP, 2002. 26–42. Print.

Kagelmann, H. Jürgen. "Themenparks." *Tourismuspsychologie und Tourismussoziologie*. Ed. Heinz Hahn and H. Jürgen Kagelmann. Munich: Quintessenz, 1993. 407–15. Print.

———. "Themenparks." *ErlebnisWelten: Zum Erlebnisboom in der Postmoderne*. Ed. H. Jürgen Kagelmann, Reinhard Bachleitner, and Max Rieder. Munich: Profil, 2004. 160–80. Print.

Kelman, Ari. *A River and Its City: The Nature of Landscape in New Orleans*. Berkeley: U of California P, 2003. Print.

Kenan, Randall. *Walking on Water: Black American Lives at the Turn of the Twenty-First Century*. New York: Random House, 1999. Print.

Legnaro, Aldo. "Subjektivität im Zeitalter ihrer simulativen Reproduzierbarkeit. Das Beispiel des Disney-Kontinents." *Gouvernementalität der Gegenwart*. Ed. Ulrich Bröckling, Susanne Krasman, and Thomas Lemke. Frankfurt: Suhrkamp, 2000. 286–314. Print.

Lehman, Katherine J. *Those Girls: Single Women in Sixties and Seventies Popular Culture*. Lawrence: UP of Kansas, 2011. Print.

Levine, Lawrence. "The Folklore of Industrial Society: Popular Culture and Its Audiences." *American Historical Review* 97.5 (December 1992): 1369–99. Print.

———. *Highbrow/Lowbrow: The Emergence of Cultural Hierarchy in America*. Cambridge, MA: Harvard UP, 1988. Print.

Lewis, Peirce F. *New Orleans: The Making of an Urban Landscape*. Cambridge, MA: Ballinger, 1976. Print.

———. *New Orleans: The Making of an Urban Landscape*. Second ed. Charlottesville: U of Virginia P, 2003. Print.

Lightweis-Goff, Jennie. "'Peculiar and Characteristic': New Orleans's Exceptionalism from Olmsted to the Deluge." *American Literature* 86.1 (2014): 147–69. Print.

Lindenauer, Leslie J. *I Could Not Call Her Mother: The Stepmother in American Popular Culture, 1750–1960*. Lanham: Lexington, 2014. Print.

Lopes, Paul. *The Rise of a Jazz Art World*. Cambridge: Cambridge UP, 2002. Print.

Lowe, John. *Calypso Magnolia: The Crosscurrents of Caribbean and Southern Literature*. Chapel Hill: U of North Carolina P, 2016. Print.

———. "Introduction: Creole Cultures and National Identity after Katrina." *Louisiana Culture from the Colonial Era to Katrina*. Ed. John Lowe. Baton Rouge: Louisiana State UP, 2008. 1–21. Print.

MacDonald, Dwight. "A Theory of Mass Culture." *Mass Culture: The Popular Arts in America*. Ed. Bernard Rosenberg and David Manning White. New York: The Free P, 1957 [1953]. 59–73. Print.

McCullough, Kate. *Regions of Identity: The Construction of America in Women's Fiction, 1885–1914*. Stanford: Stanford UP, 1999. Print.

McKee, Kathryn, and Annette Trefzer. "Preface: Global Contexts, Local Literatures: The New Southern Studies." *American Literature* 78.4 (2006): 677–90. Print.

McMahon-Coleman, Kimberley, and Roslyn Weaver. *Werewolves and Other Shapeshifters in Popular Culture*. Jefferson, NC: McFarland, 2012. Print.

Meisel, Perry. *The Myth of Popular Culture from Dante to Dylan*. Malden: Wiley-Blackwell, 2010. Print.

Miller, Toby. "Introduction: Global Popular Culture." *The Routledge Companion to Global Popular Culture*. New York: Routledge, 2015. 1–10. Print.

Moore, Alexander. "Walt Disney World: Bounded Ritual Space and the Playful Ritual Center." *Anthropological Quarterly* 53.4 (1980): 207–19. Print.

Noonan, Mark J. *Reading the* Century Illustrated Monthly Magazine: *American Literature and Culture, 1870–1893*. Kent: Kent State UP, 2010. Print.

Ohmann, Richard. *Selling Culture: Magazines, Markets, and Class at the Turn of the Century*. London: Verso, 1996. Print.

———. "Where Did Mass Culture Come From? The Case of Magazines." *Berkshire Review* 16 (1981): 85–101. Print.

Ostendorf, Berndt. "The Mysteries of New Orleans: Culture Formation and the Layering of History." *New Orleans and the Global South: Caribbean, Creolization, Carnival*. Ed. Ottmar Ette and Gesine Müller. Hildesheim: Georg Olms, 2017. 275–94. Print.

---. *New Orleans: Creolization and All That Jazz*. Innsbruck: StudienVerlag, 2013. Print.

---, ed. *Transnational America: The Fading of Borders in the Western Hemisphere*. Heidelberg: Winter, 2002. Print.

Parker, Holt N. "Toward a Definition of Popular Culture." *History and Theory* 50 (2011): 147–70. Print.

Peacock, James L. *Grounded Globalism: How the U.S. South Embraces the World*. Athens: U of Georgia P, 2007. Print.

Percy, Walker. "New Orleans Mon Amour." *Signposts in a Strange Land*. Ed. Patrick Samway. New York: Farrar, Straus and Giroux, 1991 [1968]. 10–22. Print.

---. "Why I Live Where I Live." *Signposts in a Strange Land*. Ed. Patrick Samway. New York: Farrar, Straus and Giroux, 1991 [1980]. 3–9. Print.

Piazza, Tom. *Why New Orleans Matters*. New York: HarperCollins, 2005. Print.

Radway, Janice. "What's in a Name? Presidential Address to the American Studies Association, 20 November 1998." *American Quarterly* 51.1 (1999): 1–32. Print.

Ralph, Julian. "New Orleans, Our Southern Capital." *Harper's New Monthly Magazine* 86.513 (February 1893): 364–86. Print.

Ramsey, Paul J. "Introduction: Popular Culture, Learning, and the Left." *Learning the Left: Popular Culture, Liberal Politics, and Informal Education from 1900 to the Present*. Ed. Paul J. Ramsey. Charlotte, NC: IAP, 2015. vii–xvi. Print.

Regis, Helen A. "Introduction." *Caribbean and Southern: Transnational Perspectives on the U.S. South*. Ed. Helen A. Regis. Athens: U of Georgia P, 2006. 1–6. Print.

Rich, Mary Alice, and Rosalyn Story. *Wading Home: An Opera of New Orleans (Libretto)*. 2015. Unpublished, typed manuscript.

Ritzer, George. *The McDonaldization of Society: An Investigation into the Changing Character of Contemporary Life*. Thousand Oaks: Pine Forge, 1993. Print.

Roach, Joseph. *Cities of the Dead: Circum-Atlantic Performance*. New York: Columbia UP, 1996. Print.

Rowe, John Carlos, ed. *The New American Studies*. Minneapolis: U of Minnesota P, 2002. Print.

---, ed. *Post-Nationalist American Studies*. Berkeley: U of California P, 2000. Print.

Sachleben, Mark, and Kevan M. Yenerall. *Seeing the Bigger Picture: American and International Politics in Film and Popular Culture*. New York: Lang, 2012. Print.

Schickel, Richard. *The Disney Version: The Life, Times, Art and Commerce of Walt Disney*. New York: Simon and Schuster, 1968. Print.

Schroeder, Fred H. "The Discovery of Popular Culture before Printing." *Popular Culture Theory and Methodology: A Basic Introduction*. Ed. Harold E. Hinds, Jr., Marilyn F. Motz, and Angela M.S. Nelson. Madison: U of Wisconsin P, 2006 [1980]. 49–54. Print.

Schudson, Michael. "The New Validation of Popular Culture: Sense and Sentimentality in Academia." *Popular Culture Theory and Methodology: A Basic Introduction*. Ed. Harold E. Hinds, Jr., Marilyn F. Motz, and Angela M.S. Nelson. Madison: U of Wisconsin P, 2006 [1987]. 85–106. Print.

Siemerling, Winfried. *The New North American Studies: Culture, Writing and the Politics of Re/cognition*. New York: Routledge, 2005. Print.

Smith, Anthony Burke. *The Look of Catholics: Portrayals in Popular Culture from the Great Depression to the Cold War*. Lawrence: UP of Kansas, 2010. Print.

Smith, Jon, and Deborah Cohn. "Introduction: Uncanny Hybridities." *Look Away! The U.S. South in New World Studies*. Ed. Jon Smith and Deborah Cohn. Durham, NC: Duke UP, 2004. 1–19. Print.

Smith, Thomas Ruys. *Southern Queen: New Orleans in the Nineteenth Century*. London: Continuum, 2011. Print.

Sotirin, Patricia J., and Laura L. Ellington. *Where the Aunts Are: Family, Feminism, and Kinship in Popular Culture*. Waco: Baylor UP, 2013. Print.

Souther, J. Mark. *New Orleans on Parade: Tourism and the Transformation of the Crescent City*. Baton Rouge: Louisiana State UP, 2006. Print.

Stahl, Roger. *Militainment, Inc.: War, Media, and Popular Culture*. New York: Routledge, 2010. Print.

Stanonis, Anthony J. *Creating the Big Easy: New Orleans and the Emergence of Modern Tourism, 1918–1945*. Athens: U of Georgia P, 2006. Print.

Starr, S. Frederick. "Introduction: The Man Who Invented New Orleans." *Inventing New Orleans: Writings of Lafcadio Hearn*. Ed. S. Frederick Starr. Jackson: U of Mississippi P, 2001. xi–xxvii. Print.

Storey, John. "'Expecting Rain': Opera as Popular Culture?" *High-Pop: Making Culture into Popular Entertainment*. Ed. Jim Collins. Oxford: Blackwell, 2002. 32–55. Print.

———. *From Popular Culture to Everyday Life*. New York: Routledge, 2014. Print.

———. *An Introductory Guide to Cultural Theory and Popular Culture*. Athens: U of Georgia P, 1993. Print.

———. *Inventing Popular Culture: From Folklore to Globalization*. London: Blackwell, 2003. Print.

———. "The Social Life of Opera." *European Journal of Cultural Studies* 6.1 (2003): 5–35. Print.

Sublette, Ned. *The World That Made New Orleans: From Spanish Silver to Congo Square*. Chicago: Lawrence Hill, 2008. Print.

Szeman, Imre, and Susie O'Brien. *Popular Culture: A User's Guide*. Hoboken: Wiley, 2017. Print.

Taylor, Helen. *Circling Dixie: Contemporary Southern Culture through a Transatlantic Lens*. New Brunswick, NJ: Rutgers UP, 2000. Print.

Thomas, Lynnell L. *Desire & Disaster in New Orleans: Tourism, Race, and Historical Memory*. Durham: Duke UP, 2014. Print.

Thompson, Mark L. "Locating the Isle of Orleans: Atlantic and American Historiographical Perspectives." *New Orleans in the Atlantic World*. Ed. William Boelhower. London: Routledge, 2010. 151–79. Print.

Tropp, Laura, and Janice Kelly, eds. *Deconstructing Dads: Changing Images of Fathers in Popular Culture*. Lanham: Lexington, 2016. Print.

Usner, Jr., Daniel H. "Between Creoles and Yankees: The Discursive Representation of Colonial Louisiana in American History." *French Colonial Louisiana and the Atlantic World*. Ed. Bradley G. Bond. Baton Rouge: Louisiana State UP, 2005. 1–21. Print.

Vidal, Cécile, ed. *Louisiana: Crossroads of the Atlantic World*. Philadelphia: U of Pennsylvania P, 2014. Print.

Wallace, Mike. "Mickey Mouse History: Portraying the Past at Disney World." *Radical History Review* 32 (1985): 33–57. Print.
Ward, Martha. "Where Circum-Caribbean Afro-Catholic Creoles Met American Southern Protestant Conjurers: Origins of New Orleans Voodoo." *Caribbean and Southern: Transnational Perspectives on the U.S. South*. Ed. Helen A. Regis. Athens: U of Georgia P, 2006. 124–38. Print.
Watson, Elwood, and Marc E. Shaw, eds. *Performing American Masculinities: The 21st-Century Man in Popular Culture*. Bloomington: Indiana UP, 2011. Print.
Weiner, Robert G., B. Lynn Whitfield, and Jack Becker, eds. *James Bond in World and Popular Culture: The Films Are Not Enough*. Second ed. Newcastle upon Tyne: Cambridge Scholars, 2011. Print.
White, Elisa Joy. *Modernity, Freedom, and the African Diaspora: Dublin, New Orleans, Paris*. Bloomington: Indiana UP, 2012. Print.
Williams, Raymond. "On High and Popular Culture." *Popular Culture: Critical Concepts in Media and Cultural Studies*. Vol. 1: History and Theory. Ed. Chris Rojek. London: Routledge, 2012 [1974]. 171–76. Print.
Zboray, Ronald J., and Saracino Zboray. "The Changing Face of Publishing." *The Oxford History of Popular Print Culture*. Vol. 6: US Popular Print Culture 1860–1920. Ed. Christine Bold. Oxford: Oxford UP, 2012. 23–42. Print.

1 Scribner's Illustrated New Orleans

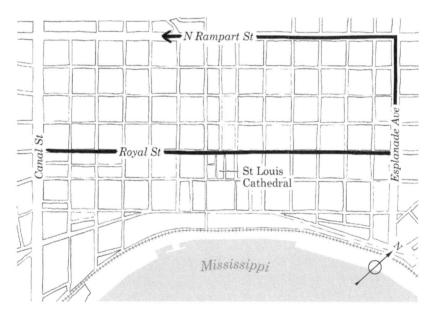

Figure 1.1 Lafcadio Hearn's tour of "The Scenes of Cable's Romances."
Source: Drawn by Polichronios Vezirgenidis.

"A Gentleman of Bayou Têche"

Perhaps one of the most fascinating pieces of Kate Chopin's short fiction is "A Gentleman of Bayou Têche," written in 1893. In this story, Mr. Sublet, an artist "looking for bits of 'local color' along the Têche," proposes to draw a Cajun fisherman and to publish the picture – in the Cajun's words – in "'one fine "*Mag*'zine"'" (319). The Cajun first agrees to pose for the drawing, then refuses for fear of being ridiculed, but eventually yields, "with shy and child-like pleasure" (324), when Sublet allows him to name the picture. "A Gentleman of Bayou Têche" can be described as a local-color story about local color – about its production (by non-local artists), its reception (by local subjects), its aesthetics, and, most importantly, its ethics. Indeed, several early critics, including David Steiling, Kate McCullough, and Judith Fetterley and Marjorie Pryse, viewed Chopin's story as an ironic comment on the local-color writer and a clever critique of the genre of local-color writing, particularly of the way it actively stages and commodifies the local.[1]

Mr. Sublet, however, is a visual artist, not a writer, and the story offers no inherent reason why we should read it as a metaphor. Later critics, including Tom Lutz and myself, have thus regarded "A Gentleman" as a celebration rather than a critique of local-color writers and writing – a celebration, however, that comes at the expense of local-color visual artists and visual art. In Lutz's view, Chopin stages a *paragone*, or contest of local-color art forms, from which writing emerges as victorious. Lutz convincingly argues that "A Gentleman" is:

> about art more than it is about Cajuns, and about literary art in particular. Anyone can come down to the bayou on a quick hunting vacation like Mr. Sublet and take a picture of a local character. But only the literary artist has the kind of perspective necessary to represent what is lost and gained, by all concerned, in the cross-cultural encounter. Only the literary artist can write from both the inside and the outside.
> (30)

Local-color writing (in the shape of Chopin's story) triumphs over local-color drawing (in the shape of Sublet's picture), then, because the former allows the artist to represent the local character both from his own and from the outsider's perspective, whereas the latter has to resort to writing (in the shape of the picture's title or caption) to achieve such a balanced, multiperspective view. Drawing on Lutz's analysis, I have argued elsewhere that Chopin uses her story to poke fun at local-color illustrators such as Edward W. Kemble (see Freitag, "Rencontres" 411). Not least thanks to his illustrations for Mark Twain's *Adventures of Huckleberry Finn* (1885), Kemble had become famous as, in his own words, a "delineator of the South, the Negro being my specialty" although he had "never been further south than Sandy Hook [New Jersey]" ("Illustrating" 32). Kemble then decided that "it was high time for [him] to go and see what the real article looked like" and, equipped with a camera, visited several plantations, "noting the local color" (32).[2] According to this reading, then, "A Gentleman" throws a dubious light on certain local-color illustrators and criticizes them for their careless, superficial, and touristic approach to their subjects.

Chopin (or her editors) had enough taste and good sense to not publish "A Gentleman" in "'one fine "*Mag*'zine,"'" let alone with illustrations: the story was first printed in Chopin's first collection *Bayou Folk* (1894), which Houghton, Mifflin and Company released without any illustrations whatsoever (except for the Riverside Press's colophon). "Azélie," by contrast, another of Chopin's stories featuring Cajuns and also written in 1893, appeared in the December 1894 issue of the *Century* – certainly "'one fine "*Mag*'zine"'" – and with three illustrations by artist Eric Pape[3] before it was reprinted in Chopin's second collection *A Night in Acadie* (1897). Chopin may not have thought highly of local-color visual art in general and of illustrators like Mr. Sublet in particular, but she could not – and may not have wanted to – entirely escape the exigencies and established procedures of the late-nineteenth–century literary marketplace. In Gilded Age America, local-color stories such as "Azélie" – as well as other short stories, novels, and poems – frequently appeared with illustrations in literary magazines before they were collected or reprinted in book form. Prior magazine publication, publishers believed, helped promote the sales of hardcover editions – which is why the major publishing companies had established or acquired literary monthlies in the first place.[4] And with the exception of some of the older, more conservative titles, such as the *Atlantic Monthly*, illustrations constituted, in Gib Prettyman's words, one of the magazines' "primary sources of competitive distinction" (26). Only a "lunatic," the enterprising literary businessman Fulkerson in William Dean Howells's *A Hazard of New Fortunes* (1890) acknowledges, "would start a [magazine] in the twilight of the nineteenth century without illustrations" (7).

To editors and illustrators, a literary genre such as local color, with its detailed descriptions of local and regional landscapes and the customs, speech, and dress of their inhabitants, and with its general emphasis on the "picturesque," must have seemed especially suited for illustration.[5] In late nineteenth-century literary magazines, local-color stories were not only frequently accompanied by illustrations, however; they were also surrounded by a distinctive mix of what long-time *Century* editor L. Frank Tooker has called the typical ingredients of "the traditionally perfect magazine of the day" (320): serialized novels; poems; essays on such issues as art, science, technology, and travel; a variety of recurring editorial departments; and advertisements, all of them often illustrated themselves. Like local-color illustrations, some of these features were especially close to local-color fiction – not only regarding their placement in the magazine, but also methodologically and with respect to their contents. Bill Hardwig, for instance, argues that local color particularly resonated with contemporary travel writing:

> local-color fiction of the era closely mirrors travel writing . . . in form, content, and purpose. In some ways, the methodological overlap between the genres makes sense. These two modes of writing shared the central objective of translating [a region] to a readership unfamiliar with [it].
>
> (3)[6]

However close they were to the local-color stories alongside which they appeared in the magazine, all of these various features had, at least potentially, an impact on how contemporary magazine readers perceived local color.

It is all the more surprising, then, that until very recently, studies of local-color fiction have completely ignored the original periodical context of local color. Basing their readings on reprints of the stories in collections (mostly arranged according to individual authors; see, for instance, Chopin's aforementioned volumes *Bayou Folk* and *A Night in Acadie*), most critics have placed local color, as Hardwig notes in *Upon Provincialism* (2013), "in larger literary and historical contexts, such as Gilded Age expansion, US imperialism, Howellsian realism, and the beginnings of American naturalism" (152).[7] Hardwig maintains, however, that local color can be more profitably understood in the context of Gilded Age periodical culture and should therefore be critically re-situated and re-evaluated within this context (see 152). This is exactly what I will attempt to do in the following. More precisely, I will take a periodical studies approach to New Orleans local color published in *Scribner's Monthly, an Illustrated Magazine for the People* (later renamed *The Century Illustrated Monthly Magazine*), in order to analyze the various ways in which these local-color stories "call and respond" (Noonan, *Reading* xvi) to other literary, journalistic, and pictorial texts about New Orleans (as well as to other features) published in the same or in other issues of the magazine.

Such a retracing of the textual and pictorial networks established by one Gilded Age periodical around the city of New Orleans will inevitably reveal the variety of and the occasional tensions between the individual texts' literary and pictorial perspectives on the urban space, its history, its future, its culture, and its inhabitants. Like any other magazine, *Scribner's/Century* was held together by an editorial formula. In fact, in the case of *Scribner's/Century*, it was one particular aspect of this formula – namely, the periodical's explicit openness to and welcoming attitude toward submissions from and about the South in the name of post-Civil War sectional reconciliation and national integration – that, among other factors, contributed to the surprisingly large number of representations of New Orleans in its pages. But of course, this editorial formula could not prevent the fact that the various textual and visual representations were not uniform in the ways they approached the city, neither within themselves – as, for instance, in the case of illustrated features, where the writer's point of view did not necessarily correspond to that of the visual artist – nor among each other. Indeed, such a complete uniformity was never even intended by the magazine, as is evidenced by at least one instance in which a writer was actively encouraged to submit her retort to another writer's supposedly "false" representation of New Orleans and its people.[8] It is precisely this at times harmonious, at times disharmonious polyvocality of the various literary, journalistic, and pictorial texts that together make up what I call here "Scribner's Illustrated New Orleans," then, that I seek to examine in the following.

"Scribner's Illustrated New Orleans" does not only stand for a large variety of intertextual and intermedial relationships, however. Equally important are the numerous interpersonal relationships that crystallized around the magazine. This network of persons included, first and foremost, the authors and artists who created the texts and illustrations about New Orleans published in *Scribner's/Century*, but also a multitude of other people who were involved in the production of the magazine in less visible ways: editors, art editors, editorial assistants, wood engravers, managers, and printers. Some of these people were entirely new to the world of magazine publishing; others were well experienced at their respective professions. Some of them were New Orleanians; others were not. Some of them had met in person (and in New Orleans!) to exchange their views on their work or even to collaborate on a New Orleans-related magazine feature; others had merely read or seen each other's work or had never even corresponded. Some of them were deeply invested in how the city should be represented textually and pictorially; for others, New Orleans was but a stopover between other projects. What brought them all together were the magazine and their individual contributions to "Scribner's Illustrated New Orleans."

While I will concentrate on the intertextual or intermedial and interpersonal networks that formed around the various New Orleans-related features printed in *Scribner's/Century* in the following, I will, occasionally, also look beyond the pages of the magazine. As I have already intimated, magazine publication was often but a stepping stone toward book publication; indeed, almost all of *Scribner's/Century*'s New Orleans-related features were later reprinted in book form, mostly by the magazine's current and former parent companies (Century Company and Charles Scribner's Sons, respectively). On their way from the magazine to the book, however, some of these features were significantly altered: texts were edited or rewritten, illustrations were repositioned or added, and existing texts – as well as existing texts and illustrations – were newly recombined. New, different images of New Orleans emerged in the process, and new people joined the network, adding their own perspectives and views of the city to the existing ones. While I will not even attempt to include and discuss the entire history of the post-periodical publication of *Scribner's/Century*'s material on New Orleans, I will nevertheless draw, at various points, on some of these post-periodical texts to substantiate and enlarge my arguments.[9]

Thus conceptualized, "Scribner's Illustrated New Orleans" comprises such well-known and trailblazing late-nineteenth–century literary and pictorial representations of New Orleans as the Louisiana chapters of the famous "Great South" series of travel sketches, the local-color stories later collected as *Old Creole Days* and *Balcony Stories*, the novella "Madame Delphine," the novel *The Grandissimes*, and the pictures of Creole slaves dancing the Bamboula in Congo Square. It includes work by such well-known writers and illustrators as George Washington Cable, Grace E. King, Lafcadio Hearn, Edward W. Kemble, and Joseph Pennell. All of these people and their texts and pictures had something to say about New Orleans, and they all had their own distinct views on the city. What they all have in common, however, is that they depicted the city as French and that they represented the city's Frenchness as past. Indeed, these textual and pictorial portrayals of French New Orleans substantially differ from the late-nineteenth–century representation of other U.S. regional cultures (particularly in local color) by completely "pastifying" (Assmann 4) them.[10] Much local-color writing from the Gilded Age uses a nostalgic or elegiac tone to "tell local cultures into a history of their supersession by a modern order now risen to national dominance" (Brodhead, *Cultures* 121), thus containing cultural difference and diversity by hierarchically ordering cultures according to not only spatial categories ("local/regional" vs. "national/cosmopolitan"), but also temporal categories ("old" vs. "new/modern"; see Freitag, "Rencontres" 410). As Jason Arthur writes in *Violet America*, local color "is a genre whose job it is to verify the imminent disappearance of its subject" (xi). Late-nineteenth–century representations of New Orleans, particularly those published in *Scribner's/Century*, however, go further by actually being set in the past (at the time of the Louisiana Purchase, for instance, or during the Reconstruction era) and, hence, completing the process of "pastifying" regional cultures that regionalist writings from e.g., New England, the Midwest, and the Appalachians, most of which are set in the present (see Brodhead, *Cultures* 120; Foote 6), had merely begun. Half a century before the first New Orleans Comprehensive Zoning Ordinance (1929) declared the city's French Quarter a "special historic district" and thus used urban planning to "pastify" or musealize Creole culture (see Klopfer 319), "Scribner's Illustrated New Orleans" employed both fictional and non-fictional writing, as well as illustrations, to depict the city's past as French and the city's French as past.

At the same time, most of the representations of New Orleans in *Scribner's/Century* also exhibit what Bill Hardwig considers typical of all local color; namely, a "radical engagement with the cultural anxieties of the era" (16). Precisely through pastifying New Orleans Creoles and their culture, "Scribner's Illustrated New Orleans" engages the present, offering more or less veiled allusions to and encrypted comments on ongoing political, economic, and cultural transformations such as Reconstruction, Redemption, and, more generally, the "race question." Ultimately, then, "Scribner's Illustrated New Orleans" is characterized by a complex temporality that employs multimedial portrayals of the pastness of French New Orleans to point to the present.

Periodical Studies and the Rhizomatic Turn

In *Social Stories: The Magazine Novel in Nineteenth-Century America* (2003), Patricia Okker notes that the first periodical to have been called a magazine was the London-based *Gentleman's Magazine* (first published in 1731). Its founder Edward Cave, Okker writes, selected the term "to accent the new magazine's identity as a compilation" and to emphasize that "the new periodical was to serve as a warehouse" (1). Indeed, the term magazine, Sammye Johnson and Patricia Prijatel remind us, "comes from the Arabic *makhazin*, which means warehouse or storehouse" (3). According to Okker, however, the illustration on *The Gentleman's Magazine*'s title page – a hand holding a bouquet of flowers – as well as the periodical's motto – "e pluribus unum" – underscored the idea that this magazine "was a whole greater than the sum of its parts" (1).

This idea – namely, that more than just compilations of individual, independent features, periodicals constitute a distinct form of publishing and thus call for distinct analytical approaches and methodologies – forms the central premise of periodical studies. Following Frank Luther Mott's seminal five-volume, Pulitzer Prize-winning *History of American Magazines* (1930–1968) and John Tebbel's slightly less ambitious *The American Magazine: A Compact History* (1969), periodical studies did not fully establish itself in the United States until the early 1990s with the first calls for distinct, holistic approaches to periodicals from both journalism scholars (see Abrahamson) and cultural critics (see Price and Smith), the founding of the Research Society for American Periodicals in 1990, and the establishment of the journal *American Periodicals* in 1991. The early and mid-1990s then saw the publication of several impressive studies particularly of nineteenth-century magazines, among them Ellen Gruber Garvey's *The Adman in the Parlor: Magazines and the Gendering of Consumer Culture* and Richard Ohmann's *Selling Culture: Magazines, Markets, and Class at the Turn of the Century* (both 1996),[11] as well as the digitization and online publication of some major nineteenth-century American periodicals in the "Making of America" project, a collaboration between Cornell University and the University of Michigan started in 1995.[12] A decade later, programmatic articles by scholars such as Judith Yaross Lee (2005) and Sean Latham and Robert Scholes (2006) contributed to further defining and theorizing periodical studies. And again, almost ten years later, John Fagg, Matthew Pethers, and Robin Vandome, in the introduction to a special issue of *American Periodicals* (2013), proclaim what could be termed a rhizomatic turn in periodical studies. Having noticed "an incipient trend toward the analysis of periodical culture . . . in terms of the network idea" (100), Fagg, Pethers, and Vandome delineate "two of the primary ways in which periodicals themselves exemplify network" (101):

> On the one hand, the material object that is a single periodical provides an intertextual network of juxtaposed objects, while the network is extended through the linking of issues within a series. This material and textual network forms a basis for interpretation and criticism. By emphasizing the interconnected nature of the periodical form, individual texts, authors, and titles can be re-evaluated in terms of their larger position within an intertextual network. On the other hand, the institutional networks of periodicals (composed of their contributors, editors, publishers, and printers, as well as distributors and readers) also form important, though sometimes scarcely visible, factors in their production and dissemination. This second, institutional periodical network forms the basis for a more sociological approach to print culture.
>
> (101)

Fagg, Pethers, and Vandome thus invite periodical scholars to examine, on the one hand, "linguistic" texts along and in conjunction with all the "bibliographical codes" (McGann 57) that immediately surround them in periodicals,[13] and, on the other hand, the relationships between various periodical actors involved in the production, distribution, and reception of a magazine.

I would like to make three points here. First, without seeking to diminish Fagg, Pether, and Vandome's contribution to the theorization of periodical studies, I would like to point out that the idea of (intertextual and institutional or interpersonal) networks is hardly new to – but rather cuts to the core of – periodical studies. Already in the mid-2000s, for instance, Lee, as well as Latham and Scholes, pointedly rejected a view of magazines as mere "containers of discrete bits of information" (Latham and Scholes 517) or "aggregations of otherwise autonomous works" (521), calling instead for an investigation of the "rich, dialogic" (528) nature of periodicals and the "interrelations among [their] contents" (Lee 199).[14] Especially Lee also calls for a serious exploration of the "means of production" (198) that characterize periodical publications. Rather than following the "Great Man . . . school of history" (197) that focuses on the lives and accomplishments of individual editors and authors, periodical scholars should, Lee maintains, "examine the published periodical as the result of a collaboration among editors, contributors, readers, and other stakeholders of a particular time and place" (198).[15] Already for Lee, and Latham and Scholes, then, the analysis of the interrelations or networks among periodical contents in periodical studies is ideally complemented by an investigation of the interrelations or networks among periodical actors.[16]

Second, while I fully agree with Fagg, Pethers, and Vandome on the relevance of the network idea for periodical studies, I believe that great care must be taken to distinguish between the various forms of intertextual and interpersonal relationships that ultimately make up these networks, because the latter are neither symmetrical nor free from (occasionally institutionalized) power imbalances. With respect to the material network that makes up the magazine, for instance, critics need to generally distinguish between intertextual and interpictorial relationships on the one hand (i.e., relationships between linguistic texts and between pictures) and intermedial relationships on the other hand (i.e., relationships between texts and graphic material). Graphic material, in turn, may be intimately bound to one specific text (e.g., illustrations) or not (e.g., decorative page borders and fleurons). While the latter may be used as mere space-fillers, however, the former have to be regarded as "collaborators in total meaning production" (Skilton 313). Occasionally it may be difficult to analytically separate texts and graphics, as, for instance, in the case of article mastheads and decorated initials, where text and image merge into what W.J.T. Mitchell has called an "imagetext" (89n9).

Leaving aside the distribution and reception of a periodical, the interpersonal or institutional network that produces the magazine is also characterized by a large variety of relationships between its individual elements; i.e., the periodical actors – editors, art editors, and business managers, for instance – undoubtedly occupy positions of power, as they ultimately determine what makes it into the magazine and what does not. Especially before the rise of the half-tone in the mid-1890s, however, when most illustrations were reproduced as woodcuts,[17] even such an intermediary craftsman as a wood engraver occasionally enjoyed a relative position of power: "Engravers might also add their own touches; if given a large expanse of sky, for instance, an engraver would often be free to determine the layout and texture of the clouds" (Schulman 16). Elizabeth Robins Pennell notes that it was not until the 1880s and 1890s that "the perfect facsimile" became the ideal of engravers (*Pennell* 38).

Finally, and for reasons that I have already mentioned, it may sometimes prove both useful and interesting to extend periodical material and institutional networks beyond the magazine and to the post-periodical (i.e., book) publication of periodical material, as well as to the reprinting of book material in a periodical. These extended networks – one could call them transperiodical networks – include book versions of texts that differ from the periodical versions in merely slight, but sometimes significant ways: as I have shown elsewhere, changing the position of an illustration in relation to the text, for instance, can make a remarkable difference (see Freitag, "Treachery" 26). And occasionally – for example, when the book version of a periodical text is accompanied by illustrations by a different artist – these transperiodical networks also include new, additional actors.

Equally revealing and interesting is a slightly different form of transperiodical networks; namely, networks that do not go beyond the periodical to examine or compare periodical and book versions of the same text, but networks that read periodical features from different magazines which are related to each other through form, content, etc.[18] In *Upon Provincialism*, for instance, Hardwig reads Southern travel writing and local color from vastly different publications – national periodicals such as the *Atlantic Monthly* and the *Century*, but also local newspapers like the New Orleans-based *Daily City Item* – in order to point to their shared strategies and goals. I agree with Mark J. Noonan, however, that one should not treat all nineteenth-century periodicals "as if they were essentially interchangeable" ("Review" 102; see also Foster 304). As with periodical and pre- or post-periodical book publications, differences in, for instance, the publication's self-conception or editorial formula and self-positioning on the market or target audience must not be ignored. This is why in the following analysis, I will focus on one periodical only: *Scribner's/Century*.

Interpersonal Networks and "Scribner's Illustrated New Orleans"

While, as I have sought to argue, the concept of periodical networks should not be applied indiscriminately, I am nevertheless convinced that it constitutes an extremely valuable tool for periodical studies in general and for an examination of the depiction of New Orleans in *Scribner's/Century* in particular. And while discussing interpersonal and intertextual or intermedial networks separately may appear somewhat artificial (and may result in some reiterations), I am nevertheless convinced that in the case of "Scribner's Illustrated New Orleans," this strategy constitutes a rewarding approach as it allows us to concretely answer very distinct questions. The concept of the interpersonal network, for example, helps us explain the remarkable frequency with which the magazine published New Orleans-related items. Although a large variety of Gilded Age magazines and newspapers featured articles and stories about the city, *Scribner's/Century* seems to have been particularly invested in both New Orleans and the larger region of the South, and especially from the 1870s to the 1890s.[19] One scholar even argues that:

> the magazine during the entire period of [Richard Watson] Gilder's editorship [i.e., from 1881 to 1909] led all northern periodicals in publications by southern writers [and that in relation to other American regions, the editor-in-chief published] a disproportionate amount of southern fiction.
>
> (H.F. Smith 55; 86)[20]

In a September 1881 editorial, *Scribner's/Century* itself pointed to the fact that "no less than seven articles contributed by Southern writers appeared in a recent number of *Scribner*," merely to illustrate the "large number of Southern contributions to the magazines" in general (N.N., "Southern" 785), and in 1890, Gilder wrote in a letter that a northern author had asked him "when [he] was going to give the North a chance" in his magazine (qtd. in Cyganowski 197).

Critics have speculated widely about the possible reasons for *Scribner's/Century*'s peculiar predilection for Southern themes and writers in general, and for the strong presence of New Orleans in the magazine in particular. As for the South, Alice Fahs, for example, has suggested that there were external "political and cultural imperatives" (219) to give a voice to the recently defeated region, imperatives that should have applied, however, to all periodical and other publications. Several scholars, including Janet Gabler-Hover and Mark J. Noonan, have argued that just like it self-consciously assumed the role of a cultural steward, custodian, and arbiter on various other matters (see Noonan, *Reading* x; 14; 110), *Scribner's/Century* also had an explicit "agenda of reconciling regional differences" (157), an "ethical motive of reconciling North and South" (Gabler-Hover 240). Already in 1916, Algernon Tassin had claimed that the periodical "had not only opened its doors to Southern writers, but it had gone to them and invited them to come in" (296). And indeed, in "The Nationalizing of Southern Literature," a speech printed in *The Christian Advocate* in 1890, Gilder claims that:

> It is well for the South to be able to tell its own story of its life, of its aspirations, its failings, its failures, its achievements, before and during and since the civil war. . . . It is well for the North, it is well for the nation, to hear in poem and story all that the South burns to tell of her romance, her heroes, her landscape, yes, of her lost cause, one of the greatest, most touching tragedies in the history of humanity.
>
> (442)

Rather than exclusively a matter of editorial formula, some scholars have maintained that *Scribner's/Century*'s focus on the South was at least partly also the result of a shrewd business decision. Arthur John, for instance, points out that in stark contrast to the personal convictions of Josiah G. Holland, *Scribner's/Century*'s founding editor-in-chief, "the magazine's earliest references to the South were in terms of tolerance and amity" (39). John speculates that the "passage of time may have mellowed Holland's outlook on the rebels, but perhaps a more potent factor was his new responsibility as editor of a periodical that aimed to win a national audience" (39). Herbert F. Smith explains: "Founded after the war, the magazine escaped the onus of Abolitionism that fell upon *The Atlantic Monthly* and *Harper's*. A series of articles on "The Great South" by Edward King . . . made *Scribner's Monthly* the most popular magazine in the South" (55). Significantly, it was the periodical's business manager Roswell Smith who had projected the "Great South" series (see Johnson 96), and as it ran, "new subscriptions came in by the thousands as, postwar, *Scribner's* was the first northern journal welcomed into southern parlors" (Noonan, *Reading* 20).[21]

Certainly, all of these factors played a role in the strong presence of the South in the pages of *Scribner's/Century*, but what about the more specific case of New Orleans? Bill Hardwig has argued that along with Appalachia, the city played a central role in late-nineteenth–century periodical regional fiction and travel writing about the South both because it served as a "physical point . . . of entry into the South" (15) and because its distinct cultural makeup could be used synecdochically to express the entire region's cultural difference from the North: "[d]ue to their geographical roles as 'ports of entry,' [New Orleans and Appalachia] become symbols of the South's cultural disjuncture from the rest of the nation" (15). Though convincing, Hardwig's argument nevertheless suffers from a lack of attention to the specificity of each periodical or, more precisely, to the particular institutional or interpersonal networks that sustained each individual magazine.

Elsewhere, I have suggested that the various journalistic, literary, and visual representations of New Orleans published in *Scribner's/Century* are all linked by what Henry Jenkins has described as "participatory culture,"[22] with consumers (readers) turning into producers (writers and artists) and vice versa, and with the magazine functioning as a site of convergence for different visions of the city (see Freitag, "Convergence"). Drawing on the concept of (trans)periodical interpersonal networks, I would like to slightly modify my argument here and point out to what extent "Scribner's Illustrated New Orleans" depended upon personal or "virtual" contacts and encounters between editors, writers, artists, engravers, and others involved in the production of the magazine.

Some of these encounters were purely accidental, such as, for instance, Edward King's "discovery" of George Washington Cable in 1873: together with illustrator James Wells Champney, King was in New Orleans during the carnival season of that year to gather material for the "Great South" series of travel sketches, which would eventually start in the July 1873 issue of *Scribner's*.[23] While in the city, King and Champney met George Washington Cable, who at the time was merely "[k]nown locally for his journalistic work with the *Picayune* and for his interest in local history" (Noonan, *Reading* 73) and who covered the 1873 carnival parade by the Mistick Krewe of Comus for the *Picayune* (see Rubin 13). According to Turner and John, Cable had already sent clippings of his "Drop Shot" column in the *Picayune* to the Charles Scribner Company (the book publisher) in 1871, but "that publishing house, perhaps dubious about encouraging a recent rebel" – Cable had been a private in the Confederate army – "had not been forthcoming" (John 64; see also Turner, *Cable*

46–7). Cable's encounter with King would change that. In a letter to Fred Lewis Pattee from 1914, Cable remembers:

> Edward King came to New Orleans almost at the beginning of his tour of the South and we became acquaintances and friends. I asked him where to send some stories – two or three – which I had just written and he himself read and sent two to Dr. Holland . . . . Then Gilder . . . wrote me, and my lifetime acquaintance with both the *Century* and Charles Scribner's Sons began.
>
> (qtd. in Ekström 49)

Throughout the summer of 1873, King continued to write letters to Cable, praising and encouraging him and telling him about his own efforts to turn the attention of the magazine editors to Cable's writings (Ekström 49–51), efforts which ultimately proved successful. Cable's first submission, a story titled "Bibi," was rejected;[24] in October 1873, however – a month before King's first article on New Orleans from the "Great South" series appeared – the magazine printed "'Sieur George: A Story of New Orleans."

From that moment on, Cable became a regular contributor to *Scribner's/Century*. The magazine would not just print everything Cable submitted – the story "Posson Jone'," for instance, was turned down "because of the scene of the drunken minister fighting the animals in the circus arena" (Johnson 123; see also H.F. Smith 67), the first two drafts of *Dr. Sevier* were rejected as too didactic, as was the manuscript that eventually became *John March, Southerner* (see Biklé 212–3; and John 160–1; 164). But "'Sieur George" was followed by five more stories in *Scribner's* until 1876;[25] *The Grandissimes*, "Madame Delphine," and *Dr. Sevier* were serialized between November 1879 and October 1880, May and July 1881, and November 1883 and October 1884, respectively; and from November 1887 to March 1888, *Century* serialized "Au Large," which was part of Cable's "Cajun" trilogy but which was partly set in New Orleans. With respect to non-fiction, *Scribner's/Century* printed, among others, a series of historical articles about Louisiana Creoles between January 1883 and July 1883, articles on Creole slave dances and songs in February and April 1886, and Cable's famous essays "The Freedman's Case in Equity" and "The Silent South" in January and September 1885, respectively. Cable's historical anecdotes of Louisiana, finally, some of which are set in New Orleans,[26] were serialized under the title "Strange True Stories of Louisiana" between November 1888 and October 1889.

Cable's success with the magazine also paved the way for his success with the Scribner book firm. Most of Cable's New Orleans-related material that had appeared in *Scribner's/Century* was eventually reprinted in book form by Charles Scribner's Sons, with the magazine and the book firm sometimes harmonizing their publication schedules to stimulate sales. For example, after rejecting the project at first (see Ekström 54; 58), the company eventually published a collection of Cable's stories (including "Posson Jone'") under the title *Old Creole Days* in 1879. *The Grandissimes* and "Madame Delphine," by contrast, came out in book form with Scribner's in 1880 and 1881, respectively, the same year they had been serialized in the magazine. "Madame Delphine" was then included in the 1883 republication of *Old Creole Days*, which "happened" to coincide with the publication of an article by Lafcadio Hearn on Cable's short stories in the November 1883 issue of *Century*.[27] The year 1884 saw Scribner's releasing *The Creoles of Louisiana*, a slightly rearranged and extended version of Cable's historical essays which had run in the magazine the year before. In 1885, Scribner's issued Cable's essay "The Convict Lease System," which had appeared in the magazine in February 1884 during the serialization of *Dr. Sevier*, together with "The Freedman's Case in Equity," published in *Century* in January 1885, and "The Silent South," published in the magazine in September 1885, under the main title *The Silent South*. *Dr. Sevier* itself was not published in book form by Scribner's until 1888, after it had first been released in Boston by J.R. Osgood in 1884. In 1888, Scribner's also issued the volume *Bonaventure*, which collected Cable's "Cajun" trilogy, consisting of "Carancro," "Grande Pointe," and "Au Large." One year later, Scribner's published *Strange True Stories of Louisiana*. Finally, after many cheaper reprintings and almost simultaneously with the "Tarryawhile" edition of Cable's collected fiction (1898; see Turner, *Cable* 313), Scribner's brought out profusely illustrated luxury editions of *Old Creole Days* and *The Grandissimes* in 1897 and 1899, respectively (previous book editions of these works had contained either frontispieces or no illustrations at all).

Edward King, having been credited with discovering George Washington Cable, once remarked that Cable "discovered himself, and would have dawned upon the world had there never been any 'Great South' scribes in New Orleans, to hear his mellifluous reading of his delightful sketches" (qtd. in Turner, *Cable* 52). That may have been true, but the editors and accountants at *Scribner's/Century* and Charles Scribner's Sons must have been delighted that Cable "discovered himself" in the presence of one of their writers.[28]

Somewhat less remunerative for the Scribner publishing universe, though perhaps equally momentous for nineteenth-century New Orleans literature, was another accidental encounter, which also took place in New Orleans. In her autobiography, *Memories of a Southern Woman of Letters*, Grace Elizabeth King not only remembers Edward King's visit to New Orleans and his "discovery" of Cable (49–50), but also her own meeting with *Century*'s editor-in-chief Gilder during the World's Industrial and Cotton Centennial Exposition in New Orleans in 1885.[29] By that time, Cable had already published *Old Creole Days*, *The Grandissimes*, "Madame Delphine," and *Dr. Sevier*. Grace King, by contrast, had never written or published any fiction in her life. Walking with King after a dinner, Gilder asked her about "the inimical stand taken by the people of New Orleans against George Cable and his works" (60). King remembers:

> I hastened to enlighten him to the effect that Cable proclaimed his preference for colored people over white and assumed the inevitable superiority – according to his theories – of the quadroons over the Creoles. He was a native of New Orleans and had been well treated by its people, and yet he stabbed the city in the back, as we felt, in a dastardly way to please the Northern press.
>
> (60)[30]

According to King, Gilder simply answered: "Why, . . . if Cable is so false to you, why do not some of you write better?" (60). "The shot," King notes, "told" (60), and the very next day, she wrote a story titled "Monsieur Motte." Although first rejected by the *Century*, it was published in the *New Princeton Review* in January 1886. King continued to write and publish, mostly in *Harper's Magazine* (although this magazine was, King writes, "not a welcome visitor to New Orleans since the Confederate War," 63), but when *Harper's* rejected King's "Balcony Stories" in 1891, King sent them to the offices of *Century*, which published them from December 1892 through October 1893. The stories appeared in book form in 1893 under the title *Balcony Stories*, though not with Charles Scribner's Sons, but with Century Company, then the magazine's parent company.

King's association with Century Company, however, much like the encounter with Gilder that initiated her career as a writer, turned out to be a one-time affair: despite *Century*'s urgings (see Bush, "Introduction" 23), King never again published in the magazine or with the book company. When in 1925 she added two more stories – namely, "Grandmama" and "Joe" – to the 14 pieces (including the introductory sketch "The Balcony") that originally made up the collection, the volume had moved to Macmillan. Already the first new edition had not been issued by Century Company anymore, but by Graham in New Orleans in 1914. And yet Century Company had managed to be the first to publish what would eventually become King's most famous depictions of New Orleans.

It is significant that both Edward King and Champney's encounter with Cable in 1873, as well as Gilder's encounter with Grace King in 1885, initially resulted in submissions to *Scribner's/Century* – namely, Cable's "Bibi" and King's "Monsieur Motte" – that were rejected by the editors. Recommendations by one of the magazine's writers and even personal encounters with its editor-in-chief stimulated and encouraged novices in the magazine business like Cable and King to start writing and submit their works to the editorial offices, but they did not guarantee automatic access to the periodical: ultimately, it was the editors who decided what would be printed in *Scribner's/Century* and what would not. Although the institutionalized power of the editors' position within the magazine's interpersonal network may appear obvious and self-evident, actually asserting this power sometimes required careful diplomacy and a delicate choice of words, especially as the periodical's network grew and started to include individuals who themselves enjoyed a position of power in the Gilded Age literary marketplace.

This is delightfully illustrated by a humorous letter from Gilder to Mark Twain, written in 1886. Twain had apparently recommended a manuscript to Gilder, but the latter felt Twain had somewhat overstepped a line. Addressing his letter to "Samuel L. Clemens, Esq., Editor The Century Magazine, Hartford, Conn.," Gilder writes:

> My dear Editor:
>
> Leman's paper shall have strict attention in this office. But I don't know whether it can be made to suit all the editors of "The Century." There is Howells, for instance; he has been editor of "The Century" for several years. He has his own way of looking at things and may not like it. Stedman, also, is a distinguished editor of "The Century;" and how can I tell whether he will like what Leman does? So, after I have got through with it, you see it will have to run the muck of Clemens, Howells, Stedman, and, according to the Newport paper, Mr. Roswell Smith also. All these persons are editors of "The Century," . . . . If I were the editor of "The Century," as you are, I would write more for my own magazine. If you will send on a contribution from your own pen I will try to get the other above-named editors to agree to it, and we will keep Mark Twain's boom booming.
> (qtd. in Cyganowski 216)

Through a fascinating mix of thinly veiled irritation and flattering cajolery, Gilder manifestly asserts his own power as editor-in-chief, putting Twain in his place, but simultaneously acknowledges Twain's position as a valued contributor. Introducing a number of prominent writers whose works had appeared in *Scribner's/Century* – William Dean Howells, Edmund Clarence Stedman – as well as business manager Roswell Smith as the periodical's "editors," Gilder ironically identifies the pressures put upon him and his editorial decisions from various sides, letting Twain know that he is by no means the only one trying to make his weight felt.[31] And of course, Twain was not just anyone. Edward King may have described himself as a "worm crawling before the Scribnerian throne" when he tried to plead Cable's case in *Scribner's/Century*'s offices (qtd. in Ekström 50), but Twain had just let Gilder print three excerpts of *Adventures of Huckleberry Finn* (in the December 1884 and the January and

February 1885 issues of *Century*) – a risk (despite Gilder's editing),[32] but also a coup for Gilder. Yet the editor makes it clear that what he wants from Twain is not advice on how to run the magazine, but submissions. The magazine's interpersonal network was a hierarchical one, within which Gilder, as editor-in-chief, occupied a top position.

Whereas some personal encounters between members of the network that sustained "Scribner's Illustrated New Orleans" were purely accidental, like the one between King, Champney, and Cable and the one between Gilder and King, others had been arranged by the magazine. This particularly applies to personal encounters between writers and illustrators who collaborated on an illustrated feature: it was the magazine that decided, for instance, to pair journalist Edward King off with artist James Wells Champney and send them on an extended tour of the South for the "Great South" series of travel sketches (published in installments from July 1873 to December 1874 in *Scribner's* and in revised and slightly extended form by the American Publishing Company in 1875).[33] It is unclear, however, who exactly chose King and Champney. As I have already mentioned, Roswell Smith projected the undertaking, and it is to him that King dedicated the book version (see King, *The Great South* n.p.). Josiah G. Holland, editor-in-chief of the magazine at the time, had known King "as a boy in Springfield, Massachusetts, where he went to work for Samuel Bowles's *Springfield Republican*" (John 40). By 1873, however, King, who was only 25 at the time, had already become well-known and distinguished as a journalist: in 1868, he had published *My Paris: French Character Sketches*, a series of articles originally written for the *Springfield Republican* and the *Boston Transcript*. Champney, in turn, who was five years older than King, was almost certainly selected by the magazine's art superintendent, Alexander W. Drake. He may have been suggested to Drake by King: as Champney had studied art in Paris in 1867, around the time King was there to gather material for "his Paris," there is a possibility that the two had met before, but there is no evidence for this (see Rainey 197). Neither do we know anything about how the two worked together: King and Champney traveled together for a considerable time in early 1873,[34] but neither of them left any recollections of their collaboration, neither in print nor in the Century Company Records.

Even less is known about the arranged encounter between Eugene V. Smalley and Edward W. Kemble in 1885, which resulted in two illustrated articles on the World's Industrial and Cotton Centennial Exposition in New Orleans in 1884–1885, published in the May and June 1885 issues of *Century*. Smalley had traveled to New Orleans to gather material for the articles in early 1885, shortly after the opening of the Exposition on 16 December 1884: in his first article, he identifies 1 February 1885, as the time of writing (see Smalley, "New Orleans" 13). Kemble, in turn, as I mentioned earlier, had become noted for his illustrations to Twain's

Adventures of Huckleberry Finn, excerpts of which were being serialized in *Century* while Smalley was in New Orleans. According to Francis Martin, Jr. ("Kemble" 185), Gilder sent Kemble to New Orleans to illustrate Smalley's articles in March 1885, but several of Kemble's pictures are dated "Feb' 85" (see, for instance, Smalley, "New Orleans" 10) – only one illustration in the second article seems to have been drawn in March (see Smalley, "In and Out" 193). While there is no positive evidence for this, it seems reasonable to assume that the magazine had arranged for Smalley and Kemble to travel to the exposition together.

Toward the end of his first article on the Exposition, Smalley writes that he hopes "to return to these two significant departments [the department of the colored race and the Women's Department] when they shall be more fully arranged than they are at this date (February 1st)" ("New Orleans" 13). Smalley apparently did remain in New Orleans long enough to see the two departments completed, for his second article features one section on "The Colored Department" ("In and Out" 192-4) and "The Woman's Department" ("In and Out" 188-9), respectively. None of Kemble's illustrations refer directly to these sections, however, and we do not know when exactly Kemble left New Orleans: neither he nor Smalley left any record of their collaboration.

By contrast, in his spirited autobiography *The Adventures of an Illustrator* (1925), artist Joseph Pennell writes in much detail about his various encounters with the writers whose works he illustrated, among them William Dean Howells and Henry James.[35] Given that in general, Pennell does not seem to have been too enthusiastic about writer-artist collaborations – "Now it is all very well for the author to select subjects [for illustration]," he writes, "but I have, in a lifetime of experience, scarce found an author who had the faintest idea of what could be illustrated. After a few attempts to conform to and carry out their wishes, I generally end by ignoring them" (170) – his account of his meeting with George Washington Cable in New Orleans in 1882 is surprisingly positive: the chapter in which he writes about this encounter is entitled "A Delightful Memory of a Delightful Winter in a Charming City with a Charming Author" (93). In late 1881, the editors had asked Pennell to travel to New Orleans and meet with Cable in order to illustrate his series of historical articles on Creoles, which would eventually appear – with illustrations by Pennell – in *Century* in 1883 (see earlier). Pennell, who was only 21 at the time and had just published his first drawings in *Century* in July 1881, considers this his "first big commission" (84). Nevertheless, even at the time Pennell had apparently already made up his mind about how a collaboration with a writer should work. The Century Company Records contain an undated typewritten list of "Illustrations suggested by Geo. W. Cable," obviously for the history of the Creoles and meant for Pennell (CCR I, 14).[36] If Pennell ever received Cable's suggestions he, indeed, "end[ed] up by ignoring them."

As soon as Pennell arrived in New Orleans, Cable, Pennell remembers, took him on a walking tour through the French Quarter, pointing out to Pennell where his short stories are set: "I was pitchforked right into France from Philadelphia. Cable began to take me about, . . . all over the Creole town, his town, to Madame Delphine's, to Jean à Poquelin's [sic]" (J. Pennell 94). Later, Pennell would spend his days drawing by himself in and around the city: "Those were delightful days I spent drawing in courts, on plantations, atop the levee, up the bayous . . . . All day I worked, stopping only to buy fresh bananas for lunch" (94). Cable had told Pennell the title of his manuscript (93) and had perhaps given him his list of suggestions for illustrations, but there is no indication that he had ever given Pennell anything to read, neither the census report on which *The Creoles of Louisiana* was based and which Cable had finished in September 1881,[37] nor (portions of) the actual manuscript, which Gilder had asked him to write in June 1881 (see Ekström 85). Elsewhere in his autobiography, however, Pennell claims that "[i]f the manuscript is ready, or the book to be illustrated has been issued, I read it carefully, which is more than most professional illustrators do" (170). Indeed, letters from Pennell to his later wife confirm that he had read *Old Creole Days* and *The Grandissimes* even prior to arriving in New Orleans (see E.R. Pennell, *Life* 52; 54). After a few months in the city, Pennell returned home to finish his drawings, for, as he himself writes, "I could not then do everything from nature as I try to now. I had made many sketches and studies, carrying out the good ones, trying to correct the bad, and several etchings, which had to be printed" (J. Pennell 102). This kept Pennell busy during the remainder of 1882 – both Arlin Turner (*Cable* 128) and Kjell Ekström (86) cite problems with Cable's manuscript for the fact that the articles were not published in *Century* until the January 1883 issue, but Pennell's pictures were not ready, either.

While in New Orleans, Pennell also drew five pictures of the settings of Cable's short stories and his novella "Madame Delphine." These pictures were not included in *The Creoles of Louisiana* (neither the magazine nor the book version); instead, they were printed with an article by Lafcadio Hearn on "The Scenes of Cable's Romances," which appeared in the November 1883 issue of *Century* and which was quite obviously intended to promote the new edition of *Old Creole Days* (now including "Madame Delphine") that Charles Scribner's Sons brought out that year. While Hearn's article itself does not mention the new edition, one of Pennell's pictures, captioned "Café des Exilés" (the title of one of Cable's stories) shows a small poster on a fence that rather unambiguously invites readers of the article to "Read Old Creole Days" (see 45). Fittingly, it was this picture that was chosen as the frontispiece of the new edition (see Cable, *Old Creole Days* n.p.).[38] In his autobiography, Pennell mentions the Hearn article – "Mr. Edward L. Tinker pointed out to me that Lafcadio Hearn wrote an article about [Cable's short stories] in *The Century*"

(99) – but he claims that "I do not remember ever seeing him" (99). According to Arlin Turner (*Cable* 195), Pennell did meet Hearn during his time in New Orleans, but at this point, Pennell's pictures were still to be accompanied by "a paragraph on each to be written by Cable" (J. Pennell 119). In a letter from April 1882, Pennell proposes to the magazine's art superintendent Alexander W. Drake an article consisting of "from seven to a dozen full page autographic things," with Pennell's drawings and Cable's texts etched on the same copper plate (see E.R. Pennell, *Life* 64). By October 1883, the project had moved from Cable to Hearn: in a letter to H.E. Krehbiel from that month, Hearn complains about the "beastly changes" made to his text by the *Century* editor (qtd. in Bisland 283). Obviously, then, when Pennell and Hearn met in 1882, they never discussed their collaboration – they did not even know they were collaborating at this point.

This is but one of several cases in the context of "Scribner's Illustrated New Orleans" in which writers and illustrators never worked together but "on paper"; that is, when their texts and pictures were printed together in the magazine. Apart from "The Scenes of Cable's Romances," other such cases include Cable's articles on Creole slave dances and songs as well as his "Cajun" trilogy, all illustrated by Kemble; the "Balcony Stories," illustrated by various artists; and the illustrated luxury editions of *Old Creole Days* and *The Grandissimes*, which feature pictures by Albert Herter. Cable's articles "Creole Slave Dances: The Dance in Place Congo" and "Creole Slave Songs," for instance, appeared in *Century* in February and April 1886, together with 20 illustrations by Kemble. There is no conclusive evidence, however, that Cable and Kemble ever met to discuss the two features; the illustrator simply seems to have been given the writer's text and asked to illustrate it. The manuscript itself had been long in the making: a first version had been sent to the editors as early as August 1884 (Turner, *Cable* 227); in June 1885, Cable asked his editor for the revised manuscript because he thought he would "fall to work on that next" (CCR I, 14). Kemble's pictures, in turn, are mostly signed "'85," and one may safely assume that they were made during Kemble's and Smalley's visit to the New Orleans exposition (see earlier). In fact, Sublette claims that the "frequently reprinted image of dancing [in Place Congo] was made during Kemble's only visit to New Orleans in 1885" (120).[39] Only three of Kemble's drawings are actually signed "New Orleans," however,[40] and the one Sublette refers to, a full-page illustration entitled "The Bamboula" (Cable, "Slave Dances" 524), is not among them. Wherever this picture – along with the others not signed "New Orleans" – was made, it was not drawn from nature: as many scholars have pointed out (see, for instance, Southern and Wright 34), neither Cable nor Kemble could have eye-witnessed the dancing described and depicted in the articles, as it had been banned in the 1840s already. While Cable had "borrowed" his material from various textual sources,[41] Kemble, in turn, simply seems to have relied on Cable's text, which has prompted one scholar to describe Kemble's "The Bamboula" as a "reconstruction" (Roach 65).

Published in *Century* in 1892–1893, Grace King's "Balcony Stories" were accompanied by decorated initials, tailpieces, and mastheads, as well as a total of 17 illustrations,[42] twelve of which were drawn by Albert E. Sterner. Otto H. Bacher – who together with Sterner would be among the founding members of the Society of Illustrators in New York City in 1901 (see Best 120) – Robert Frederick Blum, Kenyon Cox, and Eric Pape are the other artists who worked on the "Balcony Stories." It seems that each illustrator was assigned to work on one or several stories, but while the pictures for the first batch of stories, printed from December 1892 to February 1893, were all done by Sterner, he only provided pictures for half of the illustrated stories that formed the second batch, published from June to October 1893. The other illustrated stories from the second series – namely, "Anne Marie and Jeanne Marie," "One of Us," "Grandmother's Grandmother," and "The Old Lady's Restoration" – went to Bacher, Cox, Blum, and Pape, respectively. Whatever the reasons for this decision – Sterner may have been unavailable to do all the stories due to scheduling conflicts or *Century*, complying with its own guidelines for illustrations (see later), may have wanted to go for more variety in illustrators – neither King nor her biographers ever mention the illustrations. The "encounter" between King and her illustrators evidently took place on paper and through the magazine's art department only.

Judging from published sources, the same applies, finally, to the luxury editions of Cable's *Old Creole Days* and *The Grandissimes*, which Charles Scribner's Sons brought out in 1897 and 1899, respectively. Already in 1879, Cable had proposed to the editors of *Scribner's* to let Allen C. Redwood illustrate *The Grandissimes*, but they had "thought the expense greater than the gain" (Turner, *Cable* 110).[43] Almost two decades later, the publisher seemed to consider the market ready for illustrated versions of Cable's first two books. The two handsome arts-and-crafts–style volumes are identical in design and feature Japanese-inspired covers (one of them reproduced in B. Evans 147), gilt edges, and photogravures – at the time a particularly expensive method for reproducing drawings (see Jussim 303) – in which text and image sometimes merge (see Freitag, "Treachery" 30–1). Cable, however, apparently never directly communicated with the illustrator, Albert Herter.

Yet the process of simply assigning artists to illustrate accepted manuscripts was by no means unusual – in fact, it was rather the rule at *Scribner's/Century*, particularly with respect to fiction. Kemble himself remembers that after he was engaged by W. Lewis Fraser, *Century*'s art manager,[44] to work exclusively for the magazine, "all the stories from those charming writers of the South, Thomas Nelson Page, James Lane Allen, Harry Stilwell Edwards, Richard Malcom [sic] Johnson and

George W. Cable, were placed in my hands for picture work" ("Illustrating" 32). The procedures of having a feature illustrated were relatively standardized: once a manuscript was accepted for publication, a specific artist, chosen mostly by the magazine's art department, was commissioned to illustrate it (see John 182).[45] The artist received the manuscript to be illustrated and/or a list of subjects (see J. Pennell 82). Like writers (see H.F. Smith 26), artists were paid upon the acceptance of their works (see J. Pennell 99–100). All illustrations were then scrutinized by the editors for factual errors and discrepancies with the text (see Tooker 85–7) – with sometimes the picture and sometimes, especially when deadlines had to be met, the text being changed to avoid incongruities: editor L. Frank Tooker writes in his *Joys and Tribulations of an Editor* (1924) that "times beyond reckoning, when the pictures were received too late to make alterations, I have changed the text to gloss over the eccentricities of illustrators" (87). In addition, before it went to press the makeup of each issue of the magazine had to pass "tests" in which the illustrations were checked for, among others, the following criteria: "variety in subject," "variety in artist," "are pictures interesting?," "to whom?," "compare with last month," "artistic quality," and "copyrights" (Johnson 140).

Except in special cases, then, the writers whose texts were to be illustrated played but a marginal role in the magazine's production process of illustrations, with control over the final product being shifted to the editors. Whereas Twain, for instance, had not only worked closely with Kemble on *Adventures of Huckleberry Finn*, commenting on his work, selecting scenes for illustration, and even writing the captions himself (see Briden; David 62n50), *Scribner's/Century* sometimes sent the work of illustrators to authors for approval,[46] although this does not seem to have been the rule and it remains unclear when exactly (for which authors, illustrators, and/or kinds of texts) this was done.[47]

More importantly, the artists themselves had but limited control over their work: a famous illustrator like Pennell may have "never paid the slightest attention, if possible" (J. Pennell 82) to the list of subjects for illustration given to him by authors or by Drake, yet ultimately, and as with texts, it was the editors – particularly the editor-in-chief and the heads of the art department – who decided what would and what would not be printed in the magazine. If highlighting the power of the editors' position within the magazine's interpersonal network and, hence, the institutionalized power imbalances within this network, may appear banal, the following anecdote illustrates the full implications of these imbalances. Discussing Champney's illustrations for the "Great South" series, Sue Rainey writes:

> Champney's depictions of [non-Anglo-American] people are frequently sensitive individual portraits. Unfortunately, many of his drawings were distorted either in the redrawing by Sheppard or

others, or in the engraving, so that the facial expressions are changed or the individuals become types – even caricatures. For example, the central figure in Champney's drawing ["Negro Children on Balcony"/"Peeping Through"] was altered in the wood engraving . . . so that he became the kind of racial stereotype some readers would find amusing.

(204)

In this particular case, then, at least four people were involved in the production of the picture:[48] Champney, who did the original; an office artist, probably W.L. Sheppard (see Rainey 206), who redrew the sketch on the woodblock; the wood engraver, who cut Sheppard's drawing; and an editor, who told Sheppard and/or the engraver to alter Champney's original.[49]

These alterations, however, not only included a mirroring of the drawing – for some reason, Sheppard failed to redraw the sketch on the woodblock in reverse, so that the printed version looks like a mirror image of the original – they also involved changing the facial features of the picture's central character by blowing up the little African-American boy's lips to almost twice their size and making his eyes appear much more bulging. Whether these changes were, as Rainey suggests, indeed intended to inject some "humor" into the picture or whether this was but another case of making the image match the text – King's manuscript is not free from stereotypical depictions of Southern blacks (see, for instance, Romine 59) – is impossible to know. In any case, the changes almost seem to render the very idea of "The Great South" absurd: why spend more than $30,000 (see N.N., "Great South" 248) to send a writer and an artist on a tour of the South in order to get first-hand and "authentic" impressions if what ultimately counts is the editors' idea of the South? Champney, of course, had no control over these alterations, and once they were printed, he had no choice but to accept them.

If, due to their institutionalized power, the centrality of the magazine's editors in the interpersonal network of "Scribner's Illustrated New Orleans" is hardly surprising, however, the relative prominence of two other people within this network requires some further explanation. Roswell Smith officially occupied the post of *Scribner's/Century*'s business manager from the foundation of the magazine in 1870 to his death in 1892, which, interestingly, coincided with what has been called the "ten-cent-magazine revolution" (see e.g., Mott, *History* Vol. 4 (recte) 46), a major realignment of the late-nineteenth–century American periodical market that marked the beginning of the end of comparatively expensive literary monthlies such as *Scribner's/Century*. Along with Josiah G. Holland, Smith had originally conceived of the concept of the magazine (see Gladden 311), and he was also the man behind the foundation of Century Company in 1881, which made the magazine completely independent of the Scribner book firm (see John 103–108; he also served as Century Company's president). Experimenting with new marketing and business techniques, Smith contributed considerably to the success of the magazine and the companies behind it. Smith:

> was a master of systemizing the operations of *Scribner's* and planning its strategies. His introduction of prepaid postage and inexpensive, large-scale advertising, insistence on numerous illustrations, and willingness to spend huge sums of money for visionary projects . . . quickly propelled *Scribner's Monthly* into a dominant position in family magazine publishing.
>
> (Noonan, *Reading* 7)

One of Smith's "visionary projects" was, of course, "The Great South." This monumental series of illustrated travel reports not only included one of the first detailed discussions of New Orleans in *Scribner's/Century*, however; its positive impact on the magazine's circulation had definitely shown that features from or about the South paid off and perhaps made submissions from Southern writers just a little more welcome in the editorial offices. And, although Smith could not have foreseen that, "The Great South" brought *Scribner's/Century* the talent of George Washington Cable. Editor Robert Underwood Johnson later suggested that "a tablet should be erected to [Smith] in one of the Southern States" (96) for projecting "The Great South," but a similar tablet in the magazine's offices in New York City would not have been out of place, either.

Cable, in turn, occupies another central node within the interpersonal network of "Scribner's Illustrated New Orleans." Indeed, with the exception of the magazine staff, he was, in one way or another, connected to more individuals within this network than anyone else: Cable personally knew Gilder, Smith, Edward King, Hearn, Champney, and Pennell; his writings were published along with illustrations by Pennell, Kemble, and Herter; and he, albeit indirectly, introduced Grace King to the literary world in general and to *Scribner's/Century* in particular. Apart from the fact that he lived in New Orleans until his move to Massachusetts in 1885, Cable's manifold connections were mainly due, of course, to his extraordinarily prolific contribution to "Scribner's Illustrated New Orleans." Cable was but one of several late-nineteenth–century authors who wrote about New Orleans – other prominent voices of fiction included those of Grace King, Kate Chopin, Lafcadio Hearn, Ruth McEnery Stuart, and Alice Dunbar-Nelson. With the exception of Dunbar-Nelson, all of these writers appeared in *Scribner's/Century* at some point; although, as in the case of Chopin, Hearn, and Stuart, it was not with their (most famous) writings on New Orleans that they were represented in the magazine. Cable, by contrast, had not only "discovered Creole New Orleans for literature" (Turner, *Cable* iii), he was entirely the magazine's "own find"

(Rubin 62) and almost exclusively published in this periodical from the beginning of his writing career in 1873 to the late 1880s. In addition, virtually all of his many contributions to *Scribner's/Century* were related to New Orleans – his Cajun stories being the only exceptions. Finally, Cable's work was also remarkably heterogeneous: he published short stories, novellas, novels, and historiographies, as well as essays on culture and politics.

Hence, and in light of the fact that other New Orleans-related features published in the magazine were somehow related to Cable as well – for example, Hearn's illustrated article on Cable's writing and, in a slightly different way, Grace King's illustrated stories – the frequency with which New Orleans appeared in *Scribner's/Century* was mainly due to Cable's long-standing association with the periodical. Within the periodical or, rather, within the intertextual/intermedial network that constitutes "Scribner's Illustrated New Orleans," however, Cable's writings nevertheless compete with, and call and respond to, many other textual and pictorial depictions of the city. It is on the various connections between these texts and pictures, rather than on those between their creators, that I will concentrate in the following. Pointing out discrepancies and convergences between the individual works, I will trace the ongoing intertextual and intermedial discussion about New Orleans in *Scribner's/Century* in order to reveal its complex temporal dynamics; that is, the ways in which these various texts and pictures employ New Orleans's French past to engage the city's present and future.

Intertextual Networks and "Scribner's Illustrated New Orleans"

Doors to the Past, Windows to the Future: "Old and New Louisiana"

Among the first New Orleans-related features that were published in *Scribner's/Century* were "Old and New Louisiana" (November 1873) and "Old and New Louisiana – II" (December 1873), the second and third installment, respectively, of Edward King and James Wells Champney's "The Great South" series of travel sketches, which had started in the July 1873 issue with "The Great South: The New Route to the Gulf." The titles of the two articles are somewhat misleading: the greater part of King's text focuses on New Orleans – its history, its sights, its peoples, its trade, its finances, and its politics[50] – and almost all of the 68 illustrations that accompany the two texts in the magazine depict buildings, people, and scenes in and around the city.

The articles' textual and pictorial focus on urban Louisiana – and, more specifically, on New Orleans – is not particularly unusual in the context of "The Great South" as a whole.[51] Yet "Old and New Louisiana" somewhat differs from the rest of "The Great South" in other matters. In *Traveling South* (2005), John Cox notes: "The study of travel literature . . . should question less what exactly travel literature *is* or what it *describes* but, rather, what travel literature *does* – what cultural, social, political, or ideological work is performed by those texts" (15; emphasis original). While opinions about what kind of "cultural, social, political, or ideological work" the "Great South" series exactly performs have changed considerably over time, most commentators and critics have viewed the series as deeply invested in the future of the United States, either as a newly reunited nation or as an ambitious imperial power.

In his *Remembered Yesterdays* (1923), for instance, editor Robert Underwood Johnson considers the series "the first high note of nationalism struck by the magazine" (96), as it "contributed materially to the promotion of good feeling between the lately hostile sections" (97).[52] Since the mid-2000s, critics have offered quite different views, although they, too, have considered "The Great South" as concerned with the future of the nation: for example, scholars such as Jamie Winders and Jennifer Rae Greeson have argued that by framing the South in colonialist terms, King and Champney's series prepared the ideological ground for the rise of discourses and practices of U.S. imperialism toward the end of the nineteenth century. Relying, among others, on Mary Louise Pratt's concept of the "capitalist vanguard" (see Pratt 146–55) and Edward Said's concept of "Orientalism" (see Said), both Winders and Greeson note that "The Great South" highlights the South's economic potential and, simultaneously, the inability of the "natives" to exploit this potential, thus creating a "moral imperative" for the occupation and exploitation of the region by the United States (see Greeson, "Expropriating" 505; Winders 391).[53] This "imperial framing of the South within northern travel narratives" (Winders 391) and especially within "The Great South," in turn, positioned the occupied South as a "rehearsal or a training ground" (Greeson, "Expropriating" 515; see also Winders 405) for U.S. expansion into the hemisphere in the late nineteenth and early twentieth centuries.

For Winders, however, the relationship between the North and the South in "The Great South" and similar travel writings is always but "imperfectly imperial" (Winders 391), as, for instance, Southern white "natives" and bustling Southern cities such as Atlanta complicated any attempts to depict the region in straightforwardly colonialist terms (395–6). By contrast, Greeson views "The Great South" as directly following the "basic ideological contour" of contemporary English travel writing about Africa ("Expropriating" 498). Greeson takes her cue from the periodical connection between Edward King and Henry Morton Stanley, the journalist who in 1871 had "discovered" British explorer David Livingstone in present-day Tanzania for the *New York Herald*. Having seen off Stanley on his way to Africa and Livingstone, King wrote two articles about the expedition for *Scribner's*/*Century* (titled "An Expedition with

Stanley" and "How Stanley Found Livingstone"), which appeared in November 1872 and January 1873, half a year before "The Great South" began serialization in the magazine ("Expropriating" 496–500).[54]

Greeson could have employed another periodical connection to also substantiate the second part of her argument; namely, that the South, as portrayed in "The Great South," is not only used for the "projection of imperial power *within*" (Greeson, "Expropriating" 499; emphasis original), but also *outside* the United States, a rehearsal on domestic territory for more ambitious imperial projects. Five years after "The Great South," *Scribner's/Century* featured another travel series, entitled "Brazil." Written by Herbert H. Smith and running from May to December 1879, "Brazil" consists of six articles that discuss, among other topics, economic opportunities for U.S. tradesmen and investors in Brazil. In the first installment of the series, "The Metropolis of the Amazons," for example, Smith and his companions dream up "sunset towers" and "air-castles" (66) of future prosperity and wealth in the region around the eponymous metropolis of Pará that are reminiscent of the "industrial reverie" Pratt associates with the early nineteenth-century "capitalist vanguard" in *Imperial Eyes* (150). Like the other articles in the "Brazil" series, "The Metropolis of the Amazons" is illustrated by none other than James Wells Champney, and his drawings of the Pará market, harbor, theater, parks, and of the various "types" the travelers encountered there, are strikingly similar in content and tone to his illustrations for "Old and New Louisiana." For Champney, "The Great South" was indeed a rehearsal on home ground for a later project on foreign territory.

Certain elements of a specifically colonialist approach, including economic "reveries" and urgent calls for Northern investment and immigration, can also be found in the depiction of Louisiana in "The Great South."[55] However, King also pointedly diverges from the colonialist approach: not only does he comment on the "sturdy strength" and "reserve energy" of the native Louisianians ("Old and New" 10), as well as their "praiseworthy ambition" ("Old and New II" 149), thus stressing that they are far from being unable or unwilling to exploit Louisiana's economic potential, he also actively discourages his readers from investing in the state. Quoting "a prominent historian and gentleman of most honorable Creole descent" ("Old and New" 12)[56] as "alleg[ing] that [people at the North] should not alter their determination [to not invest in Louisiana] so long as the present condition of politics prevailed" (13) and citing several examples of dramatically declining property values in New Orleans and the rest of the state (21), King identifies Reconstruction politics, in the shape of incompetent black legislators and unscrupulous white carpetbaggers, as the ultimate source of Louisiana's economic stagnation in general and the lack of capital and immigrants in particular (22). King therefore advocates putting an end to Northern intervention in Southern politics in order to facilitate Northern intervention in the

Southern economy. Such a return to the rule of the white elite would also, King writes, prevent further political turmoil:

> There is no rebellious spirit in Louisiana against the United States – no desire to undo the war's legitimate results; but there is a gradual accumulation of indignation against the plunderers, who have been numerous in the State, which bodes something very like the ugly form of revolution.
>
> (22)

With the "negro" being "protected as thoroughly as needs be" (22), King notes, things should now go back to "normal" so that Louisiana can finally become "Paradise Regained" (1).

As its title indicates, "Old and New Louisiana" is not, however, only concerned with the nation's or the state's future (the "Paradise Regained" or the "new" Louisiana from the article's title). "You must know much of the past of New Orleans and Louisiana to thoroughly understand their present" (3), King writes at the beginning of the first article, and especially in this feature, he and Champney spend considerable space and effort informing the reader about this past. More specifically, they establish the state and particularly the city as a chronotope of Frenchness, a complex intermingling of local urban space, French exoticism, and pastness.

"Old and New Louisiana" opens with a spectacular, almost full-page article masthead, which shows, at the bottom, a bizarre group of anthropomorphized animals and other weird creatures gathered in a swamp (1). The scene, which has reminded several commentators of the work of British illustrator John Tenniel (see Rainey 198; Greeson, *South* 245), simultaneously refers to "the fantastic creations of untutored fancy" with which "Indian legend peopled every nook and cranny of the Territory" (2) and the "*outré* masks" (26) of the New Orleans carnival, which King and Champney describe and depict in great detail toward the end of the article (23–6; see especially Champney's illustration of the "Masquerade at the Varieties Theater" [30]). More importantly, the masthead immediately sets the tone for the characterization of Louisiana and New Orleans as a fairy-tale wonderland – Rainey (198) points out that Tenniel illustrated Lewis Carroll's "Alice in Wonderland" books – whose geographical location is, at best, murky and that is set in a vague past. Indeed, the first paragraph of King's text describes Louisiana's former "immense limits" (2) and presents the area's history as a series of romantic fairy-tale and adventure stories from a different time: "[Louisiana] has been in turn the plaything of monarchs and the bait of adventurers. Its history and tradition are leagued with all that was romantic in the eighteenth century. . . . What wonder . . . that it is so richly varied, so charming, so unique?" (2).

The beginning of the second paragraph then constitutes an attempt at narrative and thematic control. Replacing the rapture of the first paragraph with a matter-of-fact, truncated style, King firmly situates himself and the reader in time and space: "Six o'clock, on Saturday evening, in the good old city of New Orleans" (2). Yet the past and, concomitantly, the fairy-tale discourse invariably force their way into the text again: the sound of the bells of the St. Louis cathedral remind King of Don Andre Almonaster, "*once upon a time* 'perpetual regidor' of New Orleans," and thus "seem to call up visions of the quaint past" (2; emphasis added). Time and again, in the following pages, the sights and sounds of present-day New Orleans – and specifically of the French Quarter – "call up" such "visions of the quaint past": walking from Jackson Square through the older parts of the city, King writes, "one may readily call to mind the curious changeful past of the commonwealth and its cosmopolitan capital; for there is a visible reminder at many a corner, and on many a wall" (4). Indeed, as, according to King, the city has changed but little since 1723 (4), a glimpse of it simultaneously offers a glimpse into the past: "I like to stand in these Louisianian byways, and look back on the progress of French civilization in them" (6). With every street and building invoking legends and memories of the past (16), the city becomes a chronotope and the visitor a time-traveler.

The arrangement of text and illustrations supports this notion of the city's chronotopicity, this "intrinsic connectedness" (Bakhtin 84) of the local urban space and the past: King's lengthy and detailed account of the history of New Orleans from the founding of the settlement in 1718 to the present (4–10) is accompanied by depictions of sights and scenes in the present-day French Quarter, thus underlining the present-day city's pastness. To be sure, there are also illustrations of historical persons, namely, a portrait of Bienville (8), the second governor of Louisiana, and a "brace of old Spanish governors" (11), both of them provided by Gayarré, as King acknowledges in a footnote ("Old and New II" 134). The other pictures, however, depict present-day New Orleans. Following the article masthead, the first illustration (2) appropriately shows the St. Louis cathedral, whose bells, as King states on the same page, "seem to call up visions of the quaint past" (see earlier). The illustrations on the following pages continue this "Catholic" theme, showing scenes of alms-giving (3) and of a black child dipping her hand into a holy water font (4), as well as depictions of the Archbishop's Palace and garden (5) and the new Ursuline convent (10). A second "series" of thematically linked pictures, this time focusing on Jackson Square, starts with an illustration of the Cabildo (6) and continues with the Jackson statue (7) and a scene at the corner of the square (9). Some of the buildings and sites depicted in the illustrations may be historical – "antique," as King calls them (2) – but Champney shows them as they appear in the present: the picture of the Archbishop's Palace features a horse-drawn streetcar passing in front of the edifice, that of the Cabildo, an American flag on top of the building, and in the scene "on the corner of Jackson Square" four children are gathered around an advertising column. Yet the combination of present-day views of New Orleans and a historiographical account of the city's past inevitably ascribes a pastness to the place. Just as they do for King when he stands "in these Louisianian byways" in 1873 New Orleans and "look[s] back on the progress of French civilization in them" (6), present and past also mingle and merge for readers of "Old and New Louisiana" when they are confronted, on the very same page, with pictorial renderings of the present-day city and a textual account of the place's past.[57]

Yet New Orleans is characterized not only as a chronotope by King and Champney, but also and more specifically as a chronotope of Frenchness. Right after King has described the sound of St. Louis cathedral's six o'clock bells and their capacity to evoke the past, he again firmly situates himself and the reader in the present: "Now the sunlight mingles with the breeze" (3). We are back in the present, on a "Saturday evening, in the good old city of New Orleans" (see earlier), and King tells the reader to look around:

> See! a black-robed woman, with downcast eyes, passes silently over the holy threshold; a blind beggar, with a parti-colored handkerchief wound about his weather-beaten head, hears the bustling of her gown, and stretches out his trembling hand for alms; the market-women hush their chatter as they near the portal; a mulatto lazzaroni is lounging in the shade of an ancient arch, beneath the old Spanish Council House.
>
> (3)

King adopts the perspective of the flaneur, who leisurely walks through the city and records his impressions of the urban spectacle in (semi-)public spaces such as squares, streets, and markets (see Benjamin). Yet what he discovers here is not, as in the examples cited above, New Orleans's pastness, but the city's foreignness and exoticism, its un-Americanness and Europeanness: "this is not an American scene, and one almost persuades himself that he is in Europe" (3). In both parts of "Old and New Louisiana," King time and again stresses the French Quarter's foreignness or, more specifically, its Frenchness. "Step off from Canal Street ... some bright February morning," he tells the reader, "and you are at once in a foreign atmosphere. Three paces from the corner have enchanted you; ... this might be Toulouse, or Bordeaux, or Marseilles!" (10). Shopkeepers live above their shops, "as in foreign cities" (10); the awning of a little café is "drawn down exactly as in France" (10); the "lazy negro," who appears at first to represent "a touch of Americanism, perhaps," speaks French (10); and the theater's play-bill is "in French, of course" (11). At the end of his description of the French market ("Old and New II" 156–7), too, King notes: "Coming out from the markets into the French quarter's venerable streets, ... one rubs his eyes, and feels almost certain that he is not in America" (157).

Perhaps somewhat surprisingly, Champney's illustrations do not seem to fully exploit the text's exoticism. To be sure, the relatively short description of the French market is accompanied by a series of no fewer than eight engravings of the various sights and types to be found there ("Old and New II" 145–57). Yet King's flanerie through the French Quarter ("Old and New" 10–12) is neither illustrated with street scenes reminiscent of cities in southern France, nor with pictures of little cafés with awnings. Instead, following the Catholic-themed illustrations and the impressions of Jackson Square at the beginning of the article, Champney offers but one drawing of "an old Spanish house on Royal Street" (9) and, apart from that, impressive views of mostly neoclassical buildings in the Quarter – the St. Louis Hotel (12), the U.S. Branch Mint (13), the old Louisiana Bank (17), and the St. Charles Hotel (19), where King and Champney stayed (see Drake and Jones xxxvn50) – that would not have looked entirely out of place in any other city in the United States. King, too, brings up the French Quarter's foreign atmosphere only to immediately add that "ten minutes of rapid walking will bring [one] to streets and squares as generically American as any in Boston, Chicago, or St. Louis" ("Old and New" 3) and that one "has only to enter some of the restaurants on the American side of Canal Street, where the piles of oyster shells, and the odor of Washington pie, will quickly awaken him from his delusion [of not being in America]" ("Old and New II" 157). Mapping "cultural difference onto distinct neighborhoods" (Bramen 160), King and Champney tell readers that whenever they start to feel too much like strangers in their own country in the French Quarter, they can quickly escape to nearby places of reassuringly familiar Americanness.

King not only stresses that New Orleans's foreignness or Frenchness is spatially limited to the French Quarter, however. More importantly, he also interweaves the Quarter's Frenchness and its pastness, thus depicting it as a chronotope of Frenchness. This becomes most obvious in the following juxtaposition from the beginning of "Old and New Louisiana":

> You may compass the perfection of contrast in a brief time here. Yonder is the archbishop's palace: stand upon one side of it, and you seem in a foreign land; stand upon the other, and you catch a glimpse of the rush and hurry of American traffic of to-day along the levee.
> ("Old and New" 3)

Having established New Orleans's pastness (through the "visions of the quaint past" evoked by the sound of the bells [2]) and its Frenchness (through his flaneuresque description of Jackson Square, culminating in his exclamation "this is not an American scene" [3]) separately and individually, King now proceeds to inextricably link the two. The American present – in the shape of "the rush and hurry of American traffic of to-day" – is implicitly contrasted here with a foreign past, with the result that the two, foreignness/Frenchness and pastness, appear as indissolubly bound up with each other. New Orleans's past is characterized as un-American and French; conversely, the city's French are characterized as past.

King's pastifying of French New Orleans, his depiction of the French Quarter as a chronotope of Frenchness, becomes even more intense as the text moves on, with French New Orleans receding further and further into the past. In a manner reminiscent of Harriet Beecher Stowe's *Oldtown Folks* (1869), which describes traditional New England life as "rapidly fading away" (1), King at first claims that New Orleans's "older colonial landmarks" are "fast disappearing" ("Old and New" 3). "The imprint of French manners and customs will," he adds confidently, "long remain, however; for it was made lasting by two periods of domination" (3). A mere three pages later, however, King declares these "manners and customs" as officially past: "I like to stand in these old Louisianian byways, and look back on the progress of French civilization in them, *now that it has been displaced by a newer one*" (6; emphasis added). The "battle of race with race, of the picturesque and unjust civilization of the past with the prosaic and leveling civilization of the present" (2), of which King spoke in the first paragraph of his article, seems to be definitively over. Indeed, on the following page, King once again reassures the reader that, presumably since they have been politically and culturally displaced, firmly belong to the past, and no longer pose a threat even in one of their former strongholds, "[w]e can well afford to feel friendlier towards the French now than did our ancestors when they were encroaching on the northwest" (7).

Exactly what kind of "cultural, social, political, or ideological work" does King's pastifying of French New Orleans perform, however; what is the function of his depiction of New Orleans as a chronotope of Frenchness? Greeson has suggested that with its focus on the colonial history of Louisiana and the latter's changing European masters, "Old and New Louisiana" explores the "global context of the nation's domestic possession of Louisiana" ("Expropriating" 506). This, however,

> becomes the first step in conceptualizing a hemispheric expansion of the US that may be signally distinguished from competing European designs on Spanish America. King's intensive focus on Louisiana and its past allows for a rehearsal of US acquisition and administration of a previously colonial, semi-tropical American territory, and the Gulf Coast location of New Orleans easily directs the acquisitive gaze of his readers yet farther south.
>
> (506–507)

In short, King and Champney contribute to portraying Louisiana and New Orleans as America's very own Orient (see Makdisi) and as its gateway to the South. Like the rest of "The Great South," the two installments share the series' overall ideological and political concerns with the imperial future of the nation. That may be true, but in the context of *Scribner's/Century*'s intertextual network, "Old and New Louisiana" has yet another function: simultaneously providing important historical and social background information on New Orleans and creating a textual gap – that is, a readerly desire to hear more about the city – the two articles introduce and whet the reader's appetite for the New Orleans-related features that immediately surround them in the periodical – namely, George Washington Cable's "Old Creole Days" stories, two of which appeared right before ("'Sieur George," October 1873) and after ("Belles Demoiselles Plantation," April 1874) "Old and New Louisiana."

In his first article, King depicts French New Orleanians as a generally isolated and reclusive people. People in the French Quarter, he writes, "seem to have a total disregard of the outside world . . . . They seem as remote from New York or Washington as if limitless oceans rolled between" (12). Note that King's observations about New Orleans's French Quarter – and New Orleans's French – are mostly based on public spaces and events: Jackson Square, the streets of the Quarter, the French market, the carnival parades and balls. There is but one exception, one single instance in which King allows us a short glimpse into a more private space. Strolling through the French Quarter and describing the buildings with their large and "massive" street doors leading into "stone-paved court-yards" (10), King notes:

> Sometimes, through the portal, you catch a glimpse of a delicious garden, filled with daintiest blossoms, purple and white and red gleaming from the vines clambering over a gray wall; rose-bushes, with grass about them strewn with loveliest petals; symmetrical green bosquets, and luxuriant hedges, arbors, and refuges, trimmed by skillful hands; banks of verbenas; bewitching profusion of peach and apple blossoms; dark green of the magnolia; in a quiet corner, the rich glow of the orange in its nest among the thick leaves of its parent tree; the defiant palmetto, the frost-fearing catalpa, and a mass of rich bloom which laps the senses in slumbrous delight, when – suddenly the door closes behind some dark-haired, flashing-eyed, slender Creole girl, clad in black, and your paradise is lost, while Eve remains inside the gate!
>
> (10)

As Michael T. Taussig has noted, "precapitalist societies acquire the burden of having to satisfy our alienated longings for a lost Golden Age" (7). Behind the massive street door, King has caught a glimpse of a wonderful, multicolored, paradisiacal fairy-tale world, the "Paradise Lost" as which he has identified "Louisiana to-day" in the first sentence of his article (1) and the curious wonderland depicted by Champney in the lower part of his article masthead (1). Immediately upon discovering this hidden world, however, King has the Creole girl rudely shut the door upon readers, leaving them wondering who she was, where she went, and what else might possibly be going on behind this and other closed doors in the French Quarter. Edward King would not tell readers (perhaps he could not), but George Washington Cable would.

Peeping Behind Closed Doors: "Old Creole Days"

Published just a month before the first installment of "Old and New Louisiana," "'Sieur George: A Story of New Orleans," Cable's first contribution to *Scribner's/Century* and, hence, to "Scribner's Illustrated New Orleans," begins with a scene that is at once strikingly similar to and strikingly different from the one described by King:

> In the heart of New Orleans stands a large four-story brick building, that has so stood for about three-quarters of a century.... Under its main archway is a dingy apothecary-shop. On one street is the bazaar of a *modiste en robes et chapeaux* and other humble shops.... A peep through one of the shops reveals a square court within, hung with many lines of wet clothes, its sides hugged by rotten staircases that seem vainly trying to clamber out of the rubbish.... The building is a thing of many windows, where passably good-looking women appear and disappear, clad in cotton-gowns, watering little outside shelves of flowers and cacti, or hanging canaries' cages.
>
> (739)

As in King's text, readers find themselves in present-day New Orleans and in the French Quarter (complete with signs in French); as in King's text, they catch a glimpse into the hidden courtyard of one of the buildings; and as in King's text, they see, for a very brief moment, some of the building's inhabitants. Unlike King, however, Cable ultimately does not leave readers in the dark about the people who live in this building and about what is going on behind its façade. To be sure, he does not simply reveal this information straightforwardly, either. Instead, maintaining the atmosphere of concealment, secrecy, and partial visions that characterizes the story's opening (as well as King's courtyard scene), Cable merely allows readers to join Kookoo, the building's landlord and the story's focalizer, in peeping through half-opened doors (742), keyholes (743), and windows (745), and in eavesdropping from hidden places under the stairs (741), to find out about the contents of the mysterious hair-trunk in 'Sieur George's apartment (see Cleman, *Cable* 26–7). The fact that the trunk is not a treasure chest, as Kookoo had long assumed (740; 744), but rather contains the remnants of a tragic life given over to gambling, as he and readers learn toward the end of the story (745), should have been clear from the beginning: a treasure may have fit into the luxuriant paradise that King discovers behind the massive street doors of the French Quarter, but a trunk full of the sad remains of lost hopes and dreams – namely, losing lottery tickets – seems much more appropriate for Cable's hidden courtyard, whose "rotten staircases that seem vainly trying to clamber out of the rubbish" (739) imply all sorts of decay and failure.

With its emphasis on degeneration and portending tragedy on the one hand, and on concealment and voyeurism on the other hand, as well as with the parallel it draws between the physical state of a French Quarter building and the fates of its inhabitants, the beginning of "'Sieur George" not only points to the remainder of that story, however. It also sets the tone for the five other New Orleans stories by Cable that *Scribner's/Century* would publish in the following three years (with the last story, "Café des Exilés," featured in the March 1876 issue of the magazine) and that, another three years later, in 1879, would appear in collected form with Charles Scribner's Sons as *Old Creole Days*. Indeed, like "'Sieur George," almost all of these stories begin with detailed descriptions of buildings in the present-day French Quarter, whose decaying façades, closed shutters, and high walls and fences simultaneously hide and, in one way or another, externalize or mirror the stories of their owners or tenants (see, among others, Ekström 105; Petry, *Genius* 18; and Nagel 51). Through peeps, glimpses, and sideway glances behind the surface of the façades – usually over the shoulder of one of the protagonists – readers gradually learn about these stories (see Cleman, *Cable* 25–6),[58] which, more often than not, turn out to be tragic or disastrous, involving moral corruption ("'Sieur George"), severed family ties ("'Tite Poulette"), infectious diseases ("Jean-ah Poquelin"), and illegal gunrunning ("Café des Exilés").

In the intertextual network of "Scribner's Illustrated New Orleans," the revelation of these tragedies constitutes the most obvious way in which Cable's short fiction "responds" to the "call" made by King's travel writing: both writers guide their readers through the present-day French Quarter and point out sites and buildings that appear to contain a story.[59] Yet whereas King simply moves on after the door has been shut to his inquisitive gaze, leaving readers wondering and guessing, Cable, pushing the limits of the flaneur's superficial urban vision, allows his readers to penetrate, along with his voyeuristic characters, the surfaces of the visible city and at least partially reveals the histories and voices of its residents.[60] Next to "'Sieur George," the most paradigmatic of Cable's stories in this sense are "'Tite Poulette" and "Jean-ah Poquelin," published as the writer's third and fourth pieces in the magazine in October 1874 and May 1875, respectively. Particularly with respect to the themes of concealment and peeping, however, both texts complicate, each in its own way, the formula established by "'Sieur George," and thus indicate further ways in which Cable's fictions "respond" to King's travel writing. Most importantly, Cable, too, pastifies French New Orleans.

Just like the beginning of "'Sieur George,'" the first paragraphs of "'Tite Poulette" contain the description of a French Quarter building – in this case, a building that leads the narrator/guide to "guess that it is a remnant of the old Spanish Barracks" (674). Here, too, the building's general air of concealment and secrecy – its "big, round-arched windows in a long, second-story row, are walled up" and one "might stand about on the opposite *banquette* for weeks and never find out [who lives there now]" (674) – simultaneously hides and exposes the precarious social and economic situation of its (former) residents (see Petry, *Genius* 103; Elfenbein 37–8). And here, too, we join one of the characters – in this case, "rosy-faced, beardless young Dutchman" Kristian Koppig (674) – in peeping, from his conveniently located dormer window, at the building in order to find out about the story it contains. The readers' initial alignment with Koppig's voyeuristic perspective (in the course of the story, Cable will occasionally shift the angle of narration; see Cleman, *Cable* 34) is further stressed in the illustrated book version of "'Tite Poulette," published in 1897 by Charles Scribner's Sons. Indeed, the first of the altogether three pictures which illustrator, portraitist, and muralist Albert Herter created for this story is placed right above its printed title and shows a young man with his back turned to the viewer – presumably Koppig – peering through the latticed shutters of a dormer window at something below – presumably the mysterious building opposite the street (see Cable, *Old Creole Days* 137).[61] While we cannot see what Koppig is looking at, his position aligns our gaze with his.

Yet, in "'Tite Poulette," Cable's spectatorial strategies are far more complex than in "'Sieur George." First of all, in this case, the residents of the building, Zalli/Madame John and the eponymous 'Tite Poulette, know that they are being watched by Koppig and even react to his peeping. Indeed, while at first, they merely wonder "'If he saw us last night!'" (677) when they discover him sitting at his dormer window, 'Tite Poulette soon sets up a little garden on the windowsill for the sole purpose of strategically displaying herself at the window:

> [I]t was odd to see, – dry weather or wet, – how many waterings per day those plants could take. ['Tite Poulette] never looked up from her task; but I know she performed it with that unacknowledged pleasure which all girls love and deny, that of being looked upon by noble eyes.
>
> (678)

Moreover, knowing that not all eyes may be as "noble" as Koppig's, the two women peep back. As the description of their building in the opening paragraph already indicates, the hidden gaze is by no means unidirectional in this story: the "big, round-arched" windows of the structure may have been "walled up," but "two or three from time to time have had smaller windows let into them again, with odd little latticed peep-holes in their batten shutters" (674). The city may cast furtive glances at the building and at Zalli/Madame John and 'Tite Poulette, but far from remaining mere objects of the gaze, they return the peeping, observing, for instance, Koppig (677), the manager of the *Salle de Condé* (678), or the two of them interacting (679). Peeping back – whether through the latticed shutters of their home or through the satin mask that Zalli/Madame John used to wear for the quadroon balls (675) – has been economically and socially vital for the two women (see Petry, *Genius* 103).

Koppig's peeping, in turn, develops from an almost unconscious act into a bold spectatorship, with the result that he turns from an interested, but disconnected, passive onlooker into an agent actively involved in the drama. Watching 'Tite Poulette waiting for Zalli/Madame John to return from her Sunday dance performances, "slow-thinking" Koppig at first never even notices "that he staid at home with his window darkened for the very purpose" (676). Later, however, after he has lost his job and has started spending entire afternoons at his dormer window peeping at the building across the street (678), Koppig "prepare[s] to become a bold spectator" of the encounter between the manager of the *Salle de Condé* and Zalli/Madame John (679). The scene that follows features a complex criss-crossing of furtive peeps and direct gazes between Koppig, 'Tite Poulette, Zalli/Madame John, and the manager, with both Koppig and the manager as well as Koppig and 'Tite Poulette looking directly at each other, Koppig observing 'Tite Poulette peeping at Zalli/Madame John from her window, and 'Tite Poulette and Zalli/Madame John peeping at Koppig and the manager (679). By the end of the scene, Koppig has irrevocably crossed the line from observer to participant.

In King's courtyard scene, as well as elsewhere in King's accounts, this line is never crossed. Walking through the streets of the French Quarter, King may observe its inhabitants and explicitly invite readers to "See!" ("Old and New" 3), he may even describe the eyes of the Creole "Eve" as "flashing" (10), but throughout the two texts he remains strangely invisible to the city and its residents. Not so in "'Tite Poulette," where the city returns the gaze and where Cable dramatizes the role of the observer, putting him on the stage: not only do Zalli/Madame John and 'Tite Poulette, but also the manager, peep and stare back at Koppig, Koppig also interacts with them, verbally and otherwise, and thus becomes directly engaged with and part of the city. Unlike King, he is even allowed to pass through the gate of the mysterious building (682), where at the end of the story he finds his "Eve" – namely, 'Tite Poulette. In Cable's story, the paradise is not lost.

In "Jean-ah Poquelin," Little White also crosses the line from passive observer to active participant, though ultimately to no avail. Like "'Sieur

George" and "'Tite Poulette," "Jean-ah Poquelin" is, as John Cleman has pointed out, "structured as an indigenous mystery leading to a dramatic revelation" (*Cable* 37), but the role of the voyeur-turned-participant is somewhat different in this story. To be sure, similar to Kookoo and Koppig, Little White initially peeps at Jean-ah Poquelin's old colonial plantation house in order to expose the secret of the building or, rather, to prove that there is no secret in the first place: "'I tell you frankly,'" he admits, "'I go into this more to prove [Poquelin] innocent than with any expectation of finding him guilty'" (96). However, when he discovers that there is a secret, after all, he stops peeping – tellingly, he "shut[s] his eyes in his hands" (97) – and starts acting in order to help the former Creole planter, slave-trader, and smuggler hide what is going on behind the façade of the building rather than in order to reveal its mystery.

When the secret does get exposed at the end of the story, the "dramatic revelation" is neither, as in "'Sieur George,'" the result of furtive peeps, hidden glimpses, and sideway glances, nor, as in "'Tite Poulette,'" the result of direct gazes. Instead, it is the result of an aggressive invasion of and an open trespassing upon Poquelin's estate (specifically by the municipal authorities' levelers, rodsmen, and road constructors [92] and the mob of "[t]wo or three hundred men and boys" [99] who charivari old Poquelin), two acts that in the story are explicitly related to a historic change – namely, the U.S. takeover of Louisiana in 1803. Thus, it is neither Poquelin's secret itself nor its revelation, but the way this revelation dramatizes the passing of the colonial French order and rule following the Louisiana Purchase that allows us to see how Cable's short fictions respond in yet another way to King's accounts: like King, Cable stresses the pastness of the French Creoles.

I am not referring here to what Jennifer Rae Greeson has called the "generic 'local color' reading of Cable's fiction" – namely, the idea that "Jean-ah Poquelin" as well as Cable's other stories simply document "a regionally specific way of life already lost to the standardizations of modernity at the poignant moment of its imminent demise" ("Expropriating" 507). Of course, the opening paragraph of the story and the "acute tension" it creates "between the 'newly established American Government' and the old Creole order" (Petry, *Genius* 91), the fact that Poquelin's house is "half in ruin" (Cable, "Poquelin" 91; see Egan n.p.) and that he himself is "'[t]he last of his line'" (91), and, most importantly, the aggressive encroachment upon Poquelin's estate by the growing city which brings about the revelation at the end of the story – all stress the slow but sure disappearance of the French way of life in New Orleans. Yet there is a crucial difference between Cable's story and the writings of other local colorists. Indeed, other works of local color that record such moments of the passing of regional cultures in the face of a newly risen modern order are mostly set in the present (see earlier). In "Jean-ah Poquelin," by contrast, the moment of passing has already passed; in fact, viewed from the time of writing, it passed long ago, at the beginning of the nineteenth century.[62] This is true for Cable's short stories in general: not only do most of them, in one way or another, revolve around or allude to the demise of the French rule in New Orleans (see particularly the ending of "'Sieur George," "Belles Demoiselles Plantation," and "Madame Délicieuse"), they are all set in the past. In a letter to Scribner, Armstrong & Co., written in February 1878, Cable dates his stories as follows: "Jean-Ah Poquelin, 1805; 'Tite Poulette, 1810; Posson Jone', 1815; Belles Demoiselles Plantation, 1820; Madame Délicieuse, 1830; Café des Exilés, 1845; 'Sieur George, 1850" (qtd. in Biklé 58). Hence, as already indicated by some of the titles Cable originally proposed for the collection of his short fictions (especially "Jadis," "The Old Regime," and "Créoles du Vieuxtemps"; see Biklé 58–9) and the title that was eventually chosen ("Old Creole Days"), Cable's New Orleans stories, like King's travel accounts, describe the city's French as past.

Moreover, and again like the text and pictures of "Old and New Louisiana," the stories also characterize the city's past as French. As he shifts almost imperceptibly from the descriptions of buildings in the present-day French Quarter, with which he opens his stories, to the gradual revelations of the fates of the former French inhabitants of these buildings, which comprise the stories proper, Cable ascribes an undeniably French pastness to the area. "'Sieur George" and "'Tite Poulette" are cases in point: the buildings are described in the present tense, but the narrator switches to the past tense for the Creole stories that follow.[63] As in King's account, then, where sights and sounds in the present-day French Quarter "seem to call up visions of the quaint past" ("Old and New" 2) and where one may stand in byways and "look back on the progress of French civilization in them" (6), Cable's stories interweave Frenchness and pastness to depict the city as a chronotope of Frenchness.

The strategy Cable uses to establish the pastness of French New Orleans in "Jean-ah Poquelin" (as well as in his short fiction in general) – dramatizing the moment of their passing, and setting this moment in the distant past – directly links this text to Cable's next contribution to "Scribner's Illustrated New Orleans," namely, his novel *The Grandissimes*, serialized from November 1879 to August 1880: it is certainly no coincidence that Jean-ah Poquelin makes a cameo appearance in chapter XLIV of the novel (see ahead). There is a crucial difference, however, in how the two texts morally evaluate the irrevocable passing of the French colonial order. For Greeson, the ending of "Jean-ah Poquelin" constitutes both a narrative inexorability and a solution that is depicted as "morally for the best" ("Expropriating" 509) – with respect to the narrative, "outside control of Louisiana" and the ensuing exposure of Poquelin's secret are inevitable since without them, "there would be no plot" (509). Morally, the U.S. takeover is vindicated, Greeson argues, because "Cable generally subordinates thorny conflicts over political control and property ownership to cultural clashes between his Creoles and their US occupiers" (509).[64]

In fact, however, as scholars such as John Cleman (*Cable* 38–9), Alfred Hornung (238), and Jonathan Daigle have pointed out, the story is by no means as unambiguous about the U.S. takeover, the related "imported virtues" (Cable, "Poquelin" 95) of materialist and civic progress and improvement, the ensuing revelation of Poquelin's secret, and, hence, about itself, its own telling, as Greeson claims it is. Daigle, for instance, argues that when Little White sees the truth – and immediately covers his eyes with his hands (97) – he has not only uncovered Poquelin's secret, but also recognized "his own complicity in the cycle of exploitation" (Daigle 17). The same applies to the mob and, implicitly, the readers, once they learn Poquelin's secret at the end of the story: they finally know now what Poquelin and Little White have so desperately tried to conceal, but at what price? Readers, too, may come to the conclusion that Poquelin was "'a better man, with all his sins, than [they; i.e., readers] will ever be'" (Cable, "Poquelin" 100). Again, Albert Herter's illustrations for the 1897 version of *Old Creole Days* are revealing here: in his third and final illustration for "Jean-ah Poquelin," Herter has the men in the mob turn their backs upon the viewer (see following 130). Aligning their gaze with that of the mob-men upon Poquelin's dead body and his brother, Herter depicts the reader as one of them. *The Grandissimes*, by contrast, not only leaves readers in no doubt as to which side they are supposed to take in the conflict between French Creoles and Americans, the novel also employs the pastifying of French New Orleans to blur the dividing line between past and present.

Times of Crises, Crises of Temporality: The Grandissimes

In chapter XLIV of *The Grandissimes*, first published as part of the novel's penultimate installment in the July 1880 issue of *Scribner's*, readers meet an old "friend" whom they had first encountered over five years before. Right after he has finally decided to eat yet another fruit from the tree of "'ow dead fathe's mistakes'" (Cable, *Grandissimes* 194 [20.2])[65] and has therefore restituted Fausse Rivière Plantation to Aurora and Clotilde Nancanou, Honoré Grandissime goes to Canal street, the upper boundary of the city, where one "could think aloud . . . with impunity" (389 [20.3]), to ponder the state of New Orleans society. Beyond the street, the narrator notes,

> the open plain was dotted with country-houses, brick-kilns, clumps of live-oak and groves of pecan. . . . At one or two points the sky was reflected from marshy ponds. Out to westward rose conspicuously the old house and willow-copse of Jean Poquelin.
>
> (389 [20.3])

According to Robert O. Stephens, the reference to Cable's short story "Jean-ah Poquelin," published five years before in the May 1875 issue of the magazine, serves to add to the atmosphere of "witchlore and voodoo" that pervades the novel, but also to identify the period in which *The Grandissimes* is set as one of economic and social transition, a time of crises for French New Orleans ("Saga" 5). These are, however, by no means the only connections between *The Grandissimes* and "Jean-ah Poquelin" in particular and Cable's other "Old Creole Days" stories in general. The novel also replicates the basic structure or motif of the stories: just as most of the stories do, *The Grandissimes* confronts readers with a mystery or secret and allows them to join one of the characters, who is intent on solving and who eventually manages to solve the riddle.[66] Yet whereas in the stories, of course, the mysteries in question merely involve the residents of one particular building in New Orleans, in the novel it is the city as a whole, the entire "Community of New Orleans" (Cable, *Grandissimes* 582 [19.4]), that constitutes the riddle. And whereas Little White, Koppig, and Kookoo start investigating the secrets they are confronted with more or less out of sheer curiosity, Frowenfeld has no other choice: placed as he is "in a situation of financial and social insecurity," the study of New Orleans and its inhabitants are "not merely an interesting exercise but also part of his survival" (Tipping 66). Indeed, as Honoré points out to him during their first encounter already, Frowenfeld "cannot affo'd" to remain outside and ignorant of this community (Cable, *Grandissimes* 252 [19.2]). Finally, whereas in the stories the mysteries are hidden behind decaying façades, walled-up or shuttered windows, and high walls and fences, in *The Grandissimes* the secret is metaphorically contained in a mysterious book, complete with a "brightly illuminated title-page" (582 [19.4]).

The book metaphor is exceptionally apt, since it links the gradual revelation of the secret, Frowenfeld's "reading" of the book of New Orleans, to the experience of the readers of *The Grandissimes*, thus directly aligning them with Frowenfeld. For instance, when Frowenfeld resolves to begin with "the perusal of this newly found book, the Community of New Orleans" in chapter XVIII, he already knows:

> he should find it a difficult task – not only that much of it was in a strange tongue, but that it was a volume whose displaced leaves would have to be lifted tenderly, blown free of much dust, re-arranged, some torn fragments laid together again with much painstaking, and even the purport of some pages guessed out.
>
> (582 [19.4])

Up to this point, roughly a third into the novel, Frowenfeld has spent most of his time failing to understand his fellow New Orleanians, both linguistically and culturally (see Hochman 530). "He tried hard to understand it, but could not" (102 [19.1]), "The tenant did not understand" (254 [19.2]), "[Palmyre's speech] was not understood" (260 [19.2]), "He smiled his ignorance and shook his head" (374 [19.3]) – these and numerous similar comments are sprinkled throughout this part of the text. To Frowenfeld, Dr. Keene's stories about New Orleans appear as "little more than a thick mist of strange names, places and events" that leaves him "befogged" (103 [19.1]); in the book version, he complains about not being able to distinguish between the various Grandissimes (40), he constantly finds himself bewildered and surprised (Cable, *Grandissimes* 256 [19.2]), becomes "brain-weary," "involved among shadows, and going from bad to worse, seemed at length almost to gasp in an atmosphere of hints, allusions, faint unspoken admissions, ill-concealed antipathies, unfinished speeches, mistaken identities and whisperings of hidden strife" (380 [19.3]).

Readers of *The Grandissimes*, more likely than not, know how he feels. Mostly due to Cable's characteristically allusive and sometimes enigmatic style, which contemporary reviewers had already complained about,[67] there is, as John Cleman points out, "too much ... for a first-time reader to grasp" in the novel's opening scenes ("Art" 399). But, Cleman continues, "this is precisely the situation facing Frowenfeld. The trouble the reader has in peering behind the dance masks is exactly the problem faced by Frowenfeld in his attempt to understand the culture where he has chosen to live" (399). Hence, while other critics have stressed Frowenfeld's connection to the author (Daigle, for instance, calls him "Cable's mouthpiece on social issues" [26]), Jenny Franchot argues that the "bewildered immigrant and suitor" "stands in for Cable's postbellum, implicitly Northern reader" (514), and that his "reading" experience, his gradual initiation into New Orleans society, parallels that of the reader (see Cleman, *Cable* 51).[68] This parallelism is further underlined by the near simultaneity of the intradiegetic time of the events narrated in the novel and the rhythm of its serial publication in *Scribner's*: *The Grandissimes* was published in twelve monthly installments from November 1879 to October 1880; this very closely corresponds to the time of the action, which runs from September (1803; see Cable, *Grandissimes* 97 [19.1]) to "while it is yet summer" (in 1804; see 812 [20.6]). In between, while neither being strictly linear nor evenly paced, the narrative nevertheless more or less follows the publication schedule. By Chapter IX (set on 24 December 1803, and published in the December 1879 installment; see 254 [19.2]), the narrative has caught up with the time of publication, only to lag behind again in Chapter XXX (set in early March 1804 and published in May 1880; see 24 [20.1]), but it eventually catches up through a five-month jump in time in Chapter XLVI (set in August 1804 and published in August 1880; see 527 [20.4]).

The formal parallel between the past time of the action and the present time of publication/reading already points to the more general alignment or even conflation of past and present in *The Grandissimes*. In "The Mulatto in *The Grandissimes*," Thomas H. Fick and Eva Gold argue that Cable's abundant use of hybrid characters and character doubles across racial and gender boundaries provokes "not only a category crisis (whereby our habitual categories do not work), but a crisis of category (where the act of categorization itself is called into question)" (72). With respect to the category crisis, Fick and Gold are mostly concerned with gender and race, noting that at the masked ball in Chapter I, for instance, the cross-dressers (most notably the white, male, Anglo-American Dr. Charlie Keene in the guise of the African Creole-speaking "Indian queen" Lufki-Hamma) "indicate a destabilization of comfortable binarity" in gender and especially race relations (71).[69] Yet the masked ball scene also and simultaneously establishes the destabilization of yet another category – namely, that of time or, more precisely, the clear separation between past and present (see Clark 603). The dancers are dressed, after all, as their own (or, in the case of Keene, as their friends') ancestors; that is, their doubles across the boundary between past and present (see Railton 206–207). In the case of Aurora Nancanou, who at the ball wears the costume of a "*Fille à la Cassette*" (Cable, *Grandissimes* 98 [19.1]), this is confirmed at the end of Chapter XXV, aptly titled "Aurora as a Historian," when she shows a puzzled Frowenfeld a painting of her grandmother and playfully adds: "'Dass one *fille à la cassette*, . . . my gran'-muzzah; *mais*, ad de sem tam id is [my daughter] Clotilde. . . . Clotilde is my gran'-mamma'" (699 [19.5]). For Frowenfeld, history may constitute, as Stephanie Foote has pointed out, "a logical, linear progression" (108). For the Creoles, however, the past is always present (in the case of Aurora and Clotilde, literally so: Aurora's daughter *is* also her grandmother), determining their identity as well as their actions, and it is precisely the Creoles' presentification of their past that ultimately seals their pastification in the novel.

Indeed, *The Grandissimes* portrays French New Orleans as constantly looking backward, as obsessed with its own past and fiercely resolved to repeat it: "It early attracted the apothecary's notice, in observing the civilization around him, that it kept the flimsy false bottoms in its social errors only by incessant reiteration" (Cable, *Grandissimes* 690 [19.5]). Honoré Grandissime, with his usual perceptiveness about his own people, agrees, identifying tradition – namely, "'that old trhaditional prhinciple'" of the "'unity of ow family'" – as the "'secrhet of ow existence'" (195 [20.2]).[70] Clinging to established notions and convictions rather than moving forward, however, French New Orleans has hopelessly fallen out of touch with the times: not only in fashion (see 373 [19.3]), but in all other respects, too, and especially regarding questions of race and slavery, Creole society is, Frowenfeld bluntly notes, "'sadly in arrears to the civilized world'" and "'entirely unprepared and disinclined to follow the course of modern thought'" (697 [19.5]), defending "views of human relations which the world is abandoning as false" (701 [19.5]). Honoré, the merchant, takes an economic approach, but again agrees: "'The shadow of the Ethiopian,'" he says, "'drhags us a centurhy behind the rhes' of the world! It rhetahds and poisons everhy industrhy we got!'" (703 [19.5]).

Cable's diagnosis of the "cultural lag" (Swann 258) of French New Orleans society finds its most impressive articulation in the novel's curiously ambivalent and metamorphic portrait of Agricola Fusilier. First introduced to the reader as an awe-inspiring "large, heavily built, but well molded and vigorous man" with the "front of a bull" and "the beard of a prophet" (Cable, *Grandissimes* 256 [19.2]), Agricola soon reveals himself to be, in Etienne de Planchard de Cussac's words, the "arch-Creole" and "guardian of tradition" who "remembers past offences, keeps feuds alive, maintains all the nice distinctions elaborated by the colonial past, and thus paralyses the evolution of his community toward democracy" ("'Gothic'" 141). In fact, as one of his last actions in the novel, he writes a fiery pamphlet in which he attacks "the miserable school of imported thought which had sent its revolting influences to the very Grandissime hearth-stone" (Cable, *Grandissimes* 814 [20.6]). While Cable still depicts him with a surprising amount of sympathy – his constant misreadings of Frowenfeld's character and attitudes make Frowenfeld's protests look weak and ineffectual rather than Agricola imperceptive (see 198 [20.2]) – he also makes it unmistakably clear that Agricola is hopelessly anachronistic, blocks social progress, and that his death therefore constitutes a necessity if French New Orleans ever wants to catch up with the "civilized world": "'waid till Agricola Fusilier ees keel,'" Honoré Grandissime f.m.c. tells Frowenfeld when the latter tries to lecture him about how to elevate the free quadroons (25 [20.1]), and when Agricola is actually stabbed to death by none other than Honoré Grandissime f.m.c., the narrator refers to him as "the aged high-priest of a doomed civilization" (818 [20.6]).[71] Agricola's last words – "'Louis – Louisian – a – for – ever!'" (820 [20.6]) – may point to the future, then, but right before, his harangue against the "Yankee Government" and "the doctrine of equal rights" (819 [20.6]) once again inextricably links him with New Orleans's irrevocably lost colonial past.

Agricola, then, is doomed almost from the beginning, and so is the society whose atavism he personifies (see Rubin 85). Indeed, references to stasis, decay, and death in connection with French New Orleans society abound in *The Grandissimes*; "throughout the novel," Tipping writes, "the perceptive reader receives, through the imagery, the impression of a society constantly under threat and in danger of collapse. The formless menace of the swamp is always in the background" (78). Perhaps the earliest of these references can be found in Chapter II, where the narrator describes the Louisiana landscape as a "land hung in mourning, darkened by gigantic cypresses, submerged; a land of reptiles, silence, shadow, decay" and comments on how the horizon is "shut out" by "funereal swamps" (Cable, *Grandissimes* 100 [19.1]). The swamp imagery is taken up again by Dr. Keene when he describes Creole pride as "as lethargic and ferocious as an alligator" and as "preposterous, apathetic, fantastic," and "suicidal" (110 [19.1]).[72] Hence, French New Orleans's obsession with the past directly leads to its passing.

Not only is French New Orleans passing, as in "Jean-ah Poquelin," then; as in the short story, the moment of passing has long passed. Constantly comparing New Orleans at the time the novel is set to the city at the time of the novel's publication, the narrator keeps reminding readers that *The Grandissimes* tells of people and events long gone. The Grandissime mansion, for instance, "is quite gone" now (841 [19.6]), but the building that housed the Veau-qui-tête restaurant "still stands on the corner of Chartres and St. Peter streets" (202 [20.2]), and so do the former residence of Governor Kerlerec and the house that "reminds one of a man with spectacles standing up in an audience, searching for a friend who is not there and will never come back" – if, of course, "they were not pulled down yesterday" (841 [19.6]). The city's inhabitants, too, have changed: men used to give such bows "as we see now only in pictures" (382 [19.3]), and "in later times, under the gentler influences of a higher civilization, [the] old Spanish-colonial ferocity [of the Grandissimes] was gradually absorbed by the growth of better traits. . . . The Creole character has been diluted and sweetened" (820 [20.6]). If Edward King, in "Old and New Louisiana," and Cable's narrator, in the "Old Creole Days" stories, walk through present-day New Orleans and discover visions and stories "of the quaint past," Cable's narrator in *The Grandissimes* takes readers through past New Orleans and points out the roots of the present.

This applies, as we have seen, to buildings and people, but most importantly to social issues, which indicates yet another way in which the past and the present are conflated in the novel. In his review of *The Grandissimes*, published anonymously in *Scribner's Monthly* only three months after the last installment of the novel had appeared there, H.H. Boyesen could not "help suspecting Mr. Cable of a benevolent intention to teach his Southern countrymen some fundamental lessons of society and government, while ostensibly he is merely their dispassionate historian" (160). Ever since then, virtually no self-respecting critical article about the novel has failed to mention its allegorical dimension, which, through often surprisingly explicit interjections such as "(We have a *Code Noir* now, but the new one is a mental reservation, not an enactment.)" (Cable, *Grandissimes* 853 [19.6]), establishes parallels between the Louisiana Purchase and (the end of) Reconstruction.[73] Probably no one has put it more succinctly than Daniel Aaron, who wrote: "Cable's Creoles talk and think like the post-War die-hards" (qtd. in Turner, *Essays* 235). Due to its intention "to deal honestly with the complexity of Southern racial experience," Louis D. Rubin has characterized *The Grandissimes* as "the first 'modern' Southern novel" (78). In the context of "Scribner's Illustrated New Orleans," however, Cable's novel constitutes the first text to employ a complex temporality, which pastifies French New Orleans in order to engage the present.

More Complex Temporalities: "Madame Delphine"

If *The Grandissimes* harkens back to "Jean-ah Poquelin," then the following contribution to "Scribner's Illustrated New Orleans," Cable's novella "Madame Delphine," serialized in three installments from May–July 1881, returns to the themes, motifs, and narrative strategies of "'Tite Poulette," which had first been published in *Scribner's* almost seven years before, in October 1874. Compared to "'Tite Poulette," "Madame Delphine" may have, as James Nagel writes, "much richer character development, a deeper emotional conflict for the widowed mother, significant secondary issues, and a much more complex thematic structure" (28). The two texts are nevertheless, as Catharine Savage Brosman has argued, like "two sides of a dyptich" as they "both portray a quadroon mother and her daughter, alike caught in the trap . . . of the law that forbade whites to marry anyone with black ancestry" (95).[74]

That the two texts are thus linked is already suggested by the publication history of "Madame Delphine": following its serialization in the magazine, where Cable is identified in each installment as the "Author of 'Old Creole Days,' and 'The Grandissimes,'" the novella was first published as an independent volume in 1881 by Charles Scribner's Sons. Two years later, however, "Madame Delphine" was added to Cable's collection *Old Creole Days*, which, of course, also contained "'Tite Poulette." Reversing the order in which the stories had been written, Cable had decided to open this version of *Old Creole Days* with "Madame Delphine" (see Nagel 28), while "'Tite Poulette" only comes as the sixth text in the book.[75] In 1896, Charles Scribner's Sons released "Madame Delphine" as an independent volume again, but added a preface by Cable in which he confirmed the connection between the short story and the novella. Indeed, the preface identifies "Madame Delphine" as the answer to an anonymous letter sent to Cable by a "poor quadroon . . ." (vii) who had read "'Tite Poulette." The letter-writer, Cable notes, urged him to:

> change the story, even yet, and tell the inmost truth of it. Madame John lied! The girl was her own daughter; but like many and many a real quadroon mother, as you surely know, Madame John perjured her own soul to win for her child a legal and honorable alliance with the love-mate and life-mate of her choice.
>
> (vii)

The 1881 magazine version of "Madame Delphine" contains no such preface, but the similarities and parallels between the story and the novella are quite obvious from the beginnings of the two texts: in both cases, Cable starts with descriptions of seemingly abandoned, yet inhabited, buildings in the present-day French Quarter of New Orleans, descriptions which are later followed by shifts back to the early nineteenth century – 1810 in the case of "'Tite Poulette" (see earlier); 1821–1822 in the case of "Madame Delphine" (see 27 [22.1] and 192 [22.2])[76] – and the stories of the buildings' former inhabitants, in which, as the buildings' almost impenetrable shutters, fences, and walls already indicate, concealment, secrecy, and voyeurism play significant roles. At the same time, however, the opening of "Madame Delphine" also evokes Edward King's wanderings through the French Quarter in "Old and New Louisiana." Like King, Cable's narrator directly addresses readers as "you" and leads them through the French Quarter, past "[m]any great doors" that are "shut and clamped and grown gray with cobweb" (22 [22.1]), until at some point Cable's guide-narrator, too, lets the tourist-readers catch a brief glimpse of a hidden paradise and an Eve:

> [S]ometimes you get sight of comfort, sometimes of opulence, through the unlatched wicket in some *porte-cochère* – red-painted brick pavement, foliage of dark palm or pale banana, marble or granite masonry and blooming parterres . . . . The faces of the inmates are in keeping – a sad proportion of the passengers in the street are dingy and shabby; but just when these are putting you off your guard, there will pass you a woman – more likely two or three – of patrician beauty.
>
> (22 [22.1])

In addition, like King, Cable's narrator establishes a contrast between "the activity and clatter" of Canal street and the American sector of the city and the "ancient and foreign-seeming" atmosphere of the French Quarter (22 [22.1]), thus depicting it, precisely as King does, as a chronotope of Frenchness. One may even be tempted to identify Cable's tourist-reader as the Edward King of 1873, who, after all, and like Cable's "you," came to New Orleans during the "time of the carnival," stayed at the St. Charles Hotel, and let himself be guided through New Orleans by Cable (see earlier).

References to the pastness and passing of French New Orleans abound in the first chapter – Cable describes the French Quarter as a "region of architectural decreptitude, where . . . upon everything has settled down a long Sabbath of decay" (22 [22.1]) – and are further reinforced and confirmed in the following through the shift back to the "first quarter of the present century," the "golden age" of "the free quadroon caste of New Orleans," and the actual story of Madame Delphine (23 [22.1]). But

Cable also and simultaneously characterizes the impression of pastness – the entire story of "Madame Delphine," in fact – as the fulfillment of the tourist-reader's specific desire for local color. John Cleman has pointed out that in "Madame Delphine," the narrator assumes his role of a French Quarter tour guide in a more direct and open manner than in "'Tite Poulette" or Cable's other "Old Creole Days" stories (*Cable* 84). The same applies to the figure of the reader, who is explicitly identified as "a lover of Creole antiquity" who, "in fondness for a romantic past," still calls Royal Street "the Rue Royale" (22 [22.1]). On several occasions, Cable makes a point of mentioning that neither in the present nor in the past would the local population understand the reader's particular interest in the buildings and people the story discusses: "not that they would not tell [you who lives there], but they cannot grasp the idea that you wish to know" (22 [22.1]), he notes with respect to the reader's question about the present inhabitants of Madame Delphine's house, and with respect to Madame Delphine herself:

> She was never pointed out by the denizens of the quarter as a character, nor her house as a "feature." It would have passed all Creole powers of guessing to divine what you could find worthy of inquiry concerning a retired quadroon woman.
>
> (23 [22.1])

By contrast, Cable and his guide-narrator know what their tourist-readers want, and they are willing to give it to them, but they also wish to make a point. Unlike *The Grandissimes*, "Madame Delphine" contains no explicit authorial comments or interjections that would establish a parallel between the past of the "golden age of the quadroons" and the present of the post-Reconstruction era. Nevertheless, several scholars have insisted on such an allegorical reading of "Madame Delphine," too, among them Louis D. Rubin (53) and John Cleman. The latter writes: "Cable clearly targets not only the Code Noir of the 1820s, when the story is set, but also the segregation laws that were created in the aftermath of Reconstruction, when the story was written" (*Cable* 91). According to this interpretation, then, "Madame Delphine," too, employs a complex temporality, which uses the pastness of French New Orleans to point to the post-Reconstruction, post-French present. Given the complete lack of explicit authorial comments on diachronic social and political parallels, however, how could such a reading be justified?

The key lies, I suggest, in the ultimate consequences of the solution that Cable offers to the central conflict of the story, consequences that are never explicitly mentioned in the text. Madame Delphine's perjuring herself may not "figs [i.e., fix]" the law itself, but since everyone else accepts her story – whether they actually believe it or not (see Petry, *Genius* 45–6) – it nevertheless allows her daughter Olive to get married to Vignevielle. Cable has thus written, as Cleman has pointed out, "a story of successful 'passing' and hence a story of undetected or, at least, erased transmission of the 'taint of the tarbrush' across the color line" (*Cable* 93). Yet, while Cable tells us what happened to the quadroon couple who eventually moved in with Madame Delphine, following their story down to the present (442 [22.3]), he never lets us know what happened to Olive and Vignevielle or their children. Just like the descendants of the quadroon couple, they must live somewhere in the New Orleans of 1881, among the "activity and clatter of a city of merchants," undetected, as fully white people, as a living subversion of the color line that contemporary social customs and laws were so desperately trying to maintain. The fictional "romantic past" of "Madame Delphine" engages the present, then, by exposing contemporary racial attitudes as being based on a mere fiction.

Pictures From the Past: "The Creoles of Louisiana"

After having published Cable's *Old Creole Days* stories, his novel *The Grandissimes*, and his novella "Madame Delphine," the magazine now called *Century* – the change in ownership and name (see earlier) had taken place in November 1881, shortly after the serialization of "Madame Delphine" – must have felt that it was time for an appraisal; Cable was, after all, "the monthly's first discovery" (John 163). Of course, *Scribner's* had routinely and dutifully reviewed Cable's works as soon as they had been published in book form by the magazine's then sister company, Charles Scribner's Sons. These reviews had appeared in the "Culture and Progress" sections of the issues of July 1879 (*Old Creole Days*), November 1880 (*The Grandissimes*), and September 1881 ("Madame Delphine"), and were strictly concerned with the respective publications. George E. Waring's article "George W. Cable," featured in the main part of the February 1882 issue, by contrast, also provided information on Cable himself, his biography, his working methods, and even his looks:

> Personally, Mr. Cable is a small, slight, fragile looking man, thirty-seven years old. He is erect, bright and frank, with a strong head, and a refined, gentle face. His hair and beard are dark, and his large hazel eyes are expressive.
>
> (Waring 602)

Readers could compare Waring's description with Timothy Cole's monochrome of Abbott H. Thayer's portrait of Cable that served as the issue's frontispiece and that also featured Cable's autograph (see Turner, *Cable* 112). *Century* clearly knew how to build up a new star.

Waring's profile not only sought to create Cable's public image as an emerging literary celebrity, however, but also to promote the next Cable feature to be published in the magazine. Toward the end of his article, Waring describes Cable as "the first authority in all matters, light or grave, relating to the people and the history of Louisiana" and, in this context, particularly praises Cable's latest achievement:

> For more than a year past [Cable] has devoted himself almost exclusively to the preparation of a history of New Orleans, which is now being published by the Census Office in connection with the social statistics of that city, and, except so far as relates to the mere enumeration, he has collected the statistical information himself. He might well rest his reputation for thorough and judicious historical and descriptive work on this production alone.
>
> (604)

A page later, Waring even inserts a direct quote from this "census history of New Orleans," a brief paragraph on the general character of the Louisiana Creoles. The article's specific interest in and emphasis on this particular Cable text was no accident: it was Waring himself who had originally asked Cable to write a historical sketch of New Orleans for the Tenth U.S. Census Report (see Turner, *Cable* 112; Powell 21–2). Moreover, by the time Waring's profile of Cable appeared in February 1882, artist Joseph Pennell, then at the very beginning of his career, had already spent at least a month in New Orleans (see E.R. Pennell, *Life* 53–4), with Cable as his local guide, illustrating the writer's altogether six articles on the history of the Louisiana Creoles which were based on the census history and which *Century* would eventually publish the following year (see earlier). To be sure, Waring's article does not *explicitly* alert readers to this forthcoming Cable feature in the magazine, but this may have been due to the fact that both the text and the illustrations were delayed (see earlier) and that a precise date of publication could not yet be communicated.

When the first of Cable's articles, complete with Pennell's illustrations, was eventually published under the title "Who Are the Creoles?" in January 1883, it followed on the heels of yet another series of articles on American history written by a man who had previously been known mainly for his literary work. In 1879, Gregory M. Pfitzer notes, Edward Eggleston, author of *The Hoosier Schoolmaster* (1871) and other regionalist novels, "surprised family and friends . . . with the announcement that he planned to abandon the writing of fiction altogether to devote himself for the remainder of his days to a broad historical study of American social life" (192). Three years later, in November 1882, *Century* published some of the first results of Eggleston's decision, an illustrated article on "The Beginning of a Nation," which would be followed by "The Planting of New England" in January 1883, the same issue that also contained Cable's "Who Are the Creoles?"[77] Pfitzer discusses Eggleston's turn from fictional to historiographical writing in the context of late-nineteenth-century popular histories, whose main characteristics were attractive packaging and illustration, a lack of footnotes and bibliographic material, and, perhaps most importantly, the extensive use of "literary strategies for treating the past" (6; 9; 7). In fact, Pfitzer notes, most of these popular histories were written by poets and novelists: "Houses such as Scribner's, Appleton's, and Collier's sought out only those authors whose names were familiar enough to readers to sell books. These writers rarely had formal training as historians," but they possessed "rhetorical gifts that were valued by many middle-class readers who viewed fiction and history as inextricably linked" (4).

Cable's historiographical work on the Creoles (both the magazine articles as well as the volume into which they were collected in 1884, entitled *The Creoles of Louisiana* and published by Charles Scribner's Sons) partially fits into this pattern, too: for the magazine and for the book (and, hence, just as for its first publication in the Census; see Powell 26), Cable's original manuscript was shorn of its countless footnotes and references.[78] Also, Cable's writing came with maps, reproductions of portraits of historical figures, and Pennell's attractive illustrations. As a contemporary review attests (qtd. in Turner, *Essays* 68), the book version was sometimes even bound in an "alligator" paper, thus offering the reader, as Brad Evans has formulated, "the fantasy of fragments from the physical record of the peoples under textual observation" (101). By contrast, scholars have pointed out content-related parallels rather than stylistic continuities between Cable's fictional and his historiographical texts.[79] John Cleman, for instance, writes that "the history presented in *The Creoles of Louisiana*, a narrative of the rise and fall of Creole civilization, is essentially the same history – pointedly a moral history – that underlies *Old Creole Days*, *The Grandissimes*, and *Madame Delphine*" (*Cable* 96–7). Indeed, to diligent readers of Cable's fiction, and particularly of *The Grandissimes*, his depiction of the Creoles as a people whose main characteristics were shaped by the triple "evil influences" ("Plotters and Pirates" 853) of a "soil of unlimited fertility," a "luxurious and enervating climate," and the "habit of commanding a dull and abject slave class" ("Who" 395), must have seemed somewhat familiar. And this is hardly surprising: as Cable himself later stated, he had welcomed Waring's offer as an opportunity "to write historically of a people whom I was accused of misrepresenting in fiction" ("My Politics" 16).

Equally unsurprising is the centrality with which (French) New Orleans figures in Cable's history – after all, the text was originally conceptualized as a historical sketch of the city rather than of the "Creoles of Louisiana." To be sure, Cable initially identifies all of "the country lying between the mouth of Red River on the north and the Gulf marshes of the south, east of the Têche and south of Lakes Borgne, Pontchartrain, and Maurepas, and the Bayou Manchac" ("Who" 386) as the "home" of the Creoles.

The reader can locate all of these places on the "Map of Louisiana" with which the first article opens and which also indicates the distribution of the "Anglo-American" and "French Speaking" population in the region (see 384). Already the next two illustrations in the article, however, narrow the focus down to the city of New Orleans: the third illustration offers a "location chart" that indicates the distance of New Orleans from several cities of the Americas and the Caribbean (among them San Francisco, New York, and Havana; see 386); the second illustration, which was also used as the frontispiece of the book version, depicts what has since become an iconic view of the St. Louis cathedral and the Presbytère, both partly hidden by the bushes and trees of Jackson Square, much like Champney's second illustration for "Old and New Louisiana" had done a decade earlier (although Pennell suggests rather than clearly draws the contours and details of the buildings; see E.R. Pennell, *Pennell* 10).

And indeed, the rest of *The Creoles of Louisiana* (both the magazine and the book version) is almost exclusively concerned with New Orleans. Starting with Chapter III, entitled "The Creoles' City," Cable traces, in an almost strictly chronological manner, the development of the community from the founding of the settlement in 1718 to the sanitary reforms following the yellow fever epidemic of 1878, with the notable exceptions of the Battle of New Orleans, the Civil War, and the period of Reconstruction.[80] The earlier parts of this account are, by necessity, mostly set in the French Quarter and around Jackson Square. Here, and as King had done, Cable repeatedly switches to the present in order to stress the pastness (and foreignness) of the area, asserting, for instance, that:

> [f]ew who know its history will stand to-day in Jackson square and glance from its quaint, old-fashioned gardening to the foreign and antique aspect of the surrounding architecture . . . without finding the fancy presently stirred up to . . . recall the humbler town of Jean-Baptiste Lemoyne de Bienville, as it huddled about this classic spot when but ten years had passed since the first blow of the settler's ax had echoed across the waters of the Mississippi.
> ("Who" 388; see also "End" 643; or "Gate" 218)

Pennell's illustrations support Cable's textual strategy. To be sure, as in the case of "Old Canal on Dauphine Street. A Restoration" ("Who" 398) or "The Cabildo of 1792" ("End" 646), the pictures occasionally offer views of what the city must have looked like at the time about which Cable was writing. Generally, however, Pennell depicts the present-day French Quarter and invites readers to let their "fancy" be "stirred up to recall" the past. The picture of the St. Louis cathedral even does so explicitly through its caption ("The Cathedral and the Old Place d'Armes, New Orleans"; "Who" 385), which refers to Jackson Square by its former colonial name.[81]

Eventually, however, the text reaches the 1850s, when the American quarter replaced the French Quarter as the "center and core of the whole city" ("Gate" 224). Cable "illustrates" this development by describing a "small steel-engraved picture of New Orleans," in which the Vieux Carré is "pushed out of view, and the lately humble Faubourg Ste. Marie fills the picture almost from side to side" (224). Yet in contrast to Cable's ekphrastic illustration, Pennell's pictures continue to focus on the French Quarter, depicting, for instance, "The Old Bank in Toulouse Street" (229) or the "Old St. Louis Hotel (Afterward the State House)" (230) – much like Champney's illustrations for "Old and New Louisiana." This is not to argue that from Champney to Pennell, and from 1873–1883, the pictorial discourse about New Orleans in *Scribner's/Century* did not change: where Champney had concentrated on the neoclassical buildings of the "modern" French Quarter (see earlier), Pennell, as the captions already indicate, primarily shows the colonial buildings of the "old," the "historic" Quarter. Where Champney had Americanized and "modernized," Pennell Frenchifies[82] and pastifies, blurring the line between past and present, and in one of the next contributions to "Scribner's Illustrated New Orleans," Pennell would also help to blur the line between fact and fiction.

Cable Country: "The Scenes of Cable's Romances"

In November 1883, only four months after the conclusion of the "Creoles of Louisiana" series, *Century* offered its readers yet another Cable feature; namely, the first installment of the author's new novel, *Dr. Sevier*, which would run until October 1884. The header of the piece identifies Cable as the "Author of 'Old Creole Days,' 'The Grandissimes,' 'Madame Delphine,' etc." (54 [27.1]),[83] but readers of this first installment must have soon noticed that the novel somewhat differed from Cable's earlier fiction. To be sure, the setting is once again New Orleans, but as in the "small steel-engraved picture of New Orleans" that Cable had described in one of his historical articles to illustrate the fact that by the 1850s the Vieux Carré no longer constituted the center and core of the city (see earlier), the French Quarter is "pushed out of view":

> Number 33 1/2, second floor, front, was the office of Dr. Sevier. . . . Canal street, the city's leading artery, was just below at the near left-hand corner. Beyond it lay the older town, not yet impoverished in those days, – the French Quarter.
>
> (54 [27.1]; in fact, the beginning of the novel is set in 1856)

Accordingly, Creoles and quadroons, speaking Cable's by then famous "French-English" (W. Evans), make their appearance (for example, Madame Zénobie and Narcisse), but they are all minor characters and their presence in the novel steadily declines from the first installment onward. Other non-Anglo-American characters, each with his or her own dialect,[84] fill their ranks, e.g., Germans (the Reisens), Italians (Raphael Ristofalo), or Irish (Kate Riley). Rather than as French, then, *Dr. Sevier* depicts New Orleans as a multiethnic (albeit predominantly Anglo-American) city.

If nineteenth-century readers missed the slight change in Cable's fiction, modern Cable critics certainly did not. Arlin Turner, for instance, comments that *Dr. Sevier* "broke from the pattern of Cable's earlier fiction" (*Cable* 160) and John Cleman argues that "the diminishment of local-color features and . . . the broadened range of ethnic stereotypes makes the novel seem less regional than national, not a New Orleans but an American novel" (*Cable* 111; see also Rubin 134–5; and John 160). As if to counterbalance the new "Americanness" of Cable's fiction, *Century* published yet another Cable-related feature in the November 1883 issue, one that heavily stresses the "Frenchness" of the author's earlier writings. "The Scenes of Cable's Romances," written by Lafcadio Hearn and illustrated by Joseph Pennell, simultaneously constitutes an attractive magazine article and a shrewd cross-promotional piece that served simultaneously the interests of periodical publishing (specifically the *Century*) and book publishing (particularly Charles Scribner's Sons), as well as those of mass tourism (especially the World's Industrial and Cotton Centennial Exposition). And while it generally continues the "pastifying" of French New Orleans in "Scribner's Illustrated New Orleans," the temporality of its portrayal of New Orleans comes, as I will show, closer than ever before to that of the depiction of other "regional" cultures in this magazine in particular and in late-nineteenth–century local-color writing in general.

Combining recountings of key scenes of Cable's "Old Creole Days" stories,[85] "Madame Delphine," and *The Grandissimes* with bits of local history and folklore (e.g., Père Antoine, the Lafitte brothers, and Cayetano's Circus), and a verbalized "Vieux Carré walking map" (Fertel 84), the main part of "The Scenes of Cable's Romances" takes readers on a short tour through the French Quarter, from the corner of Canal and Royal Streets past the St. Louis cathedral and Jackson Square to the corner of Royal Street and Esplanade Avenue, then to the corner of Esplanade and Rampart Street and down Rampart to Congo Square (see Figure 1.1). Along the way, the narrator or tour guide points out various "sights," always indicating their location first (sometimes even including the precise street address), then describing the building or the square in great detail, and finally, with the help of direct quotes from Cable's texts and from the latter's private collection of Creole folk songs, identifying the location as the setting of one of the Cable's "romances" or of a place associated with a prominent figure of New Orleans folklore. Drawn while the artist visited New Orleans to illustrate the "Creoles of

Louisiana" series (see earlier), Pennell's pictures focus on the settings of Cable's shorter texts and are generally placed close to Hearn's descriptions of the respective buildings.

Within the *Century*, "The Scenes of Cable's Romances" constituted the first of a two-part series of illustrated articles on the "scenes" of popular American authors: in July 1884, the magazine published "The Scenes of Hawthorne's Romances," written by Julian Hawthorne and illustrated by Harry Fenn.[86] The two articles, however, also formed part of a larger, transnational cultural trend in the late nineteenth century that has been described as "literary tourism"; that is, "the practice of visiting places associated with literary figures or celebrities, whether these places are associated with the life of the author or associated with his or her fictional creations" (H.I. Lowe 6).[87] Especially in Britain, as Nicola J. Watson has observed, the period between the late 1880s and the 1920s witnessed "a slew of publications" aimed at (armchair) literary tourists (169). These books and magazine articles, Watson explains, "typically tie verifiable topography, whether rural or urban, primarily to an author's works, rather than to authorial biography, and they are almost invariably associated with novelists" (169).[88] Seeking to "map the imaginary onto the actual" (201), such publications sought to brand and popularize specific locales as "literary countries" (169).

Both Cable's literary work and Lafcadio Hearn must have seemed almost ideal for a "literary country" publication about New Orleans. Not only did virtually all of Cable's writings to date feature scenes set in the comparatively restricted and easily accessible area of the French Quarter,[89] as has already been discussed, but Cable's narrators themselves often already assumed the role of a tour guide (see earlier). Hearn, in turn, was just as familiar with New Orleans as he was with Cable's depictions of it: having moved from Cincinnati to New Orleans in 1877, Hearn had become deeply interested in and fascinated with Creole folklore and customs, and published a large number of sketches on life in the city in local newspapers such as the New Orleans *Item* or the *Cincinnati Commercial*, but also in *Harper's Weekly* (see Starr). A personal friend of Cable's (the two men used to "stroll . . . through the Old Quarter" several times a week [Cott 155] and collected Creole songs together [J. Lowe, *Calypso* 171]), he also wrote several reviews of Cable's *The Grandissimes* for the *Item* (see Ekström 69; and Turner, *Cable* 101n15), as well as an article on "The Original Bras-Coupé" (also for the *Item*; see Stephens, "Missing Arm" 392–3).

Moreover, a "literary country" publication on Cable's New Orleans seemed especially opportune in late 1883:[90] that year, as I pointed out earlier, Charles Scribner's Sons reissued Cable's *Old Creole Days* (now including "Madame Delphine"). Even more importantly, in February 1883, Congress had approved an act "to encourage the holding of a World's Industrial and Cotton Centennial Exposition in the year eighteen hundred and eighty-four" (Congress). Though these details were not specified by the act, the exposition was to be hosted by the city of New Orleans in the area now occupied by Audubon Park and was scheduled to open on 1 December 1884 (T.R. Smith 139; 145). Organizing an exposition was a fairly common strategy of urban tourism destination development in Gilded Age America (see Stanonis 15) and the Cotton Centennial was expected to draw up to four million visitors to New Orleans (Gotham 46).[91] Apart from promoting the new edition of *Old Creole Days* to *Century* readers and generally stressing, as Waring had already done, Cable's profile as the leading expert on New Orleans, then, "The Scenes of Cable's Romances" also aimed at capitalizing on the raised public awareness of the city as a potential tourist destination by establishing the French Quarter as "Cable Country."

The text's goal of inducing (literary) tourism to New Orleans has, however, a double impact on the temporality of its depiction of the city. On the one hand, by inextricably linking the French Quarter with Cable's fictions, all of which are set in the distant past, Hearn, too, pastifies the city. On the other hand, lest readers should postpone their travel plans, Hearn repeatedly points out that "Cable Country" is rapidly disappearing – right before his eyes, in fact – and, hence, takes an almost stereotypical "local color" approach to the city that markedly contrasts with earlier approaches to French New Orleans in *Scribner's/Century*.

Of course, establishing New Orleans as an attractive destination for literary tourists depended on convincing readers that a tour through the French Quarter would actually transport them to the imaginary geography of Cable's fictional past. Hearn therefore points out that "[e]ach one of [Cable's] charming pictures of places" was "painted after some carefully selected model of French or Franco-Spanish origin" and asserts that "[g]reatly as the city has changed since the eras in which Mr. Cable's stories are laid," these models could still be found and identified in the "old creole quarter," where they are haunted by Cable's "delightful phantoms" (40). Later, Hearn goes even further and deliberately blurs the boundary between fact and fiction: rather than merely claiming that a specific building served Cable as the model for the setting of his short story "'Sieur George,'" for instance, he writes: "This is the house where 'Sieur George so long dwelt" (42). The accompanying picture of the building even overcomes the temporal distance, with the caption simply identifying the building as "'Sieur George's" (42). Rather than merely "map[ping] the imaginary onto the actual," as other "literary country" publications may have done, then, "The Scenes of Cable's Romances" fuses fact and fiction. Whereas in the companion piece, Julian Hawthorne stresses that the "scenes of Hawthorne's novels are not . . . accessible by earthly travel" (397), Hearn ultimately claims just that – namely, that the geographical and temporal settings of Cable's romances *can* be accessed by walking through the French Quarter.

However, even in "Cable Country," as Hearn simultaneously and somewhat paradoxically claims, time does not stand still. Just as so many "local-color" texts about the nation's various regional cultures did at the time (see earlier), and unlike previous texts in "Scribner's Illustrated New Orleans," "The Scenes of Cable's Romances" portrays French New Orleans not only as past, but also as passing: to be sure, "one may *still* wander at random [through the Vieux Carré] with the certainty of encountering eccentric façades and suggestive Latin appellations at every turn" (40; emphasis added), but already at the beginning of the tour, at the corner of Canal and Royal streets, "one observes with regret numerous evidences of modernization. American life is invading the thoroughfare" (41; note how modernity and Americaness are jointly opposed to the pastness of the French Quarter). As the tour continues, Hearn steadily increases the drama: the "Café des Réfugiés" is still there, but "may be torn away at any moment" (43); to Madame Delphine's house, "architectural additions" have already been made which have "greatly diminished" the picturesqueness of the building (44); and "[s]carcely a week ago, from the time at which I write," the "Café des Exilés" was "ruthlessly torn away" (45). Fans of Cable's romances, the text implies, better hurry up and travel to New Orleans before it is all gone. And, as we will see, some of them did.

Fair People: "The New Orleans Exposition"

It is, unfortunately, nearly impossible to determine the exact impact of "The Scenes of Cable's Romances" on New Orleans (literary) tourism in general and attendance at the World's Industrial and Cotton Centennial Exposition in particular.[92] Instead of the projected 4 million, only 1.16 million visitors attended the event (see Gotham 46). Many of those who came, however, "showed more interest in the scenes [Cable] had employed than in the displays at the exposition grounds" (Turner, "Reformer" 136). And at least some "used [Hearn's] article" – either the original magazine version or the version reprinted in the *Historical Sketch Book and Guide to New Orleans and Environs* (1885)[93] – "as a guide to the scenes and houses Cable had described" (Turner, *Cable* 195). The practice seems to have been common enough for Rebecca Harding Davis to satirize it in *Harper's New Monthly Magazine*: in the third installment of her travel narrative *Here and There in the South* (serialized in *Harper's* from July–November 1887), Davis has Mrs. Ely, a Northern visitor to the Cotton Centennial, promenading the "Boulevard Esplanade,"

> looking out for Mr. Cable's creoles, and regarding every old man with white hair and black eyes with awe as a possible Grandissime. She made vain pretences of asking her way from people whom she

fancied were Legrees, or Madame Delphines, or Texan cow-boys; but they all turned out to be from Duluth or Chicago.
(601; Hearn's tour indeed includes Esplanade Avenue)

Among the visitors to the New Orleans Exposition was also *Century* reporter Eugene V. Smalley, who had been writing articles on various topics for the magazine since 1881. Smalley's two features about the Cotton Centennial – "The New Orleans Exposition" and "In and Out of the New Orleans Exposition," both published toward the end of the fair in May and June 1885, respectively – constitute the core of *Century*'s rather extensive coverage of the exposition, which also included two "Open Letters" by Richard Nixon, the secretary for the exposition's board of managers (published at the beginning of the fair in December 1884 and after its end in November 1885), an "Open Letter" by Marion A. Baker, editor of the New Orleans *Times-Democrat* (printed in July 1885 as a comment to Smalley's second article), and a cartoon in the May 1885 "Bric-À-Brac" section by Edward Kemble, who also provided most of the illustrations for Smalley's articles.

From 1873 (the year of the "World Exposition" in Vienna) to 1893 (the year of the "World's Columbian Exposition" in Chicago), *Scribner's/Century* not only steadily increased the amount of magazine space devoted to world's fairs,[94] but the focus of the coverage changed, too: whereas, for instance, the two articles on the 1878 "Exposition Universelle" in Paris (published in December 1878 and June 1879, and entitled "Art at the Paris Exposition" and "The Fine Arts at the Paris Exposition," respectively) mainly concentrate on the works of art on exhibition in Paris and on the architecture of the fair buildings, Smalley's articles also discuss the Cotton Centennial as an event. Thus "The New Orleans Exposition" opens with a reflection on the ongoing popularity of the "medium" of world's fairs (3); and the following section, comprising about a fourth of the article, is devoted to the "ideas which lay back of the New Orleans Exposition" and an account of "how the show itself was brought into existence" (4), including precise information on the financial organization of the fair. Later, Smalley describes in great detail the technical facilities of the exposition, praising the effectualness of the buildings and their floor plans (8; 10); the size and capacity of the power engines, pumps, and boiler and filtering plants that provided the fair with electricity, steam, and water (8); the convenience of the elevator system (8); and the overall effect of the newly introduced electric lighting system: "Never before has a world's fair been brilliantly illuminated throughout at night" (12).[95] Hence, much of "The New Orleans Exposition" is concerned less with the fair's exhibits themselves than with their framing.

To be sure, one may speculate that Smalley merely used this material as a filler since, as he himself writes, "not until about the 1st of February [the time he wrote the first article; see 13] were all departments of the fair brought into a tolerably complete state" (7).[96] Yet even in his second article, Smalley not only writes about the exposition's now completed "Women's" and "Colored Department[s]" ("In and Out" 188; 192), "Brazilian Coffee" (196), and "Belgium at the Fair" (197), but also dedicates a section of his text to "Types and Oddities":

> The visitors themselves are as well worth seeing as the show. To sit on a bench on one of the broad aisles of the Main Building, . . . and observe the passing throng, is to my mind the best part of the sight-seeing at the fair.
>
> (194)

It is these "types and oddities," moreover, that dominate Kemble's illustrations for both "The New Orleans Exposition" and "In and Out of the New Orleans Exposition."

From his debut in the magazine – his illustrations for the excerpts of Twain's *Adventures of Huckleberry Finn*, which were published in December 1884 and January and February 1885 (see earlier) – Kemble had distinguished himself as both a humorist and a figure drawer. Indeed, during the following years, when he was under exclusive contract with *Century*, Kemble not only provided illustrations for Southern local-color stories by such writers as Joel Chandler Harris, but also regularly contributed cartoons to the monthly's "Bric-À-Brac" section. Kemble's talent for humoristic figure drawing also becomes apparent in his illustrations for Smalley's Cotton Centennial articles. All of these depict people at the fair (either visitors or exhibitors), with the exhibits themselves being frequently pushed into the background and often not shown at all, and nearly all of them have a humorous touch.[97] In fact, there is virtually no difference in tone between these pictures and the Kemble cartoon featured in the May 1885 issue, which is also set at the fair (Kemble, "Exposition").

At least one of Kemble's "fair people" pictures also directly contributes to the pastifying of French New Orleans in "Scribner's Illustrated New Orleans." According to Gotham, "the construction of knowledge about local [New Orleans] culture took several forms" at the Cotton Centennial (55). Among others, Gotham argues, these forms included the collection of New Orleans "cultural artifacts and historic memorabilia" displayed at the Women's Department and the Louisiana Women's Exhibit (57; see also T.R. Smith 151). Smalley, in his second article, obviously considers the Women's Department more a relaxation area than a part of the "real" exhibition ("In and Out" 188), but in the

"Types and Oddities" section of the text, he describes yet another local "cultural artifact":

> The Creole Louisianian (by which term, let it be explained for the hundredth time for the benefit of persistent ignorance, is meant, not a mulatto, but a native white of French or Spanish ancestry) is short of stature, slight of frame, with a curious mixture of languor and vivacity in manner, carefully dressed, very polite, and with small interest in the doings of the world outside his own State.
> (195)

Small wonder, then, that Davis's Mrs. Ely is "looking out for Mr. Cable's creoles" – they constitute an exhibit in themselves. Kemble's accompanying illustration, in turn, resonates with the traditional iconography of international expositions, which "fostered countless stereographs and photographs of foreign, nonwhite racial and national typologies from their ethnological displays or living villages" (Rabinovitz 120). As with most of Smalley's other "types and oddities," Kemble also produced a picture of "the Creole Louisianian": "Creoles," as the illustration is captioned, depicts a young woman in an elegant dress and an elderly man in a long coat and a top hat that makes him almost as tall as the woman. The pair is standing outside beneath a moss-draped live oak[98] and seems to be posing for the artist: both are looking directly at the reader/viewer, and the man has assumed the classic "hand-in-waistcoat" pose (192). What is particularly interesting about the illustration is not, however, the appearance of the pair – in fact, they do not look manifestly different from the mass of unidentified fairgoers depicted in the picture "The Promenade" on the following page – but rather its position in relation to the text. Instead of on the same page as Smalley's description of the "Louisianian Creole," "Creoles" appears earlier in the text, above a paragraph in which the writer describes the sugar-planters of antebellum times:

> They were a gentle, luxurious, hospitable race, and were rudely shaken by the storm of war and the emancipation of the slaves. . . . Many of the old, influential families have perished . . . . There is still enough left, however, of the old planting life behind the levees on the rivers and bayous, where . . . the pillared porches of old mansions gleam through the foliage of orange-trees.
> (192)

Even if only by loose association with Smalley's description of the remnants of the antebellum South, hidden behind levees and orange-trees and slowly but surely disappearing, French New Orleanians are once again pastified.

Folklore and Folklorism: "The Dance in Place Congo" and "Creole Slave Songs"

When the World's Industrial and Cotton Centennial Exposition opened on 16 December 1884, George Washington Cable had been on his famous lecture tour with Mark Twain for over a month already.[99] As in his earlier solo platform performances,[100] Cable not only read from his published works in his part of the tour program, but also sang songs from his extensive collection of old "Creole" melodies.[101] Some material from this collection had already found its way into Cable's early fiction: although Scribner, Armstrong & Co. had rejected his idea of "quoting from [old Creole songs] at the head of each story" in the 1879 collection of *Old Creole Days* (Biklé 59; see Turner, *Cable* 227; and Hochman 524), Cable weaved fragments of lyrics and staff notations of songs into *The Grandissimes* (see, for instance, 846 [19.6]). In a footnote to "The Scenes of Cable's Romances," Lafcadio Hearn, too, had quoted the lyrics of a "*chanson créole*" from Cable's private collection (46). The song quoted by Hearn ("C'est Michié Cayétane"), as well as three of the songs included in *The Grandissimes* ("Dé Zabs," "Ah! Suzette," and "Anoqué"; see 847 [19.6], 852 [19.6], and 856 [19.6]),[102] eventually reappeared in "Creole Slave Dances: The Dance in Place Congo" and "Creole Slave Songs," Cable's "ethnographic" (G. Jones 128) essays printed in the *Century* in February and April 1886.

The two articles, visually highly attractive – the musical notations and the illustrations, which at least in one case also included staff notation (see "Slave Songs" 823), considerably enlivened the *Century* pages – and particularly "The Dance in Place Congo," are perhaps most notable for their curious role in the early historiography of jazz. As both Bryan Wagner and Randall Sandke have noted, the (false) claims that the dancing and music-making in New Orleans's Congo Square lasted into the 1880s and thus "'midwifed into existence what we know as jazz'" (Roth qtd. in Wagner 98) – claims made by such early histories of the jazz tradition as Frederic Ramsey, Jr. and Charles Smith's *Jazzmen* (1939) or Marshall Stearn's *The Story of Jazz* (1956) – can all be ultimately traced back to Cable's *Century* articles (as well as to a similar article written in 1883 by Lafcadio Hearn for the *New York World*; see Wagner 97–8; and Sandke 44–5). However, whereas Wagner maintains that "Congo Square was created as a myth by misdating and misreading the writings of George Washington Cable" (10), Sandke argues that Cable himself was at fault, calling "The Dance" "chimerical" and an "outright fraud" (46; 45). A close analysis of the text reveals that "The Dance in Place Congo" is, in fact, no fraud but instead merely draws on the narrative conventions and the temporal manipulations of the author's fiction in particular and "Scribner's Illustrated New Orleans" in general.

Indeed, the overall structure of "The Dance in Place Congo" replicates that of Cable's "Old Creole Days" stories and specifically "Madame Delphine": the narrator takes his readers on a tour through the French Quarter and, once they have reached the desired spot, subtly shifts back to the past to tell the story associated with this particular place. In the case of "The Dance," the tour starts at "St. Louis Cathedral, looking south-eastward – riverward – across quaint Jackson Square, the old Place d'Armes" (517), from where the narrator leads readers "north-westward, straight, and imperceptibly downward . . . toward the rear of the city" to a public square: "That is the place. . . . That is Congo Square" (517–8). The narrator then shifts back to a past he somewhat hazily identifies as "the early days," "[b]efore the city outgrew its flimsy palisade walls" (518–9) – to when Congo Square was known as the titular "Place Congo." Intensifying (and racializing) the contrast between Jackson and Congo Square that he had already hinted at by leading readers "downward" and "toward the rear of the city" (see Cowan 162), the narrator notes that back then, the two squares were at opposite ends of the city in more than just the geographical sense:

> The white man's plaza had the army and navy on its right and left, the court-house, the council-hall and the church at its back, and the world before it. The black man's was outside the rear gate, the poisonous wilderness on three sides and the proud man's contumely on its front.
> (518)

Whereas in his earlier fiction, Cable had frequently contrasted the French Quarter with the American sectors of New Orleans, "The Dance" thus depicts the city's geography as polarized along racial lines.

The "story" the narrator then proceeds to tell is that of the Sunday afternoon slave dances in Congo Square. Yet instead of simply describing the gatherings, Cable gives readers the illusion of actually attending a dance, with the narrator, still acting as a tour guide, explaining and commenting upon what is happening: "So we must picture it now if we still fancy ourselves spectators on Congo Plains. The bamboula still roars and rattles, twangs, contorts, and tumbles in terrible earnest, while we stand and talk" (525). To create this sense of immediacy and presence, Cable switches into the present tense for much of the account, as he had sometimes also done in his short fiction, and replaces the truncated, almost monotone sentences he had used in the beginning ("[T]he gathering was a weird one. The negro of colonial Louisiana was a most grotesque figure. He was nearly naked"; 522) with a breathless, run-on enumeration flanked by imperatives:

> See them; wilder than gypsies; wilder than the Moors and Arabs whose strong blood and features one sees at a glance in so many of them; gangs – as they were called – gangs and gangs of them, from

this and that and yonder direction; tall, well-knit Senegalese from Cape Verde, black as ebony, with intelligent, kindly eyes and long, straight, shapely noses; Mandingoes, from the Gambia River, lighter of color, of cruder form, and a cunning that shows in the countenance; . . . . See them come!

(522)

Throughout the text, the narrator uses imperatives to tell readers to see, hear, and notice specific details of the spectacle (see, for instance, 523) and propels the account forward with exclamations ("Now for the frantic leaps! Now for the frenzy! Another pair are in the ring!"; 523) and by pretending to ignore what will happen next ("Will they dance to that measure? Wait! A sudden frenzy seizes the musicians"; 523).

To be sure, Cable not only admits that at least some of his account is based on pure speculation ("But I can only say that with some such slow and quiet strain the dance *may* have been preluded"; 523; emphasis added; see also 521–2), he also clearly states that "[a]ll this Congo Square business was suppressed at one time; 1843, says tradition" (527). Hence, Cable never sought to maintain "the fiction that the dances in Congo Square continued up to his present day, the mid-1880s," as Sandke claims he does (47), but the illusion of immediacy and presence created in "The Dance" must have given later jazz historians the impression that "Cable was writing about performances that he saw with his own eyes" (Wagner 98).

Kemble's illustrations – especially his frequently reprinted, full-page portrayal of slaves dancing "The Bamboula" (524) – may have further contributed to these misreadings of Cable's text: like some of his other pictures for "The Dance" and "Creole Slave Songs," "The Bamboula" is signed "Kemble 1885," which may have led some readers to assume that Kemble had been an eyewitness to the dancing scene depicted, just as he had been an eyewitness to the scenes portrayed in his illustrations for Smalley's Cotton Centennial articles (see earlier). More importantly, the background of "The Bamboula" shows, as Ned Sublette has pointed out (120), an anachronistic combination of city palisades (according to Cable, still existing "in Spanish days" [517], but since removed) and the new "straight" spires of St. Louis cathedral (constructed in 1850 to replace the "sloped" roofs of the colonial structure completed in 1794). While the spires unambiguously locate the dancing in (or behind) the city of New Orleans, they also suggest that the spectacle took place sometime after 1850.[103]

Yet "The Dance in Place Congo" and "Creole Slave Songs" not only document what happened in "the early days"; Cable also traces the continuation of the musical tradition into the present. "Ah! Suzette," for instance, one of the songs discussed in "Creole Slave Songs," came into

Cable's hands "from a Creole drawing-room in the Rue Esplanade." He explains:

> How many ten thousands of black or tawny nurse "mammies," ... holding *'tit mait'e* or *'tit maitresse* to their bosoms, have made the infants' lullabies these [songs], will never be known. Now and then the song would find its way through some master's growing child of musical ear, into the drawing-room.
>
> (809)

As Gavin Jones has argued in *Strange Talk*, Cable's essays thus chart "the cross-cultural transmission of the aesthetic products of African America" (118) to the white community, thereby "undermin[ing] white-Creole claims to cultural separateness and purity" (119). Moreover, and as Wagner has pointed out (94), Cable not only represents but also reenacts cultural syncretisms[104] – that is, he not only charts "the cross-cultural transmission" of the Creole slaves' musical tradition, but also takes an active part in it, through his fiction, through his platform performances, and, most importantly, through his two essays. In the process, however, he pastifies his material, just as he had earlier presentified the slave dances.

Although the staff notation and the lyrics of "Dé Zabs" included in *The Grandissimes* may have prompted some musically minded readers to sing the song, Cable still mainly *represents* the cross-cultural transmission of slave songs in his novel. Indeed, almost a third of the songs included in *The Grandissimes* are sung by the white Creole Raoul Innerarity to a white Creole audience, during the "Fête de Grandpère" (see 846–7 [19.6]).[105] With his platform performances (both solo and with Mark Twain), by contrast, Cable himself becomes a cultural transmitter, a white, non-Creole New Orleanian performing the songs for a white, non-New Orleanian Northern audience. In "The Dance" and "Creole Slave Songs," finally, Cable not only acts as a cultural transmitter again, he also allows and encourages his readers themselves to continue the tradition. "Now sing it!" he tells the overwhelmingly non-Creole, non-New Orleanian readership of the *Century* ("Slave Songs" 808), and the staff notations, complete with arrangements and lyrics, of the altogether twelve songs at the end of the two articles actually allow readers to follow Cable's call.

Cable's essays, then, are not only "ethnographic" or folkloric, but also folkloristic.[106] As Michael A. Elliott has argued, however, it is precisely this combination of ethnographic and folkloristic approaches in Cable's essays – Elliott speaks of the "language of professional observation" – that "leads the writer to treat the songs as relics from the past" (60). Indeed, throughout "Creole Slave Songs," Cable stresses that the individual songs are "very old" (813), "from the last century most likely" (821), or "genuine antiques" (823). In addition, toward the end of the article, Cable compares himself to a "sapper . . . and miner" (823). By constantly stressing the age of the songs and characterizing the transcription and translation of the music as pioneer work, Cable turns his act of transmission, folklorization, and popularization into one of preservation. In other words, even though they may no longer be sung in their original folk contexts, the songs themselves are far from being "endangered" – with Cable performing them on stage and *Century* readers in their drawing-rooms, they may, in fact, be more popular than ever before. Nevertheless, their interest and popularity depend on their quaintness, foreignness, and age. The music, as Cable writes in "The Dance," "does survive" (525), but only as an "antique."

Revisiting Cable's New Orleans: "Strange True Stories of Louisiana"

Cable again drew on his personal collection of Louisiana folklore for his next contribution to "Scribner's Illustrated New Orleans," the travel accounts, life writings, tales, and anecdotes serialized in *Century* as "Strange True Stories of Louisiana" from November 1888 through October 1889 and collected under the same title by Charles Scribner's Sons (with added illustrations) in 1889.[107] Much like "The Dance in Place Congo" and "Creole Slave Songs," "Strange True Stories" can be regarded as a folkloristic "recycling" (De Caro 4; 87) of what at least in the cases of some of the altogether seven "stories" constitutes genuine folklore material: the story of "Attalie Brouillard," for instance, is, as Cable writes at the beginning of that tale, a "bit of lawyers' table-talk" and "vouched for stoutly, but only by tradition" (749). Likewise, as he notes in the introductory essay "1888: How I Got Them," the history of the so-called haunted house in Royal Street "is known to thousands in the old French quarter" (114; in the story itself, Cable makes a similar statement, see 590) and the tale of "Françoise" has come to him "after innumerable recountings by word of mouth to mother, sisters, brothers, friends, husband, children, and children's children" (111). If Cable's collecting, writing down, and publishing these bits of Louisiana folklore in a popular national magazine constitutes a folkloristic act (see De Caro 4), however, the introduction itself, with its accounts of how Cable received and researched the material and with its comments on how he is going to use it in "Strange True Stories," self-consciously focuses on the actions and roles of the folklorist and can thus be considered meta-folkloristic.

Moreover, far from merely continuing the folkloric/folkloristic discourse of "The Dance" and "Creole Slave Songs" (and partially drawing on the same sources; see "How I Got Them" 114), Cable's "Strange True Stories" – both the individual stories as well as the collection as a whole – also establish intertextual connections to the author's other previous contributions to *Scribner's/Century*.[108] Most importantly, perhaps, Cable's "little museum of true stories" ("How I Got Them" 113) complements his earlier history of the "Creoles of Louisiana." As Griffith T. Pugh has observed,

> the oldest of the true stories dates back more than a hundred years from the time of Cable's writing, and the most recent has its setting in the time of the Civil War. For the most part the scenes of the action are in Louisiana, in both its urban and its rural areas. The characters are of all classes from slaves and ignorant swamp-dwellers to wealthy aristocrats of noble descent.
>
> (37)

Taken together, then, the "Strange True Stories" form "a more or less chronological overall narrative of the city and the wider region(s)" (Robinson 97) that refracts the "official" historical narrative told in "Creoles of Louisiana" into the "private" histories of its individual protagonists.

Among the individual stories, it is undoubtedly "The 'Haunted House' in Royal Street" that creates the densest intertextual network with Cable's other writings. This is hardly surprising: published in August 1889 as the fifth of the seven "Strange True Stories," "The 'Haunted House'" has been considered not only "the masterpiece of the collection and one of the most powerful and effective stories Cable wrote" (Cleman, *Cable* 145), but also the one story "most overtly to feature the personal imprint of Cable himself . . . as an actively controlling presence" (Robinson 103). Sometimes Cable simply weaves the names of the protagonists of his earlier fictions into the narrative. Stressing the popularity of the story (and thus confirming its status as "folklore"), for instance, he writes near the beginning:

> There are fifty people in this old rue Royale who can tell you their wild versions of this house's strange true story against any one who can do this present writer the honor to point out the former residence of 'Sieur George, Madame Délicieuse, or Dr. Mossy, or the unrecognizably restored dwelling of Madame Delphine.
>
> (590)

Cable also points out the settings of some of his other writings without, however, directly mentioning them: the "old calaboose" (from *Dr. Sevier*; 592), Congo Square (from "The Dance in Place Congo"; 592), and the place of the "yearly rendezvous of the voodoos" (from "Creole Slave Songs"; 596).

In addition, "The 'Haunted House'" features both themes and narrative strategies that readers of Cable's (and also Hearn's) contributions to "Scribner's Illustrated New Orleans" have long been familiar with.

The "intense jealousy between the Americans and the Creoles" (593) and Cable's explicit critique of slavery and segregation (593; 600), for example, may remind readers of the central conflicts of *The Grandissimes*. The story of Marguerite's passing (601) evokes Cable's "quadroon diptych" of "'Tite Poulette" and "Madame Delphine," but also and especially "A Life-Ebbing Monography," the 1871 *Times-Picayune* article about "a white man who opened a vein in his arm and inserted the blood of a fair mulatto so that he could then legally marry her" (Turner, *Cable* 50) which Turner and Elfenbein have attributed to Cable (see earlier). And the letter in which Cable's friend predicts a surge in visitors to the house if its story was known – quoted in the very text that makes this story known to hundreds of thousands of *Century* readers – raises the issue of New Orleans (literary) tourism and thus evokes "The Scenes of Cable's Romances."

As to narrative strategies, Cable's narrator once more acts as a tour guide at the opening of the story, leading readers through the Vieux Carré and down Royal Street to the entrance of the "haunted house" as well as into its rooms, the attic, and to the belvedere (590–2). Before we enter the house, however, the narrator predictably stresses its closed shutters and their "hostile impenetrability" (590), which, as in Cable's "Old Creole Days" stories, hide and simultaneously externalize the building's (past) mysteries. And not very surprisingly, the "haunted house" also features "a small, damp, paved court," entirely hidden from view "save from one or two neighboring windows" (591) – a perfect setting for both secret tragedies and the furtive peeps and hidden glances that eventually expose and reveal them (593).

Finally, "The 'Haunted House'" also employs the complex temporal structure that had already distinguished *The Grandissimes* and "Madame Delphine." The story's opening paragraph at first depicts New Orleans as a contemporary and future-oriented city:

> When you and – make that much-talked-of visit to New Orleans, by all means see early whatever evidences of progress and aggrandizement her hospitable citizens wish to show you; New Orleans belongs to the living present, and has serious practical relations with these United States and this great living world and age.
>
> (590)

Readers who had been looking forward to enjoying a typical Cable story and were somewhat disconcerted by these unfamiliar tones must have been very relieved when they arrived at the next two sentences, which through the use of a contrastive conjunction reintroduce the time-honored practice of pastifying the French Quarter: "*And yet* I want the first morning walk that you two take together and alone to be in the old French Quarter. Go down Royal street" (590; emphasis added).[109]

Cable again seems to depart from his own script when the narrator, after having given the tour of the French Quarter and having switched back to the antebellum past for the story of Madame Lalaurie, does not end the tale there, but instead proceeds to tell yet another, postbellum episode of the building's history. Yet here, too, Cable moves through familiar terrain: in *The Grandissimes* (and also, in a way, in "Madame Delphine"; see earlier), the pastness of French New Orleans had served as a foil for the post-Civil War, post-French present, with Cable using narratorial comments to establish parallels between antebellum slavery and postwar segregation. Such comments can also be found in "The 'Haunted House'" (see, for instance, 597), but it is mainly the successive telling of two episodes from the house's history that establishes the parallels here:

> The image of the house as "a ghost-ridden monument" to the "horridest possibilities" of slavery . . . becomes an effective device for linking the Southern past to the "dark romance" of Cable's own day: the fundamentally, if not so visibly, brutal actions of the White League in trying to enforce segregation.
>
> (Cleman, *Cable* 143)

Hence, "The 'Haunted House'" is only superficially "two different narratives," as Philip Butcher maintains (100); below the surface, it is the same narrative taking place all over again, in the same setting.

Thus, revisiting the characters, settings, themes, and narrative strategies of the writer's previous New Orleans-related features in the magazine, "The 'Haunted House'" in particular and the "Strange True Stories" in general constitute an appropriate coda to Cable's contribution to "Scribner's Illustrated New Orleans."[110] What mainly distinguishes this coda from Cable's earlier writings is, of course, his insistence on the truthfulness of the tales: whenever he can, Cable mentions precise dates, places, and names – details his narrator had more often than not professed to have forgotten in his earlier texts – and provides readers with sources and proofs of the tales' authenticity: court records, letters, and eyewitness reports. Indeed, Cable spends much of the introductory "How I Got Them" on telling readers not "how he got them," but how he verified and authenticated his "natural crystals" (110), these "'true things that have never had and shall not have a literary tool lifted up against them'" (113). The book version also enlists the illustrations in this rhetoric of truth: made, as the "List of Illustrations" insists, "from photographs of the originals" (n.p.), and thus relying on the "presumption of veracity that gives all photographs authority" (Sontag 6), they show the manuscripts, court records, letters, etc., on which the tales are supposedly exclusively based.

Several critics have wondered what lies behind Cable's insistent claims to have given the "truth" only, especially since, as my reading of "The 'Haunted House'" has already shown, these claims are so obviously exaggerated. Alice Hall Petry, for instance, considers the "Strange True Stories" an intellectually pleasing, though aesthetically not particularly satisfying, experiment to "argue that (1) what we understand by the term 'truth' is at best unreliable and that (2) its unreliability is due largely to the words used to record and convey it" ("Limits" 29). Instead of viewing the collection as an entirely serious endeavor, Owen Robinson, by contrast, argues that Cable is merely "having fun" (99) with his readers by "playfully" engaging with the problems of authenticity that he has posed himself (98). There are numerous passages in "The 'Haunted House'" that indicate that Cable is indeed trying to tease readers as much as he can: the narrator repeatedly claims to "leave the ground for what we know to be authenticated fact" (590), to be "dealing with plain fact and history" (591), and "not to plead one cause or another" (598). And yet the story is full of undocumented information, rumors, hearsay, digressions, morals, and pleadings, always marked as such, but nevertheless included in the text.[111] At least in "The 'Haunted House,'" then, Cable has it both ways, telling what he considers to be the "bare facts," but also liberally adding gossip, rumors, and his own opinions, just as he had done in his earlier writings. Hence, the story squarely contradicts Cable's statement in his introduction that he has "learned to believe that good stories happen oftener than once I thought they did" (110). As "The 'Haunted House'" with its reassembling of elements from earlier Cable texts illustrates, what he seems to have learned instead is what it takes to turn a "true story" into "good art" (110).

Past No More: "Balcony Stories"

Cable's "Strange True Stories" were followed by yet another story collection with an introductory frame: the "Balcony Stories," serialized in the magazine from December 1892 through October 1893, collected as *Balcony Stories* by Century Company in 1893, and written by none other than Grace E. King. As described in her memoirs, the politically and socially conservative King had severely criticized Cable's depiction of race relations in New Orleans in general and his portrayal of New Orleans Creoles in particular, and had been challenged by *Century*'s editor-in-chief Gilder to correct Cable if he was so "false" to her (see earlier). Critics have debated to what extent King's fictional oeuvre met that challenge, with some scholars arguing that King somewhat sidestepped the issue by focusing on the lives of (Southern) women rather than on the defense of the Creoles in her stories (see, for instance, A.G. Jones 127) and others suggesting that at least sometimes, the author's professed convictions notwithstanding, King's texts show a less than unquestioning "support of Old South values" (Hardwig 141; see also Kuilan 100). According to critics, then, a general comparison of Cable's and King's fictions does not reveal the clear contrast that the two writers' stark differences in political opinions may have led one to expect.

Within the more restricted context of *Scribner's/Century* and "Scribner's Illustrated New Orleans," however, where King's "Balcony Stories" directly "responded" to Cable's "Strange True Stories," contrasts become more readily apparent: for instance, the introduction to King's collection, simply called "The Balcony," lyrically evokes the intimate, dreamy, and romantic atmosphere of a summer night in the South, when women in "vague, loose, white garments" "sit and talk together" on balconies, with "the stars breaking the cool darkness, or the moon making a show of light – oh, such a discreet show of light! – through the vines" (279). The stories these women tell to each other in "low, soft" voices – the very stories we are about to read – are both personal and highly individual since they are based on the storytellers' own "[e]xperiences, reminiscences, episodes . . . from other women's lives" and since each storyteller "has a different way of picking up and relating her stories, as each one selects different pieces, and has a personal way of playing them on the piano" (279). Hence, whereas Cable's "1888: How I Got Them" had insisted on the textuality, factuality, and "truth" of the "strange true stories," "The Balcony" rather stresses the orality, individuality, and fictionality of the "Balcony Stories"; instead of Cable's written and/or printed first-hand accounts, official documents, and verified reports, "which have never had and shall not have a literary tool lifted up against them" (see earlier), readers get memories, hearsays, and rumors, passed on orally and arranged, "dramatize[d] and inflect[ed]" (279), according to the individual storyteller's preferences and style. While Cable's introductory sketch relates a meta-folkloristic story (see earlier), "The Balcony" tells, as Kate Falvey notes, "the story *of* storytelling" (207; emphasis original).[112]

The stories that follow largely confirm this. Indeed, as James Nagel has pointed out, "much of what is reported" in the various "Balcony Stories" is "uncertain, the product of gossip and speculation" (64). In "La Grande Demoiselle," for instance, the descriptions of the protagonist's scandalously decadent life in antebellum times are all introduced by the phrase "It was said that" and the narrator concludes: "But it must be remembered that this is all hearsay. When one has not been present, one knows nothing of one's knowledge; one can only repeat" (324). Likewise, concerning certain details in "The Story of a Day," the narrator remarks: "Of course one must supply all this from one's own imagination or experience" (232). In "A Crippled Hope," much of Little Mammy's early story is based on "tradition or the old gray-haired negro janitor" (376; see Nagel 74). And finally, the story of "The Old Lady's Restoration" is itself that of a rumor – namely, the rumor that upon the reported restoration of her lost fortune (a report that is never verified in the story), the old lady would return to her former luxurious lifestyle: "Where the news came from nobody knew, but everything was certified and accepted as facts, although, as between women, the grain of salt should have been used" (727).

Moreover, several stories contain metafictional comments that highlight the text's origins in storytelling practices. "The Story of a Day," for instance, begins with a note by the narrator that draws the listener's/reader's attention away from the story itself and toward the art of telling it: "It is really not much, the story; it is only the arrangement of it, as we would say of our dresses and our drawing-rooms" (230). Later on, the narrator again comments on her portrayal of the events: "And so, with all its grace of curve and bend, and so – the description is longer than the voyage – we come to our first stopping place" (232). And in both "La Grande Demoiselle" and "A Crippled Hope," the descriptions of antebellum life in New Orleans are compared to other fictions, to the "perfervid pictures of tropical life, at one time the passion of philanthropic imaginations" (323) in the former and to the *Arabian Nights* (375) – itself, of course, a story collection on storytelling – in the latter story.

Even more importantly, Cable's and King's collections also contrast with respect to the temporal dynamics of their depictions of New Orleans: both "Strange True Stories" and "Balcony Stories" are characterized by a complex temporality, but where Cable – at least in "The 'Haunted House'" – underlines the continuity between antebellum and post-Reconstruction New Orleans with respect to racial discrimination, King – at least in the early "Balcony Stories" – focuses on the social transformations and reversals in race and class hierarchies brought on by the Civil War and Reconstruction, as well as their material, emotional, and psychological repercussions on Southern women. The later stories then increasingly transcend the narrow temporal and socio-political context of Reconstruction and, while still focusing on New Orleans women, dramatize social, material, and emotional reversals that are not connected to the Civil War and Reconstruction. The collection thus steadily universalizes its themes, creating a "narrative of community" (Zagarell; see Hanrahan) that finds its formal equivalent in the storytelling circle on the balcony, which *Century* readers are invited to join. Hence, the balcony becomes a place that, instead of pastifying New Orleans, connects the city with the rest of the nation.

Thus, "The Balcony" not only links readers with the women on the balcony, but also with each other. On the one hand, as they read the stories, particularly female readers – men, King points out, "are not balcony sitters" (279) – find themselves placed on the balcony, listening to the women telling their individual tales. On the other hand, Michael Lund has compared the gatherings described in "The Balcony" to the "virtual" gatherings of hundreds of thousands of readers upon the publication of each new issue of *Century* (or any other magazine, for that matter): "The repeated comings together of many storytellers and listeners – balcony-sitters or periodical audience – provided opportunities to gather value from the tales of others and to invest meaning in one's own stories" (81). For Lund, "The Balcony" thus symbolizes the social connections that could be made "in a new, rapidly growing, urban industrial society" "through the new media of magazines" (80).

It is mainly through its themes, though, that "Balcony Stories" brings together readers – Northern and Southern women, and even men. The introduction rather vaguely identifies "other women's destinies" as the general topic of balcony stories: "what God has done or is doing with some other woman whom they have known – . . . that is what interests the women who sit of summer nights on balconies" (279). Most critics agree, however, that the collection more precisely revolves around social, economic, and psychological reversals in the lives of Southern women, reversals brought about by the Civil War and Reconstruction (see, among many others, Falvey 204).[113] *Century* readers were not entirely unfamiliar with this subject: in an article entitled "Southern Womanhood as Affected by the War" and published slightly more than a year before the first installment of the "Balcony Stories" was printed (that is, in November 1891), Wilbur Fish Tillett argued that

> [a]mong the many changes that have taken place in the Southern States and among Southern people within the past thirty years, some of which are the direct result of war, and others the simple and natural development of the times, there is none more significant and worthy of notice than the change that has taken place in the condition, the life, and the labor of Southern women.
>
> (9)

Seeking to "compare and contrast the life, and condition, and work of woman as they are now in the South with what they were in ante-bellum times" (9), Tillett had sent out a detailed questionnaire with four questions to "some half-dozen representative Southern women" selected "from the range of his acquaintances in three different States" (10). The article reprints both the questionnaire (10–11) and selections from the answers Tillett received.

Appearing a year later, the "Balcony Stories" almost seem like somewhat delayed, fictional answers to Tillett's questionnaire. This particularly applies to the first three stories in the collection, which all focus on French New Orleanian women and the ways they cope with the sudden loss of financial means and social status due to the war: "A Drama of Three" (published along with "The Balcony" in December 1892), "La Grande Demoiselle" (January 1893), and "Mimi's Marriage" (February 1893). On the surface, "A Drama of Three," for instance, appears to be mainly concerned with the aristocratic old General B – the son of a wealthy plantation owner who now, "under the new régime" (281), unknowingly depends on the charity of Journel, the grandson of the plantation's former overseer.[114] Although the eponymous "drama" of rent day has reaffirmed the loss of his former social and financial status with monthly regularity for five years now, the general's undiminished view of himself as "the man to whom the bright New Orleans itself almost owed its brightness" (282) and his pointless threats to Journel and Pompey clearly demonstrate that he still lives in his antebellum days of glory. But the drama is a farce to Journel only. To the General's wife, Madame Honorine, it rather constitutes a tragedy. While her husband does not even care who it is that owes him so much to send him money every month – in fact, the anonymous notes rather reinforce his self-importance (see 282) – the question is a constant source of jealous anxiety to "Madame la Générale":

> It is very little consolation for wives that their husbands have forgotten, when someone else remembers. Some one else! Ah, there could be so many some one elses in the General's life, for in truth he had been irresistible to excess. But this was one particular some one else who had been faithful for five years. Which one?
>
> (282)

Judith Fetterley and Marjorie Pryse have pointed to Honorine's complicity in maintaining the General's sense of superiority (296), but rather than criticizing or mocking Madame, as it does with her husband, King's story asks particularly female readers to empathize with her. Both Honorine's ongoing and still explicitly erotic admiration for her husband and the pangs of jealousy she suffers are depicted as emotions shared by all (elderly) wives:

> Ah, to the end a woman loves to celebrate her conquest! . . . If one could look under the gray hairs and wrinkles with which time thatches old women one would be surprised to see the flutterings, the quiverings, the thrills, the emotions, the coals of the heart-fires which death alone extinguishes, when he commands the tenant to vacate.
>
> (280)

Moreover, the narrator makes a point of mentioning that Journel "never saw Madame Honorine" (282), thus probably implying that he would not play his little joke on the General if he only knew what it does to Honorine. Hence, in contrast to what critics such as Hanrahan (230) or Nagel (64) have assumed, "A Drama of Three" is less concerned with the General's reaction to the social and economic reversals of postbellum society but puts Honorine center stage, unearthing and exploring her reaction, which has remained hidden to everyone else. From the very beginning of the "Balcony Stories," then, King focuses on the role(s) of women in the drama of Reconstruction.

The second story continues to highlight the female perspective and intensifies the contrast between pre-war and Reconstruction times, but leaves, as Nagel has pointed out, the "emotional dimension of the transition ... unexpressed" (68). Instead, "La Grande Demoiselle" concentrates on the economic and social fall of the eponymous protagonist, which is symbolized through her clothing: rather than silk dresses from Paris with buttons "of real gold and silver" (324), she now wears a "plain, coarse, cottonade gown. The negro women about her were better dressed than she" (327); and rather than being the center of New Orleans society, she now hides her face behind a "green barege veil" (326). The narrator's most explicit critique is not directed against the Demoiselle's antebellum arrogance and excesses, however, but against (Southern) men: "And, after all, a woman seems the quickest thing forgotten when once the important affairs of life come to men for consideration" (324). It is only old Champigny, one of the many *"nouveaux pauvres"* (326), who comes to her rescue.

Similarly, "Mimi's Marriage" does not so much ridicule the narrator's naïve dreams of marrying a "handsome *brun*" (493), dreams from the time "'before the war'" (495), as criticize a (male-dominated) society that has left women thoroughly unprepared for the postbellum world: "'I prayed to God to help me, to advise me,'" Mimi admits. "'I could not teach – I had no education; I could not go into a shop – that would be dishonoring papa'" (494). God answers Mimi's prayers in the shape of a less than handsome *blond*, but she ultimately shows a pragmatism that she considers typical of women: "'Men ought not to be subjected to the humiliation of life; they are not like women, you know. We are made to stand things'" (495). Mimi's brief but violent crying attack after her wedding, too, is brushed aside rather lightly as part of the experience of all brides: "'it occurs to me, that if you examined the blue bows on a bride's *négligée*, you might always find tears on the other side'" (496).

Generalizations such as these already contribute to universalizing King's portraits of Creole New Orleanian women in the postbellum era, making them easily relatable not only to Southern, but also to Northern, female readers. Moreover, even in these early "Balcony Stories" references to the war and Reconstruction – which, after all, constitute the "salient transformational events in the background" (Nagel 81) of these stories – are curiously vague and infrequent. In "A Drama of Three," for instance, the old General merely speaks of "'the new régime'" (281); in "Mimi's Marriage" the "old times, 'before the war'" are compared to "this age" (495); and in "La Grande Demoiselle," the narrator introduces the topic as follows: "Well! Everyone knows what happened after '59. There is no need to repeat" (324).[115] James Nagel has evoked Ernest Hemingway's "iceberg principle" to account for King's handling of the socio-political context of the "Balcony Stories": "In *Balcony Stories*, published three decades before Hemingway's work, King is remarkably subtle in instilling

[an] unexplained background beneath the surface of her fiction, a crucial element that is never stated but only implied in context" (63).

In the stories that follow, however, even the tip of the iceberg disappears – in fact, the emotional, financial, and social reversals that the female protagonists experience in the majority of the later "Balcony Stories" are no longer connected to the Civil War and Reconstruction at all. This thematic shift is underlined by a three-month hiatus in the serialization of the collection: after the installment containing "Mimi's Marriage" (February 1892), no new "Balcony Stories" appeared until the June 1893 issue of *Century*, which featured "The Story of a Day." Yet in contrast to the first three "Balcony Stories," this lyrical piece is not set in Creole New Orleans but in the rural, mythical landscape of the Acadians and seems to take place, as Lori Robison argues, "out of any clear sense of time" (64). While thus lacking the specific socio-political context of "A Drama of Three," "La Grande Demoiselle," and "Mimi's Marriage," "The Story of a Day" is nevertheless connected to these earlier stories through the portrayal of a reversal in a French Louisianian woman's life, in this case, the tragic death of Adorine's fiancé Zepherin. The illustration strategy used by artist Albert E. Sterner for this story – the first picture depicting Adorine before (233) and the second one after (234) the death of Zepherin – further stresses this connection: like "The Story of a Day," "La Grande Demoiselle" and "Mimi's Marriage," too, are accompanied by pairs of pictures that contrast scenes from "before" and "after" the respective reversal in each story (that is, scenes from before and after the Civil War).

With the notable exception of "A Crippled Hope" (July 1893), the remaining stories of the collection revolve around reversals that are disconnected from the Civil War and Reconstruction: in Jeanne Marie's realization that "she had never known her twin sister at all" (374; in "Anne Marie and Jeanne Marie," July 1893), in the "Dugazon *manquée*"'s goodbye to the stage of the New Orleans opera (544; in "One of Us," August 1893), in the unnamed convent's girl's meeting with her mother ("The Little Convent Girl," August 1893), in the tragic death of the husband of "grandmother's grandmother" (in the eponymous story, September 1893), the slow financial decline of the "old lady" ("The Old Lady's Restoration," September 1893), the reconciliation between "Amour" and "Divine" ("A Delicate Affair," October 1893), and, finally, in Pupasse's confession ("Pupasse," October 1893), the socio-political context of the first three stories does not play any role whatsoever. And even in "A Crippled Hope," the war is again depicted in a highly indirect and impressionistic fashion:

> There came a night. . . . Alarm-bells rang in the streets, but [Little Mammy] did not know them for alarm-bells; alarm brooded in the dim space around her, but she did not even recognize that. . . .

Morning came. . . . At nightfall a file of soldiers entered. . . . You divine it. The negro-trader's trade was abolished, and he had vanished in the din and smoke of a war which he had not been entirely guiltless of producing.

(378–9; see also Robison 66)

As in the first three "Balcony Stories," the reader is called upon to decode what the narrator merely alludes to.

Hence, in the course of serialization, the complex temporality of "A Drama of Three," "La Grande Demoiselle," and "Mimi's Marriage" (as well as "A Crippled Hope"), which contrasts the antebellum with the immediate post-Civil War period, is replaced with the atemporality of the later stories, a timelessness that substantially contributes to the increasing thematic broadening of the collection: though mostly set in French New Orleans, the reversals depicted in the later stories are such as, the texts imply, could happen to all women, anytime, anywhere in the United States.[116] At one point in "The Balcony," the stories are described as revolving around "old times, old friends, old experiences" (279). Yet in contrast to virtually all of the other texts and pictures that constitute "Scribner's Illustrated New Orleans," the later "Balcony Stories" do not pastify, but instead universalize (or at least nationalize) French New Orleans: both formally and thematically, the collection works, as Hanrahan has pointed out, "to connect the women gathered on the balcony to the rest of America" (238) and envisions a city that is "fully reconciled to the rest of the nation, distinct yet also joined" (233). With King's "Balcony Stories," then, the intensely local and almost quintessential New Orleans space that is the balcony becomes, at least with respect to women, a microcosm of the nation and French New Orleans is released from the past.

Conclusion

In June 1893 – *Century* had just resumed the serialization of King's "Balcony Stories" and featured "The Story of a Day" in its current issue – the first issue of *McClure's Magazine* appeared. Named after its co-founder Samuel Sidney McClure, who less than a decade before had briefly worked for both the De Vinne Press (*Scribner's/Century*'s long-time printer of choice; see Tichenor) and Century Company,[117] *McClure's* constitutes one of two periodicals that Arthur John has considered as "especially linked to the *Century*'s loss of readership" in the 1890s (235; circulation had indeed dropped from an all-time high of 222,000 in 1887 to 150,000; see Noonan, *Reading* 178). More often, scholars name *McClure's* alongside the *Ladies' Home Journal* (begun as an independent publication in 1883), *Cosmopolitan* (started in 1886), and *Munsey's* (begun in 1889) as part of an entire group of new monthly magazines that revolutionized[118] the U.S.

mass periodical market during the late 1880s and early 1890s, initiating the economic decline of older quality monthlies such as *Century* (see, for example, Garvey 9; Johanningsmeier, *Fiction* 16; or Sumner 30). Richard Brodhead explains:

> These magazines were significantly cheaper than the older kind of monthly – fifteen cents or even a dime, as in the case of *Munsey's*, as against a quarter or thirty-five cents. They could be cheaper because they financed themselves in a different way: instead of supporting themselves by subscription fees, they dropped fees, built massive circulations, then sold space to advertisers at a price based on the size of the audience the advertiser could thereby reach, using advertising revenue as their financial base.
>
> ("Literature" 475; see also Zboray and Zboray 32)

Yet, it was not only with respect to business matters that *Century* found itself under pressure. The blend of fiction, poetry, and feature articles on nature, technology, and literature, as well as numerous illustrations, that the inaugural issue of *McClure's* offered its readers (among others, "A Dialogue between William Dean Howells and Hjalmar Hjorth Boyesen," an article on "Where Man Got His Ears," and a short story by Joel Chandler Harris, all of them copiously illustrated) was not remarkably different from the contents of a typical *Century* issue at the time and targeted a similar readership. Nevertheless, as Noonan writes, in the 1890s, the older magazine conceived of itself, "perhaps more so than ever before, as a steadfast beacon in a sea of pending violence, lowered standards, and changing attitudes." Thus refusing to change with the times, however, *Century* would soon begin "to lose its dominance as *the* cultural arbiter" (*Reading* 178). By 1893, then, the magazine had reached and passed its zenith, both economically and socio-culturally.

While the story of the *Century* would continue into the twentieth century (it was not until 1930 that the periodical was merged with *The Forum*), the story of "Scribner's Illustrated New Orleans" virtually came to an end in 1893: *Century* continued to publish Southern and Louisiana fiction and articles (the December 1893 issue, for instance, would feature the first installment of Mark Twain's *Puddn'head Wilson*; a month later, *Century* would publish Kate Chopin's "A No-account Creole"), but following King's "Balcony Stories," no new and significant New Orleans-related features appeared in the pages of the magazine until the late 1920s, when Lyle Saxon joined the illustrious ranks of "Scribner's Illustrated New Orleans," contributing stories and articles to the magazine and publishing several non-fiction books, among them *Fabulous New Orleans* (1928), with the Century Company (see e.g., J.W. Thomas 65–6; 78; 89–122). Cable's "Père Raphaël," published in August 1901 as a companion story to "Posson Jone'" (which had never even been printed in the magazine) was a pale, sentimental shadow of his earlier fiction;[119] and despite being urged to, Grace King would not contribute to *Century* again (see earlier).

For precisely two decades, however (from the publication of Cable's "'Sieur George: A Story of New Orleans" in October 1873 to that of King's "Pupasse" in October 1893), *Scribner's/Century* had printed an astonishing amount of New Orleans-related content, both fictional and non-fictional, both textual and pictorial, both by well-established writers and artists and by newcomers, as well as both by New Orleanians and by others. Judging by the sheer number of his contributions to the magazine, as well as by his numerous and multifarious connections to other contributors, the most prominent among these writers and artists was undoubtedly George Washington Cable, although even he had to submit to the institutionalized power of a Richard Watson Gilder or a Roswell Smith. Nevertheless, "Scribner's Illustrated New Orleans" is as much the work of Cable as he is, in a way, the product of the magazine.

With respect to content, certainly one of the most remarkable aspects of *Scribner's/Century*'s depiction of New Orleans – particularly given the variety of textual and pictorial genres included, and the number of periodical actors involved, as well as the enormous variety of the latter's backgrounds and of their relationships to the city – is its consistency with respect to Frenchness and pastness: virtually all of the New Orleans-related features published by *Scribner's/Century* portray the Crescent City as French and simultaneously pastify French New Orleans. Writing and drawing the city's Frenchness off into the past, rather than merely portraying it as passing, the texts and pictures that constitute "Scribner's Illustrated New Orleans" thus contribute to the unique position of New Orleans on the map of local-color settings in late-nineteenth–century American literature as the only place where a "deviant" culture has been *fully* contained from a temporal perspective.

This imaginative and aesthetic containment can be viewed as a sociocultural corollary of the territorial-political containment of the city through the Louisiana Purchase, and is indeed sometimes employed to set the stage for further territorial and imperialistic expansions of the United States, as, for instance, in King's "The Great South." More frequently, however, the pastified Frenchness of New Orleans is used to point to contemporary local, regional, and national issues, for example via stressing the continuity of racial and caste-related discrimination in the South across the divide between French past and post-French present (perhaps most prominently in Cable's "The 'Haunted House' in Royal Street") or via dramatizing the reversals brought about by this divide (as in King's early "Balcony Stories"). In the context of local-color studies, then, the complex temporality of much of "Scribner's Illustrated New Orleans" manifestly contradicts assumptions about the nostalgic, reactionary character of local color and related genres and art forms. Though often much less overtly so, "Scribner's Illustrated New Orleans" nevertheless engages the present as much as the past.

In the context of periodical studies, my analysis of "Scribner's Illustrated New Orleans" has sought to complement the reading of periodical content with an account of the interrelations between periodical actors. More specifically, this chapter has complicated ideas about the institutional or interpersonal and intertextual networks that sustained popular periodical publications in late-nineteenth–century America, stressing institutionalized and other hierarchies in interpersonal networks as well as distinguishing between intermedial and intertextual/interpictorial relationships and generally extending these material networks beyond the pages of the magazine itself to pre- and post-periodical book publication. Thus, building and reflecting upon the rhizomatic turn in periodical studies, however, "Scribner's Illustrated New Orleans" also problematizes notions of individual authorship and autonomous genres and oeuvres in periodical publishing.

From the 1870s to the 1890s, in both the table of contents and in the magazine itself, *Scribner's/Century* accorded the "social prestige of authorship" (Cordell, "Reprinting" 418) more and more liberally.[120] Thus, identifying the respective contributions of more and more individuals to the magazine as a whole, *Scribner's/Century* also tacitly acknowledged the essentially collaborative nature of periodical publishing. Simon Cooke has examined the illustrations appearing in British illustrated periodicals in the 1860s as "the result of a series of collaborations" (37) between artist, engraver, author, editor, and publisher, but the same also applies to "Scribner's Illustrated New Orleans" and to (illustrated) magazines in general. As Amy Tucker has noted, the format manifestly "undermine[s] the unitary concept authorship" (158).

Similarly, what the juxtapositions of and the dialogues between the various fictional (local-color), historical, folklor(ist)ic, and travel writings about New Orleans published in *Scribner's/Century* tell us is, as Richard Brodhead has pointed out, "that nineteenth-century literary genres we are used to thinking of as freestanding were not autonomous in their original cultural production but formed mutually supportive parts of a concerted textual program" (*Cultures* 131). As, for instance, the pastifying of French New Orleans in King's "The Great South" series of travel sketches is echoed in Cable's short fiction, as well as in his articles about Creole history and folklore, the lines between the various textual genres or modes become blurred.

Much the same can also be said, finally, about the individual contributions. Indeed, while my discussion of the intertextual network of "Scribner's Illustrated New Orleans" may be structured according to individual textual features, the analyses have shown that the "total" meaning of these features depends not merely on the texts themselves, but also and to a significant extent on all the "bibliographical codes" (McGann 57) that surround them in the periodical. This applies, first and foremost, to the accompanying illustrations and their captions, but often enough also to other, seemingly more "distant" textual and graphic features. With texts and pictures thus bound together – both literally and metaphorically – in the magazine, the idea of autonomous oeuvres becomes rather difficult to sustain in the periodical context. The illustrated magazine constitutes a "*Gesamtkunstwerk,*" a total artwork, and needs to be studied as such.

In the "Le Bat en Rouge" souvenir shop at Disneyland's New Orleans Square, a copy of French chiromancer Jean Belot's *Œuvres* (1640) – opened so that customers can admire Belot's detailed palm-reading chart – decorates the top of a merchandise display shelf, along with vials, skulls, a mortar, a little cauldron, and other items popularly associated with New Orleans voodoo. A little further down the street, a display window located next to the "Mlle. Antoinette's Parfumerie" shop contains, almost hidden among numerous old flacons, a colorful trade card from the New York-based fragrance manufacturer Theodore Ricksecker that was distributed to visitors of the 1884–1885 New Orleans Cotton Centennial Exposition. Together with the other set pieces and the architecture, music, retail products, foods, and drinks, as well as rides featured at New Orleans Square, the book and the card locate the temporal setting of the area in a vaguely French nineteenth-century past.

Illustrated books and magazines and nineteenth-century print products have not only served as mere props for the depiction of New Orleans at Disneyland, however: an illustrated article about "The Magic Worlds of Disney" by Robert de Roos, published in the August 1963 issue of *National Geographic*, features a photograph of designer Herbert Ryman working on a preliminary sketch for New Orleans Square, scheduled to open at the Anaheim theme park three years later. Lying on Ryman's drawing table is a copy of the February 1953 issue of *National Geographic*, which, the caption informs us, Ryman uses to design the "lacy ironwork" of the "[b]alconied buildings of New Orleans Square" (174).[121] Indeed, in *Fairground Attractions: A Genealogy of the Pleasure Ground* (2012), Deborah Philips claims that the genres and iconographies established through popular illustrated publishing played an integral role in shaping the landscapes of theme parks in general and Disneyland in particular: "The categories which Disneyland employs to divide the spaces of the park are those of the popular literary genres identifiable from the moment of the mass reproduction of texts and images" (32). In the case of New Orleans, Disney's depictions of the Crescent City in its themed commercial spaces specifically build on the idea of the city as disseminated in the pages of *Scribner's*/*Century*, translating the latter into three dimensions.

Finally, there are also more abstract connections or analogies between "Scribner's Illustrated New Orleans" and "Disney's Immersive New

Orleans": composed of various individual elements realized in different media and created by frequently unnamed individuals in more or less intensely collaborative ways, theme parks, too, can be conceived of as total artworks. Much like *Scribner's/Century*'s tables of contents list specific "elements" (articles, poems, editorial departments, and illustrations), Disneyland visitor guides and the attraction posters displayed in the park's entrance area readily identify individual experiences and services (rides, shows, restaurants, shops, and service areas). And through the so-called "Main Street Windows" – tributes to specific individuals involved with the creation of Disney theme parks that are painted on the windowpanes of buildings in Disneyland's Main Street section (see Heimbuch) – certain "contributors" (architects, designers, artists, or composers) are even accorded the "social prestige of authorship." However, in contrast to the texts and images analyzed in "Scribner's Illustrated New Orleans," the depictions of New Orleans to be discussed in "Disney's Immersive New Orleans" have constantly changed and thus require a different diachronic or historical approach. And this is precisely the reason why my tour of "Disney's Immersive New Orleans" will start neither at Disneyland nor in New Orleans, but at the "Historama" in Europa-Park, Germany's most-visited theme park.

Notes

1. McCullough, for instance, reads "A Gentleman" as "a metaphor for the North's consumption of Southern Local Color fiction" (198) and as an "ironic self comment" by Chopin on her position as a local-color artist (200). Similarly, Steiling has argued that the story uses "the techniques of the local-color school to deconstruct and transcend the limitations of the local-color writer" (200). And Fetterley and Pryse consider "A Gentleman" a "narrative of resistance" to the exploitation of regional subjects by local-color writers (*Writing* 241). Chopin, of course, as has been noted by many critics, "refused to be considered a local colorist and resented being compared to [George Washington] Cable and Grace King" (Seyersted 83).
2. According to Francis Martin, Jr. ("To Ignore" 672), this trip took place in 1888. As we will see, however, Kemble visited New Orleans as early as 1885.
3. Pape (1870–1938) was a San Francisco-born painter and scenic designer who had studied art in New York and Paris and who worked as an illustrator for such magazines as *McClure's*, *Scribner's*, *Cosmopolitan*, *Collier's*, *The Saturday Evening Post*, and *Life* (see Reed 79). Pape was also one of the illustrators for Grace King's "Balcony Stories" (as "F[rederick] S. M[oritz] Pape").
4. In 1885, one book publisher claimed before a Senate committee studying the question of international copyright: "It is impossible to make the books of most American authors pay, unless they are first published and acquire recognition through the columns of the magazines" (qtd. in Mott, *History* Vol. 1 3). Virtually all of the major late-nineteenth–century literary monthlies were directly owned by or connected to, and also named after, a prominent publisher: Hurd & Houghton (later Houghton, Mifflin) had acquired

the *Atlantic Monthly* in 1873; Charles Scribner Company owned a minority share of Scribner and Company, which started *Scribner's Monthly* in 1870. After Scribner and Company became independent in 1881, renaming itself Century Company (the magazine became *Century Magazine*), Charles Scribner's Sons started another magazine, *Scribner's Magazine*, in 1886. The House of Harper owned an entire array of magazines that addressed different target audiences: *Harper's New Monthly Magazine* (started in 1850), *Harper's Weekly* (established in 1857), *Harper's Bazaar* (a women's magazine launched in 1867), and *Harper's Young People* (started in 1879). Other house magazines which were named after their parent companies were *Putnam's Monthly*, *Lippincott's Magazine*, and *Appleton's Journal* (see Meyer 16–7; Ohmann, "Diverging" 103–104).
5. Indeed, older critical analyses of local color repeatedly emphasized the similarities between the literary genre and drawing and painting, describing local-color texts as "genre-painting of a sort" (Tooker 214), "exotic word painting" (Kreyling 114), and "illustrative landscape literature loosely woven into a fictional plot" (Silber 73). In fact, the very term "local color" was borrowed from a technical term in painting (see Braddock 103).
6. The connection between travel writing and local-color fiction has been emphasized by a number of critics, among them Archie Green (84), Richard Brodhead (*Cultures* 125–31), John D. Cox (194–5), Jennifer Rae Greeson (*South* 251), and Amy Tucker, who speaks of "the clash between two competing forms of realism in the late nineteenth-century popular press, documentary and fictional" (164).
7. These analytical practices have also been reflected in anthologizing practices. Anthologies of local-color writing have often grouped together stories according to specific regions or even the gender of the authors. See, for example, Judith Fetterley and Marjorie Pryse's *American Women Regionalists: A Norton Anthology* (1992), Elizabeth Ammons and Valerie Rohy's *American Local Color Writing, 1880–1920* (1998), or Barbara C. Ewell, Pamela Glenn Menke, and Andrea Humphrey's *Southern Local Color: Stories of Region, Race, and Gender* (2002).
8. The writers in question were Grace Elizabeth King and George Washington Cable, and the point of disagreement between the two was the portrayal of New Orleans's French Creoles. The incident will be discussed in more detail later.
9. The "Scribner's" in "Scribner's Illustrated New Orleans" not only refers to the original name of the magazine, then, but also to the name of the publishing house and its one-time sister company.
10. In her book *Zeit und Tradition* (1999; "time and tradition"), Assmann identifies two diametrically opposed cultural strategies related to time:

> "Presentifying" constitutes a temporal strategy that pulls the seemingly inaccessible into the accessibility of the present, thus opening it up for change; through "pastifying," by contrast, something is pushed into the past in order to close it off from re-evaluation or change.
>
> (4; my translation)

I will elaborate on the precise functions of the "pastifying" of French New Orleans in "Scribner's Illustrated New Orleans" later.
11. See also, for instance, Frankie Hutton's *The Early Black Press in America, 1827–1860* (1992), Gerald J. Baldasty's *The Commercialization of the News in the Nineteenth Century* (1992), Matthew Schneirov's *The Dream of a New Social Order: Popular Magazines in America, 1893–1914* (1994),

Helen Damon-Moore's *Magazines for the Millions: Gender and Commerce in the* Ladies' Home Journal *and the* Saturday Evening Post, *1880–1910* (1994), Ellery Sedgwick's *The* Atlantic Monthly, *1857–1909: Yankee Humanism at High Tide and Ebb* (1994), and Patricia Okker's *Our Sister Editors: Sarah J. Hale and the Tradition of Nineteenth-Century American Women Editors* (1995).

12. See https://babel.hathitrust.org/cgi/mb?a=listis&c=1930843488 and http://quod.lib.umich.edu/m/moagrp/. On the possibilities and challenges of working with digitized archives of nineteenth-century magazines, see, amongst others, Latham and Scholes; Mussell; and Cordell, "Digital."

13. These codes include, as Charles Johanningsmeier has noted, "pre-publication advertising; the headlines for [the printed text], its placement on the page; its typography; the accompanying illustrations; their captions; and the other printed materials that appeared nearby in the periodical" ("Understanding" 598). Latham and Scholes particularly emphasize the importance of advertising (see 521–8), a bibliographical code that for reasons of space I am forced to completely ignore in my analysis.

14. Going back in time even further, already in *America's Continuing Story: An Introduction to Serial Fiction, 1850–1900* (1993), Lund had evoked the idea of a magazine as an intertextual network (17–20). Indeed, the article by Latham and Scholes has itself been criticized for its "rhetoric of newness" (DiCenzo 22).

15. In a literature review about methodological issues in periodical studies for the *Routledge Handbook of Magazine Research* (2016), however, Kathleen L. Endres found that since 1990 researchers have "most frequently focus[ed] on the *content* of periodicals. As a consequence, these researchers – regardless of discipline – use content analysis as their method" (60). "Scribner's Illustrated New Orleans" can thus also be seen as a contribution to broadening the focus of recent research on periodical publications.

16. In addition, Latham and Scholes call for yet another sort of network:

> If we really wish to understand magazines in all their complexity and specificity . . ., periodical studies will have to synthesize these scattered areas of interest into collaborative scholarly networks built around these objects [i.e., magazines]. Such a collective effort can provide the diversity of expertise needed to describe the richness of periodical culture and to generate more effective critical and historical tools for analyzing its riches.
>
> (530)

17. According to Tebbel and Zuckermann (75), the first half-tone plate appeared in *Century* in 1884, and by the mid-1890s half-tones accounted for a third of the pictures in the magazine.

18. Andrew Thacker uses the term "cross-fertilization" to describe the networks of connections between periodicals (20).

19. Indeed, out of the 276 issues that were published in the first 46 volumes of *Scribner's/Century* between November 1870 and October 1893, at least 63 (or almost 23 percent) contained at least one feature that focused on New Orleans. Features taken into consideration here include: Cable's stories later collected as *Old Creole Days* (published from October 1873 to March 1876), his novel *The Grandissimes* (serialized from November 1879 to October 1880), his novella "Madame Delphine" (May to July 1881), his series of historical articles later collected as *The Creoles of Louisiana* (January to July 1883), his novel *Dr. Sevier* (serialized from November

1883 to October 1884), his contribution to the "Battles and Leaders of the Civil War" series (April 1885), his articles on Creole slave songs and dances (February/April 1886), his story "Au Large" (November 1887 to March 1888), four of the "Strange True Stories of Louisiana" (May, August, September, and October 1889), and his "Open Letter" on the White League of New Orleans (April 1890), the "Old and New Louisiana" installments of Edward King and J. Wells Champney's "The Great South" series (November/December 1873), Lafcadio Hearn's article on "The Scenes of Cable's Romances" (November 1883), Eugene V. Smalley's articles on the Cotton Centennial Exposition (May/June 1885), and Grace E. King's stories later collected as *Balcony Stories* (December 1892 through October 1893).
20. Charges of regional favoritism from various directions against the magazine were not uncommon, however. As Cyganowski has pointed out, "sometimes simultaneous charges claimed that Scribner's was dominated by eastern, southern, and northern writers and opinions" (32; see also H.F. Smith 20).
21. Johnson, in his *Remembered Yesterdays*, however, rejects this idea: "We were accused of 'catering to a Southern audience,' but surely there was little business advantage to be derived from a region so near bankruptcy as the shattered South of that day" (96–7).
22. In *Convergence Culture: Where Old and New Media Collide* (2006), Jenkins introduces the concept of "convergence culture," which seeks to capture the characteristic circulation of media content across different media platforms in contemporary culture. This circulation depends, Jenkins argues, on participatory culture, a blurring of the strict dividing line between media producers and media consumers to the point that the two roles can no longer be clearly distinguished and whereby media consumers routinely turn into media producers and vice versa:

> some ideas spread top down, starting with commercial media and being adopted and appropriated by a range of different publics as they spread outward across the culture. Others emerge bottom up from various sites of participatory culture and getting pulled into the mainstream if the media industries see some way of profiting from it.
>
> (257)

The concept of participatory culture, then, stresses the accessibility and, hence, popularity of (new) media platforms.
23. Several scholars maintain that "The Great South" started with the first of the "Old and New Louisiana" installments in November 1873 (see Noonan, *Reading* 63; Greeson, *South* 244; Hardwig 80), but the July 1873 issue of *Scribner's* features an article entitled "The Great South: The New Route to the Gulf," written by King, which may be described as a prologue to the series (see King, "New Route").
24. "Bibi" was even rejected twice by *Scribner's/Century*, and also by *Appleton's* and the *Atlantic*. A revised version would later be published, of course, as part of *The Grandissimes* (see Wagner 79).
25. These were: "Belles Demoiselles Plantation" (April 1874), "'Tite Poulette" (October 1874), "Jean-ah Poquelin" (May 1875), "Madame Délicieuse" (August 1875), and "Café des Exilés" (March 1876). Apart from "Bibi" and "Posson Jone'," three more stories were rejected by the *Scribner's/Century* editors: "Dr. Goldenbow," "Hortensia," and "Ba'm o'Gilly" (see Ekström 52).
26. These are: "Salome Müller" (May 1889), "The 'Haunted House' in Royal Street" (August 1889), "Attalie Brouillard" (September 1889), and the beginnings of "War Diary of a Union Woman in the South" (October 1889).

27. Ekström (59n58) notes that attempts were made to have the first release of *Old Creole Days* coincide with the beginning of the serialization of *The Grandissimes* in the magazine.
28. Noonan, for instance, insists on Cable's "role in making *Scribner's* a household name" (*Reading* 81).
29. The exposition itself would be the topic of two articles by Eugene V. Smalley, a frequent contributor to *Century* in the 1880s, which were printed in May and June 1885 (see later).
30. King's journal entry on Cable confirms that she especially resented Cable's unfavorable depiction of whites. She writes: "The highest virtues he gives blacks means moral degradation for whites – but the whites faltering from these Cable-imposed standards are impaled" (*To Find My Own Peace* 5).
31. Gilder's irritation may have been spurred by a certain amount of self-doubt. After 20 years as an editor, he would describe the "editor's hell [as] paved with rejected manuscripts which he wishes he had accepted" (qtd. in Cyganowski 225).
32. See, for instance, Noonan, *Reading* 161–2. Cyganowski claims that Gilder's "censoring" of the excerpts of *Adventures of Huckleberry Finn* "has consistently attracted more critical attention than any instance of actual dispute and acrimony between author and editor" (210).
33. In a December 1874 "Topics of the Time" editorial, the magazine stated that "[w]e formally conclude, with this issue, the series of papers that have been running through the MONTHLY, entitled 'The Great South'" (N.N., "Great South" 248). "There are some papers still remaining," the editorial goes on, "but they relate to parts of the South with which the North is measurably familiar, and they will form a portion of a new series on American Life and Scenery, to be produced during the coming year" (248). In fact, however, the magazine would only print one more paper from "The Great South," an article on "Baltimore: The Liverpool of America" in April 1875 (see also Drake and Jones xxxin32).
34. In his "Preface" to the book version of *The Great South*, King writes that the Scribner party toured the South "during the whole of 1873, and the Spring and Summer of 1874" (i) and that Champney accompanied him "during the greater part of the journey" (ii). Drake and Jones offer a chronology of the tour (xviii-xxix) and note that "Champney did not accompany the *Scribner's* expedition in the late spring and early summer of 1873 nor at all in 1874" (xxxii). In mid-February of 1873, however, King and Champney arrived together in New Orleans, registering at the St. Charles Hotel (xxxvn50).
35. A letter from Pennell to Robert Underwood Johnson archived in the Century Company Records shows that the artist had originally proposed this book to the Century Company in 1909 (see Century Company Records, Series I, Box 76). Century apparently declined, as the volume was eventually published with Little, Brown in 1925.
36. Henceforth, quotations from letters and manuscripts in the Century Company Records, archived at the New York Public Library, will be referred to as CCR, with the Latin numbers referring to the series and the Arabic numbers referring to the box where the source is located.
37. Cable had been asked early in 1880 to contribute a history of New Orleans to the Tenth U.S. Census Report. The 313-page manuscript (including 647 footnotes) which he eventually submitted appeared in slightly abridged form in 1882 in *History and Present Condition of New Orleans, Louisiana, and Report on the City of Austin, Texas* (see Turner, *Cable* 360) and was also included, in 1887, in *Report on the Social Statistics of Cities: Part II, The Southern and Western States* (see Powell 21–2; Cleman, *Cable* 95). In

addition to *The Creoles of Louisiana*, this manuscript also served as the basis for Cable's 1884 article on "New Orleans" in the *Encyclopedia Britannica* (see Powell 27).

38. It is unclear, of course, whether Pennell himself included this poster in his drawing or whether it was added later by the engraver, R.C. Collins, identified in the lower right corner of the printed picture.
39. At least in theory, then, Kemble and Cable could have met in New Orleans: in early March, 1885, Cable briefly returned to the city from his lecture tour with Mark Twain before he went back to New England again (see Turner, *Cable* 185; 208). Kemble, in turn, appears to have remained in New Orleans at least until early March: one of his illustrations for Smalley's "In and Out of the New Orleans Exposition" is dated "March 1885" ("The Promenade"; see 193).
40. The three are: "A Field-Hand" (Cable, "Slave Dances" 520), "The Calaboose" (Cable, "Slave Dances" 528), and "A Nurse Mammie" (Cable, "Slave Songs" 810).
41. Among them were Médéric Louis Elie Moreau de Saint-Méry's *Description topographique, physique, civile, politique et historique de la partie française de l'isle Saint-Domingue* (1798) and the journal entries of Benjamin Latrobe from 1819, which included sketches of drums being played transversally, exactly as they appear in Kemble's pictures (Latrobe's sketches are reproduced in Epstein 98). Kemble may thus have relied on Latrobe, as well as on Cable's text.
42. While the initials, tailpieces, and mastheads were dropped for the book version, Century Company's 1893 edition of *Balcony Stories* features 16 of the 17 illustrations that were also printed in the magazine.
43. According to Arlin Turner, Redwood had come to New Orleans in May 1879, "hoping especially to illustrate Cable's stories" (*Cable* 110). While this plan did not come through, his sketching among the Acadians would eventually result in an illustrated article on "The Acadians of Louisiana," written by R.L. Daniels and accompanied by seven illustrations by Redwood, which was published in the January 1880 issue of *Scribner's*, right after the third installment of *The Grandissimes*.
44. John notes that in the early 1880s, Roswell Smith installed Fraser as "art manager" to support Alexander W. Drake, the magazine's "art superintendent":

> The division of power between these two chiefs was not explicit, but Fraser evidently handled layouts and helped Drake in negotiations with illustrators; Drake spent more time supervising the production and printing of the wood engravings that he had done so much to improve.
> (181)

45. There is no evidence that *Scribner's/Century* accepted unsolicited work or that the magazine had writers illustrate engravings (that is, had fiction or poetry commissioned to accompany pictures), a practice apparently common with American magazines in the 1840s (see Patterson 87–118).
46. This is confirmed, for instance, by a 1891 letter from Edward W. Kemble to the editors of the Atlanta *Constitution*. Defending his illustrations of Clare de Graffenried's article "The Georgia Cracker in the Cotton Mill," printed in *Century* in February 1891, against criticism from the *Constitution*, Kemble notes that:

> [a]s each story is illustrated the drawings are sent to the author with a printed slip attached requesting the criticism of the writer upon the picture and changes are made accordingly. Are we to conclude that these

intelligent writers in the midst of their material have allowed this "procession of [misrepresentations] to parade through the magazines from year to year," when a word could have "shelved" them?

(CCR I, 53)

See also Johnson 383; and Kemble, "Illustrating" 32.
47. Of course, writers commented on the illustration of their texts once they had been published. In his *Remembered Yesterdays* (1923), editor Robert Underwood Johnson quotes from a letter from Joel Chandler Harris, written in 1884:

> Mr. Frost's illustrations are inimitable. They are so true to the spirit of the text that they seem to be an echo of my own mind. . . . I have but one criticism to make and that is in the shape of a regret that Mr. F. did n't represent Mizzers Staley telling Free Joe's fortune.
>
> (383)

48. The picture can be found in King, "Southern Mountain Rambles" 17. It is reproduced, along with Champney's original sketch, in Rainey 205–206.
49. Some artists drew directly on the woodblock. With the introduction, in the late 1870s, of photoxylography, a process in which the picture was photographed directly onto the woodblock, originals no longer had to be redrawn on the woodblock by a mediating office artist (see Watrous 21; Scholnik 54; Brown 174; 298n69; Noonan, *Reading* 16–7).
50. In the book version of "The Great South," where the material is subdivided into eight chapters, this is also reflected in the chapter headings. These are: "Louisiana Past and Present"; "The French Quarter of New Orleans – The Revolution and Its Effects"; "The Carnival – The French Markets"; "The Cotton Trade – The New Orleans Levees"; "The Canals and the Lake – The American Quarter"; "On the Mississippi River – The Levée System – Railroads. The Fort St. Philip Canal"; "The Industries of Louisiana – A Sugar Plantation. The Teche Country"; and "The Political Situation in Louisiana" (see King, *Great South* ix).
51. As W. Magruder Drake and Robert R. Jones note in their introduction to the 1972 reprint of *The Great South*, the series "fully treats urbanization in the South. Nearly half of the chapters focus on southern cities and towns, and portions of other chapters deal with urban matters" (xliv).
52. Paul Buck, in *The Road to Reunion* (1937), similarly describes "The Great South" as an important tool of postwar sectional reconciliation (130–2; see also Drake and Jones xxi; and Greeson, "Expropriating" 502).
53. In *Traveling South* (2005), John Cox makes a remarkably similar argument about Frederick Law Olmsted's travel writings about the South (141–64).
54. Moreover, King's second article, "How Stanley Found Livingstone," a thinly disguised advertisement for the American edition of Stanley's book *How I Found Livingstone* (1873), published by the magazine's sister company Scribner, Armstrong & Co., appeared in the same issue of *Scribner's/Century* as the second installment of the two-part travel series "New Ways in the Old Dominion: The Chesapeake and Ohio Railroad," which does for the Virginias what "The Great South" would later do for the entire South.
55. At the very beginning of the first part of "Old and New Louisiana," King writes about the state's "unlimited . . . possibilities" (1), and in the second article, he concludes that "[c]apital can make the 'Pelican State' more powerful than Holland, and can build cities in it more beautiful than Old Venice" (156).
56. Almost certainly Creole historian Charles Gayarré, on whom King extensively relied for information (see Drake and Jones xxx).

57. According to Shannon Lee Dawdy, King and Champney tread familiar ground here. "From its early colonial days," she writes, "the city has been depicted as 'ancient'" (5; see also 31–3; 78).
58. Indeed, peeping is so omnipresent in Cable's short fictions that Alice Hall Petry has identified the "benevolent voyeur" (*Genius* 17) as a distinctive character type in these stories.
59. Several scholars, including James Robert Payne (4) and Etienne de Planchard de Cussac ("*Old Creole Days*" 115), have stressed the narrator's role as a tourist guide in Cable's stories.
60. See Railton 204. Matthew Paul Smith has recently stressed the contrast between Cable's "geographic and ethnographic precision" and his "narrative indeterminacy" (85), but my point here is to underline to what extent Cable, despite his allusive style, went beyond King.
61. A reproduction of this illustration can be found in Freitag, "Treachery" 30. For more on Albert Herter, see Freitag, "Treachery" 30–1n23.
62. This difference was not properly recognized even in Cable's own times. When Yale University awarded an honorary Master of Arts to him in 1883, it did so "with the desire of recognizing publicly the eminent success which you have achieved in embalming in literature a unique phase of American social life which *is* rapidly passing away" (qtd. in Biklé 85; emphasis added).
63. In "Jean-ah Poquelin," by contrast, both the description of Poquelin's gothic plantation house and the rest of the story (with the exception of the four paragraphs that constitute its climax; see 99–100) are in the present tense, as the building has since been removed. The description nevertheless refers to present-day New Orleans when the narrator notes that the Poquelin house was located "a short distance above what is now Canal Street" (91).
64. It is in this sense that Greeson establishes yet another parallel between King's and Cable's writings: in both, she argues, the United States appears "poised to redeem the rest of the ostensibly non-national, non-English-speaking, 'semitropical' American south from its long colonial history" ("Expropriating" 512).
65. The figures in square brackets refer to the volume and the number of the issue of *Scribner's Monthly* in which the quote appeared.
66. In addition, from the very beginning of the serialization of the novel, Cable had been paratextually identified in the header of each new installment as the "author of 'Old Creole Days.'"
67. In a December 1880 review for the *Nation*, for instance, W.C. Brownell writes:

> Everything is cleared up in due time, and you don't mind being mystified, of course, but the uncertainty is annoying; the narrator comes to have the air of caressing what he has to tell, of fondling it and letting you get glimpses of it, but retaining it long and handing it over wholly to your inspection at last with wistful regret. This shows respect for what he is engaged upon, but it is a kind of *espièglerie* that is essentially not admirable and is plainly something to be outgrown.
>
> (qtd. in Turner, *Essays* 18)

In his September 1880 review for the New Orleans *Item*, Lafcadio Hearn emphasized the parallel between the reader and Frowenfeld by using, as Cable had done, mist imagery:

> There is, therefore, a certain vagueness about the work. But it is an artistic vagueness, like the golden haze of an Indian summer softening

outlines and beautifying all it touches. The old streets seemed clouded with a summer mist.

("Grandissimes" 167)

68. By implication, *The Grandissimes* stands for the "newly found book" that Frowenfeld resolves to study. And indeed, just like the "brightly illuminated title page" of that book, the title page of the 1899 illustrated book version of *The Grandissimes* shows the Nancanous (as well as, in the background, Charlie Keene and Honoré Grandissime) at the masked ball (see 1).
69. This is perhaps much less surprising than it may appear: from the very beginning of the novel, New Orleans is described as a "hybrid city" (Cable, *Grandissimes* 101 [19.1]).
70. Indeed, the past that the Creoles are so preoccupied with is one entirely of their own making. As Agricola points out, "'h-tradition is much more authentic than history!'" (104 [19.1]).
71. Ironically, as the much-criticized ending of *The Grandissimes* indicates, Cable himself was similarly unable to imagine a just society that includes the quadroons (see, among many others, Foote 118).
72. Likewise, Honoré tells Governor Claiborne that his community is "*just* the kind" to commit suicide (380 [19.3]; emphasis original).
73. Some critics have extended this reading to Cable's short fiction, arguing that the stories, too, function as veiled allegories of the author's own time. With respect to the stories collected in "Old Creole Days" in general, see, amongst others, Egan; Hornung; Payne; and Planchard de Cussac, "*Old Creole Days*." With respect to "Jean-ah Poquelin" in particular, see Turner ("Use of the Past" 515). In contrast to *The Grandissimes*, however, the short stories contain no explicit political comments on the present.
74. The diptych may, in fact, originally have been a triptych: Arlin Turner discusses an anonymous article published in the *Times-Picayune* on 24 December 1871 which "recounts from old records the story of a white man who opened a vein in his arm and inserted the blood of a fair mulatto so that he could then legally marry her" (*Cable* 50). The "description of the scene, the turn of the language, the indirection in such phrases as 'the year eighteen hundred and something beyond,' the avowal that there is no moral" (50–1), Turner argues, all allow us to attribute the article to Cable (see also Elfenbein 30). He concludes that "A Life-Ebbing Monography," as the article is called, seems "to belong to the ancestry" of "'Tite Poulette" and "Madame Delphine" (51). For Stephens, the article represents the first "stage in [Cable's] preparation" of "Madame Delphine," later followed by "'Tite Poulette" and *The Grandissimes* ("Compromise" 82).
75. In "The Treachery of (Local) Colour," I have speculated about the impact of the order in which the stories were printed on their reception: readers, having read "Madame Delphine" first, may have perceived "'Tite Poulette" as a mere repetition, immediately assuming that like Madame Delphine, Madame John, too, lied about her having adopted the girl (29–30).
76. The figures in square brackets refer to the volume and the number of the issue of *Century* in which the quote appeared.
77. Eggleston would publish nine more articles on American colonial history in the next few years in *Century*, the last one, "Church and Meeting-House before the Revolution," appearing in April 1887.
78. "The Beginning of a Nation" came with an apologetic footnote, in which Eggleston seeks to explain the absence of references in his writing:

> It is not advisable to cumber a magazine page with multitudinous references to authorities. I regret that the exigency of the present form

prevents me from giving credit in all the cases in which I happen to be indebted to living writers, and particularly where my obligation is to the industrial special student.

(61)

No such explanatory footnote accompanied Cable's articles or *The Creoles of Louisiana*.
79. Powell sees Creole historian Charles Gayarré's writings, which Cable drew upon, as stylistically more closely related to fiction than Cable's: "the historian's history is often more novelistic than that of the novelist" (26).
80. In the book version, the Battle of New Orleans is discussed in a separate chapter that was not included in the magazine version (Cable, *Creoles* 189–202). As for the Civil War and Reconstruction, Cable wrote in the fifth article, entitled "The Great South Gate":

> By and by a cloud darkened the sky. Civil war came on. . . . Arming, marching, blockade, siege, surrender, military occupation, grass-grown streets, hungry women, darkened homes, broken hearts, – let us not write the chapter; at least, not now. The war passed. The bitter days of Reconstruction followed. They, too, must rest unrecounted. The sky is brightening again.
>
> (231)

Later, Cable partially filled these omissions with his novel *Dr. Sevier*, serialized in *Century* from November 1883 to October 1884 and partly set during and after the Civil War, as well as with his article "New Orleans before the Capture," published as part of the *Century*'s "Battles and Leaders of the Civil War" series in April 1885.
81. In the book version, the caption was changed to "Jackson Square, New Orleans, Formerly the Place d'Armes" (Cable, *Creoles* n.p.).
82. Or perhaps Latinizes, since several of Pennell's illustrations show what the captions identify as "Spanish" buildings.
83. Again, the figures in square brackets refer to the volume and the number of the issue of *Century* in which the quote appeared.
84. Erik Redling has thus described *Dr. Sevier* as "the most polygraphic novel in American literature" (196).
85. Including "Posson Jone'," which had been rejected by *Scribner's* but was included in the book version of *Old Creole Days* (see earlier).
86. Further related articles include "The Salem of Hawthorne" (also written and illustrated by Hawthorne and Fern and published in May 1884) as well as Rose G. Kingley (text) and Alfred Parsons and Homer Martin's (illustrations) "George Eliot's County," published in July 1885.
87. For a more inclusive definition of "literary tourism," see Croy.
88. Unlike "The Scenes of Cable's Romances," however, "The Scenes of Hawthorne's Romances" also discusses places associated with Nathaniel Hawthorne's life, such as his one-time home, The Wayside. In Cable's case, this would have been problematic, as the author was not only still alive, but also still living in New Orleans (he did not move permanently to New England until October 1885; see Turner, *Cable* 223). Of course, as Melanie Smith, Nicola Macleod, and Margaret Hart Robertson have pointed out, "many places are both the home of the writer and the inspiration for the work" (109).
89. Watson explains: "Tourism associated with literary countries" could be "rather strenuous because of the sheer size of the tracts of country an author could describe over the course of a whole career" (169). This certainly did not apply to Cable at this point.

90. The publication of "The Scenes of Hawthorne's Romances" in July 1884 was equally timely, coinciding as it did with the 80th anniversary of Hawthorne's birthday.
91. According to Gotham, the 1884 World's Industrial and Cotton Centennial Exposition was: "the first exposition marketed and promoted by railroads, hotels, and other industries to stimulate travel and advertise cities as exotic locales and tourist attractions" (46).
92. That the French Quarter had already become – and to a certain extent still remains – "Cable Country," is, however, undeniable. In *Life on the Mississippi* (1883), Mark Twain had asserted that "[i]n truth, I find by experience, that the untrained eye and vacant mind can inspect [this ancient quarter of New Orleans] and learn of it and judge of it more clearly and profitably in [Cable's] books than by personal contact with it" (310–11). Hearn himself had claimed in "The Scenes of Cable's Romances" that when he first arrived in New Orleans, his:

> impressions of the city . . . were oddly connected with memories of "Jean-ah Poquelin." That strange little tale had appeared in this magazine a few months previously; and its exotic picturesqueness had considerably influenced my anticipations of the Southern metropolis, and prepared me to idealize everything peculiar and semi-tropical that I might see.
>
> (40)

Hearn's memory was somewhat mistaken: according to Cott (117), Hearn had arrived in New Orleans in November 1877, but "Jean-ah Poquelin" had already been published in *Scribner's* in May 1875. Today, "Madame John's Legacy" is still listed as a "French Quarter Attraction" on the official tourism site of the city of New Orleans (see www.neworleansonline.com/directory/location.php?locationID=1268), although the website's description of the attraction does not reference Cable's short story. For more on this building, see Dawdy 48–51.

93. The *Sketch Book* was one of altogether three volumes issued by the New York publisher Will H. Coleman in 1885 to capitalize on the Cotton Centennial. Edited and compiled by "several leading writers of the New Orleans press," as the title page claims, it reprinted Hearn's *Century* essay with only minuscule alterations. Pennell's pictures were reprinted, too, although they were heavily altered and no longer directly accompanied Hearn's text but were scattered throughout the volume (Elizabeth Robins Pennell claims that the illustrations were pirated; the pictures, then, were probably altered to mask the copyright infringement; see *Life* 73–4). For more on the *Sketch Book*, see Turner, *Cable* 198; and Stevenson 143. The other two books published by Coleman were Hearn's ethnographic collections of Creole proverbs and recipes, *Gombo Zhèbes: Little Dictionary of Creole Proverbs* and *La cuisine créole: A Collection of Culinary Recipes*. According to Stevenson, none of the three books did very well commercially (144).
94. Not very surprisingly, expositions organized within the United States generally received more attention in the magazine than those hosted by foreign countries. Nevertheless, the contrast between the short notice on the Vienna Exposition published in the "Culture and Progress Abroad" section in March 1872 and the huge number of articles about the Chicago fair printed from March 1892 through July 1894 is revealing.
95. According to Smalley, then, already the 1884 Exposition constituted a "perfect city" (Gilbert).

96. On the exposition's countless organizational and other difficulties, see, for instance, T.R. Smith 145–7.
97. Only two of the illustrations that accompanied the two articles do not focus on people (namely, the decorated initial for "The New Orleans Exposition," which shows the Main Building, and the picture of the Horticultural Hall; see "New Orleans" 3; 4), and these were not drawn by Kemble, but by staff artist E.J. Meeker.
98. Presumably on the exposition grounds; in his first article, Smalley had praised the grounds with their "groups and avenues of stately, wide-spreading live oaks hung with a profusion of the trailing gray tree-moss" ("New Orleans" 13).
99. The tour had started on 5 November 1884, in New Haven, Connecticut, and would eventually conclude in Washington, DC, on 28 February 1885. For a complete tour schedule, see http://twain.lib.virginia.edu/huckfinn/tourschd.html.
100. In his February 1882 profile of Cable in the *Century* (see earlier), George E. Waring had already commented on Cable's talent for singing "curious old slave songs" (604).
101. For a representative sample program from 1885, see http://twain.lib.virginia.edu/huckfinn/hfprogrm.html.
102. In the magazine version of *The Grandissimes*, the music of "Dé Zabs" was erroneously printed with the lyrics of a different song (see 846 [19.6]); this mistake was corrected in the book versions.
103. Similarly, in "Creole Slave Songs," Cable switches into the present tense to give readers the impression of being eyewitnesses to a voodoo dance:

> Presently the ceremonies become more forbidding. They are taking a horrid oath, smearing their lips with blood of some slaughtered animal, and swearing to suffer death rather than disclose any secret of the order, and to inflict death on any who may commit such treason. Now a new applicant for membership steps into their circle, there are a few trivial formalities, and the Voodoo dance begins.
>
> (818)

Here, too, Kemble's full-page illustration of the dance, signed "Kemble 85" (816), supports this impression.
104. Wagner refers, of course, to Cable's reassembling of the various sources he used for his two articles, but the same applies to the author's account of the "survival" of the music.
105. Later, Raoul even performs a duet with Clemence (see 703 [20.5]). The other songs are sung by Don José Martinez's overseer (also white; see 856 [19.6]), Clemence (see 380 [19.3]; 583 [19.4]; and 384 [20.3]), and Bras-Coupé (see 852 [19.6]).
106. In *Folklore Recycled*, Frank De Caro writes that in contemporary society, "folklore is not experienced in its usual performative contexts but through some sort of recycling: as literature and elite art, in special performance venues, as tourist symbols, elite decorative objects, or nationalistic propaganda" (4). De Caro's definition of "folklorism" as referring to "the 'life' folklore has beyond folk contexts" (4) triply applies to Cable's essays, which, first, discuss the folkloristic "life" of the Creole songs in white Creole circles, second, put the songs into the context of a popular national magazine, and, third, promote the performance of these songs in the homes of the periodical's readers.
107. In September 1889 and in April 1890, *Century* additionally published two "Open Letters" by Cable in which he responds to the doubts some

118   *Scribner's Illustrated New Orleans*

readers had expressed about the tales' authenticity (see Cable, "Open Letters: Strange True Stories" and "Open Letters: The White League"). These letters were not reprinted in the book version, although Cable did add footnotes to some of the contested passages.

108. In addition, there are also intertextual connections between the individual stories themselves; see, for instance, Cable, "'Haunted House'" 593; or Robinson 106.
109. The pastifying of the French Quarter can, of course, be read as an intertextual connection between "The 'Haunted House'" and virtually all the other texts that comprise "Scribner's Illustrated New Orleans," but the explicit contrast established here between the old French part and the modern rest of the city also and specifically recalls Cable's "Cajun" trilogy, which has not been discussed here since only the last chapters of the third part, "Au Large" (serialized from November 1887 through March 1888), are set in New Orleans. In one of these chapters, however, a character called Mr. Tarbox tells his two friends:

> I'll be with you day after to-morrow. You can't be ready for me before then, and you and your father can take Sunday to look around and kind o' see the city [New Orleans]. But don't go into the down-town part; you'll not like it; nothing but narrow streets and old buildings with histories to 'em, and gardens hid away inside of 'em, and damp archways, and pagan-looking females, who can't talk English, peeping out over balconies that offer to drop down on you and then don't keep their word; everything old-timey, and Frenchy, and Spanishy; unprogressive – you would n't like it. Go uptown. That's American. It's new and fresh. There you'll find beautiful mansions; mostly frame, it's true, but made to look like stone, you know. There you'll see wealth! There you'll get the broad daylight – "the merry, merry sunshine, that makes the heart so gay"; see?
>
> (348 [35.3])

110. Indeed, the "Strange True Stories of Louisiana" would remain Cable's last New Orleans-related publication in the magazine until August 1901, when *Century* printed "Père Raphaël," a companion story to "Posson Jone'" (which had not even been published in *Scribner's/Century*, but in *Appleton's Journal* in April 1876). By then, however, *Century* – and, in a way, Cable, too – were long past their zenith. In between, the only other Cable feature in the magazine was "The Gentler Side of Two Great Southerners" (published in December 1893), which relates two anecdotes about Robert E. Lee and Stonewall Jackson. See also ahead.
111. On several occasions, for instance, the narrator makes a statement that clearly violates his self-imposed mission of "dealing with plain fact and history" and then backpedals immediately, calling himself to order: "The moral of the two stories – if you care to consider it – is the same: . . . . However, morals can wait" (593).
112. According to Taylor, King wrote "The Balcony" at the request of Gilder, who thought that some of the stories were "perhaps too strong meat . . . for public ears" (Gilder qtd. in Taylor 66). Somewhat ironically, in 1905, King, together with John R. Ficklen, published a school textbook entitled *Stories from Louisiana History*, which, as the preface of that book proclaims, features stories that "are true in every particular. Not a single detail has been introduced from the realm of fiction" (n.p.).
113. Especially early critics relate this to King's biography: Robert Bush, for instance, notes that as "a member of a disfranchised patrician family [King]

was most conscious of how defeat in war had created the topsy-turvy world of Reconstruction in which most of the established values and standards of society had been overturned" ("Introduction" 4).
114. Robert Bush has suggested that the character of the General is modeled upon King's mentor and friend, the Creole historian Charles Gayarré (see, for instance, *King* 144).
115. It is these vague references that, according Douglas J. McReynolds, make the "Balcony Stories" also relatable to male readers: "by couching stories of passion and repressed sexuality in racial and Civil War terms, King begins to open the female experience to that portion of the reading public which would otherwise find it inscrutable" (216).
116. This universalization is confirmed by the growing diversification of the French Louisianian cast in the later stories: whereas the first three texts concentrate on New Orleans Creoles, the later pieces also feature poor Acadians ("The Story of a Day") and Gascons ("Anne Marie and Jeanne Marie") as well as quadroons ("The Little Convent Girl") and African Americans ("A Crippled Hope").
117. As McClure writes in his autobiography (serialized in his own magazine and actually written by Willa Cather), at the time "a connection with the *Century Magazine* was the uttermost limit of my ambition" (84). Nevertheless, he only stayed a few months at either company, and in October 1884 founded his newspaper syndicate service (87).
118. As has already been pointed out, Frank Luther Mott speaks of the "ten-cent magazine revolution" (Mott, *History 4* Vol. 4 (recte) 46).
119. Cable kept sending manuscripts to *Century*'s offices, though. In a letter to Gilder from 10 March 1906, he thanked the editor-in-chief for returning an obviously rejected story, commenting self-deprecatingly that he wishes his "critical faculties were not so slow to see things which they see so clearly after it is too late" (CCR I, 14). People at *Century* had not completely forgotten him either: in a letter to then editor-in-chief Robert Underwood Johnson from 5 January 1911, the magazine's long-time art superintendent, Alexander W. Drake, suggested an illustration showing "little George Cable in a high-chair, reading one of his stories" (CCR I, 28).
120. In the first issue of *Scribner's*, the table of contents merely lists the names of contributing authors; in the magazine itself, texts and illustrations are published "anonymously." A decade later, both authors and illustrators are identified in the table of contents, but in the magazine, texts and pictures generally remain nameless. By 1893, however, the *Century* printed the names of writers, illustrators, and even engravers along with their respective contributions (see also Tassin 293; Johnson 87–8; and John 147). Interestingly, Gilder apparently did not consider the naming of (well-known) contributors essential to the magazine: in a letter to Maurice Thompson from 1886, he writes:

> What makes a magazine "go" in a business and moneyed point of view, is not the individual writers . . . . I would guarantee to start a magazine next year and make it a success without the use of a single well-known name in literature – simply by the combination – if I had the right kind of publishers.
>
> (qtd. in Gilder, *Letters* 395)

Gilder's view had not kept him from publishing, in the first issue of the new *Century* five years earlier, Mark Twain's "A Curious Experiment" along with the writer's name, whereas all the other features in this issue remained anonymous. Twain's name must have been too well known and, hence, too valuable for the magazine to be merely hidden in the table of contents.

121. The February 1953 issue of *National Geographic* had indeed featured an illustrated article about "New Orleans: Jambalaya on the Levee" by Harnett T. Kane and Justin Locke. In the photograph of Ryman, the copy is turned to pp. 154–5 of that article. The photograph of Ryman, then, intends to tell readers at least as much about the "magic worlds of Disney" and how they are created as about the magazine in which it was published, as it stresses *National Geographic*'s role as an important research tool, an easily accessible source of rare information. In fact, to further emphasize the documentary role of the magazine, *National Geographic* combined the picture of Ryman with one of Walt Disney in his studio library. The caption reads: "'A truly invaluable research tool,' Disney calls the *National Geographic*. 'We use it all the time.' Here he pulls out an issue in the studio library and from it gleans information on period costumes needed in a forthcoming film" (De Roos 174).

Bibliography

Abrahamson, David, ed. *The American Magazine: Research Perspectives and Prospects*. Ames: Iowa State UP, 1995. Print.

Ammons, Elizabeth, and Valerie Rohy, eds. *American Local Color Writing, 1880–1920*. New York: Penguin, 1998. Print.

Arthur, Jason. *Violet America: Regional Cosmopolitanism in U.S. Fiction since the Great Depression*. Iowa City: U of Iowa P, 2013. Print.

Assmann, Aleida. *Zeit und Tradition: Kulturelle Strategien der Dauer*. Cologne: Böhlau, 1999. Print.

Bakhtin, Mikhail. "Forms of Time and of the Chronotope in the Novel: Notes toward a Historical Poetics." *The Dialogic Imagination: Four Essays*. Ed. Michael Holmquist. Trans. Caryl Emerson and Michael Holmquist. Austin: U of Texas P, 1981. 84–258. Print.

Benjamin, Walter. "On Some Motifs in Baudelaire." *Illuminations: Essays and Reflections*. Ed. Hannah Arendt. Trans. Harry Zohn. New York: Schocken, 2007. 155–200. Print.

Best, James J. *American Popular Illustration*. Westport, CT: Greenwood, 1984. Print.

Biklé, Lucy Leffingwell Cable. *George W. Cable: His Life and Letters*. New York: Charles Scribner's Sons, 1928. Print.

Bisland, Elizabeth. *The Life and Letters of Lafcadio Hearn*. Vol. 1. Boston: Houghton, Mifflin, 1906. Print.

Boyesen, Hjalmar Hjorth. "Cable's 'Grandissimes'." *Scribner's Monthly* 21.1 (November 1880): 159–61. Print.

Braddock, Alan C. *Thomas Eakins and the Cultures of Modernity*. Berkeley: U of California P, 2009. Print.

Bramen, Carrie Tirado. *The Uses of Variety: Modern Americanism and the Quest for National Distinctiveness*. Cambridge, MA: Harvard UP, 2000. Print.

Briden, Earl F. "Kemble's 'Specialty' and the Pictorial Countertext of *Huckleberry Finn*." *Mark Twain Journal* 26.2 (1988): 2–14. Print.

Brodhead, Richard. *Cultures of Letters: Scenes of Reading and Writing in Nineteenth-Century America*. Chicago: U of Chicago P, 1993. Print.

———. "Literature and Culture." *Columbia Literary History of the United States*. Ed. Emory Elliott. New York: Columbia UP, 1988. 467–81. Print.

Brosman, Catharine Savage. *Louisiana Creole Literature: A Historical Study*. Jackson: UP of Mississippi, 2013. Print.

Brown, Joshua. *Beyond the Lines: Pictorial Reporting, Everyday Life, and the Crisis of Gilded Age America*. Berkeley: U of California P, 2002. Print.

Buck, Paul. *The Road to Reunion 1865–1900*. Boston: Little, Brown and Company, 1937. Print.

Bush, Robert. *Grace King: A Southern Destiny*. Baton Rouge: Louisiana State UP, 1983. Print.

———. "Introduction." *Grace King of New Orleans: A Selection of Her Writings*. Baton Rouge: Louisiana State UP, 1973. 3–31. Print.

Butcher, Philip. *George W. Cable*. New York: Twayne, 1962. Print.

Cable, George Washington. "1888: How I Got Them." *Century* 37.1 (November 1888): 110–14. Print.

———. "Au Large." *Century* 35.1 (November 1887)–35.5 (March 1888). Print.

———. "Battles and Leaders of the Civil War: New Orleans before the Capture." *Century* 29.6 (April 1885). 918–22. Print.

———. "Belles Demoiselles Plantation." *Scribner's Monthly* 7.6 (April 1874): 739–47. Print.

———. *Bonaventure*. New York: Charles Scribner's Sons, 1888. Print.

———. "Café des Exilés." *Scribner's Monthly* 11.5 (March 1876): 727–36. Print.

———. "The Convict Lease System." *Century* 27.4 (February 1884): 582–99. Print.

———. "Creole Slave Dances: The Dance in Place Congo." *Century* 31.4 (February 1886): 517–32. Print.

———. "Creole Slave Songs." *Century* 31.6 (April 1886): 807–28. Print.

———. *The Creoles of Louisiana*. New York: Charles Scribner's Sons, 1884. Print.

———. *Dr. Sevier*. *Century* 27.1 (November 1883)–28.6 (October 1884). Print.

———. "The End of Foreign Dominion in Louisiana." *Century* 25.5 (March 1883): 643–54. Print.

———. "The Freedman's Case in Equity." *Century* 29.3 (January 1885): 409–18. Print.

———. *The Grandissimes: A Story of Creole Life*. *Scribner's Monthly* 19.1 (November 1879)–20.6 (October 1880). Print.

———. *The Grandissimes: With Illustrations by Albert Herter*. New York: Charles Scribner's Sons, 1899. Print.

———. "The Great South Gate." *Century* 26.2 (June 1883): 217–32. Print.

———. "The 'Haunted House' in Royal Street." *Century* 38.4 (August 1889): 590–601. Print.

———. "Jean-ah Poquelin." *Scribner's Monthly* 10.1 (May 1875): 91–100. Print.

———. "Madame Délicieuse." *Scribner's Monthly* 10.4 (August 1875): 498–508. Print.

———. "Madame Delphine." *Century* 22.1 (May 1881)–22.3 (July 1881). Print.

———. "My Politics." *The Negro Question: A Selection of Writings on Civil Rights in the South*. Ed. Arlin Turner. New York: Norton, 1958 [1888]. 1–25. Print.

———. *Old Creole Days*. New York: Charles Scribner's Sons, 1879. Print.

———. *Old Creole Days*. New York: Charles Scribner's Sons, 1883. Print.

———. *Old Creole Days: With Illustrations by Albert Herter*. New York: Charles Scribner's Sons, 1897. Print.

———. "Open Letters: Strange True Stories of Louisiana." *Century* 38.5 (September 1889): 798–99. Print.

———. "Open Letters: The White League of New Orleans." *Century* 39.6 (April 1890): 958–59. Print.

———. "Plotters and Pirates of Louisiana." *Century* 25.6 (April 1883): 852–67. Print.

———. "Preface." *Madame Delphine*, by George Washington Cable. New York: Charles Scribner's Sons, 1896. v–viii. Print.

———. "'Sieur George: A Story of New Orleans." *Scribner's Monthly* 6.6 (October 1873): 739–45. Print.

———. "The Silent South." *Century* 30.5 (September 1885): 674–91. Print.

———. *Strange True Stories of Louisiana*. New York: Charles Scribner's Sons, 1889. Print.

———. "'Tite Poulette." *Scribner's Monthly* 8.6 (October 1874): 674–84. Print.

———. "Who Are the Creoles?" *Century* 25.3 (January 1883): 384–98. Print.

Century Company. *Century Company Records*. New York Public Library MssCol504.

Chopin, Kate. *The Complete Works of Kate Chopin*. Ed. Per Seyersted. 2 vols. Baton Rouge: Louisiana State UP, 1969. Print.

Clark, William Bedford. "Cable and the Theme of Miscegenation in *Old Creole Days* and *The Grandissimes*." *Mississippi Quarterly* 30.4 (1977): 597–610. Print.

Cleman, John. "The Art of Local Color in George W. Cable's *The Grandissimes*." *American Literature* 47.3 (1975): 396–410. Print.

———. *George Washington Cable Revisited*. New York: Twayne, 1996. Print.

Congress. "Act of Congress Creating the World's Industrial and Cotton Centennial Exposition." *Library of Congress* (N.D.). www.loc.gov/resource/rbpe.2070190c/. Web.

Cooke, Simon. *Illustrated Periodicals of the 1860s: Contexts and Collaborations*. New Castle: Oak Knoll, 2010. Print.

Cordell, Ryan. "Reprinting, Circulation, and the Network Author in Antebellum Newspapers." *American Literary History* 27.3 (Fall 2015): 417–45. Print.

———. "What Has the Digital Meant to American Periodicals Scholarship?" *American Periodicals* 26.1 (2016): 2–7. Print.

Cott, Jonathan. *Wandering Ghost: The Odyssey of Lafcadio Hearn*. New York: Knopf, 1991. Print.

Cowan, William Tynes. *The Slave in the Swamp: Disrupting the Plantation Narrative*. New York: Routledge, 2013. Print.

Cox, John D. *Traveling South: Travel Narratives and the Construction of American Identity*. Athens: U of Georgia P, 2005. Print.

Croy, Glen. "Literary Tourism." *Tourism: The Key Concepts*. Ed. Peter Robinson. London: Routledge, 2012. 119–21. Print.

Cyganowski, Carol Klimick. *Magazine Editors and Professional Authors in Nineteenth-Century America*. New York: Garland, 1988. Print.

Daigle, Jonathan. "The Social Gospel in Evolutionary Time: George Washington Cable's 'Perhaps Unwise Love'." *ESQ: A Journal of the American Renaissance* 59.1 (2013): 1–47. Print.

Daniels, R.L. "The Acadians of Louisiana." *Scribner's Monthly* 19.3 (January 1880): 383–92. Print.

David, Beverly R. *Mark Twain and His Illustrators*. Vol. 1: 1869–1875. Troy: Whitston, 1986. Print.

Davis, Rebecca Harding. "Here and There in the South: III. Along the Gulf." *Harper's New Monthly Magazine* 75.448 (September 1887): 593–605. Print.

Dawdy, Shannon Lee. *Patina: A Profane Archaeology*. Chicago: The U of Chicago P, 2016. Print.

De Caro, Frank. *Folklore Recycled: Old Traditions in New Context*. Jackson: UP of Mississippi, 2013. Print.

De Roos, Robert. "The Magic Worlds of Disney." *National Geographic* 124.2 (August 1963): 159–207. Print.

DiCenzo, Maria. "Remediating the Past: Doing 'Periodical Studies' in the Digital Era." *ESC* 41.1 (March 2015): 19–39. Print.

Drake, W. Magruder, and Robert R. Jones. "Editors' Introduction." *The Great South*, by Edward King. Ed. W. Magruder Drake and Robert R. Jones. Baton Rouge: Louisiana State UP, 1972. xxi–lxii. Print.

Egan, Joseph J. "'Jean-ah Poquelin': George Washington Cable as Social Critic and Mythic Artist." *Markham Review* 2.3 (1970): N.P. Print.

Eggleston, Edward. "The Beginning of a Nation." *Century* 25.1 (November 1882): 61–83. Print.

Ekström, Kjell. *George Washington Cable: A Study of His Early Life and Work*. New York: Haskell, 1966. Print.

Elfenbein, Anna Shannon. *Women on the Color Line: Evolving Stereotypes and the Writings of George Washington Cable, Grace King, Kate Chopin*. Charlottesville: UP of Virginia, 1989. Print.

Elliott, Michael A. *The Culture Concept: Writing and Difference in the Age of Realism*. Minneapolis: U of Minnesota P, 2002. Print.

Endres, Kathleen L. "Methodological Issues: Interdisciplinarity Is the Key." *The Routledge Handbook of Magazine Research: The Future of the Form*. Ed. David Abrahamson and Marcia R. Prior-Miller. New York: Routledge, 2016. 51–64. Print.

Epstein, Dena J. *Sinful Tunes and Spirituals: Black Folk Music to the Civil War*. Urbana: U of Illinois P, 1977. Print.

Evans, Brad. *Before Cultures: The Ethnographic Imagination in American Literature, 1865–1920*. Chicago: U of Chicago P, 2005. Print.

Evans, William. "French-English Literary Dialect in *The Grandissimes*." *American Speech* 46.3–4 (1971): 210–22. Print.

Ewell, Barbara C., Pamela Glenn Menke, and Andrea Humphrey, eds. *Southern Local Color: Stories of Region, Race, and Gender*. Athens: U of Georgia P, 2002. Print.

Fagg, John, Matthew Pethers, and Robin Vandome. "Introduction: Networks and the Nineteenth-Century Periodical." *American Periodicals* 23.2 (2013): 93–104. Print.

Fahs, Alice. "Northern and Southern Worlds of Print." *Perspectives on American Book History: Artifacts and Commentary*. Ed. Scott E. Casper, Joanne D. Chaison, and Jeffrey Groves. Amherst: U of Massachusetts P, 2002. 195–222. Print.

Falvey, Kate. "'The Structures or Ruins of Life': Gothic Dislocation and Woman-Made Community in Grace King's *Balcony Stories*." *Narratives of Community: Women's Short Story Sequences*. Ed. Roxanne Harde. Newcastle: Cambridge Scholars, 2007. 196–216. Print.

Fertel, Rien. *Imagining the Creole City: The Rise of Literary Culture in Nineteenth-Century New Orleans*. Baton Rouge: Louisiana State UP, 2014. Print.

Fetterley, Judith, and Marjorie Pryse. *Writing Out of Place: Regionalism, Women, and American Literary Culture*. Urbana: U of Illinois P, 2003. Print.

Fick, Thomas H., and Eva Gold. "The Mulatto in *The Grandissimes*: Category Crisis and Crisis of Category." *Xavier Review* 21.1 (2001): 68–86. Print.

Ficklen, John R., and Grace E. King. *Stories from Louisiana History*. New Orleans: Graham, 1905. Print.

Foote, Stephanie. *Regional Fictions: Culture and Identity in Nineteenth-Century American Literature*. Madison: U of Wisconsin P, 2001. Print.

Foster, Travis M. "How to Read: Regionalism and the *Ladies' Home Journal*." *The Oxford Handbook of Nineteenth-Century American Literature*. Ed. Russ Castronovo. New York: Oxford UP, 2012. 292–308. Print.

Franchot, Jenny. "Unseemly Commemoration: Religion, Fragments, and the Icon." *American Literary History* 9.3 (1997): 502–21. Print.

Freitag, Florian. "Rencontres Américaines: Encounters between Anglo-Americans and French Americans in Kate Chopin's Short Stories." *Amerikastudien/American Studies* 58.3 (2013): 409–26. Print.

———. "Scribner's Illustrated New Orleans: Convergence Culture and Periodical Culture in Late 19th-Century America." *Convergence Culture Revisited*. Ed. Claudia Georgi and Brigitte Glaser. Göttingen: Universitätsverlag Göttingen, 2015. 95–110. Print.

———. "The Treachery of (Local) Colour: Representations of Skin in Illustrated Louisiana Local Colour Stories." *Probing the Skin: Cultural Representations of Our Contact Zone*. Ed. Caroline Rosenthal and Dirk Vanderbeke. Newcastle upon Tyne: Cambridge Scholars, 2015. 12–39. Print.

Gabler-Hover, Janet. "The North-South Reconciliation Theme and the 'Shadow of the Negro' in *Century Illustrated Magazine*." *Periodical Literature in Nineteenth-Century America*. Ed. Kenneth M. Price and Susan Belasco Smith. Charlottesville: UP of Virginia, 1995. 239–56. Print.

Garvey, Ellen Gruber. *The Adman in the Parlor: Magazines and the Gendering of Consumer Culture, 1880s to 1910s*. New York: Oxford UP, 1996. Print.

Gilder, Richard Watson. *The Letters of Richard Watson Gilder*. Ed. Rosamond Gilder. Boston: Houghton Mifflin, 1916. Print.

———. "The Nationalizing of Southern Literature. Part II – After the War." *The Christian Advocate* (10 July 1890): 441–42. Print.

Gladden, Washington. "Roswell Smith: Biographical Sketch." *Century* 44.2 (1892): 310–13. Print.

Gotham, Kevin Fox. *Authentic New Orleans: Tourism, Culture, and Race in the Big Easy*. New York: New York UP, 2007. Print.

Green, Archie. "Graphics 45: The Great South." *JEMF Quarterly* 14 (1978): 80–85. Print.

Greeson, Jennifer Rae. "Expropriating *The Great South* and Exporting 'Local Color': Global and Hemispheric Imaginaries of the First Reconstruction." *American Literary History* 18.3 (2006): 496–520. Print.

———. *Our South: Geographic Fantasy and the Rise of National Literature*. Cambridge, MA: Harvard UP, 2010. Print.

Hanrahan, Heidi M. "Grace King's *Balcony Stories* as a Narrative of Community." *Narratives of Community: Women's Short Story Sequences*. Ed. Roxanne Harde. Newcastle upon Tyne: Cambridge Scholars, 2007. 218–40. Print.

Hardwig, Bill. *Upon Provincialism: Southern Literature and National Periodical Culture, 1870–1900*. Charlottesville: U of Virginia P, 2013. Print.
Hawthorne, Julian. "The Scenes of Hawthorne's Romances." *Century* 28.3 (July 1884): 380–97. Print.
Hearn, Lafcadio. "The Grandissimes." *The Writings of Lafcadio Hearn*. Vol. 1. Boston: Houghton Mifflin, 1922 [1880]. 166–70. Print.
———. "The Scenes of Cable's Romances." *Century* 27.1 (November 1883): 40–47. Print.
Heimbuch, Jeff. *Main Street Windows: A Complete Guide to Disney's Whimsical Tributes*. N.P.: Orchard Hill, 2014. Print.
Hochman, Brian. "Hearing Lost, Hearing Found: George Washington Cable and the Phono-Ethnographic Ear." *American Literature* 82.3 (2010): 519–51. Print.
Hornung, Alfred. "George Washington Cable's Literary Reconstruction: Creole Civilization and Cultural Change." *Creoles and Cajuns: French Louisiana – La Louisiane française*. Ed. Wolfgang Binder. Frankfurt: Lang, 1998. 229–46. Print.
Howells, William Dean. *A Hazard of New Fortunes*. New York: Oxford UP, 1990 [1890]. Print.
Jenkins, Henry. *Convergence Culture: Where Old and New Media Collide*. New York: New York UP, 2006. Print.
Johanningsmeier, Charles. *Fiction and the American Literary Marketplace: The Role of Newspaper Syndicates, 1860–1900*. New York: Cambridge UP, 1997. Print.
———. "Understanding Readers of Fiction in American Periodicals, 1880–1914." *The Oxford History of Popular Print Culture*. Vol. 6: US Popular Print Culture 1860–1920. Ed. Christine Bold. Oxford: Oxford UP, 2012. 591–609. Print.
John, Arthur. *The Best Years of* The Century: *Richard Watson Gilder*, Scribner's Monthly, *and* Century Magazine, *1870–1909*. Urbana: U of Illinois P, 1981. Print.
Johnson, Robert Underwood. *Remembered Yesterdays*. Boston: Little, Brown, 1923. Print.
Johnson, Sammye, and Patricia Prijatel. *The Magazine from Cover to Cover*. New York: Oxford UP, 2007. Print.
Jones, Anne Goodwyn. *Tomorrow is Another Day: The Woman Writer in the South, 1859–1936*. Baton Rouge: Louisiana State UP, 1981. Print.
Jones, Gavin. *Strange Talk: The Politics of Dialect Literature in Gilded Age America*. Berkeley: U of California P, 1999. Print.
Jussim, Estelle. *Visual Communication and the Graphic Arts: Photographic Technologies in the Nineteenth Century*. New York: Bowker, 1983. Print.
Kane, Harnett T., and Justin Locke. "New Orleans: Jambalaya on the Levee." *National Geographic* 103.2 (February 1953): 143–84. Print.
Kemble, Edward W. "At the New Orleans Exposition: Extremes Meet." *Century* 30.1 (May 1885): 175. Print.
———. "Illustrating Huckleberry Finn." *American Studies Journal* 40 (1997 [1930]): 30–34. Print.
King, Edward. *The Great South: A Record of Journeys in Louisiana, Texas, the Indian Territory, Missouri, Arkansas, Mississippi, Alabama, Georgia, Florida, South Carolina, North Carolina, Kentucky, Tennessee, Virginia and Maryland. By Edward King, Author of "My Paris," with Illustrations from Sketches by J. Wells Champney*. Ed. W. Magruder Drake and Robert R. Jones. Baton Rouge: Louisiana State UP, 1972 [1875]. Print.

———. *My Paris: French Character Sketches*. Boston: Loring, 1868. Print.
———. "The New Route to the Gulf." *Scribner's Monthly* 6.3 (July 1873): 257–88. Print.
———. "Old and New Louisiana." *Scribner's Monthly* 7.1 (November 1873): 1–32. Print.
———. "Old and New Louisiana – II." *Scribner's Monthly* 7.2 (December 1873): 129–60. Print.
———. "Southern Mountain Rambles: In Tennessee, Georgia and South Carolina." *Scribner's Monthly* 8.1 (May 1874): 5–33. Print.
King, Grace Elizabeth. "Anne Marie and Jeanne Marie." *Century* 46.3 (July 1893): 372–74. Print.
———. "The Balcony." *Century* 45.2 (December 1892): 279–80. Print.
———. *Balcony Stories*. New York: Century, 1893. Print.
———. "A Crippled Hope." *Century* 46.3 (July 1893): 374–79. Print.
———. "A Delicate Affair." *Century* 46.6 (October 1893): 884–89. Print.
———. "A Drama of Three." *Century* 45.2 (December 1892): 280–82. Print.
———. "Grandmother's Grandmother." *Century* 46.5 (September 1893): 722–24. Print.
———. "La Grande Demoiselle." *Century* 45.3 (January 1893): 323–27. Print.
———. "The Little Convent Girl." *Century* 46.4 (August 1893): 547–51. Print.
———. *Memories of a Southern Woman of Letters*. Freeport, NY: Books for Libraries, 1971 [1932]. Print.
———. "Mimi's Marriage." *Century* 45.4 (February 1893): 493–97. Print.
———. "Monsieur Motte." *New Princeton Review* 1 (January 1886): 91–133. Print.
———. "The Old Lady's Restoration." *Century* 46.5 (September 1893): 724–27. Print.
———. "One of Us." *Century* 46.4 (August 1893): 544–46. Print.
———. "Pupasse." *Century* 46.6 (October 1893): 889–94. Print.
———. "The Story of a Day." *Century* 46.2 (June 1893): 230–35. Print.
———. *To Find My Own Peace: Grace King in Her Journals, 1886–1910*. Ed. Melissa W. Heidari. Athens: U of Georgia P, 2004. Print.
Klopfer, Nadine. *Die Balkone von New Orleans: Städtischer Raum und lokale Identität um 1900*. Bielefeld: Transcript, 2013. Print.
Kreyling, Michael. "After the War: Romance and the Reconstruction of Southern Literature." *Southern Literature in Transition: Heritage and Promise*. Ed. Philip Castille and William Osborne. Memphis: Memphis State UP, 1983. 111–25. Print.
Kuilan, Susie Scifres. "The 'All-Seeing Eye' in Grace King's *Balcony Stories*." *Songs of the Reconstructing South: Building Literary Louisiana, 1865–1945*. Ed. Suzanne Disheroon-Green and Lisa Abney. Westport: Greenwood, 2002. 99–108. Print.
Latham, Sean, and Robert Scholes. "The Rise of Periodical Studies." *PMLA* 121.2 (March 2006): 517–31. Print.
Lee, Judith Yaross. "From the Field: The Future of *American Periodicals* and American Periodicals Research." *American Periodicals* 15.2 (2005): 196–201. Print.
Lowe, Hilary Iris. *Mark Twain's Homes and Literary Tourism*. Columbia: U of Missouri P, 2012. Print.

Lowe, John. *Calypso Magnolia: The Crosscurrents of Caribbean and Southern Literature*. Chapel Hill: U of North Carolina P, 2016. Print.

Lund, Michael. *America's Continuing Story: An Introduction to Serial Fiction, 1850–1900*. Detroit: Wayne State UP, 1993. Print.

Lutz, Tom. *Cosmopolitan Vistas: American Regionalism and Literary Value*. Ithaca, NY: Cornell UP, 2004. Print.

Makdisi, Ussama. "Ottoman Orientalism." *The American Historical Review* 107.3 (2002): 768–96. Print.

Martin, Jr., Francis. "E.W. Kemble." *American Book & Magazine Illustrators to 1920*. Ed. Donald Dyal, Catherine A. Hastedt, and Steven E. Smith. Detroit: Gale Research, 1998. 182–90. Print.

———. "To Ignore Is to Deny: E.W. Kemble's Racial Caricature as Popular Art." *The Journal of Popular Culture* 40.4 (2007): 655–82. Print.

McClure, S.S. [Willa Cather]. "My Autobiography." *McClure's Magazine* 42.4 (February 1914): 76–87. Print.

McCullough, Kate. *Regions of Identity: The Construction of America in Women's Fiction, 1885–1914*. Stanford: Stanford UP, 1999. Print.

McGann, Jerome. *The Textual Condition*. Princeton: Princeton UP, 1991. Print.

McReynolds, Douglas J. "Passion Repressed: The Short Fiction of Grace King." *Rocky Mountain Review of Language and Literature* 37.4 (1983): 207–16. Print.

Meyer, Susan E. *America's Great Illustrators*. New York: Abrams, 1978. Print.

Mitchell, W.J.T. *Picture Theory: Essays on Verbal and Visual Representation*. Chicago: U of Chicago P, 1994. Print.

Mott, Frank Luther. *A History of American Magazines*. Vol. 1: 1741–1830. Cambridge, MA: Harvard UP, 1957 [1930]. Print.

Mott, Frank Luther. *A History of American Magazines*. Vol. 4: 1885–1905. Cambridge, MA: Harvard UP, 1957. Print.

Mussell, James. *The Nineteenth-Century Press in the Digital Age*. London: Palgrave Macmillan, 2012. Print.

N.N. "Topics of the Time: 'The Great South' Series of Papers." *Scribner's Monthly* 9.2 (December 1874): 248–49. Print.

N.N. "Topics of the Time: Southern Literature." *Scribner's Monthly* 22.5 (September 1881): 785–86. Print.

Nagel, James. *Race and Culture in New Orleans Stories: Kate Chopin, Grace King, Alice Dunbar-Nelson, and George Washington Cable*. Tuscaloosa: U of Alabama P, 2013. Print.

Noonan, Mark J. *Reading the* Century Illustrated Monthly Magazine: *American Literature and Culture, 1870–1893*. Kent: Kent State UP, 2010. Print.

———. "Review: *Upon Provincialism: Southern Literature and National Periodical Culture, 1870–1900.*" *American Periodicals* 24.1 (2014): 100–02. Print.

Ohmann, Richard. "Diverging Paths: Books and Magazines in the Transition to Corporate Capitalism." *A History of the Book in America*. Ed. Carl F. Kaestle and Janice A. Radway. Chapel Hill: U of North Carolina P, 2009. 102–15. Print.

———. *Selling Culture: Magazines, Markets, and Class at the Turn of the Century*. London: Verso, 1996. Print.

Okker, Patricia. *Social Stories: The Magazine Novel in Nineteenth-Century America*. Charlottesville: U of Virginia P, 2003. Print.

Patterson, Cynthia Lee. *Art for the Middle Classes: America's Illustrated Magazines of the 1840s*. Jackson: UP of Mississippi, 2010. Print.

Payne, James Robert. "Emergence of Alternate Masculinity in George Washington Cable's 'Sieur George' and 'Belles Demoiselles Plantation'." *American Literary Realism* 32.3 (2000): 244–55. Print.

Pennell, Elizabeth Robins. *Joseph Pennell: An Account by His Wife Elizabeth Robins Pennell Issued on the Occasion of a Memorial Exhibition of His Works*. Washington, DC: Government Printing Office, 1927. Print.

———. *The Life and Letters of Joseph Pennell: With Illustrations*. Vol. 1. Bouverie House: Ernest Benn, 1930. Print.

Pennell, Joseph. *The Adventures of an Illustrator*. Boston: Little, Brown, 1925. Print.

Petry, Alice Hall. *A Genius in His Way: The Art of Cable's 'Old Creole Days'*. Rutherford: Fairleigh Dickinson UP, 1988. Print.

———. "The Limits of Truth in Cable's 'Salome Müller'." *Papers on Language and Literature* 27.1 (1991): 20–31. Print.

Pfitzer, Gregory M. *Popular History and the Literary Marketplace 1840–1920*. Amherst: U of Massachusetts P, 2008. Print.

Philips, Deborah. *Fairground Attractions: A Genealogy of the Pleasure Ground*. London: Bloomsbury, 2012. Print.

Planchard de Cussac, Etienne de. "The 'Gothic' Strategy of G.W. Cable in *The Grandissimes*." *Caliban* 33 (1996): 137–46. Print.

———. "*Old Creole Days* de G.W. Cable ou les dessous secrets d'un mariage heureux entre la nouvelle et la couleur locale." *Nouvelles du Sud: Hearing Voices, Reading Stories*. Paris: Ecole Polytechnique, 2007. 113–22. Print.

Powell, Lawrence N. "Introduction." *The New Orleans of George Washington Cable: The 1887 Census Report*, by George W. Cable. Ed. Lawrence N. Powell. Baton Rouge: Louisiana State UP, 2008. 1–35. Print.

Pratt, Mary Louise. *Imperial Eyes: Travel Writing and Transculturation*. London: Routledge, 1992. Print.

Prettyman, Gib. "Harper's Weekly and the Spectacle of Industrialization." *American Periodicals* 11 (2001): 24–48. Print.

Price, Kenneth M., and Susan B. Smith, eds. *Periodical Literature in Nineteenth-Century America*. Charlottesville: UP of Virginia, 1995. Print.

Pugh, Griffith T. "George Washington Cable as Historian." *Writers and Their Critics: Studies in English and American Literature* 19 (1956): 29–38. Print.

Rabinovitz, Lauren. *Electric Dreamland: Amusement Parks, Movies, and American Modernity*. New York: Columbia UP, 2012. Print.

Railton, Ben. *Contesting the Past, Reconstructing the Nation: American Literature and Culture in the Gilded Age, 1876–1893*. Tuscaloosa: U of Alabama P, 2007. Print.

Rainey, Sue. "Images of the South in *Picturesque America* and *The Great South*." *Graphic Arts & the South: Proceedings of the 1990 North American Print Conference*. Ed. Judy L. Larson and Cynthia Payne. Fayetteville: U of Arkansas P, 1993. 185–215. Print.

Redling, Erik. "Mikhail Bakhtin and the Boundaries of Postmodernism: From Polyphony to Polygraphy." *Redefining Modernism and Postmodernism*. Ed. Sebnem Toplu and Hubert Zapf. Newcastle upon Tyne: Cambridge Scholars, 2010. 192–98. Print.

Reed, Walt. *The Illustrator in America, 1860–2000*. Third ed. New York: The Society of Illustrators, 2001. Print.

Roach, Joseph. *Cities of the Dead: Circum-Atlantic Performance*. New York: Columbia UP, 1996. Print.

Robinson, Owen. "Truly Strange New Orleans: The Unstable City in George Washington Cable's *Strange True Stories of Louisiana*." *European Journal of American Culture* 26.2 (2007): 97–108. Print.

Robison, Lori. "'Why, Why Do We Not Write Our Side': Gender and Southern Self-Representation in Grace King's *Balcony Stories*." *Breaking Boundaries: New Perspectives on Women's Regional Writing*. Ed. Sherrie A. Inness and Diana Royer. Iowa City: U of Iowa P, 1997. 54–71. Print.

Romine, Scott. "Literature and Reconstruction." *The Cambridge Companion to the Literature of the American South*. Ed. Sharon Monteith. Cambridge: Cambridge UP, 2013. 54–71. Print.

Rubin, Louis D. *George W. Cable: The Life and Times of a Southern Heretic*. New York: Pegasus, 1969. Print.

Said, Edward W. *Orientalism*. New York: Pantheon, 1978. Print.

Sandke, Randall. *Where the Dark and the Light Folks Meet: Race and the Mythology, Politics, and Business of Jazz*. Lanham: Scarecrow, 2010. Print.

Scholnik, Robert J. "Scribner's Monthly and 'The Pictorial Representation of Life and Truth' in Post-Civil War America." *American Periodicals* 1.1 (1991): 46–96. Print.

Schulman, Vanessa Meikle. "'Making the Magazine': Visuality, Managerial Capitalism, and the Mass Production of Periodicals, 1865–1890." *American Periodicals* 22.1 (2012): 1–28. Print.

Seyersted, Per. *Kate Chopin: A Critical Biography*. Baton Rouge: Louisiana State UP, 1969. Print.

Silber, Nina. *The Romance of Reunion: Northerners and the South, 1865–1900*. Chapel Hill: U of North Carolina P, 1993. Print.

Skilton, David. "The Relation between Illustration and Text in the Victorian Novel: A New Perspective." *Word and Visual Imagination: Studies in the Interaction of English Literature and the Visual Arts*. Ed. Karl Josef Höltgen, Peter M. Daly, and Wolfgang Lottes. Erlangen: Universitätsbund, 1988. 303–25. Print.

Smalley, Eugene V. "In and Out of the New Orleans Exposition (Second Paper)." *Century* 30.2 (June 1885): 185–99. Print.

———. "The New Orleans Exposition." *Century* 30.1 (May 1885): 3–14. Print.

Smith, Herbert F. *Richard Watson Gilder*. New York: Twayne, 1970. Print.

Smith, Herbert H. "The Metropolis of the Amazons." *Scribner's Monthly* 18.1 (May 1879): 65–77. Print.

Smith, Matthew Paul. "The Civil War's Literary Aftershocks: George Washington Cable." *New Orleans: A Literary History*. Ed. T.R. Johnson. Cambridge: Cambridge UP, 2019. 82–95. Print.

Smith, Melanie, Nicola Macleod, and Margaret Hart Robertson. "Literary Tourism." *Key Concepts in Tourist Studies*. Ed. Melanie Smith, Nicola Macleod, and Margaret Hart Robertson. Los Angeles: Sage, 2010. 108–11. Print.

Smith, Thomas Ruys. *Southern Queen: New Orleans in the Nineteenth Century*. London: Continuum, 2011. Print.

Sontag, Susan. *On Photography*. New York: Farrar, Straus and Giroux, 1977. Print.

Southern, Eileen, and Josephine Wright. *Images: Iconography of Music in African-American Culture, 1770s–1920s*. New York: Garland, 2000. Print.

Stanonis, Anthony J. *Creating the Big Easy: New Orleans and the Emergence of Modern Tourism, 1918–1945*. Athens: U of Georgia P, 2006. Print.

Starr, S. Frederick, ed. *Inventing New Orleans: Writings of Lafcadio Hearn*. Jackson: U of Mississippi P, 2001. Print.

Steiling, David. "Multi-Cultural Aesthetic in Kate Chopin's 'A Gentleman of Bayou Têche'." *Mississippi Quarterly* 47.2 (1994): 197–200. Print.

Stephens, Robert O. "Cable's Bras Coupé and Mérimée's Tamango: The Case of the Missing Arm." *Mississippi Quarterly* 35.4 (1982): 387–405. Print.

———. "Cable's Grandissime Saga." *American Literary Realism* 20.1 (1987): 3–17. Print.

———. "Cable's *Madame Delphine* and the Compromise of 1877." *Southern Literary Journal* 12.1 (1979): 79–91. Print.

Stevenson, Elizabeth. *The Grass Lark: A Study of Lafcadio Hearn*. New Brunswick: Transaction, 1999. Print.

Stowe, Harriet Beecher. *Oldtown Folks*. London: Sampson Low, Son & Marston, 1870 [1869]. Print.

Sublette, Ned. *The World That Made New Orleans: From Spanish Silver to Congo Square*. Chicago: Lawrence Hill, 2008. Print.

Sumner, David. E. *The Magazine Century: American Magazines Since 1900*. New York: Peter Lang, 2010. Print.

Swann, Charles. "*The Grandissimes*: A Story-Shaped World." *Literature and History* 13.2 (1987): 257–77. Print.

Tassin, Algernon. *The Magazine in America*. New York: Dodd, Mead, 1916. Print.

Taussig, Michael T. *The Devil and Commodity Fetishism in South America*. Chapel Hill: U of North Carolina P, 1980. Print.

Taylor, Helen. *Gender, Race, and Region in the Writings of Grace King, Ruth McEnery Stuart, and Kate Chopin*. Baton Rouge: Louisiana State UP, 1989. Print.

Tebbel, John William. *The American Magazine: A Compact History*. New York: Hawthorn, 1969. Print.

Tebbel, John William, and Mary Ellen Zuckermann. *The Magazine in America: 1741–1990*. New York: Oxford UP, 1991. Print.

Thacker, Andrew. "General Introduction: 'Magazines, Magazines, Magazines!'" *The Oxford Critical and Cultural History of Modernist Magazines*. Vol. 2: North America, 1894–1960. Ed. Peter Brooker and Andrew Thacker. Oxford: Oxford UP, 2012. 1–28. Print.

Thomas, James W. *Lyle Saxon: A Critical Biography*. Birmingham, AL: Summa, 1991. Print.

Tichenor, Irene. *No Art without Craft: The Life of Theodore Low De Vinne, Printer*. Boston: Godine, 2005. Print.

Tillett, Wilbur Fish. "Southern Womanhood as Affected by the War." *Century* 43.1 (November 1891): 9–16. Print.

Tipping, Schölin. "'The Sinking Plantation-House': Cable's Narrative Method in *The Grandissimes*." *Essays in Poetics* 13.1 (1988): 63–80. Print.

Tooker, L. Frank. *Joys and Tribulations of an Editor*. New York: Century, 1924. Print.

Tucker, Amy. *The Illustration of the Master: Henry James and the Magazine Revolution*. Stanford: Stanford UP, 2010. Print.

Turner, Arlin, ed. *Critical Essays on George W. Cable.* Boston: Hall, 1980. Print.

———. *George Washington Cable: A Biography.* Baton Rouge: Louisiana State UP, 1966. Print.

———. "George W. Cable's Beginnings as a Reformer." *The Journal of Southern History* 17.2 (1951): 135–61. Print.

———. "George W. Cable's Use of the Past." *Mississippi Quarterly* 30 (Fall 1977): 512–16. Print.

Twain, Mark. *Life on the Mississippi.* New York: Harper & Brothers, 1901 [1883]. Print.

Wagner, Bryan. *Disturbing the Peace: Black Culture and the Police Power after Slavery.* Cambridge, MA: Harvard UP, 2009. Print.

Waring, George E. "George W. Cable." *Century* 23.4 (February 1882): 602–605. Print.

Watrous, James. "The New School of American Wood-Engraving." *American Printmaking: A Century of American Printmaking, 1880–1890.* Madison: U of Wisconsin P, 1984. 20–27. Print.

Watson, Nicola J. *The Literary Tourist: Readers and Places in Romantic and Victorian Britain.* Basingstoke: Palgrave Macmillan, 2006. Print.

Winders, Jamie. "Imperfectly Imperial: Northern Travel Writers in the Postbellum South, 1865–1880." *Annals of the Association of American Geographers* 95.2 (2005): 391–410. Print.

Zagarell, Sandra A. "Narrative of Community: The Identification of a Genre." *Signs* 13.3 (1988): 498–527. Print.

Zboray, Ronald J., and Saracino Zboray. "The Changing Face of Publishing." *The Oxford History of Popular Print Culture.* Vol. 6: US Popular Print Culture 1860–1920. Ed. Christine Bold. Oxford: Oxford UP, 2012. 23–42. Print.

2 Disney's Immersive New Orleans

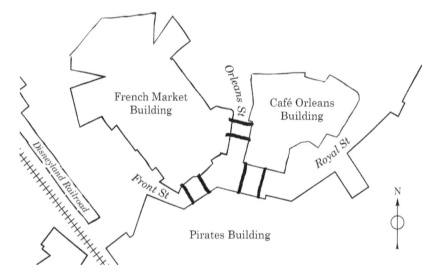

Figure 2.1 New Orleans Square (Disneyland).

Source: Adapted by Polichronios Vezirgenidis from *Your Guide to Disneyland: Summer 1977*.

"Europa-Park Historama"

Unlike most of the other rides, shows, restaurants, and shops in Europa-Park (Rust, Germany), the "Historama" is not themed to one of the various European countries and regions that are represented in the individual "lands" of this theme park.[1] Instead, this "revolving theater" show (six seating areas, arranged in a ring, rotate around six slice of pie-shaped stationary stages) is themed to Europa-Park itself – its rides, shows, and, most importantly, its history. In the "Historama" waiting area, for instance, visitors find photographs, newspaper clippings, scale models of buildings and rides, old visitor guides, and other artifacts and memorabilia from the park's opening in 1975 to more recent years, most of them displayed in glass cases and all dutifully labeled. In the main show, the waiting area's museal mode of display is replaced with multimedia presentations that use film clips, laser projections and animated timelines, as well as lights, music, and special effects, to tell the histories of the park and its sister company, the ride manufacturer Mack Rides, in both reverse (show scene 1) and forward (show scene 2) chronological order.

To be sure, and as I have argued elsewhere, the "Historama" story about the development of Europa-Park and Mack Rides is both highly selective and heavily edited for the purposes of self-promotion and brand-building: from their humble beginnings as a wagon manufacturer in 1780 and a small regional park in 1975, respectively, the company and the park are depicted as steadily progressing to develop into a successful, innovative ride designer and into Germany's largest theme park (see Freitag, "Autotheming" 143–4). Hence, the "Historama" versions of the histories of Europa-Park and Mack Rides not only replicate the ones told by the visitor guides, illustrated coffee table books, and DVDs sold in the park's various souvenir shops or, for that matter, the ones told on the park's and the company's websites,[2] adapting them into the genre or medium of the theme park show. They also reflect in a more general way the selective, teleological, and affective manner in which history and historical themes have usually been depicted in theme parks. Particularly with respect to Disney theme parks, this manner used to be criticized as "Mickey Mouse history" (Wallace) or "Distory" (Fjellman 59) for its multiple omissions and general "politics of historical erasure" (Giroux 34).[3] More recently, however, and spurred by a loss of faith in the idea of an "objective history" even among historians (see Carlà 25), theme park histories have also been praised for their broad popularization of historical themes as well as for their educational potential (see, for instance, Francaviglia, "History" 71; and Hjemdahl 106).

What is much more important here, however, is that as probably the first theme park ride themed to theme park history,[4] the "Historama" focuses on and even celebrates an aspect of the sites that is usually almost completely silenced at the parks: indeed, while frequently depicting themes from the past and applying techniques of "Theme Aging" to make elements appear older than they actually are (see Younger, *Theme Park Design* 185), theme parks generally make enormous efforts to carefully hide their own aging process and history from visitors. These efforts include using durable materials such as fiberglass rather than "authentic" ones like wood to avoid weathering as well as following rigid maintenance schedules to erase the inevitable signs of wear and tear by high levels of frequentation, but also subtly integrating new additions into the existing theme park landscape, e.g., by operating plant farms to make sure that "any horticulture added to the theme park appears to have been there for years preceding its addition" (314). And except for extremely rare cases in which theme parks choose to commemorate or pay tribute to former attractions (e.g., Disneyland planting characters from the closed "Country Bear Jamboree" show as "easter eggs" into the "The Many Adventures of Winnie the Pooh" ride that replaced it), so-called theming palimpsests – situations "in which themes from different eras are visible in the same spaces" (Lukas, "Politics" 282) – can usually be attributed to budget limits rather than to deliberate design decisions. Hence, while Giroux's comment about theme parks' "politics of historical erasure" may also be true for the depiction of history in the parks, it applies even more fundamentally to theme parks' approach to their own history.

Yet of course, theme parks do change over time, in both highly obvious and barely noticeable ways, and due to a large variety of factors both within and outside of the control of the industry. Apart from natural wear and tear, these factors include: changing trends in themes (resulting in e.g., rethemed rides, restaurants, shops, or entire areas; see Younger, *Theme Park Design* 391); changing tastes in theme park design styles (leading to, for example, the addition of explicit storylines to dark rides that formerly operated with implicit or low stories; see Younger, "Traditionally Postmodern" 78); changes in building codes or other safety, health, and labor regulations (manifesting themselves in, for instance, the addition of safety rails to ride tracks; see Weiss, "Alice"); changing operational and managerial strategies (e.g., switching from heavily themed shops offering niche products to high volume stores selling generic souvenirs; see Younger, *Theme Park Design* 347); sudden changes in economic conditions and drastically falling visitor numbers (resulting in, for example, the temporary closure of individual rides, shows, restaurants, shops, or hotels; see Koenig 317); broader cultural changes (leading to, for instance, the removal of elements that have, over time, come to be perceived as potentially offensive to visitors; see Francaviglia, "Frontierland" 176); and, perhaps most importantly, visitors' ever-increasing expectations, as well as high levels of competition in the industry (manifesting themselves in e.g., reimagined or "plussed" rides and the regular addition of new attractions and shows; see Younger, *Theme Park Design* 391; and Cornelis 225–7).

At one point, virtually all theme parks and their various themed areas, as well as their individual elements, have been subjected to the impact of several or even all of these factors and have therefore undergone more or less subtle changes. Indeed, even the "Historama" has a history: before it became the home of the "Historama" show in 2010, the cone-shaped building located between the "Russia" and the "The Netherlands" sections of Europa-Park was known to visitors as the "Chocoland," a brand space dedicated to a well-known German chocolate brand. Opened in 1990 and painted in the company colors, the "Chocoland" featured, among other elements, a café serving hot chocolate, a shop selling the company's entire product range, an interactive experience where children could fabricate chocolate, and "Das Lila Geheimnis" ("The Purple

Secret"), a revolving theater show about the history of chocolate. For Europa-Park's 35th anniversary in 2010, the shop, the interactive experience, and all references to chocolate were removed, the building was repainted in the colors of the European flag, and the show was rethemed to no longer tell the history of chocolate, but that of Europa-Park (see N.N., "Themenbereich Chocoland"). Hence, the addition of the "Chocoland" in 1990 and its 2010 retheming as the "Historama" reflect the growing importance of brands and of the theme park *as* a brand in Europa-Park in particular and in the themed entertainment industry in general (see Freitag, "Autotheming" 144).

But the history of the "Historama" goes back even further: prior to 2010, most of the artifacts displayed in the waiting area were part of the "Mack Rides Ausstellung" ("Mack Rides Exhibition"), a small and rather inconspicuous company museum located in the "Italy" section of Europa-Park. With the retheming of the "Chocoland" and the transfer of the exhibition to the new "Historama," the museum was converted into the loading station of the Leonardo da Vinci-themed suspended flight ride "Volo da Vinci" (see N.N., "Mack-Rides Ausstellung"). The ride system of the revolving theater show, in turn, was based on the "Carousel of Progress," a show about the constant improvement of domestic life through electric appliances originally designed by WED Enterprises[5] for the General Electric pavilion at the 1964–1965 New York World's Fair and subsequently moved to the "Tomorrowland" section of Disneyland (see Strodder 95–7). The "longer" history of the "Historama" testifies, then, to the more consistent and rigorous application of theming in Europa-Park, which could apparently no longer tolerate the incongruity of a German ride manufacturer's and theme park operator's company museum in an Italian-themed space, to the spread of ride technologies (the revolving theater) and related contents (the model of a teleological, progressive history) across theme parks and continents, as well as, finally, to the multiple and complex connections between world's fairs and theme parks.

Somewhat surprisingly, however, and quite in contrast to the depiction of history in theme parks, the history of theme parks themselves has been largely ignored in theme park criticism. To be sure, much has been written about the origins of the theme park in European pleasure gardens, state and county fairs, amusement parks and piers, world's fairs etc. (for a very early example, see Nye 63–6). Also, several critics have offered broad overviews of the economic development of the theme park industry, with, for example, H. Jürgen Kagelmann identifying four distinct historical phases (409; see also Adams; Davis, "Theme Park"; and Clavé 3–92). More recently, Deborah Philips has explored the roots of the most common theme park themes in other visual media, and David Younger has provided a unique look at the history of theme park design styles (see Philips; and Younger, "Traditionally Postmodern"). Finally, and with respect to individual parks, scholars have concentrated – like theme park criticism in general (see Raz 31; Clavé xvi) – on Disney's American parks and particularly Disneyland, examining in great detail the planning, financing, and construction of the company's first theme park and the contributing social, cultural, and economic factors (see, for instance, Adams 102; 163–4; Marling, "Disneyland"; Zukin 223; Avila; and Mittermeier). By contrast, and especially considering the amount of scholarly material published on (Disney) theme parks in general, in-depth diachronic studies of individual parks, themed areas, rides, or other elements have been extremely rare.[6]

Thus, already in the mid-1990s, Alan Bryman complained about the "textualist" approach of most studies of (Disney) theme parks: "The various commentators by and large viewed the parks as constituting texts to be interpreted and understood. As texts they have been seen as ripe with meaning and significance." Yet, Bryman immediately adds:

> the parks are not inert texts. Walt [Disney] always said that the parks would never be finished, and he and his successors have been true to this belief. Not only have new attractions been continually added (while others have been dropped), but also many have been changed and redesigned.
>
> (*Disney* 83)

Consequently, Bryman calls for interpretations that shift and evolve along with the parks (*Disney* 83), and this is exactly what I would like to attempt in "Disney's Immersive New Orleans." More precisely, "Disney's Immersive New Orleans" employs a historical approach to theme parks to trace the ever changing and continuously developing depiction of New Orleans in what Aldo Legnaro has called the "Disneyzone" (286), that is, the totality of themed spaces designed, owned, and/or operated by the Walt Disney Company,[7] from the opening of Disney's first theme park, Disneyland (Anaheim, California) in 1955 to the present.

On the one hand, such a diachronic approach to Disney's New Orleans-themed spaces will necessarily include the individual histories of the various spaces as they have evolved over time and in response to the numerous internal and external factors influencing the development of theme parks in general (see earlier). Delineating the stories of each of Disney's various New Orleans-themed spaces separately, "Disney's Immersive New Orleans" will thus contribute to the larger histories of the respective parks and resorts to which these individual spaces belong. On the other hand, and perhaps even more importantly, "Disney's Immersive New Orleans" will also encompass a comparative study of Disney's various New Orleans-themed spaces as they have been planned, constructed, and opened in succession, each new one inevitably building and reflecting upon its predecessor(s). Therefore, the chapter will also trace the broader evolution and continuous adaptation of the theme or image of New Orleans within the "Disneyzone." Combining the micro-histories of Disney's various New Orleans-themed spaces and the macro-history of Disney's spatial depiction of the city, "Disney's Immersive New Orleans" thus seeks to explore continuities and shifts both within and across the company's parks and resorts over a period of more than 60 years.

As in "Scribner's Illustrated New Orleans," I will occasionally leave the "Disneyzone" proper in order to consider other New Orleans-related artifacts produced by the Walt Disney Company – illustrated books, movies, TV shows, video games, etc. – as well as New Orleans-themed and other spaces designed, owned, and/or operated by theme park companies other than Disney. As even my admittedly short and rather superficial history of Europa-Park's "Historama" has already intimated, theme park histories often cut across media and operators, and this also applies to "Disney's Immersive New Orleans." Indeed, in the case of a multimedia entertainment giant that relies as heavily on the effects of cross-divisional synergy as the Walt Disney Company does (see Wasko 70–83 for a case study), discussing Disney's theme parks apart and in isolation from the company's other products is well-nigh impossible. Likewise, given the enormous impact of Disney on the theme park industry (see Clavé 99–100) as well as the increasing spread of theme park technologies and design principles to other commercial and non-commercial spaces since at least the 1990s (see Gottdiener, *Theming* and ahead), considering what Sheldron Waldrep has called "architectural give-and-take[s]" (222) between Disney and other private and public spaces is almost imperative.

Thus conceptualized, "Disney's Immersive New Orleans" comprises virtually all of the individual "modules," as well as the various sorts of "theatra" (Mitrasinovic 120) that make up a typical theme park environment: rides (dark and transportation rides); live entertainment venues (theaters, found theaters, and focal points; see Younger, *Theme Park* 373); waiting, resting, and play areas; food outlets (table service, counter service, and quick service restaurants, as well as vending carts, bars, and private clubs); merchandise outlets (shops, carts, and retail entertainment); exhibition spaces; service areas (bathrooms etc.); and even overnight accommodations (hotel rooms and private apartments), all of them organized in "lands," "sublands," and resort hotels. The chapter includes spaces in the three most-visited theme park resorts in the world (namely, Disneyland, Walt Disney World, and Tokyo Disneyland; see Rubin 10), located in three of the four largest global theme park clusters (California, Florida, and Japan; see Clavé 56), as well as spaces originally developed during three of the four most important historical phases of theme park design (namely, "Traditional," "Presentational," and "New Traditional" style design; see Younger, "Traditionally Postmodern"). Finally, it comprises such iconic rides and (in)famous restaurants as "Pirates of the Caribbean"[8] and "Aunt Jemima's Kitchen," as well as such short-lived and quickly forgotten shops and shows as "Le Bayou Magique" and "Teddy and Kenny."

Much like the texts and images in "Scribner's Illustrated New Orleans," the spaces discussed in "Disney's Immersive New Orleans" are consistently set in the past. Yet whereas the "pastifying" of New Orleans has been identified as precisely what sets New Orleans local-color fiction and related texts apart from other textual and visual depictions of U.S. regional cultures in late-nineteenth–century popular publishing, in twentieth-century and twenty-first–century theme park design, "pastifying" constitutes one of the most common strategies to depict specific themes. Instead, what is particularly remarkable about Disney's depictions of the city and its past is their gradual "Frenchifying" over time: from Disneyland's "New Orleans Street" (1955–1962) and "New Orleans Square" (opened in 1966) to the New Orleans-themed area of Tokyo Disneyland's "Adventureland" (opened in 1983) and "Disney's Port Orleans Resort – French Quarter" at Walt Disney World Resort (opened in 1991), Disney's New Orleans-themed spaces increasingly focus on French New Orleans and specifically the French Quarter. Hence, during the same time period when the city of New Orleans sought to concentrate tourism in the Vieux Carré in a process that J. Mark Souther has referred to as the "Disneyfication of New Orleans" ("Disneyfication"), Disney theme parks and resorts concentrated their "meta-versions"[9] of New Orleans tourism on the French Quarter. Here, too, then, the city's past has been increasingly depicted as French, and the city's French as past.

Toward a Historical Turn in Theme Park Research

From the very beginning of scholarly research on theme parks in the late 1960s to the early 1980s, contributions to the critical debate came from all over the (Western) world and from a wide array of scholarly disciplines and intellectual traditions (see Bryman, *Disney* 81), as the following list of some of the first studies of theme parks illustrates: Richard Schickel's biographical *The Disney Version: The Life, Times, Art and Commerce of Walt Disney* (1968); Christopher Finch's medial analysis and Louis Marin's semiotic reading of Disneyland in the former's *The Art of Walt Disney from Mickey Mouse to the Magic Kingdoms* and in the latter's *Utopiques: Jeux d'espaces* (both 1973); Umberto Eco's postmodernist-inflected "Viaggio nell'iperrealtà" through California and Florida ("Travels in Hyperreality"; originally printed in 1975 in the Italian magazine *L'espresso*); Millicent Hall's "Theme Parks: Around the World in 80 Minutes" (1976) and Richard V. Francaviglia's "Main Street, U.S.A.: The Creation of a Popular Image" (1977), both published in the American scholarly journal *Landscape: A Magazine of Human Geography*; Michael R. Real's Marxist study of Disneyland visitors in *Mass-mediated Culture* (1977); Jean Baudrillard's analysis of Disneyland (and American culture in general) as postmodern in "La précession des simulacres" (1978); and the various articles collected in *The Journal of Popular Culture*'s "special issue" on theme and amusement parks, published in 1981. As a glance at the tables of contents of such recent edited collections on theme parks as *A Reader in Themed and Immersive Spaces* (ed. Scott Lukas; 2016) or *Time and Temporality in Theme Parks* (ed. Filippo Carlà-Uhink et al.; 2017) confirms, the disciplinary and intellectual variety of theme park research has, if anything, become even more pronounced over the years.

It is without doubt for this reason that there has yet to emerge a single, all-encompassing theory of theme parks along with a corresponding, commonly accepted methodology for their study, to say nothing of an independent field of research or discipline of "theme park studies" complete with such signs of academic institutionalization as scholarly associations or publication venues. While, as Steinecke has recently noted (46), several research paradigms have established themselves,[10] and while the past 15 years have seen the publication of a number of monographs that offer more or less comprehensive introductions to the field – including Clavé's *The Global Theme Park Industry* (2007), Lukas's *Theme Park* (2008), Steinecke's *Themenwelten im Tourismus* (2009), Lukas's *The Immersive Worlds Handbook* (2013), and Younger's *Theme Park Design & The Art of Themed Entertainment* (2016) – theme park research remains, as of yet, almost as dizzyingly heterogeneous as the parks themselves (see Nye 63).

Nevertheless, around the turn of the millennium, both Aviad E. Raz and Janet Wasko sought to establish new methodological standards for theme park research by suggesting, independently of each other, what Wasko calls an "integrated approach" (152) to the parks: in *Riding the Black Ship: Japan and Tokyo Disneyland* (1999), Raz notes that "[m]any previous studies of Disney's worlds have focused on a cultural reading of the onstage" – thus echoing Bryman's earlier complaint about the dominance of (synchronic) "textualist" approaches in theme park research (see earlier) – "while neglecting its production (by workers) and reception (by visitors and customers)." Consequently, in his study of Tokyo Disneyland, Raz proposes to "combine all three viewpoints" (6). Similarly, in *Understanding Disney* (2001), Wasko argues that "the analysis of production and consumption of Disney texts is necessary to understand their significance" and that such an "integrated approach is especially relevant in considering the Disney theme parks" (152).

Reception indeed needs to be considered an integral part of theme park research, if only because, as Ariane Schwarz has recently demonstrated in her detailed reading of the water coaster "Poseidon" at Europa-Park, the presence of visitors and their interactions have often already been "built into" the theme park landscape (see Schwarz). And of course, there have been critics who have focused on theme park audiences (Wasko offers a comprehensive, descriptive list of relevant studies for the Disney parks;

see Wasko 190–5). Likewise, while the day-to-day operational part of the "production" side of theme parks has been rather neglected by scholars – Smith and Eisenberg's "Conflict at Disneyland" (1987), Van Maanen's "The Smile Factory" (1991), and Kuenz's "Working at the Rat" (1995) are among the relevant exceptions – especially the initial planning and construction of Disneyland in Anaheim, California, have received, as I have noted earlier, much critical attention.

It is not very surprising, however, that to date, Raz's and Wasko's constitute practically the only studies to employ an "integrated" approach to theme parks – i.e., ones that *simultaneously* consider the parks themselves, their production, and their reception – and that about 15 years after Raz and Wasko, critics such as Lukas and Clément are still calling for a more nuanced, "[s]ober study of these spaces [that] will entail complex analyses of the design processes that give rise to [them] as well as consideration of the ethnographic dynamics of their use by guests" (Lukas, "Research" 168; see also Clément, *Plus vrais* 17–8). Indeed, particularly in the context of this study, one could – much like Fagg, Pethers, and Vandome have done for periodical studies – proclaim a rhizomatic turn in theme park research and thus invite theme park scholars to examine the parks, their producers, and their visitors in terms of networks between theme park spaces (what Raz calls "onstage" as well as "backstage" areas), between theme park actors (planning, design, management, and operational staff, as well as visitors), and between theme park spaces and actors.[11]

This, however, is much easier said than done. In fact, there are numerous methodological problems that potentially render an integrated or rhizomatic approach to theme parks at least difficult, if not virtually impracticable. With respect to the study of the parks themselves, let me illustrate these problems by way of an anecdote from my own research: in April 2016, during a field trip to Disneyland in Anaheim, California, I had spent less than two hours in the park taking pictures and jotting notes before I was approached by two security guards who asked me what I was doing here. The encounter was amicable, and after I had explained my project to them, they allowed me to go on with my work and wished me good luck. I do not know whether it was one of the employees or visitors who noticed me and decided to call security or whether it was park security itself that spotted me through CCTV. In any case, during the rest of my stay, I was not approached anymore, perhaps because, as I found out later, I had made it onto the briefing sheet that is distributed to the individual operational managers of the park every morning. The point here is simply that theme parks are private property and that the two security guards would have had every right to ask me to leave the premises – indeed, while the *Disneyland Park Guidemap* merely asks visitors to "[p]lease comply with park rules, signs and instructions," the park's website is much more explicit: "We reserve the right to deny admission, or to require a person already admitted to leave a Park, without refund, liability or compensation if we consider that the circumstances so require" (N.N., "Disneyland Resort Park Rules").[12] Doing research on site may thus seriously impede a theme park research project.

Similarly, while park rules do not explicitly prohibit talking to other visitors, doing on-site research on the reception of theme parks by conducting open or semi-structured, questionnaire-based interviews would quite probably be considered an "[u]nauthorized event" or engaging in an "act that may impede the operation of the Park or any associated facility" (N.N., "Disneyland Resort Park Rules") and thus a violation of park regulations – quite apart from the fact that such interviews would seriously cut into visitors' time at the park, for which they have paid considerable sums. Indeed, it is remarkable that among those scholars who have studied theme park and heritage site audiences, only Bagnall appears to have systematically "interviewed people while they were visiting the site in an attempt to avoid decontextualization" (228). Others, and particularly those concerned with Disney theme parks, have relied on off-site interviews and questionnaires (see, for instance, Real; Bryman, "Global Disney"; and Wasko, Phillips, and Meehan) or on unsystematic observation of and informal conversations with other visitors (see, for example, The Project on Disney or Fung and Lee) or even other researchers (see Carlà et al., "Research"). And due to the highly competitive nature of the theme park industry, the parks have generally been "notoriously tight-lipped" (Wasko 187) about the results of their own audience research, usually conducted late during the day when people are about to leave the site.

Finally, and with respect to the production side of the integrated or rhizomatic approach to theme parks, interviewing employees on site confronts the researcher with the same problems as interviewing visitors, in addition to the fact that such an approach would exclude employees such as administration, management, or design staff, who work in areas inaccessible to average visitors. Some researchers have thus relied on official interviews, which, naturally and if granted at all, are highly selective as to the kind of information they reveal (see, for instance, Lukas, *Immersive Worlds Handbook*; or Davis, *Spectacular Nature*) or on off-site, anonymous interviews (see, for example, Kuenz; or Koenig).

Difficulties multiply if one takes, as I have proposed to do in "Disney's Immersive New Orleans," a diachronic approach to theme parks, for neither can "past" versions of theme parks be visited and examined, nor can past visitors and employees be systematically interviewed and observed, either on site or off site. At least in theory, two types of sources on theme park pasts are available: official, authorized company histories and archives, and unofficial, unauthorized publications and documents. When writing about theme park actors, for instance, many scholars have resorted to unofficial reminiscences and recollections by or of people who visited and worked for the parks, again sometimes including researchers themselves and their families. Thus Eric Avila, for instance, writes about his mother's memories of visiting Disneyland in the late 1950s and early 1960s (141–3); and Scott A. Lukas frequently draws on his own experiences as an employee trainer at Astroworld (now closed) in Houston, Texas in the mid-1990s (see, for example, "How the Theme Park"; or "Research"). In addition, fan websites dedicated to theme park history – such as Werner Weiss's *Yesterland*; Dave DeCaro's *Daveland*; Mike Lee, Foxx Nolte, and Eric Paddon's *Widen Your World* (all dedicated to Disney's American theme parks), or Charles Denson's *Coney Island History Project* – have collected and published texts by and recordings of both theme park visitors and workers. Though often woefully incomplete, these documents offer invaluable information on how people interacted with theme park spaces and other theme park actors in the past, either in a work or in a leisure context – and sometimes in both.

Fan websites like the ones mentioned earlier, as well as unauthorized publications like Chris Strodder's *The Disneyland Encyclopedia* (second edition 2012), also provide a plethora of material – photographs, audio recordings, videos, and even digital recreations of rides and entire parks – on past versions of the parks themselves. Thus, they partially compensate for the fact that, as Mike Budd has noted, particularly The Walt Disney Company "will not usually allow researchers into its archives unless it can control or approve what they publish" (15; see also Knight 2). Disney has, of course, as Budd also mentions, produced "a constant barrage of books, articles, DVDs, new media, and other materials that promulgate the company's version of its own history" (15), including that of its parks. These official histories do provide excellent resources for (potential) studies of company historiography; when viewed as "archives" of the parks' past and compared to unofficial sources, however, they are, much like the "Historama," frequently more interesting for what they omit and silence than for what they include: Aunt Jemima's restaurants, for instance, which figure prominently in Wiener's, Francaviglia's, and Avila's accounts of Disneyland's early years (see Wiener; Francaviglia, "Frontierland"; and Avila 132–44) and which will also be discussed ahead, appear to have been almost completely excised from official Disneyland history as told in company publications such as Shannon's (see Shannon).

Also, as part of Disney's brand management, the company has released official publications by and on selected theme park actors, most notably the park designers. Profusely illustrated and expensive volumes such as *Imagineering: A Behind the Dreams Look at Making the Magic Real* (1996) or *Imagineering: A Behind the Dreams Look at Making MORE Magic Real* (2010), from Disney's own publishing division, offer glimpses into the work of Disney park designers (called "Imagineers") and thus successfully rely on what Daniel Boorstin noted in 1961 already: foreshadowing both Eco and Baudrillard by describing tourist attractions as "pseudo-events" (102), Boorstin asserts that "[i]nformation about the staging of a pseudo-event simply adds to its fascination" (38). In a similar spirit, Disney has also offered seminars that "introduce executives from a variety of organizations to its distinctive approach to human resource management and has publicized this approach more generally" (Bryman, *Disneyization* 109).

Two problems remain, however. First, even complete and unrestricted access to all archives would probably not resolve difficulties arising from the essentially collaborative nature of theme park "production" in general and (early) theme park design processes in particular. Alan Bryman has criticized Disney publications for portraying the company's animators as "a faceless mass, whistling while they work in order to realize Walt's dreams" (*Disney* 26), and to a certain extent, this also applies to their portrayal of park designers. Indeed, the two *Imagineering* volumes mentioned previously are simply signed "The Imagineers," and even such a prominent Disney designer as John Hench, to whom the company accorded a certain amount of individuality through a design book of his own (see Hench and Van Pelt) as well as a "Main Street window,"[13] (re)inscribed himself into the "faceless mass" by writing: "I look upon Walt as a conductor of one of the world's greatest symphonies, and I was part of the orchestra" (qtd. in Green and Green 63). Here, however, Disney's version of its own history appears to be at least partially accurate, for as Hench has noted elsewhere, artists often do collaborate on sketches and designs at Imagineering (see Hench and Van Pelt 19; see also Grice for examples from a theme park design company other than Walt Disney Imagineering). Hence, it is perfectly possible to attribute some elements of, for instance, the "original" Disneyland to individual designers (see Francaviglia, *Main Street* [145–63] for examples from Disneyland's Main Street section and ahead for examples from Disney's New Orleans-themed spaces). Either due to lack of data or because they actually were the result of collaborations, however, most other elements will simply have to be described as the work of "the Imagineers" or (to use, as is often done, the family name of the company's founder as a shorthand for the totality of people involved in the creation of its products) as the work of "Disney."

Second, and more fundamentally, one must also wonder whether it is at all possible to analyze (theme park) spaces that no longer exist in their original form and that, hence, one can no longer experience in person. In her introduction to *Umwidmungen: Architektonische und kinematographische Räume* (2005), for instance, Gertrud Koch argues that it is

> neither sufficient to look at a photograph, a constructional drawing, or a digital simulation of a building – nor is it sufficient to have watched a movie about a particular architectural work.... In order to understand a building, one apparently needs to walk in it, one needs to experience it in its spatial presence; .... [Visualizations of

buildings] cannot substitute for the three-dimensionality of a genuine spatial experience.

(8–9; my translation)

Koch's argument is significant and should not be brushed off lightly. It constitutes, after all, the main reason for spending much time and energy, not to mention a significant amount of (public) money, to go on field trips to theme parks when one might just as well stay in one's office and look at park maps or read online trip reports. And Koch is right, of course: theme parks (and places in general) are multisensorial environments and texts, pictures, movies, and other medial representations and simulations of them cannot adequately recreate the immersive experience they offer. Nevertheless, these representations constitute our only "entry tickets" to past theme parks, their production, and their reception, and they will therefore form the basis of many of my observations and arguments in "Disney's Immersive New Orleans."

A Multiracial Brandland: New Orleans Street (Disneyland)

The first New Orleans-themed space in the "Disneyzone" was located at Disneyland and opened along with the rest of the Anaheim park on 17 July 1955. Referred to as "New Orleans Street" on postcards (see Weiss, "Don DeFore's") and in promotional publications such as *The Disneyland News* (see N.N., "Mardi Gras"),[14] though never identified as a distinct area in visitor guides, on souvenir maps, or on signs in the park itself, the area formed a small "subland"[15] of Disneyland's Frontierland section. It consisted of a row of buildings housing two food outlets (a counter and a quick service restaurant) as well as a walkway, a bandstand, and a few decorative props. After a remodel in 1962 in preparation for New Orleans Square, then scheduled to open the following year, New Orleans Street lost much of its distinctive identity as a specifically New Orleans-themed space and started to serve as a thematic and visual segue or "cross-dissolve" (Mitrasinovic 151) between Frontierland and New Orleans Square when the latter eventually opened in 1966. Until then, however, it constituted what was probably Disney's most racially and ethnically diverse representation of New Orleans in its theme parks and, somewhat surprisingly, the only one to feature explicit references to African Americans. In fact, over time, the African-American elements of New Orleans Street became more and more prominent and eventually dominated almost the entire area: by the time it "closed" in 1962, New Orleans Street had become a veritable "chocolate city."[16]

It is probably no coincidence that Disneyland – and, hence, the "Disneyzone" – included a New Orleans-themed area from the very beginning. In "Disneyland, 1955: Just Take the Ana Freeway to the American Dream," Karal Ann Marling has suggested that much of the inspiration for the park, its themes, and its layout came from the 1948 Chicago Railroad Fair, which Walt Disney visited together with Ward Kimball, a railroad enthusiast who had been working as an animator at the Disney studios since 1934. Sponsored by "thirty-eight major American carriers" and "ostensibly honor[ing] the centenary of the first steam locomotive to enter Chicago" (Marling, "Disneyland" 180), the fair featured a narrow-gauge railroad along the tracks of which various attractions were lined up, including exhibits that "recreated in convincing atmospheric detail some exotic vacation spot best reached by train" (181): a Florida mansion, a dude ranch, a southwestern Indian village, and, indeed, an area dedicated to the French Quarter in New Orleans (see 181–3). Marling concludes that "[a]s it was built, some six years later, Disneyland owed a great deal to the 1948 Chicago Railroad Fair," from the railroad that "defined the boundaries of the park, served as the chief artery of internal transportation, and even determined the scale of the buildings adjacent to the tracks" and the organization of the park into separate "lands" that "recalled the 'village' layout in Chicago" to the "kinds of places and concepts singled out for special treatment" (185) – in short, the park's various themes.

The railroad, as well as some of Disneyland's themes – and specifically that of New Orleans – may indeed have been lifted from the Railroad Fair, as Marling suggests.[17] However, rather than replicating the Fair's "'village' layout" with its string of exhibits lining the railroad tracks "in no particular order" (Marling, "Disneyland" 181), Disney chose to subdivide the park into five sections, each of which grouped together several representations of specific and often rather disparate places or cultures (what Younger refers to as "specific lands"; see *Theme Park Design* 79) under some broader heading (resulting in what Younger refers to as an "amalgamated land"; see 79). Thus, for example, Adventureland amalgamated or fused references to the tropical forests of India, Africa, and Latin America within the thematic frame of "adventure"; and Frontierland articulated its eponymous overarching theme through such subareas as a log fort (at the entrance to Frontierland), a Western frontier town (the area surrounding the "Golden Horseshoe" saloon), the desert areas of the southwestern United States (accessible via the "Stage Coach" and "Pack Mules" rides), the setting of Mark Twain's *Adventures of Tom Sawyer* (on "Tom Sawyer Island"), an "Indian village," and New Orleans (in New Orleans Street).

In addition, there was what Nick Stanley has called "a vague geographic sense to the arrangement" (285) of the western side of the park, with the North America-themed Frontierland being located to the north of Adventureland with its references to the southern hemisphere in general and Latin America in particular (see also Disney 11; Francaviglia, "Frontierland" 162). Appropriately, New Orleans Street occupied the southernmost part of Frontierland and, hence, the juncture of "North

America" and "Latin America." Scholars like Hom have even suggested that the park's western half was unified not merely by a geographic reference, but also by a thematic focus on and the depiction of (internal and imperial) territorial expansion and colonialism (Hom 26–7; 29; see also Marin 250; and Wasko 285). With its back entrance to Adventureland almost hidden behind one of the buildings, New Orleans Street can thus be seen – much like New Orleans in Greeson's reading of Edward King's "Old and New Louisiana" (see Chapter 1) – as North America's gateway from the already successfully conquered West to "the next possible fields of action" in the south (Marin 250).[18] While there were no signs and clues in visitor guides, on maps, and in the park itself, then, visitors could identify New Orleans Street as a specifically New Orleans-themed space already from its positioning within the park layout.

Through what other means was the theme of New Orleans Street communicated to visitors, however? Disney may have borrowed the general idea of a New Orleans-themed space from the Chicago Railroad Fair, but instead of recreating (a portion of) the French Quarter, as the Illinois Central had done at the Fair – and, incidentally, as Disney would do later – the Imagineers chose a rather different approach to representing the city at Disneyland. Indeed, New Orleans Street basically consisted of a broad pedestrian walkway running southward from the "Golden Horseshoe" saloon to a place where it forked, with one branch leading further southward to Adventureland (the "back entrance" mentioned earlier) and the other branch leading across a bridge to the "Chicken Plantation" counter-service restaurant, located next to the train tracks. Bordered on one side by the Frontierland river and a bandstand and on the other side by a fenced-off lawn area with an old anchor, a patio with tables and chairs, and a block of two-story buildings,[19] the street offered wide, open views of the waterway, the lush green landscape of "Tom Sawyer Island" across the river, and the southern plantation architecture of the "Chicken Plantation" in the distance – not the closed vistas of densely built streets that one may expect from a (recreated) urban space. Moreover, apart from some very minor wrought-iron details on the bandstand and the balcony of one of the buildings, there were no architectural details that visitors could have readily associated with the Crescent City – no cobblestone pavement, no hidden courtyards, no Creole cottages and mansions, no replicas of the French Market, St. Louis cathedral, or Jackson Square. Rather, the façades blended elements from neoclassical, Southern plantation, Southwestern adobe, and Western false-front styles, with the outdoor seating area of the southernmost building even featuring a thatched roof. Hence, from a purely architectural and urban planning perspective, the area seemed to not even attempt to recreate an urban – let alone a specifically New Orleans – atmosphere, but appeared more like a southern country road.

Instead, New Orleans Street was first and foremost identified as a New Orleans-themed space through music and references to Mardi Gras, particularly during such special events as the opening ceremony of Disneyland, which was broadcast live from the park on 17 July 1955, as a 90-minute television special on ABC called "Dateline: Disneyland."[20] During the event, co-host Ronald Reagan, with a view of the just christened "Mark Twain" riverboat traveling down the Frontierland river behind him, tells viewers about:

> that romantic era when whole cities grew out of riverports. The journeying paddle wheels brought new people, new customs, and new industries to those fabulous ports of call – Pittsburgh, St. Louis, and Natchez. And the riverboat even brought a new kind of music up the river from the city where the blues were born, where the Dixieland style was king: New Orleans.
> (Jackson, Phelps, and Rich 00:37:45–00:38:16)

The camera then cuts to co-host Bob Cummings, who announces that he is standing in "a street, just like in New Orleans. The old New Orleans created [by] Walt Disney for you" and in front of "the most famous little Dixieland band in the world" (00:38:30–00:38:42), the "Firehouse Five Plus Two."[21] Dressed in their characteristic fireman costumes and accompanied by several dancers and men and women with flower baskets, the band starts marching down the patio in front of the New Orleans Street buildings before the music switches from a gay, catchy Dixieland style to a slow, titillative trumpet solo during which three "Southern belles" appear on one of the balconies, fanning themselves (00:39:56). Three of the male dancers on the patio take some flowers from the baskets, toss them to the "belles," and join them for a short dance on the balcony when the sudden ringing of a fire bell (00:40:53) announces the beginning of "Mardi Gras": the rollicking Dixieland music returns and the camera cuts to Cummings, who, with his back to the viewer, appears to be embracing and kissing a young woman. Pretending to be "caught," Cummings turns around, wipes his lips, and sheepishly apologizes: "Oh ... Haha, well folks, as you can see, I'd like to say here's the Mardi Gras forever!" (00:41:19–00:41:23) before he quickly hands over to Reagan for the introduction of the next "land" of the park.

This lively and boisterous four-minute segment of "Dateline: Disneyland" focuses almost entirely on music, dancing, and flirting, then. Except for a few shots of a balcony, viewers neither get to see much of the layout or the architecture of New Orleans Street (most of the time, the cameras just show people – musicians, dancers, and/or visitors), nor do viewers learn anything about what this area might have to offer in terms of rides, restaurants, shops, or services. Instead, both the city and the Disneyland area are primarily defined through a party atmosphere and thus imaginatively related to each other:[22] Cummings identifies New Orleans as "the spot where this beat was born" (Jackson, Phelps, and

Rich 00:38:45–00:38:47) and, in fact, jazz music can be heard throughout the entire four minutes of the presentation of New Orleans Street. Hence, at least with respect to this particular segment, "Dateline: Disneyland" invites viewers not so much to ride the rides, browse the shops, or sample the restaurants of the park, but simply to join the Mardi Gras party that has been transported from New Orleans to Disneyland.

The Mardi Gras continued at least until mid-August 1955, when New Orleans Street and its two restaurants were officially dedicated. As *The Disneyland News* reported in its September 1955 issue, the park staged another "gala New Orleans type Mardi Gras" (N.N., "Mardi Gras" 11) for this event: "The festivities began with a parade led by [Disneyland band leader] Vesey Walker and the Disneyland Band, marching the participants in the show down Disneyland's Main Street and into Frontierland to the tune of 'Come to the Mardi Gras'" (11). Following the band were, among others, actress Dorothy Lamour ("a native of the Southern city" who testified that New Orleans Street "looks exactly like the wonderful city in which I was born"), a group of Marines (also "all natives of New Orleans"), a group of Frontierland "natives" (the cast of the "Golden Horseshoe" stage show, as well as "Disneyland's full-blooded Plains Indians who make their home in Frontierland"), and the "Dixieland Jazz band" playing "'When the Saints Come [sic] Marching In'" (11). Once the parade had arrived in New Orleans Street, Lamour officially dedicated the area and "a gala Mardi Gras" (11), with street dancing to the music of the two bands followed.

Again, then, New Orleans Street – and, by implication, the city of New Orleans – are primarily associated with Dixieland jazz music and Mardi Gras celebrations. However, the *Disneyland News* also hints at what was perhaps the most important way in which the "New Orleans" theme was executed in New Orleans Street, for there were, according to the report, at least two more "celebrities" who took part in the parade, the dedication, and the gala: the Frito Kid and Aunt Jemima.[23] As Eric Avila has noted, "[c]orporate names saturated the landscape of Disneyland, from its rides and attractions . . . to its many restaurants and concession stands" (130–1), and New Orleans Street was no exception. In fact, both of the area's restaurants were operated by independent companies which had signed five-year leases (and had already advanced the first and the last year's rent):[24] Frito-Lay, which ran the "Casa de Fritos," and Quaker Oats, operator of the adjacent "Aunt Jemima's Pancake House."

Both companies made sure their corporate mascots, the Frito Kid and Aunt Jemima, enjoyed a prominent presence in the park. The Frito Kid, a young blond cowboy who was perpetually smacking his lips and served as Frito-Lay's mascot from 1953–1967 (Gabaccia 165), was featured on Disneyland's "Casa de Fritos" attraction poster as well as inside the facility in the shape of an elaborate mechanical vending machine (see DeCaro, "Casa"). The notorious character of Aunt Jemima, in turn, had first appeared "in person" at the 1893 World's Columbian Exposition in Chicago (see Avila 134) and, portrayed by several different actresses, had since represented Quaker Oats at trade fairs and in radio ads. One of these actresses, Alyene Lewis, was chosen to make daily appearances as Aunt Jemima at Disneyland's "Aunt Jemima's Pancake House," welcoming guests, posing for pictures with them, and generally providing "streetmosphere"[25] (see Manring 163). And, of course, both the Frito Kid (here impersonated by an unidentified little person) and Aunt Jemima were present at the dedication of New Orleans Street: a photograph in *The Disneyland News* shows them standing next to Dorothy Lamour as she officially dedicates the area (N.N., "Mardi Gras" 11).

To be sure, neither the Frito Kid nor Aunt Jemima were directly connected to New Orleans. The former was a cowboy, presumably from Texas, where Frito-Lay's headquarters were located, while the latter, according to "The Story of Aunt Jemima" as told on the restaurant's placemats, was from rural Louisiana (see e.g., DeCaro, "Aunt Jemima"). At Disneyland's New Orleans Street, however, the Frito Kid, Aunt Jemima, and their restaurants were combined with other "celebrities" from the past and the present in such a way that the specific blend of their racial and ethnic backgrounds precisely mirrored the racial, ethnic, and cultural makeup of the Crescent City: Aunt Jemima and her "Pancake House" obviously stood for New Orleans's African-American elements; and "Casa de Fritos" served, as a sign planted on the lawn in front of the restaurant announced, "Spanish food" (see DeCaro, "Casa"; somewhat confusingly, an advertisement painted on the "Casa" façade simultaneously billed the restaurant's fare as "Authentic Mexican Food"). New Orleans's French heritage, finally, was represented by the old anchor, which according to a plaque was "said to be from a pirate ship commanded by Jean Lafitte in the Battle of New Orleans" (see Glover), and, at least during the dedication of New Orleans Street, by Dorothy Lamour, with her Creole heritage and her French-sounding stage name (see Severo).

Hence, in addition to the positioning of the area within the park and the references to jazz music and Mardi Gras, Disney employed a cast of fictional (Aunt Jemima and the Frito Kid), historical (Jean Lafitte), and contemporary (Dorothy Lamour) "celebrities" to translate the New Orleans theme into the multiracial and multiethnic "brandland" of New Orleans Street. Jon Wiener, Richard V. Francaviglia, and Eric Avila have all commented on the racial and ethnic diversity of Disneyland's early Frontierland and have concluded that Disney thus at least tacitly acknowledged what Francaviglia calls the "multicultural makeup of the [historic] West" ("Frontierland" 177; see also Wiener 133–4; and Avila 134). Yet a closer look at the original map of this section of the park reveals that except for the Native Americans in their "Indian Village," much of this diversity was in fact concentrated in the very distinct subland of New Orleans Street, where the specific combination of references to races and ethnicities relevant to New Orleans's history helped communicate the theme of the area to visitors. The rest of Disney's West was mainly white and Anglo-Saxon.

Wiener, Francaviglia, and Avila have also argued, however, that the diversity of early Frontierland was mainly achieved through the blatant use of racial and ethnic stereotypes, and this certainly applied to New Orleans Street and particularly to Aunt Jemima – and her "Pancake House," as well. For instance, the placemats told visitors that "'before the war'" Aunt Jemima "was cook for Colonel Highbee whose Louisiana plantation was a mecca for visitors" (see e.g., DeCaro, "Aunt Jemima") – she was "obviously a slave," Wiener comments, "though the word isn't used" (133). But even after "the 'War Between the States,'" the story on the placemats continued, the "opportunity to make so many families happy with the ease and satisfaction of serving her mouth-watering pancakes" had seemed so "irresistible" to Aunt Jemima that she decided to share her famous pancake recipes with "a northern flour mill representative" (see DeCaro, "Aunt Jemima") and, one concludes, with visitors at Disneyland, where her "Pancake House" was just a stone's throw away from yet another plantation (the "Chicken Plantation" restaurant). Avila notes that apart from the "savages" in the "Jungle Cruise," the character of the former plantation slave who was still wearing her iconic bandanna and was still eager to serve people "had been one of the few black faces representing Disneyland to the public" and that "the actress playing Aunt Jemima remained one of the few black employees of Disneyland through the 1960s" (134). It is easy to understand why the restaurant is almost never mentioned in Disney's own versions of Disneyland history.[26]

At the same time, it is interesting to see how theme park actors – Disneyland visitors and employees, and especially "Aunt Jemima" Alyene Lewis herself – perceived the character at the time. According to Manring, Lewis "called herself 'the happiest person in the world'" and "became good friends with Walt Disney" (163). A former employee reports that every day before the park opened to visitors, the restaurant would serve breakfast to employees and that Walt Disney was one of the regular customers: though employed as an entertainer rather than a server, Lewis would bring Disney's order to his table herself, considering it a privilege (see DeCaro, "Aunt Jemima"). The disturbing image of an African-American actress playing a former slave and considering herself privileged to personally serve the white "master" of the place may indicate that this employee – and perhaps Lewis and Disney, too – had thoroughly internalized the character of Aunt Jemima. But then, having regular personal contact with Disney may indeed have seemed like a privilege to many of his employees, and Lewis and Disney may have struck up a genuine friendship. In another report, a former visitor remembers having his picture taken with Aunt Jemima and a "Navy buddy" around 1957:

[Aunt Jemima] came out to talk with us specifically because we were Navy men in uniform. We asked if she would step outside so we could get a picture with her, which she readily consented to. I still cherish that photo .... My buddy is long since dead, as is Aunt Jemima. But this memory, and many other cherished Disney memories, live on – and will forever.

(Finnell)

Similar to the employee's account, this touching reminiscence to a certain extent illustrates what Susan Willis has called, in a more general Disney context, "the problem with pleasure" (Willis) – namely, the fact that the "Aunt Jemima" act provided pleasurable and meaningful experiences to people, no matter what they or others may have thought at the time and what people today may think about the role itself. Indeed, designer John Hench has noted that Lewis "'did a wonderful job,... but there were protests from different organizations, and she stopped doing it'" (qtd. in Wiener 134; see also Manring 169).

Before the changing cultural climate of the 1960s had its impact on Frontierland's depiction of African Americans and Disney reconceptualized Aunt Jemima's restaurant as the "Magnolia Tree Terrace" in 1970, however, the character came to virtually dominate New Orleans Street. In 1956, "Casa de Fritos" decided to expand its business and move to a bigger location further north, where – in clear violation of the principle of geographic reference – it eventually formed the nucleus of a new Mexican "subland" with a "Mexican Imports" souvenir shop and a "Mexican bandstand" (see McKim, *1958*). In New Orleans Street, the Frito Kid was replaced by yet another celebrity, actor Don DeFore, who had already made a brief cameo on "Dateline: Disneyland" and who, in preparation for his new role as a restaurant owner and operator, had taken a business management class at UCLA Extension (see DeCaro, "Don DeFore's"). Opened in the space formerly occupied by "Casa de Fritos" in June 1957, DeFore's "Silver Banjo Barbecue" was themed, as an article in the December 1957 issue of the employee magazine *Disneylander* explained, to his father's old banjo (see DeCaro, "Don DeFore's") and contained an old jukebox.

Hence, not only did the move of "Casa de Fritos" to the northern part of Frontierland disturb the underlying geographic concept of this section of the park, but the addition of the "Silver Banjo Barbecue" also upset the careful racial, ethnic, and cultural geography of New Orleans Street, as the city's "Spanish" heritage was no longer represented in the area, leaving "Aunt Jemima's Pancake House" and Lafitte's anchor as the only permanent elements with some sort of connection, however tacit and tenuous, to the city and its history. Simultaneously, as yet another food outlet hosted by a celebrity – a former employee remembers that rather than just lending his name to the place, Don DeFore made regular appearances there (see DeCaro, "Aunt Jemima") – DeFore's restaurant perfectly fit into the "brandland" that was New Orleans Street, and it also helped strengthening the musical theme of the area.

In fact, jazz music became ever more important in New Orleans Street throughout the 1950s and early 1960s. In 1956, the "Disneyland Strawhatters," a five-piece combo usually featuring a pianist, drummer, trumpeter, trombonist, and clarinetist, started performing daily at the New Orleans Street bandstand (see Strodder 405). October 1960 then saw the premiere of the "Dixieland at Disneyland" concert series, during which Disneyland's own bands (such as the "Strawhatters") would perform alongside acts associated with the company and the park (like the "Firehouse Five Plus Two") and world-renowned jazz musicians (such as Louis Armstrong or the Dukes of Dixieland) on floating stages on the Frontierland river, with the audience watching from New Orleans Street. For the finale, J. Mark Souther reports,

> all the musicians congregated on Tom Sawyer Island as the riverboat *Mark Twain* sailed in with more than two hundred park guests holding sparklers. Roman candles and other fireworks exploded in the night sky above the island as Louis Armstrong blew "When the Saints Go Marching In."
>
> (*New Orleans* 112)

Unlike the bandstand concerts, "Dixieland in Disneyland" required a special ticket and only happened once a year (see Strodder 148), so most "regular" visitors did not get to see it. Nevertheless, the concert series, which would last in Frontierland until 1963, when it was moved to a different section of the park (148), somewhat upheld the connection between jazz music and New Orleans Street (and, hence, between New Orleans Street and New Orleans).

Even more importantly, however, around the same time, Aunt Jemima became the only permanent "inhabitant" of the area. In September 1961, and thus several months prior to the expiration of its five-year lease contract, the "Silver Banjo Barbecue" closed (see Strodder 149). A July 1961 letter from the County of Orange Health Department to Don DeFore's brother Verne, who co-managed the restaurant, indicates that the establishment would have had to undergo significant "corrections" due to "violations" in its backstage area prior to the 1962 summer season (see DeCaro, "Don DeFore's"), and the DeFores may have decided to not invest further in the place. The space vacated by the "Silver Banjo" was eventually taken over by its neighbor: in January 1962, "Aunt Jemima's Pancake House" temporarily closed to reopen again in July 1962 as the much bigger "Aunt Jemima's Kitchen" (see Strodder 62). During the remodel, all references to Don DeFore and his silver banjo were removed.

In addition, the building was repainted pink and the southern façade with its adobe-style and western false-front elements, as well as its thatch-roofed outdoor seating area, was replaced with a new wing that featured a grand entrance with a Greek Revival portico, a wrought-iron–laced balcony, and a round winter garden with a cupola on top. Inside, the rustic wooden chairs and tables with checkered tablecloths of the "Pancake House" gave way to chandeliers, ruffled curtains, potted palms, delicate wrought-iron chairs, and tables with faux marble tops (see DeCaro, "Aunt Jemima") – Aunt Jemima had somehow returned to where she originally came from; namely, a luxurious and elegant plantation in rural Louisiana. Finally, Lafitte's anchor and the bandstand were also removed during the remodel.

By summer 1962, then, Aunt Jemima and, hence, a heavily stereotyped representation of African Americans, virtually dominated New Orleans Street. Mainly due to business issues – the success of "Casa de Fritos," which encouraged management to move the concession to a bigger location, and the proposed "corrections" at "Don DeFore's Silver Banjo Barbecue," which prompted the lessees to discontinue their business – New Orleans Street had gradually lost most of its other permanent themed constituents, and the 1962 remodel of "Aunt Jemima's" had removed the rest of them, with the result that New Orleans Street had ostensibly become "Aunt Jemima Land." In fact, apart from Aunt Jemima – connected to the Crescent City, as I have argued, only in the context of its combination with the original New Orleans Street's Spanish- and French-themed elements in the first place – the position of the area at the juncture of Frontierland and Adventureland, and the new wrought-iron trims on the southern façade, as well as the yearly "Dixieland at Disneyland" events, remained as New Orleans Street's only other features somehow related to New Orleans.

Around the same time, however, Disneyland also stopped referring to New Orleans Street as New Orleans Street. Already since 1958, the Disneyland "Fun Maps" – large (30 × 44 inches), detailed, intricately labeled, and regularly updated drawings of the park from a bird's-eye perspective that were sold as souvenirs (see Strodder 185–6) – had pictured a "New Orleans Square" as a "future development" in the area right next to New Orleans Street, where the "Chicken Plantation" restaurant was located (see, for instance, McKim, *1958*; and *1961*). In 1961, visitors entering the park received handbills announcing the opening of a "New Orleans Square" two years later, in 1963 (see Surrell, *Haunted Mansion* 20); and groundbreaking for the new New Orleans-themed land had also begun in 1961 (see Kurtti and Gordon 50). Hence, by 1962, New Orleans Street was no longer considered Disneyland's (main) location for the depiction of the Crescent City within the park and the 1962 changes to the area – especially the additions to the southernmost end of the building, the one that would eventually face the new New Orleans Square – were not done to enhance New Orleans Street's original theme, but rather to ease the visual transition from Frontierland to the future New Orleans Square.

From 1955–1962, however, New Orleans Street had ensured that from the beginning, (a representation of) the city of New Orleans was an essential part of Disneyland and, hence, the "Disneyzone"; and some of its most characteristic – and most characteristically New Orleans – elements, such as good food, live jazz music, Mardi Gras celebrations, references to the city's multiracial and multiethnic heritage as well as, unfortunately, stereotypical depictions of African Americans, would resurface again in one way or another in later versions of the city in Disney's theme parks. Henceforth, however, "Disney's Immersive New Orleans" would increasingly become a French affair.

A Showcase of Theme Park History: New Orleans Square (Disneyland)

Featuring such famous and iconic rides, restaurants, and spaces as "Pirates" and the "Haunted Mansion," the "Blue Bayou Restaurant," and the almost mythical "Club 33," Disneyland's New Orleans Square today probably constitutes one of the most well-known themed environments in the world and the only independent "land" of the park to refer to an actually existing place (the city of New Orleans). Frequently considered (and advertised) as being based on the French Quarter (see e.g., Goodstein 312), New Orleans Square actually features references to both the Vieux Carré and the Garden District and thus simultaneously evokes the city's French, Spanish, and American heritage. Within the story of the increasing "Frenchifying" of "Disney's Immersive New Orleans," the area can thus be viewed as an important intermediate step: while French-themed elements dominate, New Orleans Square nevertheless constitutes a thoroughly multiethnic or multicultural space. Quite in contrast to its predecessor at the park, New Orleans Street, however, New Orleans Square cannot be considered a multiracial space, as the designers did not include any permanent and/or explicit references to African Americans and their contributions to New Orleans's cultural heritage.

Officially opened on 24 July 1966, New Orleans Square simultaneously constitutes the oldest still existing New Orleans-themed space in the "Disneyzone." Considering its age, New Orleans Square has, particularly in the context of theme parks, undergone remarkably few changes over the course of its history: as on opening day, its basic layout and roster of offerings still consist of a small park and five buildings that house three rides, five food outlets, and several souvenir shops, as well as two spaces accessible only to a limited audience (an apartment and a restaurant).[27] However, the changes that did occur – from the revision of New Orleans Square's temporal setting and certain scenes in "Pirates," as well as the reorganization of retail during the 1980s and 1990s, to the introduction of more and more self-referential elements during the 1990s and 2000s, to the various modifications to improve visitor circulation in the 1980s and 2010s – can all be linked to some of the most frequently discussed paradigms in current research on theme parks and themed environments, namely: theming's "politics of inclusion/exclusion" (Lukas, "Politics" 277) in general and the use of controversial issues through techniques of "dark theming" in particular; the conflation of entertainment and consumerism; the growing relevance of self-referential elements and/or "autotheming"; as well as the increasing privatization of public urban space through design strategies adapted from theme parks, a process sometimes referred to as "Disneyfication."

Hence, New Orleans Square can be seen not only as a theme park representation of the Crescent City and its multicultural heritage, but also as a veritable "showcase" of theme park history, a place where some of the most important issues and trends in the development of the medium, as identified by theme park researchers, have crystallized and left concrete traces in the shapes of seemingly minor changes in merchandise offerings, ride scene details, or access routes to restaurants. Perhaps most importantly, a detailed study of the history of New Orleans Square offers new insights into the long critical debate about the "Disneyfication" of public urban space. Scholars have found evidence of "Disneyfication" in North American cities as diverse as New York, Montréal, Minneapolis, and Seattle, but also in Medina, Ohio, as well as in Anaheim, Orlando, and even New Orleans. As I will argue toward the end of this section, however, in what could be described as a "feedback loop of Disneyfication" – or perhaps a classic case of a monster turning upon its creator – the 1987 redesign of the entrance to "Pirates" and the 2014 expansion of "Club 33" also brought elements of "Disneyfied" urban spaces back to the Disney parks and specifically to the simulated urbanity of New Orleans Square.

From New York to Anaheim: Imagineering the Crescent City

The pre-opening history of New Orleans Square, as well as many of the decisions that affected its final design, are inextricably linked to the 1964–1965 New York World's Fair, where Disney contributed to no fewer than four pavilions (namely, those sponsored by the State of Illinois, General Electric, Ford, and Pepsi-Cola). To be sure, the designers also took research trips to New Orleans and heavily relied on the city's architecture, history, and folklore in their concepts, yet Disney's involvement in the World's Fair had an almost equal impact on the ultimate shape of the area and particularly that of its two signature rides: the "Great Moments with Mr. Lincoln" show created for the World's Fair's Illinois pavilion and the "Carousel of Progress" ride designed for the GE pavilion substantially contributed to the development of audio-animatronic (robot) technology, while Ford's "Magic Skyway" and the "it's a small world" ride created for the Pepsi-Cola pavilion allowed the designers to experiment with new and more efficient ride systems, all of which would eventually play central roles in both the "Pirates" and the "Haunted Mansion" rides at New Orleans Square. Simultaneously, work on the Fair (as well as the death of Walt Disney in 1966) also caused significant delays in the development of the "land," which would not be complete until the debut of the "Haunted Mansion" in 1969.

Indeed, New Orleans Square had been almost a decade in the making before it opened as Disneyland's first new "land" since the park's debut in 1955. Already in 1957, teams of designers – including Herbert Ryman, who would later become the leading designer of the Square's general layout and its façades – were sent on research trips to New Orleans and "came back with snapshots of the French Quarter" (Marling, "Imagineering" 115).[28] A first general sketch of the area, drawn by Sam McKim the same year, shows a roughly triangular square with a central fountain, bordered by the already existing "Chicken Plantation" restaurant on the western side, a somewhat dilapidated mansion labeled "Haunted House" on the southern side, and, on the eastern side, a long block of city buildings with wrought-iron balconies containing, according to the labels pasted onto the sketch, a "thieves market" and a "wax museum" devoted to pirates (see Kurtti and Gordon 49–50). A remarkably similar layout appeared a year later in the park's 1958 "Fun Map," also drawn by McKim, where the area was identified as a "future development" located between Adventureland, New Orleans Street, and the train tracks (see McKim, *1958*). And in an article for *True West* magazine, also published in 1958, Walt Disney announced the creation of "a Louisiana Purchase section, where we'll reproduce the New Orleans French Quarter, together with a fantastic Haunted House filled with all manner of delightful ghosts" (12).

From the very beginning, then, the concepts for New Orleans Square featured numerous references to the architecture of the French Quarter and to myths and folklore popularly associated with New Orleans in general and with the Vieux Carré in particular – indeed, the inspiration for the "Haunted House" and the pirate "wax museum" may have come straight out of the pages of *Scribner's/Century*, particularly George Washington Cable's "Jean-ah Poquelin" (1875) and "The 'Haunted House' in Royal Street" (1889) with their allusions to ghosts and the supernatural as well as Cable's "Madame Delphine" (1881) and "Plotters and Pirates of Louisiana" (1883) and their evocation of pirates and privateers. These basic architectural and thematic references would be kept for the final design, although the details of the overall layout and of the "Haunted House"'s exterior were still shifting: by 1961, when groundbreaking was begun, the façade of the "Haunted House" had been completely redesigned to resemble a Southern urban mansion with a carefully landscaped garden (see the sketches by Ken Anderson reprinted in Surrell, *Haunted Mansion* 13; and 21) and the building had been moved from the extreme southern to the extreme northern end of New Orleans Square, where it was separated from the rest of the area by the (already existing) Frontierland train station.

Thus, however, New Orleans Square had been effectively split into two distinct sections: a southern part themed to the French Quarter, containing the pirate wax museum, as well as the "thieves market," and evoking both the city's French and Spanish heritage; and a northern part consisting of the "Haunted House," whose design was ostensibly based on a Victorian mansion in Baltimore, Maryland (see Baham 12–3), but which was actually supposed to refer to New Orleans's Garden District and thus evoked New Orleans's Anglo-American heritage (see Hobbs 93). The new layout first appeared in the "Fun Maps" in 1962, which showed the redesigned and renamed "Haunted Mansion" located to the north of a horseshoe-shaped complex that featured numerous balconies and contained the wax museum (now referred to as "Pirates of the Caribbean"), the "thieves market," and a new element, the "Blue Bayou Mart" (see McKim, 1962). That same year, an article published in the *Los Angeles Times* announced the opening of New Orleans Square in 1963 (see N.N., "\$7 Million") and indeed, in 1963, at least the exterior of the "Haunted Mansion" was finished.

Yet, work on the New Orleans Square construction site had virtually come to a halt, and a sign posted in front of the "Haunted Mansion" attempted to humorously explain the delay by pretending the park was still looking for "ghosts and restless spirits" interested in taking up residence at Disneyland (see Surrell, *Haunted Mansion* 20). In fact, however, rather than "casting" ghosts, WED Enterprises had shifted from finishing the plans for New Orleans Square to designing the four rides Walt Disney had agreed to contribute to the State of Illinois, General Electric, Ford, and Pepsi-Cola pavilions at the 1964–1965 New York World's Fair. According to a biographer, Disney's involvement in the World's Fair was mainly motivated by four goals: to "try out Disney ideas on an East Coast audience," to "generate money by working for large corporations and designing their exhibits," to "create attractions that could be brought back to Disneyland," and to "focus on the development of new ways to design and execute rides and displays" (Krasniewicz 132–3).

With respect to New Orleans Square, the last goal was undoubtedly the most significant and consequential one. Before work on the World's Fair began, both the "Pirates" attraction and the "Haunted Mansion" had been conceptualized as walk-through experiences featuring wax figures (in the case of "Pirates") and tableaux animated with special effects (in the case of the "Haunted Mansion"; see Surrell, *Pirates* 18–20; and *Haunted Mansion* 15). With the perfection of audio-animatronics for the Illinois and Pepsi-Cola pavilions, however – according to a press release, a "grand combination of all the arts," including "the three-dimensional realism of fine sculpture, the vitality of a great painting, the drama and personal rapport of the theater, and the artistic versatility and consistency of the motion picture" (qtd. in Schickel 327) – Disney decided to make the wax figures and tableaux come to electronic life: in 1963, articles in the *Los Angeles Times* and *National Geographic* announced the use of audio-animatronic robots in both "Pirates" and the "Haunted Mansion" (see N.N., "Tiki Room"; and De Roos 207).

Whereas the inclusion of audio-animatronics in the New Orleans Square attractions was thus highly publicized from the very beginning, the introduction of new ride systems, also based on technology originally developed for the World's Fair, was rarely mentioned in the press, probably because it was primarily motivated by operational concerns about the low capacity of walk-through attractions (see Surrell, *Haunted Mansion* 30). In order to handle the masses of visitors expected at the Fair's Pepsi-Cola and Ford pavilions,[29] Disney had developed two innovative and efficient ride systems: a so-called flume ride system using "a flat bottomed boat in a channel of water . . ., pushed along by a current" (Younger, *Theme Park Design* 426) for Pepsi-Cola's "it's a small world," and an endless transit system based on rotating tires embedded in a track for Ford's "Magic Skyway" (somewhat ironically, then, the Ford automobiles used as ride vehicles in the "Skyway" did not move by themselves; see Younger, *Theme Park Design* 419). After first considering the flume ride system for both "Pirates" and the "Haunted Mansion," it was eventually decided to use it only for the former, while the latter would feature a continuously moving, looped chain of ride vehicles called "Omnimover" (see Younger, *Theme Park Design* 420–1), a "direct descendant of the [ride system] developed for Ford's Magic Skyway" (Surrell, *Haunted Mansion* 30).[30]

Once the World's Fair attractions were up and running in April 1964, WED designers turned their attention back to New Orleans Square, with Dorothea Redmond now in charge of interior designs and Herbert Ryman responsible for the façades and the overall layout (see Surrell, *Pirates* 19; and 21). Among many other sketches, Ryman created, in 1964, a large watercolor and pen and ink concept painting called "The Square" (reproduced in Gordon and Mumford 182–3), which is notable for a number of reasons. First, it illustrates how Ryman had reorganized the layout of the Square's "French Quarter" section, splitting up the huge show building for "Pirates," the "thieves market," and the "Blue Bayou" into several smaller structures with, as the artist comments, "winding streets curving out of view [to] arouse people's curiosity and invite them in to explore" (Gordon and Mumford 182). Second, the two buildings at the center of the painting closely resemble – but do not exactly reproduce – the architecture of the Cabildo and the Presbytère, the two colonial structures flanking the St. Louis cathedral and facing Jackson Square in New

Orleans (cf. the arches on the first floor, the central pediment, the mansard roofs, and the cupolas), while the space between the two buildings is filled with trees and smaller buildings with wrought-iron balconies rather than with a structure evoking the cathedral. Finally, the foreground of the picture shows a landscaped area with benches and planters surrounded by black, ornate iron railings.[31]

"The Square" thus points to a number of important changes in the design of New Orleans Square that occurred during the last, post-World's Fair stage of the area's planning history: unlike New Orleans Street, the new "land" and particularly its "French Quarter" section would actually seek to create an atmosphere of urbanity by positioning a number of irregularly shaped buildings at odd angles in order to create several "winding" streets with closed vistas. Also in contrast to New Orleans Street, the façades of New Orleans Square would newly recombine specific elements of well-known, actually existing New Orleans structures such as the Cabildo and the balconied buildings on Royal Street to form what Filippo Carlà-Uhink and I have elsewhere described as "abstractions" or "amalgamations of typical features associated with [a particular] type of building in its most recognizable forms" (245). Finally, Ryman's painting indicates the use of a park-like area, reminiscent of Jackson Square and nowadays informally referred to as "Magnolia Park" (see Strodder 256), to visually separate New Orleans Square's "French Quarter" from its "Garden District" section.

By 1965, then, almost eight years after the first concept sketch had been drawn and more than two years after the originally projected opening date, the general plans for New Orleans Square had been completed and the Disneyland marketing department shifted into high gear: full-page ads, illustrated with Ryman's "The Square" and placed, among others, in the *Los Angeles Times*, announced the opening of the Square for the 1966–1967 season; and in a January 1965 episode of his weekly television show, Walt Disney showed off scale models of the "French Quarter" section, as well as the "Haunted Mansion." Both the ads and the television show highlight the "winding streets" and the "courtyards" of the "French Quarter" section, where visitors can find "fine shops" and "restaurants serving exotic foods" (N.N., "Ad 1965"; Luske, "Anniversary" 00:08:54–00:09:17), but they also prominently feature the two rides, with, for instance, Walt Disney taking Disneyland ambassador Julie Reihm through a mock-up of "Pirates" (00:12:00–00:13:15; N.N., "Ad 1965").

As the designers still had to work on the details of the two rides, however, and presumably also to spread the novelty draw of the new "land" and its signature attractions,[32] it was decided to open New Orleans Square in three stages: the shops and restaurants of the "French Quarter" would debut on 24 July 1966, "Pirates" on 19 April 1967, and the "Haunted Mansion" on 12 August 1969. Thus, however, the park simultaneously depicted the area as being composed of three main elements, with each element evoking one of New Orleans's (former) rulers: France (the shops and restaurants of the "French Quarter" with their French names),[33] Spain ("Pirates" with its vague setting in the "Spanish Main"),[34] and the United States (the "Haunted Mansion" with its "Garden District" setting).

The Crescent City on Screen: Opening New Orleans Square

To publicize the opening of the park's latest addition, the Disneyland marketing department placed ads in local newspapers such as the *Los Angeles Times*, published articles in promotional magazines such as *Vacationland* and the *Disney News*,[35] and distributed press kits (see, among others, N.N., "Ad 1966"; N.N., "New Orleans Square"; N.N., "All New for '66!"; and N.N., *Profile*, respectively). Above all, however, the successive openings of the individual "parts" of New Orleans Square – the "French Quarter" section, "Pirates," and the "Garden District" section with the "Haunted Mansion" – were each marked by intricately choreographed and elaborately staged ceremonies and performances that were, of course, widely covered by the local press, but also and especially by Disney's own weekly show on national television. Even more so than during the opening of New Orleans Street in "Dateline: Disneyland" eleven years earlier, Disney thus effectively used the park's telegenic landscapes as a setting for sophisticated screen productions, particularly for the openings of "Pirates" and the "Haunted Mansion." Moreover, and again even more so than for the opening of New Orleans Street, Disney also employed celebrities and music, especially for the openings of the "French Quarter" section and the "Haunted Mansion," to generally create interest in the shows, but also to define the respective target audience for each of the individual "sections" of New Orleans Square and, perhaps most importantly, to establish each section's specific "ethnic" identity.

In *Populuxe* (1986), Thomas Hine describes Disneyland as "a place that was like walking into a movie." The designers of the park, Hine notes, "did not think as architects; [but] in very literally cinematic terms" (151). Elsewhere, I have built on Hine's remarks to develop a systematic categorization of the complex and multifarious intermedial relationships between movies and (Disney) theme parks (see Freitag, "'Like Walking'"). In the present context, however, I am using them simply to point to the fact that like elsewhere in the park, designer Herbert Ryman – who was originally an art director and illustrator for MGM, Twentieth Century Fox, and Disney Studios (see Strodder 370) – included techniques borrowed from the construction of movie sets (e.g., "forced perspective")[36] into his plans for New Orleans Square, not only for economic and psychological reasons (see Younger, *Theme Park Design* 330–1), but perhaps also because he knew that starting with the opening ceremonies, New

Orleans Square would in fact also be used as a set for TV productions. New Orleans Square was designed for visual effect, to be looked at either by the human eye or by the mechanical eye of the camera.

The new "land" made its first appearance on the small screen on 18 December 1966, in "Disneyland around the Seasons," a special episode of *Walt Disney's Wonderful World of Color*, Disney's weekly TV show on NBC.[37] Reviewing (and, of course, promoting) the additions to Disneyland made during the previous season (among them "Great Moments with Mr. Lincoln," "it's a small world," and the "Primeval World," all of them relocated to Disneyland from the New York World's Fair), "Disneyland around the Seasons" also features footage from the official opening of New Orleans Square's "French Quarter" section, which had taken place five months before, on 24 July. The highlights of that ceremony – dedication speeches by Walt Disney and by New Orleans's then mayor, Victor Schiro – had already been widely covered by the local press: in an article entitled "'Looks Just Like Home': Mayor of Real New Orleans Praises Disneyland Replica" and published the day after the opening, for instance, the *Los Angeles Times* focuses on how "plainly enchanted" and impressed Schiro was with the "authentic" visuals, smells, foods, and especially sounds offered by New Orleans Square. Concerning the "highly-trained staff," Schiro is quoted as having said "in his soft accent": "'They pronounce it New Olyuns . . . . Not Noo Orleans'" (McPhillips). Apparently not satisfied with Schiro's assessment alone, the *Orange Daily News* had sent Bill Carney, "who is presently Sports Editor and a staff writer for the Daily News, [but] originally from New Orleans and lived there for 22 years," to cover the event (Carney). Carney fully corroborates Schiro's remarks by judging New Orleans Square "another triumph for Disney in factual and delightful portrayal of America's rich history and heritage" (Carney).

"Disneyland around the Seasons," too, stresses the authenticity of New Orleans Square's depiction of the Crescent City, particularly with respect to its architecture: over long and medium shots of the buildings, Walt Disney's voice-over asserts that "[t]he original architecture and atmosphere of old New Orleans of the 1850s has [sic] been retained. The narrow, winding streets, intimate courtyards, and the iron-laced balconies are authentic in every detail" (Luske, "Seasons" 00:24:27–00:24:45). Already in the mid-1980s, critics such as Mike Wallace noted that while more or less freely admitting to "whitewashing" history in the parks, the "Disney people . . . also insist they are bringing out deeper truths. John Hench, a leading member of the organization, expanded on this in an interview, explaining that Disney sought to recapture the *essence* of a period" (36; emphasis original). At least in the case of the opening of New Orleans Square, however, Disney neither admits to having "improved" upon history nor resorts to concepts of a "deeper truth" or a historical "*essence*," but quite simply asserts that its representation of New Orleans at the park is "authentic in every detail." Allusions to the contrary, although they were made at the time,[38] were not officially released.

At the same time, "Disneyland around the Seasons" also borrows heavily from "Dateline: Disneyland" in that here, too, New Orleans and its representation at Disneyland are imaginatively linked via (live) jazz music, albeit to a different effect. "New Orleans," Disney asserts in his voice-over, "was the birthplace of marching jazz bands. Here in Disneyland's New Orleans Square, the tradition is an everyday occurrence" (Luske, "Seasons" 00:26:38–00:26:46). Viewers see (and hear) a six-piece, all-white Dixieland band – possibly an enlarged version of the "Strawhatters" – led by two black singers and dancers, marching down the streets of New Orleans Square past visitors as well as a "southern belle" who is waving at the musicians from one of the iron-laced balconies. The parade eventually arrives at the patio of the "French Market Restaurant," where it climbs a small stage and continues to play and dance for the audience seated at their tables. Disney comments: "Diners in French and Creole sidewalk cafés are entertained in true Dixieland fashion" (00:27:12–00:27:18). While building, much like "Dateline: Disneyland" did, upon the popular association of New Orleans with jazz music performed live in public spaces, New Orleans Square's parade is spirited, but decidedly more orderly and sedate than the wild, boisterous, and explicitly sensual Mardi Gras of New Orleans Street. This time, rather than invading the (New Orleans) street, the carnival is, eventually, safely confined to the stages of New Orleans Square.

Also in contrast to "Dateline: Disneyland," "Disneyland around the Seasons" actually tells its viewers about the various offerings of New Orleans Square and specifically its shops, but does so in a way that once again characterizes the new "land" as much more calm and refined than its predecessor. Over shots of artists manufacturing silk and stained-glass flowers and of children admiring jewelry and antiques, such as an old-fashioned coffee mill or a brass model ship, Disney notes: "The quaint shops offer treasures from all over the world. Craftsmen create articles in silver, stained glass, and many other materials" (Luske, "Seasons" 00:25:50–00:25:59). The countless shots of children goggling at high-end merchandise through shop windows confirm rather than undermine the general sense that New Orleans Square – or, rather, its "French Quarter" section – is, in fact, no place for children at all, but instead addresses an adult audience interested in tasteful merchandise and elegant dining. New Orleans Square's "French Quarter" thus depicts the city's French past as reassuringly exotic and, at the same time, as enticingly sophisticated.

The opening of "Pirates" was also featured a few months after the actual event, which had taken place in April 1967, in a special episode of *Walt Disney's Wonderful World of Color* that promoted the latest additions to the park (among them, once again, rides relocated from the World's Fair).

Entitled "Disneyland: From the Pirates of the Caribbean to the World of Tomorrow" and aired on 21 January 1968, the program combines old New Orleans Square-related footage from previous episodes (notably the 1965 "Anniversary" show that featured scale models of the area, and the 1967 "Disneyland around the Seasons" show that covered the opening of the "French Quarter")[39] with new images from the "Pirates" opening press event. After repeating the by now familiar statements concerning the "faithful[ness]" of Disney's "recreation" of New Orleans and the "sheer elegance" of its shops, restaurants, and overall design (Luske, "Pirates" 00:11:26–00:12:34), host and Disneyland ambassador Marcia Miner is joined by whom she calls her "friends Captain Hook and Mr. Smee from *Peter Pan*" to state that "at the Walt Disney Studio, we've always been partial to pirate stories" and to thus introduce the new ride (00:12:56–00:13:12).

The emphasis on Disney's supposedly long-standing penchant for pirates is probably meant to somewhat counterpoise the slightly un-Disneyesque and – at least by today's standards – downright controversial scenes from the opening that viewers were about to see: the basic plot of the press event revolves around Disneyland's "Sailing Ship Columbia," with a crew of reporters and special guests aboard, being attacked and overtaken by a group of pirates who make the sailors walk the plank and the hostesses distribute the ship's cargo of "rum" to the reporters (Luske, "Pirates" 00:13:14–00:15:25). With the press in tow, the pirates then land in New Orleans Square, kill the two colonial soldiers who guard the entrance to "Pirates," batter the doors open, and thus clear the way for the public (00:15:26–00:16:29). Finally, viewers of *Walt Disney's Wonderful World of Color* get to watch a full ride-through of the attraction, which alternates between close-ups of the ride scenes and reaction shots of the visitors (00:16:30–00:25:49).

Some of the more disturbing scenes from the press event include the pirates killing the sailors and the soldiers, but especially the pirates carrying the screaming hostesses over their shoulders as well as beating and poking at them with their swords, acts later repeated by the audio-animatronic pirates in the ride. Shots of the "killed" soldiers getting up again as well as of smiling and laughing hostesses are interspersed to indicate that everything is happening "in good fun," but could also be interpreted, of course, and particularly in the latter case, as signifying that the women actually enjoy the violence. Hence, the elaborately staged opening of "Pirates" characterizes the Spanish-themed section of New Orleans Square – in direct contrast to the "French Quarter" section previously opened – as a male-dominated and action-filled, morally ambiguous, and ultimately transgressive space that even at the time was considered somewhat incongruous in the context of the entire park (see Malnic; indeed, "Pirates" would be significantly toned down in the following; see ahead).

For the opening of the "Haunted Mansion," finally, Disney switched tactics: to be sure, viewers of "Disneyland Showtime," which promoted the new attraction and aired on 22 March 1970, almost seven months after the original opening of the ride in August 1969, also got to watch a short documentary about the making of the "Haunted Mansion," as well as a full ride-through with, again, shots of the ride scenes alternating with reaction shots of visitors (see Wiles 00:36:40–00:41:43; and 00:42:28–00:46:48, respectively). Rather than staging a press event and sending camera crews to cover it for the show, however, the writers and producers created a shrewd cross-promotional venture in the shape of a comedy set at the park and starring actors Kurt Russell and E.J. Peaker as well as the Osmond Brothers (all playing themselves). Indeed, the razor-thin plot of "Disneyland Showtime" – the Osmonds are supposed to give a concert at the park, but the youngest brother, Donny Osmond, is much more interested in seeing the new "Haunted Mansion" than in rehearsing and thus wanders off, which prompts the others to scour the park for him – offers plenty of opportunities for Russell, Peaker, and the Osmonds to display their singing talents and, simultaneously, for Disneyland to showcase its picturesque landscapes and rides: Peaker, for instance, performs "Walking Happy" aboard the "Mark Twain" riverboat (00:16:30–00:19:03) and the Osmonds, who had actually started their professional career at Disneyland and had already appeared on Disney's show in 1962 (see Osmond 33), sing Creedence Clearwater Revival's "Down on the Corner" while riding the bus down Main Street, U.S.A. (00:04:50–00:06:53).

After Disney had targeted mature and primarily female visitors looking for high-end shopping and sophisticated dining in "Disneyland around the Seasons" and a predominantly male audience looking for action and adventure in "Disneyland: From the Pirates of the Caribbean to the World of Tomorrow," "Disneyland Showtime" thus employed the popularity of Beaker, Russell, and particularly the Osmonds to position the "Haunted Mansion" – and, in fact, Disneyland in general – as an attractive destination for a gender-neutral and young (child and teenage) demographic. Any subversive potential that the idea of a "Haunted House" at Disneyland may have – much like "Pirates," the ride somewhat diverges from the atmosphere of optimism and reassurance that pervades the rest of the park – is more than offset by the program's overall comedic tone. However, while the show features several scenes set in New Orleans Square's "French Quarter" section – Donny, along with the characters of Brer Bear and Brer Fox,[40] dances to the music of the "Strawhatters" and the "Royal Street Bachelors"[41] (see Wiles 00:07:45–00:08:44; and 00:11:52–00:12:30, respectively) – no attempt whatsoever is made to connect the ride to its New Orleans Square setting. By 1970, Disney apparently no longer felt the need to explain the internal "logic" of the park to its audience.

Cleaning Up the Streets: New Orleans Square in Changing Cultural Climates

At the same time, and starting shortly after the opening of New Orleans Square already, Disney apparently did consider it necessary to adjust its portrayal of New Orleans to the public's changing notions of political or social acceptability and appropriateness. As commercial enterprises that depend on attracting a maximum amount of visitors in order to be economically successful, theme parks have always been careful to select themes that are easily recognizable to as many people as possible, but also to avoid themes (or aspects of a theme) that might offend or alienate potential customers (see Carlà and Freitag 244). In the history of theme parks, these "politics of inclusion/exclusion" (Lukas, "Politics" 277) have frequently inspired both the use of particularly racial or ethnic stereotypes (due to their recognizability) and, with changing times, their later removal (due to their offensiveness). Indeed, while scholars have continued to criticize especially the Disney parks' politics of theming – Wasko considers this "fashionable sport of 'Disney bashing'" as largely responsible for the "boom in 'Disney studies'" from the 1990s onwards (4) – numerous examples from their history and that of other theme parks illustrate how vital the idea of "appropriateness" has been to the sites and how they have constantly adapted to changing perceptions of what exactly constitutes an "offensive" depiction. With respect to Disneyland's Frontierland, for instance, these examples include the retheming of "Aunt Jemima's Kitchen" to the "Magnolia Tree Terrace" in 1970 (see earlier), but also the renaming of the "Indian War Canoes" to "Davy Crockett Explorer Canoes" in 1971, as well as the opening of the ride's race- and gender-specific hiring practices in 1971 and 1995, respectively (see Wiener 134).

With respect to neighboring New Orleans Square, the issues thus addressed over the years have likewise involved the representation of racial minorities (African Americans), but also the general depiction of the South as well as the portrayal of violence against women. Whereas some of the alterations at New Orleans Square motivated by changing cultural climates, however, were instantly noticeable at the park and have therefore been widely discussed both in the press and among fans, others were more subtle, often affecting the representation of New Orleans Square in promotional publications rather than the park landscape itself, and have thus only rarely been acknowledged by visitors, journalists, or critics. Taken together and notwithstanding the continuing criticism of the company's politics of theming, these alterations nevertheless testify to Disney's sensitiveness to such critiques – a sensitiveness that is, undoubtedly, primarily motivated by concerns about the company's corporate image and profitability, but that still has translated into concrete changes of even such iconic rides as "Pirates."

Some of the first changes, taking place in 1969 and thus a mere two seasons after the opening of the "French Quarter" section, concerned the depiction of African Americans at New Orleans Square. Quite in contrast to its predecessor, New Orleans Street, the "land" has featured no explicit and/or permanent references to African Americans and their contributions to the multicultural makeup of New Orleans.[42] With the by then considerably enlarged "Aunt Jemima's Kitchen" right next door (at least until 1970; see earlier), including a specifically African-American–themed space in New Orleans Square, may have seemed somewhat redundant to the designers. However, as part of its original "streetmosphere" entertainment program, the "Royal Street Bachelors," an all-black jazz trio led by clarinetist Jack McVea, and "Teddy and Kenny," two young African-American boys (probably in their early or mid-teens) dressed up as shoe-shiners, would roam around New Orleans Square, frequently together, entertaining visitors with their live music and dancing.

Both the "Bachelors" and "Teddy and Kenny" were featured prominently in promotional material about New Orleans Square and particularly in the TV specials dedicated to the openings of the "French Quarter" section and the "Haunted Mansion."[43] Whereas the "Bachelors" appear to have been newly formed explicitly for New Orleans Square, however, the characters of "Teddy" and "Kenny" had already shined shoes prior to 1966 on Main Street, U.S.A. (see DeCaro, "Teddy and Kenny"), thus partly disproving frequent critical statements about the "exclusion of African Americans and their history from the representational syntax" of that "land" (Avila 135). The original "Bachelors" continued to regularly perform in New Orleans Square until the death of banjoist Harold Grant in 1985 and the retirement of McVea in 1992 (see DeCaro, "Bachelors"; Strodder 368), but according to entertainment guidebooks distributed at the park, a jazz trio with the same name still entertains visitors at New Orleans Square in 2020. By contrast, after "dancing and shining in New Orleans Square from 10:00 a.m. to 6:00 p.m." daily during the summer season and on weekends and holidays during the winter season until fall/winter 1968, "Teddy and Kenny" disappeared from the "Entertainment" sections of Disneyland visitor guides in summer 1969.[44] By the time Donny Osmond danced to the music of the "Bachelors" in "Disneyland Showtime" (1970; see earlier), the trio was no longer accompanied by Teddy and Kenny, but by Brer Bear, Brer Fox, and the Three Little Pigs.

Child labor issues aside, it is easy to see why Disney discontinued the "Teddy and Kenny" act around the same time as, elsewhere in the park, it replaced "Aunt Jemima," the "Indian War Canoes," and, incidentally, the "Indian Village" with its live dance performances (see Wiener 134) – but also why, much like "Aunt Jemima," the two shoeshiners have been virtually excised from "official" histories of Disneyland. Drawn, as they were, from "tradition[s] of racial stereotyping in the national culture" rather than having been invented by Disney (Avila 135), the bellicose Native

Americans and the subservient black mammies and shoeshine boys were included in the park for their easy recognizability, but removed as soon as Disney felt they would hurt rather than foster business.

As in the case of Alyene Lewis (the actress who played "Aunt Jemima"), however, it is also interesting to see how the characters have been perceived by the performers themselves. Talking about the four years he worked as "Teddy" alongside Kenny "Kenny" Bell before outgrowing the role and playing one of the Three Little Pigs, Teddy Miller, for instance, above all remembers roaming the park and riding the rides for free while being watched over by the "Royal Street Bachelors," who would make sure the two young performers would save some of their tips (see DeCaro, "New Orleans Square"). Hence, emphasizing the feelings of camaraderie and responsibility among New Orleans Square's African-American performers, but especially the fun he had while working for the park, Miller once again raises "the problem with pleasure" (as well as the possibility that he may have danced with Donny Osmond after all, though not in his role as "Teddy," but as one of the "Three Little Pigs").

Around the same time it removed "Teddy and Kenny" from New Orleans Square (as well as other stereotypical depictions of African and Native Americans from neighboring Frontierland), Disneyland also slowly started shifting the temporal setting of the "land." In contrast to New Orleans Street, which, following the story of "Aunt Jemima" (see earlier), was located in a decidedly vague, postbellum past, New Orleans Square was originally set at a precise point in time: both the ads placed in the *Los Angeles Times* as well as the descriptive *Profile* distributed to the press for the 1966 opening of the "French Quarter" section located the new "land" in the year 1850. The ad, for instance, invited readers to take "a trip back through time to the New Orleans of 1850" (N.N., "Ad 1966") and in its description of the "Blue Bayou," the *Profile* noted how "[w]rought iron furnishings and candlelight contribute to the Louisiana, 1850, flavor" of the restaurant (N.N., *Profile* 10). In the park itself, a U.S. flag flown atop the "Pirates" building features 30 stars and has thus indicated to observant visitors that New Orleans Square is set somewhere between 4 July 1848 (the year the 30-star-flag became the official flag of the United States after the addition of the 30th star for the newly admitted state of Wisconsin) and 4 July 1851 (the year the 31st star was added for the admission of California).[45] Originally, then, the Square depicted antebellum New Orleans.

It may not be very surprising that in its portrayal of 1850 New Orleans, Disney failed to make a single reference to slavery in general and the city's then role as the hub of the interstate slave trade in particular (as depicted in "Scribner's Illustrated New Orleans" in, for instance, Grace E. King's "A Crippled Hope"; see Chapter 1). In fact, the only allusion to slavery is decorously hidden in the opening description of "New Orleans, the 1850's" in the 1966 *Profile* of New Orleans Square, which characterizes

New Orleans as "a city of contrasts" where "[t]heatres provided the most sophisticated entertainment as domestics danced the ritualistic bamboula and colinda at stage doors" (N.N., *Profile* 1–2; the designers may not have read King's "A Crippled Hope," then, but they must have heard of Cable's "Creole Slave Dances"). What *is* surprising, by contrast, is that among all the other "Distories" and cases of "historical erasure" identified by critics in the Disney parks, the omission of slavery in New Orleans Square appears to have been almost completely ignored by critics.[46]

Disney, however, must have become aware of the fact that New Orleans Square's utter silence on the subject of slavery had an increasing potential for controversy, for over the years, the temporal setting of New Orleans Square has been rendered more vague and, even more importantly, generally been pushed to the postbellum period: a 1975 *Vacationland* article on the "French Market Restaurant," for instance, speculates that "[l]unch may have been like this 125 years ago in New Orleans" (N.N., "Fine Food" 13) and thus still locates the "land" in 1850. By the early 1980s, however, the *Vacationland* contributors and the script writers of *A Day at Disneyland*, a souvenir video sold in the park's shops, had shifted to the more ambiguous expression "mid-nineteenth century" (see N.N., "Profile" 5; and Elliott 00:05:32–00:05:41). The 2015 "New Orleans Square at Disneyland Park Fact Sheet," published on the park's official website, finally, is even more vague, locating the Square simply "in the 1800s" (N.N., "Fact Sheet").

In the park itself, additions to the décor have contributed to muddling the originally precise temporal setting of New Orleans Square. By 2007, for instance, while the 30-star U.S. flag was still flown atop the "Pirates" building, "triple flags" – featuring the contemporary flags of the United States, France, and Spain – had appeared on several New Orleans Square balconies (see DeCaro, "New Orleans Square"), thus setting the "land" in an ahistorical, fantastic time in which it is governed by all of its former and present "rulers" at the same time.[47] Indeed, the "Pirates of the Caribbean Show Information Guide," an internal reference memo that I was shown (but not allowed to photocopy) during one of my research trips to New Orleans Square in April 2016, confirms that "New Orleans Square is truly a timeless land, where the past and the present blend together in perfect harmony."

Simultaneously, and even more importantly, minor changes to New Orleans Square signage and architecture have pushed the "land" forward into the early twentieth century: already in 1997, both the signs of the newly opened "Jewel of Orleans" store, as well as a plaque mounted in the "Court of Angels," first introduced art deco elements to New Orleans Square (see DeCaro, "New Orleans Square" and "Court of Angels"). In 2013–2014, during the expansion of the "Club 33" restaurant (see ahead), large stained-glass screens decorated with art deco floral motifs were installed to close off the "Court of Angels" from the general public (see DeCaro, "Club 33 Pg. 2"), thus reinforcing the new temporal setting of New Orleans Square in the "art deco" period. While there remains a certain feeling of nostalgia for the Old South – the musical sheets displayed on one of the balconies suggest that Dan D. Emmett's "Dixie's Land" is a favorite among the musicians "living" in New Orleans Square – the "land" has generally been pushed, then, from its original antebellum setting toward the period of the 1910s and 1920s. Remaining true to its "politics of inclusion/exclusion," Disney, rather than "filling in" the representational blanks of the original New Orleans Square, has preferred to move the temporal setting of the "land" to a point in time when the park can no longer be accused of "historical erasure."[48]

The year 1997 also saw significant changes being made to the "Pirates" ride which were not related to the portrayal of African Americans or the Old South in New Orleans Square, however, but rather to the depiction of women. With the ride's basic plot revolving around a band of pirates attacking and burning a seaport in the Spanish Caribbean, critics have felt the need to account for the presence of "Pirates" and its "dark theming"[49] in the generally reassuring and optimistic environment of Disneyland almost from the very start – in fact, the debut of "Pirates" in 1967 roughly coincided with the beginnings of academic research on (Disney) theme parks (cf., for instance, the publication of Schickel's *The Disney Version* in 1968). Some, such as Umberto Eco, have related the inclusion of the supposedly incongruous "Pirates" to the imperatives of the entertainment industry: "The ideology of America," Eco writes, "wants to establish reassurance through Imitation. But profits defeat ideology, because the consumers want to be thrilled not only by the guarantee of the Good but also by the shudder of the Bad" (57). Others, including Elizabeth and Jay Mechling, as well as Susan Aronstein, have argued that the ride serves as a negative example, a deliberate "counterpoint to the ideal" represented elsewhere in the park (Mechling and Mechling 175; see also Aronstein 67). Still others, such as Priscilla Hobbs, finally, have viewed "Pirates" (as well as the "Haunted Mansion") as an attempt to symbolically and imaginatively contain the "growing counterculture movements" of the 1960s (99–100).

As has been pointed out by Louis Marin in 1973 already, however, "Pirates" is, in fact (and in stark contrast to the performance staged for its opening; see earlier), quite explicit in its condemnation of the behavior of its protagonists and thus perfectly fits into the park's "morality play" (Real 48). Opening with scenes of pirate skeletons lying on their accumulated treasures over the sounds of a disembodied voice proclaiming that "dead men tell no tales," the ride tells its story, Marin correctly notes,

> in a reverse chronological order; the first scene in the tour-narrative is the last scene in the "real" story. And this inversion has an ethical meaning: crime does not pay. The morality of the fable is presented

before the reading of the story in order to constrain the comprehension of the fable by a preexisting moral code.

(254)

During a 1997 refurbishment on the occasion of the ride's 30th anniversary, designers Eddie Sotto and Bob Baranick reinforced the message by adding another scene with skeletons, heaps of treasures, and the warning voice at the very end of the ride. Sotto explains: "When you make that subtle hint at the end . . ., you get what it really means. Then you are not obliged to sanitize the fun of the show so much" (qtd. in Younger, *Theme Park Design* 145).

Other scenes from "Pirates" *were* "sanitized" during this refurbishment, however, most notably the notorious "wench-chasing" scene (roughly located about ten minutes into the 15-minute ride). In the original version, three pirates were each chasing a young woman, while, in an attempt at a comic reversal, a fourth pirate was chased by a much fuller-figured woman.[50] After Richard Schickel had first criticized the scene in 1968 (329–30), the number of complaints from scholars started to increase in the early 1990s (see, for instance, Adams 146; Fjellman 228). Following the 1997 renovation, only one pirate was still chasing a woman, who was now holding a plate of food, while the other three, carrying various kinds of foodstuffs, were now chased by the women with brooms and rolling pins – implying that the pirates were no longer after the women themselves, but merely the contents of their pantries. Widely covered by the press (see e.g., Dickerson), the changes met with strong reactions from both the designers of the original version as well as fans: X. Atencio, the lyricist of the "Pirates" theme song, for instance, derided the new version as "Boy Scouts of the Caribbean" and during a 2000 special event, the revised scene was booed by the audience (see N.N., "23 Questions"; Moseley). Hence, Disney's attempt to stall criticism from one camp only led to new complaints from others. While nobody has seemed to miss "Teddy and Kenny" or the original temporal setting of New Orleans Square, the reactions to the 1997 "Pirates" refurbishment either show that by that time, the ride had gained a "cult" status that made any changes seem like a sacrilege (see also ahead), or, perhaps, that some critiques of Disney's "politics of theming" were (still) regarded as less justified than others. Undeterred, Disney has nevertheless continued to update its depiction of women in "Pirates."[51]

New Orleans Mall: Shopping in the Crescent City

Some of the other changes that were made to New Orleans Square during the period from the 1960s to the 1990s were even more directly concerned with issues of profitability. Theme park scholars agree that next to revenues from admissions and food and beverage facilities, merchandise outlets (shops, carts, and retail entertainment) constitute one of the parks' key sources of income (see, for instance, Clavé 356; or Bryman, *Disneyization* 81).[52] At the same time, merchandise outlets also significantly contribute to the atmosphere and theming of the parks and their individual "lands," both through their décor, which includes exterior façades and interior decoration, but also the costumes of the clerks, as well as through the products on sale. This deliberate intermingling or conflation of consumption and immersion has been criticized almost from the very beginnings of academic research on theme parks: scholars such as Marin, Eco, Fjellman, Gottdiener, and Bryman have all argued that by being offered in a themed environment, the merchandise sold at the parks is loaded with meanings beyond its mere use value, which turns the shops into places for the exchange of symbolic content as well as money, and the act of buying into a way of participating in the show (see Marin 247; Fjellman 161–7; Gottdiener, *Theming* 74; Bryman, *Disneyization* 34). Perhaps Eco put it most succinctly: "you buy obsessively, believing you are still playing" (43).

A detailed look at the history of merchandising at Disney parks in general, and at New Orleans Square in particular, suggests, however, that this general view needs to be somewhat qualified, especially for the period prior to the 1990s. As David Younger has pointed out:

> [f]or the first few decades of Disneyland's . . . operation, Merchandising was . . . utilizing Contributory Per Capita Operation [which] allowed individual stores to make a loss as long as the overall Merchandising department made a profit. While high capacity stores supported them, this allowed a number of smaller stores which contributed to the guest experience in theme. . . . [The latter] operated as loss leaders, purely for the show, providing niche objects which, while being for sale, would rarely actually be bought.
>
> (*Theme Park Design* 347)

Younger's strict dichotomy between high-capacity stores operated solely for profit and niche stores operated "purely for the show" may seem slightly oversimplified, but rightly insists on the fact that each merchandise outlet was expected to perform according to its own individual set of prioritized (material and non-material) goals. In an attempt to increase profitability during the early 1990s, however, Disney parks merchandising switched from contributory to "Independent Per Capita Operation," which "judges stores on a dollars per square foot basis in which each shop had to be independently profitable" (Younger, *Theme Park Design* 347). The effects of this fundamental switch in managerial strategies, which made profitability the main reason for a store's existence, became immediately noticeable in New Orleans Square.

When its "French Quarter" section opened in 1966, New Orleans Square featured a total of seven shops, as well as three outdoor vending locations (a flower stall and portrait artists, both located in the "Court of Angels," as well as a bookstand, located in the "Royal Court"). Hence, although the smallest "land" in terms of area size, New Orleans Square nevertheless comprised the second-highest number of retail outlets in the entire park, right after Main Street, U.S.A. with its 14 shops and numerous vending carts. In contrast to the latter section, however, which also featured shops and stands that mainly sold "generic" Disney souvenirs (for instance, the "Emporium," "Main Street Gifts," and the "Souvenir Stands"), New Orleans Square's retail outlets mainly consisted of craft demonstrations (so-called "retail entertainment"; see Younger, *Theme Park Design* 353) that manufactured and offered "diegetic" merchandise:[53] at "Laffite's [sic] Silver Shop," for instance, "a metal craftsman . . . makes silver charms and other jewelry on order from customers" (N.N., *Profile* 5–6); at "Cristal d'Orleans" a glass blower "specializing in creating bottles of all sizes and shapes" provides "a continuous show" for visitors (6); at "Mlle. Antoinette's Parfumerie" a "perfumer will blend special fragrances to compliment a guest's personality, complexion and type" (7); and in the "Court of Angels," artists "in corduroy smocks, sandals and black berets set up their easels [to] paint portraits of guests" (7). In addition, New Orleans Square's roster of shops also included the "One-of-A-Kind Shop" and "Le Forgeron," two antique stores focusing on furniture and stained-glass objects, respectively. Although visitor guides dutifully listed these locations as "Shops and Stores," Disney was certainly right in considering them at least partly also as attractions or, as the *Profile* of New Orleans Square describes them, as "Adventures in Shopping" (4). "Playing" did not necessarily translate into "buying obsessively" here, but also into watching the craftsmen and browsing the shelves.

It is unknown how much money New Orleans Square's retail outlets exactly made (or lost), but it seems safe to assume that overall, they did not exactly constitute gold mines for the park: in a 1979 article in the employee magazine *The Disneyland Line*, then Disneyland stage supervisor Jack Oynett maintains that "people will often come out to Disneyland for the sole purpose of acquiring something from [the 'One-of-A-Kind Shop']" (qtd. in DeCaro, "One of A Kind"), but David Koenig quotes a former Magic Kingdom store manager as saying that the "Olde World Antiques" shop (the Florida park's equivalent of Disneyland's "One-of-A-Kind Shop," located in the New England-themed Liberty Square) "made about $100,000 a year – but spent $1 million!" (111). The fact that Disney nevertheless continued to operate the store for over 20 years shows that at least in this case, the shop's contribution to the theme of the "land" was considered more important than its balance sheets.

In the mid-1990s, however, the implementation of "Independent Per Capita Operation" at Disneyland's Merchandise department began to show its effects in the streets of New Orleans Square. To be sure, some changes had already taken place prior to the switch in managerial strategies: starting in 1975, "Le Forgeron" underwent various transformations and finally became the "Mascarade d'Arlequin" hat shop in 1988. Moreover, two locations that had previously not been used for retail had been converted into stores: in 1980, the "Pirates Arcade Museum," an arcade located next to the exit of "Pirates," had reopened as "Pieces of Eight," a classic "attraction store"[54] (see Strodder 332); and in 1987, the space above the entrance to "Pirates," originally intended as a private apartment for Walt Disney, had become the "Disney Gallery" (see Solomon, "Behind-Scenes" and "Designs"). Finally, in 1988 "Laffite's [sic] Silver Shop" closed to make way for an expansion of "Café Orléans."

These changes, however, seem negligible compared to what happened in the 1990s. The first "victim" of "Independent Per Capita Operation" was the "One-of-A-Kind Shop" in 1996: after experiments with "reproductions and more generic gift items" (Strodder 313) rather than genuine antiques had apparently proven unsuccessful, "Le Gourmet" moved from further down the street into the extremely prominent location at the entrance to New Orleans Square. At the original location of "Le Gourmet," Disney opened "La Boutique de Noel," a store offering holiday ornaments all year round. These were apparently so popular that in 1998, Disney also transformed the neighboring "Mascarade d'Arlequin" into an ornament shop ("L'Ornement Magique"; see Strodder 249), resulting in the awkward but apparently profitable situation of having two similarly themed shops right next to each other. The second shop to go was "Mlle. Antoinette's Parfumerie" with its custom-blended fragrances, which in 1997 was replaced by "Jewel of Orleans," a shop that in contrast to "Laffite's Silver Shop" did not feature craft demonstrations but "merely" sold vintage jewelry (see Strodder 227–8).

Generally, under the new profit-driven regime, shops have come and gone faster and faster: in 2001, "Le Gourmet" was replaced by "Le Bat en Rouge," an "attraction store" for the "Haunted Mansion." A mere five years later, "Le Bat en Rouge" moved to the former "La Boutique de Noel" location at the back of New Orleans Square, thus making way for "Port Royal," another "attraction store" for the "Haunted Mansion" (once again, then, two highly similar stores – "Port Royal" and "Pieces of Eight" – were located right next to each other). In 2009, "L'Ornement Magique" became "Le Bayou Magique," a shop themed to Disney's animated movie *The Princess and the Frog*, which was released the same year;[55] and in 2011, "Jewel of Orleans" once again became "Mlle. Antoinette's Parfumerie." Clearly, Disney has wasted no time moving or replacing underperforming stores to maximize profits in each location.

In addition to an increasingly rapid turnover in shops, other major effects of the implementation of "Independent Per Capita Operation" were the loss of most retail entertainment locations, a growing focus on attraction- and movie-related merchandise, and the outsourcing of shops carrying "diegetic" merchandise to lessees. As of 2020, the only store in

New Orleans Square to still feature craft demonstrations – as well as the only shop to have continuously operated in the same spot since 1966 – is "Cristal d'Orleans."[56] "Cristal d'Orleans," however, has never been managed by Disney but by a lessee, namely, Arribas Brothers, a Florida-based family business that following the 1964–1965 New York World's Fair has been collaborating exclusively with Disney and today operates a total of eleven outlets in five of the company's theme park destinations in Anaheim, Orlando, Tokyo, Paris, and Shanghai (see Arribas; see also Fjellman 166). Much like "Cristal d'Orleans," the Arribas Brothers' first shop (see Strodder 122), each outlet features craft demonstrations by glass blowers and offers personalized gift items such as engraved glass objects.

The only two other New Orleans Square stores still offering "diegetic" merchandise apart from "Cristal d'Orleans" – namely, "Mlle. Antoinette's Parfumerie" and "La Mascarade d'Orleans" (the former hat shop) – are now also operated by or in cooperation with well-known lessees. When "Mlle. Antoinette's Parfumerie" reopened in 2011, it became one of altogether three retail locations operated in partnership with the Paris-based luxury conglomerate LVMH at the U.S. Disney parks (the other two being located, quite appropriately, in the "France" pavilion at Walt Disney World's EPCOT).[57] Staffed by both Disney and LVMH employees (the latter including store manager Mary Hamilton Lipsie), "Mlle. Antoinette's Parfumerie" now exclusively sells men's and women's fragrances from the LVMH family of brands, including Dior, Guerlain, and Givenchy. Unlike at the EPCOT locations, however, where large logos in the stores advertise the various brand names, the LVMH connection is not readily identifiable at New Orleans Square.

By contrast, since 2015, a prominent sign above the entrance to "La Mascarade d'Orleans" has informed visitors that the shop now exclusively carries jewelry by the popular Pandora company. As in the case of Arribas's "Cristal d'Orleans" and LVMH's "Mlle. Antoinette's Parfumerie," "La Mascarade d'Orleans" is but one of several Pandora retail locations at Disney's (domestic) theme parks (another one can be found on Main Street at Walt Disney World's Magic Kingdom) and forms part of a "strategic alliance" between the jewelry company and Disney. This alliance began in 2014 and also includes special collections of Disney-themed jewelry (see Pandora). With Arribas, LVMH, Pandora, and the "attraction stores," then, New Orleans Square has, in a way, again become the "brandland" that once was New Orleans Street.

Autotheming: From Disney's New Orleans to Disney's Disney's New Orleans

Disney's return to external and internal brands in New Orleans Square's lessee outlets and "attraction stores," respectively, can not only be seen as the result of a switch in managerial strategies at the park's Merchandise department, however. Especially the addition of "attraction stores" also illustrates the growing thematic self-referentiality of theme parks in general and New Orleans Square in particular. Elsewhere, I have argued that for at least two decades, "theme parks have increasingly relied on theme parks and their historic antecedents (trolley parks, amusement piers, and county fairs) as themes for rides, shops, restaurants, and entire themed areas" (Freitag, "Autotheming" 141; see also Clavé 79). Such cases of "autotheming," as I have called them, can be regarded as subsets of what Beardsworth and Bryman have termed "reflexive" theming, a trend in which "the thematic elements are internally generated and then continuously reproduced" (Bryman, *Disneyization* 18).[58] While reflexively themed and/or autothemed spaces can be found in many theme parks all over the world (see Freitag, "Autotheming" for examples from North American, European, and Asian parks), they seem to be especially popular in parks owned by multimedia entertainment corporations such as Disney and NBCUniversal, where they are often used to cross-promote the companies' various media franchises (e.g., movies, TV shows, or, indeed, theme park rides).

Yet reflexive theming and autotheming are more than just effective marketing tools. Drawing on "internally generated" brands, franchises, and images, as well as – in the most extreme cases – exclusively on themselves rather than on external thematic sources, reflexively themed and especially autothemed spaces raise today's theme parks to a level of hyperreality or simulation that the original proponents of these concepts, Umberto Eco and Jean Baudrillard, had imagined either only in theory or in jest. Baudrillard, for instance, had originally considered Disneyland a *"simulation of the third order"* ("it masks the *absence* of a profound reality"; *Simulacra* 12; and 6; emphases original). Roughly ten years later, he saw the opening of the movie-themed Disney-MGM Studios theme park at Walt Disney World as "[o]ne more spiral in the simulacrum" and jokingly added: "One day they will rebuild Disneyland at Disneyworld" (*Cool Memories II* 42). One can only wonder what Baudrillard would say now that his prediction has, in a way, come true: to be sure, there is no Disneyland at Walt Disney World (or vice versa), but both parks feature rides, shops, restaurants, shows, and parades whose theming refers to nothing but the parks themselves, either directly or via Disney's representations of the parks in other media. These spaces are indeed "pure simulacra," having "no relation to any reality whatsoever" (Baudrillard, *Simulacra* 6). And many of them can be found in New Orleans Square.

Indeed, there are numerous examples for how, like the city of New Orleans, New Orleans Square has become "nostalgic for itself" (Dawdy 110). Among the earliest are the "attraction stores" "Pieces of Eight," "Le Bat en Rouge," and "Port Royal," opened in 1980, 2001, and 2006, respectively. Through their décor and their themed merchandise, these retail outlets directly refer to the two signature attractions of the "land,"

"Pirates" and the "Haunted Mansion." "Pieces of Eight," for instance, located next to the exit of "Pirates," not only features generically pirate-themed decorations and products, such as ship parts, swords, or skull-and-bones flags,[59] but also reproduces specific elements from the ride: props, taglines, as well as entire scenes. Already the shop's logo, a painting of a treasure chest ready to be buried on a beach, recalls the first scene that visitors see when they enter the "Pirates" building.[60] An identical copy of the Spanish treasure map featured in that scene can also be found in a glass case in the store. Moreover, the shop's clerks wear the same costumes as the employees working at the ride, and its soundtrack includes, among others, the "Pirates" theme song, "Yo Ho (A Pirate's Life for Me)." Finally, some of the merchandise sold at "Pieces of Eight," including T-shirts and decorative plates, reproduces the logo of "Pirates" and artwork from the ride's attraction poster, as well as the ride's tagline, "dead men tell no tales."

Similarly, the neighboring "Port Royal" store contains numerous elements from the "Haunted Mansion," from the reproductions of the "changing" portraits originally created by Marc Davis for the ride's waiting area (see Surrell, *Haunted Mansion* 76-7) that decorate the store's walls, to the distinctive pattern of the wallpaper designed by Rolly Crump for the ride's "corridor" scene (see Surrell, *Haunted Mansion* 95) that is emblazoned on some of the T-shirts and top hats sold at the shop (the top hats simultaneously refer to the costumes of the "Haunted Mansion" ride operators). The autotheming of "Le Bat en Rouge," in turn, refers to the "Haunted Mansion Holiday," a seasonal retheming of the "Haunted Mansion" that has combined elements of the regular version of the ride and Tim Burton's film *The Nightmare before Christmas* (1993; co-produced and distributed by Disney) since 2001. Originally merely accompanied by a small souvenir cart, the "Haunted Mansion Holiday" overlay proved so popular that it eventually received its own permanent "retail spin-off" in 2002 (Strodder 242).

Just as some of New Orleans Square's stores are themed to its rides, some of New Orleans Square's themed balconies refer back to its stores. For example, in addition to an elaborate mirror and a chaise longue, the balcony above "Mlle. Antoinette's Parfumerie" also features two small shelves loaded with decorative perfume bottles that complement both the interior decoration and the merchandise of the store below (and that supposedly indicate that Mlle. Antoinette lives right above her shop). The musical instruments and easels displayed on some of the other balconies in New Orleans Square may indicate, in turn, that the open spaces below them were at some point used as "found theaters" (Younger, *Theme Park Design* 373) for the portrait artists and the performances of the "Royal Street Bachelors," respectively.

In 2006, Disney created what today probably constitutes New Orleans Square's most famous and most widely discussed autothemed space.

Around the turn of the millennium, the company had released several feature films that all bore the titles of and were more or less directly inspired by some of Disney's theme park rides, including *Mission to Mars* (2000), *The Country Bears* (2002), and *The Haunted Mansion* (2003).[61] While most of these movies proved commercial failures, Gore Verbinski's *Pirates of the Caribbean: The Curse of the Black Pearl* (2003) performed so spectacularly at the box office that Disney not only decided to produce no fewer than four sequels (2006–2017), but also to add characters and story elements from the movie series to the Disneyland attraction that originally inspired it.[62] The retrofitted version of "Pirates" was officially opened on 24 June 2006, to coincide with the premiere of the first sequel, *Pirates of the Caribbean: Dead Man's Chest* (2006), which was also held at New Orleans Square.

The circle of remediation leading from "Pirates" (the ride) to *Pirates* (the movies) and back has been discussed by a number of critics, among them Petersen, Jess-Cooke, Hom, Aronstein, and, most recently, Schweizer and Pearce, as well as Younger ("Traditionally Postmodern"). In the context of a historical approach to "Disney's Immersive New Orleans," two issues seem particularly important. On the one hand, and as has been pointed out by Younger, the 2007 changes to "Pirates" imposed a linear plot – namely, one inspired by the movies – on what had originally been a mere series of vignettes held together by nothing but "the set-up of 'pirates attack and loot a town'" ("Traditionally Postmodern" 65; see also Younger, *Theme Park Design* 93; 99). The shift from "implicit" to "explicit" storylines, however, has been considered one of the key characteristics of "New Traditional Style Design," a theme park design style that, largely due to cost factors, appeared to have gone out of fashion in the early 1990s, but that made a comeback in the early 2000s with projects such as the revised "Pirates" (76–81; see also Aronstein 69; and Petersen).

On the other hand, "plunder[ing] from itself, then adapt[ing] to accommodate its new form," the rethemed "Pirates" ride also represents, as Schweizer and Pearce have argued, an "ideal case study" of "auto-textual poaching" (95) or (as I have called it) "autotheming." Indeed, whereas the original version had been "cobbled together from several different sources across multiple media" (98), including movies such as Disney's own *Treasure Island* (1950), as well as from history (see the paintings of historical pirate figures in the ride's waiting area), as of 2007, "Pirates" has no longer pointed to any outside referent, but exclusively to (a remediation of) itself. The result is, once again, a "pure simulacrum," which is then carried over into spaces such as "Pieces of Eight" (see earlier).

Yet the most extreme cases of autotheming in New Orleans Square can be found in the restaurants and "private" spaces of the "land." After having been renamed "Café Orléans" in 1972 and having been expanded in 1988 (see earlier), the eatery once known as "The Creole Café" underwent yet another transformation in 2006, when it was converted into a table service restaurant and when numerous framed paintings and drawings were added to the walls. In contrast to the huge tile murals decorating the walls of the neighboring "French Market Restaurant," however, which depict historical scenes of New Orleans (Jackson Square "Anno 1803" and the river bend "Anno 1805"), the pictures at "Café Orléans" exclusively show scenes of – "Café Orléans"! Displaying selected concept sketches from the restaurant's various renovations, "Café Orléans" is now themed to nothing but itself and its own history.

Similarly, "Club 33," New Orleans Square's private bar and restaurant, had always been a "showplace for rare Disney mementos" (Johnson OC B1), with, for instance, concept sketches of Adventureland rides decorating the walls of the "jungle exploration"-themed "Trophy Room" (see OC B6). In the 2000s, however, framed old photographs of Walt Disney and a painting of him enjoying a cup of coffee at the restaurant replaced the Adventureland sketches and concept drawings of New Orleans Square (including Ryman's "The Square"), while a painting of the "Royal Street Bachelors" were added to "Club 33"'s bar and entrance areas (see DeCaro, "Club 33"). Following the 2013–2014 expansion of the club (see also ahead), the designers installed another painting of the "Bachelors," more concept sketches of the Square and its rides, and paintings expanding the fictional history of the latter (e.g., a sketch of the "Haunted Mansion" before it became haunted), thus turning "Club 33" into even more of an autothemed space (see DeCaro, "Club 33 Pg. 2").

The neighboring "Dream Suite," a 2,600 square foot overnight accommodation that in 2007 replaced the "Disney Gallery" (see above), finally, constitutes a doubly autothemed space: the main hallway is decorated with Dorothea Redmond's concept sketches for the "Suite" (or, rather, its original version as a private apartment for Walt Disney), and each of the individual rooms is dedicated to one of Disneyland's "lands" (the front parlor being the "New Orleans Square" room; see DeCaro, "Dream Suite"). This is, then, perhaps the true "heart" of Disneyland – an apartment themed to the various sections of the very park it is located in. Rather than "rebuild[ing] Disneyland at Disneyworld," as Baudrillard had predicted, Disney has quite simply rebuilt Disneyland at Disneyland.

Feedback Loops of Disneyfication

"Club 33" and the "Dream Suite" also stood at the center of the two biggest construction projects in the history of New Orleans Square: the reconfiguration of the plaza in front of the entrance to "Pirates" in 1987 and the expansion of "Club 33" in 2013–2014.[63] Both of these projects were essentially concerned with crowd flow issues, but, as I will argue, they also contributed to intensifying the socio-spatial stratification of people at Disneyland in general and of the park's visitors in particular.

Interestingly, they did so using design strategies adapted from urban entertainment or downtown revitalization projects which, in turn, had drawn on the architecture of (Disney) theme parks to create particular sanitized and consumer-friendly urban experiences, and which therefore have been regularly referred to as "Disneyfied places" (see, for instance, Kolb 1). What happened at New Orleans Square in 1987 and 2013–2014 may be described, then, as a feedback loop of Disneyfication, a process of "architectural give-and-take" (Waldrep 222) in which specific elements of urban planning and design used for social screening and "spatial apartheid" (Boddy 140) have traveled from theme parks to downtowns and – in heavily intensified form – back. As a result, much like public urban space has been penetrated by privatized "Disneyfied" places, the simulated public spaces of Disneyland and especially New Orleans Square are now pierced by (even more) simulated private or "hyper-Disneyfied" places that are restricted to a narrowly circumscribed audience mostly based on class and income. Art imitates life imitating art.

The discussion about the relationship between public urban space and theme parks probably constitutes one of the most intensive and interesting ones in scholarly research on themed and immersive environments. In very general terms, this debate has moved from early appraisals of the parks and resorts as "truly remarkable experiment[s] in urban technology and urban psychology" (Finch 430–1), particularly by architects and urban planners, to much more critical assessments, especially by cultural critics, of the parks' roles as models, catalysts, and agents in the increasing privatization of public urban space from the early 1980s onwards. For example, in what has probably become one of the most frequently used quotes about Disneyland (at least in Disney's own publications on the park; see Koenig 22), planner and developer James W. Rouse remarked in a keynote delivered at the Seventh Urban Design Conference, organized by Harvard's Graduate School of Design in 1963:

> I hold a view that might be somewhat shocking to an audience as sophisticated as this – that the greatest piece of urban design in the United States today is Disneyland. If you think about Disneyland and think about its performance in relation to its purpose; its meaning to people – more than that, its meaning to the process of development – you will find it the outstanding piece of urban design in the United States.
>
> (qtd. in Bright 29)[64]

Early commentators such as Rouse and later critics such as Fjellman and Mitrasinovic have extolled Disney theme parks both for their innovative and efficient infrastructure, as well as for their attractive and harmonic design: "Here we have an efficient movement system in an atmosphere of optimum cleanliness and security that provides a pleasurable experience for varied socio-economic groups while making a profit without polluting the environment" (Mitrasinovic 239; see also Fjellman 185–97). Some scholars have gone so far as to suggest that the parks and specifically their small town-themed Main Street, U.S.A. sections were deliberately conceived as model solutions to the urban problems of Los Angeles (see Marling, "Disneyland" 185; and "Imagineering" 169–70; Carosso 70), New York City (see Findlay 63; Mitrasinovic 183), and the modern industrialized American metropolis in general (see Bierman 283; Avila 119–20; Cross and Walton 181).[65]

When, however, by the early 1980s, North American cities increasingly started to adapt and implement theme park design strategies in the context of, for instance, downtown revitalization and urban entertainment projects, especially cultural critics also began to worry about the social and political effects of the spread of the "theme park model" and, in turn, to criticize the parks' alternative visions of urbanity. Variously referring to the process as the "theme-park-ification" (Dear and Flusty 417) or, most commonly, the "Disneyfication"[66] of the city and identifying the resulting urban spaces as, for instance, "variations on a theme park" (Sorkin, "Introduction"), "urbanoid environments" (Goldberger), "non-place urban realms" (Carosso), or simply "Disneyfied places" (Kolb), critics have examined theme park-inspired forms of urbanity in a large variety of cities in both the United States and Canada. Examples include, of course, James W. Rouse's own Faneuil Hall in Boston (1976) and Harborplace in Baltimore (1980), as well as similar "festival marketplaces" in other cities (see Boddy; Bloom 150–79; Francaviglia, *Main Street* 169–80; Bryman, *Disneyization* 36), but also shopping malls such as West Edmonton Mall in Edmonton (1981; see Crawford), sports and congress venues such as the Angel Stadium of Anaheim and the Anaheim Convention Center (1966 [as Anaheim Stadium] and 1967; see Findlay 100–102; Vollmar; Siegel), and "New Urbanist" projects such as the town of Seaside, Florida (1981; see Reisenleitner). Through its involvement in, for instance, downtown revitalization projects in Seattle (1985–1989) and New York City (the 1995 redesign of Times Square), as well as through the development of the "New Urbanist" community of Celebration at Walt Disney World (1996), Disney itself has entered the realm of urban planning not only as a provider of ideas and a catalyst, but also as an active agent (mostly via its "Disney Development Company" division, founded in 1984 and merged with Walt Disney Imagineering in 1996; see, among others, Warren, "Demise"; and Roost).

What most scholars have criticized these and other "Disneyfied" urban spaces for is, first, the replacement of "authentic" urban culture with a mere simulation of it; second, the focus on consumption; and finally, as well as most importantly, the increasing privatization of public space and the ensuing socio-spatial segregation and loss of civil rights and liberties. Indeed, although they may often visually imitate public urbanity,

"Disneyfied" places are *private* spaces. Privately owned, privately developed, privately operated, they have the power to exclude the chaos of contemporary life [and] demonstrations and other functions of the political marketplace" (Orvell 244; emphasis original). Gottdiener, for instance, has noted how what he calls the "new city simulations" employ security forces, video surveillance, and "defensive architecture" "to filter and control the crowd" (*Theming* 180–1), thus excluding marginalized persons and social groups. "Nonconforming" behavior – i.e., almost any activity not related to consumption – is excluded, too: as Mitrasinovic has pointed out, "[o]nly a few states in the United States currently still guarantee the right of free speech in [privately owned, publicly accessible spaces]" (265). Hence, the "Disneyfication" of the city has been interpreted as a direct assault on democracy: "Constitutional guarantees of free speech and of freedom of association and assembly mean much less if there is literally no peopled public place to serve as a forum in which to act out these rights" (Boddy 125).

These observations have also led critics to (re-)examine the urbanism of (Disney) theme parks, especially of those areas with a "city" theme, such as Main Street, U.S.A.[67] Indeed, numerous scholars have pointed out that as private spaces that merely borrow the forms and the language of the public realm to simulate urbanity, theme park "mock towns" (Gottdiener, *Theming* 119) such as Main Street, U.S.A. engage, much like "Disneyfied" spaces, in both social screening and a suspension of democracy: in addition to video surveillance and security forces (barely noticeable until you start taking too many pictures; see earlier), theme parks mainly use admission fees and grooming codes (the former increasingly so, the latter decreasingly so) to filter out poor and other undesired customers.[68] With respect to free speech, theme parks are similarly uncompromising: when on 6 August 1970, members of the "Youth International Party" started marching down Main Street, U.S.A. (as well as engaging in other political activities), Disneyland started to evict them and eventually shut down.[69] The reason is simple: in terms of urban planning, accessibility, and civil rights and liberty, Main Street is not a street, just as "Disneyland isn't a city" (Marling, "Imagineering" 176).

It is against the background of this critical discussion that I would like to examine the 1987 and 2013–2014 structural changes to New Orleans Square. Unlike Disneyland's Main Street, U.S.A., New Orleans Square features no simulations of such key institutions of civic life as a city hall, a firehouse, or a police station (the "New Orleans Square/Frontierland Train Station" forms the only possible exception).[70] Nevertheless, like Main Street, New Orleans Square, too, constitutes a "mock town," a private place masquerading as public space: the separation of walkways into paved streets and cobblestone sidewalks (the latter actually made of stamped concrete; see Younger, *Theme Park Design* 320), the street signs (with street names of actual streets in New Orleans, including Esplanade,

Royal, Front, and Orleans streets) and house number plaques (partly inconsistent), as well as the street furniture used in New Orleans Square (lampposts, benches, and trashcans) all suggest that the "land" – or, at least, its "French Quarter" section – forms part of a public urban realm and is thus accessible to anyone. In fact, of course, the streets of New Orleans Square are private and only open to those who have paid admission at Disneyland's entrance and who abide by the park's rules.

In addition to mock public spaces, however, New Orleans Square's "French Quarter" has, from its very beginnings, also featured simulations of semi-public and private spaces, which, although their design may suggest otherwise, have been either accessible to all visitors, prohibited to all visitors, or restricted to select visitors. These include such typically New Orleanian semi-public spaces as balconies and courtyards, "backstage" areas like kitchens, stock rooms, and employee break rooms, as well as the apartment above the entrance to "Pirates" and the "Club 33" restaurant and bar. For example, although the large iron grill gates at the entrances to the "Royal Courtyard" and the "Court of Angels" may have signaled to visitors that these are private spaces, the gates had always been kept open and everyone had been welcome to explore – at New Orleans Square, then, Edward King could have followed his "dark-haired, flashing-eyed, slender Creole girl" through the portal and into the "stone-paved court-yard" (10). By contrast, in order to exclude visitors from "backstage" areas, Disney has, among others, relied on an architectural system of spatial stratification: New Orleans Square's central kitchen as well as a small staff area, for instance, are located below ground level (see Koenig 58; and Mannheim 156n25), whereas one of the main stock rooms was located above the "French Market Restaurant," accessible to employees only via stairways and an enclosed bridge that connects the "Pirates" building with the "French Market" building. Hence, the spatial layering of people at New Orleans Square simultaneously constituted a social stratification, with (regular) visitors on the ground level and employees (also) below and above them.

New Orleans Square's system of the socio-spatial stratification of visitors and employees was significantly expanded and refined for Walt Disney World's Magic Kingdom (opened in 1971), where an entire system of service and staff tunnels pervades the ground below the park (see Fjellman 189; Sorkin, "See You" 230). However, it may have also inspired, or at least contributed to the further spread of, the "analogous" or "parallel" cities of bridges and tunnels in, for example, Minneapolis, Calgary, and Montréal that Trevor Boddy as well as Vincent James and Jennifer Yoos have examined in "Underground and Overhead: Building the Analogous City" (1992) and *Parallel Cities: The Multilevel Metropolis* (2016).[71] Though originally intended and promoted as "devices to beat the environmental extremes of heat, cold, or humidity that make conventional streets unbearable" (Boddy 124) – and thus as urban centers' response to the increasing competition from suburban shopping malls (see James and Yoos 94) – from the early 1960s onwards, these networks of overhead bridges and underground tunnels between downtown blocks have increasingly been used, Boddy shows, as "a refuge not just from the elements, but from the social climate" (140) of the streets. Hence, as other "Disneyfied" places, the "analogous city" also contributed to an "increasing race and class stratification" (139) within the urban realm, exacerbating "problems of social fragmentation, segregation, and political expression" (James and Yoos 152).

From the "analogous" or "parallel cities" and/or Walt Disney World's Magic Kingdom, the "Disneyfied" system of socio-spatial stratification was re-imported to New Orleans Square in heavily intensified (because much more visible) form in 1987 and 2013–2014. Here, too, it was originally intended to simply make people more comfortable, but eventually became a means of social differentiation, though this time not between employees and visitors, but between different classes of visitors. For example, by the mid-1980s, the plaza in front of the entrance to "Pirates" was almost perpetually overcrowded: too small to handle the long lines for the ride as well as the masses of people seeking to go to Adventureland, Frontierland, and the back of New Orleans Square, it had become a notorious bottleneck in the park (see Younger, *Theme Park Design* 298). In order to improve crowd flow, Disney in 1987 lowered the waiting area for "Pirates" to below ground level and installed an overhead bridge: henceforth, visitors interested in riding "Pirates" had to pass through one of two tunnels to get to the lower-level waiting area, while everyone else had to use the bridge. Moreover, the designers added two flights of stairs to the "Pirates" building in order to lead visitors away from the plaza and into the newly opened "Disney Gallery" on the building's second floor.

Initially, then, the spatial stratification of visitors on the "Pirates" plaza simply layered people according to their intended destinations in the park – below ground level for "Pirates," above ground level for the "Gallery," ground level for the rest – and did not carry any social connotation whatsoever. To the contrary, since the "Gallery" opened up the formerly private apartment above the entrance to "Pirates" to the general public,[72] one could even argue that the reconfiguration of the plaza generally contributed to a social "de-stratification" of visitors. Things changed in 2007, however, when in the context of a marketing campaign, the "Gallery" was once again transformed into a private apartment, the auto-themed "Dream Suite" (see earlier). Since then, the staircases have only been open to contest winners; Disney managers, celebrities, and other "special guests" who have been invited by Disney to spend a night at the "Dream Suite" (see Strodder 451; Abrams); and visitors who are willing to pay as much as $15,000 for a private dining experience (see Kubersky). Hence, plainly visible as they are to everyone passing by, the staircases became, in 2007, the first signs of Disneyland's increasing socio-spatial differentiation between "regular" and "special" visitors.

More such signs appeared in 2013–2014, when Disney renovated and significantly expanded "Club 33," the private club located next to the "Dream Suite" on the second floors of the "Pirates" and the "Café Orleans" buildings. Inspired by the executive lounges at the 1964–1965 New York World's Fair, "Club 33" had welcomed members to its elegantly designed bar and restaurant since the opening of New Orleans Square in 1966 and constituted the only place in the park to serve alcohol. Membership was limited to a few hundred, yet open to anyone who could afford the membership fee of $5,000 (in 1984) and the additional annual dues (see Johnson OC B6). Occasionally, the club also served as a location for special events, such as the opening of the "Haunted Mansion" in 1969 (see earlier). Members would enter the club through an inconspicuous door located next to the "Blue Bayou Restaurant" and access the main dining room via a small overhead passageway that connected the "Pirates" and the "Café Orleans" buildings and that was hidden behind a street corner.[73]

When in 2013–2014, Disney decided to turn the stock room above the "French Market" into an additional dining room for "Club 33" in order to increase the club's capacity (and the revenues from club membership fees and dues), however, the company no longer tried to hide "Club 33":[74] the small passageway was significantly widened and equipped with large picture windows; similar picture windows appeared elsewhere in "Club 33," offering impressive views from inside the club not only of New Orleans Square, but especially of the "Fantasmic!" nighttime spectacular, which takes place on and across the neighboring "Rivers of America." At the same time and especially at night, however, the new picture windows also allow "regular" visitors glimpses into the new facilities from down below. Online reviewers have angrily commented on this, complaining that Disney now dangles the "Club 33" experience in front of visitors like a carrot, trying to get them to spend even more money at the park (see, for instance, DeCaro, "Kool Aid"). Far from making "a determined effort either to erase, or at least render unimportant, our awareness of class distinctions in the park" (Harwood 52), then, Disney now underlines its differentiation between "regular" and "special" guests by allowing them to observe each other.

Moreover, "Club 33" also received a new, highly prominent and ostentatious entry: the (open) iron grill doors at the entrance to the "Court of Angels" were replaced with stained-glass screens in order to close the courtyard for "regular" visitors and to use it as the club's new entrance and lobby. In a strange case of what can only be called the simulated privatization of simulated public space, the courtyard, a private space originally designed to evoke a (semi)public place, was redesigned to represent a private space, accessible only to the most affluent among Disneyland's visitors. Hence, rather than offering counterpoints to or providing model solutions for the problems of real cities, Disneyland's "mock" cities have started emulating the very processes of privatization and, concomitantly, social screening at "Disneyfied" places that they themselves had inspired.

And they have done so using the very same architectural means as "Disneyfied" places: in order to connect the original "Club 33" with the new dining room above the "French Market Restaurant," a new, extremely prominent overhead bridge was installed between the "Café Orleans" and the "French Market" buildings. With the expanded passageway between the "Pirates" and the "Café Orleans" buildings and the new bridge between the "Café Orleans" and the "French Market" buildings, then, a network of instantly noticeable bridges now links all of the blocks in New Orleans Square's "French Quarter" on the second-floor level, thus forming a simulated "analogous city" in the Square's simulated "downtown" (see Figure 2.1). Much like the staircases leading to the "Dream Suite," New Orleans Square's network of bridges thus represents a "hyper-Disneyfied" space: a (re-)adaptation of both the system and the concrete forms of the socio-spatial stratification of people in "Disneyfied" public spaces, which were originally adapted from Disney theme parks. At New Orleans Square, then, "Disneyfication" has, in essence and form, come full circle.

Repetition With a Difference: French Quarter Land (Tokyo Disneyland)

Following Disneyland's New Orleans Square (1966), the "Disneyzone" did not witness the addition of another New Orleans-themed space until the unnamed French Quarter-themed "subland" of Tokyo Disneyland's Adventureland opened along with the rest of that park on 15 April 1983. Entering Tokyo Disneyland's "French Quarter Land," as it will be referred to here, visitors familiar with Disneyland's New Orleans Square may feel a vague sense of déjà vu: in fact, French Quarter Land is nothing but a partial and slightly modified reproduction of New Orleans Square's "French Quarter" section and mainly consists of almost exact copies of that area's "Pirates" and "Café Orleans" buildings. Within the larger story of "Disney's Immersive New Orleans," then, the opening of French Quarter Land marked one further step in the ongoing "Frenchifying" of Disney's depiction of the Crescent City in its themed spaces: with New Orleans Square's "Garden District" section having been completely dropped, French Quarter Land "merely" evokes the Crescent City's Spanish and French heritage (via the "Pirates" ride and the shops and restaurants that make up the rest of the area, respectively).

The individual history of French Quarter Land, in turn, comprises two distinct phases: the story of the pre-opening transfer and transformation of California's New Orleans Square to Tokyo and into French Quarter

Land; and the story of the development of French Quarter Land from 1983 onwards. Both of these phases are marked by interesting parallels to and divergences from the California "model." For instance, although the designers re-used some of New Orleans Square's building plans for Tokyo Disneyland, French Quarter Land nevertheless had, from the very beginning, its own unique identity. Apart from the absence of a "Garden District" section, this identity was principally shaped by architectural responses to the comparatively harsh Tokyo climate, subtle influences of the "Presentational Style" then prevalent in theme park design (see Younger, "Traditionally Postmodern" 69–74), and, perhaps most importantly, the relocation of the "subland" on the geographic and symbolic map of the park: unlike New Orleans Square, French Quarter Land is not set between Adventureland and Frontierland, but between World Bazaar (Tokyo Disneyland's equivalent of Main Street, U.S.A.) and the Caribbean-themed "subland" of Adventureland.

Hence, and like Tokyo Disneyland in general, the modified and relocated New Orleans Square that was French Quarter Land on opening day may have seemed, upon first sight, like a mere repetition, but was, in fact, what Deleuze has called a repetition "qui comprend la différence" (see Deleuze 36), a repetition with a difference. This also applies to the later history of French Quarter Land: since its opening, the "subland" has undergone its own unique set of historical changes and developments, including, for example, the addition of the "Theatre Orleans" open-air theater in 2001. At the same time, however, much of the post-opening history of French Quarter Land – the gradual shift of the temporal setting of the "subland" to the postbellum period, for instance, but also the move away from retail entertainment and "diegetic" merchandise in its stores, as well as the increase in autothemed spaces – has paralleled that of New Orleans Square, with the result that here, too, one may speak of "repetitions with a difference."

The pre-opening, planning history of French Quarter Land is, of course, inextricably linked to that of Tokyo Disneyland in general. Unlike later Disney theme park destinations located outside of the United States, such as Disneyland Paris (opened in 1992), Hong Kong Disneyland Resort (2005), and Shanghai Disney Resort (2016), Tokyo Disney Resort (1983) is not (co-)owned and operated by the Walt Disney Company, but by the Urayasu, Japan-based Oriental Land Company (OLC). OLC was founded in 1960 as a partnership between Mitsui Real Estate Development and Keisei Electric Railway in order to reclaim land off the coast of Urayasu and to use the landfill for, among other things, a "major recreational facility" (Raz 23; see also Koenig 189). When reclamation work was almost completed, OLC approached Disney, and in 1979, after five years of difficult negotiations, the two companies signed a contract according to which Disney, in return for designing the facility and continuously providing advice and expertise on how to run it, would receive licensing fees from OLC based on the sale of admissions, merchandise, and food, as well as on incomes from sponsorship deals (see Raz 27; Bryman, *Disney* 47; Laemmerhirt 74).[75] Construction began in December 1980, and a little over two years later, Tokyo Disneyland officially opened (see Raz 28).

Possibly inspired by the virulent debates about Disneyland Paris and the Americanization of France (see Freitag, "Amerikanisierung"), much of the scholarly literature on Tokyo Disneyland – at least those texts published in English – has sought to demonstrate that the park, including its production by OLC employees and its reception by Japanese visitors, does not constitute an example of American cultural imperialism, but rather a case of Japanese cultural appropriation.[76] Indeed, Brannen, Van Maanen ("Displacing"), Yoshimoto, Raz, Bryman ("Global Disney"), and, most recently, Laemmerhirt have all argued that it was precisely by actively importing an almost exact copy of Disneyland and then producing and consuming it in unique ways, that the Japanese have made Tokyo Disneyland their own. Van Maanen, for example, explains that:

> [m]ost observers of modern Japan note the country's penchant for the importation of things foreign . . . . The choice of imports is, however massive, highly selective. From this perspective, the consumption of foreign goods in Japan seems less an act of homage than a way of establishing a national identity by making such imports their own through combining them in a composite of all that the Japanese see as the "best" in the world.
>
> ("Displacing" 16)

Similarly, Yoshimoto uses the concept of "internationalization" to point out that Tokyo Disneyland "perfectly fits in with the nativist discourse valorizing the selective hybridity of Japanese culture" (197). The park supposedly serves as a "differentiating device, whereby the Japanese can marvel at the spectacle of their cultural adaptability" (Clément, "Review" 20).

There exists, in fact, much evidence to suggest that OLC managers insisted on an "authentic" American and Disney experience, and explicitly asked Disney's designers to refrain from "localizing" the park: for instance, an OLC representative told Brannen that the company "really tried to avoid creating a Japanese version of Disneyland" (216); and designer Marty Sklar remembers that the "'Japanese told us from the beginning, "Don't Japanese us"'" (qtd. in Mitrasinovic 83). Preoccupied as it was with the planning of EPCOT at Walt Disney World (opened in October 1982), Disney, in turn, was unwilling to invest too much of the company's creative resources into the Tokyo park. As another member of the Tokyo planning and design team recalls, Card Walker, then CEO and chairman of Walt Disney Productions, "'was very specific that internally EPCOT was to have design priority over Tokyo Disneyland as

EPCOT was a Disney investment.'" Hence, Tokyo Disneyland "'was to be based on existing attractions with minimal new design work'" (qtd. in Koenig 189).

The result of these corporate decisions was a park that, at least upon first sight, indeed appears to be "[n]early a carbon copy of the 'original' Disneyland" (Yoshimoto 190). Nevertheless, as several scholars have pointed out, more or less prominent adjustments and changes were made for climatic, legal, cultural, and stylistic reasons: due to Japan's cold winters and rainy summers, for instance, World Bazaar was covered with a huge glass cupola, thus turning Disneyland's Main Street, in yet another example of the "feedback loop of Disneyfication," into a huge indoor shopping mall with a "small town" theme (see Brannen 222; Laemmerhirt 80–1). Legal regulations for trains in Japan necessitated a rerouting of the "Disneyland Railroad," which in Tokyo encircles merely the western half rather than the entire park and hence visually separates Westernland (Japan's version of Frontierland) from the rest of Disneyland (see Brannen 219; Raz 35). The renaming of Main Street, U.S.A. (to World Bazaar) and Frontierland (to Westernland) can, in turn, be attributed to cultural differences (i.e., to the lack of such concepts as "main street" and the "frontier" in Japanese culture; see Laemmerhirt 77; and 80), as can be the changes to the "Jungle Cruise" ride and the addition of the "Cinderella Castle Mystery Tour" and "Meet the World" rides (see Raz 33–8; 38–50; and 50–60, respectively). Finally, Younger has pointed out how changing tastes in theme park design styles, and particularly the rise of the so-called "Presentational Style," have contributed to modifications in the general layout of Disneyland for the Tokyo park:

> The wide walkways that allow open vistas between lands, and layout decisions that allow, for example, the "Country Bear Theater" to face Snow White Grotto, make far more sense when we understand that Walt Disney Imagineering was no longer explicitly seeking immersive design which requested suspension of disbelief. The block color walkways were intended to be symbolic rather than literal.
> ("Traditionally Postmodern" 72)

Far from being "[n]early a carbon copy of the 'original' Disneyland," then, Tokyo Disneyland can be much more accurately described as a "selective replication and rearrangement of Disneyland in Tokyo" (Raz 15) or, indeed, as a "repetition with a difference."

This is also and especially true for French Quarter Land. To be sure, among the factors discussed previously, only Japan's comparatively harsh climate and the rise of the "Presentational Style" significantly affected the shape and look of the "subland" on opening day: in order to protect visitors from inclement weather, California's outdoor waiting line for "Pirates" was moved indoors into a newly added side wing of the

"Pirates" building. And in accordance with the "Presentational Style" preference for wide, open spaces and vistas, the plaza in front of the "Pirates" building was significantly enlarged and cleared of all the planters and street furniture that visually break up the area in California.[77] By contrast, the most important differences between New Orleans Square and French Quarter Land – namely, the removal of the "Garden District" section and the recategorization and repositioning of the area as a "subland" of Adventureland – can rather be attributed to marketing considerations.

In their promotional material, as well as in their layout planning, theme parks use what David Younger has called "anchors" – "attractions, lands, or other popular elements known to guests before they arrive and which they seek out" – in order to first draw visitors to and then spread them throughout the sites (*Theme Park Design* 252). Whereas, however, in the mid-1960s, New Orleans Square had, in itself and even without its two signature rides, been considered a draw, to the point that it received its own opening ceremony (see earlier), by the time Tokyo Disneyland was being designed, "Pirates" and the "Haunted Mansion" had become such popular and prominent "brands" that Disney judged them better "anchors" than New Orleans Square as a whole. This is confirmed by a 1981 preview brochure, as well as by a 1982 promotional film, both of which explicitly mention the names of the two rides (see N.N., *Tokyo Disneyland* 3–4; and N.N., *Disneyland Comes to Tokyo* 00:12:26; and 00:08:35) while remaining completely silent about New Orleans.

Such marketing considerations ultimately led, however, to the removal of New Orleans Square's "Garden District" section. While Raz asserts that Tokyo Disneyland is "primarily modeled on" the Magic Kingdom of Walt Disney World (32), rather than on Disneyland in California, it seems that whenever there were both a California and a somewhat different Florida version of a particular ride, restaurant, shop, etc., the designers invariably chose whichever version they considered superior. In the case of "Pirates," this turned out to be the California original rather than the Florida variation of the ride. The latter was, in fact, nothing but a slightly abridged version of the former that was somewhat hastily added to the Magic Kingdom's Adventureland section in 1973 after numerous visitors had complained about its absence from the park's 1971 opening-day roster of attractions (see Surrell, *Pirates* 54–5). This reaction, without a doubt, underlined the potential of "Pirates" to function as an "anchor," so when faced with the decision of whether to work with the California original or the abridged Florida version of the ride, the designers of Tokyo Disneyland ultimately opted for the original, along with its "French Quarter" surroundings.

In the case of the "Haunted Mansion," by contrast, it was the Florida version that eventually made the trip to Japan. For the Magic Kingdom, which featured no New Orleans-themed area (see ahead), the exterior of Disneyland's "Haunted Mansion" had been completely redesigned to resemble a pre-Revolutionary Gothic manor house in the lower Hudson River Valley and to thus fit in with the ride's new surroundings, the New England-themed Liberty Square (see Surrell, *Haunted Mansion* 36–7). It was this newer, Florida version of the "Haunted Mansion" that was chosen for Tokyo Disneyland, where for both visual and thematic reasons it was placed in the Fantasyland section rather than in French Quarter Land (see 38–9).[78] With no ride or other element left to support the "Garden District" section, however, that area was simply dropped and New Orleans Square found itself reduced to a "subland" exclusively themed to New Orleans's French Quarter.

The position of this "subland" within Tokyo Disneyland was also mainly determined by the role of "Pirates" as an "anchor" for the park. Arguably, French Quarter Land would have perfectly fit in with Tokyo Disneyland's Westernland section, where, according to the promotional film, the "sound of Dixieland jazz" emanates from the "Mississippi paddle wheel steamboat 'Mark Twain'" as it "round[s] the bend" of the "Rivers of America" (N.N., *Disneyland Comes to Tokyo* 00:19:54–00:20:01). Privileging the "Caribbean" theme of "Pirates" over the "New Orleans" theme of the entire "subland," however, the designers ultimately decided to integrate French Quarter Land into Adventureland, which, again according to the promotional movie, offers an "authentic blending of the Tropics, the South Seas, and the Caribbean" (00:11:22–00:11:27). It was only on the specific geographical position of the "subland" *within* Tokyo's Adventureland that the "Crescent City" theme and, more precisely, its distinctly urban look and atmosphere, had an impact: unlike the U.S.-based Disney parks, where Adventureland can only be accessed via "Central Plaza," Tokyo Disneyland also offers visitors a direct route to Adventureland (as well as Tomorrowland) from World Bazaar (see Younger, *Theme Park Design* 257). In order to smoothen the visual segue between this indoor mock town and Adventureland, the designers added wrought-iron balconies and other details to the World Bazaar façades closest to the Adventureland entrance and placed French Quarter Land right next to them, thus creating an urban-themed transition zone between the two "lands" in the southeastern corner of the park.

Overall, then, the "repetition with a difference" of New Orleans Square in Tokyo Disneyland had precisely the "deterritorializing" effect that Deleuze and Guattari have ascribed to the process in *A Thousand Plateaus* (see 360): shorn of its Anglo-American-themed "Garden District" section and moved as far away as possible from the U.S.-themed Westernland and into Adventureland, New Orleans, as represented in French Quarter Land, has cut virtually all ties with the U.S. territory. The Stars and Stripes flown atop the "Pirates" building alone reminds visitors of the fact that what is represented here is actually a U.S. city. Hence, whereas Tokyo Disneyland seeks elsewhere, as originally requested by

OLC, "to create the illusion that the visitors are in the United States" and therefore depicts non-U.S. locales – including, indeed, Japan – as exotic (Laemmerhirt 78), in French Quarter Land, (a part of) the United States itself has been exoticized.

The U.S. flag on top of "Pirates" is remarkable for other reasons, as well. The 1982 promotional video had rather vaguely described French Quarter Land's "Blue Bayou Restaurant" (a copy of New Orleans Square's "Blue Bayou") as evoking "an atmosphere reminiscent of the Mississippi River plantations in the America of the 1800s" (00:12:04–00:12:10). When Tokyo Disneyland opened a year later, however, the flag allowed visitors to much more precisely locate the "subland" in time: featuring 23 stars, it indicated that French Quarter Land was set somewhere between 4 July 1820 (when two stars were added to the official flag of the United States for the admission of Alabama and Maine) and 4 July 1822 (when a 24th star was added for the newly admitted state of Missouri). It is unclear why, at a time when Disneyland in Anaheim had already started pushing the temporal setting of New Orleans Square toward the postbellum years (see earlier), the designers of the original French Quarter Land went in the opposite direction, locating the "subland" even earlier in the antebellum period than the California "land" that served as its model.

In 2001, however, Tokyo Disneyland eventually decided to join Disneyland in its efforts to "clean up the streets" of the French Quarter: when in that year the former "Adventureland Stage" outdoor theater reopened as the "Theatre Orleans," it not only featured a new, thematically appropriate show called "Mickey's Adventureland Mardi Gras" (see the 2001 "Tokyo Disneyland Show and Parade Guidebook"),[79] but also a completely redesigned stage building whose architecture perfectly matched that of French Quarter Land and that, most importantly, pushed the temporal setting of the "subland" to the postbellum period: in bright, gilded numbers, the lettering on the façade announces that the building was constructed in 1881. As of 2020, however, the temporal relocation of French Quarter Land has remained Tokyo Disneyland's only concession to changing cultural climates and notions of "appropriateness": just as their California counterparts did from 1967–1997, and as they have done in Tokyo since 1983, for instance, French Quarter Land's "Pirates" are still chasing young women (rather than vice versa) in the ride's "wench-chasing" scene – although this may say more about the "cult" status of "Pirates" than about cultural climates in Japan.

In other respects, too, the history of French Quarter Land since 1983 has followed that of New Orleans Square, but always with a difference. For instance, when the "subland" first opened, most of its shops and stores focused on retail entertainment and/or sold "diegetic" merchandise, including pirate-themed merchandise at "The Golden Galleon," jewelry at "Laffite's [sic] Treasure Chest," fragrances at "La Petite Parfumerie," hats and caps at the "Le Marché Bleu" stand, and food items as well as kitchen accessories at "Le Gourmet." Retail entertainment in the shape of interactive experiences and craft demonstrations was provided by "Blackbeard's Portrait Deck," where visitors could dress up as pirates and have their picture taken in front of a "ship" or a "treasure" background, as well as, from April 1986 onwards, by "Cristal Arts," where Arribas Brothers manufactured and sold their signature glass and crystal items. Until the late 1990s, French Quarter Land's roster of merchandise outlets remained basically unchanged, yet by the time the implementation of "Independent Per Capita Operation" at the U.S. Disney parks in general and at New Orleans Square in particular had shown its first signs of financial success, OLC – perhaps encouraged by Disney, which due to its licensing contract had, of course, a vital interest in increasing merchandise sales at the Japanese park – decided to emulate Disney's Merchandise departments.

The first original French Quarter Land shop to go was "Laffite's Treasure Chest," which in 1999 made way for an expansion of "Cristal Arts." In July 2007, "Blackbeard's Portrait Deck" and "Le Gourmet" were replaced by "Pirate Treasure" and "Party Gras Gifts," respectively, which sell smaller pirate-themed ("Pirate Treasure") and more generically Disney-themed ("Party Gras Gifts") gift items, including pens, key rings, and the like. At Tokyo Disneyland, too, then, one can observe a general move away from retail entertainment and "diegetic" merchandise. Yet whereas at New Orleans Square this has led to an increasing reliance on lessees (see earlier), Tokyo Disneyland still mainly offers its own merchandise in French Quarter Land stores, even at "La Petite Parfumerie," where instead of Dior, Guerlain, or Givenchy, one finds "Tinker Bell" soap, "Minnie Mouse" bath salt, and "100 Acre Wood" hand wash. This can be related to the Japanese custom of buying "omiyage" – small gifts from travelers to those at home that must, however, "have a legitimating 'trade mark' of the place where it was bought" (Raz 67; see also Laemmerhirt 81–5). The tradition of "omiyage" also explains the comparatively small size of most merchandise available at French Quarter Land – with many of the products at "La Petite Parfumerie," for instance, being sold in travel-size containers – as well as the success of "cult merchandise" (Younger, *Theme Park Design* 352) such as Disney pins, which, quite in contrast to New Orleans Square, can be found in virtually every store in French Quarter Land.

Finally, and just as in New Orleans Square, changes in the shops and stores of the "subland" also contributed, among other things, to a marked increase in autothemed spaces in French Quarter Land. To be sure, with "The Golden Galleon" and "Blackbeard's Portrait Deck," Tokyo Disneyland had featured, from the very beginning, two merchandise outlets themed to pirates and located right next to each other. Compared to the "Portrait Deck" with its more or less generic pirate theme, however, the "Pirate Treasure" shop that replaced it in 2007 has included, in both its interior design and in its merchandise, much more specific references to the ride as whose "attraction store" it functions, from the "Pirates" theme song used in the space's soundtrack to the "Pirates" logo (though not the tagline, which for linguistic reasons had to be altered; see Surrell, *Pirates* 59) emblazoned on T-shirts, flags, and mugs. "Pirates" itself became an autothemed space when in 2007 Tokyo Disneyland added, much like Disneyland in California had done the year before (see earlier), characters and story elements from the "Pirates" movie franchise to the ride. And around the same time, autothemed elements also appeared in the indoor waiting area of the attraction, where gild-framed design sketches of the attraction (both of the Tokyo "original" as well as of the retrofitted, autothemed version) now decorate the heretofore bare walls.

The most interesting case of self-referential theming in connection with French Quarter Land, however, is one of "across-the-parks" autotheming (see earlier) and debuted in summer 2017. In order to stimulate overnight stays and thus increase profits, Tokyo Disneyland added, similar to other Disney theme park destinations at the time (see Disney California Adventure in Anaheim, opened in 2001, and Walt Disney Studios Park in Paris, opened in 2002), a so-called "second gate" in 2001.[80] One of the original design principles of Tokyo DisneySea, as the new park was called, was to avoid redundancy: "'Do not poach, or do not cannibalize on, any of the experiences in Tokyo Disneyland,'" was the direction given to designer Steve Kirk (qtd. in Younger, *Theme Park Design* 198). "As such," Younger notes, "elements such as a pirate themed land were considered, but dropped due to the redundancy that would have existed with *Pirates of the Caribbean*" (198). Nevertheless, in a press release published on 21 September 2016, OLC announced a new "special event" at Tokyo DisneySea for the 2017 summer season: a stage show, along with "[s]pecial merchandise and menu items, as well as decorations inspired by the special event [that] will transform [Tokyo DisneySea] into a world of the Disney film *Pirates of the Caribbean*" (N.N., "Exciting Offerings" 3). The ongoing success of the movie series has ensured that 34 years after the opening of French Quarter Land, Tokyo Disneyland and its designers still consider "Pirates" an "anchor."

Yet there is one aspect of the "internal" history of French Quarter Land that, perhaps somewhat surprisingly, has never had an equivalent in New Orleans Square – namely, the increasing (and quite literal) "carnivalization" of the "subland" from the early 2000s onwards. While, as I have tried to show, the original conception and design of French Quarter Land had been mainly determined by "Pirates," both the debut of "Mickey's Adventureland Mardi Gras" in 2001 and the opening of "Party Gras Gifts" six years later can be read as deliberate attempts to strengthen the "New Orleans" theme of the "subland."[81] In both cases, however, the thematic link to the Crescent City is established via references to Mardi Gras: several of the stage show's performers, for instance, were dressed in the traditional Mardi Gras colors (purple, gold, and green), and during the finale, Mickey appeared as "Rex," the king of Carnival. At "Party Gras Gifts," in turn, the tops of the display shelves are decorated with strings of beads, carnival masks, and framed black-and-white photographs of Mardi Gras parade floats. Of course, the use of Mardi Gras elements in the depiction of New Orleans at French Quarter Land harkens back to the very beginnings of "Disney's Immersive New Orleans," notably the opening ceremonies of New Orleans Street in 1955 and of New Orleans Square's "French Quarter" section in 1966 (see earlier). The new "Mardi Gras" theme may have also been inspired, however, by the next addition to the list of New Orleans-themed spaces in the "Disneyzone," a place that not only culminated the gradual "Frenchifying" of "Disney's Immersive New Orleans," but that has also chronotopically identified the Crescent City with Mardi Gras, turning the one-day event into a permanent built environment: Walt Disney World's Port Orleans – French Quarter Resort.

Every Day a Fat Tuesday: Port Orleans – French Quarter Resort (Walt Disney World)

Opened on 17 May 1991 as "Disney's Port Orleans Resort," Disney's Port Orleans – French Quarter Resort, as it has been officially referred to on signage and in promotional material since April 2000, was the first New Orleans-themed space in the "Disneyzone" and, hence, in "Disney's Immersive New Orleans," that was not directly part of a theme park. Instead, the 1,008-room hotel constitutes one of more than 20 themed resorts and campsites owned and operated by the Walt Disney Company at Walt Disney World near Orlando, Florida.[82] Billed as a "moderate" (rather than a "value" or "deluxe") resort, Port Orleans was one of the first hotels opened in the context of Disney's strategic effort to massively increase both the number and range of accommodation offerings at Walt Disney World, an effort that saw the addition of roughly one resort per year during the late 1980s and 1990s, until the downturn in tourism caused by the 9/11 terrorist attacks put a halt to further plans.

Like several of the other resorts constructed during this phase (for example, the Caribbean Beach Resort, opened in 1988, and the Port Orleans – Riverside Resort, Port Orleans's rural Louisiana-themed sister resort, opened in 1992), Port Orleans was not designed by Walt Disney Imagineering, but by Fugleberg Koch, a Winter Park, Florida-based design firm specializing in hospitality, mixed-use, and commercial projects, with the overall development of the Walt Disney World resorts overseen and coordinated by the Disney Development Company (see Clavé 278; see also earlier). The theme that Fugleberg Koch's principal in charge of the project, Robert Koch, eventually created for the resort, and that was chosen by Disney via a design competition (see N.N., "Portfolio"), was that of "New Orleans's French Quarter on Mardi Gras." Indeed, both the general layout of the hotel as well as all of its individual "units" – from the central check-in/restaurant/retail complex and the seven more or less identical guest room buildings to the outdoor pool, the man-made river, and the various parks and squares between the buildings – feature countless references to French New Orleans, the French Quarter, and Mardi Gras.

Somewhat ironically, then, it was left to an outside design company to bring the gradual "Frenchifying" of "Disney's Immersive New Orleans" to its ultimate, logical conclusion: 36 years after the opening of the "multiracial brandland" of New Orleans Street at Disneyland, the company finally opened a space that through its design exclusively identified the Crescent City as French. What is perhaps even more interesting, however, is how the theme of Port Orleans, and especially its chronotopical aspect that inextricably links the city with one particular day of the year, is performed and brought to life at the site by the resort's employees, both during such special events as the "Mardi Gras Pargo Parade," organized each year on Mardi Gras, as well as in their day-to-day interactions with visitors at the front desk, in the lobby, and in the resort's various other spaces. In fact, as visitor patterns show, even New Orleanians accept and embrace Port Orleans as a place "perfect for celebrating Mardi Gras anytime" (Bshero) and in particular for celebrating Mardi Gras on Mardi Gras itself.

Interestingly, before the opening of Port Orleans, Disney had consciously avoided the theme of New Orleans at Walt Disney World. At the Magic Kingdom park (opened in 1971 as the first phase of the Florida complex), for instance, Disneyland's New Orleans Square and "Pirates" were dropped and the "Haunted Mansion" was relocated to a new, colonial New England-themed "land" called Liberty Square (see earlier). "The designers," David Koenig explains, "thought that Central Florida was too close to the real New Orleans and the real Caribbean for there to be interest in a faux New Orleans Square or Pirates of the Caribbean" (46). Likewise, although in a 1982 interview with the employee magazine *Eyes & Ears*, Dick Nunis, then president of outdoor recreation at Walt Disney World, had announced "'a beautiful New Orleans hotel'" in the Walt Disney World Village area (qtd. in N.N., "Chattin'"), the hotel was never built, presumably for the same reasons.

Theme park scholars such as Bryman, Kolb, Steinecke, Younger, and Steinkrüger have identified the rationale behind the designers' original decision to dispense with the theme of New Orleans at the Florida complex as the principle of thematic "externality" or "opposition." In *Sprawling Places*, Kolb notes that:

> the reference to what is outside the themed place is a constitutive element in the place. Though they pretend to offer total absorption

in their themes, themed places rely on a continual awareness of the outside and their difference from it.

(112)

From this, Steinkrüger concludes that the source of an immersive space's theme is not just "typically ... external to the institution or object to which it is applied," as Bryman had argued in *The Disneyization of Society* (15), but that "spatial, temporal or worldly externality is a *necessary condition* for a space to be perceived as a themed space": "To be recognizable as a theme the represented times, spaces, and worlds have to become 'other' times, spaces, and worlds" ("Other Times" 88; emphasis added). Similarly, Younger defines "opposition" as a design principle that is not only used within theme parks to emphasize specific details, but also to heighten the contrast between the theme park and its surroundings: "One of Disneyland's ... successes is credited as being its lush recreation of the Mississippi river in the dry, urban, desert environment of Southern California" (*Theme Park Design* 165). Steinecke, finally, has considered the extreme contrast between the theme and the geographic and cultural features of the location as one of the two principal characteristics that set apart themed hotels from "conventional" ones (96).

While at Walt Disney World, the principle of "externality" or "opposition" may have initially prevented the construction of New Orleans Square in the Magic Kingdom and the New Orleans-themed hotel in the Village area, the late 1980s and early 1990s witnessed the addition of several spaces themed to the Crescent City and more generally to the South: rides (for example, "Splash Mountain" in the Magic Kingdom, 1992), water parks (Typhoon Lagoon, 1989), but especially hotels (among others, the Grand Floridian Resort, 1988, the Old Key West Resort, 1991, and, of course, Port Orleans and its sister resort, 1991–1992; see Waldrep 205). It was these Southern-themed resorts, in fact, that marked the beginning of the "frantic hotel expansion" (Koenig 284) at Walt Disney World, an expansion that the company's then new CEO Michael Eisner, following an "accelerating hybrid consumption strategy" (Bryman, *Disneyization* 60), had launched in order to increase revenues from the Florida complex's hotel, but also its food and beverage as well as its merchandise divisions.

When Walt Disney World first opened in 1971, it featured only two hotels (the Contemporary and the Polynesian Resort), both of them luxury resorts. A third facility, the "Disney Inn" golf resort, was opened in 1973.[83] However, by the mid-1980s, Disney thought that:

> too many theme park visitors were staying off property and that as a result the company was losing a huge revenue stream. Also, if people went off Disney property at the end of the day, they would be less likely to be spending their money in theme park restaurants and on merchandise.
>
> (Bryman, *Disneyization* 59–60)

In order to "'get you there, keep you there, and . . . make sure you spend all your money with them,'" as one of Disney's former vice-presidents has summarized the company's new "Orlando philosophy" (qtd. in Bryman, *Disneyization* 60), Disney started to greatly increase and diversify the number of hotels on property, opening roughly one resort per year during the period from 1988–2004 – mostly deluxe and moderate resorts at first (among them Port Orleans), but from 1994 onwards, also and increasingly, value resorts (see Clavé 279). In addition to such amenities as free, direct transportation, as well as early access to the theme parks (see Bryman, *Disneyization* 60), the new Disney hotels also offered theming to differentiate themselves from off-property, non-Disney resorts. Yet whereas the themes of Walt Disney World's first hotels were inextricably linked to those of the Magic Kingdom (with, for instance, the Contemporary Resort mirroring Tomorrowland and the Polynesian Resort reflecting Adventureland), many of the new hotels were themed to the South, thus apparently breaking the "externality" principle.

Far from suggesting that Disney had simply abandoned thematic "opposition," however, the increasing turn to Southern themes at Walt Disney World in the late 1980s rather indicates that the principle of "externality" was radically redefined to reflect the Florida complex's gradual development into a multi-day, multi-gate "global theme park" (Mitrasinovic 106) with an increasingly international clientele. To be sure, Walt Disney World had not "been planned solely by the population-radius parameters or conventional trade area analyses" (107) and had thus relied, unlike Disneyland in Anaheim, on a non-local audience from its very beginnings. However, with two theme parks and several smaller nature and water parks, the complex had, by the mid-1980s, reached the "critical mass of facilities necessary for attracting a significant volume of international tourism" (106) and, hence, an audience to whom the U.S. South presumably appeared as no less exotic or "external" than Walt Disney World's other, non-local themes. Consequently, rather than as the opposition between an immersive space's themes and its location, "externality" was redefined at Walt Disney World as the contrast between its themes and the place(s) of origin of its visitors, thus also allowing for the inclusion of Southern- and specifically New Orleans-themed spaces.[84]

In the case of Port Orleans, however, Disney still preserved some degree of "traditional" "externality" by locating the space in a place and at a time that can be defined as "other." Instead of promoting the hotel as a representation of the Crescent City, as the company had done in the case of New Orleans Street, New Orleans Square, and French Quarter Land (see earlier), for instance, Disney introduced Port Orleans to visitors as a unique place, a city remarkably similar to, but nevertheless distinct from New Orleans. Indeed, from 1991–1999, visitors arriving at Port Orleans received a copy of the *Sassagoula Sentinel*, an eight-page tabloid-format fictional newspaper that not only contained practical information about the hotel (e.g., the opening hours of the restaurants), but also several illustrated articles about the history of the site (see N.N., "Document Downloads"). According to this history, the settlement of Port Orleans was founded in 1704 by two French explorers, Pierre d'Orr and Philippe Leane, at the mouth of the Sassagoula river (N.N., *Sassagoula Sentinel* 1). Although it soon developed into "the main trading and commerce center for the entire region" (8) and a "diverse cosmopolitan city" (2) with a distinct architecture, a unique cuisine, and "a music that defied classification" (7), Port Orleans was handed over to Spain in 1763 as part of a war settlement (2). The city briefly became a French possession again, before in 1823 [sic], it was sold to the United States as part of the Louisiana Purchase (8).

Combining historical actors and episodes from New Orleans's past (France, Spain, the United States, the cession to Spain, and the Louisiana Purchase) with evidently fictional characters (Orr and Leane), as well as intertextual references to fictional representations of the Crescent City (the "clever bellowing" of Port Orleans's street vendors, for example, may remind readers of Clémence from Cable's *The Grandissimes*; see N.N., *Sassagoula Sentinel* 8), the *Sassagoula Sentinel* and its history of Port Orleans could be described as a whimsical piece of "historiographic metafiction" (Hutcheon 5), an entertaining, self-conscious, postmodern parody of (New Orleans) historiography. At the same time, however, the history also constitutes a classic "Distory" – a thoroughly sanitized, whitewashed version of the Crescent City's history that has been stripped of all references to interracial conflicts, slavery, segregation, the Civil War, plagues, pirates, and hurricanes, among other things.

Promoting Port Orleans as New Orleans's happier "Other," a city that enjoyed all of the Crescent City's "positive" aspects while never having experienced the latter's darker sides, conveniently allowed Disney to forestall any potential discussions about (mis)representing New Orleans and its past. Even more importantly, the depiction of Port Orleans as a distinct space with its own history and character also significantly increased the "externality" factor of the hotel for both local and international visitors. Nevertheless, the company does not seem to have been particularly invested in the history of Port Orleans. Not only has this story left virtually no traces in the physical space of the hotel;[85] already in the *Sentinel* itself, Disney somewhat paradoxically reverted to more traditional promotional discourses, with, for instance, the welcome message printed in the newspaper's "Guest Information Supplement" inviting visitors to "sample an authentic taste of the French Quarter – its cuisine, its fanciful nature and its charm" (3). And after the *Sentinel* had been replaced with a rather conventional info package in 1999, Port Orleans's fictional history has only survived in an internal memorandum that urges employees to "bring the story to life" and communicate it to visitors (N.N., *Bringing*).[86]

By contrast, the various architectural, performative, and other manifestations of the hotel's temporal setting have, if anything, intensified and increased over the years. Compared to that of the other spaces in "Disney's Immersive New Orleans," Port Orleans's location in time is at once more hazy and more precise: while a particular year, decade, or even century are nowhere unambiguously identified (according to its menus, "Bonfamille's Café" was established "in the early 1900s," yet Disney's official website describes the hotel as generally "evok[ing] the Antebellum era"; N.N., "Port Orleans Resort"), the month and even the day are clearly established: "Every day's a Fat Tuesday here!" (N.N., "Port Orleans Resort"). Mardi Gras or, more generally, carnival can, of course, be characterized as a time that is quintessentially "other"[87] and thus ideal for establishing a sense of "externality" as well as a festive holiday atmosphere, which is precisely why Disney had previously used the "Mardi Gras" theme for such scripted special events as the opening ceremonies of New Orleans Street and New Orleans Square's "French Quarter" section (see earlier). Before Port Orleans, however, the company had never attempted to adapt the event into a permanent immersive environment (Tokyo Disneyland's "Party Gras Gifts" would not open until 16 years later), so it is particularly interesting to see how Fugleberg Koch responded to the challenge.

Port Orleans is, first of all, a New Orleans-themed space, and of all the New Orleans-themed spaces in the "Disneyzone," it constitutes without doubt the most literal interpretation of the Crescent City or, more precisely, its French Quarter: located on a bend of the (man-made) Sassagoula River, the hotel is laid out in a dense grid pattern, with the seven guest room buildings, the central check-in/restaurant/retail complex, the pool area, and the five parks or squares forming a total of nine rectangular blocks organized in two rows. Each of the guest room buildings comprises three stories and is surrounded by outside walkways (or "balconies") that are decorated with wrought-iron trims. "Fractional architecture" is used to suggest that the buildings are actually blocks made up of several smaller, individual structures. The walkways running between the blocks and squares are paved with cobblestones and lined with black iron street lamps, hitching posts, and street signs, although as in New Orleans, the names of the streets are also indicated by blue and white tiles embedded in the walkways. The pool area, located in the center of the first row of blocks and separated from the river only by a graveled "carriage path," is surrounded by live oaks and an ornate iron fence that is closely modeled on the one around New Orleans's Jackson Square. Covered by a glass roof and featuring an ornate fountain, the hotel's main lobby, finally, has been designed to look like an outdoor courtyard and is surrounded by brick façades behind which visitors can find the front desk, the shop, and the bar, as well as the hotel's two restaurants.[88]

The French Quarter is not only evoked through Port Orleans's general layout and architecture, however, but also through references that address the auditory, gustatory, and olfactory senses: Dixieland jazz music – more specifically, the Preservation Hall Jazz Band's 1988 album *New Orleans, Vol. 1* and Lionel Hampton's *Greatest Hits* (1996) – can be heard throughout Port Orleans's indoor and outdoor public areas (see N.N., "Music"). The "Scat Cat's Club" also offers live music during the evenings, although in 2013 the bar's long-time resident musician, jazz saxophonist and vocalist, Elliott Dyson, was replaced by a changing variety of acts, among them Jason Thomas and Billy Varnes, who had previously performed at EPCOT's "Canada" pavilion with the rock band "Off Kilter" (N.N., "Scat Cat's").[89] At the neighboring "Sassagoula Floatworks and Food Factory" counter-service restaurant, visitors can enjoy such New Orleans or French Quarter classics as jambalaya, po'boys, café au lait, and beignets (see Bshero). And right across, "Jackson Square Gifts & Desires" offers Creole cookbooks, Café du Monde coffee and beignet mixes, Aunt Sally's pralines, and seasonings and mixes from the "Louisiana" brand.

By contrast, Port Orleans features surprisingly few "reflexive" references to Disney's other New Orleans-themed spaces and movies: framed prints of Herbert Ryman's "The Square" can be found in a corner of the lobby and in some of the guest rooms, and during a recent renovation, huge playing cards with the images of Tiana and Naveen (from Disney's 2009 animated movie *The Princess and the Frog*) were added to the décor of the counter-service restaurant (see ahead; according to employees, Tiana also regularly appears as a walkaround character at the hotel). Autothemed elements are even rarer: amidst black-and-white drawings of the French Quarter (somewhat reminiscent of Joseph Pennell's illustrations for *Scribner's/Century*), a watercolor painting of the hotel's main building – perhaps the one Port Orleans building that with its huge glass roof least evokes the architecture of the French Quarter – adorns the walls of "Jackson Square."[90]

Instead, much of the theming of the hotel is dedicated to Mardi Gras. The traditional Mardi Gras colors (purple, gold, and green) can be found almost everywhere at Port Orleans: on bedspreads in the guest rooms, on rugs and chairs in the lobby, on signs throughout the resort, on employee uniforms, and even on floor tiles in the counter-service restaurant. Likewise, low-relief tiles in the common bathrooms, restaurant menus, and the signs above the hotel's main entrance (which represent the logo of Port Orleans's fictional carnival organization, the "Krewe of Port Orleans") all feature silhouettes of Mardi Gras masks, while huge Mardi Gras parade float masks and props, bought from warehouses in New Orleans, are hanging, appropriately enough, from the ceiling of the "Sassagoula Floatworks and Food Factory." Finally, Mardi Gras characters and revelers – in the shape of paintings and statues – populate the front desk area, the lobby, the restaurant, and especially the pool area: a mural depicting a Mardi Gras ball, for instance, serves as the background for the registration desks; mannequins dressed like jesters and apparently designed by Blaine Kern Studios (see N.N., "Fun Facts")[91] provide photo opportunities in the lobby, the restaurant, and at the entrance to the pool area; and on the walkway to the pool, a group of anthropomorphized alligators with musical instruments has organized a small Mardi Gras parade.

Moreover, Port Orleans also offers its visitors all the necessary accessories to become Mardi Gras revelers themselves: for example, beads, coins, and balloons in the Mardi Gras colors are freely available at the front desk (see ahead); cocktails, Mardi Gras Fritters, and "King Cakes" (actually little Bundt cakes with purple, green, and gold frosting) are offered at the bar, the pool bar, and the restaurant; and "Jackson Square" sells hard liquor and Mardi Gras-themed shot glasses (advertised, in a nod to Disney's reputation as family-friendly, as "toothpick holders"), as well as beautifully detailed, handmade papier-mâché carnival masks. The latter are particularly interesting, as they are actually not related to the New Orleans carnival at all: in fact, the masks are designed and manufactured by Balocoloc, a Venice, Italy-based family business that for several years has been operating a carnival mask store at the "Italy" pavilion at Walt Disney World's EPCOT park on a lessee basis. As the Balocoloc employee in charge of the EPCOT store informed me during my field trip to Walt Disney World in May 2016, the masks are produced in batches, and the ones destined for sale at Port Orleans use the same basic designs as the ones offered at the "Italy" pavilion, with only the colors being adjusted to the familiar purple, green, and gold.

Yet above all, Port Orleans's "Mardi Gras" theme is brought to life through the hotel's employees and their interactions with visitors. It is perhaps for this reason that the critical response to the hotel has been rather negative: Sheldon Waldrep, for instance, has argued that like most of the other "moderate" resorts opened at Walt Disney World during the 1980s and 1990s, Port Orleans represents "a sort of zero degree of theming or, simply, minimalistic theming in which the sparest of narrative effects are employed" (203). Solely based as it is on the hotel's architecture and its interior decoration (what Raz has called the "onstage"; see earlier), Waldrep's assessment completely ignores the "production" of themed spaces by their employees and, more specifically, the various ways in which the Port Orleans staff performs or celebrates Mardi Gras for and with visitors on both a daily and a yearly basis. As I have tried to argue throughout "Disney's Immersive New Orleans," however, aspects of production and reception should form an integral part of research on immersive spaces in general and theme parks in particular, and Port Orleans is a case in point.

Indeed, the hotel's employees seek to immerse visitors into the theme of "Mardi Gras" from the very beginning of the latter's stay at Port Orleans: upon checking in at the front desk, for instance, especially younger visitors are given Mardi Gras beads, coins, and balloons (handing out beads to adults has proven problematic, however, as some have reacted by lifting their shirts).⁹² At regular intervals, and especially when there are a lot of children in the registration area, the front desk team also interrupts their work for short Mardi Gras "parades," during which the hotel's regular soundtrack (see earlier) is replaced with Disney versions of current pop hits and the employees lead visitors on an impromptu parade through the lobby.⁹³ From October 2012 through June 2013, additional children's Mardi Gras parades were staged every afternoon in the pool area as part of the hotel's regular poolside recreation schedule. Occasionally, these afternoon parades were preceded by "Mardi Gras" crafts activities, during which children could, among other things, decorate their own carnival masks. Since 2010, finally, Port Orleans has also employed a so-called "greeter": dressed in a purple suit with a green bowtie and a golden sash and wearing an oversized purple top hat with green and golden feathers, Arneil, who has been with the company for more than 30 years, roams Port Orleans's lobby in order to welcome visitors to the hotel, give out coins and beads, lead the front desk Mardi Gras parades, and generally provide "streetmosphere."

Hence, through the hotel's architecture, interior decoration, food and beverages, merchandise, and especially via the daily interactions between employees and visitors, Mardi Gras forms an integral part of Port Orleans and its unique temporality. As I have argued with Filippo Carlà-Uhink, Sabrina Mittermeier, and Ariane Schwarz, theme park temporalities can generally be described as complex temporalities that comprise and combine various different temporal layers ("Introduction" 12). Among the latter, one may distinguish between, first, those times and temporalities that "originate within the parks themselves and are thus unique to them"; second, those "that can be categorized as 'external' since they lie beyond the influence of the parks"; and, third, those "that may be external but that are nevertheless consciously employed by the parks" (12). Similar to tourist seasons, civil and/or religious holidays like Christmas, Halloween, and, indeed, Mardi Gras belong to the third group, as the parks cannot control them but nevertheless integrate them into their yearly cycles of festivities (13) – usually via holiday seasons that are stretched out over a period of several weeks (see Carlà et al., "Formierung" 336–40). In the case of Port Orleans's Mardi Gras, however, the "external" holiday has been stretched out even further, over the entire year; and instead of merely integrating it, Port Orleans produces Mardi Gras, day after day after day. The holiday has thus been fully taken over by the themed space and become an essential part of the latter's very identity.⁹⁴

This does not mean, however, that the "real" Mardi Gras goes unobserved at Port Orleans. Quite to the contrary, perhaps the most important way in which the hotel's employees perform or celebrate Mardi Gras for and with its visitors occurs on Mardi Gras itself: since 2006, Port Orleans has organized a yearly "Mardi Gras Pargo Parade," for which volunteers from the hotel's individual divisions (front desk, housekeeping, custodial, food and beverage, retail, maintenance, etc.) dress up "pargos" (small electric vehicles usually used for the transportation of goods and employees) as Mardi Gras parade floats according to a previously chosen theme. The latter usually, though not always, has some connection to Disney – over the last few years, pargo parade themes have included "Disney Heritage through the Decades" (2012), "Walt Disney World Sweets and Treats" (2018), and "Past Walt Disney World Attractions" (2020); but also "Celebrating the Holidays" (2014), "Music" (2015), and "Board Games" (2016). On Mardi Gras itself, the individual teams line up the decorated pargos/parade floats and drive them along a predetermined route from Port Orleans – Riverside Resort (where the pargo garage is located) to Port Orleans – French Quarter Resort, with the members of each team walking behind their respective float and distributing beads, coins, and candy to the crowds along the parade route. At Port Orleans, the parade usually stops for a brief ceremony, during which prizes are awarded for the "best themed," the "most creative," and the "best all-around" floats, before returning to the garage. The celebrations continue with a Mardi Gras ball in the Port Orleans lobby, which includes a King Cake eating contest, visits from Disney characters, and dancing to live music.

In a 2009 press release, Disney itself has described Port Orleans's annual Mardi Gras as "'an excellent way to engage our [visitors] in celebrating with our [staff]'" (qtd. in N.N., "Port Orleans Celebrates"); and in fact, employees at the hotel, each of whom had participated in the parade and the ball at least twice, confirmed how much they, their colleagues, and the visitors enjoyed the yearly festivities. At the same time, the press release also notes that the event is "'meaningful and representative of our theme at Disney's Port Orleans Resort.'" Indeed, while Mardi Gras at Port Orleans constitutes both a creative team-building and morale-boosting activity for employees and a fun event for visitors (both the parade as well as the Mardi Gras ball are announced on the hotel's official recreation schedule), it is also intended to further reinforce the hotel's thematic connection with Mardi Gras. As an event that clearly provides a significant amount of pleasure for everyone involved, but also uses the employees' volunteer work in order to add to the visitors' immersive experience (as well as to strengthen the staff's identification with their workplace), however, the festivities once again illustrate the "problem with pleasure."

The press release, of course, merely stresses that the event "'is a[n] [employee] favorite every year, and they enjoy interacting with our [visitors] during the parade, some of whom time their vacations each year to Mardi Gras'" (qtd. in N.N., "Port Orleans Celebrates"). The latter point, too, has been confirmed by employees at the hotel. Even more interestingly, they reported that during the Mardi Gras season, about a third of the hotel's rooms are booked by repeat visitors from New Orleans and the surrounding area, most of whom have been regularly visiting Port Orleans on Mardi Gras for several years. Somewhat ironically, however, it is not primarily in order to celebrate Mardi Gras at Port Orleans that many of these New Orleanian visitors travel to Walt Disney World during the carnival season, but rather because they wish to avoid the Crescent City during this time of the year and/or because they rent out their homes to tourists who come to New Orleans for carnival. Hence, in terms of tourism flows, New Orleans's Mardi Gras simultaneously functions as a pull and a push factor, as during the season the massive influx of tourists from elsewhere to the Crescent City (see Gotham 171–2) routinely generates another, significantly smaller but still noticeable flow of tourists from New Orleans to Port Orleans.

Nevertheless, the hotel's "French Quarter on Mardi Gras" theme – or, rather, the way this theme has been turned into a built environment – does play a role in New Orleanian visitors' decision to spend their Walt Disney World vacation at Port Orleans: due to its French Quarter-inspired, dense grid layout, the hotel constitutes one of the complex's most compact resorts, and like other visitors, New Orleanians enjoy the short walks from their rooms to the restaurant and the pool. And since they often bring along King Cakes (actual ones, not Bundt cakes) for the Mardi Gras ball, Port Orleans, by a curious turn of circumstances, does in fact offer "an authentic taste of the French Quarter" and Mardi Gras – at least once a year.

Conclusion

For his "Travels in Hyperreality," Umberto Eco deliberately went, within the space of 24 hours, "from the fake New Orleans of Disneyland to the real one" (44):

> I was coming from the recreated New Orleans of Disneyland, and I wanted to check my reactions against the real city, which represents a still intact past, because the Vieux Carré is one of the few places that American civilization hasn't remade, flattened, replaced.
>
> (29)

When "Travels in Hyperreality" was published in the Italian magazine *L'espresso* in three installments in late 1975, however, the French Quarter had long been turned into the focal point of New Orleans tourism and was well on its way to become what in the very same year Pierce F. Lewis called a "Creole Disneyland" (38):[95] already "in the 1950s under Mayor deLesseps S. Morrison," J. Mark Souther writes, "the city government sought to make the Vieux Carré clean, safe, and attractive for tourists" ("Making" 120). Morrison's successor in office, Victor Schiro – the very Schiro who had been Walt Disney's guest of honor at the 1966 opening of the "French Quarter" section of Disneyland's New Orleans Square – continued his predecessor's efforts to create "a suburban-like atmosphere where tourists would feel comfortable" (120). But it was under the mayorship of Maurice Edwin "Moon" Landrieu that, according to Souther, the "Disneyfication" of the French Quarter eventually took off with the construction of several "Disneyfied" places: "In 1970, shortly after Landrieu took office, he announced a plan to turn three of the streets surrounding Jackson Square into a pedestrian mall" (*New Orleans* 166). Soon, the newly flagstone-paved St. Peter, St. Ann, and Chartres streets were filled with "artists, street musicians, fortune tellers, and sideshows" rather than cars (167). Five years later, and only a few months before *L'espresso* would print Eco's texts, the historic French Market reopened as a "'festival marketplace' along the lines of San Francisco's Ghirardelli Square . . . and the James Rouse Company's transformation of Boston's Quincy Market" (168). Hence, when "Travels in Hyperreality" finally appeared, at least parts of the French Quarter had already been "remade, flattened, replaced," and the contrast between the "fake New Orleans of Disneyland" and "the real one" was no longer quite as clear-cut or pronounced as Eco had thought it was.

But it was not just the Crescent City that was increasingly concentrating on the French Quarter in order to accommodate tourists. Indeed, around the same time that New Orleans sought to turn the Vieux Carré into the city's main tourism spot through e.g., the creation of "Disneyfied" spaces, Disney theme parks and resorts, too, started to focus more and more on the French Quarter in their spatial depictions of the city: from Disneyland's New Orleans Street (1955) to the Anaheim park's New Orleans Square (1966) to Tokyo Disneyland's French Quarter Land (1983) to Walt Disney World's Port Orleans – French Quarter Resort (1991), with every new New Orleans-themed "land," "subland," or resort opened in the "Disneyzone," the Vieux Carré and French New Orleans would play a more and more prominent role in "Disney's Immersive New Orleans."

This was by no means a coincidence. As New Orleans's city administrations increasingly made the promotion of tourism their priority (see Souther, *New Orleans* 159), and as the level of competition in the theme park industry continued to grow, city planners – as well as theme park designers – strove to transform the city and Disney's representations of it, respectively, into places that corresponded as closely as possible to tourists' preconceived notions of what (a trip to) New Orleans should be like. It is in this sense that we can speak of New Orleans tourism as "popular culture tourism" (Geraghty, Lundberg, and Ziakis 1241): due to such textual and visual representations of New Orleans as, for instance, the various fictional, historical, ethnographic, and travel writings and their accompanying illustrations printed in *Scribner's/Century*, the French Quarter had, as Souther correctly notes, long "connoted New Orleans" in the popular mind (*New Orleans* 8; see also Souther, "Disneyfication" 804). The "Disneyfication" of the Vieux Carré and the simultaneous "Frenchifying" of "Disney's Immersive New Orleans" suggest that both the Crescent City and Disney employed the Vieux Carré to give tourists exactly what they had come to see.

To be sure, one could also read Disney's growing embrace of the Frenchness of New Orleans – as opposed to a broader, more culturally diverse depiction of the city – as yet another indication of the company's desire and efforts to avoid controversy. Given the parallel developments in New Orleans and the "Disneyzone," however, I contend that authenticity may be identified as the central factor that has shaped the development of Disney's representation of the Crescent City in its theme parks and resorts. Authenticity is used here not in its "conventional understanding as something historically accurate and consisting of genuine fabric" (Holtorf 33), of course, but rather in the negotiable, gradable, and radically subjective sense ascribed to the term by scholars of tourism from the late 1980s onwards (see Cohen). Instead of an intrinsic characteristic of a given object or place, authenticity in this sense denotes an appearance of credibility and genuineness that, if successful, engenders an experience of recognition. Perhaps Wayne Curtis put it most succinctly when he defined the authentic as "something that looks as you imagine it might" (qtd. in Lukas, *Theme Park* 139). Yet whereas the city of New Orleans has always had to negotiate between vastly different concepts or ideas of what constitutes "authentic New Orleans" (locally, historic preservation and "Disneyfication" have met with quite different responses; see Gotham 142–68; Dawdy 55–61), the designers of "Disney's Immersive New Orleans" were free to focus on adapting popular images of the Crescent City and to thus meet visitors' expectations toward "authentic" experiences in immersive spaces (already Eco had warned readers that in New Orleans, they may risk feeling "homesick for Disneyland"; 44).

In a way, authenticity has also played a role in the micro-histories of some of the various components of "Disney's Immersive New Orleans," particularly in that of Disneyland's New Orleans Square. In fact, as the oldest still existing New Orleans-themed space in the "Disneyzone," New Orleans Square has, at least for some theme park actors, acquired something of an authenticity of its own over the years.[96] Consequently, changes to New Orleans Square such as the "hyper-Disneyfication" of the "land" during the 2013–2014 expansion of "Club 33" sparked controversies that were remarkably similar to the ones caused by the "Disneyfication" of New Orleans's French Quarter (see earlier). In addition, however, "Disney's Immersive New Orleans" has shown that the individual histories of New Orleans Street, New Orleans Square, French Quarter Land, and Port Orleans have also been shaped by numerous other factors, including changing trends in themes (e.g., the rise of autotheming at New Orleans Square); changing tastes in theme park design styles (for instance, the impact of the "Presentational Style" on the design of French Quarter Land); changes in building codes or other safety, health, and labor regulations (cf. the closure of the "Silver Banjo Barbecue"); changing operational and managerial strategies (for example, the implementation of "Independent Per Capita Operation"); sudden changes in economic conditions (e.g., the end of Walt Disney World's hotel expansion); and broader cultural changes (among others, the shift of New Orleans Square's temporal setting or the 1997 renovation of California's "Pirates").

Describing exactly how and why the spatial depiction of the Crescent City in Disney's theme parks and resorts has evolved, on both a macro-level as well as a micro-level, has only been one of the goals of "Disney's Immersive New Orleans," however. Above all, and much more fundamentally, this chapter has sought to generally problematize the notion that (Disney) theme parks and resorts constitute "inert texts" (Bryman, *Disney* 83) and has thus called for historical approaches to theme parks that critically address the numerous and manifold ways in which these spaces have constantly shifted and changed over time. While much has been written about the origins of the theme park in general and of Disneyland in particular, tracing the later development of this and other parks has been left, all too often, to the companies themselves. For purposes of self-promotion and branding, however, the latter have, as in the case of Europa-Park's "Historama," merely produced highly selective and heavily edited – in short, theme park – versions of their own pasts. Methodological problems notwithstanding, restoring the "historical erasures" of these theme park "Distories" can be, as "Disney's Immersive New Orleans" has hopefully shown, both fruitful and illuminating, and should thus form an integral part of the critical study of themed and immersive spaces.

This also applies to the production of theme parks by design, management, and operational staff, as well as to their reception by visitors. Although particularly in the context of a diachronic approach to theme parks, the study of theme park actors, too, confronts the researcher with serious methodological difficulties, "Disney's Immersive New Orleans" has nevertheless sought to build upon and continue Raz's and Wasko's pioneering studies by simultaneously considering Disney's New Orleans-themed spaces themselves, their production, and their consumption. The results may suggest rather than exhaust the potential of such an "integrated" or rhizomatic approach, but as the stories of Aunt Jemima, Teddy and Kenny, and Port Orleans's "Mardi Gras migrants" have illustrated, analyses that exclusively focus on the "onstage" may fail to capture the various different meanings that theme park spaces take on for different people at different times. Indeed, the theme park needs to be conceived of as a network, a place of interaction between spaces, between people, and between spaces and people, and it should also be discussed as such.

Predictably, the events of Hurricane Katrina were not referenced or acknowledged in any official way at Disney's New Orleans-themed spaces.[97] In the Crescent City, meanwhile, the storm and the debate about the post-Katrina future of New Orleans had rekindled old fears of a "Disneyfication" of the city that were expressed in numerous newspaper articles and speeches (see Parmett; Gotham 2–3), but also in such public performances as the 2014 parade of Krewe du Vieux, perhaps New Orleans's most irreverent carnival organization. For this parade, which rolled through Marigny and the French Quarter on 15 February 2014, the Krewe of sPANk, one of the altogether 17 sub-organizations of Krewe du Vieux, designed a particularly original float: in front of a miniature St. Louis cathedral, a papier-mâché figure of New Orleans mayor Mitchell J. Landrieu, dressed in a "New Orleans Will"[98] T-shirt and wearing Mickey Mouse ears, had replaced Andrew Jackson on the horse of the Jackson monument as he welcomed Mardi Gras revelers to what the huge banner above him, printed in the characteristic Disneyland font, identified as "Disneylandrieu." Maps of "Mitchey Mayor's Gentrified Kingdom," handed out by Krewe of sPANk members wearing Mickey Mouse ears during the parade, were closely modeled on Disneyland's visitor guides and promised "a happy, quiet and appropriately sanitized experience for you and your entire family" (Krewe of sPANk).[99]

As the following chapter will illustrate, however, "Disneylandrieu" was by no means the first or the last time that one of Krewe du Vieux's parade floats in particular, or a public performance in general, had raised the issue of the future of post-Katrina New Orleans. And at least some of these public performances would radically alter the depiction of New Orleans in popular culture, turning it from an exceptional into an exemplary city.

Notes

1. As of 2020, these include (going from the main entrance at the extreme northern end to the hotel section at the extreme southern end of the park): Germany, Italy, France, Ireland, Switzerland, Greece, England, Russia, Luxembourg, the Netherlands, Austria, Scandinavia, Spain, Portugal, and Iceland. See Rubin (11) for attendance figures from 2018 and Dawid and Schwarz for recent analyses of Europa-Park.
2. See http://corporate.europapark.com/en/company/historie/ and www.mack-rides.com/en/company/history/index.html, respectively.
3. Alan Bryman, also discussing Disney theme parks, explains: "What we find in the parks is a reconstruction of the past which exaggerates positive elements and plays down or altogether omits negative ones. Two techniques which influence the depiction of the past are humour and omission" (*Disney* 127). According to Bryman, it is above all problems caused by corporations, issues related to class, race, and gender, and problems involving any sort of conflict that are silenced in theme parks (129–34).
4. Particularly at Disney theme parks, park anniversaries have often inspired temporary decorations, parades, and shows that also reference park history

(see Freitag, "Autotheming" 144). As a theme park *ride* about theme park history, however, the "Historama" is unique.
5. The company responsible for the design of Disney theme parks, renamed Walt Disney Imagineering in 1986 (see Sklar).
6. Exceptions include Hildebrandt's study of Cedar Point, Davis's history of SeaWorld San Diego (Davis, *Spectacular Nature*), Wiener's, Francaviglia's, and Avila's accounts of the early history of Disneyland's Frontierland (Wiener; Francaviglia, "Frontierland"; Avila 132–5), Francaviglia's comparison of the "Main Street" sections at Disneyland and The Magic Kingdom at Walt Disney World (Francaviglia, "Main Street U.S.A."), and Rahn's history of Disneyland's "Snow White" ride.
7. As of 2020, the "Disneyzone" comprises five theme park resorts, each with at least one theme park and at least two hotels; three standalone resorts that, together with several locations at the theme park resorts, form the "Disney Vacation Club" timeshare program; and the Disney Cruise Line, with four ships and a private port of call.
8. Henceforth, "Pirates of the Caribbean" will be referred to as "Pirates."
9. According to Charles Carson, Disney theme parks "represent idealized visions of guests' *vacation experiences*" of the cultures and places they depict:

> It is not enough that a visitor to a Disney theme park should experience (what s/he believes to be) a foreign 'land'; Disney ensures that what visitors see of that land is what they would want to see on an actual vacation there.
>
> (232; emphasis original)

See also Köck 14.
10. Steinecke mentions, amongst others, McDonaldization, Disneyfication, and postmodernism (46–8).
11. In fact, both Lukas and Clément do just that by suggesting the use of Actor-Network Theory in the study of themed and immersive spaces (see Lukas "Research" 167; and Clément, *Plus vrais* 21). Interestingly, Alexander C.T. Geppert has recently proposed to reconceptualize exposition studies as the study of "exhibitionary networks" (4; see also ahead).
12. As if to prove my point, Lukas tells anecdotes of encounters with security guards that were apparently much less amicable than mine (see "Research" 159–60).
13. "Main Street windows" are tributes to specific individuals involved in the creation of Disney theme parks that are painted on the windowpanes of buildings in Disneyland's Main Street section (see Heimbuch).
14. Billing itself the "official publication [of] Disneyland California" in its masthead, *The Disneyland News* was a tabloid-sized, illustrated mock newspaper published monthly from July 1955 through March 1957 (and sporadically afterwards). Edited by Marty Sklar, who later became president of Walt Disney Imagineering, it contained "news" about the park and was sold for 10 cents a copy on newsstands and by newsboys in the Main Street section of Disneyland (see N.N., "The Disneyland News"). A collection of scans of *The Disneyland News* front pages can be found on http://keeline.com/DLmagazines/Disneyland_News/index. html.
15. According to David Younger, sublands are "small areas within a [theme park] land that are grouped by a further subtheme beyond that of the land itself" (*Theme Park Design* 294).
16. In a controversial speech given on Martin Luther King, Jr. Day, 2006 – and, hence, only a few months after Hurricane Katrina had destroyed much

of the city – New Orleans's then mayor Ray Nagin had stated that New Orleans would be "chocolate at the end of the day" (qtd. in Hackenesch 75).
17. Many commentators have speculated about the origins of Disneyland's themes in particular and the overall theme of the park in general. Marling's genealogical approach is very closely related to that of Deborah Philips, who traces Disneyland's themes back to "those of the popular literary genres identifiable from the moment of the mass reproduction of texts and pictures" (32; see earlier). Most scholars, however, have followed Walt Disney, who suggested in an interview that "there's an American theme behind the whole park" (qtd. in Giroux 36), and have analyzed Disneyland as an affirmative projection of specifically American – read Protestant, middle-class, Midwestern, capitalist, technologized – mythologies, images, and values (see, for instance, Marin 240–1; Real 341; M.J. King 120; Gottdiener, *Postmodern* 112–3; and Prager and Richardson 204). In addition, Gottdiener has also offered an autobiographical or psychological reading of the park, viewing it as "the personalized self-expression of its creator" (*Postmodern* 114–5), while Hobbs sees "the map of the park [as] a map of the American psyche" (23) at large. Rather than by such "manifestation themes" (Younger, *Theme Park Design* 75–7) as "America" or "Walt Disney (the person)," designer John Hench has identified the park as being unified by the "dramatic themes" (Younger, *Theme Park Design* 77) of "reassurance" and "optimism" (see Bright 237; Hench and Van Pelt 56). Although they are frequently based on versions of the park that have since undergone dramatic alterations, cases can be made for all of these interpretations: as Gottdiener has noted, "no single interpretation can capture the symbolic experience of the park" (*Postmodern* 116).
18. Next to geography and politics or ideology, a structure along the axes of "reality/fantasy" and "space/time" (see Marin 252) and the topology of the human brain (Bukatman 65) have been invoked to account for the overall layout of Disneyland and the precise positioning of its individual "lands."
19. Actually just one building which the designers, using a technique called "fractional architecture," made appear to look like a collection of three smaller buildings; see Younger, *Theme Park Design* 332.
20. For the role of television in general and ABC in particular in the financing and pre-opening promotion of Disneyland, see, for instance, Findlay 60–1. For one of the earliest accounts of the structural relationship between television and theme parks, see Hall (5). See also Telotte.
21. Composed of several Disney animators, among them the already mentioned Ward Kimball as leader, this popular Los Angeles-based band "combined hard-driving two-beat Dixieland with regular infusions of vaudeville-style comedy" (Fairweather) and had recorded their first LP six years before, in 1949, with Good Times Jazz.
22. In fact, before the term "theme park" had established itself, Disneyland was sometimes referred to as an "atmospheric park" (see, for example, Schickel 22).
23. Aunt Jemima had, in fact, already made a brief cameo during the opening television special in July: as the "Firehouse Five Plus Two" marched down New Orleans Street, she joined the parade for a dancing solo (Jackson, Phelps, and Rich 00:39:48–00:39:57), although her connection to New Orleans Street was left unexplained. The off-camera announcer simply introduced her with: "And there's Aunt Jemima!"
24. The role of corporate sponsors and lessees in the financing of early Disneyland was almost as important as that of television and ABC; see, among others, Schickel 306. See also Younger, *Theme Park Design* 346.

25. See Manring 163. According to David Younger, "streetmosphere" refers to "a type of street theater within a theme park that attempts to portray the fictional inhabitants of the themed area" (*Theme Park Design* 368).
26. The only two exceptions I could find are Jason Surrell's books about "Pirates" and "The Haunted Mansion," both published by Disney Editions (see Surrell, *Pirates* 15; and *Haunted Mansion* 12).
27. More precisely, "Pirates," the "Haunted Mansion," and the "New Orleans Square/Frontierland" station of the "Disneyland Railroad" in terms of attractions; the "Creole Café" (renamed Café Orleans" in 1973), the "French Market Restaurant," the "Royal Street Veranda," the "Blue Bayou Restaurant," and the "Mint Julep Bar" in terms of food outlets; and, in 2020, "Port Royal," "Pieces of Eight," "Le Bat en Rouge," "Mlle. Antoinette's Parfumerie," "Cristal d'Orleans," and "La Mascarade d'Orleans" in terms of shops. Concerning the numerous changes in New Orleans Square retail, see ahead.
28. Goodstein maintains that Ryman never went to New Orleans, but instead used Harnett T. Kane and Justin Locke's article "New Orleans: Jambalaya on the Levee" (published in the February 1953 issue of *National Geographic*) as his primary source (313). See also earlier.
29. In fact, as Lawrence R. Samuel has noted, "[w]ith the exception of GM's Futurama and the Vatican's exhibit, Disney-created pavilions turned out to be the most popular at the Fair, with often a two or more hour wait to get into any of them" (110).
30. Incidentally, although both technologies were originally developed for other rides, audio-animatronic robots (as symbols of the "hyperreality" of Disney theme parks) and the Omnimover system (as an example of the intermedial connection between the parks and the movies) would become invariably associated with "Pirates" and the "Haunted Mansion" in early Disney criticism (see, for instance, Eco 44; and Finch 414–5), which partly accounts for the relative prominence of New Orleans Square in these texts.
31. "The Square," like many of the Ryman's other works, has since been regularly printed in Disney's publications on its parks (see, for instance, The Imagineers 63) and reproductions of it can be found in several of Disney's New Orleans-themed and other spaces (e.g., in the lobby of Disney's Port Orleans – French Quarter at Walt Disney World Resort, and on the second floor of the Disneyland Hotel at Disneyland Paris). The painting has also achieved distinction as the "first piece of Disney artwork to inaugurate the State Department's Art in Embassies Program" and was displayed in the U.S. Embassy in Paris in the late 1980s (see Gordon and Mumford 180).
32. In "Time and Temporality in Theme Parks: The Economic Impact of Immersion," Pieter Cornelis discusses a case study in which the addition of an immersive attraction to a theme park caused "a 12.3 [percent] impact on the number of visitors in the first year," but only an 8.0 percent impact in the second year (234). By spreading out the opening of New Orleans Square and its individual rides, Disneyland obviously sought to retain the "first-year-impact" over a period of several years.
33. On opening day, most of the shops and restaurants in the "French Quarter" section featured French words or allusions to French and French-American culture in their names. Examples include "Le Gourmet," "Cristal d'Orleans," "Mlle. Antoinette's Parfumerie," "Le Forgeron," "Le Chapeau," the "Creole Café," and the "French Market Restaurant" (see, for instance, N.N., *Profile*).
34. See, for instance, the attraction poster (reprinted in Handke and Hunt [46]) or the inscriptions on the buildings in the little town attacked by the pirates during the ride, which are all in Spanish.

35. *Vacationland*, formerly called *Disneyland Holiday*, was a free quarterly originally edited, like *The Disneyland News*, by Marty Sklar. From 1957 through the 1980s, it was distributed "to motels and hotels throughout the Southwest in an attempt to reach travelers on their way to Los Angeles" (Findlay 79). Also a quarterly, the *Disney News*, later renamed *Disney Magazine*, was "the official magazine for Magic Kingdom Club family" and was published from 1965–2005.
36. David Younger notes that the:

> heights of New Orleans Square . . . building stories begin at 13 feet at ground level, required to hold the stores, 8 feet 9 inches above that, and then 7 feet 11 inches on the top floor, although units like Club 33 [located on the second floor] mean the interior scale does not match the external one.
>
> (*Theme Park Design* 331)

37. Originally called *Disneyland* (1954–1959) and *Walt Disney Presents* (1959–1961), the show had been renamed following its move from ABC to NBC (and from black-and-white to color) in September 1961 (see Telotte).
38. In fact, McPhillips reports in his article that in response to Schiro's assertion that New Orleans Square "'looks just like home,'" Disney quipped: "'Well, . . . I'd say it's a lot cleaner'" (McPhillips; see also Schickel 338–9). Significantly, however, while "Disneyland around the Seasons" briefly included footage from the speeches (00:25:00–00:25:14), the original sound was replaced by Disney's voice-over.
39. Possibly lest the reuse should become too obvious, some of the old footage was mirrored; see, for instance, Luske, "Pirates" 00:11:26–00:11:38.
40. Until the opening of "Splash Mountain" in 1989, these two characters from Disney's 1946 live-action/animated movie *Song of the South*, which was loosely based on Joel Chandler Harris's "Uncle Remus" stories (see Sperb), were frequently associated with New Orleans Square (see, for instance, N.N., "Profile" 5; and 8), most probably because of the movie's "deep South" setting.
41. Similar to the "Strawhatters," this jazz trio, originally comprised of Jack McVea (clarinet), Harold Grant (banjo), and Herb Gordy (bass), had been regularly performing at New Orleans Square since 1966 (see Strodder 367–8; see also ahead).
42. The "voodoo balcony," a themed balcony located across from the New Orleans Square visitor bathrooms (and thus in an area with a considerable amount of pedestrian traffic) that is decorated with wooden masks and spears, a skull, wind chimes, and a shelf with all sorts of flasks and from which emanate the sounds of voodoo chants, constitutes the only possible exception.
43. For instance, a New Orleans Square publicity shot from 1966 or 1967 shows Teddy and Kenny shining Mickey Mouse's huge black shoes (see N.N., "Kenny, Teddy, and Mickey"), and a picture of the "Bachelors" playing in front of the "Blue Bayou" illustrates a 1975 *Vacationland* article on the restaurant (N.N., "Blue Bayou" 17). In "Disneyland around the Seasons," Teddy and Kenny make a brief cameo, dancing to the music of the Dixieland band as the latter parades through the streets of the "French Quarter" (see Luske, "Seasons" 00:26:21–00:26:25); and "Disneyland Showtime" features a scene in which Donny Osmond, Brer Bear, and Brer Fox dance to the music of the "Bachelors" (see earlier).
44. A collection of visitor guides from various Disney parks is available on http://disneyparksearchive.com.

45. McDougall maintains that the flag features 31 stars (244n55), which would set New Orleans Square somewhere between 4 July 1851, and 4 July 1858, but old pictures (see, for instance, DeCaro, "New Orleans Square") as well my own research from 2016 confirm that there have always been only 30 stars on the flag.
46. Goodstein seems to be the only exception. In "Southern Outposts in the Magic Kingdom," she writes: "The racial and social discrimination implicit in New Orleans historical collective were blanks in the Disney version of the city, left to be filled in – or tacitly accepted – by the visitor" (311).
47. In older pictures and videos, the "triple flags" never appear. By 2016, however, they had all been removed again, except for, somewhat appropriately, the one on the balcony of the "Royal Court" building on 21 Royal Street. The flags must have been removed during the expansion of "Club 33" (see ahead).
48. Interestingly, the amount of time by which the temporal setting of New Orleans Square has been shifted (about seven decades, from 1850 to the 1920s) almost corresponds to the amount of time by which the "land" has actually aged (exactly half a century, from 1966 to 2016). My argument is, of course, that the designers have not made New Orleans Square undergo a "natural" aging process, but that they have attempted to avoid theming controversies.
49. According to Scott A. Lukas, "dark theming" "draws on previously taboo themes like violence, death, and genocide to provocatively organize a space in a thematic way" ("Themed Space" 17; see also Lukas, "Controversial Topics"; and "Dark Theming").
50. The effect was achieved by setting the four pairs of figures on spinning turntables.
51. In 2018, Disney changed yet another "Pirates" scene that has frequently been criticized for its controversial depiction of women; namely, the "bride auction" scene, which occurs right before the "wench-chasing" scene. Rather than depicting a male pirate auctioning off the town's women, the scene now shows a female pirate asking the townspeople to surrender their valuables (see Fisher).
52. As in general, precise figures are notoriously hard to obtain, and particularly so for the Disney parks. As Fjellman already pointed out in 1992, the Walt Disney Company "reports its consumer products revenues separately from its theme park and resorts revenues. It is unclear how much merchandising is included in the latter reporting category" (428n40). Several sources estimate that revenues from retail outlets represent about 20–25 percent of the overall income of theme parks (see, for instance, Desgue; and Martín).
53. Younger defines "diegetic" merchandise as "those items that would diegetically be available to citizens of the story-world the land presents," such as "wands and butterbeer in a *Harry Potter* land" (*Theme Park Design* 351). In the case of New Orleans Square, this included antique furniture (at the "One-of-A-Kind Shop"), household decorations (at "Cristal d'Orleans" and "Le Forgeron"), kitchen accessories (at "Le Gourmet"), jewelry (at "Laffite's Silver Shop"), fragrances (at "Mlle. Antoinette's Parfumerie"), and hats (at "Le Chapeau"), as well as books and newspapers, candy, and flowers (at the stalls). In fact, "Mlle. Antoinette's Parfumerie" and the "One-of-A-Kind Shop" were no doubt inspired by the French perfumeries and antique stores in New Orleans that, according to Shannon Lee Dawdy, negotiate the city's Frenchness and pastness on a local level (see 96–101; 127).
54. According to Younger, an "attraction store" is "the theme park cliché of a gift shop attached to the exit of an attraction, included in the hope of

capturing some of the enthusiasm of exiting riders and converting that into merchandise sales" (*Theme Park Design* 348). Prior to the opening of "Pieces of Eight," New Orleans Square had not featured any "attraction stores," which is particularly surprising given the enormous popularity of the two signature rides of the "land."
55. For more on *The Princess and the Frog*, see the Conclusion.
56. The portrait artists also still offer their talents, but have moved to a location opposite the "Blue Bayou" restaurant following the closure of the "Court of Angels" in 2013–2014.
57. Already "Jewel of Orleans," which both followed and preceded "Mlle. Antoinette's Parfumerie" in this location from 1997–2011, had been owned and operated by a lessee, namely, the family-owned "Dianne's Estate Jewelry" (see Strodder 227–8; and Tully).
58. "Reflexive" theming is self-referential in that company logos and brands provide the main sources of theming (see Bryman, *Disneyization* 18). Autothemed spaces are much more specific, as they refer to individual themed spaces created by a company (regardless of whether that space employs an internal or an external theme).
59. Additional decorations, e.g., on the tops of merchandise shelves, include leather-bound copies of such "ocean"-themed novels as Melville's *Moby-Dick* and Hemingway's *The Old Man and the Sea*. With the latter having been published in 1952, one may wonder whether the temporal setting of New Orleans Square has once again been pushed forward in time.
60. The logo of "Le Coffre du Capitaine," the "attraction store" for "Pirates" opened at Disneyland Paris's Parc Disneyland in 1992, features a nearly identical painting. Since the Paris version of "Pirates" does not feature such a scene, one may argue that the autotheming of "Le Coffre du Capitaine" refers not so much to Parc Disneyland's "Pirates" as to Disneyland's "Pieces of Eight." There are several more such examples of "across-the-parks" autotheming at Parc Disneyland (see, for instance, N.N., "Design"), but also at Tokyo Disneyland (see ahead).
61. Already in 1997, Disney had produced a TV movie based on and set at "The Twilight Zone Tower of Terror," a ride at Walt Disney World's Disney-MGM Studios park.
62. The existing "Pirates" rides at Walt Disney World's Magic Kingdom and Tokyo Disney Resort's Tokyo Disneyland later underwent similar changes (see ahead). Shanghai Disneyland Park's "Pirates" ride, opened along with the rest of the resort in 2016, has contained references to the movie series from the very beginning.
63. Another major construction project involved the transformation of "Esplanade Street," the walkway separating New Orleans Square from the Frontierland river, into a terraced viewing area (commonly referred to as a "focal point"; see Younger, *Theme Park Design* 307) for the "Fantasmic!" nighttime spectacular, which premiered in May 1992 (see Strodder 162–3).
64. For similar quotes by such architects, urban planners, and architectural critics as Charles Moore, Robert Hall, Peter Blake, Paul Goldberger, and Robert Venturi, all from the mid-1960s to the mid-1970s, see M.J. King 122–3; and 126; Wallace 42; J. Adams 142; and Clément, "Review."
65. Findlay correctly points out that "[l]ittle evidence exists . . . that suggests that Disney originally intended the Anaheim park as a model by which to reform urban planning" (105). By the mid-1960s, however, when he was planning Walt Disney World and its "Experimental Prototype Community of Tomorrow (EPCOT)," urban planning and design had clearly become an issue for Disney. In a promotional movie in which he outlined the Florida

project, Disney noted: "'I don't believe there's a challenge anywhere in the world that's more important to people everywhere than finding solutions to the problems of our cities'" (qtd. in Fjellman 114). And in 1982, the year EPCOT eventually opened, designer John Hench argued:

> [I]n modern cities you have to defend yourself constantly and you go counter to everything that we've learned from the past. You tend to isolate yourself from other people. . . . You tend to be less aware. You tend to be more withdrawn. This is counter-life . . . you really die a little. . . . I think we need something to counteract what modern society – cities have done to us.
>
> (qtd. in Findlay 67)

66. Coined by Richard Schickel in 1968, the term "Disneyfication" originally referred to "that shameless process by which everything the studio later touched, no matter how unique the vision of the original from which the studio worked, was reduced to the limited terms Disney and his people could understand" (220). Among the first to use it in the context of urban planning were Francaviglia, "Main Street U.S.A." 146; Warren, "Disneyfication"; and Klugman 103.
67. Steinecke (8) is among the few who have included urban culture in their lists of the most popular themes in themed environments, and rightfully so.
68. Findlay quotes "one early official" of Disneyland who recalled that in the beginning, "'[t]he *only* reason for *any* price was to keep undesirables out'" (81; emphases original). With respect to grooming standards, the Disneyland website today informs customers that:

> [w]e reserve the right to deny admission to or remove any person wearing attire that we consider inappropriate or attire that could detract from the experience of other Guests. Visible tattoos that could be considered inappropriate, such as those containing objectionable language or designs, are not permitted.
>
> (N.N., "Disneyland Resort Park Rules")

As a 1968 article in the *Los Angeles Times* attests, Disneyland used to be much stricter:

> One more word about Disneyland. It is a private enterprise of a very special sort. Julie Christie once arrived in a miniskirt and was told to leave. Hippies aren't welcome. One female star, then appearing in a Disney film, arrived in a mini one day with her long-in-the-locks boyfriend. There was quite a flap, but they finally got in. Not the best philosophy for welcoming people, but Disneyland may be worth a lowered hem and a haircut.
>
> (Warga)

69. The day went down in Disneyland history as "Yippie Day" (see Strodder 451–2). Today's park rules prohibit the "distribution of printed or recorded materials of any kind," as well as "[u]nauthorized events, demonstrations or speeches, or the usage of any flag, banner or sign . . . to incite a crowd" (N.N., "Disneyland Resort Park Rules"). Things are different at Parc Disneyland in Paris, where in 2001, I personally witnessed a strike by the employees of the park's entertainment division along the parade route in the park.

70. Of course, none of these "institutions" on Main Street, U.S.A. have ever been operational: the building labeled "city hall" serves as an information center for visitors, the Victorian fire truck at the fire station is not functional, and the police station building has always been but an empty shell.
71. In fact, although in their book they trace the idea as far back as the fifteenth century, to Leonardo da Vinci and his proposed "ideal city" (see James and Yoos 143; 230), James and Yoos specifically identify "the 1939 World's Fair in New York and the World Expos of the 1950s and 1960s" (95) as some of the sources of the "parallel city" in North America. It is not entirely inconceivable, however, that just like Disneyland's Main Street section inspired the revitalization of American small-town main streets (see Francaviglia, *Main Street* 178), New Orleans Square contributed to the further spread of "analogous" or "parallel cities."
72. Just as he had already included a few rooms for himself and his family in Disneyland's Main Street section, Walt Disney had also planned to install a private apartment above the entrance to "Pirates" as a place to entertain important guests (see Solomon, "Beginnings"). Although Disney died before construction was completed, the apartment was finished and, until 1974, used by a Disneyland sponsor, the Insurance Company of North America, to host VIP receptions. Afterwards, and until it was transformed into the "Disney Gallery" store in 1987, the apartment was used for office space (see DeCaro, "Disney Gallery").
73. Strictly speaking, then, New Orleans Square had used a system of sociospatial stratification of visitors from its very beginning, and the 2013–2014 renovation was a change of degree rather than of kind: the new "Club 33," with its ostentatious entrance and the prominent overhead bridges (see ahead) is simply much more noticeable from the outside than before.
74. For a schematic drawing of the "Club 33" expansion, see N.N., "Club 33 Expansion."
75. Japanese audiences had already been widely familiar with Disney in general and with Disneyland in particular: Mitsushiro Yoshimoto reports that the "Disneyland" TV show had successfully aired on Japanese television from 1958–1967 (189).
76. In fact, most of the studies of Tokyo Disneyland written in English were published after 1992, the year Disneyland Paris was opened. In Japan, in turn, Raz notes, the "tremendous success of [Tokyo Disneyland] has . . . spawned a thriving genre of 'how does it really work' books [that] explain the success of [the park] in terms of its human resource management and service manuals" (9).
77. As the original width of the "street" between the "Pirates" and the "Café Orleans" buildings – a mere 15 feet, according to Strodder (306) – was left unchanged, however, French Quarter Land feels much more intimate and distinct than New Orleans Square.
78. Interestingly, the preview brochure lists the "Haunted Mansion" as part of "Westernland" (see N.N., *Tokyo Disneyland* 4), while the promotional movie depicts the ride in its "Fantasyland" segment (see N.N., *Disneyland Comes to Tokyo* 00:08:36). Apparently, the attraction was moved during the planning process.
79. All information on the history of French Quarter Land since 1983 has been gathered from the Tokyo Disneyland "Expert's," "Shoppers'," and "Parade and Show Guidebooks" in the author's personal collection. Copies of these "Guidebooks," which are written in both Japanese and English, are frequently sold on ebay and other websites. Additional reference material was provided by the staff of TDRExplorer.com, an unofficial fan website.

80. Younger (*Theme Park Design* 284) defines a "second gate" as:

    the sequential opening of [an] additional theme park . . . to a resort. . . . The addition of a second (or subsequent) theme park is a major expansion for a resort, with many theme parks initially expanding through smaller additions, such as Hotels, Retail Entertainment Centers, Water Parks, Boutique Parks, and other Upcharge Attractions.

    The concept of "multi-gate resorts" was first introduced in the 1970s by Walt Disney World, during what Kagelmann has called the "boom phase" of theme parks ("Themenparks" 409; see also Clavé 248–9). Most of Disney's "second gates" were opened, however, at the beginning of the twenty-first century (see Younger, *Theme Park Design* 284).
81. After a three-year run, "Mickey's Adventureland Mardi Gras" was eventually replaced by "Minnie Oh! Minnie," which contains no references to New Orleans or Mardi Gras.
82. See the list provided by Clavé (279), which does not mention, however, the Old Key West Resort (opened in 1991) and the Saratoga Springs Resort (2004), both of which are part of the "Disney Vacation Club" timeshare program. Since the publication of Clavé's book, Disney has added one more resort, the Art of Animation Resort (2012). Furthermore, there are a number of hotels located on the site that are neither owned nor operated by the company, including the Michael Graves-designed Walt Disney World Dolphin and Walt Disney World Swan Resorts (both opened in 1990).
83. Renamed "Shades of Green," the hotel was acquired by the U.S. Department of Defense in 1996 and has since exclusively served members of the U.S. armed forces and their families as part of the U.S. Army Family and Morale, Welfare and Recreation program (see N.N., "Shades of Green").
84. Likewise, when in 2001 Disney started to develop its Anaheim property into a "global theme park" by adding a "second gate" as well as several hotels, the company consciously chose specifically local, Californian themes for both the new park (called Disney's California Adventure) and the new hotels (Disney's Grand Californian Hotel and Disney's Paradise Pier Hotel).
85. The fictional names on the street signs throughout the hotel (see ahead), a sign at the counter-service restaurant, and the teller's windows at the front desk constituted the only exceptions. The latter two, however, have since been removed.
86. It is, of course, quite impossible to determine to what extent this is actually done, although several of the front desk employees to whom I talked during my field trip in May 2016 readily shared the story without being prompted to do so.
87. In *Problems of Dostoevsky's Poetics*, Bakhtin notes that "the laws, prohibitions and restrictions which determine the system and order of normal, i.e. non-carnival life are for the period of carnival suspended" (101).
88. In contrast to the "Sassagoula Floatworks and Food Factory," Port Orleans's counter service food outlet, "Bonfamille's Café," a table service restaurant, had only been open on a highly irregular basis from 2000–2019, before the space was integrated into the "Scat Cat's Club" (see N.N., "Port Orleans History").
89. Before coming to Port Orleans, Dyson, in turn, had regularly performed at Universal Studios Florida. These and other biographical details point to the relevance of theme parks and resorts to Orlando's music scene.
90. The picture, prints of which are also for sale at the shop, is the work of Larry Dotson, a Celebration, Florida (i.e., Walt Disney World)-based artist

who has produced a large number of paintings of Disney's themed spaces. Much like the products of Arribas Brothers, Dotson's works are exclusively sold at the Disney parks and via the artist's website (see N.N., "About Larry").
91. Founded in 1947, Blaine Kern Studios have been one of New Orleans's leading Mardi Gras parade float designers and have also designed Mardi Gras-themed and other props and sculptures for such immersive spaces as the Luxor hotel and casino in Las Vegas (see Gotham 179–80). Interestingly, in 1959, Walt Disney had offered Kern a job as a parade float designer for Disneyland, but Kern preferred to stay in New Orleans (see Sampson).
92. Information on the "production" and "reception" of Mardi Gras at Port Orleans was provided by Port Orleans employees during my field trip to Walt Disney World in May 2016. As far as possible, the information obtained has been verified by comparing it to the hotel's recreation schedules, which are available on www.portorleans.org.
93. "Front desk dances" are a regular feature of the hotels at Disney's theme park resorts and can also be observed, for instance, at the hotels at Disneyland Resort Paris. The "Mardi Gras" theme of Port Orleans's dances is, however, unique to the site.
94. The resort thus constitutes a material manifestation of one of the two ways in which tourists, according to Shannon Lee Dawdy, perceive Mardi Gras: "as a continuous space-time in which the distinction between Mardi Gras the event and New Orleans the place collapses" (40).
95. Already in 1968, Walker Percy had warned of the Vieux Carré turning into a "Disneyland Francaise" (16).
96. Already in "Authenticity and Commodification in Tourism," Cohen remarks that "[n]ew cultural developments may also acquire the patina of authenticity over time – a process designated a[s] 'emergent authenticity'" (371) – and specifically cites Disney theme parks as an example (380).
97. Nevertheless, the company did try help the Crescent City recover from the disaster through such "charitable acts" as the organization of a special exhibit of original Disney artwork at the New Orleans Museum of Art in 2009–2010 (see Parmett).
98. Launched in January 2014, "New Orleans Will" is a civic pride campaign organized and run by the New Orleans Convention and Visitors Bureau.
99. Scans of the "Disneylandrieu" map, which was designed by Krewe of sPANk member "Wendar the Magnificent," can be downloaded from the website of *Gambit*, a New Orleans city magazine, at www.bestofneworleans.com/blogofneworleans/archives/2014/02/17/krewe-of-spanks-dizneylandrieu-brochure-the-pdf-download.

Bibliography

Abrams, Natalie. "Inside Disneyland's Magical Dream Suite and Walt Disney's Private Apartment!" *Entertainment Weekly* (2 February 2016). www.ew.com/article/2016/02/12/disneyland-dream-suite-walt-apartment-photos. Web.
Adams, Judith A. *The American Amusement Park Industry: A History of Technology and Thrills*. Boston: Twayne, 1991. Print.
Aronstein, Susan. "Pilgrimage and Medieval Narrative Structures in Disney's Parks." *The Disney Middle Ages: A Fairy-Tale and Fantasy Past*. Ed. Pugh Tison and Susan Aronstein. New York: Palgrave Macmillan, 2012. 57–74. Print.
Arribas. "Our Story." *Arribas Brothers* (N.D.). www.arribas.com/our-story. Web.

Avila, Eric. *Popular Culture in the Age of White Flight: Fear and Fantasy in Suburban Los Angeles*. Berkeley: U of California P, 2004. Print.

Bagnall, Gaynor. "Consuming the Past." *Consumption Matters: The Production and Experience of Consumption*. Ed. Stephen Edgell, Kevin Hetherington, and Alan Warde. Oxford: Blackwell, 1996. 227–47. Print.

Baham, Jeff. *The Unauthorized Story of Walt Disney's Haunted Mansion*. N.P.: Theme Park P, 2014. Print.

Bakhtin, Mikhail. *Problems of Dostoevsky's Poetics*. Trans. R.W. Rotsel. Ann Arbor: Ardis, 1973. Print.

Baudrillard, Jean. *Cool Memories II: 1987–1990*. Durham: Duke UP, 1996. Print.

———. "La précession des simulacres." *Traverses* 10 (1978): 3–37. Print.

———. *Simulacra and Simulation*. Trans. Sheila Faria Glaser. Ann Arbor: The U of Michigan P, 1994 [1981]. Print.

Bierman, James H. "Disneyland and the 'Los Angelization' of the Arts." *American Popular Entertainment: Papers and Proceedings of the Conference on the History of American Popular Entertainment*. Ed. Myron Matlaw. Westport, CT: Greenwood, 1979. 273–83. Print.

Bloom, Nicholas Dagen. *Merchant of Illusion: James Rouse, America's Salesman of the Businessman's Utopia*. Columbus: The Ohio State UP, 2004. Print.

Boddy, Trevor. "Underground and Overhead: Building the Analogous City." *Variations on a Theme Park: The New American City and the End of Public Space*. Ed. Michael Sorkin. New York: Hill and Wang, 1992. 123–53. Print.

Boorstin, Daniel J. *The Image; Or, What Happened to the American Dream*. New York: Atheneum, 1961. Print.

Brannen, Mary Yoko. "'Bwana Mickey': Constructing Cultural Consumption at Tokyo Disneyland." *Re-Made in Japan: Everyday Life and Consumer Taste in a Changing Society*. Ed. Joseph J. Tobin. New Haven: Yale UP, 1992. 216–34. Print.

Bright, Randy. *Disneyland: Inside Story*. New York: Harry N. Abrams, 1987. Print.

Bryman, Alan. *Disney and His Worlds*. London: Routledge, 1995. Print.

———. *The Disneyization of Society*. London: Sage, 2005. Print.

———. "Global Disney." *The American Century: Consensus and Coercion in the Projection of American Power*. Ed. David Slater and Peter J. Taylor. Oxford: Blackwell, 1999. 261–72. Print.

Bshero, Rachel. "Flavors of New Orleans Arrive at Sassagoula Floatworks and Food Factory at Disney's Port Orleans Resort." *DisneyParksBlog* (18 November 2016). https://disneyparks.disney.go.com/blog/2016/11/flavors-of-new-orleans-arrive-at-sassagoula-floatworks-and-food-factory-at-disneys-port-orleans-resort/. Web.

Budd, Mike. "Introduction: Private Disney, Public Disney." *Rethinking Disney: Private Control, Public Dimensions*. Ed. Mike Budd and Max H. Kirsch. Middletown, CT: Wesleyan UP, 2005. 1–33. Print.

Bukatman, Scott. "There's Always Tomorrowland: Disney and the Hypercinematic Experience." *October* 57 (1991): 55–78. Print.

Cable, George Washington. "Creole Slave Dances: The Dance in Place Congo." *Century* 31.4 (February 1886): 517–32. Print.

———. *The Grandissimes: A Story of Creole Life*. *Scribner's Monthly* 19.1 (November 1879)–20.6 (October 1880). Print.

———. "The 'Haunted House' in Royal Street." *Century* 38.4 (August 1889): 590–601. Print.

———. "Jean-ah Poquelin." *Scribner's Monthly* 10.1 (May 1875): 91–100. Print.

———. "Madame Delphine." *Century* 22.1 (May 1881)–22.3 (July 1881). Print.

———. "Plotters and Pirates of Louisiana." *Century* 25.6 (April 1883): 852–67. Print.

Carlà, Filippo. "The Uses of History in Themed Spaces." *A Reader in Themed and Immersive Spaces*. Ed. Scott A. Lukas. Pittsburgh, PA: ETC, 2016. 19–29. Print.

Carlà, Filippo, and Florian Freitag. "Ancient Greek Culture and Myth in the Terra Mítica Theme Park." *Classical Receptions Journal* 7.2 (2015): 242–59. Print.

Carlà, Filippo, Florian Freitag, Gordon Grice, and Scott A. Lukas. "Research Dialogue: The Ways of Design, Architecture, Technology, and Material Form." *A Reader in Themed and Immersive Spaces*. Ed. Scott A. Lukas. Pittsburgh, PA: ETC, 2016. 107–12. Print.

Carlà, Filippo, Florian Freitag, Sabrina Mittermeier, and Ariane Schwarz. "Zur Formierung der komplexen Zeitlichkeit von Themenparks." *Zeiten der Form – Formen der Zeit*. Ed. Michael Gamper et al. Hanover: Wehrhahn, 2016. 317–41. Print.

Carlà-Uhink, Filippo, Florian Freitag, Sabrina Mittermeier, and Ariane Schwarz. "Introduction: The Complex Temporalities of Theme Parks." *Time and Temporality in Theme Parks*. Ed. Filippo Carlà-Uhink, Florian Freitag, Sabrina Mittermeier, and Ariane Schwarz. Hanover: Wehrhahn, 2017. 9–16. Print.

———, eds. *Time and Temporality in Theme Parks*. Hanover: Wehrhahn, 2017. Print.

Carney, Bill. "Disneyland Adds New Orleans Charm." *Orange Daily News* (28 July 1966): A4. Print.

Carosso, Andrea. "America's Disneyland and the End-of-the-Century Cityscape." *Revue Française d'Etudes Américaines* 83 (January 2000): 64–75. Print.

Carson, Charles. "'Whole New Worlds': Music and the Disney Theme Park Experience." *Ethnomusicology Forum* 13.2 (2004): 228–35. Print.

Clavé, Salvador A. *The Global Theme Park Industry*. Wallingford: CABI, 2007. Print.

Clément, Thibaut. "'Locus of Control': A Selective Review of Disney Theme Parks." *InMedia* 2 (2012). http://inmedia.revues.org/463. Web.

———. *Plus vrais que nature: Les parcs Disney ou l'usage de la fiction dans l'espace et le paysage*. Paris: Presses Sorbonne Nouvelle, 2016. Print.

Cohen, Eric. "Authenticity and Commoditization in Tourism." *Annals of Tourism Research* 15 (1988): 371–86. Print.

Cornelis, Pieter. "Time and Temporality in Theme Parks: The Economic Impact of Immersion." *Time and Temporality in Theme Parks*. Ed. Filippo Carlà-Uhink, Florian Freitag, Sabrina Mittermeier, and Ariane Schwarz. Hanover: Wehrhahn, 2017. 223–39. Print.

Crawford, Margaret. "The World in a Shopping Mall." *Variations on a Theme Park: The New American City and the End of Public Space*. Ed. Michael Sorkin. New York: Hill and Wang, 1992. 3–30. Print.

Cross, Gary S., and John K. Walton. *The Playful Crowd: Pleasure Places in the Twentieth Century*. New York: Columbia UP, 2005. Print.

Davis, Susan G. *Spectacular Nature: Corporate Culture and the Sea World Experience*. Berkeley: U of California P, 1997. Print.

———. "The Theme Park: Global Industry and Cultural Form." *Media, Culture and Society* 18 (1996): 399–422. Print.
Dawdy, Shannon Lee. *Patina: A Profane Archaeology*. Chicago: The U of Chicago P, 2016. Print.
Dawid, Anka. "Poseidon, Pommes und Piraten: Zum Unterhaltungswert der Archäologie im Europa-Park Rust." *Museumsblatt* 38 (2005): 26–30. Print.
De Roos, Robert. "The Magic Worlds of Disney." *National Geographic* 124.2 (August 1963): 159–207. Print.
Dear, Michael J., and Steven Flusty. "The Spaces of Representation." *The Spaces of Postmodernity: Readings in Human Geography*. Ed. Michael J. Dear and Steven Flusty. Oxford: Blackwell, 2002. 415–18. Print.
DeCaro, Dave. "Aunt Jemima/New Orleans St." *Davelandweb* (N.D.). http://davelandweb.com/frontierland/auntjemima.html. Web.
———. "Casa de Fritos/Rancho Del Zocalo." *Davelandweb* (N.D.). http://davelandweb.com/casadefritos/. Web.
———. "Club 33." *Davelandweb* (N.D.). http://davelandweb.com/club33. Web.
———. "Club 33 Pg. 2." *Davelandweb* (N.D.). http://davelandweb.com/club33/index2.html. Web.
———. "Court of Angels." *Davelandweb* (N.D.). http://davelandweb.com/neworleanssquare/courtofangels.html. Web.
———. "Disney Gallery." *Davelandweb* (N.D.). http://davelandweb.com/neworleanssquare/disneygallery.html. Web.
———. "Disneyland Dream Suite." *Davelandweb* (N.D.). http://davelandweb.com/dreamsuite/. Web.
———. "Don DeFore's Silver Banjo BBQ." *Davelandweb* (N.D.). http://davelandweb.com/silverbanjo/. Web.
———. "Kool Aid at Club 33, Pt. 1." *Daveland* (29 July 2014). http://davelandblog.blogspot.de/2014/07/kool-aid-at-club-33-pt-1.html. Web.
———. "New Orleans Square." *Davelandweb* (N.D.). http://davelandweb.com/neworleanssquare/. Web.
———. "The One of A Kind Shop." *Daveland* (27 April 2013). http://davelandblog.blogspot.de/2013/04/the-one-of-kind-shop.html. Web.
———. "Royal Street Bachelors." *Davelandweb* (N.D.). http://davelandweb.com/neworleanssquare/bachelors.html. Web.
———. "Teddy and Kenny, the Shoeshine Boys." *Daveland* (15 January 2013). http://davelandblog.blogspot.de/2013/01/teddy-and-kenny-shoeshine-boys.html. Web.
Deleuze, Gilles. *Différence et répétition*. Paris: Presses Universitaires de France, 1968. Print.
Deleuze, Gilles, and Félix Guattari. *A Thousand Plateaus: Capitalism and Schizophrenia*. Trans. Brian Massumi. New York: Continuum, 2004. Print.
Desgue, Rozenn. "La boutique, un enjeu majeur pour les parcs de loisirs." *Cahiers espaces* 86 (September 2005): 130–32. Print.
Dickerson, Marla. "Flap over 'Pirates' Proves a Treasure Trove for Disney." *Los Angeles Times* (8 March 1997). http://articles.latimes.com/1997-03-08/news/mn-36020_1_walt-disney. Web.
Disney, Walt. "Frontierland." *True West* (May/June 1958): 10–13. Print.
Eco, Umberto. "Travels in Hyperreality." *Travels in Hyperreality: Essays*. Trans. William Weaver. San Diego: Harcourt Brace Janovich, 1986. 1–58. Print.

Elliott, Barry, dir. *A Day at Disneyland*. Burbank: Walt Disney Productions, 1982. Home video.

Fagg, John, Matthew Pethers, and Robin Vandome. "Introduction: Networks and the Nineteenth-Century Periodical." *American Periodicals* 23.2 (2013): 93–104. Print.

Fairweather, Digby. "Firehouse Five Plus Two." *The Rough Guide to Jazz: The Essential Companion to Artists and Albums*, by Ian Carr, Digby Fairweather, and Brian Priestley. Third ed. New York: Rough Guides, 2004. 261. Print.

Finch, Christopher. *The Art of Walt Disney from Mickey Mouse to the Magic Kingdoms*. New York: Harry N. Abrams, 1973. Print.

Findlay, John M. *Magic Lands: Western Cityscapes and American Culture after 1940*. Berkeley: U of California P, 1992. Print.

Finnell, Bill. "Posing with Aunt Jemima." *Yesterland* (3 December 2002). www.yesterland.com/auntjemimamemory.html. Web. Courtesy of Yesterland.com.

Fisher, Marla Jo. "Disneyland Reopens Pirates of the Caribbean without the Bride Auction." *Orange County Register* (8 June 2018). www.ocregister.com/2018/06/08/disneyland-reopens-pirates-of-the-caribbean-without-the-bride-auction/. Web.

Fjellman, Stephen M. *Vinyl Leaves: Walt Disney World and America*. Boulder: Westview, 1992. Print.

Francaviglia, Richard V. "History after Disney: The Significance of 'Imagineered' Historical Places." *The Public Historian* 17.4 (1995): 69–74. Print.

———. *Main Street Revisited: Time, Space, and Image Building in Small-Town America*. Iowa City: U of Iowa P, 1996. Print.

———. "Main Street U.S.A.: A Comparison/Contrast of Streetscapes in Disneyland and Walt Disney World." *The Journal of Popular Culture* 15.1 (1981): 141–56. Print.

———. "Main Street, U.S.A.: The Creation of a Popular Image." *Landscape: A Magazine of Human Geography* 21.3 (1977): 18–22. Print.

———. "Walt Disney's Frontierland as an Allegorical Map of the American West." *Western Historical Quarterly* 30.2 (Summer 1999): 155–82. Print.

Freitag, Florian. "Amerikanisierung, Lokalisierung, Branding: EuroDisney, 1992." *Transkulturelle Dynamiken: Aktanten – Prozesse – Theorien*. Ed. Jutta Ernst and Florian Freitag. Bielefeld: Transcript, 2015. 165–97. Print.

———. "Autotheming: Themed and Immersive Spaces in Self-Dialogue." *A Reader in Themed and Immersive Spaces*. Ed. Scott A. Lukas. Pittsburgh, PA: ETC, 2016. 141–49. Print.

———. "'Like Walking into a Movie': Intermedial Relations between Disney Theme Parks and Movies." *The Journal of Popular Culture* 50.4 (2017): 704–22. Print.

Fung, Anthony, and Micky Lee. "Localizing a Global Amusement Park: Hong Kong Disneyland." *Continuum: Journal of Media and Cultural Studies* 23.2 (2009): 197–208. Print.

Gabaccia, Donna R. *We Are What We Eat: Ethnic Food and the Making of Americans*. Cambridge, MA: Harvard UP, 1998. Print.

Geppert, Alexander C.T. *Fleeting Cities: Imperial Expositions in* Fin-de-Siècle *Europe*. New York: Palgrave Macmillan, 2010. Print.

Geraghty, Lincoln, Christine Lundberg, and Vassilios Ziakis. "Guerst Editorial: Exploring the Popular Culture and Tourism Placemaking Nexus." *The Journal of Popular Culture* 52.6 (2019): 1241–49. Print.

Giroux, Henry A. *The Mouse That Roared: Disney and the End of Innocence.* Lanham: Rowman & Littlefield, 1999. Print.

Glover, Erin. "Then and Now: Lafitte's Anchor at Disneyland Park." *Disney ParksBlog* (20 August 2012). https://disneyparks.disney.go.com/blog/2012/08/disneyland-park-then-and-now-lafittes-anchor/. Web.

Goldberger, Paul. "The Rise of the Private City." *Breaking Away: The Future of Cities. Essays in Memory of Robert F. Wagner, Jr.* Ed. Julia Vitullo-Martin. New York: Twentieth Century Fund, 1996. 135–47. Print.

Goodstein, Ethel S. "Southern Outposts in the Magic Kingdom: The South as a Regional Sub-Text in Disney's American Spectacle." *Visual Resources* 14 (1999): 307–19. Print.

Gordon, Bruce, and David Mumford. *A Brush with Disney: An Artist's Journey, Told through the Words and Works of Herbert Dickens Ryman.* Santa Clarita: Camphor Tree, 2000. Print.

Gotham, Kevin Fox. *Authentic New Orleans: Tourism, Culture, and Race in the Big Easy.* New York: New York UP, 2007. Print.

Gottdiener, Mark. *Postmodern Semiotics: Material Culture and the Forms of Postmodern Life.* Cambridge: Blackwell, 1995. Print.

———. *The Theming of America: Dreams, Visions, and Commercial Spaces.* Second ed. Boulder: Westview, 2001. Print.

Green, Amy Boothe, and Howard E. Green, eds. *Remembering Walt: Favorite Memories of Walt Disney.* New York: Disney Editions, 1999. Print.

Grice, Gordon. "Temporality and Storytelling in the Design of Theme Parks and Immersive Environments." *Time and Temporality in Theme Parks.* Ed. Filippo Carlà-Uhink, Florian Freitag, Sabrina Mittermeier, and Ariane Schwarz. Hanover: Wehrhahn, 2017. 241–57. Print.

Hackenesch, Silke. "'To Highlight My Beautiful Chocolate Skin': On the Cultural Politics of the Racialised Epidermis." *Probing the Skin: Cultural Representations of Our Contact Zone.* Ed. Caroline Rosenthal and Dirk Vanderbeke. Newcastle upon Tyne: Cambridge Scholars, 2015. 73–91. Print.

Hall, Millicent. "Theme Parks: Around the World in 80 Minutes." *Landscape: A Magazine of Human Geography* 21.1 (1976): 3–8. Print.

Handke, Danny, and Vanessa Hunt. *Poster Art of the Disney Parks.* New York: Disney Editions, 2012. Print.

Harwood, Edward. "Rhetoric, Authenticity, and Reception: The Eighteenth-Century Landscape Garden, the Modern Theme Park, and Their Audiences." *Theme Park Landscapes: Antecedents and Variations.* Ed. Robert Riley and Terence Young. Washington, DC: Dumbarton Oaks Research Library and Collection, 2002. 49–68. Print.

Heimbuch, Jeff. *Main Street Windows: A Complete Guide to Disney's Whimsical Tributes.* N.P.: Orchard Hill, 2014. Print.

Hench, John, and Peggy Van Pelt. *Designing Disney: Imagineering and the Art of the Show.* New York: Disney Editions, 2008. Print.

Hildebrandt, Hugo John. "Cedar Point: A Park in Progress." *The Journal of Popular Culture* 15.1 (1981): 87–107. Print.

Hine, Thomas. *Populuxe.* New York: Knopf, 1986. Print.

Hjemdahl, Kirsti Mathiesen. "History as Cultural Playground." *Ethnologia Europaea* 32.2 (2002): 105–24. Print.

Hobbs, Priscilla. *Walt's Utopia: Disneyland and American Mythmaking.* Jefferson, NC: McFarland, 2015. Print.

Holtorf, Cornelius. "The Presence of Pastness: Themed Environments and Beyond." *Staging the Past: Themed Environments in Transcultural Perspectives*. Ed. Judith Schlehe, Michiko Uike-Bormann, Carolyn Oesterle, and Wolfgang Hochbruck. Bielefeld: Transcript, 2010. 23–40. Print.

Hom, Stephanie Malia. "Simulated Imperialism." *Traditional Dwellings and Settlements Review: Journal of the International Association for the Study of Traditional Environments* 25.1 (Fall 2013): 25–44. Print.

Hutcheon, Linda. *A Poetics of Postmodernism: History, Theory, Fiction*. New York: Routledge, 1988. Print.

Imagineers, The. *Imagineering: A Behind the Dreams Look at Making the Magic Real*. New York: Hyperion, 1996. Print.

Imagineers, The, and Malody Malmberg. *Imagineering: A Behind the Dreams Look at Making MORE Magic Real*. New York: Disney Editions, 2010. Print.

Jackson, Wilfred, Stu Phelps, and John Rich, dir. "Dateline: Disneyland." *Walt Disney Treasures – Disneyland USA*. Disc 1. Los Angeles: Walt Disney Video, 2001. DVD.

James, Vincent, and Jennifer Yoos. *Parallel Cities: The Multilevel Metropolis*. Minneapolis: Walker Art Center, 2016. Print.

Jess-Cooke, Carolyn. "Sequalizing Spectatorship and Building Up the Kingdom: The Case of *Pirates of the Caribbean*, Or, How a Theme Park Attraction Spawned a Multibillion-Dollar Film Franchise." *Second Takes: Critical Approaches to the Film Sequels*. Ed. Carolyn Jess-Cooke and Constantine Verevis. Albany: State U of New York P, 2010. 205–23. Print.

Johnson, Kevin. "No Mickey Mouse Club Here." *Los Angeles Times* (8 September 1991): OC B1-OC B6. Print.

Kagelmann, H. Jürgen. "Themenparks." *Tourismuspsychologie und Tourismussoziologie*. Ed. Heinz Hahn and H. Jürgen Kagelmann. Munich: Quintessenz, 1993. 407–15. Print.

Kane, Harnett T., and Justin Locke. "New Orleans: Jambalaya on the Levee." *National Geographic* 103.2 (February 1953): 143–84. Print.

King, Edward. "Old and New Louisiana." *Scribner's Monthly* 7.1 (November 1873): 1–32. Print.

King, Grace Elizabeth. "A Crippled Hope." *Century* 46.3 (July 1893): 374–79. Print.

King, Margaret J. "Disneyland and Walt Disney World: Traditional Values in Futuristic Form." *The Journal of Popular Culture* 15.1 (1981): 116–40. Print.

Klugman, Karen. "Under the Influence." *Inside the Mouse: Work and Play at Disney World*. Ed. The Project on Disney. Durham: Duke UP, 1995. 98–109. Print.

Knight, Cher Krause. *Power and Paradise in Walt Disney's World*. Gainesville: UP of Florida, 2014. Print.

Koch, Gertrud. *Umwidmungen: Architektonische und kinematographische Räume*. Berlin: Vorwerk, 2005. Print.

Köck, Christoph. "Die Konstruktion der Erlebnisgesellschaft: Eine kurze Revision." *Erlebniswelten: Herstellung und Nutzung touristischer Welten*. Ed. Karlheinz Wöhler. Münster: LIT, 2006. 3–16. Print.

Koenig, David. *Realityland: True-Life Adventures at Walt Disney World*. Irvine: Bonaventure, 2007. Print.

Kolb, David. *Sprawling Places*. Athens: U of Georgia P, 2008. Print.

Krasniewicz, Louise. *Walt Disney: A Biography*. Santa Barbara: Greenwood, 2010. Print.

Krewe of sPANk. *Your Guide to Disneylandrieu*. New Orleans: N.P., 2014. Map.
Kubersky, Seth. "Disneyland Converts Former Dream Suite into 21 Royal Private Dining Experience." *Attractions Magazine* (26 January 2017). https://attractionsmagazine.com/disneyland-converts-former-dream-suite-21-royal-private-dining-experience/. Web.
Kuenz, Jane. "Working at the Rat." *Inside the Mouse: Work and Play at Disney World*. Ed. The Project on Disney. Durham: Duke UP, 1995. 110–62. Print.
Kurtti, Jeff, and Bruce Gordon. *The Art of Disneyland*. New York: Disney Editions, 2005. Print.
Laemmerhirt, Iris-Aya. *Embracing Differences: Transnational Cultural Flows between Japan and the United States*. Bielefeld: Transcript, 2013. Print.
Legnaro, Aldo. "Subjektivität im Zeitalter ihrer simulativen Reproduzierbarkeit. Das Beispiel des Disney-Kontinents." *Gouvernementalität der Gegenwart*. Ed. Ulrich Bröckling, Susanne Krasman, and Thomas Lemke. Frankfurt: Suhrkamp, 2000. 286–314. Print.
Lewis, Peirce F. "To Revive Urban Downtowns, Show Respect for the Spirit of the Place." *Smithsonian* 6 (1975): 33–41. Print.
Lukas, Scott A. "Controversial Topics: Pushing the Limits in Themed & Immersive Spaces." *Attractions Management* 20 (2015): 50–54. Print.
———. "Dark Theming Reconsidered." *A Reader in Themed and Immersive Spaces*. Ed. Scott A. Lukas. Pittsburgh, PA: ETC, 2016. 225–35. Print.
———. "How the Theme Park Gets Its Power: Lived Theming, Social Control, and the Themed Worker Self." *The Themed Space: Locating Culture, Nation, and Self*. Ed. Scott A. Lukas. Lanham: Lexington, 2007. 183–206. Print.
———. *The Immersive Worlds Handbook: Designing Theme Parks and Consumer Spaces*. New York: Focal, 2013. Print.
———. "A Politics of Reverence and Irreverence: Social Discourse on Theming Controversies." *The Themed Space: Locating Culture, Nation, and Self*. Ed. Scott A. Lukas. Lanham: Lexington, 2007. 271–93. Print.
———, ed. *A Reader in Themed and Immersive Spaces*. Pittsburgh, PA: ETC, 2016. Print.
———. "Research in Themed and Immersive Spaces: At the Threshold of Identity." *A Reader in Themed and Immersive Spaces*. Ed. Scott A. Lukas. Pittsburgh, PA: ETC, 2016. 159–69. Print.
———. *Theme Park*. London: Reaktion, 2008. Print.
———. "The Themed Space: Locating Culture, Nation, and Self." *The Themed Space: Locating Culture, Nation, and Self*. Ed. Scott A. Lukas. Lanham: Lexington, 2007. 1–22. Print.
Luske, Hamilton S., dir. "Disneyland around the Seasons." *Walt Disney's Wonderful World of Color* 13.14 (18 December 1966). TV show.
———. "Disneyland: From the Pirates of the Caribbean to the World of Tomorrow." *Walt Disney's Wonderful World of Color* 14.15 (21 January 1968). TV show.
———. "Disneyland's 10th Anniversary." *Walt Disney's Wonderful World of Color* 11.13 (3 January 1965). TV show.
Malnic, Eric. "Yo, Ho, Ho! Pirates Stamp out Good Guys." *Los Angeles Times* (20 April 1967): A1. Print.
Mannheim, Steve. *Walt Disney and the Quest for Community*. Burlington, VT: Ashgate, 2002. Print.

Manring, Maurice M. *Slave in a Box: The Strange Career of Aunt Jemima*. Charlottesville: UP of Virginia, 1998. Print.

Marin, Louis. *Utopics: The Semiological Play of Textual Spaces*. Trans. Robert A. Vollrath. New York: Humanity, 1984. [*Utopiques: Jeux d'Espace*. Paris: Minuit, 1973.] Print.

Marling, Karal Ann. "Disneyland, 1955: Just Take the Ana Freeway to the American Dream." *American Art* 5.1–2 (Winter-Spring 1991): 168–207. Print.

———. "Imagineering the Disney Theme Parks." *Designing Disney's Theme Parks: The Architecture of Reassurance*. Ed. Karal Ann Marling. Paris: Flammarion, 1997. 29–177. Print.

Martín, Hugo. "Theme Parks Expect New Rides to Send Merchandise Sales Soaring." *Los Angeles Times* (30 March 2011). http://articles.latimes.com/2011/mar/30/business/la-fi-theme-park-merchandise-20110330. Web.

McDougall, Russell. "Micronations of the Caribbean." *Surveying the American Tropics: A Literary Geography from New York to Rio*. Ed. Maria Cristina Fumagalli et al. Liverpool: Liverpool UP, 2013. 231–62. Print.

McKim, Sam. *1958 Fun Map*. Burbank: Walt Disney Productions, 1958. Map.

———. *1961 Fun Map*. Burbank: Walt Disney Productions, 1961. Map.

———. *1962 Fun Map*. Burbank: Walt Disney Productions, 1962. Map.

McPhillips, William. "'Looks Just Like Home': Mayor of Real New Orleans Praises Disneyland Replica." *Los Angeles Times* (25 July 1966): 3. Print.

Mechling, Elizabeth Walker, and Jay Mechling. "The Sale of Two Cities: A Semiotic Comparison of Disneyland with Marriott's Great America." *The Journal of Popular Culture* 15.1 (1981): 166–79. Print.

Mitrasinovic, Miodrag. *Total Landscape, Theme Parks, Public Space*. Burlington: Ashgate, 2006. Print.

Mittermeier, Sabrina. *A Cultural History of the Disneyland Theme Parks: Middle Class Kingdoms*. Wilmington, NC: Intellect, 2020. Print.

Moseley, Rebekah. "Report: Pirates of the Caribbean Special Event." *Laughing-Place* (26 June 2000). www.laughingplace.com/w/legacy/News-ID500940.asp/. Web.

N.N. "$7 Million to Go into Disneyland Attractions." *Los Angeles Times* (8 February 1862): A2. Print.

N.N. "23 Questions with X Atencio." *D23* (N.D.). https://d23.com/23-questions-with-x-atencio/. Web.

N.N. "About Larry Dotson." *Larry Dotson Studio* (N.D.). www.larrydotson.com/about/. Web.

N.N. "All New for '66!" *Disney News* 1.3 (Summer 1966): N.P. Print.

N.N. *Bringing Our Port Orleans Story to Life*. N.P.: Walt Disney Company, N.D. Print.

N.N. "Chattin' with Nunis, May 1982." *Progress City, U.S.A.* (29 August 2008). http://progresscityusa.com/2008/08/29/chattin-with-nunis-may-1982/. Web.

N.N. ("Mitch"). "Club 33 Expansion." *Imagineering Disney* (1 October 2013). www.imagineeringdisney.com/blog/2013/10/1/club-33-expansion.html. Web.

N.N. "Design: Oh Just Move It." *SamLand* (3 February 2010). http://samlanddisney.blogspot.com/2010/02/design-oh-just-move-it.html. Web.

N.N. "Disneyland Ad." *Los Angeles Times* (14 June 1965): E38. Print.

N.N. "Disneyland Ad." *Los Angeles Times* (4 August 1966): OC 5. Print.

N.N., dir. *Disneyland Comes to Tokyo*. Burbank: Walt Disney Productions, 1982. 16 mm Film.

N.N. "The Disneyland News." *FindingMickey* (N.D.). http://findingmickey.squarespace.com/ disneyland-facts/main-street-usa/8011622. Web.

N.N. "Disneyland Resort Park Rules." *Disneyland Resort* (N.D.). https://disneyland.disney.go.com/park-rules/. Web.

N.N. "Document Downloads." *PortOrleans.org* (N.D.). www.portorleans.org/documents.php. Web.

N.N. "Enchanted Tiki Room Opens at Disneyland." *Los Angeles Times* (20 June 1963): A12. Print.

N.N. "Exciting Offerings Coming to Tokyo Disneyland and Tokyo DisneySea in Fiscal Year 2017." *Olc.co.jp* (21 September 2016). www.olc.co.jp/en/news/tdr/20160921_01e. pdf. Web.

N.N. "Fine Food at the French Market." *Vacationland* 19.3 (Fall/Winter 1975): 13–14. Print.

N.N. "Fun Facts & Trivia." *PortOrleans.org* (N.D.). www.portorleans.org/trivia.php. Web.

N.N. "Kenny, Teddy, and Mickey." *Gorillas Don't Blog* (6 November 2011). http://gorillasdontblog.blogspot.de/2011/11/kenny-teddy-and-mickey.html. Web.

N.N. "Mack-Rides Ausstellung." *EPFans* (N.D.). www.epfans.info/?id=1534,16,&. Web.

N.N. "The Music of Port Orleans." *PortOrleans.org* (N.D.). www.portorleans.org/music.php. Web.

N.N. "New Orleans Square." *Vacationland* 10.2 (Summer 1966): 3–4. Print.

N.N. "New Orleans Square at Disneyland Park Fact Sheet." *Disneyland News* (22 April 2015).

N.N. "New Orleans Square Profile." *Vacationland* 25.2 (Summer 1981): 5–8. Print.

N.N. "New Orleans Square's The Blue Bayou Restaurant: A Little French, Spanish, & American." *Vacationland* 19.2 (Spring 1975): 17–18. Print.

N.N. "Portfolio: Disney's Port Orleans." *FuglebergKoch.com* (N.D.). www.fuglebergkoch.com/Portfolio/Project/Disney-Port-Orleans. Web.

N.N. "Port Orleans Celebrates Mardi Gras." *PortOrleans.org* (N.D.). www.portorleans.org/mardigras.php. Web.

N.N. "Port Orleans/Dixie Landings Resort History." *PortOrleans.org* (N.D.). www.portorleans.org/history.php. Web.

N.N. "Port Orleans Resort – French Quarter." *Disney.com* (N.D.). https://disneyworld.disney.go.com/resorts/port-orleans-resort-french-quarter/. Web.

N.N. *Profile – New Orleans Square – Disneyland*. Glendale: WED Imagineering, 1966. Print.

N.N. *Sassagoula Sentinel: Special Commemorative Edition. The History of Port Orleans*. N.P.: N.P., 1994. Print.

N.N. "Scat Cat's Club." *PortOrleans.org* (N.D.). www.portorleans.org/scatcats.php. Web.

N.N. "Shades of Green Booking Rules." *Shadesofgreen.org* (31 May 2011). www.shadesofgreen.org/eligibility.htm. Web.

N.N. "Themenbereich Chocoland." *EPFans* (N.D.). www.epfans.info/?id=2861,16,&PHPSESSID=dsmniwac. Web.

N.N. *Tokyo Disneyland*. N.P.: Walt Disney Productions, 1981. Print.

Nye, Russel B. "Eight Ways of Looking at an Amusement Park." *The Journal of Popular Culture* 15.1 (1981): 63–75. Print.

Orvell, Miles. "Understanding Disneyland: American Mass Culture and the European Gaze." *Cultural Transmissions and Receptions: American Mass Culture in Europe*. Ed. Rob Kroes et al. Amsterdam: VU UP, 1993. 240–53. Print.

Osmond, Donny. *Life Is Just What You Make It: My Story So Far*. New York: Hyperion, 2000. Print.

Pandora. "Press Release: Pandora and Disney Announce New Strategic Alliance." *Pandoragroup* (12 August 2014). http://investor.pandoragroup.com/common/download/download.cfm?companyid=ABEA-4ZFRFB&fileid=775808&filekey=C1F4E8D0-A467-4C3C-BBF5-EFDB00E6215A&filename=PANDORA_Press%20release_DISNEY_UK.pdf. Web.

Parmett, Helen Morgan. "Disneyomatics: Media, Branding, and Urban Space in Post-Katrina New Orleans." *Mediascape* (Winter 2012). www.tft.ucla.edu/mediascape/Winter2012_Disneyomatics.html. Web.

Percy, Walker. "New Orleans Mon Amour." *Signposts in a Strange Land*. Ed. Patrick Samway. New York: Farrar, Straus and Giroux, 1991 [1968]. 10–22. Print.

Petersen, Anne. "'You Believe in Pirates, Of Course . . .': Disney's Commodification and 'Closure' vs. Johnny Depp's Aesthetic Piracy of 'Pirates of the Caribbean'." *Studies in Popular Culture* 29.2 (2007): 63–81. Print.

Philips, Deborah. *Fairground Attractions: A Genealogy of the Pleasure Ground*. London: Bloomsbury, 2012. Print.

Prager, Brad, and Michael Richardson. "A Sort of Homecoming: An Archeology of Disneyland." *Streams of Cultural Capital: Transnational Cultural Studies*. Ed. David Palumbo-Liu and Hans Ulrich Gumbrecht. Stanford: Stanford UP, 1997. 199–219. Print.

The Project on Disney, eds. *Inside the Mouse: Work and Play at Disney World*. Durham: Duke UP, 1995. Print.

Rahn, Suzanne. "Snow White's Dark Ride: Narrative Strategies at Disneyland." *Bookbird: A Journal of International Children's Literature* 38.1 (2000): 19–24. Print.

Raz, Aviad E. *Riding the Black Ship: Japan and Tokyo Disneyland*. Cambridge, MA: Harvard UP, 1999. Print.

Real, Michael R. *Mass-Mediated Culture*. Englewood Cliffs: Prentice-Hall, 1977. Print.

Reisenleitner, Markus. "Resetting the Clock: Theme Parks, New Urbanism, and Smart Cities." *A Reader in Themed and Immersive Spaces*. Ed. Scott A. Lukas. Pittsburgh, PA: ETC, 2016. 279–87. Print.

Roost, Frank. "Synergy City: How Times Square and Celebration Are Integrated into Disney's Marketing Cycle." *Rethinking Disney: Private Control, Public Dimensions*. Ed. Mike Budd and Max H. Kirsch. Middletown, CT: Wesleyan UP, 2005. 261–98. Print.

Rubin, Judith, ed. *The Global Attractions Attendance Report 2018*. Burbank: Themed Entertainment Association (2019). www.aecom.com/wp-content/uploads/2019/05/Theme-Index-2018-4.pdf. Web.

Sampson, Wade. "The Disney/New Orleans Connection." *JimHillMedia* (6 September 2005). http://jimhillmedia.com/alumni1/b/wade_sampson/archive/2005/09/07/1277.aspx. Web.

Samuel, Lawrence R. *The End of the Innocence: The 1964–1965 New York World's Fair*. Syracuse: Syracuse UP, 2007. Print.

Schickel, Richard. *The Disney Version: The Life, Times, Art and Commerce of Walt Disney*. New York: Simon and Schuster, 1968. Print.

Schwarz, Ariane. "Staging the Gaze: The Water Coaster Poseidon as an Example of Staging Strategies in Theme Parks." *Time and Temporality in Theme Parks*. Ed. Filippo Carlà-Uhink, Florian Freitag, Sabrina Mittermeier, and Ariane Schwarz. Hanover: Wehrhahn, 2017. 97–112. Print.

Schweizer, Bobby, and Celia Pearce. "Remediation on the High Seas: A Pirates of the Caribbean Odyssey." *A Reader in Themed and Immersive Spaces*. Ed. Scott A. Lukas. Pittsburgh, PA: ETC, 2016. 95–106. Print.

Severo, Richard. "Dorothy Lamour, 81, Sultry Sidekick in Road Films, Dies." *The New York Times* (23 September 1996). www.nytimes.com/1996/09/23/us/dorothy-lamour-81-sultry-sidekick-in-road-films-dies.html. Web.

Shannon, Leonard. *Disneyland: Dreams, Traditions and Transitions*. N.P.: Kingdom Editions, N.Y. Print.

Siegel, Greg. "Disneyfication, the Stadium, and the Politics of Ambiance." *Rethinking Disney: Private Control, Public Dimensions*. Ed. Mike Budd and Max H. Kirsch. Middletown, CT: Wesleyan UP, 2005. 299–323. Print.

Sklar, Marty. "Introduction: Imagineering. A History That's No Mystery." The Imagineers and Malody Malmberg, *Imagineering: A Behind the Dreams Look at Making MORE Magic Real*. New York: Disney Editions, 2010. 10–11. Print.

Smith, Ruth C., and Eric M. Eisenberg. "Conflict at Disneyland: A Root-Metaphor Analysis." *Communication Monographs* 54.4 (December 1987): 367–80. Print.

Solomon, Charles. "'Art of Disneyland' Shows Park Beginnings." *Los Angeles Times* (5 December 1985): E4. Print.

———. "A Behind-Scenes-Look in 'The Art of Disneyland'." *Los Angeles Times* (13 August 1987): OC E1. Print.

———. "Designs for Disney Parks to Be Sold." *Los Angeles Times* (28 April 1988): OC E11. Print.

Sorkin, Michael. "Introduction: Variations on a Theme Park." *Variations on a Theme Park: The New American City and the End of Public Space*. Ed. Michael Sorkin. New York: Hill and Wang, 1992. xi–xv. Print.

———. "See You in Disneyland." *Variations on a Theme Park: The New American City and the End of Public Space*. Ed. Michael Sorkin. New York: Hill and Wang, 1992. 205–32. Print.

Souther, J. Mark. "The Disneyfication of New Orleans: The French Quarter as Facade in a Divided City." *Journal of American History* 94 (2007): 804–11. Print.

———. "Making 'America's Most Interesting City': Tourism and the Construction of Cultural Image in New Orleans, 1940–1984." *Southern Journeys: Tourism, History, and Culture in the Modern South*. Ed. Richard D. Starnes. Tuscaloosa: U of Alabama P, 2003. 114–37. Print.

———. *New Orleans on Parade: Tourism and the Transformation of the Crescent City*. Baton Rouge: Louisiana State UP, 2006. Print.

Sperb, Jason. *Disney's Most Notorious Film: Race, Convergence, and the Hidden Histories of* Song of the South. Austin, TX: U of Texas P, 2012. Print.

Stanley, Nick. "Chinese Theme Parks and National Identity." *Theme Park Landscapes: Antecedents and Variations*. Ed. Robert Riley and Terence Young. Washington, DC: Dumbarton Oaks Research Library and Collection, 2002. 269–89. Print.

Steinecke, Albrecht. *Themenwelten im Tourismus: Marktstrukturen – Marketing – Management – Trends*. Munich: Oldenbourg, 2009. Print.

Steinkrüger, Jan-Erik. "Other Times and Other Spaces: Themed Places and the Doubling of Landscape." *Time and Temporality in Theme Parks*. Ed. Filippo Carlà-Uhink, Florian Freitag, Sabrina Mittermeier, and Ariane Schwarz. Hanover: Wehrhahn, 2017. 83–95. Print.

Strodder, Chris. *The Disneyland Encyclopedia*. Second ed. Salona Beach: Santa Monica, 2012. Print.

Surrell, Jason. *The Haunted Mansion: Imagineering a Disney Classic*. Los Angeles: Disney Editions, 2015. Print.

———. *Pirates of the Caribbean: From the Magic Kingdom to the Movies*. Los Angeles: Disney Editions, 2006. Print.

Telotte, J.P. *Disney TV*. Detroit: Wayne State UP, 2004. Print.

Tully, Sarah. "Disneyland Store Prepares to Close." *Orange County Register* (2 April 2010). www.ocregister.com/news/close-242211-disneyland-prepares.html. Web.

Van Maanen, John. "Displacing Disney: Some Notes on the Flow of Culture." *Qualitative Sociology* 15.1 (1992): 5–35. Print.

———. "The Smile Factory: Work at Disneyland." *Reframing Organizational Culture*. Ed. Peter J. Frost et al. London: Sage, 1991. 58–76. Print.

Vollmar, Rainer. *Anaheim: Utopia Americana. Vom Weinland zum Walt Disney-Land. Eine Stadtbiographie*. Stuttgart: Franz Steiner, 1998. Print.

Waldrep, Sheldon. "Monuments to Walt." *Inside the Mouse: Work and Play at Disney World*. Ed. The Project on Disney. Durham: Duke UP, 1995. 199–229. Print.

Wallace, Mike. "Mickey Mouse History: Portraying the Past at Disney World." *Radical History Review* 32 (1985): 33–57. Print.

Warga, Wayne. "Studios Invite the Outsider for Inside Look." *Los Angeles Times* (13 October 1968): C13. Print.

Warren, Stacy. "Disneyfication of the Metropolis: Popular Resistance in Seattle." *Journal of Urban Affairs* 16.2 (June 1994): 89–107. Print.

———. "Saying No to Disney: Disney's Demise in Four American Cities." *Rethinking Disney: Private Control, Public Dimensions*. Ed. Mike Budd and Max H. Kirsch. Middletown, CT: Wesleyan UP, 2005. 231–60. Print.

Wasko, Janet. *Understanding Disney: The Manufacture of Fantasy*. Cambridge: Polity, 2001. Print.

Wasko, Janet, Mark Phillips, and Eileen Meehan, eds. *Dazzled by Disney?: The Global Disney Audience Project*. London: U of Leicester P, 2001. Print.

Weiss, Werner. "Alice in Wonderland: The Dark Ride with the 'Leafy Vine' Track Outside." *Yesterland* (2014). www.yesterland.com/alice.html. Web.

———. "Don DeFore's Silver Banjo Barbecue Restaurant." *Yesterland* (16 May 2007). www.yesterland.com/silverbanjo.html. Web.

Wiener, Jon. "Tall Tales and True." *The Nation* (31 January 1994): 133–35. Print.

Wiles, Gordon, dir. "Disneyland Showtime." *The Wonderful World of Disney* 16.20 (22 March 1970). TV show.

Willis, Susan. "The Problem with Pleasure." *Inside the Mouse: Work and Play at Disney World*. Ed. The Project on Disney. Durham: Duke UP, 1995. 1–11. Print.

Yoshimoto, Mitsushiro. "The Images of Empire: Tokyo Disneyland and Japanese Cultural Imperialism." *Disney Discourse: Producing the Magic Kingdom*. Ed. Eric Smoodin. New York: Routledge, 1994. 181–99. Print.

Younger, David. *Theme Park Design and the Art of Themed Entertainment*. N.P.: Inklingwood, 2016. Print.

———. "Traditionally Postmodern: The Changing Styles of Theme Park Design." *Time and Temporality in Theme Parks*. Ed. Filippo Carlà-Uhink, Florian Freitag, Sabrina Mittermeier, and Ariane Schwarz. Hanover: Wehrhahn, 2017. 63–82. Print.

Zukin, Sharon: *Landscapes of Power: From Detroit to Disney World*. Berkeley: U of California P, 2000. Print.

3 *Wading Home*'s Post-Katrina New Orleans

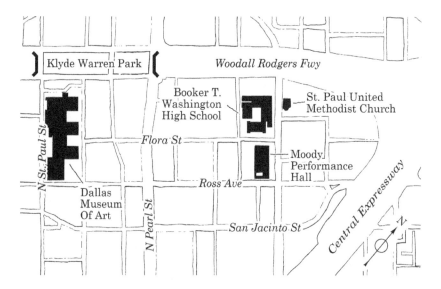

Figure 3.1 Dallas Arts District.

Source: Adapted by Polichronios Vezirgenidis from dallasartsdistrict.org/map/.

C'est Levee

On 11 February 2006, at around 7 p.m., members of Krewe du Vieux lined up on the corner of Decatur Street and Port Street in New Orleans's Faubourg Marigny neighborhood for what would become one of the most significant and famous parades in the then almost 170-year-old history of the city's carnival processions. *C'est Levee*, as Krewe du Vieux's parade was called, was perhaps as momentous as the first parade of the Mistick Krewe of Comus in 1857 – the first carnival procession in New Orleans dedicated to a specific motto or theme, organized by a carnival society ("krewe"), and restricted to the members of this society – or the first parade of what is generally known as "The Rex Organization" in

1872 – the first time Rex seized power over the Crescent City as the "King of Carnival."[1] In contrast to these – at the time – unprecedented and novel approaches to celebrating carnival in New Orleans, *C'est Levee* was part of an already well-established tradition: founded in 1987 by former members of the Krewe of Clones (itself founded in 1978), Krewe du Vieux had been marching on the third Saturday before Mardi Gras (Shrove Tuesday, the day before Ash Wednesday and the beginning of Lent) for almost two decades (see N.N., "Brief History").[2] Moreover, according to its mission statement, the krewe sees itself as the sole heir to "the old traditions of Carnival celebrations, by using decorated mule-drawn floats with satirical themes, accompanied by costumed revelers dancing in the streets [of the French Quarter] to the sounds of jazzy street musicians" (N.N., "Krewe du Vieux Mission").[3]

Indeed, as the first carnival parade after Hurricane Katrina had destroyed much of the Crescent City in late August 2005,[4] *C'est Levee* went down in Mardi Gras history not because it invented new traditions, but rather because it continued old ones: for one thing, through their sharp critique of the U.S. Army Corps of Engineers (USACE) and the Federal Emergency Management Agency (FEMA), the 17 themed floats of *C'est Levee*,[5] featuring such mottoes as "The Corpse of Engineers Presents 'A Day at the Breach'" and "K.A.O.S. Rules FEMA," kept up Krewe du Vieux's tradition of biting and trenchant political satire – as well as, in a way, the late nineteenth-century custom of using organized carnival as a "theater of protest" against the federal government (especially during and in the context of Reconstruction; see R. Mitchell, *Mardi Gras* 69; and Roach 239–81). As Keith Twitchell, Krewe du Vieux's "Poobah of Publicity," noted: "This is an opportunity to keep people aware of the damage and who's responsible for it" (qtd. in Jensen, "Vieux"). One member of the sub-Krewe of K.A.O.S. put it even more succinctly: "[Krewe du Vieux] let's [sic] Katrina and the feds have it. . . . I love the fact that all those FEMA workers staying in the [French] Quarter are going to get a load of this" (N.N., "C'est Levee").

In response to Hurricane Katrina, several of New Orleans's carnival krewes had adjusted their original parade or float themes, which had often been established before the hurricane hit the city. The Krewe of King Arthur, for instance, which paraded on 19 February 2006 on the topic of "popular periodicals," changed the theme of a float on parenting magazines to "celebrate an expected boom of Katrina babies, begotten by evacuees 'in hotel rooms with nothing to do'" (MacCash). And the Knights of Chaos, whose procession rolled on 23 February 2006, satirized the federal government's response to the Katrina disaster as "Reconstruction II," thus making the parallels between late-nineteenth–century and post-Katrina carnival's "theater of protest" even more explicit than Krewe du Vieux had done (see Godet). Krewe du Vieux itself, in turn, had not started planning for its 2006 procession until mid-October 2005, but from the very start had considered Katrina as a possible theme. "C'est Levee" – a pun on the French phrase "c'est la vie" ("that's life") – was suggested by the krewe's co-founder, former captain, and 1999 king Ray "Plaine" Kern, and decided upon by vote during a captain's meeting on 5 November 2005. The individual sub-krewes were then free to interpret the parade's main theme for their floats. Amidst national debates in which New Orleans was sometimes accused of having brought the disaster upon itself for its "sinful" ways (see, for instance, Richards 521–2), Krewe du Vieux members obviously felt it was important to make a point, name names, and articulate their point of view in what may be considered one of the city's "native" media – the carnival procession.

Yet it was not just the parade's "content" – that is, Krewe du Vieux's irreverent representation of Hurricane Katrina in general and of the federal government's response in particular – that earned *C'est Levee* its place in the history of New Orleans carnival parades. What was perhaps even more important was the parade's sheer presence in the streets of the city – i.e., the fact that *C'est Levee*, as well as Mardi Gras celebrations in general, took place at all a mere six and a half months after about 80 percent of New Orleans had been flooded, hundreds of lives had been lost, and thousands of residents had been displaced. In order to keep down expenses on crowd control, fire protection, and sanitation, a cash-strapped New Orleans City Council had shortened the parade season to eight rather than twelve days and asked krewes to "shorten their parades, use only the traditional Uptown route and pick up after themselves" (Jensen, "Carnival"; see also Godet). The krewes themselves had to cope with a lack of manpower – according to Deloughery, overall krewe membership was down 27 percent due to Katrina-related deaths and diaspora (143) – and damaged equipment – MacCash reports that the floats of both Rex's and Krewe d'Etat's parades, for instance, bore "waterlines from the post-Katrina floodwaters." In the case of Krewe du Vieux, hundreds of the organization's roughly 900 members had been displaced; the private home of then captain Susan Gibeault was flooded; the krewe's float storage facility in the Faubourg Marigny, the so-called "Den of Muses," suffered some damage; and the krewe was worried it would not find enough brass bands to accompany each of the parade's floats (see N.N., "Brief History"; and Jensen, "Vieux").

Nevertheless, the parades rolled on, over 50 of them, according to Gotham (170). In a way, they had to. Given the central role the tourism and convention industry had come to play in the local economy prior to Katrina (see, among others, Thomas), letting the world know that the city was still alive and capable of welcoming business and leisure travelers was economically vital to New Orleans, and Mardi Gras 2006, covered as it was by both national and international media, offered a perfect opportunity to do so. Local officials and editors thus vigorously supported the event, declaring it "the most anticipated Carnival season in recent memory" (N.N., "Commentary") and appealing to residents' and krewe members' sense of duty: celebrating carnival will "send out the signal that New Orleans is not dead,'" then-mayor Ray Nagin noted (qtd. in Thevenot), and the New Orleans newspaper *Times-Picayune* agreed: "It's a kick-start for a crippled economy and a test to prove to the world the city can still hold massive events" (Thevenot). Perhaps even former Krewe du Vieux king Angus Lind was only half in jest when he wrote the day before *C'est Levee* in a *Times-Picayune* editorial that "[t]his is the first Mardi Gras parade post-Katrina, and Krewe du Vieux has a very serious responsibility, which I am happy to report the members are not taking seriously at all."

Yet this "spirit of resilience" was by no means just "engineered by city officials and public editors in order to placate national public opinion ... and attract tourists back to NOLA," as Godet to some extent maintains. In the last chapter of his 2005 monograph *Performance in America*, David Román stresses the critical role the performances on New York City's Broadway played during the weeks after 9/11: "The performing arts offered people a chance to be with others and experience themselves together. In this sense, we were as much audiences for ourselves as for the performances" (253). This also and especially applies to the first celebration of carnival in post-Katrina New Orleans, particularly to the parades of Krewe du Vieux and other carnival organizations. Arthur Hardy explains:

> Every year, people meet on the same street corner to watch the parade. Every year, it's the same families. After Katrina, when you didn't see those families, you didn't know if they drowned, evacuated or if they just didn't care to come. So when people did reconnect, it was very moving. It was probably the most important Mardi Gras ever.
> (qtd. in O'Neill 91)[6]

Indeed, *C'est Levee* did not just show to the rest of the world that New Orleans was still there. Parading krewe members and celebrating spectators also showed to each other and to themselves that they were still there (or back). In this sense, the parade – including the enormous crowd it drew (see N.N., "Brief History") – was a live performance of both New Orleans's and New Orleanians' aliveness (see also R. Mitchell, "Carnival" 794).

C'est Levee was one of the first of countless live events inspired by Hurricane Katrina. Like *C'est Levee*, many of these performances took place in "found," non-theatrical spaces in New Orleans,[7] while others, such as the 2008 *Festival New Orleans*, were staged in professional venues as far away as London. Some, like *C'est Levee*, involved hundreds of experienced, but nevertheless amateur, performers from the Crescent City, while others, such as Paul Chan's *Waiting for Godot in New*

Orleans: A Play in Two Acts, A Project in Three Parts (2007), featured a more limited cast of professional actors and theater personnel from both New Orleans and elsewhere. Like *C'est Levee*, some performances were one-time affairs and part of larger performance events, whereas others, including Mackenzie Westmoreland and Michael Marks's *The Katrina Project: Hell and High Water* (2005), were independently performed more than 100 times. Some performances, like *C'est Levee*, were free and operated on a comparatively limited budget (the parade cost Krewe du Vieux about $85,000), while others, such as the 2006 *Jazz Fest*, were ticketed events involving tens of millions of dollars. Like *C'est Levee*, some were (more or less tightly) scripted, whereas others, like the Centre for Playback Theatre's performances in New Orleans in 2005, relied more on the performers' improvisational skills. Finally, like *C'est Levee*, some performances explicitly focused on Hurricane Katrina, while others, including the "HOME, New Orleans?" project's *Lakeviews: A Sunset Bus Tour* (2007), deliberately also stressed pre-Katrina life in the city.[8]

What all these performances and events had in common was that they were – like all performances – live and, as such, processual, transient, and ephemeral, disappearing forever and being irrevocably lost in the very moment they were over. In other words, unlike the numerous cultural objects or artifacts inspired by Hurricane Katrina – including novels (literary novels, pulp fiction, and young adult fiction), short stories, life writings, dramas, poems, songs, paintings, photographs, comics and graphic novels, street art (graffiti), sculptures, murals, monuments, and TV series, as well as fictional and documentary films[9] – these performances, depending as they did on the bodily co-presence of performers and audiences, could not be fixed, archived, or contained.[10] This does not mean that they are not important. Quite to the contrary: just like they did in post-9/11 New York City, as David Román has argued, live performances and events have also and again emerged as a "viable response" (239) to the events of Hurricane Katrina, not only because they offered professional artists and amateurs "an especially effective means to engage the contemporary" (1), a public forum in which to comment on tragic events that were happening at that very moment, but also because each performance created a "temporary and conditional we" (1), bringing people (back) together at a specific place and for a specific time – as performers, as audiences, and as performers and audiences. It is precisely in their constituent and inherent ephemerality, then, that a substantial part of the significance of these events and performances for post-Katrina U.S. culture is grounded.

"*Wading Home*'s Post-Katrina New Orleans" seeks to substantiate these claims by documenting and analyzing one specific post-Katrina performance: namely, the premiere of *Wading Home*, an opera written by Rosalyn Story (libretto) and Mary Alice Rich (libretto and music), which took place on 2 April 2015 at 7:30 p.m. at the Moody Performance

Hall (formerly known as the Dallas City Performance Hall) in Dallas, Texas, under the conductorship of Constantina Tsolaino and under the direction of Barbara Hill Moore (music) and Hank Hammett (stage). Based on Rich's score and Story and Rich's libretto (which, in turn, had been adapted from Story's 2010 novel *Wading Home: A Novel of New Orleans*), involving a cast of more than 40 performers (including internationally renowned baritone and multiple Grammy Award-winner Donnie Ray Albert), and drawing an enormous crowd (although the Performance Hall offers about 750 seats, numerous people had to be turned away at the doors), the premiere of *Wading Home* was remarkable in several respects. It was especially remarkable, however, for the way the fictional world represented on stage resonated with and spoke to what was happening on that particular evening in the "actual" world of the venue. Indeed, depicting Hurricane Katrina as part of a long history of racially motivated displacement and dispossession of African Americans in Louisiana and representing the future of post-Katrina New Orleans as ultimately depending on the return of African-American artists (musicians, painters, and chefs) to the city, the performance temporarily brought together a cast of mostly African-American performers (singers, musicians, and dancers), as well as a racially diverse audience in a part of Dallas that, since its development from a former "Freedman's Town" into the Dallas Arts District over the course of the twentieth century, had itself been the site of African-American displacement and dispossession. Through the performance, then, the opera's socio-political critique of Hurricane Katrina and particularly its vision for a revitalized post-Katrina New Orleans, as enacted – represented, performed – on the stage, were transferred to and directly acted out – put into action, actualized – in the context of Dallas, if only for a limited amount of time (namely, the exact duration of the performance).

In order to capture this striking concurrence of theatrical and political action, "*Wading Home*'s Post-Katrina New Orleans" will, similarly to what I have done in my brief discussion of *C'est Levee*, combine a textual or semiotic reading of the opera (as well as the novel that inspired it)[11] with an ethnographic-phenomenological reading of its premiere performance in April 2015 in Dallas.[12] The latter will include detailed looks at the history of Dallas in general and the Dallas Arts District in particular, the place of the Moody Performance Hall within this history, the personal stories of the creators of *Wading Home* (especially Story, Rich, and Hill Moore), and responses from members of the audience (including my own). Thus conceptualized, "*Wading Home*'s Post-Katrina New Orleans" draws as much on the text of the novel and the libretto/score of the opera as on studies of the history of Dallas and archival material from the Dallas Public Library, on my recordings and notes of the dress rehearsal on 1 April 2015 and the premiere, and on interviews with the creators of the performance. The chapter simultaneously contributes to the history of Dallas and especially the city's Arts District, the discussion about the performative aftermath of the Katrina disaster, and the history of the representation of (post-Katrina) New Orleans in popular culture.

With respect to the last point, however, the story of "*Wading Home*'s Post-Katrina New Orleans" is quite different from those of "Scribner's Illustrated New Orleans" and "Disney's Immersive New Orleans." Both Helen Taylor and Jennifer Gipson have noted that immediately following the events of Hurricane Katrina, the Crescent City's French heritage was newly stressed and valorized, also and particularly in post-Katrina events and performances (see, for example, H. Taylor, "After the Deluge" 498; and Gipson 182). Probably the most prominent example of this is the sub-Krewe of PAN's *C'est Levee*-float, whose motto asked then-French President Jacques Chirac to "buy us back."[13] French New Orleans also plays a relatively prominent role in Story's novel and (to a somewhat lesser extent) in Story and Rich's libretto, but ultimately became a non-issue during the premiere performance of *Wading Home*. Hence, following "Scribner's Illustrated New Orleans" and "Disney's Immersive New Orleans," "*Wading Home*'s Post-Katrina New Orleans" traces a notable decrease in the significance of French New Orleans in popular representations of the city during post-Katrina times, highlighting instead the rise of post-Katrina New Orleans as a transhistorical, national paradigm or scenario that also applies to other (U.S.) cities and periods.

Pre-Formance, Post-Formance: Research Paradigms in Performance Studies

Performances are spatially bound and temporally limited events during which specific actions are presented to an audience (see Bial and Brady) – indeed, theater director and "founding father" of performance studies, Richard Schechner, has described "performing" quite simply as "showing doing" (*Performance Studies* 28). Such a broad and inclusive definition of these terms allows not only for the discussion of a remarkably wide range of corporeal artistic and social practices and activities under the heading of "performance," including at the very least theatrical presentations (such as opera performances), rituals (such as Mardi Gras parades), games, sports, and play, but also for the identification of performance as a "key paradigm" of (human) behavior across historical periods and cultures (Schechner, "Broad Spectrum" 4–5). Performance, then, simultaneously refers to isolated events of cultural expression that have been conventionally conceived of as performances (Schechner, *Performance Studies* 38) as well as to an analytical lens through which to view and analyze specific processes or practices *as* performances (see D. Taylor 3; Bauridl and Wiegmink 157).

Later named the "broad spectrum approach" (see Schechner, "Broad Spectrum"), this expansive conceptualization of (cultural) performance and performing was first articulated by Schechner in his programmatic article "Approaches to Theory/Criticism" (1966), frequently cited today as the founding text of performance studies in North America (see, for instance, Balme 70; Bial 404).[14] In this essay, Schechner refers to ritual, theater, play, games, and sports as "the public performance activities of men [sic]" (27), but does not yet call for a general theory of (cultural) performance (although toward the end of the text, he does suggest the possibility "that a unified set of approaches will be developed that can handle *all* theatrical phenomena," 53; emphasis original). Such calls for a general theory, by both Schechner himself and others, would start to appear in the mid-1970s (see, for instance, Schechner, "Performance" 4; and MacAloon 2) and were eventually answered with the publication of several introductory monographs in the mid-1990s and early 2000s, most notably Marvin Carlson's *Performance: A Critical Introduction* (1996), Jon McKenzie's *Perform, Or Else: From Discipline to Performance* (2001), or Schechner's own *Performance Studies: An Introduction* (2002).[15]

By that time, performance studies in the United States had, in Barbara Kirshenblatt-Gimblett's words, "come of age," as indicated by the establishment of performance studies departments (starting with the renaming of NYU's Graduate Drama Department as the Department of Performance Studies in 1980), specialized journals (among others, *TDR/The Drama Review*, subtitled "A Journal of Performance Studies" since 1986), and professional associations (for example, PSi Performance Studies international, founded in 1997), as well as book series at, for instance, Routledge (see Kirshenblatt-Gimblett 26). These signs of disciplinary institutionalization notwithstanding, performance studies has consistently and vigorously refused to identify itself as a unified field, preferring self-appellations such as "interdiscipline" (Conquergood, "Caravans" 137), "postdiscipline" (Roach xii), or even "antidiscipline" (Roach qtd. in Carlson, *Performance* 189), which has prompted Jon McKenzie to argue that "liminality" itself has become the defining characteristic of and even something of a norm within performance studies (50; see also Bial 402). Yet, McKenzie has also admitted that citing not just performance studies departments, publication venues, and professional organizations, but also "genres of performance and canons of literature," "methods and disciplines," and "courses and curricula," as well as "intellectual histories," "someone researching the field from the outside might . . . comment: if it walks like a paradigm" (48). Indeed, at least among the three approaches this study draws on – periodical studies, theme park studies, and performance studies – the latter not only appears to be the most firmly institutionalized one (as of now). There are also several recurring issues or concerns that may be identified, aspects of performance that scholars have more or less routinely raised and discussed in their writings.

One of these issues or concerns involves the "liveness" – and thus, the inherent ephemerality and uniqueness – of performance events. Faced with "both the technological and social imperative for a new understanding of performance" due to the development of global communication technologies, performance studies scholars have, starting with Philip Auslander's *Presence and Resistance* (1992), increasingly redefined liveness as "simultaneity rather than [bodily] presence" (Bial 404; 409). Nevertheless, liveness – that is, the simultaneity of production and reception – is still considered the core of performance: "Performer and spectator may no longer share physical space, but they share virtual space and actual time" (Bial 409). Liveness, however, automatically implies both transience and momentariness, as well as uniqueness and unrepeatability. Based as they are on live "action, interaction, and relation" (Schechner, *Performance Studies* 30), performances leave, with the possible exception of the material objects employed in the events (such as costumes, stage sets, or props; see Fischer-Lichte, *Introduction* 22), "no visible trace" behind (Phelan, *Unmarked* 149). Performances thus create and undo themselves at the very same time; their irrevocable disappearance constitutes both their basic condition as well as their raison d'être; they become themselves, in Phelan's famous words, "through disappearance" (*Unmarked* 146; see also Fischer-Lichte, *Transformative Power* 76; and *Introduction* 22). "We have created and studied a discipline based on that which disappears," Phelan has noted elsewhere ("Introduction" 8). Moreover, as a live and "autopoietic" (Fischer-Lichte, *Introduction* 22) or, rather, "auto-destructive" event, each performance is also unique and unrepeatable, not only, as Randy Martin has claimed (188), since it would be almost impossible to recreate the exact combination of performers and theater personnel, costumes, stage sets and props, and members of the audience of a given performance event,[16] but also because even if such a "reenactment" of a given performance was attempted, particularly the internal and external reactions of the performers and the members of the audience would necessarily be altered by their previous experience of the original event.

It is perhaps due to performance's radical presentness that performance studies scholars have been so preoccupied with its antecedents or past – what John J. MacAloon has called performance's "pre-formance" (9) – as well as its aftermath or future – what could analogously be referred to as its "post-formance." In a frequently quoted article first written in 1977 and later included in his collection *Between Theatre and Anthropology* (1985), for instance, Schechner has characterized performance as "restored" or "twice-behaved" behavior ("Restoration" 35–6). Paige McGinley has specified that while both phrases suggest "a kind of doubleness or repetition,"

> "twice-behaved behavior" implies a doubleness localized to one actor: the actor in rehearsal and then in performance, for example, or the

teacher who introduces herself anew at the beginning of every semester. "Restored behavior," however, gestures toward a repetition that is not limited to a single actor. Rather, it suggests a cultural or collective repetition.

(85)

In fact, while affirming the uniqueness and non-repeatability of individual performances, performance studies scholars nevertheless widely agree that all performance draws on pre-existing "strips of behavior" (Schechner, "Restoration" 35), "pattern[s] of action" (Carlson, *Performance* 15) of unknown origin that may be as long as an entire ritual or as short as a mere gesture and that may be transferred (and recognized) across time, place, and contexts (see Schechner, "Restoration" 35; Stecopoulos 249).

In order to more fully capture the reiterative quality of performance and to expose performance's intimate relation with history and memory, Joseph Roach and Diana Taylor have developed the concepts of "performance genealogies" and the "repertoire," respectively. In *Cities of the Dead* (1996), Roach – incidentally, while discussing Mardi Gras parades – defines performance genealogies as a way of passing on and disseminating knowledge and memory through "expressive movements as mnemonic reserves," particularly in opposition to "history as it is discursively transmitted," e.g., through documents and texts (26). Similarly, in *The Archive and the Repertoire* (2003), Taylor distinguishes between "the *archive* of supposedly enduring materials (i.e., texts, documents, buildings, bones)" (19; emphasis original) and the repertoire, "which enacts embodied memory: performances, gestures, orality, movement, dance, singing – in short, all those acts usually thought of as ephemeral, nonreproducible knowledge" (20). According to Taylor, just as one way of approaching the archive is through identifying specific narratives, one method of studying the repertoire is to look at "meaning-making paradigms that structure social environments, behaviors, and potential outcomes," paradigms that she refers to as "scenarios" (27). Citing scenarios of discovery (27) and conquest (29) as examples drawn from the specific repertoire of the Americas, Taylor argues that the scenario "includes features well theorized in literary analysis, such as narrative and plot, but demands that we also pay attention to milieu and corporeal behavior such as gestures, attitudes, and tones not reducible to language" (27). Reactivating themselves by "conjur[ing] up past situations" (32), scenarios "grab the body" – that of the (social) actor and/or that of the spectator – "and insert it into a frame" (54).

This does not necessarily mean, however, that the body is not free to move: scenarios may be "formulaic structures that predispose certain outcomes" (D. Taylor 31), but, Taylor maintains, precisely because they are (re-)enacted and (re-)embodied rather than scripted (54; see also 30), scenarios also allow for "reversal, parody, and change" (31) and, hence, for subversion and resistance. Roach, too, asserts that individual performances in the genealogy may be "[i]n the service of memory, or in its betrayal" and may therefore often have "unpredictable" consequences (269). Like Taylor and Roach, several scholars have emphasized that as they recur across time and space, restored behaviors are always subject to and even encourage revision and change (see, for instance, Conquergood, "Performance Theory" 44; or Stern and Henderson 9). It is, according to Matthias Warstat, above all in this potential for revision and change that performance's agency and its (potential) impact on spectators in particular and society at large – in short, its political dimension – manifest themselves (74).

The discussion about performance's "pre-formance" is thus inextricably linked to that about its "post-formance," that is, performance's short- and long-term cultural, social, and political effects. Perhaps spurred by its inherent transience and ephemerality, performance studies scholars have long and intensely debated the question of the efficacy of performance.[17] In very general terms, this debate has focused both on the nature and the durability of performance's efficacy, with scholars distinguishing, on the one hand, between performances with a socially affirmative, restorative, and stabilizing potential and transgressive, resistant, or subversive performances, and, on the other hand, between performances with a permanent, irreversible impact on participating individuals and performances that only have a temporary effect on their audiences. Especially since the mid-2000s, scholars have become particularly interested in the exact relationship between theatrical performances – which have usually been considered potentially transgressive, but of merely temporary efficacy, as opposed to e.g., rituals – and lasting political and societal change. However, whereas some, including David Román and Jill Dolan, have conceptualized performance as a mere catalyst or, more fittingly, a mere "rehearsal" for social and political activism, others, such as Shannon Jackson and Pia Wiegmink, have explored performances and events that deliberately blur the boundaries between theatrical and political action.

Already in 1959, Goffman included performance's "influence on the observers" as a fundamental part of his definition of the term (22), although he did not further specify exactly what kind of influence or effect performances may have. Indeed, time and again, performance studies scholars have reminded themselves and each other that performance in itself is neither conservative nor counter-hegemonic and, therefore, has the potential both to "put . . . forward alternative viewpoints, showcase . . . emerging perspectives, and allow . . . for cultural dissent" as well as to "cohere to positions already widely held, and in fact serve to promote them" (Román 269). However, while generally affirming the "power of performance" (McKenzie 20) and while acknowledging that political, cultural, and social norms, models, and structures may be both reflected, confirmed, and perpetuated, but also criticized, contested, and challenged by and in performance, performance studies has, Jon McKenzie maintains, nevertheless consistently emphasized performance's subversive possibilities (30).

This marked preference for transformational rather than conservational performances among performance studies scholars, which has also been noted and reflected by, for instance, Ian Maxwell (60), may well have become something of a norm within performance studies, as McKenzie has famously suggested (50) – it certainly fits performance studies' self-conceptualization as a transgressive "antidiscipline" (see earlier). In fact, like this self-conceptualization, performance studies' particular interest in transgressive performances can be traced, according to McKenzie, to the "liminal-norm" (50); that is, the persistent use and continued relevance of liminality in general and the liminal rite of passage in particular for the field – although no longer as an object of study, as during the 1960s and 1970s (see Bial 404–406), but rather "as an *exemplar* of the entire field of objects," "guiding the selection of activities to be studied, their formal analysis, and their political evaluation" (McKenzie 37; and 50; emphasis original).

Performance studies scholars have not only debated the nature of performance's effects, however, but also its durability. Around the mid-1970s, Schechner started to identify the binary system of efficacy and entertainment as the core of performance and to distinguish between performances that effect a permanent change in their participants ("social dramas") and performances that merely effect a temporary change within their audiences ("aesthetic dramas"; see Schechner, "From Ritual" 89–90; and "Towards a Poetics" 124). This distinction later became inextricably linked with Victor Turner's differentiation between "liminal" and "liminoid" phenomena, also established in the mid-1970s, in which the former primarily refer to passage rites in tribal and pre-modern agrarian societies and the latter to the entertainments of industrial societies (including theater; see Turner, "Liminal to Liminoid" 84–6). Schechner himself, for instance, noted that "[l]iminal rituals are transformations, permanently changing who people are. Liminoid rituals, effecting a temporary change . . ., are transportations" (*Performance Studies* 72). Likewise, in a book aptly titled *The Transformative Power of Performance*, Fischer-Lichte writes that while "the liminal experience in ritual may transform the participants' social status and alter their publicly recognized identity," liminoidity "lacks two traits that apply exclusively to ritualistic liminality: first, durability (irreversibility); and second, social recognition" (176; 179).

What precisely does the temporary efficacy of liminoid phenomena and especially theatrical performances consist of, however? Since the mid-2000s, scholars such as Phyllis Scott Carlin and Linda M. Park-Fuller, but above all David Román and Jill Dolan, have stressed theatre's role as an alternative space whose (re)presentation of a different, better world may inform, inspire, motivate, provoke, catalyze, and, indeed, rehearse social activism outside the spatial and temporal limits of performance. Perhaps Dolan's concept of "utopian performatives" encapsulates this argument most succinctly: "Utopian performatives, in their doings," Dolan writes,

> make palpable an affective vision of how the world might be better. . . . The affective and ideological "doings" we see and feel demonstrated in utopian performatives also critically rehearse civic engagement that could be effective in the wider public and political realm.
> (6–7; see also Román 3; Carlin and Park-Fuller 22)

By contrast, using phrases such as "social theatre" (Schechner, *Performance Studies* 319), "socially engaged art" (Jackson 17), "activist performance" (Wiegmink 2), or "applied theatre" (Snyder-Young 4), other scholars have pointed to theatrical actions that do not just potentially inspire or "rehearse" political actions, but that deliberately "seek to bridge the gap between theatrical representation and direct political action" (Wiegmink 2). In these kinds of performances, "theatrical presentation and political action coincide and merge into one" (2).

The 2015 premiere of *Wading Home* in Dallas was, I argue, just such an event. In this performance, theatrical presentation – that is, *Wading Home*'s "utopian" vision of a post-Katrina New Orleans revitalized by returning African-American artists – and political action – namely, the gathering of African Americans in general and African-American artists in particular in a gentrified former freedman's town in Dallas – "coincided and merged into one." This is by no means to say that the premiere performance of *Wading Home* may not also have inspired, provoked, or motivated some of the individuals involved in the event – creators, performers, theater personnel, or audience members – to engage in other forms of political action following the performance. There is, indeed, almost no way of knowing about or identifying all the various political actions – in addition to the individual emotional, affective responses – that this particular performance would eventually or may still inspire in each and every one of the persons present on that evening in the Moody Performance Hall. What I seek to show in "*Wading Home*'s Post-Katrina New Orleans," by contrast, is that already during this event, political and theatrical action converged and became inseparable. On that evening, the opera's "utopia" of a better world was simultaneously enacted *in* as well as *upon* Dallas.

The key to *Wading Home*'s "post-formance," the performance's efficacy of bringing together and integrating theatrical action about post-Katrina New Orleans and political action about post-gentrification Dallas, lies in its "pre-formance," however – that is, in the particular scenario that

Wading Home "conjured up" or "reactivated" in order to represent the Katrina disaster on stage. In fact, depicting Katrina as but the most recent case in the long history of the displacement and dispossession of African Americans in the United States in general and in Louisiana in particular, *Wading Home* exposed African-American displacement and dispossession *as* a scenario that is at least as old and as central to the American experience as those of discovery and conquest identified by Taylor (see earlier). "[G]rab[bing] the bodies" of African Americans and "insert[ing] them into a frame" (D. Taylor 54) of forced diaspora and homelessness, this specific scenario may be viewed as the embodied or enacted version of a narrative that has been frequently evoked in the critical debate about Hurricane Katrina, a debate that started almost immediately following the tragic events and that I have elsewhere referred to as Katrina's "disaster discourse" (see Freitag, "Displacement" 129). In the following, I will first sketch this debate in order to then show how one of the narratives emerging from it was used in *Wading Home* – the opera, as well as the novel on which it was based – and how this narrative, in turn, resurfaced in its embodied version, as a scenario, during the 2015 performance of *Wading Home* in Dallas.

Pre-Katrina, Post-Katrina: Disaster Discourses about Hurricane Katrina

In her introduction to *Racing the Storm* (2007), Hillary Potter employs theatrical metaphors to stress the implications of U.S. race relations and racial injustice for Hurricane Katrina. "The stage was set," she writes, "and Hurricane Katrina provided a performance that allowed the nation and the world to see who the players were and that each role had not been afforded an equal part in this tragic production of social reality" (xiii). Although probably inspired by the highly publicized nature of the Hurricane Katrina disaster itself – notably the live images of mostly African Americans waiting to be rescued off New Orleans rooftops or from the Superdome – Potter's performance rhetoric is also apt insofar as much like the theoretical discourse on performance, critical accounts and analyses of events commonly referred to as "natural disasters" – storms, earthquakes, fires, and floods – also focus on both the pre-history and the aftermath of these phenomena. Indeed, while disasters themselves may be intense, yet short-lived and local, discourses and narratives about disasters reach well beyond the limited geographical and particularly temporal frames of the events at hand, reading them, as Vincanne Adams has noted, "in terms that provide a social autopsy of what went wrong before but also in the long-term aftermath" (15). Addressing questions of accountability and responsibility, but also seeking to draw lessons from the events in the interest of preventability, disaster discourses thus constitute powerful forms of critique that draw attention to fundamental shortcomings and systemic flaws in society, politics, and culture and that, in the final consequence, seriously question the "naturalness" of natural disasters.

According to Rachel E. Luft, scholars have challenged the naturalness of disasters ever since the 1980s, when "a new, constructionist school of disaster scholarship began to emphasize the preexisting social conditions that contribute to and exacerbate disaster" (506). Pointing to "the ongoing conditions of 'social vulnerability' – poverty, racism, sexism – that construct and interact with disaster" on the one hand, and characterizing these "enduring social problems as disastrous in their own right" on the other hand, this scholarship has, Luft notes, simultaneously questioned the supposed discreteness and exceptionalism of disasters. In fact, already as early as the mid-1970s, critics such as Paul Richards and Phil O'Keefe, Ken Westgate, and Ben Wisner have suggested considering vulnerability – "a vulnerability that is induced by socio-economic conditions that can be modified by man" – as the "real cause of disaster" (O'Keefe, Westgate, and Wisner 567) and have therefore proposed to "replace the term *natural* with the more appropriate term *social* or *political* disaster" (Richards qtd. in O'Keefe, Westgate, and Wisner 566; emphases original).

Such arguments and views were reiterated 30 years later in much of the disaster scholarship on Hurricane Katrina and the subsequent flooding of New Orleans. Indeed, considering how old the critical debate about the "naturalness" of natural disasters was by the mid-2000s, and how widespread, well-established, and commonly accepted its main points (supposedly) were among scholars by that time, it is quite surprising how much particularly early accounts and analyses of Hurricane Katrina felt the need to insist on the unnaturalness of the event – a fact that can perhaps only be explained by the sheer magnitude of human suffering, destruction, and hence, media attention it caused. Initial media reports tended, as Phil Steinberg has noted, to emphasize once again the Crescent City's historical, social, and cultural uniqueness, which "made it appear to some more like the nearby Caribbean . . . than like the adjacent United States" (Steinberg 3), thus tapping into what Jonathan Shapiro Anjaria has described as "the imagination of a globe divided into a First World (that works) and a Third World (that doesn't)" (187). Soon thereafter, however, both journalists and scholars started to frame Hurricane Katrina and its aftermath as the result of systemic flaws in American politics, society, and culture, supplanting narratives about New Orleans's exceptionalism with investigations of the exemplarity and, consequently, the unnaturalness of Hurricane Katrina (see Steinberg 3).[18]

The titles of two essay collections on Katrina, both published in 2006, are a case in point: *Unnatural Disaster:* The Nation *on Hurricane Katrina*, edited by Betsy Reed, and *There Is No Such Thing as a Natural Disaster*, edited by Chester Hartman and Gregory D. Squires. These two volumes were among the first of the countless critical articles, special issues, edited collections, and monographs that have been published since the 2005 events and that by and large confirm early scholarly predictions that Hurricane Katrina would become "one of the most studied disasters in U.S. history," if not in history *tout court* (Gill 613; see also Luft 501–502). Indeed, according to Luft, by 2009, no fewer than 18 academic journals had produced special issues on Katrina (see 501), and if the steady stream of scholarly writing on the disaster somewhat slowed down in subsequent years, the tenth anniversary of Katrina in 2015 occasioned a renewed academic interest in the event, as evidenced by such publications as Ron Eyerman's *Is This America?*, Bernie Cook's *Flood of Images*, Simon Dickel and Evangelia Kindinger's *After the Storm*, Mark Klinedinst's *Katrina: Ten Years After*, and Mary Ruth Marotte and Glenn Jellenik's *Ten Years after Katrina* (to which I myself have contributed a chapter; see Freitag, "Displacement"). It is not without justification (and a certain cynicism) that Clyde Woods has spoken of a veritable "research industry that arose around the Katrina tragedy" ("Les Misérables" 789).

Yet Reed's *Unnatural Disaster* and Hartman and Squires's *There Is No Such Thing as a Natural Disaster* also illustrate the fact that while generally agreeing on the unnaturalness of the events, critical analyses of Hurricane Katrina have nevertheless viewed the disaster from a large variety of competing perspectives and responded to, as Matthew B. Hackler writes, "sometimes drastically different visions of highly contested histories" (3). Indeed, the collections by Reed and by Hartman and Squires each represent one of the two most prominent discourses that eventually emerged from this "interpretive scrum" (Diamond 82); namely, neoliberalism and racism, respectively. In the introduction to their volume, for instance, Hartman and Squires quote from George W. Bush's famous speech, delivered on 15 September 2005 at Jackson Square against the backdrop of a floodlit St. Louis cathedral, in which he asserted that the poverty in the Gulf region "has its roots in racial discrimination, which cut off generations from the opportunity of America" (qtd. in Hartman and Squires 2). Asking what created the extreme disparities of the pre-Katrina world, they agree that amidst:

> plenty of racist behavior by individuals, incompetence by FEMA and other public and private bureaucracies, corruption on the part of government contractors and their partners in the public sector . . ., and other forms of malfeasance and misfeasance, by far the most potent force . . . is institutional racism.
>
> (5)

Similarly, Eric Mann, in *Katrina's Legacy: White Racism and Black Reconstruction in New Orleans and the Gulf Coast* (also published in 2006), identifies Hurricane Katrina as one among many "manifestations of the crisis of Black people in the U.S." and therefore seeks to "challenge the ideology of white supremacy that shapes national policy" (9). The volumes by Hartman and Squires, as well as Mann, were among the first to discuss Katrina in the context of racism and racial justice, and they were followed by many more, including the South End Press Collective's *What Lies Beneath: Katrina, Race, and the State of the Nation* and Hillary Potter's *Racing the Storm* (both 2007), Manning Marable and Kirsten Clarke's *Seeking Higher Ground: The Hurricane Katrina Crisis, Race, and the Public Policy Reader* (2008), Robert D. Bullard and Beverly Wright's *Race, Place, and Environmental Justice after Hurricane Katrina* (2009), and *Katrina's Imprint: Race and Vulnerability in America*, edited by Roland Anglin et al. (2010). Reviewing the critical writings on the disaster from the preceding five years in 2011, Cedric Johnson concluded that:

> [i]n the aftermath of Katrina, the racial justice frame quickly emerged as the default interpretation of this disaster in academic, journalistic, and activist circles and its centrality to public discourse shaped the kinds of responses that were crafted by progressive and liberal organizations. . . . This basic claim that racism either at the level of executive power or in the deep structures of society was the principal cause of this disaster was developed and advanced in dozens of articles, books, and conference presentations.
>
> (xxxiv)

Yet, as Andrew Diamond has rightly pointed out, the racial justice frame did not become hegemonic (82). In his introduction to Betsy Reed's *Unnatural Disaster*, for instance, Adolph Reed, Jr. argues that "those who insist on interpreting the differential impact of the storm and its aftermath in the language of racism . . . merely catalogue racially disparate outcomes, offering no larger analysis" (xvii), that the discourse of racism "clouds more than it clarifies" (xxix), and that therefore "racism is not an adequate conceptual frame for understanding the sources and dynamics reproducing the inequalities that appear most conspicuously along racial lines" (xv). According to Reed, the racial critique simply "cannot help expose or make sense of the deeper structures of neoliberal practice and ideology that underlie everything about the travesty in New Orleans, as well as the other devastated areas of the Gulf Coast" (xv). Similarly, Henry A. Giroux, in *Stormy Weather: Katrina and the Politics of Disposability* (also from 2006), has analyzed the events surrounding Katrina as:

> the consequence of a systemic, violent form of social engineering in which those populations in the United States marginalized by race and class are now considered disposable – that is, simply collateral damage in the construction of a neoliberal order.
>
> (11)

Already in 2006, then, scholars such as Reed and Giroux started to develop a different disaster discourse around Katrina, one that explicitly rejects institutional or structural racism and instead identifies neoliberal politics and practices as the main context for the hurricane and its aftermath. This line of argument has been further pursued in collections and volumes such as *The Neoliberal Deluge: Hurricane Katrina, Late Capitalism, and the Remaking of New Orleans* (2011) and *Markets of Sorrow, Labors of Faith: New Orleans in the Wake of Katrina* (2013). In the introduction to the former, editor Cedric Johnson asserts that the "contingent social and political disasters that are commonly attributed to Hurricane Katrina were rooted in the project of neoliberalization that has been transforming American life and culture over the past three decades" (xix). In the latter, author Vincanne Adams describes both the pre-history and the aftermath of Katrina as largely shaped by "what is often called *neoliberal capitalism*" (5; emphasis original). A particularly interesting take on the neoliberalism frame can be found in *Crisis Cities* (2014) by Kevin Fox Gotham and Miriam Greenberg, who compare post-9/11 and post-Katrina redevelopment efforts in New York City and New Orleans. Observing an "acceleration of a market-oriented mode of urban redevelopment . . . that became known as 'disaster capitalism'" (10) in both cities, they develop a historical, cyclical model according to which uneven, market-driven urban development generates and exacerbates socio-spatial inequalities and, hence, vulnerabilities and disasters, which, in turn, set the ground for redevelopment processes that reproduce rather than redress these vulnerabilities (see 14; 231).

Proponents of both disaster discourses on Hurricane Katrina – that of racism or racial injustice and that of neoliberalism – have often been in sharp disagreement, accusing each other of "marginalizing or depoliticizing race [by] focusing on the narrative of government failure" (South End Press Collective viii) or of failing to fully capture "the political forces at play in New Orleans" and to thus "pierce the cultural armament of late capitalism" (Johnson xxxvi), respectively. To be sure, several scholars have attempted to mediate between the two positions, with, for instance, Zeus Leonardo affirming the validity of both points of view: "The partnership between white supremacy and capitalism is best explained as a double jeopardy for many African Americans. Mobilizing and privileging one analysis over the other is like paying attention to one hand as the other hand wreaks havoc" (161). Others, such as Jordan T. Camp, Kristen L. Buras, and Clyde Woods, have emphasized "the neoliberal era's continuity with prior racial regimes" (Camp 702) instead: arguing that "neoliberalism was from the very beginning a project to achieve the restoration of *racial* power to the *white* strata of the population" (Buras 5; emphases original), these critics have traced how especially in New Orleans, the white local elite espoused a "racialized neoplantation/neoliberalism," effectively evolving into a "neoplantation" or "neo-Bourbon" bloc (Woods, "Les Misérables" 776). Through the eye of Katrina, Woods asserts, we see "the plantation oligarchy walking again in daylight" ("Katrina's World" 429).

According to Keith Wailoo, Karen M. O'Neill, and Jeffrey Dowd, it is this historical continuity, or, more precisely, the historical continuity in the impact of racism and neoliberalism on African Americans, that renders the racial discourse surrounding Katrina so powerful and resonant, particularly with African Americans themselves.[19] As Wailoo, O'Neill, and Dowd note in their introduction to *Katrina's Imprint* (2010), the experiences of black New Orleanians during and after Katrina:

> were traumatic precisely because they evoked, built on, and resonated with a troubling past for African Americans in the Gulf area and beyond. The lack of a feasible evacuation plan for poor residents of New Orleans ... reminds many of the past restrictions on African Americans' travel in the South. The visible evidence of abandoned houses ... recalls many historical moments when larger social forces displaced blacks from their homes. The diaspora of former residents of the Gulf Coast ... parallels the African diaspora of slavery.
>
> (2)

Likewise, Michael C. Dawson suggests "historical resonance[s]" as one reason why "Katrina became a strong presence in the political and artistic discourses of African Americans" (25). Even Cedric Johnson, otherwise a fierce advocate of the discourse of neoliberalism (see earlier), admits that the "racial justice argument ... still possesses a powerful symbolic resonance" (xxxvi).

Especially in local African Americans, Katrina may have evoked the experiences of black Louisianians during and after earlier storms and floods, including the Great Mississippi Flood of 1927, when at the instigation of a group of New Orleans bankers, an upstream levee was dynamited to save the city from destruction, which, however, resulted in the flooding of much of St. Bernard and Plaquemines Parishes (see Dyson, "Great Migrations?" 75). Interestingly, both proponents of the "racism/racial injustice" discourse such as Jeremy I. Levitt and Matthew C. Whitaker, as well as advocates of the "neoliberalism" discourse such as John R. Short, discuss this earlier disaster as a historical precedent that ultimately belies the historical exceptionality and uniqueness of Hurricane Katrina in both its causes and in its effects. For example, looking ahead to Katrina, Short ominously observes that this "would not be the last time that the [U.S. Army Corps of Engineers], dependent on Congressional approval and funding, aligned its policies and actions with powerful business interests" (86; see also Blakely 118). Levitt and Whitaker, in turn, note that much like almost 80 years later during Katrina, during the Great Mississippi flood, too, blacks "were displaced from their homes;

denied proper food and shelter; trapped in a dangerous disaster zone; accosted, abused, and detained unfairly by the authorities; and forced to work under dangerous circumstances for little or no pay" (13; see also Kish 672).

Beyond the rather limited context of floods and other devastations – Kish also mentions the Vanport Flood of 1948 in Oregon and Washington, as well as the Dust Bowl (see 672) – it was above all the restricted mobility and forced migration of African Americans during and after Hurricane Katrina that evoked an entire genealogy of black captivity and displacement, both in New Orleans and Louisiana, as well as elsewhere in the United States and beyond, belying the historical exceptionality of New Orleans. According to Mia Bay, for instance, the "failure of black mobility in the case of Katrina," which can be attributed to a lack of access to cars and other means of transportation, "underscores the continuing racial disparities in access to transportation across the nation" (30; see also Dyson, *Come Hell* 5–6). Several critics have reported that survivors compared the situation in the postdiluvian city and particularly in the Superdome to that on board of a slave ship (see, for example, Sublette 305; and Camp 696). The "ad-hoc evacuation" of Katrina victims to unfamiliar destinations and the "government-induced separation of family members during that process" (Peek and Weber 11), finally, evokes the troubling and traumatic history of the slave trade across the Atlantic and within the United States (see, for instance, Dickerson). It is precisely this genealogy of black displacement that Rosalyn Story condenses into the history of one particular (fictional) African-American Louisianian family in her 2010 novel *Wading Home: A Novel of New Orleans*.

Displacement and Dispossession in *Wading Home: A Novel of New Orleans*

One of the principal effects of Katrina, John Lowe notes in the introduction to *Louisiana Culture from the Colonial Era to Katrina* (2008), "has been the diaspora of coastal Americans away from the homeland they love" (3). In *Wading Home*, Rosalyn Story shows that both the threat of homelessness and actual displacement have been a ubiquitous experience of not just New Orleanians, but of Louisianians both after the hurricane and before, both in coastal areas and elsewhere. What all the cases of threatened and actual displacement depicted in the novel have in common is that they target African Americans. Combining the story of a former plantation in rural upper Louisiana with the story of pre- and post-Katrina New Orleans, *Wading Home* illustrates that phenomena as seemingly different and disconnected as nineteenth-century slavery and post-Civil War segregation, twentieth-century urban planning, twenty-first–century neoliberalism, and a "natural" disaster have had precisely the same impact on black Louisianians. Rather than causally differentiating between these various phenomena, and particularly between racism and neoliberalism, as some scholars have done, the novel highlights the continuity of their impact on the lives of Louisianian blacks across time and space, and thus explores the historical resonances of Hurricane Katrina.

Indeed, the main goal of Story's novel is to develop a disaster discourse for Hurricane Katrina that extends well beyond the geographical and temporal frames of the event and that meaningfully relates it to past and contemporary political, economic, social, and cultural structures. Moving from New Orleans to rural upper Louisiana and going precisely 150 years back in time, *Wading Home* conceptualizes Katrina as only the latest manifestation of what may be referred to as the "plantation regime"[20] and thus insists on the historicity and ubiquity of African Americans' struggle against captivity, displacement, and dispossession. The story of pre- and post-Katrina New Orleans illustrates the impact of this regime of white power on the modern Southern urban space, while the story of the former plantation takes readers back to the origins of the plantation regime in the antebellum Southern space and simultaneously depicts the threat of the regime's return to a place that, at one point in time, had managed to free itself from this racist legacy.

Yet Story's novel evokes racism and the plantation regime as a disaster discourse not only to explain the larger significance of Hurricane Katrina and to address questions of accountability, but also in the interest of preventability. Most importantly, in the context of the persistent threat of displacement of African Americans due to the plantation regime, *Wading Home* stresses the significance of remembrance and storytelling as strategies of resistance. Over the course of the novel, family stories about past displacements radically revise the main character's conception of "home," drawing his attention to the chronotopic dimension of the term, and make him aware of the need to pass these stories on to future generations. Indeed, it is stories such as these, and Rosalyn Story's, that may help to deal with, if not prevent, future "storms" – in New Orleans and elsewhere.

The Chronotopicity of Home

Wading Home mainly revolves around Julian Fortier, a 36-year-old African American who had left his hometown New Orleans for New York City in order to pursue an international career as a jazz trumpet player.[21] Julian returns to New Orleans immediately after Katrina in order to search for his father Simon, a 76-year old retired chef, who got lost during the hurricane. The novel lyrically traces Julian's evolving sense of rootedness and belonging, as during the nerve-wracking days and weeks he spends looking for Simon, he slowly reconnects with his family history; his ex-girlfriend Velmyra, an art teacher who had refused to leave for New York City with him; his music; and, most significantly, his home.

Previously, Julian had mainly regarded the stage as his home (Story, *Wading Home* 21) and New Orleans merely as "the place where he was born" and "where his father lived" (25) – but certainly not as the place where he could make the most of his musical talent: "as much as Julian loved the city, he was not about to wind up in a café in the French Quarter when he was 60, playing for scale and tips" (143). Simon, in turn, had considered Julian's lack of a "southern-boy homing instinct" as "more than heartbreaking" (84; see also 18).

Back in post-Katrina New Orleans, however, Julian starts to reflect upon what "home" means to him, slowly realizing that it constitutes a chronotopos: a place where time – in the shape of the past of family history, the present of one's identity, and the future into which the latter two must enter as memory – becomes, as Bakhtin notes, "palpable and visible" (250) and, hence, a place that provides a link between the generations. Julian now understands what Simon had tried to teach him all along; namely, that a true home "meant history, and history meant you knew who you were. It was the legend that helped decipher the map of your life" (Story, *Wading Home* 226). New York City may have offered Julian "a spot on the big stage" (34), yet it lacks these "ties of ancestral history" (226) and therefore does not qualify as a home. Consequently, it is the story of his father's, his ancestors', and his own rediscovered home that Julian starts rehearsing for his children at the end of the novel:

> He kissed his daughter's tiny head and, believing her days would be many, hoped that when the time came for him to tell her the story of the ones who came before, he would be able to remember all of it. He got up from the rocker as his girl-child lay her sleepy head on his shoulder, patted her back as her eyes closed. Let's see. *There was a Frenchman, and a beautiful African woman, with skin like midnight sky* . . . .
>
> (304; emphasis original)

While Julian, metaphorically homeless, slowly and painfully unearths his ties to his home, however, he – along with the reader – also hears the stories of a large number of African-American New Orleanians who *literally* lost their homes due to Katrina: for example, Simon's double shotgun in Tremé is rendered uninhabitable due to the flood (see Story, *Wading Home* 31). Casey, a trumpet player and Julian's best friend before he left New Orleans, got trapped in his apartment in the Seventh Ward and was "airlifted to safety by a National Guard helicopter" (35). Velmyra's family is scattered in Atlanta, Houston, and Baton Rouge (see 80). And Dereek, a young trombonist with whom Julian used to play in a band, tells how he watched from the helicopter's rescue basket as his house in the Lower Ninth Ward collapsed and floated away (see 225) – just like all the other members of the band lost their homes to flood water (see

222). Everyone, in fact, "knew someone who knew someone who'd lost a house" (62).

From its first page, *Wading Home* underlines that many of these houses had been in the hands of the same family for several generations: "Hand-built houses passed down through five generations floated away and fell apart" (1). Simon's Tremé place, for instance, had been built by Julian's grandfather "with his rock-hard hands seventy-eight years ago" (10). And Dereek's place had "lasted through four previous generations in his family" (225). More than just reflecting actual home ownership patterns in New Orleans,[22] this emphasis on continuity in home ownership over several generations suggests, particularly in the light of the novel's conceptualization of "home" as a chronotopos, that these buildings were actual *homes* to their owners and that their loss will have an enormous impact on people's future: "And the lives that survived were forever changed" (1).

Wading Home does not depict African-American homelessness solely in the context of post-Katrina New Orleans, however. As they learn more about Simon and the history of the Fortier family over the course of the novel, readers start to realize that African Americans have been threatened with displacement not only in New Orleans, but also elsewhere in Louisiana, and not only since Katrina, but ever since before the Civil War. Simon himself, for instance, has felt pressured to leave the Tremé neighborhood due to rising crime rates and poor city planning even before the storm (see Story, *Wading Home* 12–3). Simon's cousin Genevieve, in turn, is threatened with the loss of Silver Creek, a former plantation in rural upper Louisiana where she grew up together with Simon, due to the schemes of a land developer who has already acquired the land of some of Genevieve's black neighbors, most notably the Parettes (see 18–9; 104). In fact, ever since the plantation came into the hands of the Fortier family before the Civil War, the various Fortiers have had to fight to keep the land in the family (see 164; 176–7).

In the novel, then, Hurricane Katrina constitutes but one of several different instances in which black Louisianans are threatened with being displaced from their long-time homes. In an interview included in the press kit for *Wading Home*, Story tells about the genesis of the "Silver Creek" episode and explicitly identifies the loss of homes as the motif that links this episode with Katrina:

> The story of Silver Creek came from a series of articles written by a team of AP [Associated Press] writers titled "Torn from the Land," (2001) which detailed how for decades, blacks have been losing land in the rural South by the millions of acres through corporate greed, exploitative interpretation of existing land laws, and sometimes even through violence. . . . The situation in the Lower Ninth Ward of New Orleans after the flood just reinforced this for me, as there was talk of not allowing people to rebuild in those neighborhoods. All of

these situations tie in together, and amount to one thing: the tragedy of hard-working people losing the one thing they owned and could point to with pride.

(Story, "Q&A")

In *Wading Home* itself, the parallels between Katrina and the "Silver Creek" episode are first expressed through the metaphorical use of storm imagery right at the beginning of the novel. After telling about the approach of Hurricane Katrina, the narrator continues:

Upriver, though, where the winds were calmer, another storm formed under clear skies and bright sun and in the sleep-quiet darkness of night. It shaped in the clouded minds of men, gathered force with ambition, surged with greed and lust. But the uprooting of lives would be as heartbreaking as any hurricane.

(Story, *Wading Home* 1)

The storm metaphor continues to be used throughout the rest of the novel: the first signs of the land developer's attempt to get a hold of Silver Creek are described as a "storm warning" (271), and the previous attempts to dispossess the Fortier family of their land as "the blustery winds of a sometimes unkindly world" (182). Story takes up the widespread use, in criticism, of the terms "Katrina" and "storm" as shorthands for the hurricane itself and the human and technological disaster that preceded and followed it,[23] but extends this use even further in both space and time to include all instances in which black Louisianians have been threatened with displacement and dispossession.

Instead of framing the threat of losing one's home as an inevitable "natural" disaster, however, Story's extended storm metaphor embeds Katrina within the long history of the discrimination and displacement of Louisianian blacks, simultaneously de-naturalizing and racializing (or racing) the event. Indeed, although at one point the narrator speaks of hurricanes as "acts of God" (Story, *Wading Home* 242), the effects of Katrina on Tremé and on Simon's shotgun are also compared to those of World War II on Dresden: "In school, [Julian had] seen pictures of Dresden after the bomb blasts of World War II; it was the only thing he'd ever seen that was remotely similar. It couldn't have left any more destruction than this" (253). And while in the interview, Story merely speaks of "hard-working people" and in the novel some of the post-Katrina city planners who seem to consider the "close-knit black community" as "disposable"[24] are identified as having black ancestry (225–6), the divide between victims and profiteers of dispossession in *Wading Home* clearly runs along racial lines: the Fortiers and the Parettes are black, whereas the real estate developer and the planters and farmers who tried to evict Genevieve's and Simon's ancestors from Silver Creek are all white.

Hence, drawing parallels between and metaphorically linking Katrina and contemporary, as well as historical, moments when black Louisianians were displaced – or at least threatened to be displaced – from their homes by whites, Story's novel suggests that Katrina and its aftermath constitute but another illustration of the continued workings of institutionalized racism or the "plantation regime." The text shows how through antebellum slavery, post-Civil War vigilantism, and twentieth- and twenty-first–century neoliberal politics and practices, the plantation regime has dispossessed black people and regulated their mobility both before and after Katrina, and both in the Southern cityscape and in the regime's historical origin site, the rural South. In fact, Julian's evolving sense of home and rootedness in the novel stems precisely from his growing awareness of this history of dispossession and its racist context. Realizing that his ancestors have continuously been forced to defend their land and homes against whites and their racist practices, Julian understands that he and his progeny are bound to these places through the history of this fight:

> For years Julian thought Simon was imposing Silver Creek on him, the burden of a gift he didn't really want. But the gift really had been Julian's to give to his father – to steward his father's treasure, to be caretaker of what he would leave behind. His memories, his history, his home.
> (Story, *Wading Home* 179)

Katrina is thus simultaneously de-naturalized and racialized: far from being a unique event in an exceptional city, it constitutes one more in a long line of racist disasters.

In the following, I will take a closer look at the two homes of the Fortiers, the Tremé shotgun and Silver Creek, at the strategies the family has used to defend them, and at the ways in which Julian's growing awareness of the history of this fight informs his growing sense of home as a chronotopos over the course of the novel. In order to trace Julian's development as closely as possible, I will first discuss the Tremé home, where Julian grew up and where his search for the meaning of home starts, and then move on to Silver Creek, where Julian merely spent a few summers during his early childhood (see Story, *Wading Home* 84), but where he ultimately finds his way home. Learning about his family history, which spans experiences of dispossession and displacement through institutionalized racist practices from slavery to Katrina, Julian realizes that for black Louisianians, home transcends generations and continually needs to be defended.

Walking Through Tremé

When the mandatory evacuation order for New Orleans is issued on 28 August 2005, Simon decides to ignore it despite his friends' and his son's warnings: "he hadn't left for [Hurricane] Betsy [in 1965] and he wasn't leaving now" (Story, *Wading Home* 7). In contrast to many other poor, old, and black New Orleanians, Simon has several chances to leave the city before the storm – his son offers him a plane ticket to New York City (see 10) and his girlfriend Sylvia offers him a ride in her car (see 8), but he nevertheless chooses to "hold out": "he was a Fortier, and a Fortier did not leave his home to the whims of storms and thieves" (7). At this point in the novel, Simon's decision appears to be based mainly on an elderly man's stubbornness, tragic misperception of risk, and possibly exaggerated fear of vandals and looters. This decision assumes a quite different significance, however, in the light of the Fortiers' long struggle to hold on to their homes and the novel's metaphorical use of the term "storm." As readers learn later, the Fortiers indeed could not leave their homes to "storms" of any kind, lest they should lose them forever. Julian, however, has not yet learned about the family history at this point and considers Simon's behavior as merely "beyond foolhardy" (25). Whereas Julian thinks Simon does not comprehend what is at stake, precisely the opposite is true. Not yet having heard of the family history of threatened dispossession and, hence, not yet being aware of what it would mean to a Fortier to leave his home in a storm, Julian is simply unable to fully understand the reasons behind Simon's decision to "hold out." In contrast to Simon, he has not yet realized the ubiquity and pervasiveness of structural racism and the plantation regime, which may lurk behind everything – including a "natural" disaster.

The reader, by contrast, is already given a first glimpse of what motivates Simon's seemingly foolhardy and stubborn behavior. Not only is Simon attached to his Tremé home through the memory of his father and his deceased wife Ladeena: "Abandon the house built with his father's own sweat and muscle, the place where he's spent forty years with Ladeena . . . ? It's complicated" (11). More importantly, describing Simon's daily routine since his retirement and before the storm, which includes a walk through the neighborhood along "the five-block circle to Field's Grocery and around the school yard and the Mount Zion Baptist Church" (13), the narrator also shares that Simon has felt pressured to abandon his home even before the approach of the hurricane:

> Friends chided him for daring to walk in a neighborhood that, though once safe, now had been all but taken over by young boys with a loathsome skulk in their walk and hooded, futureless eyes. . . . And that wasn't the only way the neighborhood had changed; the tight-knit black community, so rich in history, had been broken in two by the wrecking ball. It had been almost forty years, but he still longed for the old days when the neighborhood was whole, before they'd built the awful freeway that sliced through his beloved Treme like a surgeon's amputating knife. Before the shade of the majestic

live oaks, perfect for parade watching, gave way to the shadows of a concrete overpass.

(13)

To be sure, there is nobody who has literally forced Simon to sell his home and leave the neighborhood. Yet the city officials' negligence of and indifference toward Tremé, which becomes evident in poor urban planning, notably the construction of the elevated Interstate 10 above Claiborne Avenue in the late 1960s, and in the failure to address rising poverty and crime rates, have created social conditions in which Simon feels pressured to at least regulate his mobility and suspend his daily walks, if not to relocate altogether. Simon ignores his friends' warnings to no longer take his daily walks and refuses to give up his neighborhood, however, just as he will later ignore the mandatory evacuation order and Julian's advice to leave the city and refuse to "leave his home to the whims of storms and thieves":

> Simon walked anyway, head high, defiant, never mind the freeway shadows and the glaze-eyed boys. He used the cane to steady his feet, but if need be, he could swing it like a cutlass. This was *his* neighborhood. He reclaimed it with each stubborn tap of his cane, and nobody – not street thugs nor the thieving city planners – was going to take it away.
>
> (13; emphasis original)

Similar to his decision to "hold out" after the mandatory evacuation order has been issued, Simon's daily walks through Tremé before the storm have to be seen as a way of "reclaim[ing]" his space and defending his home against the plantation regime, here in the shape of the neoliberal practices of city officials and authorities.

Indeed, Simon's walks are singularly reminiscent of Michel de Certeau's strategy of re-claiming the urban space through walking in the city, a strategy de Certeau discusses in his essay "Walking in the City," originally published as a chapter of *The Practice of Everyday Life* (1984). In the context of Simon's walks through Tremé, the elevated Interstate 10 corresponds to the 110th floor of the World Trade Center, with which "Walking in the City" opens, in that it provides a panoramic perspective from which one can distance onself from the city. As de Certeau argues, the "panorama-city" (93) allows one to "be a solar Eye, looking down like a God," and perhaps most importantly, to make "the complexity of the city readable" (92). The text created by the bird's eye's perspective of the city, from the World Trade Center as from the freeway is, however, according to de Certeau, a "projection that is a way of keeping aloof, by the planner urbanist, city planner or cartographer" (92–3). By contrast, rather than opening the city to specific reading strategies, the practice of walking in the city, not from an elevated point of view but down below in the streets, writes the city. The urban flaneur's footsteps, de Certeau writes, "give their shape to spaces. They weave places together" (97).

Simon's walks through the neighborhood thus have to be seen as a spatial urban practice – indeed, a performance – that squarely contradicts and defies the planned vision of the city, a vision that has been made possible by the construction of and the panorama perspective available from the elevated freeway. Whereas the freeway continues to "slice . . . through . . . Treme like a surgeon's amputating knife" (Story, *Wading Home* 13), Simon, with each daily walk, "weaves" the neighborhood back together, giving it its former shape once more. As a flaneur who walks where he should not walk, Simon again and again subverts and defies the pre-Katrina planned vision of Tremé and undermines the plantation regime by recreating "his" neighborhood and making it "whole" again through the act of walking.

Likewise, after having gotten trapped in his attic by the rising flood and having been airlifted to the Convention Center, Simon "sweet-talk[s] an emergency vehicle driver . . . to give him a ride to the highway" (262) and starts walking the approximately 100 miles to Silver Creek, where years before he had told Julian he would be in case of an emergency (see 66–7). Again, faced with conditions that seek to regulate his mobility – here, the authorities' failure to provide adequate transportation out of the city immediately following the flood – Simon simply walks. Just as Simon's decision to "hold out" during the hurricane and his walking through the dangerous Tremé neighborhood, his walking away from the relative safety of the Convention Center could be attributed to mere foolhardiness and poor risk judgment (indeed, on his way to Silver Creek, Simon quickly loses consciousness and gets hospitalized; see 262–3). Again, however, it has to be seen as a way of undermining the plantation regime, which restricted and controlled post-Katrina black mobility in New Orleans without providing viable alternatives. While he may endanger his health and even his life, Simon's walking asserts his control over his own mobility – and thus, his citizenship and freedom.

Exploring Family History in Silver Creek

Julian, in the meantime, is unaware of all this as he still tries to locate Simon, hindered as he is by the inadequate and insufficient information policy, as well as by the generally catastrophic response by the authorities to the Katrina disaster. He has, however, learned of another case of threatened dispossession in the Fortier family; namely, of the fact that Silver Creek has been sold: "The Fortier land – gone. Two hundred and some acres of the most beautiful and fertile land in Louisiana, in his father's family since before the Civil War, handed off to strangers" (Story, *Wading Home* 103). At this point in *Wading Home*, Julian's relationship to his father's childhood home is ambiguous at best: he simply cannot "understand his father's obsession" with what he considers "a stretch of flat, lifeless land" (84). Tellingly, when Julian thinks about driving to Silver Creek after Katrina because he hopes to find his father there, he has to ask for the way (see 68; and 105). Hence, when Julian learns that Silver Creek has apparently been sold, he is upset mainly because he knows how much the land means to his father, not because he himself cares about the place (see 103).

Like his reaction to Simon's decision to "hold out" when the hurricane approaches New Orleans, Julian's indifference toward Silver Creek can be attributed to the fact that he is unaware of the history of threatened displacement connected with the land. Returning to Silver Creek to find his father, he notices the beauty of the landscape (see 100), and he also remembers his father's stories about the history of the place:

> It was when Julian was about eleven that the stories began about the Silver Creek land. . . . Simon told Julian how his grandfather Moses, a freed slave turned sharecropper, had inherited the land from his former master and mulched it with sweat and blood. It had first been left to Jacob, Simon's father, and Jacob's first cousin, Maree, and then, upon their deaths, to the next generation of Fortiers – Maree's daughter Genevieve and Simon.
>
> (82–3)

The memory of these stories, which focus exclusively on the continuity of ownership, merely evoke and reinforce in Julian the idea that this is his father's home, however. The stories do not manage to convince Julian that in a chronotopic sense, this is his home, too, and that he must defend it for his own sake.

This radically changes when Genevieve tells Julian the entire history of the place.[25] Genevieve essentially repeats Simon's story; she adds, however, two crucial details which establish Silver Creek as a space that managed to purge itself of institutionalized racism and the plantation regime and, simultaneously, as a space that time and again has been threatened by racist practices. It is these details about the history of Silver Creek that help Julian grasp the significance of the recent sale of the land, reconsider his relationship to the former plantation, and start fighting for the place.

First, Julian learns that his great-grandfather Moses was not just a former slave of Jean Michel, the original owner of Silver Creek, but also the latter's second son: after the death of his first wife, Jean Michel had secretly married Claudinette, one of his slaves, who soon gave birth to Moses and who had agreed to the marriage in return for the freedom of all of her children (see Story, *Wading Home* 162). When Moses's white half-brother from Jean Michel's first marriage runs away due to a local brawl, Jean Michel decides to leave the entire estate to Moses (see 167). Genevieve's revelation inscribes *Wading Home* into the tradition of what George B. Handley has identified as "postslavery literature." According to Handley, postslavery fictions focus on genealogy and family history in order to move "away from a fixation on the more formal manifestations of slavery and into the more complex social relations before and after its legal abolition" (3). One central thematic and structural element of postslavery fictions is, Handley notes, genealogy: "by following biological links across races, sexes, and generations, family history exposes the genealogical ideologies that have concealed evidence of sexual contact across racial and class lines in order to protect a white elite patrimony" (3).

Tracing the history of Silver Creek, *Wading Home* exposes evidence of sexual contact across racial lines and even locates this evidence on the map of the estate: Genevieve leads Julian to Claudinette's cabin. Claudinette, Genevieve explains,

> insisted her lover Jean Michel build her a place where they could meet on equal terms, a place of her own that was neither slave quarters – reminding her of her station – nor plantation house, reminding her of his.
>
> (Story, *Wading Home* 175)[26]

The fact that Claudinette's cabin is the only building left from the antebellum days, while both the slave quarters and the main cottage have disappeared, functions as a signifier of the end of the plantation regime. There is literally no place for the plantation regime on this plantation. Silver Creek can serve as a place of identification and a home for Simon and the entire family precisely because ever since "Simon's great-grandfather, the Frenchman, had bequeathed it to his black son Moses" (18), it has no longer been haunted by this system of white power. Rather than as the historical epicenter of white racism, its regulations of black mobility, and its tradition of exploiting and dispossessing black people, *Wading Home* conceptualizes Silver Creek as a plantation that even before the formal demise of slavery, expelled the racist ideology it had helped to create.

On the one hand, this helps to explain Simon's unrestrained praise for and his idealized notion of Silver Creek – he refers to it as "a piece of paradise" (3) and "a perfect piece of land" (8) – which echoes, along with the threat of dispossession, the simultaneously idyllic and elegiac tone of other "plantation fictions" (see Grammer). Yet what makes Silver Creek a paradise is not only the beauty of the landscape, but its freedom from the plantation regime. On the other hand, it also becomes perfectly understandable that after the storm, Simon wants to leave New Orleans to go to Silver Creek. Escaping the city where the plantation regime threatens to regulate his mobility and to dispossess him, he seeks a place where he knows this white power system does not rule and cannot reach him.

Julian, in turn, learns that he needs to preserve this "paradise" not only because it constitutes a legacy of a past without the plantation regime, but simultaneously because it offers a key to a future without structural racism. For Genevieve not only tells him how Silver Creek came into the hands of the Fortiers, she also relates how the plantation regime has, time and again, threatened to force its way back onto the plantation. Jean Michel, for instance, had initially refused to give the land to Moses out of fear of people's reaction to this violation of the regime:

> John Michel had witnessed the heedless pride, the erect walk and upturned head of his son. Black skin, a straight spine, an unbowed head and eyes that looked straight on at white men – all were an open invitation to trouble. Make him a landowner too? John Michel shook his head.
>
> (Story, *Wading Home* 164)

Moses nevertheless obtains and manages to hold on to the place; yet his son Jacob faces the very threats that his grandfather had predicted:

> After John Michel died . . ., white men had simply seen Moses as a black man stewarding his dead white master's land, and pretty much let him be. Not so with Jacob. He was a black man tending his own land, the best land in the parish, and he was living well. That had been his crime. . . . And it was not long afterward the fires started: first the barn, then the shed. They weren't accidents, [Genevieve] believed, but acts of spite.
>
> (176–7)

Using "every trick they could think of" (168), but most conspicuously the barn fire, the white farmers and planters threatened to displace Jacob from his home. The fire – a seemingly natural but actually a man-made disaster – subtly connects this episode to New Orleans and Katrina, establishing parallels between turn-of-the-century rural and twenty-first–century urban Louisiana. Most importantly, however, it helps Julian grasp the significance of the recent sale of the land. Indeed, after having heard Genevieve's story, Julian recognizes that this sale constitutes only the latest manifestation of the plantation regime, although rather than resorting to physical violence and property damage in order to dispossess his family, those who try to displace the Fortiers now employ neoliberal logic and legal tricks.[27] Simultaneously, Genevieve's story helps Julian come, in her words, "all the way home" (159); that is, realize that Silver Creek is also his home and that like his ancestors did, he needs to defend it against the plantation regime: "A few years ago, none of this would have mattered to him. But everything was different now" (210).

The solution to the Silver Creek episode – an olographic will by Jacob,[28] discovered in the family Bible that had almost gotten lost in the aftermath of the flood – again defies the plantation regime by using its very own strategies against it. In the case of the Tremé home, Simon literally reclaims his space by countering the regime's spatial practices of displacing African Americans – through the construction of the elevated freeway and the general neglect of the neighborhood – with the spatial practice of walking. The family Bible, which contains the names and dates of birth of the various Fortiers, as well as Jacob's will, re-claims the family's space by rectifying the regime's exclusionary genealogical practices that had almost prevented Moses from owning the estate in the first place and that were later used to justify attempts at dispossessing Jacob. At the same time, the Bible constitutes a legal document that ultimately helps to defy the plantation regime's attempt to use legal loopholes in order to dispossess African Americans: "An 'olographic' will . . . was as good as any in a Louisiana court of law. [The real estate developer] protested mightily, pouring money and energy into getting the decision overturned, but to no avail" (Story, *Wading Home* 288).

Wading Home does not end with this will, the court scene, or the renovation of Simon's Tremé shotgun, however, but with Julian beginning to rehearse the story of Silver Creek for the day when he will tell it to his children (see Story, *Wading Home* 304). Not only has this story awakened Julian's sense of home in connection with New Orleans and especially with Silver Creek, its written fixation in the family Bible has also assured the Fortiers' continued ownership of Silver Creek during the latest of the plantation regime's repeated attempts at displacement and dispossession. Julian's rehearsing this story, then, bespeaks his intention to both instill a "homing instinct" in his children and prepare them for future attacks of the plantation regime, in the shape of literal or metaphorical storms. For, as his reflections on the cyclicity of time at the end of the novel indicate – "endings become beginnings" (304) – he may sense that the storm is not over.

Art and the Future of the City in *Wading Home: An Opera of New Orleans*

In March 2013, about two and a half years after Rosalyn Story's *Wading Home: A Novel of New Orleans* had been published, Dallas-based violin teacher and composer Mary Alice Rich came up with the idea of adapting the novel into an opera. A long-time friend of Story (the two had first met in 1981 when they both played the violin in the Tulsa Philharmonic), Rich had undergone treatment for cancer shortly before, which made her realize that if she wanted to embark on as ambitious a project as writing her first opera, she "had better get started."[29] In a blog post for her publisher, Story has admitted that while to her,

> the story of post-Katrina New Orleans seemed perfect fodder for a novel, a theater piece with classically trained singers, an orchestra

and a children's chorus, performed on an opera stage before an audience, was the furthest thing from my mind.

(Story, "Wading Home")

Rich, however, not only felt that Story's writing was "so lyrical ... it would lend itself to opera" (Rich qtd. in Weeks), she also convinced Story that the novel "had all the requisite drama, intrigue, and musical possibilities of an opera, with all the attendant elements: heroes, adversaries, obstacles, and a life-changing journey fraught with moments of tragedy and triumph" (Story, "Wading Home"). Eventually, Story granted Rich permission to adapt the novel and, starting in August 2013, also joined Rich to collaborate on the libretto. Together with Story and with feedback from her composition coach Winston Stone, a jazz musician and clinical professor at UT Dallas's School of Arts and Humanities, Rich completed the libretto and the piano vocal score of the proposed opera in February 2014 and began orchestrating the work for full chamber orchestra. By the end of summer, the score and the libretto were mainly finished, although both were extensively revised between August 2014 and the premiere performance of *Wading Home: An Opera of New Orleans* in April 2015.[30]

As an opera with an original English-language libretto, an opera about jazz musicians and including jazz elements in the score, as an opera featuring an almost exclusively African-American cast of characters in lead singing roles and dealing with racial issues, and as an opera inspired by Hurricane Katrina, *Wading Home* can look back on long and sometimes surprisingly rich traditions in the more than four-century-old history of opera.[31] Rather than situate the work within these traditions, however, the following reading of Rich and Story's opera will primarily discuss *Wading Home* as an adaptation of Story's eponymous novel to see how it elaborates upon the Katrina disaster discourse developed in the text. Moreover, as a consequence of my training in literary and cultural studies rather than in musicology,[32] I will mainly focus on one of the two "dramatic texts" (Hutcheon and Hutcheon, *Art of Dying* 14) that constitute opera – namely, the libretto (the other one being the score). Tracing the development from fiction to libretto, then, this section will illustrate the contribution of literary and cultural studies to the transdisciplinary venture of opera studies.

As an adaptation of *Wading Home* (the novel), *Wading Home* (the opera) is first and foremost notable for its extreme condensation: indeed, the libretto contains much fewer plot lines, characters, and scenes than the novel. While, as will be shown, these changes can be explained as reflecting the characteristic medial requirements of opera, others indicate a substantial reworking of the very contents of the novel during the process of adaptation: although much like *Wading Home* (the novel), *Wading Home* (the opera) seeks to expose the role of the plantation regime in the continued displacement of African-American Louisianians, Rich and Story's libretto insists, much more so than Story's novel does, on the role of the arts in the rebuilding of New Orleans and thus in the prevention of future "storms."

Reading Opera

As a "hybrid," "composite," or "meta-medium" – that is, as an art form that encompasses and integrates various media conventionally viewed as distinct, in this case music, poetry, drama, visual art, and sometimes dance (see Rajewsky 203; Wolf 253; Geppert 3) – opera "cries out," as Linda and Michael Hutcheon have stated (*Desire, Disease, Death* 5), for transdisciplinary approaches that engage at the very least musicology, literary and cultural studies, and theater and performance studies (see, for instance, Imhof and Grutschus 11). Until the 1970s, however, opera criticism was clearly dominated by musicologist perspectives (see Balme 19; Balestrini 23), a fact that can be attributed to the long and widely assumed centrality of music to opera's complex fusion of art forms and semiotic systems. Even as late as 1988, and in the introduction to an edited collection that sought to problematize the assumed centrality of music to opera and to redress the resulting disciplinary imbalance in opera studies, Arthur Groos still affirmed the "primacy of music" and intimated that he "would scarcely be interested in opera were it not for the music" (1).

Leaving aside for the moment issues concerning the actual performance of opera, which will be taken up again in the following section of "*Wading Home*'s Post-Katrina New Orleans," the scholarly privileging of music or the score in opera criticism has come primarily at the expense of the libretto, long disparaged as the sub-literary and uninteresting "little book" that its very name implies it is (see Hutcheon and Hutcheon, *Desire, Disease, Death* 6). This is all the more ironic since, as Linda and Michael Hutcheon have pointed out elsewhere, it was "to allow the words to be heard" that the art form known today as opera was developed in late sixteenth-century Florence in the first place ("Jazz" 24). Following Patrick J. Smith's *The Tenth Muse: A Historical Study of the Opera Libretto* (1970), however, numerous literary critics, including Gary Schmidgall, Catherine Clément, some of the contributors to *Reading Opera* (1988; ed. Groos and Parker) and *Opera through Other Eyes* (1994; ed. Levin), Linda and Michael Hutcheon, Albert Gier, and Nassim Balestrini, have sought to reposition the libretto as a by no means autonomous, but nevertheless integral and equal part of opera:

> In opera the libretto's actual words are clearly as important as the music, especially today with the use of surtitles. The story they tell

> is enacted and embodied on stage, even as the music provides additional meaning and impact through its connotative and expressive powers.
>
> (Hutcheon and Hutcheon, *Bodily Charm* 27)

Scholars have suggested a large variety of critical approaches to opera libretti from the distinctive perspective of literary studies: Linda and Michael Hutcheon, for instance, argue that as a "theatrical script designed to be set to music," the opera libretto "should be read for its combination of words, dramatic narrative (plot, characters), and stage directions and other mise-en-scène instructions" (*Desire, Disease, Death* 7). Similarly, according to Arthur Groos, libretti may be read as verbal artifacts, as "texts for musical realization," but also as adaptations of literary works (10). While not applicable to all libretti, the latter aspect has also been stressed by Balestrini, who considers adaptations into libretti as part of the reception history of literary works (15–6). Most of these suggestions will be taken up in the following, although I will focus on how the libretto of *Wading Home: An Opera of New Orleans* adapted and re-accentuated the specific disaster discourse of Hurricane Katrina developed in *Wading Home: A Novel of New Orleans*.

From Fiction to Libretto

In *Literature as Opera* (1977), Gary Schmidgall stresses the "large number of operas, some of them among the greatest in the repertory, that are based upon literary masterpieces" (23). In her *From Fiction to Libretto* (2005), Balestrini counts more than 250 operas that have been adapted from nineteenth-century American fiction alone, including "narratives that have been regarded as classics and more recently rediscovered texts" (5; see also 1). And in "Adaptation and Opera" (2017), Linda and Michael Hutcheon call opera "the Ur-adaptive art" (305). However, Schmidgall, Balestrini, and Hutcheon and Hutcheon also point to some of the implicit "rules" underlying virtually any translation from fiction to libretto, rules that directly result from the practical prerequisites of the libretto as a performance script. First and foremost among these is the need to condense and compress:

> The available performance time and its management in opera affect the process of adapting a literary source into a workably structured libretto. The librettist-adapter usually reduces a much longer text to a rather brief libretto, as singing consumes more time than speaking the same lines.
>
> (Balestrini 34; see also Schmidgall 19; Hutcheon and Hutcheon, "Adaptation" 309)

Hence, plots are generally simplified and stripped of sub-plots, characters are reduced in number and arranged "in easily understandable constellations," and scenes are cut or combined (Balestrini 34; see also Hutcheon and Hutcheon, *Desire, Disease, Death* 8).

This also applies to the adaptation of *Wading Home*. As they have both stated in my conversations with them, Rich and Story were very well aware of the need to trim and pare down, and at some point Rich decided "to take out the entire story line centered around Matthew Parmenter's character." In the novel, Julian believes that Parmenter, a famous New Orleans restaurant owner and Simon's former employer, has cheated Simon out of a home in the more expensive, but safe Garden District neighborhood by selling the Fortier family recipe for red beans and rice to grocery store chains (see Story, *Wading Home* 40). The conflict is eventually solved when after his death Parmenter bequeaths his own Garden District mansion to Simon (233). With the omission of the Parmenter plotline in the libretto, however, the story not only loses several colorful and distinctly New Orleanian characters – including Parmenter himself ("a cross between a tall Santa Claus and an avuncular Confederate general," 50), his deceased wife Clarisse (a "real New Orleans socialite," 52), and their attorney Cedric Cole (an attractive, affable African American in his late forties; see 189) – but the number of solo singing roles is brought down to seven: Simon (baritone), Julian (baritone), Velmyra (soprano), Sylvia (mezzo soprano), Casey (baritone), Simon's unnamed Latina nurse at the hospital (mezzo soprano), and Kevin (tenor), the real estate developer's grandson and the only white character in the opera.

Perhaps even more importantly, due to the cut of the Parmenter plotline, Rich and Story were also forced to omit the memorable and, once again, typically New Orleanian scene of Parmenter's jazz funeral, in which Julian, leading the band into a rendition of "Just a Closer Walk with Thee," after his long injury finally "felt it, somewhere in the middle of all that sound. He was a player again. He was back" (Story, *Wading Home* 229). In order to fill the emerging plot hole and to make up for the loss of local color, which particularly Story sorely regretted, the two librettists first moved Julian's "comeback" to a different scene of the novel that was, however, kept in the libretto – namely, Julian's impromptu playing session with Casey. The stage directions for this scene clearly indicate its significance in the story: "As [Julian and Casey] play together, [Julian] gains confidence. Then, Julian confidently cues the new upbeat tempo. When they finish, stage audience applauds and Julian truly smiles for the first time in the opera" (Rich and Story 24 [II,3]).[33] Moreover, Rich integrated the famous gospel song played by Julian during the funeral into the score of the opera, with "Just a Closer Walk with Thee" both serving as the "theme" of the flooding and the destruction of New Orleans (see 3 [I,1] and 26 [II,4]), and, in an "upbeat 'second line' version . . . played by the brass band & percussion," as the music for bowing (see 40–1 [following II,8]).

Another one of the "rules" governing the transfer from fiction to libretto is concerned with what may be referred to as dramatic pacing. Rich and Story's libretto comprises two acts of almost equal length (each takes up about 20 pages in the typed version of the libretto and contains a little more than 400 lines of text to be sung or spoken), which are subdivided into nine and eight scenes, respectively. Like the first chapter of the novel, Act I opens with a scene set in Simon Fortier's double shotgun in Tremé in late August 2005, thus introducing the "Hurricane Katrina" plotline (Rich and Story 1–3 [I,1]). By contrast, the dramatic end of Act I is marked by the news of the sale of Silver Creek (20 [I,9]), which is revealed much earlier in the novel (namely, at the end of Chapter 9, roughly a third into the text). The first scene of Act II returns to the topic of Hurricane Katrina, with Simon awakening from a coma in a "[d]arkened hospital room" (20 [II,1]) after he had tried to escape the flooded city to get to Silver Creek, whereas readers of Story's novel are long kept in ignorance of Simon's fate after the storm and do not learn about his precise whereabouts until almost at the end, in Chapter 21. In the last scene of Act II, which revolves around the discovery of the olographic will that restores the Silver Creek property to the Fortier family (38–9 [II,8]), however, the libretto once again joins the narrative order and structure of the novel, where the will is retrospectively discussed in the epilogue, set two years after the events of the main story (see Story, *Wading Home* 287–8). Hence, the libretto starts and ends much like its source text, although between, Rich and Story have moved the major peripeteic events of the plot – i.e., the sale of Silver Creek and Simon's rescue – to strategically important positions in the dramatic structure (namely, the end of Act I and the beginning of Act II), which leads to a dramatic increase of suspense right before the intermission, a veritable cliff-hanger.

Simultaneously, this partial reordering of plot elements establishes a certain formal symmetry and balance with respect to *Wading Home*'s two central plotlines, which focus on the Fortier family's two homes: the beginnings of both Act I and II are concerned with Simon and, by implication, with the Tremé double shotgun and the forced migration of African Americans in New Orleans during and after Hurricane Katrina, whereas the ending of each act revolves around Silver Creek and the displacement and dispossession of black Southerners in rural Louisiana both before and after the storm. This formal symmetry dramatically supports the libretto's principal message: much like the novel, the opera depicts Hurricane Katrina as but another instance in which black Louisianians are forced to leave their long-time homes, thus establishing a parallel between the impact of events commonly categorized as "natural disasters" and that of neoliberal practices specifically targeting African

Americans. In the opera, too, Simon knows that he must not leave his home unless he should lose it forever: "Everybody sayin, 'Get out now!['] But/I am stayin! That's my vow! (Raises and shakes his fist)" (Rich and Story 2 [I,1]).

Wading Home's disaster discourse on Hurricane Katrina is reflected not only in the libretto's structure, however, but also in its language. Rich stated in one of my conversations with her that she merely "got the rough draft [of the libretto] started" but that eventually Story "came in to give it sophistication, more fully bringing forth her poetic voice." Story herself has maintained that adjusting the language, she focused primarily on issues related to "black southern colloquial speech . . . as well as the 'slang-u[s]age' of black jazz musicians," but clearly also some of the novel's more general lyricism and layered use of language found its way into the libretto, either through Rich's original draft or via Story's revisions. For example, as in the novel, in the libretto, too, the metaphorical use of the word "storm" simultaneously de-naturalizes Katrina and points to an entire history of instances in which the Fortiers have been threatened with being displaced from their homes. Over the course of the first scene, "It's just another storm" (1 [I,1]), the deceptively simple line sung by Simon with which the opera begins, comes to refer to "all kinds of storms," to the personal blows experienced by Simon and his deceased wife Ladeena ("Remember our son's fragile start? When he was born with a tiny hole/in his heart"), but also and more importantly, to Julian's and Simon's "ancestors'/history of strife": "Those Fortiers/ . . . fought for/our land, too!" (2 [I,1]). Reiterated by Simon no fewer than seven times in this scene (and, at one point, repeated three times in succession; see 2 [I,1]), "It's just another storm" may thus, much like Simon's cooking, at first appear to merely reflect the elderly man's increasing need to "calm [his] fears" before the storm (1 [I,1]). However, what the line ultimately reveals is that Simon knows exactly what is at stake: Hurricane Katrina is indeed "another storm," that is, yet another serious threat to the Fortiers' ownership of their homes.

Finally, the link between Hurricane Katrina and other "storms" is confirmed through the use of the chorus. Representing "the Fortiers of all the years" invoked by Simon shortly before (2 [I,1]), the chorus appears for the first time toward the end of the opening scene of Act I. Just as Simon starts to repeat "It's just another storm" one more time, the stage directions ask for the light on Simon "to dim to nothing. Lighting changes to represent darkness with lightning flashes" (3 [I,1]), thus indicating, on the one hand, the moment the hurricane hits the city and, on the other hand, the return of the ancestors from the past. "How? Who? Why?" the chorus wonders in both English and Zulu and asks for help (3[I,1]), which already suggests that the storm and the subsequent flooding of the city constitute an attack on the Fortiers that can be compared to the as yet unspecified past "storms" endured by the family. The chorus of the ancestors reappears in the last scene of Act I, which is set on Silver Creek and during which Julian explains to Velmyra how the former plantation came into the hands of the Fortiers (16–9 [I,9]), and then again in the fourth scene of Act II, when Julian and Velmyra visit the destroyed Lower Ninth Ward.[34] Hence, the ancestors are alternately evoked in the context of Silver Creek (the Fortier home they had actually defended in the past) and in the context of New Orleans (the other Fortier home that Simon is fighting for in the present), which ultimately implies that past and present fights against displacement in both New Orleans and elsewhere – and thus the impacts of past metaphorical storms and present actual storms on black Louisianians – are really one and the same.

From Past Storms to the Future of the City

It is primarily through the use of the chorus of the ancestors, then, that *Wading Home* explores the historical dimension of African-American displacement and dispossession in both rural and urban Louisiana. The novel, of course, employs extensive flashbacks to tell readers about the Fortier family's past fights for the land against the plantation regime, including both the fight of Moses, Jacob, and Genevieve against the white farmers, planters, and real estate developers who tried to evict them from Silver Creek (see Story, *Wading Home* 161–8; and 171–80), and Simon's fight for his Tremé home against the urban planners, city officials, and authorities who have considered the neighborhood community as disposable (12–3). The libretto, by contrast, does not reveal too many details about these struggles, neither through the chorus's lines ("We fought and died," 26 [II,4]) nor through its actions on the stage ("The entire ancestor chorus, . . . in white dressing gowns, enters the actual stage. They walk in from opposite directions holding candles, and meet in the center, led by Claudinette and Jean Michel," 16 [I,9]). Even more importantly, while the novel spends considerable time delineating the antebellum world of French rural Louisiana, a world in which love across racial lines eventually triumphs over institutionalized racism to create a space free from the plantation regime, the libretto devotes but four lines to "the old Frenchman, my/great-great grandfather Jean/Michel, [lying] next to the midnight-/skinned beauty he loved so well" (17 [I,9]). Already but evoked in a flashback in Story's novel, the topic of the Frenchness of Louisiana and New Orleans becomes even less prominent in Rich and Story's libretto. Neither are French New Orleans and Louisiana "pastified" here, nor are New Orleans and Louisiana's past "Frenchified," Frenchness simply does not play much of a role anymore.

Rather than to (also) reveal the details of the Fortiers' past and their struggles to hold on to their homes, the presence of the ancestors on the stage mainly serves to remind the audience and the characters, especially Julian, of the mere fact that African-American displacement has by no means been a recent phenomenon in Louisiana and that therefore "home," for black Louisianians, represents a chronotopos. For example, toward the end of Act I, the ancestors directly address Julian to tell him about Silver Creek:

> This is your land, right where you
> Stand. From man to man, down to
> You. This is your right, all in
> Your sight. For this you fight.
> It's up to you. This is your
> Family, and your legacy. Please
> Promise me you'll take care of it
> All.
> (18 [I,9])

"Home" not only constitutes a legacy from the past, however, but also and simultaneously an obligation toward the future. To emphasize the role of the future in the chronotopicity of home, *Wading Home* employs yet another chorus; namely, the chorus of the children of the city, which joins the chorus of the ancestors whenever the latter appears in the New Orleans scenes of the opera. At the end of the first scene of Act I, for instance, right after the hurricane has hit the city and the chorus of the ancestors has entered the stage to plead for help, the lightning flashes are replaced by projected images of "a raging hurricane, trees bending, water slashing, [and] actual footage of Hurricane Katrina" and the children's chorus starts singing "Just a Closer Walk with Thee" to mourn the death of the city and the lost lives of its inhabitants (3 [I,1]). This scene perfectly illustrates *Wading Home*'s conceptualization of "home" as a chronotopos: rather than repeating "It's just another storm," his signature line from the opening scene, yet again in its entirety, Simon breaks off after "another." The missing word, "storm," is then enacted on the stage through lighting effects and projections; and the consecutive appearances of the ancestors and the children explore the full dimension of the devastation of the city: it is not just the home of those living there in the present that is being destroyed, but also a past and a future home. Likewise, right after the chorus of the ancestors has reprised "Just a Closer Walk with Thee" to commemorate the devastation and the deaths in the Lower Ninth Ward in the fourth scene of Act II, the children's chorus appears to survey the destruction. Here, the children even enter into a dialogue with the ancestors: "Chorus (addressing the children): This is your land . . ./ Children's Chorus: Right where we stand./Chorus: We fought and died,/ Children's Chorus: Side by side" (26 [II,4]).

Moreover, the children's chorus also appears several times without being accompanied by the chorus of the ancestors, though always in scenes set in New Orleans. The first of these "solo" entrances of the children occurs in the sixth scene of Act I, during a gathering at Sylvia's cottage in the Uptown neighborhood of New Orleans. Referring to the note from Simon which she found in the previous scene and which indicates that Simon had managed to escape from Tremé, Sylvia declares that "there is hope in our/town!" and is immediately backed by the children: "We'll build the city again. We'll/bring it back again. All city-wide,/ showing our pride, building our/city again" (11 [I,6]). In the second part of the Lower Ninth Ward scene (II,4), the children appear again without the ancestors, and again they bring up the topic of the future of New Orleans. Prompted by Velmyra's questions to Julian, "And what about the children?/Who will teach them?" (27 [II,4]), they affirm their need for guidance in "build[ing] the city again": "Who will share with/us? . . . Who will help us know/ . . . Things that help us grow? Here we/are. Who will paint the future?" (28 [II,4]).

The topics of the post-Katrina future of New Orleans and the need to guide the city's children, especially through teaching arts and music to them, are already inextricably linked in Story's novel, of course. In Chapter 20, for instance, Velmyra and Julian discuss the chances of New Orleans "coming back" after Hurricane Katrina, and Velmyra vehemently defends people who, like Casey or herself, have decided to stay in or move back to the city in spite of the devastation: "'What if everybody with talent, with potential, left? Who would teach the kids art and music, who'd give them the opportunities we had?'" (Story, *Wading Home* 246). Moreover, the epilogue informs readers that Velmyra and Julian:

> gradually converted many of the unused, light-filled rooms of [Matthew Parmenter's Garden District] mansion into a nursery, a music studio, a recording studio, a painting studio, and an activity room for a nonprofit they formed called Living Dreams, a program for teaching art and music classes to the returning but still at-risk children of the struggling city.
>
> (295)

Both of these scenes or details have been kept and, partly because of the omission of the Parmenter plotline, combined in the libretto: it is, in fact, the conversation between Velmyra and Julian about the future of the city that prompts the second "solo" appearance of the children's chorus in the fourth scene of Act II (see earlier). And while the children are "coloring with crayons on sketch pads" and wondering "[w]ho will paint the future" with and for them, Velmyra "walks among them, smiling over their shoulders at what they are drawing, [and] bending to offer helpful pointers," thus already showing Julian and the audience what the planned nonprofit may look like (27–8 [II,4]).

Especially due to the extensive visual and vocal presence of the children, not only in this particular scene, but throughout the entire libretto, however, questions about the future of the city and about the role of the arts in this future figure much more prominently in *Wading Home* than in the libretto's source text, where the children do not even appear as characters and where the focus is more on walking and storytelling as strategies of resistance that may help to prevent future "storms" in both urban and rural Louisiana (see earlier). Employing the children's chorus to insist on the relevance of the arts in the post-Katrina revitalization of New Orleans, *Wading Home* joins a number of critics and artists who have invoked culture as an essential tool for reconstructing the city (see, for instance, Le Menestrel and Henry 180; or the voices gathered in Porter 594). In this sense, it is highly significant that during the opera's finale – a quintessential brindisi praising love, music, forgiveness, and, last but not least, "red beans and rice"[35] – not just Velmyra and Julian, but all the adult characters pledge to "teach ... our children": in *Wading Home*, this is the only way to "start over" and to "build [the city] again" (40 [II,8]).

In Chapter 16 of *Wading Home* (the novel), Casey tells Julian about his wife, who after Hurricane Katrina has decided to permanently leave the city and move to Dallas. "'I told her to call me when she came to [her senses],'" Casey adds, "'*Dallas*, man. Can you believe that? Where am I gonna play in Dallas?'" (197; emphasis original). While Casey's remark points to the very real problems of New Orleans musicians and artists who were forced to find new employment in the cities they had (been) evacuated to (see, for instance, Le Menestrel and Henry 182–4), Rich and Story had the good sense to not use Casey's words in the libretto, at least not in the version of the libretto that was used for the premiere performance of *Wading Home: An Opera of New Orleans* on 2 April 2015 at the Moody Performance Hall in the Dallas Arts District. Nevertheless, the topic of the relevance of young, African-American artists and musicians to the reconstruction of post-Katrina New Orleans and, more generally, the question of the role of the arts in the revitalization of (U.S.) cities, did play a pivotal role in the premiere production of *Wading Home*.

As I have noted before, there is, of course, almost no way of knowing about the individual emotional, affective responses that the first performance of *Wading Home* may have elicited in each and every one of the persons present on that evening in the Moody Performance Hall, or of identifying the various meanings that each and every one of the individual members of the production team, the cast, the audience, or the theater personnel may have ascribed to or found in this specific event. Yet it is also undeniable that *Wading Home*'s vision of a post-disaster New Orleans revivified by the arts emphatically resonated with virtually all aspects of the performance, including, among others, the biographies of its creators and its cast, the history and the location of its venue, and even the ethnic and racial composition of its audience. It is the concurrence of these particular places and people that not only enabled Rich and Story's libretto (as well as Rich's score) to come to life on the stage, but that also and simultaneously allowed this "utopian performative" to become a reality, however briefly, in the context of the city of Dallas. Indeed, as I intend to show in the following ethnographic-phenomenological reading of the premiere performance of *Wading Home*, the event not only represented how a city marked by the displacement and dispossession of African Americans *could* be revitalized through the arts, it actually *did* use the arts to effectuate such a revitalization at the very place where it was performed. Enacting – performing, depicting – Rich and Story's utopia of a resuscitated Crescent City on the stage and directly acting out – putting into action, actualizing – this vision by transferring it to the context of Dallas, the premiere performance of *Wading Home* thus combined theatrical and political action into an "activist performance." Precisely through its combination of theatrical and political action, however, the premiere performance of *Wading Home* also stressed parallels between (the history of African-American displacement and dispossession in) New Orleans and Dallas, thus depicting the Crescent City as exemplary rather than exceptional.

From New Orleans to Dallas: *Wading Home* on Stage

Sometime in February 2014 – Mary Alice Rich was about to complete the libretto and the piano vocal score of *Wading Home: An Opera of New Orleans* – Rosalyn Story suggested to her friend that they put the soon-to-be-finished work on stage in Dallas. Rich liked the idea, and by May, Story had secured basic funding for the production in the shape of a $40,000 grant from the Sphinx Organization, a Detroit-based national nonprofit institution dedicated to the development of black and Latino classical musicians (see ahead). Story went on to approach two other friends, the Meadows Foundation Distinguished Professor of Voice at Southern Methodist University, Barbara Hill Moore, and internationally renowned baritone and multiple Grammy Award-winner Donnie Ray Albert, to serve as the musical director for the production and to play the role of Simon, respectively. On 10 November 2014 (Rich had meanwhile finished orchestrating the score for full chamber orchestra), the newly assembled production team consisting of Story, Rich, and Hill Moore heard the first auditions for the rest of the singing roles and also began to look for a stage director, stage manager, publicist, production designer, conductor, choreographer, performing pianist and other orchestra musicians, as well as rehearsal accompanists. Production schedules and budget plans were made, remade, and finalized, and mid-December 2014 saw the first "table-read" rehearsal with cast and piano. This "table-read" was followed by approximately twelve more rehearsals between mid-February and the end of March 2015. During the same time, the production team wrote press releases, gave interviews, set up special accounts on social media, and put together the twelve-page program. On 1 April

2015, the dress rehearsal took place at the Moody Performance Hall, and on 2 April, at 7:30 p.m., the big night had finally arrived.[36]

"It's been a long journey from printed page to opera stage," Story summarizes the production process in a blog post for her publisher. In fact, it took Story and her colleagues but 14 months to put *Wading Home* on stage and, as she also points out in the post, to thus "mak[e] history": "To our knowledge, never in recent history had an opera with a cast of mostly African-American artists and employing African-American cultural themes been conceived, created, and performed in Dallas, Texas" (see Story, "Wading Home"). From the variety or vaudeville shows presented in Dallas's Deep Ellum district in the 1890s (see Govenar and Brakefield 49) to *The Arrival of the Negro*, J. Berni Barbour's "race operetta" performed on 17 and 18 December 1925 at the Dallas City Hall Auditorium,[37] and from the various gospel, jazz, and other black musicals produced by the Dallas-based The Black Academy of Arts and Letters from 1977 onwards (see Mayo and Holt 114–51; see also ahead) to the 2013 performances of *The Gershwins' Porgy and Bess* hosted by the Winspear Opera House at the AT&T Performing Arts Center in the Dallas Arts District (see N.N., "Lexus"),[38] Dallas audiences have had numerous opportunities to enjoy musical theater featuring black talent and dealing with African-American themes. A classical opera about blacks written and produced by Dallasites and performed by mainly African-American artists in Dallas, however, was indeed an unprecedented event in the history of the city.

The fact that the journey "from printed page to opera stage" was not long does not mean that it was not arduous, however. In the blog post for her publisher, Story freely admits that as composer, co-librettists, and co-producers, she and Rich found themselves "in unchartered territory . . . and often wondered if [they] had gotten in over [their] heads" (Story, "Wading Home"). In my conversations with them, Rich, Story, and Hill Moore have offered more details about the particular challenges they encountered during the production process: rehearsal time was extremely limited, and scheduling rehearsals for people traveling from the Fort Worth area and from far south Dallas after work proved difficult. Several times, rehearsals had to be rescheduled due to singers' illnesses and Dallas's winter ice storms. Finding adequate, affordable, and available rehearsal space turned out to be a challenge, as well. Hill Moore's institution, Southern Methodist University (SMU), eventually opened its doors to the *Wading Home* team, but since the cast involved many individuals who were not affiliated with SMU, the production had to be declared Hill Moore's faculty project in order to avoid insurance issues. When rehearsals did take place, the general complexity of the score, as well as the fact that parts of it were still being developed or revised as the composer began to hear the music in the voices of the chosen singers, challenged both the performers and Hill Moore, who, along with Rich, did most of the conducting during rehearsals.

Money constituted another serious challenge. Opera is, as Linda and Michael Hutcheon have pointed out, "an expensive art form to produce" (*Art of Dying* 7), and in a "grass roots" production such as the premiere of *Wading Home*, budgeting becomes an art form in itself. Unplanned expenses and cost overruns continuously forced the producers to come up with creative solutions: "With barely enough funding to compensate singers and orchestra and rent the performance space [for the dress rehearsal and the premiere performance], there was," Hill Moore recalls, "little room to budget imaginative staging." The team therefore decided to "semi-stage" the opera, using lighting effects, minimal props, and slide projections against the upstage wall rather than full sets, and to bill the event as a "workshop premiere" (see Weeks). At the same time, and like virtually all the other aspects of the performance as well, even the production's finances reflected the opera's emphasis on the revitalizing and healing effects of the arts.

Money to Fill the Air With Music: Production Finances

In addition to a grant from Sam Holland, Dean and Professor of Music at SMU's Meadows School of the Arts, and donations of time and talent from members of the cast and the production team (see N.N., "Local Residents"), funding for the premiere of *Wading Home* mainly came in the shape of a $40,000 MPower Grant by the Sphinx Organization awarded to Rosalyn Story in May 2014. The MPower Grant is part of an entire set of scholarships in Sphinx's "Artist Development" program and was launched to empower Sphinx alumni to achieve specific career objectives, with grants ranging "based upon the scope, need and nature of each competitive application" and averaging an amount of $25,000 (see N.N., "MPower"). The "Artist Development" program, in turn, is one of Sphinx's four main initiatives – the other three being "Education and Access," "Performing Artists," and "Arts Leadership" – which are all designed to further the main goal of the organization: to "transform lives through the power of diversity in the arts" (see N.N., "Sphinx Organization").

Founded in 1997 by Aaron P. Dworkin, who in 2015 was appointed the dean of the University of Michigan's School of Music, Theatre & Dance after having been former U.S. President Barack Obama's first appointment to the National Council on the Arts in 2011,[39] the Sphinx Organization and its mission were inspired by Dworkin's own life experiences as an African-American violinist. As Dworkin also notes in his autobiography, *Uncommon Rhythm* (2011), he specifically sought to address "the stark under-representation of people of color in classical music" (qtd. in N.N., "Sphinx Backgrounder" 1). In addition to scholarships for more or less established artists, such as the MPower Grant, the Sphinx Organization therefore also dedicates a significant part of its annual income of over $5 million (in 2016–2017; see N.N., "Year in Review" 7) to introducing young African-American and Latino children to classical music through its "Education and Access" initiatives. The "Ouverture" program, for instance, provides "free violin lessons to elementary school students in underserved communities," the "Sphinx Performance Academy" reaches out to gifted and aspiring young musicians of color with an "intensive summer chamber music and solo performance program," and "Classical Connections" offers an "in-school beginning-level interactive music curriculum focused on the string instrument family and contributions by composers of color" (see N.N., "What We Do" 1). Sphinx thus reaches over 100,000 students in 200 schools across the nation each year (see N.N., "Sphinx Backgrounder" 2) and has had, along with similar nonprofits, an impact on the U.S. classical music scene that is truly remarkable: Sphinx estimates that during the 18 years from 1998–2016, the number of black and Latino members in American orchestras has risen from 2.7 percent to 4.3 percent (see N.N., "Year in Review" 26–7).[40]

Although it did not directly contribute to the budget of the premiere of *Wading Home*, The Black Academy of Arts and Letters (TBAAL) was also instrumental in bringing the opera before the public: via its general mailing list, which reaches an impressive 50,000 persons nationwide (see Mayo and Holt 151), the Dallas-based arts institution helped publicize the event particularly among African-American Dallasites, and was thus at least partly responsible for the fact that the cast played not only in front of a full house, but also in front of one of the most diverse audiences the Moody Performance Hall had ever seen (see ahead). Established in 1977 as the Junior Black Academy of Arts and Letters and with "a personal investment of $250 in the home of its founder Curtis King" (Mayo and Holt 115), TBAAL now constitutes, according to Sandra M. Mayo and Elvin Holt's *Production History of Black Theatre in Texas* (2016), the "longest-running and most financially established" of all black theater groups in Dallas as well as being "one of the most progressive cultural arts centers in the country" (xiii; 118), serving over 650,000 patrons each year and managing a budget of over $2 million (15 percent of which comes from Dallas's Office of Cultural Affairs; see 147).

While TBAAL describes itself as a "multi-discipline" organization and seeks to "promote, cultivate, foster, preserve and perpetuate the African, African American and Caribbean Arts and [L]etters in the Fine, Visual, Performing and Cinematic Arts" (N.N., "About Us"), theater, and especially musical theatre, has always played a major role in the activities of the institution. One of TBAAL's first productions was, indeed, Dallas playwright Bob Ray Sanders's musical *Blues on 125th Street* in 1978 (see Mayo and Holt 152); and over its 30-year history, the academy has continued to rely on gospel, jazz, and popular musicals, "often featuring celebrities of stage and screen" (131), to bring in large audiences, to various rented venues in the city of Dallas at first and from 1989 onwards to TBAAL's own two new theaters in the Dallas Convention Center (the 1,750-seat Naomi Bruton Theatre and the 250-seat Clarence Muse Café Theater; see 144).

Starting with the 1982–1983 season, the academy has also put special emphasis on developing and nurturing young audiences and talent in the realm of the performing arts. In addition to its annual Summer Youth Arts Institute, which produces musical classics for Dallas children (see Mayo and Holt 145–6), TBAAL also serves "more than 50,000 youth in its Art and Education programs" (N.N., "About Us") such as Young Gifted Black Artists, which seeks to "further enrich selected youth who display exceptional artistic qualities in the performing arts" by offering them performance opportunities and master classes (see N.N., "Education"). In recognition of its educational services, TBAAL annually receives more than $150,000 in funding from the Dallas Independent School District (see N.N., "Education).

The contributions of the Sphinx Organization and TBAAL to the premiere of *Wading Home* were, of course, prominently acknowledged on the title page of the program, copies of which were freely distributed to all audience members on the night of the performance. Yet just as they benefited from organizations dedicated to the future of the (classical) arts, the producers of the opera also wished to give back to the community. Thus, while admission to the premiere was free, the program asked for freewill donations to the New Orleans-based The Roots of Music organization and to the Dallas-based Bruce R. Foote Memorial Foundation – two other nonprofits that seek, each in its own way, to transform African-American and Latino lives through classical music. Large glass boxes set up in the lobby of the Moody Performance Hall on the night invited cash donations, but the program also indicated an address to which additional contributions could be mailed after the premiere.

The younger of the two organizations, The Roots of Music, almost seems to have been conceived as a direct reply to Velmyra's questions to Julian in the fourth scene of Act II of *Wading Home*: "And what about the children?/Who will teach them?" (Rich and Story 27 [II,4]). Indeed, Derrick Tabb, a professional musician who was born and raised in New Orleans's Tremé neighborhood and has served as a marching band drum instructor at middle school and high school levels in New Orleans, co-founded The Roots of Music in 2007 both to "improv[e] the life choices of youth in New Orleans" and to celebrate and preserve the city's "great cultural and musical heritage" (see N.N., "Our Team"). As Tabb noted in an interview on the occasion of him being named a "Top 10 CNN Hero" in 2009,

> When Katrina hit, the music stopped in New Orleans. . . . The Katrina generation is a bunch of kids that are dealing with a lot; not having

a house is a lot to deal with. . . . In New Orleans right now, it's a lot easier to get a gun than an instrument. The vision I had would actually teach them discipline, community. . . . I stepped in and started this program because I honestly didn't think that nobody knew what the kids needed.

(N.N., "Heroes Tribute" 00:01:20–00:03:28)

The Roots of Music thus seeks to simultaneously address several of New Orleans children's basic needs by combining free music instruction, free academic tutoring, and free meals. Co-founder Allison Reinhardt describes a typical day at The Roots of Music:

[T]he kids come to the program, we pick them up at their schools, they arrive and they go straight to homework tutoring. We have Tulane University and Xavier University providing us with academic mentors and they actually help the kids with their homework. They do that for the first half of the program, and then they break up into their music section and they go to their music class and learn music. And for the last 15 minutes of the program we eat dinner together.

(N.N., "The Roots of Music" 00:02:22–00:02:47)

Starting with 42 children in the program, The Roots of Music had grown to an enrollment of more than 125 students by the end of 2015 and keeps nurturing their future and, at the same time, that of New Orleans's musical and performance legacy. During Mardi Gras 2020 alone, and among many other appearances, The Roots of Music Marching Crusaders contributed to the parades of the krewes of Freret, King Arthur, Bacchus, and Proteus.[41]

In a way, the Bruce R. Foote Memorial Foundation continues the work of The Roots of Music, although it focuses on a different kind of music and a different city. Named after baritone, long-time chair of the voice faculty of the University of Illinois (1933–1970), and member of the voice faculty at SMU (1970–1985), Bruce R. Foote, the organization was founded in 1995 in order to honor and carry on Foote's career-long dedication to the recruiting and mentoring of minority students. Hence, the foundation's mission is "to encourage and support students with a background that has been historically under represented in the advanced pursuit of classical vocal study" (N.N., "About Bruce Foote"). Twelve-month scholarships are awarded to students matriculated in the Graduate and Artist Certificate programs at SMU based on their talent, career potential, and financial need. In addition, the Bruce R. Foote Memorial Foundation "awards significant financial assistance throughout the year to singers – regardless of gender, race or ethnicity – for excellence in singing" (N.N., "About the Scholarship"). Finally, the organization has also administered the Rae and Ed Schollmaier Family Foundation Awards, which from 2000–2011 allowed African, European, and Latin American young talent to study classical singing at SMU, and the Rosemary Haggar Vaughan and David M. Crowley Summer Study Awards, which have supported SMU voice students "for community service in music" (see N.N., "Summer Study Awards").

Bruce R. Foote and the awards and scholarships presented by the foundation that bears his name have played a significant role in the careers of several individuals involved in the premiere production of *Wading Home*. Lauren Pinzás, who played the role of Simon's young nurse, for instance, was the recipient of a Rosemary Haggar Vaughan and David M. Crowley Summer Study Award; Paul André Doucet, who played Julian's trumpeter friend Casey, was awarded Foote Foundation scholarships from 2001–2003; and Bronwen Forbay, who played Velmyra, was a Schollmaier Scholar at SMU from 2002–2004. Both Donnie Ray Albert, who sang the role of Simon, and Barbara Hill Moore, who served as the production's music director, are former students of Foote (see N.N., "About Bruce Foote"). Perhaps even more importantly, Hill Moore has been the founder and the President of the Board of the Bruce R. Foote Memorial Foundation. Her work for the organization serves as an example of the dedication of the entire production team, including Hill Moore, Rich, and Story, to nurturing young talents in classical music and to thus ensure the future of the arts.

Passing on Traditions: The Production Team

In her overview of post-Katrina performances in New Orleans, New Orleanian performance scholar and artist Anne-Liese Juge Fox criticizes other researchers for not distinguishing between "'Katrina art' made by New Orleanians for New Orleanians" and "response art made by others outside of New Orleans for national audiences that are not local audiences" (25). Using *The Breach* (2007), a play written by "*three East Coast playwrights*" (45; emphasis original), but also Paul Chan's *Waiting for Godot in New Orleans: A Play in Two Acts, A Project in Three Parts* (2007) as examples, Fox raises the question of whether non-New Orleanian "outsiders" can or should attempt to represent Hurricane Katrina and its aftermath on the stage: "there are ethical implications in this . . . making and showing art inspired by the disaster" (25). Christopher Wallenberg notes that like Fox, many New Orleanian performing artists "have expressed serious reservations about the idea of non-natives telling the city's story" (59). He, too, cites *The Breach* and *Waiting for Godot in New Orleans* as examples of plays that "have rankled some in the artistic community" (57) and whose creators and organizers have been accused of being "'carpetbagging' outsiders" (59).

Of course, the creators and producers of the premiere performance of *Wading Home*, none of whom hails from the Crescent City,[42] were very aware of these discussions: for instance, while frankly admitting that she herself is not from New Orleans and has no direct connections with the city "other than having visited many times over the years and finding it to be one of the most fascinating places [she has] ever seen" (Story, "Wading Home"), Story, in one of my conversations with her, has also suggested that she would not necessarily consider herself an "outsider" either:

> My great-great-grandfather, enslaved before and during the Civil War on a South Carolina plantation, was first recognized as a free man after the war and set up his first homestead as a "self-owned" individual in Homer, Louisiana. In the 1800s, my ancestors moved with their masters from South Carolina to Alabama, then to Louisiana, before eventually settling in Arkansas. But it was in Louisiana that my great-great-grandfather, Moses, first breathed air as a free man. This means a lot to me, as Louisiana represents the beginning of my family's story as free American citizens. The first time I visited Louisiana, I felt that connection.

Moreover, during the same conversation, Story also articulates her belief that New Orleans is "not necessarily the sole province of only those who live there, or are from there":

> Some would posit that only those in New Orleans would know what New Orleanians have gone through [during and after Hurricane Katrina]. That's true. But we don't need to justify our "right" to create a story based on an experience which happened outside of our immediate realm of familiarity. The fact is that all of history is fair game to every creative mind. That said, we do have a responsibility to research, respect, and humble ourselves to the truth that took place.

Debates about the ethics of (stage) representations of Hurricane Katrina by and/or for people who "merely" followed the tragic events from afar are particularly pertinent to the study of the premiere of *Wading Home* if the disaster itself is considered the main theme of the performance. If, however, we think of the premiere as being mainly concerned with the revitalization of the city and the undoing of African-American displacement and dispossession through the arts, as I have suggested here, then the creators and producers of the Dallas performance of *Wading Home* are by no means "outsiders": indeed, as the biographies of Story, Rich, and Hill Moore illustrate, each member of the production team has long been intensely dedicated to passing on the traditions of classical music to young African-American and other minority talents. As they themselves experienced the difficulties of getting access to the world of classical music in the course of their lives, Story, Rich, and Hill Moore, too, and each in her own way, have sought to provide answers to Velmyra's questions of "And what about the children?/Who will teach them?" (Rich and Story 27 [II,4]).

Born and raised in Kansas City as the daughter of two factory workers, Rosalyn M. Story, for example, had wanted to study piano as a child but her family could not afford it. When she was around 10 years old, however, free violin lessons, including instruments for loan, became available at her public elementary school and she immediately signed up, also because, as she has noted elsewhere, her mother had always wanted her to play the violin: "She had seen an orchestra when she was a kid and she thought if she ever had a daughter she wanted her to play in that orchestra" (Adkins 00:00:41–00:00:47). Three years later – and thus at a comparatively late age – Story started taking private violin lessons and seriously considering music as a professional career. After majoring in music at university, Story landed her first symphony job immediately following her graduation. She played in the Tulsa Orchestra (where she met Mary Alice Rich; see earlier) and in the Kansas City Symphony before she eventually joined the Fort Worth Symphony Orchestra, for which she has been playing in the violin section for more than 25 years now.

While playing for the Tulsa Orchestra in the early 1980s, Story also started writing for *The Oklahoma Eagle*, a local weekly newspaper focusing on the African-American community, since, as she told me in one of our conversations, she "had always been a great lover of literature and journalism." An assigned piece on black spinto soprano and Oklahoma native Leona Mitchell, published in the *Eagle* in 1985, got Story interested in the history of African Americans in classical music in general and in opera in particular. In 1986, she wrote an article about black divas for *Essence*, and it was from this article that she "was able to get a book contract on the history of the black opera singer." *And So I Sing: African American Divas of Opera and Concert* was eventually published with Warner in 1990 and went on to inspire the 1999 documentary *Aida's Brothers and Sisters: Black Voices in Opera and Concert* (see Schmidt-Garre and Schroeder), in which Story also appears as featured narrator.

Story has not just sought to raise awareness of the trailblazers for African-American women in classical music and opera through her journalism, however; she has also worked to open doors for new talents: for several years, Story has been a violinist with the Sphinx Orchestra, "which accompanies many talented competitors in Sphinx's annual competition for black and Hispanic string instrumentalists" (Story, "Wading Home"; it was her work for the Sphinx Orchestra that made Story eligible for the Sphinx MPower Grant; see earlier). In addition, after Hurricane Katrina, Story also volunteered several times to work in Habitat for Humanity's "Musicians' Village," a rebuilding project dedicated to constructing homes for displaced musicians in New Orleans's Upper Ninth Ward (see N.N., "Musicians' Village"). Hence, even before depicting the return of black artists to post-Katrina New Orleans on the stage (as well as making African-American musicians and other people return to the Dallas Arts District) in *Wading Home*, Story also helped to quite literally pave the way for displaced (African-American) musicians to come back to the Crescent City.

Composer, co-librettist, and co-producer of *Wading Home* Mary Alice Rich, in turn, grew up in Fairmont, a small town in rural Minnesota. There was, she remembers,

> not a strong cultural tradition of classical music [there], so we were lucky to have an orchestra program with excellent teachers in our public school. When I was 16, I had an opportunity to take private violin lessons . . . . At the time, I was very aware of the sacrifice it was for my family to pay the $3.50 for each lesson. They never complained, and when it came time to buy a better violin, my father carefully wrote the check for three hundred dollars as if it were three million.
>
> ("Rich")

After graduating from the University of Illinois with bachelor's and master's degrees in violin performance, Rich played in professional orchestras in Tulsa, Dallas, and Fort Worth for ten years until in 1992 focal dystonia forced her to end her career as a professional violinist and turn to composing instead.[43] Now a published composer of orchestral music – her works have appeared with Neil A. Kjos and Fountain Park, among others – Rich has won the Texas Orchestra Directors Association annual Composition Contest no fewer than three times (see N.N., "About Mary Alice Rich").

While she was still performing with professional orchestras, Rich already taught violin at Texas A&M University–Commerce, and she still maintains a private teaching studio in Dallas, where she now lives. In 1992, however, she also joined the faculty of Young Strings, a nationally recognized musical development program sponsored by the Dallas Symphony Orchestra that provides talented African-American and Latina/o string students from Dallas with instrument loans, free lessons, performance opportunities, mentoring, and career guidance (see Allen, Jabr, and Davies). Now serving over 200 students each year, Young Strings has given Rich the opportunity to share "what has been given to me from my parents and teachers. It means passing along a beautiful tradition of classical music" (Rich, "Rich").

Finally, music director and co-producer of *Wading Home* Barbara Hill Moore was born in 1942 in St. Louis, where she grew up in the Pruitt-Igoe housing projects, internationally infamous for their crime and poor living conditions (see N.N., "News"). By the age of 10, Hill Moore knew she wanted to sing and teach, so after receiving a B.S. from the University of Missouri and an M.S. as a University Fellow from the University of Illinois, she worked as a music instructor for the St. Louis Archdiocese and the St. Louis public school system. In 1969, Hill Moore became Assistant Professor of Voice at Millikin University in Decatur, Illinois, and in 1974, she started her long career as Professor of Voice at Southern Methodist University in Dallas, serving as the head of the Voice Department from 1977–1992 and becoming SMU's Meadows Foundation Distinguished Professor of Voice in 2005.

As a performer, Hill Moore has traveled the lands and the seas of the world, singing opera, jazz, spirituals, and church music in the United States, Brazil, Japan, Korea, and throughout western Europe, as well as cruising the Atlantic, the Pacific, the North Sea, and the Caribbean aboard the MS Europa on its Classical Concert Tours series. She is particularly well known to German audiences for her annual concerts of American music, her frequent performances at the Schleswig-Holstein Musik Festival and the Freiburg Zelt-Musik-Festival as well as her portrayal of the character of Jenny in *The Threepenny Opera* in Berlin (see N.N., "Biography"). Like many other black classical singers, Hill Moore "faced some who saw her skin color instead of listening to her voice," but, she notes, "I tried not to let that... eat my spirit. I would, every time I sang, prepare as much as I could, do my absolute best in the moment and never look back" (N.N., "The Distinguished Professor" 00:01:52–00:02:10).

In addition to founding the Bruce R. Foote Memorial Foundation (see earlier), Hill Moore has long worked with young classical singers in South Africa, teaching Master Classes for both students and teachers there and, in the context of the SMU Study Abroad Program which she founded in 2011, producing various American musicals with both SMU and South African students (see N.N., "Biography"). It was in the course of organizing and directing these performances, Hill Moore told me during one of our conversations, that she acquired the "unyielding faith and perseverance to *make it happen*" that were also needed to bring *Wading Home* to the stage; and it was also in South Africa that Hill Moore first met some of the cast of the Dallas premiere of *Wading Home*.

The Gershwin Principle: The Cast

In the versions used for the 2015 Dallas premiere, the libretto and the score of *Wading Home* feature a total of seven solo singing roles, five of which – namely, those of Simon, Julian, Sylvia, Velmyra, and Casey – depict African-American New Orleanians (the other two, Kevin and the unnamed "Young Nurse," represent a young white man and a young Latina woman, respectively).[44] For the premiere, all of these roles were cast with singers whose skin color and racial or ethnic background match those of the characters they portrayed; the chorus of the ancestors and the children's chorus, too, consisted exclusively of African-American singers. Hence, singers were cast not only for their vocal suitability, but also because they possessed what is called the *"physique du rôle"* – with respect to age and sex, but also with respect to race and ethnicity. The point was not, or not primarily, to bring visual realism to the stage: as Rosalyn Story told me in a conversation, one of the "greatest things" about the premiere of *Wading Home*, to her, was "that it provided singing opportunities for some of the greatest artists who are overlooked, largely because of color." She added that in the future, too, the opera "should provide opportunities for singers of color who might otherwise never, or rarely, find employment." Mary Alice Rich has echoed these sentiments, stating in a conversation that as she was scoring *Wading Home*, she was hoping that it "would open up opportunities for many more opera singers of color."

The decision of the producers to cast the premiere race-specifically, and Story and Rich's wish to have this practice continued in future productions of the opera, of course recalls George Gershwin and his stipulation, stated in his will, that his *Porgy and Bess* "must always be done by an all-black cast" (R. Elliott 45) – a casting directive that has resulted in the Gershwin estate's continued refusal to authorize productions of *Porgy* that do not observe this requirement (see Jarvis et al. 207–208n2). The choice of a race-specific cast for the premiere of *Wading Home* and the reasoning behind this choice situate the event squarely in the middle of more sociological debates about blacks in opera – including the history of racism in U.S. opera and the alternative performance opportunities that black American operatic singers have been forced to find – as well as more performance-related debates about *representations* of blackness in opera – including discussions in which traditional conceptions of opera as "essentially artificial, non-realist" (Hutcheon and Hutcheon, "Jazz" 26) contrast with acknowledgments of the growing relevance of stage verisimilitude. As performances, as events that rely on "warm, material bodies . . . with visible markers of, for instance, gender, race, and age" (Hutcheon and Hutcheon, *Bodily Charm* 25) to depict bodies similarly marked by these categories, any opera production, in fact, faces these debates.

It is certainly no coincidence that Story has felt the way she does about the casting of *Wading Home*, as both through her journalism and her work as a professional musician, she has been intimately familiar with racism and its history in U.S. classical music in general and in opera in particular. As she has written in *And So I Sing*, until well into the twentieth century, "black artists did not sing with major [U.S.] opera companies – they were not allowed" (xiv). This means neither that there were no talented African-American operatic singers in the United States nor that they did not perform, of course. Some artists went to European opera houses, "where race was a more subtle issue" (89), or performed operatic repertoire on the concert stage or, when the doors of white theaters and auditoriums remained closed to them, in church (see 172).

Elizabeth Taylor Greenfield, a freedwoman from Natchez, Mississippi, who made her recital debut in 1851 in Buffalo at the age of 27, is frequently cited as the first African American to have sung opera in concert (see, for instance, Elliott 37). Greenfield is also sometimes said to have founded the first all-black opera company in the United States, although "documentation to substantiate this assertion has not yet been found" (39). The first documented such company was the Coloured American Opera Company, "which performed Julius Eichberg's opera *Doctor of Alcantara* (1862) in Washington, DC and Philadelphia in February 1873" (39); other early black companies included the Colored Opera Company (originating in Chicago in 1886), the Drury Colored Opera Company (founded by black baritone Theodore Drury in 1889), and the Grand Creole and Colored Opera Company (1891) (see 39). While often plagued with financial difficulties (many did not survive their first production), black opera companies did offer African-American artists the rare opportunity to "publically perform major roles in their entirety and in full productions" (Ingraham, So, and Moodley 12).

Especially during the late nineteenth century, artists organized in touring black concert companies and African-American opera companies occasionally performed the same music on the same stages when they sang with companies that specialized in another performative genre, one that, ironically, was referred to at the time as "black opera" or "Ethiopian opera" (André, Bryan, and Sailor 3; Elliott 36): the minstrel show. Minstrel shows often contained "a select few operatic hits" taken from "popular English and Italian operas" (Elliott 37). Though usually performed by whites in blackface – according to Elliott, "it was the very fact that no African-American singer would ever be seen on the operatic stage that created the urge for blackface performers to parody the genre" (36) – it is not surprising that, due to the scarcity of options for performing, black operatic singers also went into minstrelsy, vaudeville, and, later, musical theater. Perhaps one of the most well-known African-American singers in this genre was Sissieretta Jones, the "Black Patti," who from 1896 onwards headed the "Black Patti Troubadours" and thus found, amidst comedic sketches and acrobatic acts, a "forum for her operatic talent" (Story, *And So I Sing* 14).

It was not until Laszlo Halasz and Rudolf Bing were appointed director of the New York City Opera and general manager of the Metropolitan Opera in 1943 and 1950, respectively, that major U.S. opera companies started to employ African-American singers. In 1945, baritone Todd Duncan, who ten years earlier had debuted the role of Porgy in *Porgy and Bess* on Broadway, became the first black artist to perform with a white company in the United States (New York City Opera); a year later, soprano Camilla Williams became the first African-American to sign a season contract with a major company (also New York City Opera; see Story, *And So I Sing* 116; 72). In 1955, contralto Marian

Anderson made her long-awaited debut at the Metropolitan Opera, the first African American to sing on the stage of the "citadel of American opera" (54); the same year, baritone Robert McFerrin became "the first black male to perform at the Met" (Hutcheon and Hutcheon, "Jazz" 25). In the wake of these historical "firsts," the 1960s "marked the first time black artists could make a living principally as singers of opera in America, without compromise in the form of musical theater or recital work" (Story, *And So I Sing* 116). Opera has thus constituted "the only area of classical performance where black employment even slightly resembles a foothold" (184), although from the mid-1990s onward, the number of African Americans on U.S. operatic stages appears to have declined again (see Cheatham 179).

In addition to the supposed unsuitability of the "black voice" for opera, one of the main arguments formerly used to bar African Americans from the opera stage was, as Wallace McClain Cheatham has pointed out, visual believability (see 184; 180). Opera's "traditional generic commitment to artifice" ("here everyone sings," Hutcheon and Hutcheon, "Jazz" 26) alone should have exposed this argument as the excuse for racism that it was. Moreover, at the same time that realism was invoked to prevent black singers from playing white operatic roles, black characters such as Sélika in Meyerbeer's *L'Africaine* and the title roles in Verdi's *Aida* and *Otello* were, and until very recently have been, regularly played by "blacked up" white singers, as were the characters of Gershwin's first black opera, *Blue Monday*, during its 1922 premiere (see Elliott 45).[45] However, with the growing influence of television and film on opera, which several critics have commented upon (see, for instance, Story, *And So I Sing* 189; and Hutcheon and Hutcheon, "Jazz" 26), a "new demand for verisimilitude in dramatic performance" (Hutcheon and Hutcheon, *Bodily Charm* 137) has made particularly attractive the hiring of black singers for black roles – as well as for other non-white roles such as that of Ulrica in Verdi's *Un Ballo in Maschera*, with "perhaps one Other [being] as good as any other Other" (Hutcheon and Hutcheon, "Jazz" 25).[46]

The casting of opera today does not just involve a "mix of political correctness, realism, and artifice" (Hutcheon and Hutcheon, "Jazz" 27), but depends, as tenor and professor of voice Curtis Ryam has pointed out, on a large variety of factors: "availability, voice typecasting, physical appearance or the possibility to create the right appearance, and money" (qtd. in Cheatham 184). And while black (and other non-white) roles, such as the inhabitants of Catfish Row in *Porgy and Bess*, historically have "ensured abundant work for black singers over the decades," setting in motion the careers of numerous black divas, "the amount of work generated by them could hardly sustain an entire career" (Story, *And So I Sing* 68; 116). Nevertheless, such roles still appear to constitute important performing opportunities for African-American operatic singers, as is evidenced by the artist biographies of the cast members of the premiere of *Wading Home*: baritone Donnie Ray Albert, who sang the role of Simon, for instance, received the first of his altogether three Grammy Awards for his interpretation of Porgy in the 1976 Houston Grand Opera production of *Porgy and Bess* (1977 Best Opera Recording); mezzo soprano Walteria Bethea, who played Simon's girlfriend Sylvia, portrayed Serena in *Porgy*, but also Ulrica in *Un Ballo in Maschera*, Alzucena in Verdi's *Il Trovatore*, and the title role in Bizet's *Carmen*; baritone Nathan De'Shon Myers, who sang the role of Julian, made his Austrian debut in 2013–2014 at the Salzburg State Theatre in the title role of Ernst Krenek's 1927 jazz opera *Jonny spielt auf*; and soprano Bronwen Forbay, who played Julian's girlfriend Velmyra, lists Bess in *Porgy* as part of her operatic repertoire (see N.N., "Donnie Ray Albert"; N.N., "Schedule"; N.N., "Bio"; N.N., "Repertoire"). While the cast members have also portrayed white operatic characters, including The Dutchman in Wagner's *Der Fliegende Holländer* (Albert), Hedwige in Rossini's *Giulielmo Tell* (Bethea), Lescaut in Puccini's *Manon Lescaut* (Myers), and the title role in Donizetti's *Lucia di Lammermoor* (Forbay), non-white roles have nevertheless figured prominently in all of their performing careers.

To be sure, considering the prominence of race in disaster discourses about Hurricane Katrina and the relevance of race to the plot of *Wading Home* (both the novel and the opera), a color-blind casting for the premiere may have been inconceivable in the first place. But the producers also sought to make a point and offer overlooked black singers a chance to perform. Thus, however, they simultaneously brought an unprecedented number of African-American artists to a classical music event in the Dallas Art District – and the diversity on the stage was also mirrored by that in the auditorium.

"Big D's Big Deed": The Audience

In one of my conversations with her, Rosalyn Story has described the Dallas premiere of *Wading Home* as "the most democratic performance" in classical music she had ever seen:

> As someone who has been in classical music performance for more than 25 years, and who is African American, I've had the chance to observe many audiences in symphony performances, chamber music, musicals, and operas. At most of the performances where I've participated as a musician, there may be as many as 90 people on stage – orchestra, chorus, vocal soloists – and as many as 2,000 in the hall. Of this number, the number of people of African descent often could be counted on one hand. . . . Early in my orchestra career I actually counted the number of black people in the audience, and rarely counted more than five or six. Depending on the music, in later years,

I might see slightly more. The audience at our premiere was very, very unusual, and we were able to cast a very wide net. . . . In short, this was the most diverse audience for opera that I have seen in my years as a professional musician.[47]

During the same conversation, Story also speculated about the reasons why so many among the 750 people in the audience – the Moody Performance Hall was filled to capacity on the night – were of African descent. Of course, some performers, particularly the members of the children's chorus, had brought family and friends. Moreover, via its database of about 50,000 nationwide subscribers, The Black Academy of Arts and Letters had helped publicize the premiere particularly among African Americans in Dallas and elsewhere in North Texas. Finally, even though the event was billed as an opera, which, as Story has noted, "might have put off a lot of people who were not familiar with the art form," the fact that it "featured black performers and dealt with themes of interest to African Americans" as well as the fact that it was free of charge may have attracted many black North Texans who had never been to an opera performance before. *Wading Home* was extremely accessible.

There was, however, also another group of (mostly) African Americans who had their own, very personal reasons to attend the premiere of *Wading Home* – namely, Hurricane Katrina evacuees to the Dallas-Fort Worth metroplex who after the storm had made the region their temporary or permanent home. In fact, during the 30-minute talkback after the premiere, which was attended by some 50 members of the audience, one person identified herself as a Katrina victim. Prompted by then general director of Fort Worth Opera Darren K. Woods, who hosted the talkback, to comment on the opera, this woman had the following to say: "I just wanna say that my last time in Dallas, I was here evacuated for Katrina. And so I'm here today and I just wanna thank you for honoring our story." It is unclear how many other Katrina survivors were among the members of the audience on that night, but already before the premiere, Story had opined in an interview with Scott Cantrell from the *Dallas Morning News* that *Wading Home* may have special resonance in Dallas: "Some 25,000 people from New Orleans are still in this area. They've added to our culture – more restaurants, New Orleans-style cooking, music ensembles that have sprung up, because of people who brought their culture with them" (Cantrell, "Ten Years").

The story of the Dallas response to Hurricane Katrina – "Big D's Big Deed," as Dave Levinthal has called it, referring to Dallas by its common nickname (1B) – still needs to be written, although glimpses of this story may be obtained from academic studies of the Katrina diaspora like Lori Peek and Lynn Weber's *Displaced: Life in the Katrina Diaspora* (2012), as well as from reports and articles in such local newspapers and magazines as the *Dallas Morning News*, the *Dallas Observer*, *D Magazine*, and the *Dallas Weekly* (a black newspaper). According to these sources, of the 1.5 million people who were displaced from the Gulf Coast after Hurricane Katrina, roughly 250,000 evacuated to Texas, among them 150,000 to Houston and about 25,000 to the Dallas-Fort Worth metroplex, including 17,000 to the city of Dallas itself (see Peek and Weber 1; Angel et al. 1; 88; and Jeffers). Among the latter were many evacuees from New Orleans and both people who had left the city before the mandatory evacuation order was issued on 28 August 2005, in order to stay with Dallas-based family and friends or in hotels, and people who were evacuated after the levees had broken on 29 August and who were flown or bused to the Dallas hospitals and shelters during the first days of September (see N.N., "Texas Hospitals"; Kennedy, "Hotel" 19).

Whether they had chosen to come to the "Big D" and arrived with vehicles, suitcases, and a certain knowledge of and contacts in the city, or whether they were forcibly taken there and had nothing but "a different sort of baggage: the traumatic experience of the Superdome" (Kennedy, "Hotel" 19), these evacuees suddenly found themselves more or less permanent residents of a place that, with respect to both its layout and its demographics, was utterly different from New Orleans: the Crescent City's compact neighborhoods contrasted perhaps as much with sprawling Dallas-Fort Worth as did the former's mid-sized, largely black population – before the storm, two-thirds of New Orleans's 437,000 inhabitants identified as African American – with the latter's 1.3 million inhabitants and its significant white and Latino communities (see Horner, "Foreign Country" 1A; Peek and Weber 6–7). No matter how out of place evacuees may have felt at first, local commentators overall agree that Dallas – in the shape of then-city manager Mary Suhm, who was charged with the city's emergency response, then-mayor Laura Miller, and Dallas citizens in general – responded rather well to the crisis. Nevertheless, city officials also made some controversial decisions and residents, as elsewhere in Texas, eventually started to show some "signs of fatigue" (Horner, "'Compassion Fatigue'"; see also Jacobson; Levinthal; N.N., "Give Us").

On Monday, 29 August – the day the levees broke in New Orleans – Dallas officials told the *Dallas Morning News* that they were expecting only about 50 evacuees who needed shelter (Flick). Given that only 53 percent of the 36,000 hotel rooms within the city limits were occupied, Phillip Jones, chief executive of the Dallas Convention & Visitors Bureau, said he did not "anticipate any problems" (Marta 3D). In fact, equipped with "carloads of supplies, pets and favorite possessions," hurricane victims had started "checking into Dallas hotels late Sunday and continued to arrive throughout Monday" (Flick), but by late Monday afternoon, there was only one family of ten in the shelter set up in East Dallas by the Dallas Area Chapter of the American Red Cross (Horner, "They're Far"). Rather than preparing for evacuees, the city still focused on sending rescue workers to Louisiana. By Tuesday morning, however, the East Dallas shelter was at capacity with 235 people, and the ARC set up a second facility in the Love Field section of the city (Horner, "They're Far").

As the magnitude of the disaster and its potential consequences were slowly becoming clearer, Dallas sprang into action: while Louisiana officials "announced they would transport all those stranded in the Superdome to Houston's Astrodome" (Hacker, "Districts" 15B), city manager Mary Suhm declared on Wednesday, 31 August, that "New Orleans' emergency is Dallas' emergency" and opened up Reunion Arena, an indoor arena close to the West End District that served as the primary home of the Dallas Mavericks and that would be able to shelter about 1,600 people, to incoming evacuees (Meyer, Young, and Levinthal 1A). Later that day, the city decided to use part of the Dallas Convention Center, also located in the downtown area and with a capacity for 1,000 people, as a backup shelter. In both cases, Dallas acted "like a landlord, while relief agencies such as the Red Cross provide[d] a spectrum of in-shelter services" (Levinthal 9B), which eventually included a field hospital, FEMA registration desks, a pharmacy, a chaplain area, a children's play area, a post office, substance-abuse meeting spots, message boards, job fairs, and tables with donated clothes, toiletries, etc. (see Trahan). Highly secured by the Dallas police – to protect both evacuees and Dallas citizens, as then-Chief David Kunkle insisted (see Levinthal and Stutz 26A) – the shelters thus became the central spots for all evacuees, whether they actually stayed there or whether they lived in hotels, with relatives and friends, or, later, in their own apartments. Once shelter operations ceased at the Convention Center and Reunion Arena on 16 September and 9 October, respectively, evacuee services were moved to a disaster recovery center, which operated until April 2006 (Hughes). Meanwhile, hotels that housed hurricane evacuees also started to offer services, with, for instance, the Quality Inn on Market Center Boulevard giving out free meals and turning its lobby into a computer center (Kennedy, "Hotel").

On the afternoon of Thursday, 1 September 2005, then-Texas governor Rick Perry came to Dallas and visited the Reunion shelter, where about 600 evacuees had registered by Wednesday night (see Menzer). Earlier that day, Perry had agreed to house 25,000 evacuees from Louisiana in Dallas, after having already accepted 25,000 for Houston and another 25,000 for San Antonio on Wednesday night and Thursday morning, respectively. Dallas officials did not learn about Perry's decision until Thursday evening, however, and then not from the governor himself, but from then-County Judge Margaret Keliher (see Levinthal and Stutz 26A). Mayor Miller panned state and federal leaders for "a lack of communication with Dallas officials," but immediately set up plans to enlarge the Convention Center shelter and to open up an additional shelter facility at the Decker Detention Center, a former hotel turned jail (N.N., "Give Us"). The latter eventually turned out to be one of the city government's more controversial decisions, as the building still served as a halfway house for convicted sex offenders and violent felons (see Meyer; Gray). Nevertheless, when the first buses with evacuees from New Orleans started arriving on Friday afternoon, they all found a place to stay, whether in one of the three main shelters, in the private homes of Dallas citizens who spontaneously volunteered to house hurricane victims (see Jacobson 1B), or in apartments that the Dallas Housing Authority had made available to evacuees (see N.N., "Give Us"). On Sunday night, more than 2,300 people stayed in the three shelters alone (Getz).

Earlier, however, the city government had made another controversial decision: on Saturday, 3 September, Mayor Miller informed the governor's office that Dallas had reached capacity and asked state homeland security officials to immediately stop sending buses to the city, which later prompted Jim Schutze from the *Dallas Observer* to editorialize that:

> Mayor Laura Miller and police Chief David Kunkle peeked out the door with a sandwich in one hand and a badge in the other. Kind of like, "Some of you can stay, but a whole lot of you have to keep on going."
>
> ("RIP" 9)

County Judge Keliher, who directed relief efforts in North Texas, however, "encouraged the governor's office to send even more," and the trek from New Orleans to Dallas continued until Sunday morning (Ramshaw, "FEMA" 9B; and "Survivors" 11A). By Monday, 5 September, more than 14,000 Katrina survivors had registered in Dallas, about 6 percent of the estimated 240,000 evacuees that Texas had taken in (Ramshaw, "FEMA" 9B). "'Looking back, there were moments where I felt we were fixin' to drown,'" Suhm told the *Dallas Morning News*, perhaps too exhausted to notice the inappropriateness of her metaphor, "'but we handled things pretty well'" (qtd. in Londono 1B).

During the following days, weeks, and months, Dallas officials and citizens cooperated to move evacuees into more permanent homes, offer them jobs, and put their children into school. Getting hurricane victims out of the shelters and hotels and into apartments was a top priority for the city, not least because operating the shelters was hugely expensive: in September 2005 alone, Dallas spent nearly $7 million to house evacuees, with police and firefighters overtime costs making up "60 percent of the Katrina price tag" (Ramshaw, "$6.8 M" 9B). Lest its solvency should be compromised, Dallas, unlike other Texas cities, refused to enter into an agreement with FEMA that would require the city to pay for evacuees' rent expenses and await reimbursement from federal sources (see Hartzel). Instead, Mayor Miller set up a private relief fund that would cover two months' rent and utilities, after which time hurricane victims received FEMA-funded rent vouchers, administered by the Dallas Housing Authority (see Batsell). "Project Exodus," as the plan was dubbed, put

Dallas somewhere in between Houston, which advanced the money for nearly 30,000 yearlong rent vouchers, and Atlanta, which "simply gave $400,000 to a homeless-services group, asking it to find housing for 50 families for six months" (N.N., "Struggle"). Nevertheless, the program was harshly criticized by Katrina survivor associations, who claimed it encouraged price gouging by landlords (see Kennedy, "Long Road").

With respect to integrating evacuees into the Dallas labor market, commentators were initially optimistic: the U.S. Department of Homeland Security and the Texas Department of Licensing and Regulation had temporarily suspended requirements for documents and professional licenses, and evacuees had arrived during a season when hiring in the service sector traditionally picks up (see N.N., "Texas Clarifies"; Shah and Case). Hurricane victims were also encouraged to start their own businesses, particularly in the restaurant sector (see Hall). Despite such initiatives and numerous job fairs, however, unemployment continued to remain high among evacuees to Dallas, as elsewhere in Texas – by May 2006, two out of three evacuees in the Dallas area were still without a job (Horner, "Foreign Country" 8A), which the press attributed to the fact that many New Orleanians did not own cars and were accustomed to a "less formal work culture" (8A), but also to discrimination against evacuees on the part of employers (Horner, "Help" 14A).

Dallas schools and colleges – both public and private – were more receptive to hurricane victims: by 1 September 2005, SMU had received about 180 students and student-athletes from Tulane University, and both SMU and the University of Texas at Dallas eventually allowed Tulane students from Dallas-Fort Worth to enroll in their classes (see Hacker, "SMU"). Likewise, Jesuit College Preparatory High School in Dallas took in students from the Jesuit High School in New Orleans (see Fischer). The majority of evacuee students enrolled in the public schools of the Dallas Independent School District, however, with evacuee student figures rising from 255 on 6 September 2005 to about 2,000 by the end of that month (see Booth; N.N., "Katrina Evacuees").

In 2006, a survey for the Texas Health and Human Services Commission found that 85 percent of Hurricane Katrina evacuees to Texas considered their current situation "about the same" (26 percent) as or even "better" (59 percent) than life before the disaster. Hence, it comes as no surprise that according to the same poll, most hurricane victims were "likely to stay – and those in the Dallas area [were] even more inclined to stay long-term": of those residing in North Texas in May/June 2006, when the survey was conducted, 56 percent thought they would still be living in the same area in May 2007, compared to 26 percent who expected to have left Texas by that time. Looking further into the future, 44 percent intended to remain in North Texas through May 2008, while only a third thought they would be living outside of the state in two years' time (see Garrett). As there are no official figures available, however, it is quite impossible to say how many evacuees to Dallas actually did stay there. In August 2006, the *Dallas Morning News* stated there were 21,000 hurricane victims in the Dallas area (see Horner, "Struggling" 14A); a year later, advocate groups estimated that "20,000 to 30,000 evacuee households still call North Texas home" (Horner, "Help" 1A); and in 2010, the Community Council of Greater Dallas estimated that "as many as 20,000" were still living in the city (Horner, "Home").

While nobody "has kept track exactly how many of the roughly 66,000 who evacuated to North Texas during Hurricane Katrina stayed for good" (Horner, "Home"), the Katrina diaspora in North Texas in general and in Dallas in particular has remained both vocal and visible over the years. Some of the New Orleans businesses who relocated to Dallas after Katrina – including spice company Zatarain's and float maker Kern Studios (see Robinson-Jacobs; Stuetz) – may have returned to the Crescent City, but RJ's Crustaceans Restaurant of New Orleans, opened shortly after Katrina in Dallas's Deep Ellum district (see Hall), continued to serve customers until at least 2015. Formal associations such as the Katrina Survivors Association of the Association of Community Organizations for Reform Now (ACORN; see Simnacher) or Dallas Area Interfaith (DAI)'s Katrina Survivors Network (see Horner, "Katrina") may have disbanded, but, as elsewhere in Texas (see Lindahl), evacuees have continued to meet informally to watch the New Orleans Saints (see Clark) or simply to enjoy a gumbo (see Hanna). Katrina survivors may have also met at the Dallas Symphony in the Arts District, which granted free admission to hurricane victims in the weeks after the disaster (see Yan). And at least one survivor came back to the Arts District for the premiere of *Wading Home* – a particularly fitting place to come to for displaced African Americans.

Another Story of Displacement and Dispossession: The Venue

Selecting a venue for the premiere of *Wading Home* was perhaps one of the most important decisions to be made during the production process. As she told me in one of my conversations with her, Rosalyn Story chose the Moody Performance Hall, located at 2520 Flora Street on the eastern edge of the Dallas Arts District, "for very specific reasons: it was the right size, had great acoustics, and was located halfway between north Dallas (mostly white neighborhoods) and south Dallas (largely black neighborhoods)." Story's decision, then, was not just based on purely technical criteria such as available seating and acoustics, but also on what may be referred to as the social or cultural identity of the performance building. As a performing artist herself, Story was well aware of the fact that "theatres mean" (Carlson, *Places* 3) – i.e., that according to their audience arrangements, audience support spaces (lobbies, staircases etc.), architecture, and especially their relationship to the surrounding urban fabric, places of performance develop specific social or cultural meanings (see e.g., Schechner, "Towards a Poetics" 114; Carlson, *Places* 2; or Van den Berg 1) – and that these meanings, consciously or not, affect "the audience's understanding and experience of the theatre event" (Carlson, *Places* 3; see also Van den Berg 16). Lest the event should be perceived as primarily geared toward either a white or a black demographic (due e.g., to its genre or its theme and cast, respectively), and thus in order to attract the widest and most racially diverse audience possible, Story deliberately chose a "neutral" venue located between north (white) and south (black) Dallas.[48]

Yet the venue's location on the *contemporary* social and racial map of Dallas only tells half the tale. The other half is a story of African-American displacement and dispossession that suggestively parallels and resonates with the one told by the opera performed on the stage of the Moody Performance Hall on the night of 2 April 2015. In fact, until at least the 1970s, it was primarily in south Dallas where white neighborhoods could be found, whereas north Dallas – that is, the area north of Ross Avenue, including the 17 blocks between Ross Avenue and Woodall Rodgers Freeway that would eventually become the Dallas Arts District – was largely populated by African Americans. Indeed, north Dallas had been the home of black Dallasites ever since the founding of Freedman's Town soon after the announcement of the Emancipation Proclamation in Texas on "Juneteenth" (19 June 1865); and it would remain "the heartland of African American culture in Dallas" (Prior and Schulte 71) until several infrastructure, housing, and zoning projects from the 1940s onward effectively contributed to the "gentrification" of the area, dispossessing and displacing blacks to south Dallas. And in this part of the tale, too, the Moody Performance Hall has played a central role.

When the Moody Performance Hall hosted the premiere of *Wading Home* in April 2015, it had only been open for about two and a half years. Although plans to build a multi-purpose performing arts venue in this location date back to the 1990s (see Wilonsky, "Dance"), it was not until Dallas citizens approved two city bond elections in 2003 and 2006, which allocated a total of $40.45 million for the design and construction of the hall, that the project finally moved ahead (see Granberry). From the beginning, the venue had been envisioned as "a quality public performance space for Dallas based emerging and mid-sized performing arts organizations" that would allow "all Dallas citizens and visitors [to] have an opportunity to experience the finest in arts and culture" (N.N., *Dallas City Performance Hall*): a technically versatile, acoustically flexible, as well as approachable and affordable venue that would fill the niche left in the Dallas Arts District by the AT&T Center's Wyly Theatre, "whose acoustics are too dry for most classical music," the AT&T Center's Winspear Opera, whose 2,400-seat auditorium is too large for most emerging and mid-sized groups, and the Meyerson Symphony, which lacks a "proscenium and stage house for theater or dance" (Cantrell, "New Venue").[49]

The intended role or civic mission of the Moody Performance Hall, with its emphasis on the local and the non-exclusive, has manifested itself in the venue's architecture and interior design, its technical infrastructure, its operating and renting policies, and even in its funding structure: like the Wyly, the Winspear, and the Meyerson, the Moody Performance Hall is owned by the city of Dallas, but it is the only performing arts venue in the Dallas Arts District that was also entirely funded and has been managed and operated by the city (through the latter's Office of Cultural Affairs; see Cantrell, "New Venue"). Once funding had been secured via the city bond elections, questionnaires were sent out to over 70 local performing arts organizations to gather information on what they expected from the new hall. Skidmore, Owings & Merrill LLP, the Chicago-based architects who were responsible for the design, along with Schuler Shook theater planners, then used this input to tailor their plans to the needs of local artists.[50] The 2013 Frank Lloyd Wright Honor Award-winning result is a beautiful, modern performance venue featuring a shoebox-shaped auditorium with a capacity of 749 seats (192 on the balcony, 557 on the main floor), a large, fully equipped stage, a back of house with offices, a greenroom, four dressing rooms, and a loading dock, as well as a comparatively spacious and open, two-story main lobby that, equipped with step-seats, doubles as a performance and meeting space for smaller events.

Conceiving of itself as "the people's building," the Moody Performance Hall seeks to attract as diverse as possible audiences, performing groups, and events. In order to encourage "social and cultural interaction from the street to the stage" (N.N., *Dallas City Performance Hall*), for instance, the building was set – in stark contrast to e.g., the neighboring Wyly Theatre and the Winspear Opera – extremely close to the street and features a huge glass façade. The expressly open and welcoming atmosphere is further enhanced by the easygoing attitude of the ushers and the relaxed house rules (patrons are allowed to bring food and drinks into the space). The large, versatile, fully equipped stage (a grid, a mechanized pit lift, an acoustical shell, orchestra and choral risers, a marley dance floor, and a grand piano are all available), as well as the much-praised, flexible acoustics (woolen banners over the walls can be adjusted to create the perfect sonic environment for either choral and chamber orchestra music or for speech, theater, and amplified music), in turn, allow the venue to host a large variety of events. The tiered rental and booking systems – Dallas-based not-for-profit arts and cultural organizations pay the lowest rates and have the first pick of dates – clearly favor local and small, emerging arts groups; and the administrative and technical staff is prepared to work with groups who have various levels of performing experience, providing whatever assistance is necessary.

To be sure, some of the Dallas arts organizations involved in the planning and design process have been concerned that the Performance Hall would not be able to "'meet the role that it was originally intended for'" – the auditorium has been criticized as too large and the rents as too high, especially for smaller groups (Cantrell, "New Venue"; see also Cantrell, "New Arts"). In response, the city introduced discount rates and, in 2017, accepted a $22 million gift from the Galveston-based Moody Foundation, $10 million of which have been used to create an endowment for small and emerging Dallas arts groups (in return, the City Council agreed to rename the venue Moody Performance Hall; see Lowry). Nevertheless, it is not only through its architecture – as Cantrell has pointed out, the hall's design marked a clear break with the "starchitecture" prevalent elsewhere in the Dallas Arts District (see "New Venue") – that the venue has sought to distinguish itself from its surroundings: according to the general manager, the intended diversity of audiences and events is also meant to counter the widespread stigma about the Arts District as an ethnocentric, monocultural area – "a place for rich white people." Somewhat ironically, the Moody Performance Hall thus comes closer than most of its neighbors to fulfilling the original vision for the Dallas Arts District as a place that "'belongs' to all groups in the city" and that makes the arts "accessible and essential to all segments of the community" (Carr et al. 31; and 1).

This vision for the Arts District was essentially a product of the late 1970s and early 1980s, when new wealth coming from "high oil prices, rising real estate appraisals, and a growing tax base" – by the mid-1970s, Dallas-Fort Worth had become the 10th largest metropolitan area in the nation – spurred a construction and planning boom in Dallas that gave the city, among others, an expanded convention center (1973), a new city hall (designed by I.M. Pei and opened in 1978), its first historic district (the West End Historic District; created in 1976), and a *Comprehensive Arts Facilities Plan* (1977) that would eventually become the basis for the Dallas Arts District (Prior and Kemper 195; see also Dillon and Tomlinson 124). At the time, several major Dallas arts institutions, most of which were located southeast of downtown in Fair Park, felt a "pressing need" (Carr et al. 4) to relocate to new quarters. Nine of these institutions banded together to sponsor an arts facilities study that was carried out by Cambridge, Massachusetts-based city planners Carr, Lynch Associates.[51] Submitted in October 1977, Carr, Lynch Associates's 50-page report considered Dallas "to be at a special moment of growth to cultural excellence" (1) and urged the City Council and the Mayor to use this "time of special opportunity" (n.p.) to implement a "comprehensive strategy for the arts in Dallas," consisting of:

(1) a coherent policy of city support for the arts, and an administrative function which will implement that policy, and coordinate public and private actions;
(2) a new arts concentration in which sites will be available as older institutions relocate and new ones emerge, and which will receive special public improvements;

(3) a positive new cultural role for Fair Park; and
(4) support for cultural activities in the local neighborhoods.

(24)

For the "new arts concentration," Carr, Lynch Associates recommended "neither a single site arts center nor any general dispersal" (2), but a concentrated network of arts institutions on the northern side of downtown Dallas, "because of the ample and less expensive sites available there, the good highway access, the relation to downtown growth" (34) as well as because – and this, the report insists, "was decisive" – other locations:

> were not socially neutral – they 'belonged' to one group or another. Any institution placed [outside of Fair Park or downtown] would be less accessible to some Dallas people, not only because of distance or lack of public transportation, but also because they might feel excluded.
>
> (30)[52]

Very much in tune with this concern for accessibility, openness, and non-exclusivity were Carr, Lynch Associates's cautioning remarks about the use of "elevated plazas or underground passages" in the new arts concentration (38) – that is, the very design elements of socio-spatial stratification employed to create the "analogous" or "parallel cities" of Minneapolis, Calgary, Montréal, and Disneyland's New Orleans Square (see Chapter 2).

City leaders were so enamored by the Carr, Lynch Associates concept that they attempted "to build the arts district in one fell swoop" (Rodrigue 105). A June 1978 city bond election asking voters for $45 million to fund, among other things, new buildings for the Museum of Fine Arts and the Dallas Symphony, failed spectacularly, however, and in another election in November 1979, citizens merely approved $27.05 million for a new museum and a concert hall site (see Rodrigue 105–107; Dillon and Tomlinson 168–9; Shulman 34–5; 42; and Arnold 17). Undeterred, in 1981 representatives of the Dallas Concert Hall, the Museum of Fine Arts, and the City of Dallas, as well as property owners in the proposed area, formed an Arts District Consortium to further plan and coordinate the project and appointed Philip O'Bryan Montgomery, Jr. Arts District Coordinator (see Sasaki Associates et al. 10; S.O. Dawson, "Dallas Arts District" 20; and "Skyscraper's" 991). Following a design competition in March 1982, the Consortium chose Sasaki Associates of Watertown, Massachusetts, as the master planner for the district. The *Urban Design Plan* that Sasaki Associates eventually submitted in August 1982 has been considered aesthetically "bland and old hat," "tired," and "stiff and unimaginative" by some later commentators (see Dillon and Tomlinson 169); yet the design firm had intuitively sensed that its clients were looking as much for an economic and marketing strategy as for a design plan and had shrewdly teamed up with consultants from Halcyon, Inc. to propose a plan that "made [e]very effort to be as financially detailed as it was design detailed" (S.O. Dawson, "Skyscraper's" 994): overall construction costs for public improvements in the district, for instance, were estimated at precisely $21,028,300 (Sasaki Associates et al. 83).

With respect to design, Sasaki Associates proposed to establish Flora Street as the central pedestrian boulevard of the district, along the length of which arts institutions would mix with restaurants, sidewalk cafés, specialty shops, and offices, as well as hotels and residential developments in three distinct, themed zones (Sasaki Associates et al. 3–6). Although generally based on the Carr, Lynch Associates report, the Sasaki Associates plan thus took a slightly different approach to the idea of the Arts District: primarily targeting "the affluent, casual metropolitan audience" (Dillon and Tomlison 169), it envisioned the area as a place where one could:

> negotiate a business deal, savor Texas chili or Coquille St. Jacques, muse over the meaning of a contemporary dance performance or an African sculpture, purchase Dallas souvenirs or additions to an art collection, or meander through trees along the street exchanging pleasantries with patrons of a sidewalk cafe.
> (Sasaki Associates et al. 39)

Accordingly, the plan recommended the use of the very "analogous" design features that Carr, Lynch Associates had explicitly warned against, from overhead skywalk systems (33) to below-grade retail areas (35).[53] To be sure, the Sasaki Associates plan still talked about the non-elite, multinational, and intergenerational atmosphere of the Arts District, but merely cited this as one of "the objectives for the district formulated by the Dallas Arts District consortium" (10) and one of the "particular concerns expressed by the responding groups" in preliminary surveys (69). And while none of the proposed "analogous" design elements ever made it past the planning stage, Robert Wilonsky, some 30 years later, nevertheless identified the Sasaki Associates plan as "the reason pieces of the Arts District have the feel of an 'exclusive elitist enclave'" ("Thirty").

In February 1983, the Dallas City Council passed the "Dallas Arts District Plan Development District Ordinance," which formally adopted the Sasaki Associates plan, and only a year later, the new, Edward L. Barnes-designed Dallas Museum of Art opened at the western end of Flora Street as the first anchor of the area. By that time, however, a real estate and banking crisis had put an end to the construction and planning boom of the 1970s (see Fulton 98–100), and it was not until 1989 that the Arts District saw a second major addition in the shape of the Morton H. Meyerson Symphony Center, designed, like the new city hall, by I.M. Pei and located two blocks down from the museum. During the following years, the empty lots along Flora Street were replaced, one by one, by the Museum of Art's Hamon Wing (1993), the Crow Collection of Asian Art (1998), the Nasher Sculpture Center (2003), the AT&T Performing Arts Center (2009), and, eventually, the Moody Performance Hall (2012), together forming what the Arts District's website proudly proclaims is "the largest contiguous urban arts district in the nation" (N.N., "About the Dallas Arts District"). Not least due to the decline in private construction during the mid-1980s, which "occurred before sufficient critical mass developed to provide the rich, varied urban experience originally anticipated" by Carr, Lynch Associates and particularly by the Sasaki Associates plan (Fulton 100), Flora Street had never become an organic, lively pedestrian boulevard with shops, cafés, and residences.[54] In more recent years, however, the tide appears to have turned with the opening of, for instance, the Museum Tower residential building between the Nasher Center and the Meyerson in 2013 and the first phase of the mixed-use HALL Arts development next to the Wyly Theatre in 2015.

Yet, the Moody Performance Hall is by no means the only institution in the Dallas Arts District that provides a home for diverse audiences and new and emerging arts organizations and artists. Just around the corner from the hall, at 1816 Routh Street, St. Paul United Methodist Church has been hosting "the longest-running free jazz series in the Dallas Arts District" (N.N., *Dallas Arts District* 13).[55] And right across the street from the Moody Performance Hall, at 2501 Flora Street, the world-renowned and award-winning Booker T. Washington High School for the Performing and Visual Arts provides Dallas students from grades 9–12 with a chance to study music, theater, dance, two-dimensional art, sculpture, and applied design (13; see Figure 3.1). Unlike the Moody Performance Hall and virtually all of their other neighbors, however, both Booker T. Washington and St. Paul – as well as the buildings that house these institutions – predate the Arts District: the high school itself, for instance, was founded in 1976 as Dallas's "Arts Magnet High School" in the context of the Dallas Independent School District's desegregation plans (see Linden 108–25; L.M. Smith 199–200; Garnett). The two-story brick building that now houses the arts high school, in turn, dates back to 1922, when it became the new home of Booker T. Washington High School, Dallas's first – and, until 1939, only – public high school for African Americans. That institution, finally, which until 1902 had simply been referred to as "Colored School No. 2" or "Dallas Colored High School," was established in 1892, four years after black students in Dallas had first enrolled for high school instruction (see Bellerophon Quill Club 6; Schiebel 11; 30; and Prior and Schulte 95; 139). Construction for the vaguely gothic-styled building that is now the home of the congregation of St. Paul United Methodist Church, in turn, had been completed by 1927 (Skipper 53), but the church itself, then called Saint Paul Methodist

Episcopal, had been founded as one of at least seven African-American churches in the area in August 1873 already (see Prior and Schulte 88–91; Skipper 37–8).

Booker T. Washington and St. Paul are the only remainders in the Dallas Arts District of what was once a veritable city within the city, complete with schools, churches, businesses, and other facilities that brought together African Americans from all over Dallas: Freedman's Town/North Dallas.[56] Starting out as a freedmen's settlement shortly after the Civil War about a mile northeast of where the Arts District is currently located (an area then outside the corporate city limits), Freedman's Town, during the 1880s, merged with several other nearby black communities such as North Dallas or Stringtown and eventually grew to form an enclave that encompassed "the entire area [between] Pearl Street and McKinney Avenue on the west, Haskell Avenue on the east, Ross Avenue on the south, and the [former freedman's, Jewish, Catholic, and Greenwood] cemeteries on the north" – currently the Uptown, Bryan Place, and Arts District neighborhoods, with the latter forming the southwestern corner of what used to be the enclave (Prior and Schulte 180). By the late 1910s, the area had become not the city's only black enclave – African-American Dallasites had always lived in "concentrated pockets" dispersed throughout the city (Fairbanks, *For the City* 40)[57] – but certainly its largest, and the "central focus of African life" in Dallas (Prior and Schulte 61):

> As the location of inordinate numbers of African American cultural organizations, churches, medical clinics, and businesses as compared to other African American communities of the city, Freedman's Town/North Dallas emerged as the principal leisure and professional center for African American Dallasites during the [Progressive Era]. Moreover, the enclave hosted the only secondary private and public schools for African Americans in the city, rendering the area a primary educational center as well.
>
> (133)

Around the same time, however, Freedman's Town/North Dallas also started to show the first signs of overcrowding and continued municipal neglect. While the enclave may have attracted African Americans from all over the city due to its various amenities, residential segregation enforced by custom and, from 1916 onwards, by a zoning ordinance that was upheld at least until 1921 (see Fairbanks, "Rethinking" 817), prevented the area from further growth: Freedman's Town/North Dallas was "virtually sealed off from expansion" by "a string of White-owned mansions along Ross Avenue" to the south, "elite, White-owned homes to the west and to the east," and the cemeteries to the north (Prior and Schulte 182). Increasingly crowded conditions – "many single-family homes had been modified for use as multiple-family dwellings" (194) – were exacerbated by the city's refusal to extend basic improvements and infrastructure to its black enclaves in general and to Freedman's Town/North Dallas in particular (see Graff 132): certain parts of Dallas had been furnished with sewer service and paved streets as early as 1899, but "African-American neighborhoods were petitioning the city for these amenities as late as the end of the 1920s" (Peter et al. vii). By 1912, garbage collection had begun in white, but not in black areas (see Gower 197). A 1925 survey of African-American housing in Dallas – carried out in black enclaves across the city, although Prior and Kemper maintain that its results also reflect conditions in Freedman's Town/North Dallas (186; see also Prior and Schulte 187) – found that more than half of all African-American homes were "barely habitable or completely unfit for habitation" (Fairbanks, *For the City* 151). Fifty percent of all-black housing did not have "gas, electricity, toilets, running water, or bath tubs" (Prior and Schulte 186); 83 percent "were on unpaved streets, and more than two-thirds had neither paved streets nor sidewalks" (186). Similar surveys from 1934, 1938, and 1940 revealed that if anything, the situation had grown even worse (see Fairbanks, *For the City* 151; and 153).

Concerned that inadequate black housing might affect the welfare of the city as a whole (as well as the image of Dallas; see Fairbanks, *For the City* 153; Prior and Kemper 185), Dallas city officials and community leaders eventually turned to slum clearance and public housing, but it was not until January 1941 that ground was broken for Dallas's first public housing project for African Americans. Located in an area of Freedman's Town/North Dallas that was considered beyond repair – namely, the area where the original Freedman's Town had been – Roseland Homes, as the project was called, would ultimately house about 650 black, carefully screened families in modernly furnished, aesthetically appealing accommodations and at low rents. Moreover, the project offered the entire community a new focal point in the shape of a spacious auditorium (see Prior and Kemper 189–90). Yet the construction of Roseland Homes also necessitated the clearance of a 191-acre site and the removal of more than 260 existing structures. Protesting against their forced displacement, the owners and renters of these buildings filed suit against the Dallas Housing Authority in 1939, but to no avail (see Fairbanks, *For the City* 159; Prior and Kemper 189). And when faced "with severely limited options, some blacks, uprooted by the slum clearance project, moved into a previously all-white area of South Dallas," residents there responded with mob violence and a series of bombings of African-American homes and businesses between September 1940 and November 1941 (Fairbanks, *For the City* 159; see also Prior and Schulte 194). As Fairbanks concludes, the public housing program "brought as many problems as solutions to Dallas blacks" (*For the City* 161).

The case of Roseland Homes to some extent already suggested the city of Dallas's generally "light regard" for black ownership (Schutze,

Accommodation 11), and it would by no means remain the only incident in which residents of Freedman's Town/North Dallas were forcibly displaced and dispossessed in the name of slum clearance, urban renewal, and general progress. Around the same time that land clearance efforts for Roseland Homes were underway, the city also started preparatory work on Central Expressway (U.S. Highway 75), the proposed six-lane link between the downtown business district and outlying residential neighborhoods which would replace the tracks of the Houston & Texas Central Railroad. Once again, black homes in Freedman's Town/North Dallas needed to make way: just as the city had invoked the federal Housing Act of 1937 to displace African Americans for Roseland Homes, it now used federal transit laws to force black property owners to sell their lots for Central Expressway (see Prior and Kemper 191). Moreover, it was not only living African Americans who were evicted by the construction project: as research undertaken in the context of the expansion of Central Expressway in the late 1980s and early 1990s revealed, the original construction project had simply paved over an acre of Freedman's Cemetery, the "principal burial ground for virtually every African American in Dallas between 1867 and 1907" (Davidson). Robert Prince, a Freedman's Town/North Dallas descendant and author of the revisionist *History of Dallas: From a Different Perspective* (1993), remembers that at the time, his family was offered $10 "for each relative whose grave could be proven to have been moved or destroyed during the construction" (N.N., *Freedman's Cemetery*). Finally, the construction of Central Expressway, which was completed in 1949, also had a disastrous impact on the community's general social and economic dynamics:

> What was envisioned by city leaders and transportation planners as a new path to and from downtown Dallas for those who lived in the affluent White neighborhoods in the northern sectors of the city became nothing less than a barrier between the western and eastern sections of North Dallas. Friends, associates, and patrons of African-American businesses literally were walled off from one another, with no easy access from one side to the other of North Dallas. Children who resided on the west side of the freeway had to cross the busy highway to attend school.
> (Prior and Kemper 191–2)

If the Central Expressway bisected the community along a north–south axis, the eight-lane Woodall Rodgers Freeway (Texas State Highway Spur 366), opened in 1962 as part of Dallas's downtown freeway loop, cut through Freedman's Town/North Dallas along an east–west axis. The construction of the Woodall Rodgers Freeway may have contributed to diverting through traffic from downtown Dallas and thus to avoiding "the paralyzing gridlock that still afflicts cities such as Phoenix" (Dillon and Tomlinson 143), but it has done so at the cost of Cochran Street, which it replaced, and which had been one of the enclave's two premier locations for stores and small businesses (see Prior and Kemper 184). Some residents, Prior and Schulte report, have considered the Woodall Rodgers Freeway "more disruptive to the community than any previous occurrence" (196), as it displaced not just businesses and residents, but also several churches as well as the Paul Lawrence Dunbar Branch Library, which had opened in 1931 as Dallas's first public library for African Americans (see 169).

The main effect on Freedman's Town/North Dallas of the construction of Roseland Homes, Central Expressway, and Woodall Rodgers Freeway was a tremendous decline in population, especially during the 1960s and 1970s. Already between 1940 and 1960, and thus "at a time when the city and county populations were expanding significantly," the enclave had lost more than 6,000 or about 30 percent of its inhabitants (Prior and Kemper 192). Some had moved to Hamilton Park, a segregated, middle-class black housing development opened in 1954 more than ten miles from downtown (see Phillips 144); others had relocated to south Dallas, most of whose white residents had joined the "white flight" to the suburbs in response to the desegregation of the public school system (see Prior and Kemper 194–5). From 1960–1980, the population of Freedman's Town/North Dallas then dropped by another 65 percent, from 14,585 to just 5,144, with the population in what would soon become the Dallas Arts District (Census Tract 17.01) having been reduced to a mere 72 (see the Census data qtd. in Prior and Kemper 193; 198; and 199). By 1980, the African-American community of Freedman's Town/North Dallas had, as Prior and Kemper have chosen to phrase it, "been 'disappeared'" (196).

In a way, then, the process of the gentrification of the former black enclave that slowly set in with the creation of the Arts District in the early 1980s did not amount, as elsewhere in Dallas and in other U.S. cities, "to 'Negro removal'" (Graff 167) – the black residents of the area had long been gone already. However, just like in other U.S. cities (New York City with its Lincoln Center remains the prime example; see Carlson, *Places* 92), the creation of a downtown arts district did lay the foundation for the urban renewal of the surrounding area, perhaps indeed, as Carlson maintains, due to the "association in the public mind developed in the eighteenth and nineteenth centuries between the monumental public theatre and elegant urban districts" (92). In fact, a 1984 "discussion document" prepared by Theatre Projects Consultants Inc. had identified "urban renewal and revitalization" as one of the primary aims and objectives of the Dallas Arts District project (Theatre Projects Consultants Incorporated 3). And it worked: bolstered later by the creation of the State-Thomas Historic District (1986), the establishment of Tax Increment Finance (TIF) Districts for the State-Thomas and Cityplace areas (in 1988 and 1992, respectively), and the creation of the Uptown Public Improvement District (PID; in 1993, renewed in 2000 and 2005), the Arts District started a process that brought the number of housing units in the former Freedman's Town/North Dallas enclave from 2,764 in 1980 to 3,143 in 2000, of which more than 75 percent had been created within these two decades – in other words, since 1980, the housing stock in the area had been almost completely renewed (see Prior and Kemper 198–9).

Uptown, Bryan Place, and the Arts District have become, Prior and Kemper have opined, "what African-American North Dallas could never have become" (207). Problems that had been ignored for decades were suddenly addressed: the TIF districts and the PID made millions of dollars available for public improvements and infrastructure; the city even extended its DART light rail system to the area (Prior and Kemper 204). Issues that had long been considered non-problematic, in turn, suddenly appeared on the agenda: in 2012, Klyde Warren Park opened over a three-block section of Woodall Rodgers Freeway, offering green spaces, a performance pavilion, a play area, food trucks, a butterfly garden as well as free events and activities to the public. Linking what is now the Arts District with what is now Uptown, the park was built, the Arts District visitor guide notes, "with connectivity in mind" (N.N., *Dallas Arts District* 9; see also Garvin 142) – a connectivity that Dallas city planners had not been too much concerned about when Uptown and the Arts District were Freedman's Town/North Dallas and when the Woodall Rodgers Freeway was Cochran Street. This is not to say that Klyde Warren Park, and the Dallas Arts District in general, are not beautiful places – they certainly are, but there is also a forgetfulness about them, a certain amnesia that, according to Michael Phillips, seems to befall Dallas whenever the city is confronted with its own past of racial strife (3). *Wading Home* shed a spotlight on this past.

The Premiere as Reprise and Rehearsal: The Night

It did so in a quite literal way: as the lights of the Moody Performance Hall's lobby shone through the venue's glass façade on the night of the premiere of *Wading Home*, they illuminated the façade of Booker T. Washington High School right across the street – especially the old, brick portion of the building that once housed Dallas's first public high school for African Americans, whereas the newer, Brad Cloepfil-designed Hamon Arts Magnet wing, opened in 2008 and off to the side, remained in the dark. Subtly, almost offhandedly, and even before the audience had entered the auditorium and the orchestra had played the first notes of the score, the premiere event thus already suggested what the opera and the performance would be all about.

But of course, *Wading Home* also shed light on the Dallas Arts District's history of African-American displacement and dispossession in a more metaphoric way. In his essay "Spatial Stories," published in *The Practice of Everyday Life* (1984), Michel de Certeau distinguishes between maps and stories as two different ways of representing space. As de Certeau argues, the map constitutes "a totalizing stage on which elements of diverse origin are brought together to form the tableau of a 'state' of geographical knowledge" (121). From this stage, however, "the operations of which it is the result or the necessary condition," – that is, the stories, tours, or itineraries that eventually produced the map – have been "pushed away," "as if into the wings" (121). Instead, the map testifies to the toponymical power of its makers, who initiate their "order of places by naming them" (130). Indeed, neither the map of Dallas that was given to me at my hotel during my stay in the city nor the map of the Dallas Arts District on the District's website that I consulted to find my way to the Moody Performance Hall on the day of the premiere told me about Freedman's Town/North Dallas, Cochran Street, or the Dallas Colored High School. Re-inventing them as "Uptown," "Bryan Place," and the "Arts District," "Woodall Rodgers Freeway" and "Klyde Warren Park," and "Booker T. Washington High School for the Performing and Visual Arts," respectively, the maps merely represented the result of "a new ordering of urban space in Dallas" (Prior and Kemper 179), "pushing away," "as if into the wings," the story behind these places and their names.

Yet, as de Certeau has famously pointed out in his essay, "[w]hat the map cuts up, the story cuts across" (129). Telling the story of African-American displacement and dispossession in rural and urban Louisiana from the nineteenth to the twenty-first century, *Wading Home* pointed to the remarkably similar story of black removal and homelessness in Dallas during the twentieth and twenty-first centuries. Hence, in a way *Wading Home* not only "pushed" from the wings and back onto the stage the history of the former center of African-American life in Dallas, the story (or, rather, the performance) also "cut across" the map of the Southern United States, inextricably linking rural upper Louisiana, New Orleans, and Dallas in a geography of black diaspora – and thus stressing the very exemplarity, rather than the exceptionality, of (post-Katrina) New Orleans.

But *Wading Home* did more than that. In "Spatial Stories," de Certeau further argues that in addition to producing the geographical knowledge out of which maps are made, stories also "organize walks," "[t]hey make the journey, before or during the time the feet perform it" (116), thus opening a "legitimate *theater* for practical *actions*," a "field that authorizes dangerous and contingent social actions" (125; emphases original). To illustrate his point, de Certeau describes and analyzes two ancient rituals or "narration[s] in acts" (124), as he also calls them: the procession of the fetiales, performed in Rome whenever the republic "'undertook any action with regard to a foreign nation,' such as a declaration of war, a military expedition, or an alliance" (124), and a ritual described in the Vedas, in which Visnu, "by his footsteps, opens the zone of space in which Indra's military action must take place" (124). Both rituals or performances, de Certeau notes, simultaneously constitute recitations and predictions, reprises of original founding acts, and rehearsals for (political or military) action (see 124–5). Similarly, envisioning the revitalization of post-Katrina New Orleans through the arts in general and through the return of African-American artists to the city in particular, *Wading Home* reprised the various acts of social activism performed by the production team – Story's work for the Sphinx Orchestra and Habitat for Humanity's "Musicians' Village," Rich's involvement with Young Strings, Hill Moore's engagement for her students – and the organizations involved in the production – the Sphinx Organization, The Black Academy of Arts and Letters, The Roots of Music organization, the Bruce R. Foote Memorial Foundation – and, at the same time, it rehearsed future activism.

Even more, rather than just representing activism on the stage and thus opening a "legitimate theater" for future actions, the premiere performance of *Wading Home*, by using the arts to gather African-American artists and black audiences – among them at least one Katrina evacuee – in an area from which African-American Dallasites had been forcibly removed, undid precisely that removal, if only for the limited time of the performance. Indeed, during those two to three hours on the night of 2 April 2015, theatrical and political action converged, as the opera's utopian vision of African-American displacement and dispossession being undone by the arts was simultaneously enacted *in* as well as *upon* the Dallas Arts District. Exposing black displacement and diaspora as a scenario that is central to the (Southern) American experience, *Wading Home* did not just imagine a counter-scenario of African-American return, but, also and at the same time, made this scenario a lived reality.

Conclusion

After the final notes of the opera had faded away, the house lights had come back on, the singers, musicians, and members of the production team had taken their well-choreographed bows – as specified in the stage directions, they were waving white handkerchiefs and dancing to an "upbeat 'second line' version of 'Just a Closer Walk with Thee' played by the brass band & percussion" (Rich and Story 40–1 [following II,8]) – and the first members of the audience had started to leave the auditorium, the "project *Wading Home*" was far from over. Already a stagehand was rearranging some chairs on the stage for the 30-minute talkback which, hosted by then general director of Fort Worth Opera Darren K. Woods, would take place immediately after the premiere. Meanwhile, backstage in the green room, a caterer was setting up drinks and a large pot of gumbo for the after-show party. On 3 April 2015, at about 11 a.m., the cast and crew were meeting again at the La Madeleine French Bakery on Mockingbird Lane, right next to the campus of Southern Methodist University, for the distribution of their payroll checks, with Rosalyn Story now acting as production accountant. Also, cash donations collected on the night before had to be counted and forwarded to The Roots of Music organization and to the Bruce R. Foote Memorial Foundation, final reports had to be written for the Sphinx Organization, and numerous congratulatory notes had to be answered.

But the performance itself was over. To be sure, there remained both material and digital traces of it, including the props used on stage (a large old Bible, a bottle of hot sauce, a steering wheel); the marked copies of the score used by the musicians and the singers; the list of people who had RSVP'd either via email or via their social media accounts; some of the twelve-page printed programs and posters; some leftover copies of *Wading Home: A Novel of New Orleans*; an "event post" on a social media website complete with pictures of and comments on the performance; countless other still pictures on people's cell phones and cameras; and even a professional sound and video recording of the entire performance that would eventually be distributed to the cast and the production team. During the days following the premiere, review articles appeared on, among others, *TheaterJones* (see Isaacs), which not only provided further material for "*Wading Home*'s Post-Katrina New Orleans," but also further evidence of the fact that something had happened on the night of 2 April 2015 in the Moody Performance Hall in the Dallas Arts District. And yet, these numerous and varied traces notwithstanding, the performance itself, the unique and unrepeatable combination of singers, musicians, technical staff, and audience members, of sights, sounds, and atmospheres, had forever disappeared and was irrevocably lost.

That, however, does not mean that the event did not matter. As "*Wading Home*'s Post-Katrina New Orleans" has sought to argue, it did matter; and it was important to different people for different reasons: to some, for instance, the premiere performance of *Wading Home* may have been particularly relevant and exciting because it was a premiere for them as well, their first opera either as a member of the audience, a cast or staff member, a (co-)producer, composer, or a librettist. To some, the night of the performance may have been important because it was the first time that they saw and heard an opera written and produced by Dallasites, dealing with issues of relevance to African Americans, and/ or with a cast of mostly black artists. Some may have found the event especially relevant because it allowed them to finally meet in person well-known or even famous musicians, singers, and writers that they had only read about, seen, or heard in the media. Others may have been to the Moody Performance Hall, the Dallas Arts District, or Dallas for their first time on that night. In fact, for some, including myself, it was virtually all of the above. And then there was at least one person to whom the premiere of *Wading Home* was particularly relevant and meaningful not only because it honored her story – that is, the story of the victims of Hurricane Katrina – but also because it brought her back to the place where she had been evacuated right after the storm and together with people who perhaps had made similar experiences of displacement and homelessness, either in New Orleans or elsewhere.

Indeed, much like the performances on New York City's Broadway during the weeks after 9/11, performances inspired by Hurricane Katrina such as *Wading Home* and *C'est Levee* were important because they offered people a chance to reconnect, "to be with others and experience themselves together" (Román 253). In the case of at least some of these performances, including *C'est Levee* and perhaps also *Wading Home*, this meant nothing less than the realization that the others were still alive. It is in this that post-Katrina performances essentially differ from other cultural artifacts inspired by the storm and its aftermath: since they do not depend on the bodily co-presence of creators and audiences, fiction, poetry, life writing and journalistic accounts, but also visual and three-dimensional art, music, as well as TV series and fictional or documentary films about Katrina and post-Katrina New Orleans can be fixed, archived, and contained, but they cannot offer their recipients such experiences of presence and aliveness. Performances, by contrast, do precisely that, yet their presence, liveness, and aliveness come at the cost of permanence, repeatability, and archivability. Indeed, their transience, momentariness, and uniqueness are what constitutes performances in the first place; performances are what they are because as soon as they are over, they are no more.

Yet before they are over, performances bring people (back) together; and this is, of course, also and precisely what *Wading Home* identifies as the key to bringing back the post-Katrina city: "What if we all felt like you?!" Velmyra asks Julian in the fourth scene of Act II of the opera when the latter defiantly claims that "folks who stay . . . are fools": "Who'd preserve our Mardi Gras, Creole food, art and his-try, jazz and blues?! . . . And what about the children? Who will teach them?" (27 [II,4]). This is *Wading Home*'s "affective vision of how the world might be better" (Dolan 6), the utopian scenario that the opera develops in order to counter the scenario of displacement and dispossession which it had pinpointed as the central experience of African-American Louisianians, both in New Orleans and elsewhere, both before Katrina and after: a return to the city in the name of the arts and the future of the children. Indeed, in its textual or semiotic reading of the opera or, more precisely, of the opera's libretto, "*Wading Home*'s Post-Katrina New Orleans" has discussed Rich and Story's work as providing the script for a "utopian performative," a performance that suggests, perhaps even promises, that beyond the diasporic past and present lies "a future that might be different" (Dolan 7), thus offering a blueprint or a critical rehearsal of that future.

As the ethnographic-phenomenological reading of the actual premiere performance of *Wading Home* on 2 April 2015 at the Moody Performance Hall in Dallas revealed, however, the event did not just rehearse the future; instead, it crossed the threshold between theatrical and political action to turn *Wading Home*'s utopian performative into a lived reality. As African-American musicians, singers, creators, and audience members returned to a part of Dallas from which they and/or their ancestors had been forcibly removed, they, too, did so in the name of the arts and – through their donations to The Roots of Music and the Bruce R. Foote Memorial Foundation – in the name of the future of the children. At the same time that it pointed to a history of African-American displacement that was singularly reminiscent of the one performed on stage, then, the premiere performance of *Wading Home* also continued a genealogy of black performance that reaches at least as far back as 1901, when the 4 July parade of the Freedman's Town/North Dallas' Colored Fair and Tri-Centennial Exposition rolled down Flora Street, bringing together black Dallasites from all over the city (see Prince 60), and it prepared the grounds for future activism in the Dallas Arts District. Through the embodied power or efficacy of performance, both the opera's scenario of African-American displacement and its counter-scenario of a return through and for the arts were transferred to and enacted in and upon Dallas. As the boundary line between theatrical and political action was blurred, so were the ones between stage and auditorium, representation and reality, setting and location, New Orleans and Dallas.

It is important to stress that the production finances, the biographies of the production team, the cast, the audience, and especially the venue and its particular atmosphere contributed at least as much, if not more, to the "activist" dimension of the premiere of *Wading Home* as the score and the libretto of the opera itself. And it is equally important to stress that some of these aspects of the performance lay only partially within or even entirely beyond the control of the production team: Story, Rich, and Hill Moore may have teamed up with The Black Academy of Arts and Letters explicitly in order to reach as many African-American Dallasites as possible, but they could at no point have predicted how many would actually find their way to the Dallas Arts District on the night. Likewise, they may have been able to foresee, but during the frenzy days before the premiere surely had no time to think about, the way the bright lights of the Performance Hall lobby would illuminate the brick façade of Booker T. Washington High School for the Performing and Visual Arts and thus direct my – and perhaps also others' – attention to the history of the building and to that of the Dallas Arts District in general. And they certainly could have neither predicted nor engineered the specific atmosphere in the Hall during the event, which was, like all atmospheres emanating from particular places, "affected by the presence of things, people, or the environmental surroundings and their ecstasies," but which nevertheless belonged "neither to objects nor to people" (Fischer-Lichte, *Introduction* 24).

All this amounts and testifies to the fact that performances – whether theatrical presentations, rituals, games, sports, or play – and their reception can be neither predicted nor controlled and that, hence, the variety of their potential meanings cannot be fully gleaned or deducted from either the scripts that supposedly regulate them or the digital and material traces that they leave behind – or, as Jill Dolan has phrased it, "[w]e write best about those performances we've been privileged to see" (9). In this sense, "*Wading Home*'s Post-Katrina New Orleans" constitutes a highly privileged account of the premiere performance of *Wading Home*, written by someone who not only attended the event, but who had also read and written about the novel that inspired it; who had access to the "script" before the performance itself; who had seen the dress rehearsal; who had communicated with the cast, the creators, and other people involved both before and after the event; and who had the time and means to conduct research, reflect, and record his thoughts and memories in the shape of a scholarly text. It is quite impossible to say what other accounts in whatever form, created by differently privileged persons, the premiere of *Wading Home* has inspired – the published reviews and the congratulatory notes sent to the production team may only represent a small fraction. It *is* possible to say, however, that the premiere of *Wading Home* inspired other performances.

Acknowledgments

An earlier version of the subchapter "Displacement and Dispossession in Wading Home: A Novel of New Orleans" was originally published as Freitag, Florian. "Displacement and Dispossession: The Plantation Regime as a Disaster Discourse in Rosalyn Story's Wading Home (2010)" in *Ten Years after Katrina: Critical Perspectives of the Storm's Effect on American Culture and Identity*. Ed. Mary Ruth Marotte and Glenn Jellenik. Lanham: Lexington, 2015. 129–51. Print. Rowman & Littlefield. All rights reserved.

Notes

1. In New Orleans, the tradition of masked individuals parading through the city in order to celebrate carnival dates back at least as far as 1837, the year the first newspaper account of such a procession was published in the *New Orleans Picayune* (see Gotham 25). Prior to 1857, parade organizers had simply "published a meeting place and a route, thereby inviting all maskers to unite" (R. Mitchell, *Mardi Gras* 24). Hence, the Mistick Krewe of Comus not only started the tradition of choosing a parade theme, it was also "the first organization to insist on the division between parade and people, maskers and audience" (24).

2. Strictly speaking, then, Krewe du Vieux's is not a Mardi Gras parade. Although in New Orleans, the carnival season lasts from 6 January (Twelfth Night, or the Feast of the Epiphany) to Mardi Gras (see Gotham 22), the parade season only starts twelve days before Mardi Gras. As Arthur Hardy, editor of the annual *Mardi Gras Guide*, explains: "They [Krewe du Vieux] are a part of Mardi Gras even though they are not a Mardi Gras parade" (qtd. in O'Neill 93).
3. It is hard to pinpoint exactly when the "old traditions" evoked in this statement were actually discontinued by other New Orleans carnival krewes. Motorized parade floats – as opposed to hand- or mule-drawn vehicles – were first introduced in the 1950s (see Stanonis, "Mardi Gras" 213). The use of satirical themes in general and political satire in particular had reached its height in the 1870s, when all-white elite krewes employed carnival processions and tableaux as a "theater of political protest" against Reconstruction (see R. Mitchell, *Mardi Gras* 69). Parading in the French Quarter, finally, was banned by a city ordinance in 1973 due to crowd control issues (see Souther 175).
4. *C'est Levee* was by no means the first post-Katrina parade in New Orleans, however. Scott S. Ellis notes that on 4 September 2005, just four days after the levees had failed, about 40 people kept up the annual tradition of staging a parade in the French Quarter on the Sunday before Labor Day to celebrate LGBT pride. Known as "Southern Decadence," this tradition had first been established in 1972 (142–4).
5. Krewe du Vieux's parades usually consist of altogether 19 floats: a title float, which bears the krewe's logo and announces the theme of this year's parade, a royalty float with this year's "king" or "queen" (usually someone who the krewe believes has contributed to the social and cultural uniqueness of the city), and 17 themed floats, each decorated by one of Krewe du Vieux's 17 sub-krewes and accompanied by a brass band and some of the sub-krewe's members in appropriate costumes, which interpret the parade's main theme. For a list of past Krewe du Vieux parade themes and royalty, see N.N., "Past Themes"; for a detailed list of *C'est Levee* float themes, see N.N., "C'est Levee."
6. There was, however, also some opposition to carnival, with some people questioning the "propriety of holding the celebration while the city still lay in ruin" (Thevenot), while others worried that it would chase away "national sympathy and thus national money" (Mitchell, "Carnival" 789). See also Jensen, "Vieux"; and Abrahams et al. 3.
7. Turning "the city's ravaged wards [into] a vast creative cultural playground and site of politically charged engagements" (H. Taylor 492), these performances can thus be classified as "environmental" or "site-specific" performances; see Carlson, *Performance* 105; and Pearson and Shanks 23.
8. Wallenberg; H. Taylor, "After the Deluge"; and A.J. Fox mention and discuss numerous post-Katrina performances in New Orleans and elsewhere. On *Festival New Orleans*, see H. Taylor, "After the Deluge" 499. On *Waiting for Godot in New Orleans*, see, among others, Chan; Jackson 210–38; Bishop 250–5; Salvaggio 109–20; and A.J. Fox 51–70; and 87–91. On *The Katrina Project: Hell and High Water*, see Saldaña 159. On *Lakeviews: A Sunset Bus Tour*, see Bowling and Carrico; and A.J. Fox, 70–91. On the 2006 *Jazz Fest*, see Porter; H. Taylor 489; and Watts and Porter 12–32. On the Centre for Playback Theatre's performances in New Orleans, see H. Fox 94; and A.J. Fox 135–75.
9. See, to give some of the most well-known examples, Jesmyn Ward's *Salvage the Bones* (2009), Tony Dunbar's *Tubby Meets Katrina* (2006), Lauren

Tarshis's *I Survived: Hurricane Katrina, 2005* (2011), some of the stories collected in Julie Smith's *New Orleans Noir* (2007), Dave Eggers's *Zeitoun* (2009), Suzanne M. Trauth and Lisa S. Brenner's *Katrina on Stage: Five Plays* (2011), Niyi Osundare's *City without People: The Katrina Poems* (2011), Dr. John's 2008 album *The City That Care Forgot*, Rolland Golden's "Desperation" (acrylic on canvas; 2006), Lewis Watts's "New Orleans Suite: A Photographic Essay" (2015), Josh Neufeld's *A.D.: New Orleans after the Deluge* (2009), Banksy's "Girl with Umbrella" (2008), the Katrina Memorial on Canal Street in New Orleans (dedicated in 2008), David Simon and Eric Overmyer's *Treme* (HBO; 2010–2013), Zack Godshell's *Low and Behold* (2007), and Tia Lessin and Carl Deal's *Trouble the Water* (2008).

10. Of course, many of these performances have been documented in one way or another. For instance, in addition to numerous verbal accounts, photographs, and videos of *C'est Levee*, a partial reenactment of the parade, including four of its original floats, was filmed for the sixth episode of the first season of HBO's *Treme* (see Anderson 00:54:46–00:57:23). The event of the parade itself, however, is irretrievably lost.

11. The "*Wading Home*" in the title of this chapter thus simultaneously refers to Story's novel, Story and Rich's opera, and the premiere performance of this opera in April 2015 in Dallas.

12. Hence, in Erika Fischer-Lichte's terms, "*Wading Home*'s Post-Katrina New Orleans" recognizes and pays attention to both the performance's "*perceptual order of representation*" and its "*perceptual order of presence*," discussing, as it will, bodies, places, and objects both as signs (characters, places, and objects within the fictional world of the opera) and as "bodily being[s]-in-the-world," actual places, and "objects in their phenomenal being" (*Introduction* 40; emphasis original; see also, amongst others, Fischer-Lichte and Roselt 248–51). In the context of opera, Linda and Michael Hutcheon have chosen a similar approach (with a special focus on bodies) for their study *Bodily Charm: Living Opera* (2000): "This book is written in the spirit of the critical recovery and rediscovery of bodies as sites of meaning – the bodies both represented and performing on stage" (xviii).

13. Accompanied by sub-krewe members dressed in Napoleon costumes and featuring bunting in the French national colors, a model of the Eiffel Tower, a krewe member dressed as Joan of Arc, and a mime artist (played by famous New Orleans blogger Ashley Morris), the float was the third float in the parade (following the title and the royalty floats) and became perhaps the most well-known part of *C'est Levee*. According to Helen Taylor, its satirical appeal to reverse the Louisiana Purchase of 1803 "affirmed a disconnect with the nation" (182) and with the federal government in particular. Indeed, the corresponding article in Krewe du Vieux's yearly carnival newspaper, *Le Monde de Merde*, contrasted "US Government concerns about the tremendous cost associated with the rebuilding and rebirth of the great city of New Orleans" with the prompt financial help offered to New Orleans by the French government immediately after the hurricane (see N.N., "Buy Us Back"). The float was also prominently featured in the reenactment of *C'est Levee* for *Treme* (see Anderson 00:55:20–00:55:36).

14. Conceptual links between theater and other kinds of social activities had already been suggested in the late 1950s by British anthropologist Victor Turner, Canadian-American sociologist Erving Goffman, and Polish-American anthropologist Milton Singer (see Turner, *Schism* xxv; Goffman 22; and Singer xii). In his essay, Schechner actually discusses Goffman's *The Presentation of Self in Everyday Life* (see 27n22); and from the 1970s

onward, he would collaborate extensively with Turner (see, for instance, Schechner, *Performance Studies* 16–9).
15. Among these, McKenzie's undoubtedly has the widest scope, as it discusses not only cultural, but also managerial and technological performance.
16. I am not talking here, of course, about a specific *production* of, for instance, a play, which is of course designed to be repeated, using the very same performers, stage sets, props, costumes, etc., evening after evening, perhaps even trying to attract a certain audience and to provoke certain responses from them (see Fischer-Lichte, *Introduction* 22).
17. This specifically applies to performance studies in the United States, where the audience has traditionally been conceptualized as an essentially passive one (see Carlson, "Dynamiken" 338–9). German *Theaterwissenschaft*, by contrast, has from its very beginnings in the early twentieth century viewed the audience as a co-creator of the performance (see, for instance, Fischer-Lichte and Roselt 239).
18. At the same time, of course, there were also scholars such as Lloyd Pratt who rejected and sought to overcome the "exception/example binary" (252).
19. Several scholars have stressed the relevance of race to public reactions to Hurricane Katrina. In "Worlds Apart: Blacks and Whites React to Hurricane Katrina," for instance, Leonie Huddy and Stanley Feldman provide a vast amount of data to support their thesis that "Hurricane Katrina elicited the kind of polarized racial reaction typically reserved for racial issues such as affirmative action and housing integration" (110). See also M.C. Dawson 21–62.
20. Drawing on Gilberto Freyre's *The Masters and the Slaves* (1946) and George L. Beckford's *Persistent Poverty* (1972), Elizabeth Russ has pointed out in her *The Plantation in the Postslavery Imagination* (2010) that this power regime constitutes a "total institution" in the sense that it includes "everything from 'a system of production (a latifundiary monoculture)' and 'a system of labor (slavery)' to 'a system of sexual and family life (polygamous patriarchalism)' and 'a system of bodily and household hygiene'" (8–9) as well as, one may add, a system of mobility and transportation. Russ's enumeration of the effects of the plantation system of the Americas underscores the continuity between the antebellum rural South and post-Katrina Louisiana: the legacy of the slaveholding plantation, Russ writes, is formed by "[t]he displacement and extermination of native populations, the forced exile and enslavement of millions of Africans, . . . the ravaging of peoples and lands" (3). The storm's disastrous environmental impact, and particularly the race-inflected regulation of mobility and the ensuing displacement of African Americans during and immediately following Katrina, inscribe the event into the ongoing history of the plantation regime. It is this continuity of antebellum institutionalized or structural racist practices in contemporary Louisiana that the term plantation regime seeks to convey.
21. All of Rosalyn Story's fiction and non-fiction books so far have revolved around African-American musicians: *And So I Sing: African-American Divas of Opera and Concert* (1990), Story's first book, is a history of black opera divas; *More Than You Know* (2004), her first novel, features a jazz saxophonist and his wife, a singer. Story herself is a violinist with the Fort Worth Symphony.
22. In the introduction to *What Is a City?* (2008), Phil Steinberg quotes a *New York Times* article from 2005, according to which:

> [c]ities are often naturally transient. New Orleans before the hurricane was not. Of 70 localities in the nation with populations of at least

250,000, New Orleans ranked second in the percentage of its American-born population born in the state – 83 percent, according to the census. . . . Consider the Lower Ninth Ward, a mostly poor, black neighborhood wiped out in the flooding. The census found that 54 percent of its residents had been in their homes for 10 years or more, according to the Greater New Orleans Community Data Center. Nationally, the figure was 35 percent.

(Levy qtd. in Steinberg 14; see also Falk, Hunt, and Hunt 120–1)

23. See, for instance, the following quote by Kai T. Erikson:

"Katrina" exploded into being in August 2005, but it does not have a defined location in the flow of time. [W]hat we mean by "Katrina" began long before the storm of that name began to take shape, and it will be an ongoing event for a long time to come. The storm is not over.

(xviii)

24. The notion of disposability links this passage with critical analyses that have connected Katrina with the politics of neoliberalism rather than racism. In addition to Henry A. Giroux (11; see earlier), see also Michael C. Dawson, who points to "the neoliberal tendency to regard needy populations, such as those that appeared so starkly after Katrina, as disposable" (x). In *Wading Home*, by contrast, neoliberal politics are depicted as only one way in which racism and racial injustice manifest themselves.
25. Genevieve claims that Julian has been "'told all this before.' . . . 'Ain't nobody blaming you for forgetting, but you been told before'" (Story, *Wading Home* 171).
26. In order to clearly identify the position of Claudinette's cabin on the plantation's map of spatialized racism, it may be useful to compare and contrast it with La Blanche's cabin in Kate Chopin's short story "Désirée's Baby" (originally published as "The Father of Désirée's Baby" in 1893). In Chopin's story, the plantation owner Armand presumably has an affair with La Blanche, a slave who lives in a cabin far away from the plantation mansion. As Chopin's main character famously notes: "Armand heard [the baby cry] the other day as far away as La Blanche's cabin" (70). As Armand does not recognize La Blanche as his partner nor their children as legitimate heirs, La Blanche's cabin, like Armand's mansion, is firmly integrated into the racist spatial politics of the plantation – if Armand and La Blanche meet there, they meet as master and slave. Claudinette's cabin, by contrast, constitutes a place where slave and master meet as lovers, a place ideologically free of the plantation regime.
27. More specifically, Nathan Larouchette, the white real estate developer who tries to take hold of Silver Creek and the adjacent properties, uses the fact that among African-American families in Louisiana, property is often handed down from one generation to the next without written wills and then owned communally by all the rightful heirs. If one of the heirs sells his share, however, the new shareholder can request that the property be auctioned to the highest bidder, and thus acquire the rest of the estate.
28. Referred to as a holographic testament outside of Louisiana, an olographic will is handwritten and does not have to be witnessed (see Friedman 171).
29. These and other details (see ahead) were shared with me during several conversations with Rich and Story conducted in person and via email from April 2015 through September 2017.

30. The following reading of *Wading Home: An Opera of New Orleans* is based on the unpublished version of the libretto that Rosalyn Story sent me via email in March 2015.
31. Balestrini maintains that although "opera in English translation or opera with an original English-language libretto remained controversial into the mid-twentieth century," English comic operas had long been performed parallel to operas in other European languages in the United States (70). With respect to jazz and opera, the combination of "these two differently racially encoded musical arts" has often been regarded "almost a contradiction in terms" (Hutcheon and Hutcheon, "Jazz" 27; see also Clarke). Nevertheless, operas about jazz musicians and/or musically borrowing from jazz have been written in both Europe and North America at least since the late 1920s (for example, Ernst Krenek's *Jonny spielt auf* [1927], D.D. Jackson [music] and George Elliott Clarke's [libretto] *Québécité* [2003], and, perhaps most famously, *Porgy and Bess* [1935], written by George Gershwin [music] and DuBose Heyward and Ira Gershwin [libretto]). (Incidentally, Rich has stated that she doesn't "pretend to have written a jazz opera" [qtd. in Weeks], although in one of my conversations with her, she also noted that she has "woven in elements of jazz – rhythms, harmonies, moods, instrumentation" as well as two actual jazz tunes [see ahead]. Reviewers of *Wading Home* have also commented on the "occasional brassy outburst" and the "jazzy episodes" in the score [Cantrell, "'Wading Home'"].) *Porgy and Bess*, in turn, probably also constitutes the most well-known opera to feature a cast of all-black characters, although its depiction of African Americans has not been considered essentially different from that of earlier operas with individual black protagonists (see André). Finally, apart from *Wading Home*, at least two other operas have been inspired by Hurricane Katrina, namely Anne LeBaron (music) and Douglas Kearney's (libretto) *Crescent City: A Hyperopera* (2012; see Maurer) and Jeanne Nathan's *The 9th Ward Improv Opera* (2015; see N.N., "CANO's").
32. Although I did enjoy several years of classical voice training as a teenager, I consider myself by no means equipped to discuss *Wading Home*'s score in a scholarly way. Some literary and cultural critics who have discussed specific operas have resorted to previous musicological analyses to supplement their distinctive disciplinary perspective on these works (see, for instance, Hutcheon and Hutcheon, *Desire, Disease, Death* xv). As *Wading Home* is a relatively recent work whose score has, to my knowledge, not (yet) received any serious scholarly attention beyond a few reviews, this has not been an option in the present case.
33. Here and in the following, the Arabic numbers refer to the page numbers of the typed libretto. The Latin and Arabic numbers in square brackets refer to the act and scene from which the quote is taken, respectively.
34. It is not entirely clear whether the chorus here represents the Fortier ancestors or the former inhabitants of the neighborhood, although some of the lines sung by the chorus in this scene (for example, "This is your land, right where you stand," 26 [II,4]) are identical to those sung by the chorus of the ancestors in the Silver Creek scene (see 18 [I,9]).
35. In opera, the term brindisi refers to a "Dionysian toast" or drinking song (see, for instance, Hutcheon and Hutcheon, *Bodily Charm* 183).
36. Again, these and other details (see ahead) were shared with me during several conversations with Rich, Story, and Hill Moore conducted in person and via email from April 2015 through September 2017.
37. The program of this production has been on display at "Facing the Rising Sun: Freedman's Cemetery," a multimedia exhibition curated by Alan

Govenar for the African American Museum of Dallas at Dallas Fair Park in 2012.
38. In June 1952, the city of Dallas had already hosted the American opening of one of the major revivals of *Porgy and Bess*, which featured William Warfield as Porgy and "prima donna assoluta" Leontyne Price as Bess (see Story, *And So I Sing* 67–8; 100; and 106).
39. Established through the National Arts and Cultural Development Act of 1964, the National Council on the Arts "advises the Chairman of the National Endowment for the Arts, who also chairs the Council, on agency policies and programs. It reviews and makes recommendations to the Chairman on applications for grants, funding guidelines, and leadership initiatives" (see N.N., "About the NEA").
40. In her *And So I Sing: African-American Divas of Opera and Concert*, published in 1990, Rosalyn Story already pointed out that in "professional symphony orchestras, of which there are hundreds in the United States, one or two black members on a roster of 85 to 105 is normal, but many orchestras employ no black players" (184).
41. The Roots of Music's social media accounts (e.g., www.facebook.com/The RootsOf Music/) inform followers about upcoming performances in New Orleans and elsewhere.
42. To my knowledge, the only person involved in the premiere of *Wading Home* who was actually born in New Orleans and lived there when Hurricane Katrina hit the city was choreographer Michelle Gibson, who now resides in Dallas. Tellingly, in its coverage of the premiere, North Texas public broadcaster KERA focused on Gibson and her story of evacuation (see Weeks).
43. Sometimes described as "violinist's cramp" or "pianist's cramp," focal (hand) dystopia is a crippling neurological condition that manifests as a loss of muscular control and thus severely limits musicians' ability to play.
44. Incidentally, with the exception of the Young Nurse, neither the libretto nor the event program explicitly and directly state the racial or ethnic heritage of any of the characters of *Wading Home: An Opera of New Orleans*. As they are clearly based on the characters in *Wading Home: A Novel of New Orleans*, however – each cast member received a copy to allow them to "establish deeper bonds" with their character (see Story, "Wading Home") – their racial or ethnic identity may be inferred from the descriptions in Story's novel.
45. Alison Kinney reports that the "Metropolitan Opera's first unblackened Otello, Latvian tenor Aleksandrs Antonenko, was in a 2015 production." The reverse case, that is, that of African-American singers wearing white makeup to play a white role, has also been documented (see Ingraham, So, and Moodley 3).
46. In fact, for their debuts at the New York City Opera and the Metropolitan Opera, Camilla Williams and Marian Anderson were casted in the non-black, but also non-white, roles of Madama Butterfly (in Puccini's eponymous opera) and Ulrica, respectively (see Story, *And So I Sing* 53–4; and Hutcheon and Hutcheon, "Jazz" 25).
47. Already in *And So I Sing*, Story had commented upon the fact that even "in cities such as New York, Philadelphia, and Washington, DC, which claim a progressive arts community as well as a sizeable black population, blacks comprise a negligible fraction of the audience at operas and classical concerts" (221). Story's observations about the audience of the Dallas premiere of *Wading Home*, in turn, were corroborated by some of Moody Performance Hall's ushers with whom I talked informally during the intermission and after the event. They also pointed out the unusually lively response of

the audience, especially during the "comedy" sections (Simon's complaints about hospital food) and during the opera's finale, when some interacted directly with the performers on stage in what Mayo and Holt have described as "traditional African call and response fashion" (6; see also 9).
48. In a different conversation, Story explained that it was precisely for this reason that she had decided against e.g., the Morton H. Meyerson Symphony Center (also located in the Dallas Arts District, but less well-known amongst black Dallasites) or one of The Black Academy of Arts and Letters facilities at the Dallas Convention Center, although other considerations, including size, acoustics, and rent costs, may have played roles, as well.
49. In fact, the Performance Hall had long been called the "third venue" in reference to the Morton H. Meyerson Symphony and the AT&T Performing Arts Center (the "first" and "second" venues, opened right next door in 1989 and 2009, respectively).
50. These and other details (see ahead) were shared with me during a conversation with Russell Dyer, general manager of the Moody Performance Hall, that took place on 28 March 2017, at the Moody Performance Hall.
51. The nine sponsoring institutions were: the Dallas Ballet, the Dallas Civic Opera, the Museum of Fine Arts, the Dallas Health and Science Museum, the Shakespeare Festival, the Dallas Summer Musicals, the Dallas Symphony Association, the Dallas Theater Center, and Theater Three (see Carr et al. 5–9). Not all of these institutions would eventually relocate to the new Arts District.
52. Janet Kutner from the *Dallas Morning News* agreed, noting that the selected site "is accessible to everyone, is nobody's turf, provides good public transportation, and might make downtown come alive 24 hours rather than just during the day" (qtd. in Arnold 16).
53. Of course, by 1982, work had already begun on the "Dallas Pedestrian Network," an "analogous" or "parallel city" in downtown Dallas conceived by "Multilevel Man" Vincent Ponte, the designer of Montréal's "Ville Souterraine" (see James and Yoos 202; 218).
54. Indeed, when I first visited the Dallas Arts District in April 2015, Flora Street seemed strangely empty during the day, even during lunch hours.
55. According to Skipper (107), in the past 30 years St. Paul has actively sought to adapt to its changing environment by identifying as an "Arts Church."
56. Other reminders, located outside of the current Arts District, are the Pythian Temple (built between 1913 and 1915) and St. James African Methodist Episcopal Church (1919–1921), both designed by Dallas-based African-American architect William Sidney Pittman (the son-in-law of Booker T. Washington), as well as Freedman's Memorial Park and Cemetery, erected in 1993 on the site of Freedman's Town's former cemetery (1869–1907; see Prince 68; Prior and Schulte 93; 144; and Davidson).
57. This makes it quite impossible to give more detailed information about Freedman's Town/North Dallas, as some statistics, including the number of blacks living in Dallas, are only available for the city at large, not for the individual pockets (see, for instance, Prior and Schulte 187).

Bibliography

Abrahams, Roger D., Nick Spitzer, Robert Farris Thompson, and John F. Szwed. *Blues for New Orleans: Mardi Gras and America's Creole Soul*. Philadelphia: U of Pennsylvania P, 2006. Print.

Adams, Vincanne. *Markets of Sorrow, Labors of Faith: New Orleans in the Wake of Katrina*. Durham: Duke UP, 2013. Print.
Adkins, Alton. "Wading Home by Rosalyn Story." *YouTube* (24 November 2010). www.youtube.com/watch?v=Jm9WhW-XKJY. Web.
Allen, Jamie, Carolyn Jabr, and Marion Davies. "Preface." *Dallas Symphony Orchestra Young Strings: Changing Lives Through Music*. Ed. Jamie Allen, Carolyn Jabr, and Richard Rejino. Dallas: Dallas Symphony Orchestra, 2012. N.P. Print.
Anderson, Brad, dir. "Shallow Water, Oh Mama." *Treme* 1.6 (16 May 2010). TV show.
André, Naomi, Karen M. Bryan, and Eric Saylor. "Introduction: Representing Blackness on the Operatic Stage." *Blackness in Opera*. Ed. Naomi André, Karen M. Bryan, and Eric Saylor. Urbana: U of Illinois P, 2012. 1–9. Print.
Angel, Ronald J., Holly Bell, Julie Beausoleil, and Laura Lein. *Community Lost: The State, Civil Society, and Displaced Survivors of Hurricane Katrina*. Cambridge: Cambridge UP, 2012. Print.
Anjaria, Jonathan Shapiro. "On Street Life and Urban Disasters: Lessons from a 'Third World' City." *What Is a City? Rethinking the Urban after Hurricane Katrina*. Ed. Rob Shields and Phil Steinberg. Athens: U of Georgia P, 2008. 186–202. Print.
Arnold, Leigh. "Arts District-Downtown: A City's Cultural Dream Come True." *A Developing Art Scene, Postwar to Present*. Ed. Ellen Hirzy. Dallas: Dallas Museum of Art, 2013. https://publications.dma.org/publication/dallas-sites#section/100. Web.
Bakhtin, Mikhail. *Problems of Dostoevsky's Poetics*. Trans. R.W. Rotsel. Ann Arbor: Ardis, 1973. Print.
Balestrini, Nassim Winnie. *From Fiction to Libretto: Irving, Hawthorne, and James as Opera*. Frankfurt: Lang, 2005. Print.
Balme, Christopher. *Einführung in die Theaterwissenschaft*. Fifth ed. Berlin: Schmidt, 1999. Print.
Batsell, Jake. "Deadline Doesn't End Cities' Katrina Role." *Dallas Morning News* (31 March 2006): 2B. Print.
Bauridl, Birgit, and Pia Wiegmink. "Toward an Integrative Model of Performance in Transnational American Studies." *Amerikastudien/American Studies* 60.1 (2015): 157–68. Print.
Bay, Mia. "Invisible Tethers: Transportation and Discrimination in the Age of Katrina." *Katrina's Imprint: Race and Vulnberability in America*. Ed. Roland Anglin, Jeffrey Dowd, Karen M. O'Neill, and Keith Wailoo. New Brunswick, NJ: Rutgers UP, 2010. 21–33. Print.
Bellerophon Quill Club of The Booker T. Washington High School. *A History of The Dallas High School for Negroes*. Dallas: Friends of the Dallas Public Library, 1991 [1938]. Print.
Bial, Henry. "Performance Studies 3.0." *The Performance Studies Reader*. Ed. Henry Bial and Sara Brady. Third ed. London: Routledge, 2016. 402–11. Print.
Bial, Henry, and Sara Brady. "What Is Performance?" *The Performance Studies Reader*. Ed. Henry Bial and Sara Brady. Third ed. London: Routledge, 2016. 58. Print.
Bishop, Claire. *Artificial Hells: Participatory Art and the Politics of Spectatorship*. London: Verso, 2012. Print.

Blakely, Edward James. *My Storm: Managing the Recovery of New Orleans in the Wake of Katrina*. Philadelphia: U of Pennsylvania P, 2012. Print.

Booth, Herb. "Texas Expecting Up to 60,000 New Students." *Dallas Morning News* (7 September 2005): 1A–20A. Print.

Bowling, William, and Rachel Carrico. "*Lakeviews: A Bus Tour* as a Vehicle for Regrowth in New Orleans." *TDR* 52.1 (2008): 190–96. Print.

Buras, Kirsten L. "Introduction: Counterstories on Pedagogy and Policy Making. Coming of Age in the Privatized City." *Pedagogy, Policy, and the Privatized City: Stories of Dispossession and Defiance from New Orleans*, by Kristen L. Buras et al. New York: Teachers College P, 2010. 1–16. Print.

Camp, Jordan T. "'We Know This Place': Neoliberal Racial Regimes and the Katrina Circumstance." *American Quarterly* 61.3 (2009): 693–717. Print.

Cantrell, Scott. "New Arts District Venue a Hit So Far." *Dallas Morning News* (26 September 2013): E1. Print.

———. "New Venue Offers Promise, Pitfalls." *Dallas Morning News* (5 August 2012): A1. Print.

———. "Ten Years after Katrina, New Opera Honors the Hurricane's Survivors." *Dallas News* (29 March 2015). www.dallasnews.com/arts/arts/2015/03/29/ten-years-after-katrina-new-opera-honors-the-hurricanes-survivors. Web.

———. "'Wading Home' Dramatizes New Orleans Family's Hurricane Katrina Experiences." *Dallas News* (16 September 2015). www.dallasnews.com/arts/arts/2015/09/16/wading-home-dramatizes-new-orleans-familys-hurricane-katrina-experiences. Web.

Carlin, Phyllis Scott, and Linda M. Park-Fuller. "Disaster Narrative Emergent/cies: Performing Loss, Identity and Resistance." *Text and Performance Quarterly* 32.1 (2012): 20–37. Print.

Carlson, Marvin. "Dynamiken und Herausforderungen von Aufführungen." *Die Aufführung: Diskurs, Macht, Analyse*. Ed. Erika Fischer-Lichte, Adam Czirak, Torsten Jost, Frank Richarz, and Nina Tecklenburg. Munich: Fink, 2012. 337–41. Print.

———. *Performance: A Critical Introduction*. Second ed. New York: Routledge, 1996. Print.

———. *Places of Performance: The Semiotics of Theatre Architecture*. Ithaca: Cornell UP, 1989. Print.

Carr, Stephen, E.G. Hamilton, Weiming Lu, Kevin Lynch, Charles Norris, and Sherry Wagner. *A Comprehensive Arts Facilities Plan for Dallas*. N.P.: N.P., 1977. Print.

Chan, Paul. "Provocation: Next Day, Same Place. After Godot in New Orleans." *TDR* 52.4 (2008): 2–3. Print.

Cheatham, Wallace McClain. "Racism and Sexism: Melodies That Continue to Soar on the Operatic Landscape." *Opera in a Multicultural World: Coloniality, Culture, Performance*. Ed. Mary I. Ingraham, Joseph K. So, and Roy Moodley. New York: Routledge, 2016. 178–90. Print.

Chopin, Kate. "The Father of Désirée's Baby." *Vogue* (14 January 1893): 70–74. Print.

Clark, Cassie. "Away, But Rooting for Home." *Dallas Morning News* (8 February 2010): B1. Print.

Clarke, George Elliott. "Jazzing Up Opera: A Defence of *Québécité*." *Opera in a Multicultural World: Coloniality, Culture, Performance*. Ed. Mary I. Ingraham, Joseph K. So, and Roy Moodley. New York: Routledge, 2016. 193–212. Print.

Conquergood, Dwight. "Of Caravans and Carnivals: Performance Studies in Motion." *TDR* 39.4 (1995): 137–41. Print.

———. "Performance Theory, Hmong Shamans, and Cultural Politics." *Critical Theory and Performance*. Ed. Janelle G. Reinelt and Joseph R. Roach. Ann Arbor: The U of Michigan P, 1992. 41–64. Print.

Cook, Bernie. *Flood of Images: Media, Memory, and Hurricane Katrina*. Austin: U of Texas P, 2015. Print.

Davidson, James M. "Freedman's Cemetery (1869–1907): Establishing a Chronology for Exhumed Burials from an African-American Burial Ground, Dallas, Texas." *African Diaspora Archaeology Newsletter* 6.4 (1999). http://scholarworks.umass.edu/cgi/viewcontent.cgi?article=1725&context=adan. Web.

Dawson, Michael C. *Not in Our Lifetimes: The Future of Black Politics*. Chicago: U of Chicago P, 2011. Print.

Dawson, Stuart O. "Dallas Arts District." *Urban Design International* 4.3 (1983): 20–23. Print.

———. "The Skyscraper's Base: Architecture, Landscape and Use in the Dallas Arts District." *Second Century of the Skyscraper*. Ed. L.S. Beedle. Boston: Springer, 1988. 989–1001. Print.

De Certeau, Michel. *The Practice of Everyday Life*. Trans. Stephen Rendall. Berkeley: U of California P, 1988 [1984]. Print.

Deloughery, Kathleen. "Is New Orleans Ready to Celebrate After Katrina? Evidence from Mardi Gras and the Tourism Industry." *Natural Disaster Analysis after Hurricane Katrina: Risk Assessment, Economic Impacts, and Social Implications*. Ed. Harry Ward Richardson, Peter Gordon, and James Elliott Moore. Cheltenham: Edward Elgar, 2008. 134–46. Print.

Diamond, Andrew. "Naturalizing Disaster: Neoliberalism, Cultural Racism, and Depoliticization in the Era of Katrina." *Hurricane Katrina in Transatlantic Perspective*. Ed. Romain Huret and Randy J. Sparks. Baton Rouge: Louisiana State UP, 2014. 81–99. Print.

Dickerson, Niki T. "The Katrina Diaspora: Dislocation and the Reproduction of Segregation and Employment Inequality." *Katrina's Imprint: Race and Vulnerability in America*. Ed. Roland Anglin, Jeffrey Dowd, Karen M. O'Neill, and Keith Wailoo. New Brunswick, NJ: Rutgers UP, 2010. 169–80. Print.

Dillon, David (text), and Doug Tomlinson (photographs). *Dallas Architecture, 1936–1986*. Austin: Texas Monthly, 1985. Print.

Dolan, Jill. *Utopia in Performance: Finding Hope at the Theater*. Ann Arbor: U of Michigan P, 2005. Print.

Dyson, Michael E. *Come Hell or High Water: Hurricane Katrina and the Color of Disaster*. New York: Basic, 2006. Print.

———. "Great Migrations?" *After the Storm: Black Intellectuals Explore the Meaning of Hurricane Katrina*. Ed. David Dante Troutt. New York: New P, 2006. 75–84. Print.

Elliott, Robin. "Blacks and Blackface at the Opera." *Opera in a Multicultural World: Coloniality, Culture, Performance*. Ed. Mary I. Ingraham, Joseph K. So, and Roy Moodley. New York: Routledge, 2016. 34–49. Print.

Ellis, Scott S. *Madame Vieux Carré: The French Quarter in the Twentieth Century*. Jackson: UP of Mississippi, 2010. Print.

Erikson, Kai T. "Foreword." *The Sociology of Katrina: Perspectives on a Modern Catastrophe*. Ed. David L. Brunsma, David Overfelt, and J. Steven Picou. Lanham: Rowman & Littlefield, 2007. xvii–xx. Print.

Fairbanks, Robert B. *For the City as a Whole: Planning, Politics, and the Public Interest in Dallas, Texas, 1900–1965*. Columbus: Ohio State UP, 1998. Print.

———. "Rethinking Urban Problems: Planning, Zoning, and City Government in Dallas, 1900–1930." *Journal of Urban History* 25.6 (1999): 809–37. Print.

Falk, William F., Matthew O. Hunt, and Larry L. Hunt. "Hurricane Katrina and New Orleanians' Sense of Place: Return and Reconstitution or 'Gone with the Wind'?" *Du Bois Review* 3.1 (2006): 115–28. Print.

Fischer, Kent. "'Come on Over and We'll Educate You'." *Dallas Morning News* (2 September 2005): 6B. Print.

Fischer-Lichte, Erika. *The Routledge Introduction to Theatre and Performance Studies*. Ed. and trans. Minou Arjomand. London: Routledge, 2014. Print.

———. *The Transformative Power of Performance: A New Aesthetics*. Trans. Saskya Iris Jain. London: Routledge, 2008. Print.

Fischer-Lichte, Erika, and Jens Roselt. "Attraktion des Augenblicks: Aufführung, Performance, performativ und Performativität als theaterwissenschaftliche Begriffe." *Theorien des Performativen*. Ed. Erika Fischer-Lichte and Christoph Wulf. Berlin: Akademie, 2001. 237–53. Print.

Flick, David. "Evacuees Land Here; Rescuers Head There." *Dallas Morning News* (30 August 2005): 8B. Print.

Fox, Anne-Liese Juge. "Restoring Performance: Personal Story, Place, and Memory in Post-Katrina New Orleans." Diss. Louisiana State University, 2013. http://digitalcommons.lsu.edu/gradschool_dissertations/967/. Web.

Fox, Hannah. "Playback Theatre: Inciting Dialogue and Building Community through Personal Story." *TDR* 51.4 (2007): 89–105. Print.

Freitag, Florian. "Displacement and Dispossession: The Plantation Regime as a Disaster Discourse in Rosalyn Story's *Wading Home* (2010)." *Ten Years after Katrina: Critical Perspectives of the Storm's Effect on American Culture and Identity*. Ed. Mary Ruth Marotte and Glenn Jellenik. Lanham: Lexington, 2015. 129–51. Print.

Friedman, Lawrence M. *A History of American Law*. Revised ed. New York: Simon & Schuster, 1985. Print.

Fulton, Duncan T. "Dallas Arts District." *Emergent Urbanism: Evolution in Urban Form, Texas*. Ed. Sinclair Black, Frederick Steiner, Marisa Ballas, and Jeff Gipson. Austin: The University of Texas at Austin, School of Architecture, 2008. 98–100. Print.

Garnett, Dana Lessard. "'Why Does This School Exist?' A Story to Share with Booker T. Students Today." *Fulfilling the Vision: Celebrating One Dallas Art School's Impact on the World*. Ed. Susan K. Elliott Hamm and Vonda Kaatz Klimaszewski. Dallas: Write Word, 2017. 10. Print.

Garrett, Robert T. "Many Set to Remain in Dallas Area, Poll Finds." *Dallas Morning News* (23 August 2006): 14A. Print.

Garvin, Alexander. *The American City: What Works, What Doesn't*. New York: McGraw Hill, 2013. Print.

Geppert, Alexander C.T. *Fleeting Cities: Imperial Expositions in* Fin-de-Siècle *Europe*. New York: Palgrave Macmillan, 2010. Print.

Getz, Jim. "Many Saying Goodbye to Area Shelters." *Dallas Morning News* (10 September 2005): 1A. Print.

Gill, Duane A. "Secondary Trauma or Secondary Disaster? Insights from Hurricane Katrina." *Sociological Spectrum* 27 (2007): 613–32. Print.

Gipson, Jennifer. "Lafcadio Hearn, Hurricane Katrina, and Mardi Gras: A Nineteenth-Century Folklorist's New Life in New Orleans." *Western Folklore* 73.2/3 (2014): 173–94. Print.

Giroux, Henry A. *Stormy Weather: Katrina and the Politics of Disposability.* Boulder: Paradigm, 2006. Print.

Godet, Aurélie. "'Resilient City'? The Double Face of the 2006 Mardi Gras Celebrations in New Orleans." *Revue électronique d'études sur le monde anglophone* 14.1 (2016). https://erea.revues.org/5389. Web.

Goffman, Erving. *The Presentation of Self in Everyday Life.* New York: Anchor, 1959. Print.

Gotham, Kevin Fox. *Authentic New Orleans: Tourism, Culture, and Race in the Big Easy.* New York: New York UP, 2007. Print.

Gotham, Kevin Fox, and Miriam Greenberg. *Crisis Cities: Disaster and Redevelopment in New York and New Orleans.* New York: Oxford UP, 2014. Print.

Govenar, Alan, and Jay Brakefield. *Deep Ellum: The Other Side of Dallas.* 1998. College Station: Texas A&M UP, 2013. Print.

Gower, Patricia Ellen. "Dallas: Experiments in Progressivism, 1898–1919." Diss. Texas A&M University, 1996. Print.

Graff, Harvey J. *The Dallas Myth: The Making and Unmaking of an American City.* Minneapolis: U of Minnesota P, 2008. Print.

Grammer, John M. "Plantation Fiction." *A Companion to the Literature and Culture of the American South.* Ed. Richard Gray and Owen Robinson. Malden, MA: Blackwell, 2007. 59–75. Print.

Granberry, Michael. "As City Performance Hall Rises, So Do the Questions." *Dallas Morning News* (6 June 2011): A1. Print.

Gray, Ed. "Dallas Jails Hurricane Evacuees." *Dallas Weekly* (16–22 November 2005): 16. Print.

Groos, Arthur. "Introduction." *Reading Opera.* Ed. Arthur Groos and Roger Parker. Princeton: Princeton UP, 1988. 1–11. Print.

Hacker, Holly K. "Districts Waiving Admission Rules for Displaced Children." *Dallas Morning News* (1 September 2005): 1B–15B. Print.

———. "SMU Opens Campus Doors to Tulane." *Dallas Morning News* (1 September 2005): 1B–15B. Print.

Hackler, Matthew B. "'Louisiana's New Oil': Planning for Culture on the New Gulf Coast." *Culture after the Hurricanes: Rhetoric and Reinvention on the Gulf Coast.* Ed. Matthew B. Hackler. Jackson: UP of Mississippi, 2010. 3–16. Print.

Hall, Cheryl. "Deep Ellum: The Little Easy?" *Dallas Morning News* (16 October 2005): 1D. Print.

Handley, George B. *Postslavery Literatures in the Americas: Family Portraits in Black and White.* Charlottesville: UP of Virginia, 2000. Print.

Hanna, Bill. "The Fire Marshall: 'Everything We Did in New Orleans, We Do It Here'." *Star-Telegram* (21 August 2015). www.star-telegram.com/news/state/texas/article31724196.html. Web.

Hartman, Chester, and Gregory D. Squires. "Pre-Katrina, Post-Katrina." *There Is No Such Thing as a Natural Disaster: Race, Class, and Hurricane Katrina.* Ed. Chester Hartman and Gregory D. Squires. New York: Routledge, 2006. 1–11. Print.

Hartzel, Tony. "Moving Day for Dozens." *Dallas Morning News* (19 September 2005): 1A–17A. Print.

Horner, Kim. "'Compassion Fatigue' Sets in after Gush of Good Will." *Dallas Morning News* (18 September 2005): 1B. Print.
———. "'Dallas Is a Foreign Country to Me'." *Dallas Morning News* (17 May 2006): 1A–8A. Print.
———. "Help for Evacuees Drying Up." *Dallas Morning News* (29 August 2007): 1A–14A. Print.
———. "Home Is Where the Heart Is." *Dallas Morning News* (29 August 2010): A1. Print.
———. "Katrina Survivors Network Continues Mission." *Dallas Morning News* (29 August 2010): A29. Print.
———. "Struggling to Get on Their Feet." *Dallas Morning News* (23 August 2006): 1A–14A. Print.
———. "They're Far from Home, and There's No Relief in Sight." *Dallas Morning News* (30 August 2005): 15A. Print.
Huddy, Leonie, and Stanley Feldman. "State of the Art: Worlds Apart. Blacks and Whites React to Katrina." *Du Bois Review* 3.1 (2006): 97–113. Print.
Hughes, Kristine. "Evacuees Say Goodbye to FEMA Family." *Dallas Morning News* (16 April 2006): 16B. Print.
Hutcheon, Linda, and Michael Hutcheon. "Adaptation and Opera." *The Oxford Handbook of Adaptation Studies*. Ed. Thomas M. Leitch. New York: Oxford UP, 2017. 305–23. Print.
———. *Bodily Charm: Living Opera*. Lincoln: U of Nebraska P, 2000. Print.
———. "Jazz, Opera, and the Ideologies of Race." *Opera in a Multicultural World: Coloniality, Culture, Performance*. Ed. Mary I. Ingraham, Joseph K. So, and Roy Moodley. New York: Routledge, 2016. 21–33. Print.
———. *Opera: The Art of Dying*. Cambridge, MA: Harvard UP, 2004. Print.
———. *Opera: Desire, Disease, Death*. Lincoln: U of Nebraska P, 1996. Print.
Imhof, Maria, and Anke Grutschus. "Medienkombination Oper: Zur Einführung." *Von Teufeln, Tänzen und Kastraten: Die Oper als transmediales Spektakel*. Ed. Maria Imhof and Anke Grutschus. Bielefeld: Transcript, 2015. 9–28. Print.
Ingraham, Mary I., Joseph K. So, and Roy Moodley. "Introduction: Opera, Multiculturalism, and Coloniality." *Opera in a Multicultural World: Coloniality, Culture, Performance*. Ed. Mary I. Ingraham, Joseph K. So, and Roy Moodley. New York: Routledge, 2016. 1–17. Print.
Isaacs, Gregory Sullivan. "Homeward Bound." *TheaterJones* (7 April 2015). www.theaterjones.com/ntx/reviews/20150407170523/2015-04-07/The-Black-Academy-of-Arts-Letters/Wading-Home-An-Opera-of-New-Orleans. Web.
Jackson, Shannon. *Social Works: Performing Art, Supporting Publics*. New York: Routledge, 2011. Print.
Jacobson, Sherry. "'Thank God for Dallas'." *Dallas Morning News* (5 September 2005): 1B–6B. Print.
James, Vincent, and Jennifer Yoos. *Parallel Cities: The Multilevel Metropolis*. Minneapolis: Walker Art Center, 2016. Print.
Jarvis, Robert M., Steven E. Chaikelson, Christine A. Corcos, and Jon M. Garon. *Theater Law: Cases and Materials*. Durham: Carolina Academic P, 2004. Print.
Jeffers, Jr., Gromer. "Storm Evacuees Know: Big D Is No Big Easy." *Dallas Morning News* (20 September 2005): 6B. Print.

Jensen, Lynne. "Carnival Finally Provides a Reason to Party: Parades Won't Be the Same, But Most Krewes Will Roll." *Times-Picayune* (18 February 2006): 01. Print.

———. "Vieux to Thrill: The Irreverent Krewe du Vieux Is Kicking Off a Carnival Season with a Parade That Will Be the First to Skewer Katrina and All It Wrought." *Times-Picayune* (11 February 2006): 01. Print.

Johnson, Cedric. "Introduction: The Neoliberal Deluge." *The Neoliberal Deluge: Hurricane Katrina, Late Capitalism, and the Remaking of New Orleans*. Ed. Cedric Johnson. Minneapolis: U of Minnesota P, 2011. xvii–l. Print.

Kennedy, Rick. "Hotel Katrina." *Dallas Observer* (1–7 December 2005): 17–31. Print.

———. "Long Road Home." *Dallas Observer* (9–15 February 2006): 17. Print.

Kinney, Alison. "Otello: Opera, Identity Politics and Blacking-Up." *The Guardian* (15 June 2017). www.theguardian.com/music/2017/jun/15/otello-verdi-royal-opera-race-identity-politics-black-talent. Web.

Kirshenblatt-Gimblett, Barbara. "Performance Studies." *The Performance Studies Reader*. Ed. Henry Bial and Sara Brady. Third ed. London: Routledge, 2016. 25–36. Print.

Kish, Zenia. "'My FEMA People': Hip-Hop as Disaster Recovery in the Katrina Diaspora." *American Quarterly* 61.3 (2009): 671–92. Print.

Le Menestrel, Sara, and Jacques Henry. "'Sing Us Back Home': Music, Place, and the Production of Locality in Post-Katrina New Orleans." *Popular Music and Society* 33.2 (2010): 179–202. Print.

Leonardo, Zeus. "Afterword: Whiteness and New Orleans. Racio-Economic Analysis and the Politics of Urban Space." *Pedagogy, Policy, and the Privatized City: Stories of Dispossession and Defiance from New Orleans*, by Kristen L. Buras et al. New York: Teachers College P, 2010. 159–62. Print.

Levinthal, Dave. "Big D's Big Deed: City Pulls It Together in a Triumph of Crisis Control." *Dallas Morning News* (13 September 2005): 1B–9B. Print.

Levinthal, Dave, and Terrence Stutz. "Dallas Gathering Resources to House 25,000 Refugees." *Dallas Morning News* (2 September 2005): 1A–26A. Print.

Levitt, Jeremy I., and Matthew C. Whitaker. "Introduction: Truth Crushed to Earth Will Rise Again. Katrina and Its Aftermath." *Hurricane Katrina: America's Unnatural Disaster*. Ed. Jeremy I. Levitt and Matthew C. Whitaker. Lincoln: U of Nebraska P, 2009. 1–21. Print.

Lind, Angus. "'C'est Levee!' Krewe du Vieux Maps 'Projected Path' for Tomorrow's Katrina-Inspired Parade." *Times-Picayune* (10 February 2006): 01. Print.

Lindahl, Carl. "Epilogue: A Street Named Desire." *Second Line Rescue: Improvised Responses to Katrina and Rita*. Ed. Barry Jean Ancelet, Marcia Gaudet, Carl Lindahl, and Ernest J. Gaines. Jackson: UP of Mississippi, 2013. 248–59. Print.

Linden, Glenn M. *Desegregating Schools in Dallas: Four Decades in the Federal Courts*. Dallas: Three Forks, 1995. Print.

Londono, Ernesto. "Texas May Airlift Some Evacuees." *Dallas Morning News* (5 September 2005): 1B–7B. Print.

Lowe, John. "Introduction: Creole Cultures and National Identity after Katrina." *Louisiana Culture from the Colonial Era to Katrina*. Ed. John Lowe. Baton Rouge: Louisiana State UP, 2008. 1–21. Print.

Lowry, Mark. "A Name Change for Dallas City Performance Hall." *TheaterJones* (24 May 2017). www.theaterjones.com/ntx/news/20170524165132/2017-05-24/A-Name-Change-for-Dallas-City-Performance-Hall. Web.

Luft, Rachel E. "Beyond Disaster Exceptionalism: Social Movement Developments in New Orleans after Hurricane Katrina." *American Quarterly* 61.3 (2009): 499–527. Print.

MacAloon, John J. "Introduction: Cultural Performances, Culture Theory." *Rite, Drama Festival, Spectacle: Rehearsals toward a Theory of Cultural Performance*. Ed. John J. MacAloon. Philadelphia: Institute for the Study of Human Issues, 1984. 1–15. Print.

MacCash, Doug. "Satire Floats: Local Krewes Take Aim at Katrina, Proving that New Orleanians' Humor Survived the Storm Intact." *Times-Picayune* (17 February 2006): 21. Print.

Mann, Eric. *Katrina's Legacy: White Racism and Black Reconstruction in New Orleans and the Gulf Coast*. Los Angeles: Frontline, 2006. Print.

Marta, Suzanne. "Hotels Try to Handle Influx." *Dallas Morning News* (1 September 2005): 1D–3D. Print.

Martin, Randy. "Staging Crisis: Twin Tales in Moving Politics." *The Ends of Performance*. Ed. Peggy Phelan and Jill Lane. New York: New York UP, 1998. 186–96. Print.

Maurer, David. "Review: The Industry's New Hyperopera Crescent City." *Culture Spot LA: A Selective Guide to the Arts in Los Angeles* (15 May 2012). http://culturespotla.com/2012/05/review-the-industrys-new-hyperopera-crescent-city/. Web.

Maxwell, Ian. "The Ritualization of Performance (Studies)." *Victor Turner and Contemporary Cultural Performance*. Ed. Graham St. John. New York: Berghahn, 2008. 59–75. Print.

Mayo, Sandra M., and Elvin Holt. *Stages of Struggle and Celebration: A Production History of Black Theatre in Texas*. Austin: U of Texas P, 2016. Print.

McGinley, Paige. "Highway 61 Revisited." *TDR* 51.3 (2007): 80–97. Print.

McKenzie, Jon. *Perform, Or Else: From Discipline to Performance*. New York: Routledge, 2001. Print.

Menzer, Katie. "Texas-Size Aid Efforts." *Dallas Morning News* (2 September 2005): 2B–6B. Print.

Meyer, Paul. "A Haven and a Halfway House." *Dallas Morning News* (11 September 2005): 1B. Print.

Meyer, Paul, Michael E. Young, and Dave Levinthal. "Dallas Open Arms to New Orleans Refugees." *Dallas Morning News* (1 September 2005): 1A–20A. Print.

Mitchell, Reid. *All on a Mardi Gras Day: Episodes in the History of New Orleans Carnival*. Cambridge, MA: Harvard UP, 1995. Print.

———. "Carnival and Katrina." *The Journal of American History* 94.3 (2007): 789–94. Print.

N.N. "About Bruce Foote." *Bruce R. Foote Memorial Scholarship Foundation* (N.D.). www.footefoundation.org/about-bruce-foote/. Web.

N.N. "About the Dallas Arts District." *The Dallas Arts District* (N.D.). www.dallasartsdistrict.org/about/. Web.

N.N. "About Mary Alice Rich." *Mary Alice Rich* (N.D.). http://maryalicerich.com/?page_id=11. Web.

N.N. "About the NEA: National Council on the Arts." *National Endowment for the Arts* (N.D.). www.arts.gov/about/national-council-arts. Web.

N.N. "About the Scholarship." *Bruce R. Foote Memorial Scholarship Foundation* (N.D.). www.footefoundation.org/about/. Web.

N.N. "About Us." *The Black Academy of Arts and Letters* (N.D.). www.tbaal.org/about/. Web.

N.N. "Bio." *Walteria Bethea* (N.D.). https://walteriamusic.weebly.com/bio.html. Web.

N.N. "Biography." *Barbara H. Moore* (N.D.). www.barbarahmoore.com. Web.

N.N. "Brief History of Krewe du Vieux." *Krewe Du Vieux* (N.D.). www.kreweduvieux.org/History.html. Web.

N.N. "Buy Us Back, Chirac." *Le Monde de Merde* 15.1 (11 February 2006): 6. Print.

N.N. "CANO's 9th Ward Improv Opera." *Creative Alliance of New Orleans* (N.D.). http://cano-la.org/9thwardimprovopera/. Web.

N.N. "C'est Levee or WWKdVD." *GulfSails* (15 January 2006). http://gulfsails.blogspot.com/2006/01/cest-levee-or-wwkdvd.html. Web.

N.N. "Commentary: Getting It." *Gambit Weekly* 27.7 (14 February 2006): 7. Print.

N.N. *The Dallas Arts District: A Visitors Guide to the Largest Arts District in the Nation, 2016/2017*. Dallas: Dallas Arts District, 2016. Print.

N.N. *Dallas City Performance Hall*. Dallas: City of Dallas Office of Cultural Affairs, 2015. Print.

N.N. "Donnie Ray Albert." *The University of Texas at Austin – Butler School of Music* (N.D.). http://music.utexas.edu/about/people/albert-donnie-ray. Web.

N.N. "Education." *The Black Academy of Arts and Letters* (N.D.). www.tbaal.org/education/. Web.

N.N. *Freedman's Cemetery*. Dallas: African American Museum, 2017. Print.

N.N. "Give Us Your Huddled Masses." *D Magazine* (December 2005). www.dmagazine.com/publications/d-magazine/2005/december/give-us-your-huddled-masses/. Web.

N.N. "Heroes Tribute: Derrick Tabb." *YouTube* (March 8, 2010). www.youtube.com/watch?v=YLQ2TonRshY. Web.

N.N. "In the Moment: 'The Distinguished Professor'." *Fox 4 News – Dallas-Ft. Worth* (5 May 2017). www.youtube.com/watch?v=5L3QNnDnrF8. Web.

N.N. "Katrina Evacuees by District." *Dallas Morning News* (23 September 2005): 9B. Print.

N.N. "Krewe du Vieux Mission." *Krewe Du Vieux* (N.D.). www.kreweduvieux.org/Mission.html. Web.

N.N. "Lexus Broadway Series: *The Gershwins' Porgy and Bess*." *AT&T Performing Arts Center* (N.D.). www.attpac.org/on-sale/2013/porgy-and-bess/. Web.

N.N. "Local Residents Mark Katrina Anniversary with Contemporary Opera." *City of Dallas* (N.D.). www.dallascitynews.net/local-residents-mark-katrina-anniversary-with-contemporary-opera. Web.

N.N. "MPower Artist Grants." *Sphinx Organization* (N.D.). www.sphinxmusic.org/mpower-artist-grants/. Web.

N.N. "Musicians' Village." *New Orleans Area Habitat for Humanity* (N.D.). www.habitat-nola.org/musicians-village/. Web.

N.N. "News and Events: From South Africa to SMU Meadows: 16 Years of Successes." *SMU Meadows School of the Arts* (11 August 2016). www.smu.edu/Meadows/NewsAndEvents/News/2016/160811-SMUinSouthAfrica. Web.
N.N. "Our Team: Derrick Tabb." *The Roots of Music* (N.D.). http://therootsofmusic.org/our-team/. Web.
N.N. "Past Themes & Royalty." *Krewe Du Vieux* (N.D.). www.kreweduvieux.org/ParadePast.html. Web.
N.N. "Repertoire." *Bronwen Forbay* (N.D.). www.bronwenforbay.com/resume/. Web.
N.N. "The Roots of Music." *YouTube* (11 May 2012). www.youtube.com/watch?v=ZemqFZo4ymc. Web.
N.N. "Rosemary Haggar Vaughan and David M. Crowley Summer Study Awards." *Bruce R. Foote Memorial Scholarship Foundation* (N.D.). www.footefoundation.org/rosemary-haggar-vaughan-and-david-m-crowley-summer-study-awards/. Web.
N.N. "Schedule." *Nathan De'Shon Myers* (N.D.). www.thenathanmyers.com/schedule.php. Web.
N.N. "Sphinx Backgrounder." *Sphinx Organization* (N.D.). http://sphinxmusic.org/attachments/Sphinx_Backgrounder.pdf. Web.
N.N. "Sphinx Organization: Year in Review 2016–2017." *Sphinx Organization* (2017). www.sphinxmusic.org/attachments/Sphinx_Annual_Report_2017.pdf. Web.
N.N. "A Struggle to Escape Shelters." *Dallas Morning News* (28 October 2005): 4A. Print.
N.N. "Texas Clarifies Rules for Hiring of Evacuees." *Dallas Morning News* (8 September 2005): 9D. Print.
N.N. "Texas Hospitals Taking in New Orleans Patients Most in Need." *Dallas Morning News* (1 September 2005): 24A. Print.
N.N. "What We Do." *Sphinx Organization* (N.D.). http://sphinxmusic.org/attachments/Sphinx_Programs.pdf. Web.
O'Keefe, Phil, Ken Westgate, and Ben Wisner. "Taking the Naturalness Out of Natural Disasters." *Nature* 260 (15 April 1976): 566–67. Print.
O'Neill, Rosary. *New Orleans Carnival Krewes: The History, Spirit and Secrets of Mardi Gras*. Charleston: History P, 2014. Print.
Pearson, Mike, and Michael Shanks. *Theatre/Archeology*. London: Routledge, 2001. Print.
Peek, Lori, and Lynn Weber. *Displaced: Life in the Katrina Diaspora*. Austin: U of Texas P, 2012. Print.
Peter, Duane E., Marsha Prior, Melissa M. Green, and Victoria G. Clow. "Management Summary." *Freedman's Cemetery: A Legacy of a Pioneer Black Community in Dallas, Texas*. Vol. 1. Ed. Duane E. Peter, Marsha Prior, Melissa M. Green, and Victoria G. Clow. Plano: Texas Department of Transportation, 2000. v-vii. Print.
Phelan, Peggy. "Introduction: The Ends of Performance." *The Ends of Performance*. Ed. Peggy Phelan and Jill Lane. New York: New York UP, 1998. 1–19. Print.
———. *Unmarked: The Politics of Performance*. London: Routledge, 1993. Print.
Phillips, Michael. *White Metropolis: Race, Ethnicity, and Religion in Dallas, 1841–2001*. Austin: U of Texas P, 2006. Print.

Porter, Eric. "Jazz and Revival." *American Quarterly* 61.3 (2009): 593–613. Print.
Potter, Hillary. "Introduction." *Racing the Storm: Racial Implications and Lessons Learned from Hurricane Katrina*. Ed. Hillary Potter. Lanham: Lexington, 2007. ix–xiii. Print.
Pratt, Lloyd. "New Orleans and Its Storm: Exception, Example, or Event?" *American Literary History* 19.1 (2007): 251–65. Print.
Prince, Robert. *A History of Dallas: From a Different Perspective*. Dallas: Nortex, 1993. Print.
Prior, Marsha, and Robert V. Kemper. "From Freedmans Town to Uptown: Community Transformation and Gentrification in Dallas, Texas." *Urban Anthropology and Studies of Cultural Systems and World Economic Development* 34.2/3 (2005): 177–216. Print.
Prior, Marsha, and Terry Anne Schulte. "Where Dignity Lives: Freedman's Town/North Dallas." *Freedman's Cemetery: A Legacy of a Pioneer Black Community in Dallas, Texas*. Vol. 1. Ed. Duane E. Peter, Marsha Prior, Melissa M. Green, and Victoria G. Clow. Plano: Texas Department of Transportation, 2000. 57–217. Print.
Rajewsky, Irina O. *Intermedialität*. Tübingen: Francke, 2002. Print.
Ramshaw, Emily. "$6.8M Spent on Evacuees." *Dallas Morning News* (21 February 2006): 1B–9B. Print.
———. "FEMA Answers City's Cry for Help." *Dallas Morning News* (6 September 2005): 1B–9B. Print.
———. "Survivors Depart Horrendous Scene." *Dallas Morning News* (4 September 2005): 1A–11A. Print.
Reed, Jr., Adolph. "Introduction." *Unnatural Disaster:* The Nation *on Hurricane Katrina*. Ed. Betsy Reed. New York: Nation Books, 2006. xiii–xxx. Print.
Rich, Mary Alice. "Mary Alice Rich." *Dallas Symphony Orchestra Young Strings: Changing Lives through Music*. Ed. Jamie Allen, Carolyn Jabr, and Richard Rejino. Dallas: Dallas Symphony Orchestra, 2012. N.P. Print.
Rich, Mary Alice, and Rosalyn Story. *Wading Home: An Opera of New Orleans (Libretto)*. 2015. Unpublished, typed manuscript.
Richards, Gary. "Queering Katrina: Gay Discourses of the Disaster in New Orleans." *Journal of American Studies* 44.3 (2010): 519–34. Print.
Roach, Joseph. *Cities of the Dead: Circum-Atlantic Performance*. New York: Columbia UP, 1996. Print.
Robinson-Jacobs, Karen. "New Orleans Businesses Make Do in Dallas Digs." *Dallas Morning News* (15 September 2005): 9D. Print.
Rodrigue, George. "The Arts District." *D Magazine* (May 1982): 102–107; 124–27. Print.
Román, David. *Performance in America: Contemporary U.S. Culture and the Performing Arts*. Durham: Duke UP, 2005. Print.
Russ, Elizabeth C. *The Plantation in the Postslavery Imagination*. New York: Oxford UP, 2010. Print.
Saldaña, Johnny. *Ethnotheatre: Research from Page to Stage*. London: Routledge, 2016. Print.
Salvaggio, Ruth. *Hearing Sappho in New Orleans: The Call of Poetry from Congo Square to the Ninth Ward*. Baton Rouge: Louisiana State UP, 2012. Print.
Sasaki Associates, Inc., Halcyon Ltd., and Lockwood, Andrews & Newman, Inc. *Dallas Arts District: Urban Design Plan*. Submitted to Dr. Philip O'Bryan

Montgomery, Arts District Coordinator, Dallas Arts District Consortium, and The City of Dallas. N.P.: N.P., 1982. Print.

Schechner, Richard. "Approaches to Theory/Criticism." *TDR* 10.4 (1966): 20–53. Print.

———. "From Ritual to Theatre and Back: The Structure/Process of the Efficacy-Entertainment Dyad." *Essays on Performance Theory, 1970–1976*. New York: Drama Book Specialists, 1977 [1974–1976]. 63–98. Print.

———. "Performance & the Social Sciences: Introduction." *TDR* 17.3 (1973): 3–4. Print.

———. "Performance Studies: The Broad Spectrum Approach." *TDR* 32.3 (1988): 4–6. Print.

———. *Performance Studies: An Introduction*. London: Routledge, 2002. Print.

———. "Restoration of Behavior." *Between Theatre and Anthropology*. Philadelphia: U of Pennsylvania P, 1985. 35–116. Print.

———. "Towards a Poetics of Performance." *Essays on Performance Theory, 1970–1976*. New York: Drama Book Specialists, 1977 [1975]. 108–39. Print.

Schiebel, Walter J.E. *Education in Dallas: Ninety-Two Years of History, 1874–1966*. Dallas: Dallas Independent School District, 1966. Print.

Schmidgall, Gary. *Literature as Opera*. New York: Oxford UP, 1977. Print.

Schmidt-Garre, Jan, and Marieke Schroeder, dir. *Aida's Brothers and Sisters: Black Voices in Opera and Concert*. 1999. Halle: Arthaus Musik, 2009. DVD.

Schutze, Jim. *The Accommodation: The Politics of Race in an American City*. Secaucus, NJ: Citadel, 1986. Print.

———. "The RIP: When Does an Evacuee Cease to Be a Guest and Become a Pain?" *Dallas Observer* (7–13 September 2006): 9–10. Print.

Shah, Angela, and Brendan M. Case. "Ripple Effect Hard to Predict." *Dallas Morning News* (9 September 2005): 1A–18A. Print.

Short, John R. *Stress Testing the USA: Public Policy and Reaction to Disaster Events*. New York: Palgrave Macmillan, 2013. Print.

Shulman, Laurie C. *The Meyerson Symphony Center: Building a Dream*. Denton: U of North Texas P, 2000. Print.

Simnacher, Joe. "Evacuees See Road Back to New Orleans by Way of D.C." *Dallas Morning News* (13 January 2006): 15B. Print.

Singer, Milton. *Traditional India: Structure and Change*. Philadelphia: American Folklore Society, 1959. Print.

Skipper, Jodi. "'In the Neighborhood': City Planning, Archaeology, and Cultural Heritage Politics at St. Paul United Methodist Church." Diss. The University of Texas at Austin, 2010. https://repositories.lib.utexas.edu/handle/2152/ETD-UT-2010-08-1884. Web.

Smith, Louise Mosley. "Booker T. Washington Arts High School." *Paul Baker and the Integration of Abilities*. Ed. Robert Flynn and Eugene McKinney. Fort Worth: TCU Press, 2003. 197–212. Print.

Smith, Patrick J. *The Tenth Muse: A Historical Study of the Opera Libretto*. New York: Knopf, 1970. Print.

Snyder-Young, Dani. *Theatre of Good Intentions: Challenges and Hopes for Theatre and Social Change*. London: Palgrave Macmillan, 2013. Print.

South End Press Collective. "Preface: Up from the Depths." *What Lies Beneath: Katrina, Race, and the State of the Nation*. Ed. South End Press Collective. Cambridge, MA: South End P, 2007. vii–viii. Print.

Souther, J. Mark. *New Orleans on Parade: Tourism and the Transformation of the Crescent City*. Baton Rouge: Louisiana State UP, 2006. Print.

Stanonis, Anthony J. "Mardi Gras." *The New Encyclopedia of Southern Culture*. Vol. 15: Urbanization. Ed. Wanda Rushing. Chapel Hill: U of North Carolina P, 2010. 213–15. Print.

Stecopoulos, Harilaos. "Western Hemispheric Drama and Performance." *A Concise Companion to American Studies*. Ed. John Carlos Rowe. Malden, MA: Blackwell, 2010. 247–62. Print.

Steinberg, Phil. "What Is a City? Katrina's Answers." *What Is a City? Rethinking the Urban after Hurricane Katrina*. Ed. Rob Shields and Phil Steinberg. Athens: U of Georgia P, 2008. 3–29. Print.

Stern, Carol Simpson, and Bruce Henderson. *Performance: Texts and Contexts*. New York: Longman, 1993. Print.

Story, Rosalyn. *And So I Sing: African-American Divas of Opera and Concert*. New York: Warner, 1990. Print.

———. "Q&A with Rosalyn Story, Author of WADING HOME." *Agate Publishing* (2010). www.agatepublishing.com/book/?GCOI=93284100441920. Web.

———. "Wading Home: From Novel to Opera, A Story of Rebirth." *Agate Publishing* (20 March 2015). www.agatepublishing.com/blog/2015/3/20/wading-home-from-novel-to-opera-a-story-of-rebirth.html. Web.

———. *Wading Home: A Novel of New Orleans*. Chicago: Agate, 2010. Print. Courtesy of Agate Publishing.

Stuetz, Mark. "Dallas Floats." *Dallas Observer* (22–28 September 2005): 16. Print.

Sublette, Ned. *The World That Made New Orleans: From Spanish Silver to Congo Square*. Chicago: Lawrence Hill, 2008. Print.

Taylor, Diana. *The Archive and the Repertoire: Performing Cultural Memory in the Americas*. Durham: Duke UP, 2003. Print.

Taylor, Helen. "After the Deluge: The Post-Katrina Cultural Revival of New Orleans." *Journal of American Studies* 44.3 (2010): 483–501. Print.

Theatre Projects Consultants Incorporated. *Dallas Arts District: Discussion Document*. N.P.: N.P., 1984. Print.

Thevenot, Brian. "Their Mardi Gras . . . Our Mardi Gras." *Times-Picayune* (19 February 2006): 01. Print.

Thomas, Lynnell L. *Desire & Disaster in New Orleans: Tourism, Race, and Historical Memory*. Durham: Duke UP, 2014. Print.

Trahan, Jason. "Good Deed: Making Sure Others Know the Lay of the Land." *Dallas Morning News* (8 September 2005): 2B. Print.

Turner, Victor W. "Liminal to Liminoid, in Play, Flow, and Ritual: An Essay in Comparative Symbology." *Rice University Studies* 60.3 (1974): 53–92. Print.

———. *Schism and Continuity in an African Society*. Oxford: Berg, 1996 [1957]. Print.

Van den Berg, Klaus. "The Geometry of Culture: Urban Spaces and Theatre Buildings in Twentieth Century Berlin." *Theatre Research International* 16.1 (1991): 1–17. Print.

Wailoo, Keith, Karen M. O'Neill, and Jeffrey Dowd. "Introduction: Katrina's Imprint." *Katrina's Imprint: Race and Vulnerability in America*. Ed. Roland Anglin, Jeffrey Dowd, Karen M. O'Neill, and Keith Wailoo. New Brunswick, NJ: Rutgers UP, 2010. 1–6. Print.

Wallenberg, Christopher. "In Katrina's Wake." *American Theatre* 27.5 (2010): 54–59. Print.

Warstat, Matthias. "Politisches Theater zwischen Theatralität und Performativität." *Die Aufführung: Diskurs, Macht, Analyse.* Ed. Erika Fischer-Lichte, Adam Czirak, Torsten Jost, Frank Richarz, and Nina Tecklenburg. Munich: Fink, 2012. 69–81. Print.

Watts, Lewis, and Eric Porter. *New Orleans Suite: Music and Culture in Transition.* Berkeley: U of California P, 2013. Print.

Weeks, Jerome. "'Wading Home': Katrina Opera Debuts at City Performance Hall." *Art+Seek* (1 April 2015). http://artandseek.org/2015/04/01/wading-home-katrina-opera-debuts-at-city-performance-hall/. Web.

Wiegmink, Pia. *Protest EnACTed: Activist Performance in the Contemporary United States.* Heidelberg: Winter, 2011. Print.

Wilonsky, Robert. "From Dance to Drama, Stage to Song, a Little Something for Everyone during City Performance Hall Opening Weekend." *Dallas Morning News* (10 August 2012): N.P. Print.

———. "Thirty Years after Sasaki Plan Created Dallas Arts District, a Call for a New Vision – and Fast." *Dallas Morning News* (19 June 2015): N.P. Print.

Wolf, Werner. "Intermediality." *Routledge Encyclopedia of Narrative Theory.* Ed. David Herman, Manfred Jahn, and Marie-Laure Ryan. London: Routledge, 2007. 252–56. Print.

Woods, Clyde. "Katrina's World: Blues, Bourbon, and the Return to the Source." *American Quarterly* 61.3 (2009): 427–53. Print.

———. "Les Misérables of New Orleans: Trap Economics and the Asset Stripping Blues, Part 1." *American Quarterly* 61.3 (2009): 769–96. Print.

Yan, Holly. "Arts Community Pitches In." *Dallas Morning News* (9 September 2005): 7B. Print.

Conclusion

Not even half a year after its Dallas premiere, *Wading Home: An Opera of New Orleans* saw its first out-of-town production. Between July and August 2015, Barbara Hill Moore, Rosalyn Story, and Mary Alice Rich had raised more than $50,000 to allow the *Wading Home* team to travel to New Orleans and to collaborate with students, faculty, and staff from Loyola University's College of Music and Fine Arts; and on 12–13 September 2015, at the tail end of a densely packed schedule of events commemorating the tenth anniversary of Hurricane Katrina, the opera was presented at Loyola's 600-seat Louis J. Roussel Performance Hall, right across from Audubon Park. For these two performances, members of the premiere cast, including Donnie Ray Albert, Bronwen Forbay, and Lauren Pinzás, were joined on stage by the Loyola Chamber Singers (as the chorus of the ancestors and the people of New Orleans) and singers from Chalmette High School (as the chorus of the children of the city). In a way, then, *Wading Home* had returned home (see N.N., "Hometown"). The curtain had hardly fallen upon the 13 September performance when the entire company traveled to Dallas for another presentation of *Wading Home* at the Moody Performance Hall on 15 September 2015 (see Cantrell, "'Wading Home'"). And this was just the beginning: in a March 2015 blog post for her publisher, Story had expressed her hope that *Wading Home* would "live far beyond [its] first performance, and [find] future audiences in New Orleans, Atlanta, Houston, and every other city where Hurricane Katrina's 250,000 evacuees now make their homes" ("Wading Home"). In fact, *Wading Home* (or excerpts from it) have since been performed not only in the New Orleans diaspora destination of Columbus, Mississippi (in 2017; see N.N., "Music by Women"),[1] but also in South Africa (in 2018; see N.N., "US Opera").

Taking *Wading Home* on tour has made, no doubt, an important contribution to keeping alive the memory of the victims of Hurricane Katrina, to commemorating "a time in [U.S.] history when a great city, faced with the possibility of extinction, was brought back from the brink," and to celebrating "New Orleans' gift to the world, and the fortitude and endurance of this great American culture" (Story, "Wading Home"). Especially when performed in the United States (as well as in South Africa), however, it is not entirely inconceivable that *Wading Home* might have also and again, as in Dallas, not just enacted its vision of a post-diasporic future on the stage, but also turned this utopian performative into a lived reality at the very place where it was presented. To be sure, and as I have pointed out several times in "*Wading Home*'s Post-Katrina New Orleans," performances, their effects, and the reactions to them can never be (fully) planned or predicted, let alone repeated. The 2015 premiere performance of *Wading Home* in Dallas was unique. What was not unique was the history of African-American displacement and dispossession that, among other factors, allowed this New Orleans opera to resonate the way it did in Dallas. Black dispossession and diaspora in the United States are not limited, as the opera itself has argued, to either urban or rural spaces, post-disaster or other times, or, as the premiere performance of the opera has shown, to either New Orleans/Louisiana or elsewhere. Indeed, what made the performance of *Wading Home*'s story reverberate in Dallas and what may make future performances reverberate in other places is not the uniqueness of New Orleans and of the conditions before, during, and after Hurricane Katrina, but their very exemplarity.

By 2015, *Wading Home* was by no means alone in stressing the exemplarity or representativeness of Katrina and New Orleans rather than their exceptionalism. For instance, the same year that saw the premiere of Rich and Story's opera also witnessed the publication of Ron Eyerman's *Is This America? Hurricane Katrina as Cultural Trauma.* Inspired by an essay written by Georgia Congressman John Lewis for the 12 September 2005 edition of *Newsweek*, as well as by a poster displayed at "Living with Hurricanes: Katrina and Beyond," a permanent exhibit at the Presbytère on Jackson Square opened in 2010, the poignant question that forms the title of Eyerman's volume refers, the author notes, "to the notion that America is different, exceptional, that such things do not happen here. It implies that Americans can do things better" (130). More precisely, in a typically American, because jeremiadic, manner (see Bercovitch), the question points to and laments the gulf between America's promise and American realities, between the American "ought" and the American "is":

> For social scientists, and of course many others, one could have easily turned the question into a statement: "This is America." The links between race and poverty are well documented. That the majority of those left behind with no means to escape an emergency in a large Southern city would be black and poor would surprise no one with any interest at all in the history of the United States.
>
> (Eyerman 124)

In the wake of Hurricane Katrina and ensuing assertions of the unnaturalness and exemplarity of the disaster (see Chapter 3), several commentators and critics similarly proceeded to challenge persistent assumptions about post-Katrina New Orleans exceptionalism: in *Down in New Orleans: Reflections from a Drowned City* (2007), for instance, Billy Sothern notes that "[t]he story of New Orleans following Hurricane Katrina is, even though it may be hard to accept, the story of America at the beginning of a new millennium" (xx). In a 2013 article Daniel H. Usner, Jr., maintains that "[t]wenty-first-century New Orleans offers many essential lessons about environmental management, urban sprawl, quality of life, public policy, race relations, governmental responsibility, and, yes, even self-representation – which apply to most American cities" (29). And in their 2014 *Crisis Cities*, Kevin Fox Gotham and Miriam Greenberg observe striking parallels between urban redevelopment in post-Katrina New Orleans and post-9/11 New York City. Some scholars have extended their views about the exemplarity of post-Katrina New Orleans even further into the city's past, with, for instance, Usner arguing that "[f]or the study of machine politics, reformism, urban sprawl, white flight, and desegregation, among other topics, the Crescent City is an essential example of major trends in twentieth-century American history" (28–9).

Such claims about New Orleans's historical and contemporary exemplarity – claims about the city's inherent Americanness, in fact – are nothing new, of course: already in 1976, Pierce F. Lewis wrote:

> In New Orleans, *as elsewhere*, blacks are relatively poor and ill-housed, and their neighborhoods are poorly attended by municipal services. Educational levels are low, crime rates high. Meanwhile, whites flee and the proportion of blacks continues to increase, as do the isolation and alienation of a population that sees itself as abandoned and abused.
>
> (95; emphasis added)

Yet it was only after Hurricane Katrina, I suggest, that comments such as Lewis's gained more widespread currency, simply because in the face of the disaster and its aftermath their veracity could not be ignored any longer – not even in popular culture. Indeed, it is significant that the newly rediscovered Americanness of New Orleans did not just manifest itself in both public and academic discussions, but also found its way into popular artifacts such as *Wading Home*.

For more than 100 years, and thus even before the New Orleans tourism industry had discovered what would eventually become its central asset, U.S. popular culture had engaged – contributed to, underwritten, and celebrated – the aura of uniqueness and exceptionalism that surrounds the Crescent City, its history, its peoples, and its culture(s). Late nineteenth-century popular print culture took the lead, capitalizing on contemporary interest in popular historiography, travelogues, and local color. Well-established American magazines such as the *Atlantic Monthly* and *Harper's Magazine* would print travel pieces and local-color sketches about Louisiana and/or New Orleans, but it was a relative newcomer on the national periodical market that offered its readers the most extensive, generically diverse, and visually attractive portrayal of the Crescent City. Indeed, starting with George Washington Cable's "'Sieur George" and Edward King and James Well Champney's "Old and New Louisiana" in late 1873, *Scribner's/Century* would, over the next two decades, dedicate more pages to New Orleans-related features, stories, serialized novels, and their illustrations than any other popular national magazine in late-nineteenth–century America. Sustained by a network of diverse periodical actors that often crisscrossed paths between New Orleans and New York City, "Scribner's Illustrated New Orleans" was, moreover, surprisingly consistent in its textual and visual portrayal of the Crescent City, and particularly so with respect to the latter's temporal dynamics: depicting the city as French and simultaneously writing and drawing this Frenchness off into the past, the periodical actors who contributed to "Scribner's Illustrated New Orleans" carved a truly unique spot for the Crescent City on the literary map of regional cultures in the late nineteenth-century United States.

The particular image or identity of the city thus established by "Scribner's Illustrated New Orleans" would resurface again in more concrete form more than half a century later at Disney theme parks and resorts in California, Florida, and Japan. The Crescent City was part of Disneyland's original roster of themes, and it would remain the only actually existing place depicted at this or any other of Disney's "castle parks"; conversely, no other theme park "empire" would dedicate as much space and effort to representing New Orleans as the "Disneyzone." Somewhat surprisingly, however, it would take Disney's designers, architects, and staff members several "attempts" and almost 40 years to translate the vision of the city introduced in the pages of *Scribner's/Century* into a three-dimensional themed space. Nevertheless, as the evolution from New Orleans Street (Disneyland) to New Orleans Square (Disneyland) to French Quarter Land (Tokyo Disneyland) to Port Orleans – French Quarter (Walt Disney World) shows, "Disney's Immersive New Orleans" would eventually move closer and closer to "Scribner's Illustrated New Orleans" – a city with a French, an exclusively French, past. Paradoxically, while the entertainment company sought to capture, in the name of tourism authenticity, what many perceived as the real, the true New Orleans, the actual city did precisely the same, with the result that the "Frenchifying" of Disney's New Orleans coincided with the "Disneyfication" of New Orleans's French Quarter.

The Vieux Carré was barely touched by Hurricane Katrina in 2005, and neither did the storm and the ensuing environmental and social catastrophe leave any marks on Disney's versions of the French Quarter. The disaster did, however, horrendously scar virtually all of the rest of

New Orleans and also affected the depiction of the city in other popular culture artifacts. In a stunning break with well-established popular discourses about New Orleans, for instance, the 2015 premiere performance of *Wading Home: An Opera of New Orleans* in Dallas replaced images of the Frenchness of the Crescent City with assertions of its historical and contemporary Americanness, both on stage – that is, in the opera itself – as well as in the way its performance resonated at the place where and with the audience in front of which it was presented. Yet *Wading Home* did even more than that: just as "Disney's Immersive New Orleans" crystallized the "Scribner's Illustrated New Orleans" concept of the Frenchness of the Crescent City into built environments, actually existing places that can be visited and enjoyed, "*Wading Home*'s Post-Katrina New Orleans" turned its staged vision of a resuscitated postdiluvian American city into a lived reality that could be experienced and celebrated.

The three pivotal moments from the history of New Orleans in popular culture that I have recounted in this book have contributed to the fact that today, after the city's Tricentennial in 2018, we are confronted with several popular "New Orleanses." In fact, around the same time *Wading Home* started going "on tour," another, very different popular New Orleans was getting ready to set sail. In November 2016, the Disney Wonder, launched in 1998 as the second ship of the Disney Cruise Line, began welcoming passengers to "Tiana's Place," the first new New Orleans-themed space in the "Disneyzone" since the opening of Disney's Port Orleans – French Quarter Resort in 1991. To be sure, with its brick walls, wrought-iron trims, and purple, gold, and green color scheme, the interior design of this restaurant very closely resembles that of the faux outdoor courtyard of the main lobby of Disney's Florida resort. And here, too, the "production" of the themed space by the employees turns every day into a Fat Tuesday: each night, in between the entrées and dessert, performers invite diners to line up for an "impromptu" Mardi Gras parade, accompanied live by a jazz combo. But "Tiana's Place" thematically draws on other versions of "Disney's Immersive New Orleans," as well. A poster on a faux portal next to the entrance sign, for instance, suggests that Disneyland's New Orleans Square may be just behind the door. Moreover, the restaurant – as well as the "French Quarter Lounge" bar, opened right next to "Tiana's Place" in September 2019 – also evoke a version of Disney's New Orleans realized in a different medium, namely, *The Princess and the Frog*, the company's animated adaptation of the classic fairy-tale set in 1920s New Orleans and released in 2009: walkaround characters from the movie greet diners at the entrance and interact with them during dinner, scenes from the movie decorate the table settings and the menus, and the name of the restaurant indicates that "Tiana's Place" is supposed to be the very eatery that *The Princess and the Frog*'s main character opens in New Orleans, across the river from Jackson Square, in the final scene of the movie.[2] Simultaneously drawing on "Disney's Immersive New Orleans," with its increasing focus on the French Quarter, and on *The Princess and the Frog*, which similarly reduces the Crescent City to the Vieux Carré (see Ferguson 1237), "Tiana's Place" once again depicts the city as exotically French.

With "Tiana's Place" and *Wading Home*, then, we have two very different popular New Orleanses simultaneously criss-crossing the globe. One of them is French New Orleans, the exceptional, unique city with a French past, familiar to us at least since the late nineteenth century, when Edward King and James Wells Champney made halt in the Crescent City on their "Great South" tour for the readers of *Scribner's Monthly*. The other one, almost diametrically opposed to the former, is American New Orleans, the exemplary, representative city characterized by conditions and developments that are also prevalent in other U.S. places, a city that we may have first encountered in popular culture in 2015, when Rosalyn Story, Mary Alice Rich, and Barbara Hill Moore put *Wading Home* on the stage of the Moody Performance Hall in Dallas. As vastly different as these – and other – popular New Orleanses may be, what is truly remarkable about them is not the fact that we may encounter them almost everywhere – in the pages of magazines, in themed spaces, on opera stages – and, in each case, easily understand and recognize them – as I have argued, their very accessibility is what makes them "popular" in the first place.

Rather, what is so striking about these popular New Orleanses is that we may also catch glimpses of them in the Crescent City itself. They may temporarily travel (back) to the place they refer to, as *Wading Home* and "Tiana's Place" have done when the former was performed at Loyola University in 2015 and when the latter anchored in the port of New Orleans in 2020 (starting that year, the Disney Wonder has offered departures from the Crescent City; see N.N., "Disney Cruise Line"). But they have also left more or less permanent traces in the city itself, whether in the "Disneyfied" parts of the French Quarter (see Chapter 2) or through the post-Katrina practices of "critical nostalgia" that Shannon Lee Dawdy sees at work elsewhere in the city.[3] To be sure, whether these glimpses of unique, exceptional, and exemplary, representative – of French and American New Orleans, in short – inspired or, rather, were inspired by popular New Orleans has occasionally become hard to tell. Yet that is precisely the point: the fact that the Crescent City has begotten these popular visions of itself and that the latter, in turn, have returned to and left an impact on the very place that generated them, speaks to the power, indeed the popularity, of both "real" and popular New Orleans.

Notes

1. According to Altman, about 900 evacuees had been sheltered in Columbus immediately after Hurricane Katrina, some of whom eventually made the city their new home.

2. See Clements and Musker 01:25:17–01:26:43. *The Princess and the Frog*, in turn, contains numerous references to "Disney's Immersive New Orleans": the band playing at "Tiana's Place," for instance, is called the "Firefly Five Plus Lou" (see Clements and Musker 01:25:40) and thus refers to the name of the "Firehouse Five Plus Two," the Dixieland band that used to play at Disneyland's New Orleans Street (see Chapter 2).
3. Drawing on Svetlana Boym, Dawdy distinguishes between "*restorative nostalgia*," which "invents traditions, maintains buildings in like-new condition, and serves nationalist agendas through heritage programs," and "*critical nostalgia*," which "selectively values past lifeways and old objects as a form of protest against the present" (6; emphasis original). With respect to post-Katrina "critical nostalgia" in New Orleans, Dawdy discusses practices of conserving "Katrina Patina" on buildings and objects (2–4).

Bibliography

Altman, Isabelle. "Columbus' Response to Katrina." *The Dispatch* (29 August 2015). www.cdispatch.com/news/article.asp?aid=44322. Web.

Bercovitch, Sacvan. *The American Jeremiad*. Madison: The U of Wisconsin P, 1978. Print.

Cantrell, Scott. "'Wading Home' Dramatizes New Orleans Family's Hurricane Katrina Experiences." *Dallas News* (16 September 2015). www.dallasnews.com/arts/arts/2015/09/16/wading-home-dramatizes-new-orleans-familys-hurricane-katrina-experiences. Web.

Clements, Ron, and John Musker, dir. *The Princess and the Frog*. Burbank: Walt Disney Studios, 2010. DVD.

Dawdy, Shannon Lee. *Patina: A Profane Archaeology*. Chicago: The U of Chicago P, 2016. Print.

Eyerman, Ron. *Is This America? Hurricane Katrina as Cultural Trauma*. Austin: U of Texas P, 2015. Print.

Ferguson, Josh-Wade. "'Traded It Off for That Voodoo Thing': Cultural Capital and Vernacular Debt in Disney's Representation of New Orleans." *The Journal of Popular Culture* 49.6 (2016): 1224–40. Print.

Gotham, Kevin Fox, and Miriam Greenberg. *Crisis Cities: Disaster and Redevelopment in New York and New Orleans*. New York: Oxford UP, 2014. Print.

Lewis, Peirce F. *New Orleans: The Making of an Urban Landscape*. Cambridge, MA: Ballinger, 1976. Print.

N.N. "Disney Cruise Line to Sail from Port of New Orleans for First Time in Early 2020." *Port Nola* (N.D.). www.portnola.com/info/news-media/press-releases/disney-cruise-line-to-sail-from-port-of-new-orleans-for-first-time-in-early-2020. Web.

N.N. "Hometown Heroes: Wading Home." *Fox 4 News* (31 August 2015). www.fox4news.com/news/fox-4-features/hometown-heroes-wading-home. Web.

N.N. "Music by Women Festival." *The W* (N.D.). www.muw.edu/musicbywomen/previous/2017. Web.

N.N. "US Opera to Be Performed in the Bay." *News24* (23 May 2018). www.news24.com/SouthAfrica/Local/PE-Express/us-opera-to-be-performed-in-the-bay-20180521. Web.

Sothern, Billy. *Down in New Orleans: Reflections from a Drowned City*. Berkeley: U of California P, 2007. Print.

Story, Rosalyn. *Wading Home: A Novel of New Orleans*. Chicago: Agate, 2010. Print.

———. "Wading Home: From Novel to Opera, A Story of Rebirth." *Agate Publishing* (20 March 2015). www.agatepublishing.com/blog/2015/3/20/wading-home-from-novel-to-opera-a-story-of-rebirth.html. Web.

Usner, Jr., Daniel H. "Colonial Projects and Frontier Practices: The First Century of New Orleans History." *Frontier Cities: Encounters at the Crossroads of Empire*. Ed. Jay Gitlin, Barbara Berglund, and Adam Arenson. Philadelphia: U of Pennsylvania P, 2013. 27–45. Print.

Index

adaptation 266–7; *see also Wading Home: An Opera of New Orleans*
Adventureland (Tokyo Disneyland) 185–94, 207, 336; "Blackbeard's Portrait Deck" 192; "Blue Bayou Restaurant" 191; "Cristal Arts" 192; "The Golden Galleon" 191, 192; "Laffite's Treasure Chest" 191; "La Petite Parfumerie" 191, 192; "Le Gourmet" 192; "Le Marché Bleu" 191; "Party Gras Gifts" 192, 193–4, 199; "Pirate Treasure" 192–3; temporal setting of 191; "Theatre Orleans" 191, 193–4; *see also* Pirates of the Caribbean (theme park attraction); theme parks; Tokyo Disneyland
Albert, Donnie Ray 237, 274, 280, 288, 333
analogous city 182–3, 185, 298, 299; *see also* Disneyfication
Atlantic Monthly 28, 106–7n4, 336
audio-animatronics *see* theming
Aunt Jemima 148–51, 152–3, 207, 210n23; *see also* New Orleans Street (Disneyland)
authenticity: in theme parks 133, 161–2, 206, 336
autotheming *see* theming

Bacher, Otto H. 46; *Balcony Stories* 46; collaboration with Grace E. King 46
Bakhtin, Mikhail 54, 217n87, 253
Battle of New Orleans: in George W. Cable's *The Creoles of Louisiana* 77; in theme parks 149
Baudrillard, Jean 138–9, 175, 178
Benjamin, Walter 55

Blum, Robert Frederick: *Balcony Stories* 46; collaboration with Grace E. King 46

Cable, George W.: "1888: How I got Them" 90, 93, 95; "Attalie Brouillard" 90, 109n26; "Au Large" 38, 39, 118n109; "Ba'm o'Gilly" 109n25; "Belles Demoiselles Plantation" 58, 64, 109n25; "Bibi" 38, 40, 109n24; *Bonaventure* 39; "Café des Exilés" 60, 64, 81, 109n25; "Carancro" 39; collaboration with Albert Herter 46; collaboration with Allen C. Redwood 46; collaboration with Edward W. Kemble 45–6; collaboration with Joseph Pennell 43–5, 75; "The Convict Lease System" 39; "Creole Slave Dances: The Dance in Place Congo" 45–6, 86–8, 91, 168; "Creole Slave Songs" 45–6, 88–90, 91, 117n103; *The Creoles of Louisiana* 39, 43–4, 74–8, 91; "Dr. Goldenbow" 109n25; "Drop Shot" columns 18n15, 37; *Dr. Sevier* 38, 78–9, 91; "Françoise" 90; "The Freedman's Case in Equity" 38, 39; "The Gentler Side of Two Great Southerners" 118n110; "Grande Pointe" 39; *The Grandissimes* 39, 46, 64–71, 86, 89, 92, 93, 198; "The 'Haunted House' in Royal Street" 90, 91–4, 96, 103, 109n26, 118n108, 156; "Hortensia" 109n25; "Jean-ah Poquelin" 60, 62–5, 65–6, 114n73, 116n92, 156; *John March, Southerner* 38; "A Life-

Ebbing Monography" 92, 114n74; "Madame Délicieuse" 64, 91, 109n25; "Madame Delphine" 71–4, 81, 87, 91, 92, 156; *Old Creole Days* 39, 44, 46, 59–65, 66, 70, 71, 86, 87, 92, 114n73; "Open Letters: Strange True Stories" 117–18n107; "Open Letters: The White League" 117–18n107; "Père Raphaël" 102–3, 118n110; "Plotters and Pirates of Louisiana" 76, 156; "Posson Jone'" 38, 39, 64, 103, 115n85, 118n110; relationship to Edward King 37–8, 39; relationship to Grace E. King 39–40, 94; relationship to Lafcadio Hearn 80; relationship to Mark Twain 86, 111n39; "Salome Müller" 109n26; and *Scribner's Monthly, an Illustrated Magazine for the People* 49–50, 74, 103, 119n119; "Sieur George: A Story of New Orleans" 38, 58, 59–60, 64, 81, 91, 336; "The Silent South" 38, 39; *Strange True Stories of Louisiana* 38, 39, 90–4, 95, 96, 109n26; "'Tite Poulette" 60, 61–2, 64, 71, 92, 116n92; "War Diary of a Union Woman in the South" 109n26; "Who Are the Creoles?" 75; *see also* local color; *Scribner's Monthly, an Illustrated Magazine for the People*; Waring, George E.
carnival *see* Mardi Gras
Century Company 30, 40, 48–9, 101, 106–7n4; *see also Scribner's Monthly, an Illustrated Magazine for the People*
Century Illustrated Monthly Magazine, The see Scribner's Monthly, an Illustrated Magazine for the People
Champney, James Wells 42, 47–8; "Brazil" 52; collaboration with Edward King 37, 42; collaboration with Herbert H. Smith 52; *The Great South* 36–7, 42, 49, 50–9, 62, 64, 70, 72, 103, 109n23, 146; "Old and New Louisiana" 50–9, 62, 64, 70, 72, 77, 78, 146, 336; "Old and New Louisiana – II" 50–9, 62, 64, 70, 72, 146; *see also* King, Edward
Chan, Paul: *Waiting for Godot in New Orleans: A Play in Two Acts,*

A Project in Three Parts 235–6, 280, 312n8
Charles Scribner's Sons 30, 38, 39, 40, 106–7n4; *see also Scribner's Monthly, an Illustrated Magazine for the People*
Chopin, Kate: "Azélie" 28; "Désirée's Baby" 315n26; "A Gentleman of Bayou Têche" 26–8; "A No-account Creole" 102
Cox, Kenyan: *Balcony Stories* 46; collaboration with Grace E. King 46

Dallas: African-American musical theater in 275, 277–8, 310; African Americans in 275, 277–8, 300–5, 310; The Black Academy of Arts and Letters 275, 277–8, 289, 318n48; Bruce R. Foote Memorial Foundation 279–80, 284; Deep Ellum 275, 294; *see also* Dallas Arts District; Hurricane Katrina
Dallas Arts District 236–7, 294–305; accessibility of 295–7, 298; Booker T. Washington High School for the Performing and Visual Arts 300–1; Dallas Museum of Arts 298, 299, 300, 318n51; development of 297–300; Freedman's Town/ North Dallas 237, 295, 301–4; Klyde Warren Park 305; Moody Performance Hall 236–7, 295–7; Morton H. Meyerson Symphony Center 295, 296, 299–300, 318n49; St. Paul United Methodist Church 300–1; Winspear Opera House at the AT&T Performing Arts Center 275, 295, 296, 318n49; Wyly Theatre at the AT&T Performing Arts Center 295, 296, 318n49; *see also* analogous city; Dallas
dark theming *see* theming
Davis, Rebecca Harding: *Here and There in the South* 82–3
De Certeau, Michel 258–9, 306–7
DeFore, Don 151–2; *see also* New Orleans Street (Disneyland)
Deleuze, Gilles 186, 190
disaster studies 245–6; *see also* Hurricane Katrina
Disney *see* Adventureland (Tokyo Disneyland); Disney Development Company; Disneyfication;

Index 343

Disneyland; Disneyland Paris; Disney's Port Orleans – French Quarter (Walt Disney World); Disney Wonder (cruise ship); Distory; Haunted Mansion (theme park attraction); New Orleans Square (Disneyland); New Orleans Street (Disneyland); Pirates of the Caribbean (theme park attraction); *The Princess and the Frog* (Disney movie); theme parks; theming; Tokyo Disneyland; *Walt Disney's Wonderful World of Color* (TV show); Walt Disney World
Disney Development Company 180, 194; *see also* Disneyfication
Disneyfication 13–14, 137, 138, 155, 178–85, 204–5, 208, 209n10, 215n66, 336; *see also* analogous city; French Quarter
Disneyland: and New York's World's Fair (1964–1965) 135; brands in 148, 174, 210n24; design of 105, 143, 144–5, 217n84; Frontierland 145, 149–50, 165, 209n6; "Fun Map" 153, 156–7; "it's a small world" 156, 158, 161; layout of 144–6, 210n18; Main Street, U.S.A. 105, 166, 172, 181, 209n6, 216n70; opening of 147–8; park rules 140–1, 181, 215n68, 215n69; promotional periodicals by 168, 172, 209n14, 212n35, 212n43; theme of 210n17; *see also* Haunted Mansion (theme park attraction); New Orleans Square (Disneyland); New Orleans Street (Disneyland); Pirates of the Caribbean (theme park attraction); Ryman, Herbert; theme parks
Disneyland Paris 186, 187, 214n60, 215n69, 218n93; "Le Coffre du Capitaine" 214n60; *see also* Pirates of the Caribbean (theme park attraction); theme parks
Disney's Port Orleans – French Quarter (Walt Disney World) 194–204, 336; "Bonfamille's Café" 199, 217n88; development of 194–5; (fictional) history of 197–8; "Jackson Square Gifts & Desires" 200, 201; layout of 199, 204; "Sassagoula Floatworks and Food Factory" 200, 217n88; "Scat Cat's Club" 200, 217n88; temporal setting of 199; *see also* Walt Disney World
Disney Wonder (cruise ship) 209n7, 337; "French Quarter Lounge" 337; "Tiana's Place" 337–8
Distory *see* popular history
Drake, Alexander W. 42, 111n44; *see also* Fraser, W. Lewis; illustration; *Scribner's Monthly, an Illustrated Magazine for the People*

Eco, Umberto 138, 169, 171, 175, 204, 206
Eggleston, Edward 75–6; *see also* popular history
Europa-Park 132–5, 139; "Historama" 132–5, 142, 207; *see also* theme parks

Federal Emergency Management Agency (FEMA) *see* Hurricane Katrina
folk culture *see* popular culture
folklorism 89–90
Fraser, W. Lewis 46; *see also* Drake, Alexander W.; illustration; *Scribner's Monthly, an Illustrated Magazine for the People*
Freedman's Town/North Dallas *see* Dallas Arts District
French Quarter: Disneyfication of 31, 138, 204–5, 336, 338; in *Scribner's/Century* 55–9, 60, 72–3, 77–8, 80, 81, 87, 92, 205; in theme parks 138, 154, 156, 158–9, 160, 185–94, 199–200, 205; *see also* literary tourism
Frito Kid 148–9; *see also* New Orleans Street (Disneyland)

Gayarré, Charles 10, 54, 112n56, 115n79, 119n114; *see also* popular history
Gershwin, George 285, 316n31; *Blue Monday* 287; *Porgy and Bess* 275, 285, 286, 287, 288, 316n31, 317n38
Gilder, Richard Watson: encounter with Grace E. King 39–40, 94; on editing 41; relationship to Mark Twain 41–2; *see also* *Scribner's Monthly, an Illustrated Magazine for the People*

Handley, George B. 261
Harper's Magazine 40, 106–7n4, 336
Harris, Joel Chandler 84, 102, 112n47, 212n40
Haunted Mansion (theme park attraction) 178, 211n30; attraction store 176; development of 156–8; opening of 159, 164, 184; at Tokyo Disneyland 189–90; at Walt Disney World 189–90, 195
Hearn, Lafcadio 10, 86, 113–14n67, 116n93; collaboration with Joseph Pennell 44–5; relationship to George W. Cable 80; "The Scenes of Cable's Romances" 39, 44–5, 79–82, 86, 92, 116n92; see also literary tourism
Herter, Albert 46, 61, 113n61; collaboration with George W. Cable 46; *The Grandissimes* 46, 114n68; *Old Creole Days* 46, 61, 65
Hill Moore, Barbara 237, 274, 275, 280, 283–4; see also *Wading Home: An Opera of New Orleans*
Holland, Josiah G. 18n16, 36, 42; see also Gilder, Richard Watson; *Scribner's Monthly, an Illustrated Magazine for the People*
Hurricane Katrina: and African Americans 245, 250–1, 253–4; Dallas response to 289–94; Federal Emergency Management Agency (FEMA) 233, 292; and neoliberalism 248–50, 251–2, 315n24; and racism 247–8, 249–50, 251–2; reception in art and popular culture 232–8, 251–63, 263–311, 280–1, 309; research on 6, 245–51; as an "unnatural" disaster 246–7, 255, 256; see also disaster studies; Story, Rosalyn; *Wading Home: An Opera of New Orleans*

illustration: and nineteenth-century magazines 28; production of 34, 46, 47, 48, 104, 111n44, 112n49; selection of illustrators 46–8; writer-artist collaborations 42–6; see also Drake, Alexander W.; Fraser, W. Lewis; intermediality; local color; *Scribner's Monthly, an Illustrated Magazine for the People*

intermediality: in magazines 34, 104; in theme parks 106, 175

jazz: historiography of 86; in theme parks 146–8, 151, 154, 162, 169, 199–200, 337

Katrina see Hurricane Katrina
Kemble, Edward W. 27, 42–3, 46–7, 84; "The Bamboula" 45–6, 88; collaboration with Eugene V. Smalley 42–3; collaboration with George W. Cable 45–6; collaboration with Mark Twain 27, 42–3, 47; "Creole Slave Dances: The Dance in Place Congo" 86–8; "Creole Slave Songs" 88–90; "In and Out of the New Orleans Exposition" 82–5; "The New Orleans Exposition" 82–5
Kern, Blaine 200–1, 218n91, 294
King, Edward 42; collaboration with James Wells Champney 37, 42; encounter with George W. Cable 37–8, 39, 41; "An Expedition with Stanley" 51–2; *The Great South* 36–7, 42, 49, 50–9, 62, 64, 70, 72, 103, 109n23, 112n50, 146, 182; "How Stanley Found Livingstone" 51–2; "Old and New Louisiana" 50–9, 62, 64, 70, 72, 146, 182, 336; "Old and New Louisiana – II" 50–9, 62, 64, 70, 72, 146, 182
King, Grace E.: "Anne Marie and Jeanne Marie" 46, 100, 119n116; "The Balcony" 40, 95, 96–7, 101, 118n112; *Balcony Stories* 40, 46, 94–101, 103; collaboration with illustrators 46; "A Crippled Hope" 95, 96, 100–1, 119n116, 167; "A Delicate Affair" 100; "A Drama of Three" 97–8, 99; encounter with Richard Watson Gilder 39–40, 94; "Grandmama" 40; "Grandmother's Grandmother" 46, 100; "Joe" 40; "La Grande Demoiselle" 95, 96, 99, 100; "The Little Convent Girl" 100, 119n116; "Mimi's Marriage" 99, 100; "Monsieur Motte" 40; "The Old Lady's Restoration" 46, 95–6, 100; "One of Us" 46, 100; "Pupasse" 100; relationship to

George W. Cable 39–40, 94; *Stories from Louisiana History* 118n112; "The Story of a Day" 95, 96, 100, 119n116; *see also* local color; *Scribner's Monthly, an Illustrated Magazine for the People*
krewes *see* Mardi Gras

Landrieu, Maurice Edwin "Moon" 205; *see also* Disneyfication; New Orleans
libretto *see* opera; opera studies; *Wading Home: An Opera of New Orleans*
literary tourism 72–3, 80, 92, 113n59, 116n92
local color: anthologies 107n7; and illustration 27, 28, 107n5; and "pastifying" 31, 53–5, 56–9, 63–4, 81–2, 92, 103, 336; research on 29; and travel writing 28, 58, 60, 104, 113n64
Louisiana Purchase: in George W. Cable's fictions 63, 70

magazine *see* periodicals
Mardi Gras: after Hurricane Katrina 208, 233–5; in *The Great South* 53; Krewe du Vieux 208, 232–3; krewes 208, 232, 279; parades 202–3, 208, 232–5, 279; The Roots of Music 278–9; in theme parks 146–8, 154, 191, 193–4, 195, 200–4, 337; *see also* Kern, Blaine; performance
mass culture *see* popular culture
McClure's Magazine 101–2
Mickey Mouse history *see* Distory
minstrelsy 286; *see also* opera

National Geographic 105, 211n28
New Orleans: as chronotope 53, 54–5, 56–7, 64, 72, 194–5, 253, 271; exceptionality of 6–8, 9–10, 15, 238, 246, 251, 306, 335–6, 338; exemplarity of 8, 14–15, 238, 246, 274, 306, 334–5, 338; home ownership in 314–15n22; research on 6–10; tourism in 9, 80–1, 138, 204–5, 234–5, 335; *see also* French Quarter; Hurricane Katrina; Landrieu, Maurice Edwin "Moon"; Mardi Gras; Schiro, Victor

New Orleans Square (Disneyland) 154–85, 336; balconies 168, 169, 176, 182, 212n42, 213n47; "Blue Bayou Restaurant" 154, 158, 167, 184, 211n27; brands in 174–8; "Café Orléans" 173, 177–8; "Club 33" 17n10, 168–9, 178, 184–5, 206, 212n36; "Court of Angels" 168–9, 172, 182, 184–5, 214n56; "The Creole Café" 177–8, 211n33; "Cristal d'Orléans" 172, 173, 174, 211n33, 213n53; development of 153, 156–7; "Disney Gallery" 173, 178, 183, 216n72; "Disneyland Strawhatters" 152, 162, 164; "Dream Suite" 178, 183–4, 216n72; "Fantasmic!" 184, 214n63; "French Market Restaurant" 162, 168, 178, 182, 185, 211n33; "Jewel of Orleans" 168, 173, 214n57; "La Boutique de Noel" 173; "Laffite's Silver Shop" 172, 173, 213n53; "La Mascarade d'Arlequin" 173; "La Mascarade d'Orléans" 174; "Le Bat en Rouge" 105, 173, 176; "Le Bayou Magique" 173; "Le Chapeau" 211n33, 213n53; "Le Forgeron" 172, 173, 211n33, 213n53; "Le Gourmet" 173, 211n33, 213n53; "L'Ornement Magique" 173; "Magnolia Park" 159; "Mlle. Antoinette's Parfumerie" 105, 172, 173, 174, 176, 211n33, 213n53; "One-of-A-Kind Shop" 172, 173, 213n53; opening of 144, 154, 159, 160–4, 194; "Pieces of Eight" 173, 176, 177; "Pirates Arcade Museum" 173; "Port Royal" 173, 176; representations of African Americans in 154, 166–7; "Royal Court" 172, 182, 213n49; "Royal Street Bachelors" 164, 166, 176, 178, 212n41; "Teddy and Kenny" 166–7, 207; temporal setting of 167–9, 207; urbanity of 181–2; *see also* Disneyland; Haunted Mansion (theme park attraction); New Orleans Street (Disneyland); Pirates of the Caribbean (theme park attraction); Ryman, Herbert
New Orleans Street (Disneyland) 144–54, 336; "Aunt Jemima's

Kitchen" 142, 152–3, 165, 166; "Aunt Jemima's Pancake House" 142, 148–51; brands in 148–9; "Casa de Fritos" 148, 151; "Dixieland at Disneyland" 152; "Don DeFore's Silver Banjo Barbecue" 151, 152, 207; "Firehouse Five Plus Two" 147, 152, 210n21, 339n2; "Magnolia Tree Terrace" 151, 165; opening of 147–8, 194; representations of African Americans in 144, 149, 150–1, 153, 154; *see also* Aunt Jemima; Defore, Don; Disneyland; Frito Kid

opera: African-American audiences of 288–9; African-American performers in 276–7, 279–80, 282, 285–7; and adaptation 266–7, 268; casting in 287; in English 316n31; Hurricane Katrina in 316n31; and intermediality 265; and jazz 316n31; libretto 265, 266–7; as popular culture 4–5, 14–15, 288–9; representation of African Americans in 285, 287–8, 316n31; *see also* Gershwin, George; opera studies; performance; *Wading Home: An Opera of New Orleans*
opera studies 265–6, 313n12, 316n32; role of libretto in 265–7, 316n32; *see also* opera; performance; performance studies

Pape, Eric 28, 106n3; *Balcony Stories* 46; collaboration with Grace E. King 46
parallel city *see* analogous city
Pei, I.M. 297, 299–300; *see also* Dallas Arts District
Pennell, Joseph: collaboration with George W. Cable 43–5, 75, 77–8; collaboration with Lafcadio Hearn 44–5; *The Creoles of Louisiana* 39, 43–4, 74–8, 200; "The Scenes of Cable's Romances" 39, 44–5, 79–82, 200
performance: activist performance 242, 244–5, 274, 307; after 9/11 235; after Hurricane Katrina 235–6, 280, 309, 312n4; definition of 238–9; efficacy of 242–5, 310; ephemerality of 236, 240, 308, 309, 313n10; relations to history and memory 240–2; utopian performative 243–4, 273–4, 307, 309, 334; venues of 294–5, 304; *see also* opera; opera studies; performance studies
performance studies 238–45; institutionalization of 239; and liminality 239, 243; *see also* opera studies; Schechner, Richard; Taylor, Diana; Turner, Victor
periodicals: and the literary marketplace 28, 106–7n4; *see also Atlantic Monthly*; illustration; *Harper's Magazine*; *McClure's Magazine*; *National Geographic*; periodical studies; *Scribner's Monthly, an Illustrated Magazine for the People*
periodical studies 32; institutionalization of 32, 239; periodical networks 30, 32–5, 41, 104
Pirates of the Caribbean (theme park attraction): at Disneyland 156–8, 159, 162–3, 168, 169–70, 175–6, 176–7, 183, 207, 211n30; at Disneyland Paris 214n60; at Shanghai Disneyland 214n62; at Tokyo Disneyland 185, 188–9, 191, 214n62; at Walt Disney World 189, 195, 214n62; *see also* Adventureland (Tokyo Disneyland); Disneyland Paris; New Orleans Square (Disneyland); Tokyo Disneyland
plantation regime 252, 256, 257, 258, 259, 261, 262, 263, 264–5, 270, 314n20; *see also* Story, Rosalyn
popular culture: and accessibility 5–6, 12–14, 40–2, 109n22, 288–9, 338; folk culture 3; mass culture 3–4, 12–13; popularization 4–5, 13
popular history: in nineteenth-century literature 75–6, 335–6; in theme parks 133, 161–2, 167–9, 197–8, 207
Pratt, Mary Louise 51, 52
Princess and the Frog, The (Disney movie) 173, 200, 337, 338
public (urban) space *see* Disneyfication

Reconstruction: in Edward King and James Wells Champney's *The Great South* 52–3; in George W. Cable's writings 70–1, 73, 77, 115n80; in Grace E. King's *Balcony Stories* 96–100; in Mardi Gras parades 233, 312n3

Redwood, Allen C.: "The Acadians of Louisiana" 111n43; collaboration with George W. Cable 46

Rich, Mary Alice 236, 263, 274–5, 283; *see also Wading Home: An Opera of New Orleans*

Rouse, James W. 179, 180; *see also* Disneyfication

Ryman, Herbert 105, 156, 158, 160; "The Square" 158–9, 178, 200

Saxon, Lyle 102

Schechner, Richard 238–9, 243; *see also* performance studies

Schiro, Victor 161, 204–5, 212n38

Scribner's Monthly, an Illustrated Magazine for the People: change in name and ownership 74, 106–7n4; decline 48, 101–2; production 40–2, 104, 119n120; and the South 29, 35–7, 49; *see also* Century Company; Charles Scribner's Sons; Drake, Alexander W.; Fraser, W. Lewis; Gilder, Richard Watson; Holland, Josiah G.; illustration; intermediality; periodicals; periodical studies; Smith, Roswell

Smalley, Eugene V.: collaboration with Edward W. Kemble 42–3; "In and Out of the New Orleans Exposition" 82–5; "The New Orleans Exposition" 82–5

Smith, Herbert H.: "Brazil" 52; collaboration with James Wells Champney 52; *see also* Champney, James Wells

Smith, Roswell 13, 37, 42, 48–9, 111n44; *see also Scribner's Monthly, an Illustrated Magazine for the People*

Sphinx Organization 274, 276–7, 282; *see also Wading Home: An Opera of New Orleans*

Stanley, Henry Morton 51–2; *How I Found Livingstone* 112n54

Sterner, Albert E. 46, 100; *Balcony Stories* 46, 100; collaboration with Grace E. King 46

Story, Rosalyn 236, 263–4, 274–5, 281, 282–3, 314n21; *And So I Sing: African American Divas of Opera and Concert* 282, 314n21, 317–18n47; *Wading Home: A Novel of New Orleans* 237, 251–63; *see also Wading Home: An Opera of New Orleans*

Taylor, Diana 241–2, 245

theme parks: and brands 133, 134–5, 174, 189; changes in 133–4, 206–7; consumption and 170–1; elements of 137, 209n15, 211n25, 213–14n54, 217n80; temporalities of 202; *see also* Adventureland (Tokyo Disneyland); Disneyfication; Disneyland; Disneyland Paris; Distory; Europa-Park; Haunted Mansion (theme park attraction); New Orleans Square (Disneyland); New Orleans Street (Disneyland); Pirates of the Caribbean (theme park attraction); theme park studies; theming; Tokyo Disneyland

theme park studies 138–9; employees and visitors in 139–41, 207; historical approaches to 135–7, 141–4, 207; institutionalization of 139, 239; and urban studies 179–81; *see also* Baudrillard, Jean; Eco, Umberto

theming: audio-animatronics 155, 157–8; autotheming 155, 174–8, 186, 192–3, 200, 208–9n4; dark theming 155, 163, 164, 169, 213n49; externality 195–8; reflexive theming 175; theme park design styles 134, 135, 137, 177, 188–9, 206–7; theming controversies 165–70, 206; *see also* Disneyland; Distory

Tillett, Wilbur Fish: "Southern Womanhood as Affected by the War" 97

Tokyo Disneyland 185–94, 214n60; differences to U.S. Disney parks 188–9; history of 186–7; layout of 190; research on 187; and Tokyo DisneySea 193; *see also*

Adventureland (Tokyo Disneyland); theme parks
tourism *see* New Orleans; theme parks
travel writing 51; *see also* local color
Turner, Victor 243, 313–14n14
Twain, Mark: *Adventures of Huckleberry Finn* 41–2, 42–3, 47, 145; *Adventures of Tom Sawyer* 145; collaboration with Edward W. Kemble 27, 42–3, 47; *Pudd'nhead Wilson* 102; relationship to George W. Cable 86, 111n39; relationship to Richard Watson Gilder 41–2

urban planning and theme parks *see* Disneyfication
urban renewal *see* Dallas Arts District
utopian performative *see* performance

Vieux Carré *see* French Quarter

Wading Home: as an adaptation of *Wading Home: A Novel of New Orleans* 264–5, 267–73, 317n44; *An Opera of New Orleans* 5, 236–7, 263–311; audience of the premiere performance of 288–9; cast of the premiere performance of 274, 280, 284–8; development of 263–4, 274; libretto of 265; linking New Orleans and Dallas during the premiere performance of 305–7, 310, 334; organization of the premiere performance of 275–6, 307–8; post-premiere performances of 333; premiere performance of 244–5, 273–4, 274–311, 337; production finances of the premiere performance of 274, 276–80; production team of the premiere performance of 274, 280–4; staging of the premiere performance of 276; timeline of the premiere performance of 274–5; venue of the premiere performance of 294–305; *see also* Hurricane Katrina; Hill Moore, Barbara; opera; Rich, Mary Alice; Story, Rosalyn
Walt Disney Imagineering *see* Disney Development Company; theming
Walt Disney's Wonderful World of Color (TV show) 159, 161–4, 212n43, 216n75; *see also* New Orleans Square (Disneyland)
Walt Disney World 174, 175, 180, 182, 187–8, 200, 209n6, 214n61, 214–15n65, 217n80; "Olde World Antiques" 172; Port Orleans – Riverside Resort 194, 203, 204; resort hotels 194, 196–7, 207, 217n82; *see also* Disney's Port Orleans – French Quarter; Haunted Mansion (theme park attraction); Pirates of the Caribbean (theme park attraction); theme parks
Waring, George E.: "George W. Cable" 74–5, 117n100
World's Fairs: New York World's Fair (1964–1965) 135, 155–6, 157–8, 161, 162, 174, 184, 211n29; World's Industrial and Cotton Centennial Exposition (1884–1885) 42, 79, 80–1, 82–5, 86, 105